Stand Up for Alabama

the MODERN SOUTH

series editors
Glenn Feldman & Kari Frederickson

STAND UP FOR ALABAMA

Governor George Wallace

JEFF FREDERICK

THE UNIVERSITY OF ALABAMA PRESS
Tuscaloosa

Typeface: Minion

∞
The paper on which this book is printed meets the minimum requirements of American
National Standard for Information Sciences-Permanence of Paper for Printed Library Materials,
ANSI Z39.48-1984.

Library of Congress Cataloging-in-Publication Data

Frederick, Jeff, 1963–
    Stand up for Alabama : Governor George Wallace / Jeff Frederick.
        p.   cm. — (The modern South)
    Includes bibliographical references and index.
    ISBN-13: 978-0-8173-1574-0 (cloth : alk. paper)
    ISBN-10: 0-8173-1574-8
  1. Wallace, George C. (George Corley), 1919–1998. 2. Wallace, George C. (George Corley), 1919–
1998—Political and social views. 3. Wallace, George C. (George Corley), 1919–1998—Influence.
4. Governors—Alabama—Biography. 5. Alabama—Politics and government—1951– 6. Political
culture—Alabama—History—20th century. I. Title.
    F330.3.W3F74 2007
    976.1′063092—dc22
    [B]

                                                                            2007008259

Contents

Preface

In many important ways, Alabama is one of the best places on earth to live. Few states possess as much natural beauty. Its lakes and rivers teem with fish, and its lush pine and hardwood forests are full of wildlife. Alabama is among a rare fraternity of states that feature both beaches and mountains. You can travel the world and not find a sweeter group of people. People still pull over out of respect for a funeral procession and if you have a flat tire you may be more likely to get help in Alabama than just about anywhere else I have ever been. Fast food does not exist in the Heart of Dixie; people engage in conversations and ask about your day and your kin even if it makes you wait a little longer for a cheeseburger. No matter where you are, a church is nearby. And the smell of fried chicken, as Johnny Cash sang about, is the smell of Sunday morning coming down. Dinner on the grounds is still a regular tradition across the state, and if you like greens cooked with bacon fat, fresh corn and tomatoes, homemade cornbread, sweet tea, and peach cobbler, the fare available in Alabama is world class. They play a little college football in the state too.

The essential goodness of so many in the state, black and white, rich but mostly poor, city and country, makes it difficult to reconcile the state's long-standing reputation. The education provided to the state's citizens has historically been far inferior to the education received anywhere else in America. Prisons, mental health facilities, and other state-run institutions have often faced federal scrutiny for failing to meet minimum standards. Most people in Alabama make less money than folks who live elsewhere in the country, and as of 2006, nothing in the offing suggests that is about to change. And being undereducated and poor in Alabama has usually been a life sentence. Over time, the state's politicians have done little to bring the state up to national averages. The history of Alabamians, then, is a history written in poverty, hard work, calloused hands, and weathered faces.

Tucked in the midst of this goodness and poverty is a legacy of racial discrimination. "I grew up in a house where the word nigger was as much a part of the vocabulary as 'hey' or 'pass the peas.'" author Rick Bragg writes in his memoir *All Over but the Shoutin'.* "If I was rewriting my life, if I was using this story as a way to make my life slickly perfect, this is the part I would change. But it would be a lie. It is part of me, of who I was, and I guess who I am." It is also the world in which George Wallace, the most important Alabama politician in the twentieth century and the most influential southern governor in the post–World War II era, grew up in. Wallace came to power at a time when white Alabamians were being challenged by civil rights protestors and the federal government to change.[1]

Wallace told white Alabamians that they were right to cling to their traditions and resist integration of any kind. "As you know," he wrote in 1966 a couple of years after the most important civil rights legislation—the Civil Rights Act of 1964 and the Voting Rights Act of 1965—became law, "here in the State of Alabama we have a law banning marriage between the races and in my judgement this law is completely valid and should remain on the books." That same year he was still fuming about the Civil Rights Act of 1964. "I think the Civil Rights Act of 1964 is unconstitutional, as the Supreme Court held in the 1880's, but the socializing, integrating, carpetbagging Supreme Court Justices are not interested in private property rights." First elected in 1962, Wallace served four elected terms and even managed to help elect his first wife, Lurleen, when the state's constitution prevented successive terms. Could race alone explain nearly twenty-five years of Wallace rule in Alabama? Surely the story is more complex.[2]

More than a few historians and authors have written about the life and times of George Wallace. The traditional perspective on the Alabama governor has focused on two issues: his civil rights intransigence and his forays into presidential politics. Both are important themes. The civil rights movement is a crystallizing event in southern history and, with the exception of the Civil War, the most important era of social change in American history. A huge corpus of monographs and biographies have documented the selfless sacrifice required to push the federal government to guarantee equality for all Americans. Within these works, Wallace is usually reduced to a static villain with little or no analysis of his broader impact on Alabama.[3]

Wallace's role as a third party presidential candidate in 1968, his 1972 run as a Democrat, and his overall impact on national politics have been the focus of the three previous biographies by Marshall Frady, Stephan Lesher, and Dan Carter. Carter's book, *The Politics of Rage,* is the most thoroughly researched and places Wallace's impact within the broader context of political shifts across the region and country. Even so, entire years of governance in Alabama are reduced to a single paragraph. None of the authors put much emphasis on state politics, administration policy, economic issues in Alabama, or on the evolving connection between Wallace and ordinary Alabamians.[4]

This book takes a different approach and attempts to answer two fundamental questions: What was George Wallace's impact on the state of Alabama? Why did Alabamians continue to embrace him over a twenty-five-year period? To answer the first question, I have used a variety of sources to document the state's performance in areas including mental health, education, conservation, prisons, and industrial development. For context, I have frequently cited comparisons between Alabama and both peer states in the South and national averages. Wallace's policies improved the state, but only in relation to Alabama's past, not in relation to peer states in the region or national averages. As a result, the state mostly treaded water, expending energy but making little progress.

To answer the second question, I have used the words of Alabamians themselves through oral history, correspondence, letters to the editor, and other sources. Alabamians, white and eventually black, supported Wallace because race was but one of his appeals. Wallace connected to Alabamians at a gut level, reminding them of their history and memory, championing their causes on the stump, and soothing their concerns about their place in the region and the nation. He appealed to a white southern brand of morality that transcended class barriers. Wallace evolved into a perpetual campaigner, a politician of such rare skill that he won the votes of most segregationists in his first term and some former civil rights demonstrators in his last. This story, if I have told it right, often focuses as much on rank-and-file Alabamians as on Wallace. To understand one, you must understand the other.

I devote little attention, despite the size of this work, to the more traditional civil rights flashpoints—the stand at the schoolhouse door at the University of Alabama, the many monumental events occurring in Birmingham in 1963, and the Selma-to-Montgomery march—as I see these events as part of a general pattern of Wallaceism. Race is a significant component of this book, but I attempt to look beyond infamous events and discover the broader themes that dominated the daily governance by the administration. In the same vein, the presidential campaigns are not a major topic of this work except to discuss their impact on the state and the governor. Because the Wallace campaign briefly thought he could win in 1976, I have documented the 1976 race more than any of the others. This defeat, occurring at the same time as the disintegration of his second marriage, the cold reality of paralysis, and shortly before a four-year absence from the governor's office, left Wallace disconsolate.

As I have worked on this project over the past several years, numerous people have asked me to compare Wallace to some other political figure. Some similarities are evident. Wallace used race in similar ways to Mississippi governor Ross Barnett and Arkansas governor Orval Faubus. Like Georgian Jimmy Car-

ter, Wallace was a tireless campaigner, at least until he was shot in 1972. President Ronald Reagan and presidential candidate Ross Perot became adept at
condensing complex problems into digestible sound bites, a skill they shared
with George Wallace. Like President Bill Clinton, Wallace could claim victory in the face of an obvious defeat and seem convincing. Louisiana governor Huey Long was another southern politician who had tremendous power
and enjoyed great popularity. Like Virginia governor Henry Howell, Wallace
launched a campaign against the utilities in his state.

But if all these comparisons had varying degrees of validity, the fact remains that Wallace was an original. "Can a former truck driver who is married to a former clerk in a dime store and whose father was a plain dirt farmer
be elected president of the United States?" a campaign flyer queried. "[George
Wallace] has pledged to fight the pseudo-intellectuals who think the average
working person—the laboring man, the professional worker, the retired person
and people in all walks of life—doesn't have sense enough to decide things for
himself." His background, approach to governance, campaign skills, and electoral longevity set him apart from any of his contemporaries. And his words
cemented a bond between him and Alabamians that survived integration, busing, recession, three marriages, paraplegia, and several national and regional
political realignments. Comparisons are not always useful, and so I offer few
in this book about Wallace.[5]

Wallace ran for governor in 1958 as a segregationist pledging to "keep Alabama southern.... I say to you that we can maintain our social order which is
complete segregation within the law—keep the peace and tranquility among
our people—and move forward in Alabama to acquire economic benefits for
all of our people regardless of their race, religion, creed, or national ancestry."
When that approach, legal strategies to combat integration, failed, he hardened his tone. Four years later he said, "I believe in blacks in black schools and
whites in white schools and anyone who believes differently should have their
head bored for a hollow horn." The imagery and rhetoric in the 1962 campaign
were defiant, physical, and unequivocal; Wallace coasted to victory. By 1982,
Wallace was courting and earning the votes of black Alabamians, a remarkable political metamorphosis. As Wallace announced his political retirement
in 1986, the Reverend Jesse Jackson was among the many politicos who offered
their own assessment: "The Wallace era has come to an end. It will have to be
reviewed by historians. It is so long and it had such high points and low points.
We find a different George Wallace of today and of twenty years ago."[6]

And so I offer this review of the Wallace years in Alabama. I confess that I
found more of everything than I thought. I found plenty of reasons to grieve
as this man of rare political gifts too often neglected opportunities to change
Alabama. Government by perpetual campaigning, a major theme of this book,

came with devastating costs. For all of Wallace's talents, he did not do enough to soften or enrich the lives of most Alabamians. "I remember being at ball games," Ernestine Abraham confided to Bragg in a *New York Times* article, "and having my parents come and get us because they had heard the Klan was coming. He could have changed that. He had the power and could have turned that tide. He didn't." I also found more to praise as this man reached out quietly at times to care for the state's vulnerable. The bombastic Wallace of the stump was actually more complicated, more thoughtful in private, sharper of mind, and occasionally more introspective than most people realize. The same man who openly excoriated federal judges and called for them to receive barbed wire enemas could be found nervously pacing when the state prepared to execute a death row inmate. When the lights were on and Wallace was in front of a microphone he came alive, thrusting and shaking with every turn of a phrase until the assembled throng burst forth with clapping hands, stomping boots, and rebel yells. When the lights were off and Wallace was alone, he could be strangely insecure and surprisingly nonconfrontational.[7]

Historians straddle a fine line between telling an interesting story for all readers to enjoy and challenging another scholar or toppling some existing interpretation. Idealistically, I have attempted to do both. Even so, I have made some choices. I focused more closely on the early years of Wallace rule in the 1960s, the time when he was most powerful and popular. His actions at this time set important precedents. The later years of his time in office are less thoroughly chronicled, largely because his incapacitation made him less vigorous and the legislature and interest groups were more powerful. I spent considerable time assessing Albert Brewer, a substantially different type of governor who was deeply interested in policy, but relatively few documenting the first Fob James administration, which I see as less of a departure from Wallace. I have avoided titillating personal details, except when they serve to explain actions of the governor and his administration, because they are of no interest to me.

White Alabama embraced George Wallace because he was one of their own. He reflected their sense of morality, their memories, their interpretation of history, and their preferred way of life. Over the course of a quarter century, both Wallace and the state made major transitions: Wallace from a man of vigor to a man confined to a chair, Alabama from defiance to assimilation to acceptance. "Maybe in his life," George Wallace Jr. suggested of the changes in his father over the years, "it was just more profound because I think suffering purifies us." While Wallace suffered from twenty-six years of paralysis, Alabama has suffered from an ineffective government dominated by elites and interest groups for most of its history. No man in the history of the state had both the opportunity and the requisite skills to reshape the quality of life as much as George

Wallace. Sadly, he did not choose to do so. As a result, Alabama was not transformed in the way other southern states were, thus condemning Alabamians to another generation or more of regressive taxes, low wage jobs, and schools that are underfunded and do not perform at national averages. "Was he a good governor," son-in-law Mark Kennedy pondered, "I guess it all depends. But I think he left an important legacy in Alabama, both good and bad."[8]

People in the state still gather at dinner on the grounds and at family reunions and in diners and pork barbeque restaurants just like they did in 1963 when George Wallace first took the oath of office. They still drink sweet tea and ruminate on the weather and the prospects of a good season for the Crimson Tide and Tiger football teams. The continuity of their lives, unfortunately, is far too revealing, for Alabama in 2006 continues to face many of the same problems it encountered in 1963. And whether that is a tribute to Wallace or a tragedy remains in the eye of the beholder.

Acknowledgments

I have discovered that the acknowledgment section of a book is far and away the most difficult part to write. No aspect of this project has produced as much fear as the certainty that I will forget to thank someone who has invested time and energy and professional care into me and this project. For the reality that the following list is sure to be incomplete, I apologize in advance. I also claim sole responsibility for any mistakes, shortcomings, or errors I may have made in this book.

Auburn University is a special place to live and work in so many ways. George Petrie's Auburn Creed seems hackneyed and maudlin until you've lived there; once you have, you believe in the place and love it. I love it in part because Wayne Flynt graciously took me in as his student, allowed me to tackle a project of this scope, and smiled when I handed him a 626-page manuscript. Wayne is a superb historian and an even better man, which is, to my way of thinking, a hefty compliment. Larry Gerber, Donna Bohanan, Tony Carey, and many others assisted my intellectual development. The university provided me with enough assistantships, fellowships, and grants to complete my research and help keep three kids in peanut butter and whole milk. The community of graduate students was unforgettable: Scott Billingsley, Jim Ross, Steve Murray, Mark Wilson, Greg McLamb, Eric and Jennifer Tscheslock, and Christian Gelzer merit special mention for offering support while tolerating poorly grilled hamburgers and backyard Wiffle ball games. Countless others helped make Auburn a better place than they found it.

Archivists at the Alabama Department of Archives and History, Auburn University, and the University of Alabama provided invaluable assistance. Among the truly professional and friendly were Ed Bridges, Norwood Kerr, Ricki Bruner, John Hardin, Cynthia Luckie, Debbie Pendleton, Nancy Dupree, Dwayne Cox, Joyce Hicks, and Donnelly Lancaster. Primary funding for this project came from Auburn University, the Friends of the Alabama Archives, and the University of North Carolina at Pembroke.

Numerous people read all or part of this work in its various forms including Sam Webb, Cynthia Bowling, Glenn Feldman, Kari Frederickson, Anne R. Gibbons, and Leah Rawls Atkins. Dan Carter provided advice on sources and Mills Thornton offered suggestions over lunch in Montgomery. The staff of the University of Alabama Press provided thoughtful and reasoned counsel.

My colleagues at the University of North Carolina at Pembroke have been a joy to work with. Charles Beem, Steve Berry, Scott Billingsley, Robert Brown, Wes Cook, Mickey Conley, Bruce Dehart, Janet Gentes, Kathleen Hilton, Julie Smith, and Mark Thompson have made work a relaxing place for collaboration and the occasional round of office golf.

I owe a special note of thanks to Terry and Marilyn Frederick, my parents, as well as John Frederick, Betsy Frederick, Jackie Mueller, Brad Mueller, and Gary and Marilyn Wilson. I can't imagine a more supportive set of kinfolk.

I am thankful, most of all, for Logan and Jack and Quinton. Nobody has taught me as much as these three; they are far better than I deserve. I dedicate this book to them and to my best friend, Melinda Frederick, whom I love and without whom I would be lost.

1

Shadows and Light

In Frank Lawrence Owsley's thirty-page contribution to *I'll Take My Stand*, he suggested a southern ethos that subsequent historians identified as little more than the defiant challenge of a young Turk looking to make his mark in a world spiraling into modernity. Owsley's work, "The Irrepressible Conflict," assessed the origins of the Civil War from a perspective considered implausible by most northerners then and now. "The South," Owsley concluded, "had to be crushed out; it was in the way; it impeded the progress of the machine." The northern industrial machine and its "doctrine of intolerance," according to Owsley, demanded that the South be whipped into submission and turned away from the agrarian society it had chosen to construct. More than military might was unsheathed against the South. "The leaders of the North," Owsley contended, "were able to borrow the language of the abolitionists and clothed the struggle in a moral garb. It was good politics, it was noble and convenient, to speak of it as a struggle for freedom when it was essentially a struggle for the balance of power."[1]

Owsley's contentions were more than just a discussion of a war that had ended sixty-five years earlier for the North but still seemed like current events to many below the Mason-Dixon line. W. J. Cash was among the first to see that Owsley and his cohorts had a "good deal more realism in them than in any of the earlier apologists and idealizers. . . . Save for the fact that they insisted on making it [the Old South] a good bit more contemplative and deeply wise than I think it was, they are much the same virtues I have myself assigned to it at its best: honor, courage, generosity, amiability, courtesy." White Alabamians and their Deep South neighbors had spent the years after Appomattox trying to regain a moral high ground that had been taken away by abolitionists, Radical Republicans, northern bankers and industrialists, and their kind. Much to the dismay of Owsley and his ilk, proponents of the New South creed and the remnant of the planter class had accepted the fate imposed by Lincoln, Grant, and

Sherman. The twentieth-century southern economy was rapidly industrial-
ized as mills and mines dotted Dixie in increasing numbers. Yet the inherent
morality that the white South claimed for its social and political institutions
did not die with the growth of factories and the gradual destruction of the
small land owner. The ramifications of states' rights evolved from justifying
slavery to maintaining segregation as Red Shirts and redeemers beat back first
Reconstruction and then Populism. In Alabama, the triumph was sealed with
the passage of the 1901 Constitution. One observer crystallized the intent of
the new constitution: "We are here to get rid of the nigger vote." That such an
endeavor was considered to have a noble purpose speaks to the ability of the
white southern power structure to construct its own moral compass.[2]

The constitution did more than just disfranchise black voters. The powerful
Black Belt and big industrialist (often called Big Mule) alliance that dominated the proceedings stripped away the votes of an estimated 35 percent of
whites between the ages of twenty-one and forty-four, created a system in
which special interests generally controlled the agenda in Montgomery, and, in
the words of historians William Warren Rogers and Robert David Ward, so-
lidified a world where "the rich, barring their own failure, would stay rich, and
the vast majority of poor Alabamians would stay poor and remain a limitation on the social progress the state could ever achieve." With the codification
of segregation and the construction of a safe political landscape, many white
Alabamians considered the Negro question effectively solved. The imposition
of lynching and other extralegal violence and the publicly stated goals of leaders such as Booker T. Washington kept Alabama's blacks consigned to a world
where occupation, education, family, and faith were more practical than social
equality or political rights.[3]

With the parameters of race so rigidly defined, a separate though often in-
terrelated attempt to build class-based coalitions slowly emerged through the
next decades. Progressivism in Alabama was a curious mixture of reform and
restriction. Prohibition, child labor laws, public health, railroad regulation,
and other ideas were proposed and some were enacted. Yet the "reformers"
were an odd mixture of business progressives, social and religious conservatives, rural folk who wanted the clock turned back instead of forward, and
middle-class do-gooders who thought associations could solve problems that
individuals could not. On balance, these reformers had very little in common
with each other, rendering Progressivism more a series of unrelated causes
than a cohesive movement.[4]

Progressivism represented the arrival of a viable if splintered middle class in
Alabama and carried with it continuing connotations of a southern morality
imbued with the notion that Alabamians could best determine Alabama's fate.
"When the issues were strictly class based," historian Wayne Flynt has con-

cluded, "such as better wages or shorter hours, only the most advanced Alabama Progressives helped, and workers usually lost. But when an issue touched a deeper moral sensibility, it won them influential allies." Men like Braxton Bragg Comer transferred their business credentials into political careers, but they had no interest in making a new Alabama for the state's underclass. Historian David Alan Harris summarized Comer's mission as serving the "new industrial-urban interests while not disturbing the traditions of the old plantation system." Comer was particularly unsympathetic to the growing labor movement and used the state National Guard to crush a Tennessee Coal, Iron, and Railroad strike in 1908. If Populism was the last gasp of the vulnerable, Progressivism was the mission statement of the middle class and their acknowledgment that outsiders should leave Alabama to Alabamians.[5]

Throughout the first three decades of the twentieth century, labor's power remained relatively weak as white primaries, election laws, and poll taxes combined with the dedication of planters and industrialists to prevent the formation of effective class and rank coalitions. World War One, a major stimulant to union growth, also fostered the slow reemergence of race as the dominant political theme. During the 1920s, the Ku Klux Klan reached its pinnacle in many states, including Alabama, and Klan candidates were often winning candidates. The best example of the Klan reaching the mainstream was the 1926 election of Klan members Bibb Graves as governor and Hugo Black as U.S. senator. Graves also benefited from the ability of his wife, Dixie, to bring newly enfranchised women to the polls. On the local level, particularly in Birmingham, the Klan was equally effective at electing members and handpicked candidates. Though their racial, anti-Catholic, and anti-Semitic prejudices were obvious, the Klan also became a major voice for a larger and more responsive government and control of corporate excesses. Simply put, the Klan, according to historian Robert J. Norrell, attracted working-class members because it more closely represented their political interests than the Big Mule–Black Belt alliance of elites.[6]

As for other poor states, the Great Depression was particularly hard on Alabamians since the line between survival and ruin was already so perilously thin. Perhaps no other description of the Depression was as candid and as revealing as the assessment of West Alabama sharecroppers made by James Agee and Walker Evans in *Let Us Now Praise Famous Men*. "To say they are forced in this respect to live like animals," Agee wrote, "is a little silly, for animals have the advantage on them on many counts." For most, the New Deal was more palliative than curative, but Franklin Roosevelt did turn the attention of the nation southward. The WPA, Fair Labor Standards Act, and other legislation opened Alabama to the possibility that class cleavages could dethrone the entrenched Big Mules. Within Alabama, the New Deal was perceived as a dan-

gerous turn of events by Birmingham's power structure. Charles DeBardeleben promised to close his Alabama Fuel and Iron Company rather than allow
unionization and instructed his employees to use dynamite if necessary to prevent United Mine Workers from gathering near his mines. "If you catch any
of the organizers in the camp," he told his men, "you know what to do with
them."[7]

DeBardeleben and his fellow industrialists had good reason to fear that
class-based politics might threaten their hold on the state. Governor Bibb
Graves removed convict labor from the Big Mule mines, raised taxes for education, created a cabinet-level Department of Labor, refused to follow the time-
honored gubernatorial tradition of calling out the National Guard to break
strikes, and openly supported Roosevelt's New Deal. Alabama's congressional
delegation was the South's most progressive, with Henry Steagall, Lister Hill,
Hugo Black, and others playing important roles in the passage of sweeping
economic reforms. As the nation inched toward war, union membership in
Alabama swelled and the possibility of black and white workers joining together to reshape Alabama reached a peak not seen since the Populist revolt.
Many Alabamians, young and old, developed a strong affinity for Roosevelt
and the New Deal. Future senator Howell Heflin remembered where he was
when Roosevelt died just as future generations would with John Kennedy. "I
was at the University of Texas at Austin," the Tuscumbia giant recalled. "I cried
like a baby. You just felt like he was a member of your family."[8]

The response to labor's strength was immediate and forceful. Unions were
branded as havens for communists and black sympathizers—a charge that reopened the quest to regain state autonomy and end federal meddling. In coming years, communism would serve as a supple brush for painting "outside
agitators," no matter their cause, as insidious schemers bent on revolution.
One Alabama farmer understood the tactic completely: "Around here, communism's anything we don't like. Isn't it that way everywhere else?"[9]

Concurrent to the growth of labor and the backlash of the Big Mules was an
effort by Alabama blacks in the World War II years to extend their civil rights.
The NAACP began voter registration drives and filed suits against restrictions,
tests, and poll taxes that had disfranchised them since 1901. The NAACP was
also active in litigation designed to protect black railroad workers from harassment and illegal termination. Blacks also pressed for housing protection and
better bus and streetcar service. This activism brought Big Mules, old planters, middle-class professionals and businessmen, and whites who worked with
their hands into a coalition against racial change. The result had ramifications
for national politics in 1948 as Alabamians found Strom Thurmond and his
Dixiecrats an acceptable alternative to the perceived racial and economic lib-

eralism of Harry Truman and the Democratic party. In the era before the civil rights revolution, Alabama politics was a country stew heated to a rolling boil with various ingredients taking their turn at the top of the pot. The rumblings of civil rights activism, taken together with Big Mule propaganda in response to the New Deal era, left one issue, race, simmering above all others. In 1954, when the Supreme Court ruled 9 to 0 in *Brown v. Board of Education* that separate school systems were inherently unequal, white supremacy and black inferiority were frozen in time as the mission statement of white Alabama politics.[10]

Numerous Alabama politicians spent the fifteen years after *Brown* attempting to "out-nigger" one another in order to get elected and reelected. And these appeals were usually enough to keep them in probate judgeships, on county commissions, and in the state legislature. But only one Alabama politician, George Wallace, realized that if race could be buttressed with other traditions—appeals to the working man and to a certain kind of southern morality—a governor could become more popular and powerful than anyone in state history. And even Wallace had to learn a painful political lesson, taught by a resounding defeat in 1958, in order to grasp this truth.[11]

The best way to get any message to voters was the tried and true friends and neighbors approach first identified in academic circles by political scientist V. O. Key. "In a sense," Key wrote in 1949, "the battle of state politics is not a battle between large party factions. It is rather a struggle of individuals—perhaps with the support of their county organizations—to build a statewide following on the foundation of local support." Once a candidate rallied the locals, he then branched out to sharpen his sectional appeal. Staunch social conservatives found their best sectional alliances in the Black Belt where African Americans dominated the population but could not register to vote. Key himself noted the demographic irony: "The backbone of southern conservatism may be found in those areas with a high concentration of Negro population."[12]

The predictability of Black Belt voters was offset by rivalries between North and South Alabama, between urban and rural, farm and industry, and interest groups and poor folk. Some of these rivalries could be muted by a strong personality. But in the world of white politics, it was difficult to bridge the gap between the very rich and the very poor. Consequently, poor folks in South Alabama might warm to Jim Folsom's call for higher old age pensions and farm-to-market roads even though he was from Cullman in North Alabama. But the Big Mules in Birmingham tolerated Folsom no more than they had Graves a decade earlier, and they partnered with the Black Belt remnant to thwart his legislative agenda. Making the entire contentious system even more ironic was the fact that all these factions were contained within one political party.[13]

Even if localism could be augmented by uneasy alliances between factions to support a particular candidate, passing legislation was another matter entirely. Interest groups such as the Alabama Power Company, Farm Bureau Federation, League of Municipalities, and later the Alabama Education Association were much more successful at preventing reform in the legislature than electing handpicked pawns. Political scientist David Martin has demonstrated that interest groups were stronger in Alabama than almost anywhere else in the region or indeed in the nation. Throughout the twentieth century, interest groups in Alabama grew in size and professionalism in order to turn back most constitutional amendments and tax reform bills that threatened their feudal domains. Further limiting the slim window of opportunity to end stagnation was a general lack of imaginative political leaders with the courage to take on the interest groups and the raw political appeal necessary to win. Folsom limited his own programs with a potpourri of personal peccadillos but was no match on his best day for interest group power plays in the legislature. The prospect of reform was limited severely by a system in which lobbyists often sat on the floor of the house and senate and used legislators for their own legal work.[14]

Even George Wallace did not have the power to threaten the entrenched powers in Alabama when he assumed office in January 1963. That would take a few months, the unfolding drama of events in Birmingham and Tuscaloosa, and the realization that Alabamians were hungry for a champion. But when civil rights demonstrators and the federal government began to peck away at white southern autonomy, Wallace found his place. Caught up in his moment in history, Wallace united white Alabama by placing the contexts of race and class in a white southern morality tale where *his* side was the aggrieved party; the national news media was a co-conspirator with Yankees, communists, and outsiders; and his course of action was nothing more than a reasonable defense of states' and southern rights. Decades of politics flavored with the lingering burden of Confederate history and an exaggerated depiction of the struggle to regain home rule made Wallaceism possible. And it mattered little to white Alabama that Wallace seemed to lose more often than he won in his battles with outsiders. Alabamians did not mind being the underdog; that was second nature. Even the great Bear Bryant, legendary head football coach at the University of Alabama, was wont to depict the Crimson Tide's foes as stronger, faster, and bigger before and after his boys whipped them. The implication for Bryant on the gridiron and Wallace in the governor's office was that Alabamians, since the day that Montgomery welcomed the birth of the Confederacy, simply had more heart.

The Path to Center Stage

In November 1967, Governor Lurleen Burns Wallace was recuperating from a two-month regimen of cobalt radiation treatments, and her husband, former governor George Wallace, was plotting the second of his forays into presidential waters. With the elected governor and her advisor preoccupied, political rivals and reporters began to question whether anyone was minding the store. Administration chief of staff Cecil Jackson informed the nay-sayers that no apology would be forthcoming. "During Mrs. Wallace's gubernatorial campaign," Jackson recalled, "it was made clear that the people of this state would be acting with her husband in attempting to have an impact on the national scene. We have always been honest and straightforward about this and the state government is in no wise being neglected."[15]

Jackson, a loyal soldier and capable advisor, wanted to reassure Alabamians that their first family was about the state's business but inadvertently revealed much more. In reality, Jackson was summarizing the first decade of Wallace rule in Alabama: passionate campaigning, an undeniable connection to white Alabamians, unmitigated national aspirations, and disinterested governance back home in Alabama. The governor's part-time approach to Alabama affairs was but one of many tragedies during a time in which blood and tears flowed freely and the past and present collided at bus depots, diners, water fountains, and on school campuses. George Wallace had the power, charisma, and political savvy to prevent his home state from becoming the Alabama that the nation and world would come to scorn. Unfortunately, he had other plans.

Wallace was not ideologically opposed to making government an instrument for empowering people and lifting them up. Born in rural Barbour County, Alabama, on August 25, 1919, Wallace, called George C. by his kin, had experienced poverty firsthand. Although Wallace and his family were middle class in Clio, Alabama, most Americans who looked at the wood frame house without electricity or indoor plumbing would have considered them poor. Mozelle Wallace cooked the family meals on a woodstove, sewed the family clothes, helped till and tend the family garden, and supplemented the family income with piano lessons for Clio's none-too-eager youth.[16]

Mozelle used her musical talents for the local Methodist Church, but her strong faith was unable to keep her husband in line. Wallace's father, known as George, exhibited the classic southern characteristics of a John Shelton Reed monograph: more religious than most, prone to resolving disputes through violence, and a bit relaxed if not lazy around the edges. George, sickly since birth, attended two years of college at Methodist Southern in Greensboro, Alabama, but found the work tedious and the social regulations stifling. Fighting was an accepted practice for resolving conflict and George Wallace was no exception. At sixteen he gashed his best friend with a pocketknife in a dispute over a girl. Years later, he threatened a Barbour County revenue official with his knife. George worked hard to acquire more farmland, but a series of events— bad mortgages, boll weevils, and low cotton prices—kept the family on the precipice of financial collapse. The economic strife was augmented by George's drinking, which the pious Mozelle could not stop. The drinking certainly did not help George's frightful health, which included lung, heart, sinus, and migraine trouble, and left him in a constant state of pain while performing non-mechanized farm work. According to historian Dan Carter, one family friend characterized George Wallace as "a little ole runty dried-up feller who was always freezin', even in the summertime."[17]

Southern traditions pass from one generation to the next on front porches and at the feet of rocking chairs where patriarchs and matriarchs regale enquiring minds with tall tales, family memories, and the essential tenets of southern history. This is not a history written on word processors by trained scholars. It is more authentic than that; it is a living, breathing heritage flowing through the capillaries and vessels of boys and girls raised to believe in the valor of the Gray, the superiority of white folk, and the untrustworthiness of Washington. Whether its called the "burden of southern history" by C. Vann Woodward or the "savage ideal" by W. J. Cash, the simple fact remains that for most of the twentieth century, history was not a textbook or a high school requirement; it was the blood and sinew of white southerners rich and poor, urban and rural, male and female, which bound them to home and hearth and region in a way few outsiders could ever understand. In this manner, the Wallace family was no different from a million other white southern families for whom words like Reconstruction and segregation carried moral, familial, and religious connotations. Little George C. learned these lessons from his father. "He talked to me," the governor later told a biographer, "until he died about those kind of things."[18]

Mozelle and George kept George C. and his three siblings—brothers, Gerald and Jack, and sister, Marianne—in line with discipline, work, and church. Mozelle expected the family to be in services whenever the doors were open and led family prayers at least once each day. George C. loved his paternal grandfather, Oscar, and spent as much time as he could with him. Oscar expected daily Scripture memorization and hoped George C. would be called to the ministry, but he was not opposed to giving his favorite grandson an occasional spanking himself. George's father used a leather razor strap to enforce family law, whereas Mozelle used switches from barren peach trees. She "whipped the livin' shit out of us," brother Gerald later recalled.[19]

But not everything was Bible drill, farm chores, and whippings. George C. did the things that Alabama boys did to pass the time: fishing, skipping rocks, inventing games of skill and chance, playing whatever sport they could find equipment for, and selling blackberries, pecans, and anything else they could to earn spending money. Southern boys, despite their obligations to house and farm, had a great deal of personal freedom in the years between the wars. Wallace learned about Clio the old-fashioned way through lots of barefoot walking and saying hey to strangers until they became neighbors and friends. George C. had very little of the awkward bashfulness that plagues many boys and renders them uncomfortable making eye contact, meeting strangers, or speaking above a whisper. He learned to play the guitar from Cass Welch, and the young governor-to-be and the black fiddler performed together at Clio square dances. All in all, Wallace was a popular and resourceful boy with a quick and agile mind and enough determination to be a 120-pound quarterback for the Barbour High Yellow Jackets.[20]

Out of this generally happy childhood in the hardscrabble realities of the Great Depression, Wallace found two consuming passions: boxing and politics. After his father brought home a pair of boxing gloves, George C. became obsessed, battering his brothers at will, then classmates and local blacks who could be recruited for brief bouts. The family staged these events indoors or out, depending on the weather, and enlisted the telephone operator to ring the house at the end of each two- or three-minute round. At one point, Wallace's boxing became the halftime show at Barbour County High basketball games. Despite his small frame, Wallace was deceptively strong and usually pummeled foes who invariably linked his stature with assumptions about his skills. Even in Golden Gloves–sanctioned matches, Wallace could be underestimated by older fighters, a foreshadowing of the contempt northern moralists, journalists, and political rivals would hold for him when he was governor. After being dropped twice and thoroughly pounded in the first round of a 1935 fight against an older opponent, Wallace used superior stamina and determination to pepper his rival mercilessly over the final two rounds and win a unanimous decision. George C. was superbly conditioned from whacking a homemade heavy bag and daily running, and learned to prosper when others lost their wits. All told, he lost only four official fights and won Alabama championships in two different weight classes. More importantly, boxing taught Wallace a series of life lessons he would never forget: bigger opponents were often overconfident and lazy; a certain amount of pain must be expected and tolerated; opponents must be dispatched without mercy; and fighters must be prepared to do whatever is necessary to win.[21]

If boxing satisfied Wallace's need for physical competition, politics invigorated his soul. His first experiences in Alabama's favorite spectator sport, politics, were running for third grade class president, watching vote counting, and listening to Barbour County's elder statesman talk politics around courthouses and town squares. At thirteen, George C. canvassed Clio on behalf of secretary of state candidate Fred Gibson. Gibson lost statewide, but carried Clio impressively thanks in part to the hard work of his youngest supporter. Little George also helped his father collect signatures and donations for the Dollar for Roosevelt Club. His interest in politics, like boxing, was stoked by dinner conversations with his father and grandfather who participated in campaigns as candidates and coordinators. Surrounded by traditional rural poverty made worse by the Depression, Wallace grew to appreciate the possibilities that an active government managed by a dynamic leader like Franklin Roosevelt could offer. Even so, for Wallace the campaign—handshaking, foot-stomping music, assembled throngs of freshly scrubbed youth and weathered field-workers, the smell of fresh barbeque smoking over a fire, and candidates thrusting closed fists and pointed fingers into the air to punctuate every line—remained the most interesting aspect of politics. He had only a broad interest in policy and no stomach for details.[22]

Generations later, young Alabamians view politics with either apathy or contempt and avoid the polls as if the ballot were laced with an infectious disease. But in the days of George C. Wallace's youth, politics was something much more; it was entertainment, an opportunity to escape the dreary realities of a life in and around the dirt, and it brought acceptance and stature. The attention and occasional adulation that a candidate or officeholder could command enticed Wallace. The political rally was a carnival and the candidate the main attraction for folks in overalls and wool hats and cotton housedresses who came to hear warnings about nefarious outsiders and promises of lower milk prices. For a boy who as a man would insist on being portrayed as the underdog fighting battles against giant monoliths, politics was the ultimate measuring stick of masculinity, intelligence, and heart. Some boys grew up hoping to be the quarterback of the Crimson Tide or a pilot or a doctor. George Wallace wanted to be governor of Alabama.[23]

At sixteen, George C. learned of an opportunity to be a page for the Alabama senate, a position requiring only the skills of an errand boy but that came with an entree to the politically powerful Black Belt senators and the well-heeled representatives of special interest groups. Wallace's father had arranged for a friend to nominate his son for one of four positions. It was up to George C., though, to outcampaign his rivals in order to win the position. After introducing him to a few members of the senate, his father returned to Barbour County, leaving the face-to-face work to his son. Though most page hopefuls relied on their nominator to use his connections, Wallace canvassed the capitol himself and within days impressed enough senators to win approval. Days after being sworn in, the precocious Wallace reminded some senators that they had promised to vote for him but instead voted for others. Though he savored his first meaningful victory, Wallace also rolled up his shirtsleeves and went to work. He developed contacts, learned the nuts and bolts of how the legislature really worked, both openly and behind closed doors, and ingratiated himself to Chauncey Sparks, Barbour County representative, Black Belt power baron, and future governor. Despite having to sleep in an insect-ridden boarding-house with hardened and weathered men twice his age, Wallace was intoxi-cated by the experience in Montgomery.[24]

In some ways, the next decade of his life was a journey through both shad-ows and light toward fulfilling political goals. After high school graduation, Wallace sold magazines door to door throughout North Carolina and Kentucky. Lesser sales reps grew weary of the heat, stray dogs, continual rejection, and despair; Wallace rose above the tedium and honed his interpersonal commu-nication and persuasion skills to the point that he sold magazines to the blind. Wallace's education at the University of Alabama was difficult; his family did not have money to pay for room and board let alone fraternity membership, the traditional seat of the student power structure. Weak-willed eighteen-year-olds would have returned home, longing for hot meals, soft beds, and familiar faces. Wallace gritted his teeth, waited tables, took on-campus boondoggling work, washed dishes, inoculated dogs against rabies and rented boardinghouse rooms. In short, he did nearly anything imaginable to keep tuition and rent paid and food in his belly. Wallace's grades were middling, partially due to his work and extracurricular activities and partially because he could not afford to buy all the necessary books. "George didn't make the Dean's List," Mozelle recalled, "he was out mixin' and minglin' with the students." Even so, Wallace hitchhiked from Clio to Tuscaloosa in 1937 with a handful of dollars and a goal; five years later he had a University of Alabama law degree, a stable of con-tacts and associates who would dot the landscape of his campaigns and ad-ministrations for the next five decades, and a confidence that he could endure any hardship, overcome any odds, and outwork any rival.[25]

With debts to pay, Wallace took a position as a truck driver then as a tool checker at a training depot for military aircraft mechanics. With the war under way in the Pacific, Wallace, like other young men brimming with patriotism, righteous indignation, and a thirst for action, longed to join up to save the world. Despite his voracious appetite for hamburger steak, southern fried vege-tables, and ketchup, he was unable to meet minimum weight requirements to join the air corps. After one enlistment rejection, Wallace stopped at a Kresge's Five-and-Dime for a quick meal but instead found his future wife, sixteen-year-old Lurleen Burns. Lurleen, naturally fun-loving, and pretty without be-ing threatening had already graduated from Tuscaloosa County High School and was honing her secretarial skills at a nearby business college until she could meet age requirements to enter nursing school. The two fell in love quickly and George began courting his future bride with regular visits to the five-and-dime and supper at the Burns's house. "She was all I could think about," Wallace later told a biographer. "There she was, olive complexioned, with auburn hair that was brown with a little tinge of reddish in it. She wanted to get married—and I did too. But we knew I'd be going into the service as a private and wouldn't be able to send her much money."[26]

Not long after Wallace began wooing Lurleen, the army air corps recruiting sergeant finally gave in and passed the still-underweight Wallace who had taken to bloating himself with water to meet weight standards. In January 1943, Wallace received his orders and caught a train for Miami. In the frenetically changing military climate of those years, Wallace trained for ten days in his suit trousers until uniforms arrived. After Miami, Wallace was sent to Arkadelphia, Arkansas, for preparatory classroom pilot training. While in Arkansas, he developed a horrific case of spinal meningitis that nearly killed him. After a painful recovery that included forced confinement to his bed, an allergic reaction to medication, and three weeks of quarantine, he was given a thirty-day leave.[27]

While on furlough, Wallace made some important decisions about his future: he wanted to get married as soon as possible and he wanted no further part of pilot training. The former was easier than the latter. George and sixteen-year-old Lurleen were married on May 22, 1943, by a Jewish justice of the peace after Janie Estelle Burns signed a waiver for her minor daughter. The wedding was so quickly planned that Mozelle Wallace was not even informed, let alone invited. Later that day, the newlyweds took a train to Montgomery to tell her and spent their wedding night in a boardinghouse room adorned with little more than a bed and a light bulb hanging from the ceiling. The circumstances surrounding the marriage were not idyllic and, though similar to a thousand other wartime marriages, proved an apt metaphor for the rest of the couple's years together. Wallace compartmentalized his marriage, separating the duties of husband and father from his political ambitions. Without a doubt George Wallace loved Lurleen, but he also willingly put himself and his career ahead of their marriage. More at home on the road campaigning than in his own household, Wallace strayed from his marriage vows, and later left the child rearing almost completely to his often exasperated wife. Nevertheless, when Lurleen died three weeks shy of their twenty-fifth anniversary, George was devastated.[28]

If the decision to marry was easily accomplished, the quest to leave pilot training was not. Wallace had practical political reasons, at least in his own mind, to wash out of Officer Candidate School and remain an enlisted man. I sensed," he later admitted, "that if I got back to Alabama and into politics, there would be far more GIs among the electorate than officers." After convincing his superiors that his bout with meningitis could resurface while in the cockpit, the Alabamian was reassigned to Amarillo where he languished for more than a year. After exercising his salesmanship on yet another sergeant, Wallace managed to gain permission to live off base with Lurleen in a rented attic. Even in such makeshift accommodations—they later lived in a converted chicken coop—the couple struggled to make ends meet. Lurleen took a job in a local retail outlet and George worked as an unloader at a defense plant during days off duty. Indicative of his tireless energy, Wallace found time in the midst of all the odd jobs and regular military duty to send Christmas cards to every family in Barbour County.[29]

Eventually, the demands for air personnel dictated a call to combat duty for Wallace and his comrades. Now a sergeant himself and a trained flight engineer, Wallace, with his crew, was dispatched to the Mariana Islands in late 1944 as the American high command prepared for the eventuality of invading Japan. Fearless in the ring, Wallace was shaking at the thought of going to war as he bid farewell to his wife and young daughter: "I really thought I would never get back alive." Throughout the summer of 1945, flight engineer George Wallace and the rest of the crew on the *Little Yutz* were dispatched on bombing runs over Japan's major industrial cities as part of General Curtis Lemay's plan to use B-29s to inflict heavy losses. Wallace was a skilled flight engineer, conserving fuel and helping the rest of the crew solve repair problems while in flight. The *Little Yutz* encountered frequent mechanical problems and kamikaze pilots, and in the immediate aftermath of the devastation of Hiroshima, Wallace decided he had flown his last mission. Exhausted by the round-the-clock pace and rattled by several close calls with death, Wallace, reduced to less than 120 pounds, told crew members, "I'm not unpatriotic, but I've done my share. I'm not going to fly any more." He was more forthright with superiors who contested his decision to stop flying: "I'm tired and I'm afraid of flying, especially in these big bombers that catch fire mighty easily—and the war's over."[30]

Eventually, Wallace was declared unfit to fly because of "severe anxiety" and spent most of the rest of his military service in a hospital. In December 1945, Sergeant Wallace was discharged from the Army Air Corps with three medals, a 10 percent disability for "psychoneurosis" battle fatigue, and a two-year-old letter from Governor Chauncey Sparks promising him a job in Montgomery. After a brief layover in Mobile, Wallace hitchhiked to Montgomery and used his contacts to land an assistant attorney general position. Eight days after being formally discharged, Wallace began working on legal briefs for the State of Alabama for $175 a month; three months later he took a leave of absence to run for a seat in the state house. A lifetime of daydreaming about a career in politics had finally become reality.[31]

Wallace's campaign for the state house featured a lot of handshaking and worn shoe leather. George, borrowing his grandfather's car when he could and walking when he could not, combed the highways and hedges, reminding locals of his grandfather's reputation and his own military service; and Lurleen was a one-woman correspondence machine, sending letters to voters for every conceivable reason: solicitation, invitation acceptance, birth, wedding, or funeral. Identifying his three chief concerns as farmers—the principal occupation of Barbour County folk—old-age pension recipients, and education, Wallace ran a safe campaign devoid of any sweeping ideas but with a progressive bent. In fact, these three issues would be a continuing thread of Wallace campaigns in Alabama. The issues were safe since the pool of voters opposed to old folks, school kids, and the state's traditional economic pursuit was shallow and the topics were perfect for loose generalities that required no exact details or plans. Race was no factor in the campaign that Wallace won without a runoff.[32]

The most electrifying figure entering state government in January 1947 was not George Wallace, but "Big Jim" Folsom. Folsom took Alabama commoners and progressives by storm with a class-based appeal that included calls for equitable reapportionment, raises for the state's beleaguered teachers, tax reform, farm-to-market roads, and elimination of the poll tax. Promising to sweep corruption and greed out of Montgomery and brandishing a corn shuck mop and wooden suds bucket as props, Folsom energized poor white Alabamians who thought him one of their own. Recognizing the appeal of the new governor, Wallace attached himself to the administration and became a minor floor leader.[33]

Though he had great appeal in the hinterlands, Folsom was a miserable administrator and fell victim to inexperience, special interest power, and personal foibles. Too ambitious to be taken down and too practical to be labeled, Wallace supported the governor when it served his own purposes and broke with him when it did not. The administration supported Wallace's idea for a two-cent liquor tax to raise money for a trade school system, and the young legislator fought for Folsom's road bond bills and increased tuberculosis hospital funding. But Wallace wanted no part of Folsom's plans to reapportion the legislature or use a constitutional convention to reform the state's regressive tax structure. In later years, Wallace would distribute voting records to reporters to prove he was never a full-blooded Folsomite. As a result of Wallace's episodic independence, Folsom used him but never fully trusted him. Programmatically, Wallace was closer to Ed Reid, director of the state's powerful League of Municipalities, than to Folsom.[34]

Wallace's years in the legislature were more about production than any predetermined philosophy. He introduced more bills than most of his peers and successfully navigated his trade school bill into law. Years later, Wallace would point to his record of industrial development as his most important accomplishment in the state house. The Wallace Act authorized municipalities to use deficit financing of plants, industrial facilities, and equipment to entice new industrial clients to the state.[35]

Wallace was twice voted one of the outstanding members of the legislature by the capitol press corps and supplemented the meager salary of a legislator with a small law practice based out of Rufus Little's Clayton drugstore. Even so, it was a Spartan existence. They lived in an attic with paper-thin walls, beset by hungry rats, and the home life was left to Lurleen who worked during the day and cared for baby daughter Bobbie Jo at night. George continued to spend his evenings networking with the powerful in Montgomery, Clayton, or wherever a conversation, poker game, or an evening about town could be found. Despite his burgeoning notoriety in Barbour County, Wallace was unable to link political contacts into a lucrative stable of clients. Of course, Barbour County folk were more likely to be destitute and in need of sliding scale fees than ready to pay top dollar to keep a barrister on retainer. More to the point, Wallace was never interested in wealth or its trappings. His preference was power.[36]

One method for increasing his power and adding money to the family checking account was leaving the legislature and running for the Third District Circuit Court judgeship. The race was a good fit for Wallace's personal ambitions on two fronts. The seat covered Barbour, Bullock, and Dale counties, which allowed him to build on strong support from Barbour while extending his future political reach elsewhere in South Alabama. It was also a midterm 1952 election, and Wallace did not have to risk his legislative post if he lost the campaign. Wallace thrashed his opponent, state senator Preston Clayton, by depicting him as too aristocratic to sympathize with ordinary folk's troubles. With three kids in tow—Bobbie Jo, Peggy Sue, and George Jr.—Lurleen insisted George use his new salary, eight thousand dollars a year, to provide more suitable accommodations.[37]

The Wallaces did purchase an old rental house near the Clayton High School, but nothing else changed. George continued to spend time and money on politics and Lurleen was left to solve the daily tasks of running a household that was chronically low on funds. On at least two occasions, Lurleen, frustrated with what her husband's authorized biographer called "virtual imprisonment," borrowed a car, drove until she found her husband at a poker game, and dropped the children off with him in total exasperation. Despite her misgivings, Lurleen continued to support her husband and even created a legal file of opinions, case law, and jury charges for quick reference while he was on the bench. If George Wallace was equal parts energy and ambition, Lurleen was equal parts resilience and grace.[38]

By all accounts, Wallace was an impartial and honorable judge, meting out punishment regardless of race and tending to favor the trampled underclass, especially when vested interests looked down on them or spoke disapprovingly of them in court. David Frost, a black man whose colorful life ran him afoul of the law on several occasions, found Wallace to be "a fair man" on the bench. Wallace resisted the suggestion of Circuit Solicitor Seymore Trammell to sentence Frost to prison for a run-in with a white man, and instead gave him a seventy-five-dollar fine. On another occasion, Wallace gave Frost a day in jail for contempt of court but hours later sent word for the sheriff to send him home. On several occasions, Wallace counseled juries to award civil damages in excess of the amount plaintiffs had requested. Black attorneys, such as Fred Gray and J. L. Chestnut Jr., received treatment from Wallace they had never experienced in other courtrooms. "George Wallace," Chestnut recalled, "was the first judge to call me 'mister' in a courtroom." Wallace embraced the judiciary; it provided an opportunity for independence and autonomy within a structure of tradition. And the nature of the court system in Alabama allowed Wallace to intercede on behalf of those who needed help. In no time, Wallace had significantly increased his popularity in southeast Alabama. Pete Turnham, a traveling salesman who would soon embark on his own forty-year career in the state legislature, remembers the acclaim Wallace received at the local diner. Wallace made the rounds in the café each day at noon, slapping backs and shaking hands and receiving the royal treatment from the assembled locals. On a subsequent visit when Wallace and Turnham ate together, the salesman noticed his two-piece fried chicken dinner featured a skimpy leg and a wing while the judge's contained two plump breasts that overlapped the plate. Had he been more interested in the scholarly side of the law, Wallace could have had a brilliant career as a jurist. But ambition—the desire to be governor—was greater than family, wealth, public service, or any other consideration.[39]

Two years after Wallace's election to the bench, race emerged as a front-burner issue. When the U.S. Supreme Court ruled that separate schools were inherently unequal and later ruled that affirmative action be taken to correct the inequality, the issue of race flowed so thoroughly through Alabama politics that even judges found themselves immersed. Over the next decade, every action taken by the federal government would be evaluated by white Alabama on the basis of whether it was an attack on southern traditions, white morality, and home rule. And in the blink of an eye, a protest movement came of age to threaten segregation from the grass-roots level and make Alabama center stage for the unfolding drama of the civil rights movement. A year after *Brown,* Folsom, in his second term, invited Harlem, New York, congressman Adam Clayton Powell to come to the governor's mansion for a cocktail. White Alabamians were aghast at the temerity of the governor opening the people's mansion to a Negro. Rosa Parks simply and symbolically told the world that dignity was more important than tradition. Twenty-six-year-old Martin Luther King molded the philosophical foundation of a movement when he organized a boycott to make Park's statement stand. Angry mobs took to the Tuscaloosa streets to prevent Autherine Lucy from integrating the University of Alabama. A weak governor, a defiant University of Alabama board of trustees, and the threat of violence kept Lucy from attending the school of her choice. Attorney General John Patterson successfully kicked the National Association for the Advancement of Colored people out of the state. Segregation, long since settled in the minds of white Alabama, was suddenly under a two-front attack from Washington and community activists everywhere.

For his part, Judge George Wallace announced that he favored his own passive resistance plan for resisting the enforcement of federal civil rights initiatives. "There is no law," Wallace asserted, "which says we must cooperate with federal authorities in the harassment of citizens. I hope no local law enforcement officials will aid in any of the investigations under pending bills." The judge announced that any FBI agents who came to his jurisdiction to investigate the exclusion of blacks from grand juries would be "arrested and put in jail for contempt of court." Wallace became a featured speaker at Citizens' Council rallies and stepped up his contacts with old colleagues in the legislature. Martin Luther King was also in the process of changing perceptions about obeying laws thought to be immoral. "In the black community," Bayard Rustin recounted to Howell Raines, "going to jail had been a badge of dishonor. Martin made going to jail like receiving a Ph.D."[40]

Only one thing was needed to bring Wallace gubernatorial-candidate credibility in the new post-*Brown* landscape: sever all public ties with Folsom. The Cullman giant, back in office after a 1954 victory without a runoff, wanted no part of the tide of massive resistance sweeping across the Deep South. According to an old Alabama saw, many folks voted for Folsom on election day, but a month after inauguration day it was nearly impossible to find someone who would admit it. As forces gradually aligned to make Alabama center stage in the unfolding civil rights drama, Folsom was now viewed by Alabamians from Woodville to Suggsville not as a savior, but as part of the problem. Two years after a landslide victory in the gubernatorial election, Folsom failed to capture a quarter of the state vote for Democratic national committeeman. In public, Wallace cited Folsom's failure to appoint Billy Watson, a Wallace political ally and confidante, to a Barbour County Department of Revenue post as his reason for shunning Folsom. Privately, it was made clear across the state that Wallace was no longer tolerating Folsom's soft stance on segregation.[41]

Wallace began planning his 1958 gubernatorial run two years before the campaign kicked off but had already spent a lifetime imagining every speech he would make on the back of a flatbed truck stage, every weathered hand he would shake, and every tow-headed boy and girl whose head he would pat in the quest for votes. "Wallace went to bed thinking about votes," former press secretary Bill Jones recalled, "and he woke up the next morning thinking about votes." Wallace had increased his name recognition throughout South Alabama and his call for passive resistance to FBI grand jury pool investigations had been picked up in the *Birmingham News, Mobile Register,* and *Montgomery Advertiser.* His 1957 appearance before a congressional committee to testify against pending civil rights legislation generated some exposure across the South. Yet his major opponent in the race, Attorney General John Patterson, had name recognition all over the state. Patterson's father, Albert, had been killed as a result of his crusading efforts to rid Phenix City, Alabama, of organized crime elements so notorious that the army warned nearby Fort Benning, Georgia, soldiers to stay away. At the time of his death, Albert had won the Democratic primary nomination for attorney general—tantamount to election in the days of one political party—and John was later tapped by the Democratic Executive Committee to assume the post. John Patterson's ascension to his father's position and the daily headlines that came from the imposition of martial law in Phenix City, the investigation and subsequent trials of criminals and elected officials, made him a household name in Alabama.[42]

Initially, the Wallace camp, uncharacteristically out of step with Alabama voters throughout the campaign, thought Bay Minette newspaper publisher Jimmy Faulkner was their most serious competition. Faulkner had earned 25.9 percent of the gubernatorial vote in 1954 finishing second to the Folsom juggernaut, but won five counties and nearly won several others. A long tradition of Alabama politics virtually dictated that the runner-up from the previous election was the undisputed front-runner in the next. But Patterson's image was further enriched by Hollywood in *The Phenix City Story,* a sensationalistic movie about his father's murder, and by the television show *This Is Your Life.* Historian Dan Carter records Wallace's exasperation at campaigning against the man and myth of John Patterson: "I'm running against a man whose father was assassinated. How'm I supposed to follow an act like that?" The resulting publicity, coupled with Patterson's racial politics placed him in the front. Yet, two weeks before the election, the disorganized Wallace campaign staff still perceived Faulkner to be their most significant threat.[43]

As much as Wallace had dreamed of capturing the governorship, his campaign was ill equipped for the challenge. Underfunded and often flying by the seat of their pants, the Wallace campaign learned painful lessons about scheduling, image, and, most importantly, message. The campaign was slow to respond to correspondence, a death blow to fund-raising and maintaining momentum on a ward-by-ward basis. Instead of targeting areas where his message would be well received, Wallace talked to every group no matter its size or location, and nearly exhausted himself during the process. Even the campaign's slogan, "Help Keep Alabama Southern," was too vague to effectively communicate its intended prosegregation statement. In 1958, Wallace was not nearly as cocksure as he would become in future years. In assessing his second-place finish in the primary Wallace expressed surprise at his performance. "I was just trying to get in the run-off," Wallace admitted, "and I made it."[44]

With the fourteen-man field thinned to two, the similarities and differences between the remaining candidates were spotlighted. Both candidates were unequivocal in their support for segregation. "You either were well grounded on that issue," Patterson later noted, "or you might as well forget it." The *Birmingham World*, a middle-class black newspaper, detected little difference between the two: "All the candidates for governor ran on the segregation issue; each trying to show how much they were out of line with obedience to the orders of the highest court in the land." Wallace announced he would close Alabama schools rather than allow them to be mixed. "If the federal courts try to integrate the schools in Dallas County," he promised Selma residents, "they're going to be pointing bayonets at empty school houses." But white voters noticed a harder edge to Patterson. Perhaps it was the lingering stigma of Wallace's old association with Folsom or his time on the Board of Trustees of Tuskegee Institute, but the reality is that many white Alabamians were not quite sure about his commitment to forestalling integration. Patterson understood this fact about Wallace implicitly. "George Wallace was considered soft on the issue in the '58 race," Patterson recalled, "and that's one of the things that beat him." Compounding this lingering notion was Patterson's crowning achievement of using an obscure technicality to force the NAACP out of Alabama.[45]

Beyond Patterson's ability to tout his segregation record was his ability to enlist the state's most socially conservative campaign labor force, the Ku Klux Klan. The Klan was closely tied to the Patterson bid, primarily through campaign director Charlie Meriwether, and Klan members traveled in and out of campaign offices on a daily basis. In terms of distributing literature, the Klan had no peer in the state. "They could blanket the state with your signs in one night," Patterson remembered. The Klan also circulated the word that Wallace was receiving the notorious bloc vote, a not-too-subtle suggestion that black Alabamians had chosen Wallace as their candidate. And while Patterson publicly announced he wanted "anybody's vote who's qualified to vote in Alabama, regardless of who he is," and refused to comment directly on Klan ties, Wallace, following the lead of trusted advisor and *Montgomery Advertiser* editor Grover Hall Jr., repudiated the Klan. "Patterson chatters about the gangster ghosts of Phenix City," Wallace charged, "while he himself is rolling with the new wave of the Klan and its terrible tradition of lawlessness." The NAACP, noting Wallace's repeated criticisms of the Klan, including a thirty-minute television special, issued a public endorsement of Wallace.[46]

In the racially charged atmosphere of 1958, Wallace was never able to gain any voter traction with speeches touting education, better medical care, and industrial development. With Patterson running to the right of Wallace on race and having achieved celebrity status due to his father's tragic death, the outcome was already decided. Wallace's last-ditch attempt to woo back social conservatives by brandishing Hugo Black as a traitor to the South only served to keep some moderates at home on election day. The attorney general captured almost 56 percent of the vote and beat the Barbour County judge by nearly 65,000 votes. Disconsolate at his defeat, Wallace quickly surmised the key factor in his defeat and vowed never to let it happen again: "No son-of-a-bitch will ever out-nigger me again."[47]

In a short time, Wallace overcame the bitterness of losing to Patterson and found a way to vault himself into the headlines with the next election still three years away. The Civil Rights Commission, a new division of the Justice Department, had been charged with investigating voter registration chicanery in the South and had limited power to seize county records. When Wallace learned that the Civil Rights Commission intended to review records in Barbour and Bullock counties, he engineered a surefire way to put himself between the Justice Department and the records. After asking colleagues to file petitions alleging voting improprieties, Wallace impounded the records and announced to anyone who would listen that he planned to impanel a grand jury to make a full investigation. Picking up the scent, the Civil Rights Commission immediately subpoenaed the records and ordered them brought to Montgomery. Wallace had baited the commission into a trap designed for no other purpose than to put himself in the headlines.[48]

John Patterson and his team of legal advisors offered professional advice on how and when to turn over records to the commission. Not surprisingly, Wallace declined their offer since he had orchestrated, at least in his own mind, exactly how he wanted the matter resolved. After being served with the subpoena, Wallace blasted the commission and promised to incarcerate any commission representative who tried to look at the records. Wallace wanted the commission to enlist Frank Johnson, a former classmate at the University of

Alabama and a federal judge in Montgomery, to order him to give up the records. Ideally, Johnson would give Wallace ten to fifteen days in jail for contempt of court and then his new prosouthern, anti-Washington image would sweep him into the governor's mansion. What could be more heroic than going to jail to preserve the concepts of states' rights and home rule?[49]

Unfortunately for Wallace, Johnson would not play ball. At a late-night meeting at Johnson's home in Montgomery, Wallace pleaded with the judge to find him guilty of contempt and sentence him to a small amount of jail time. Johnson, according to his biographer, cared little for Wallace's ultimate political goals and vowed to give him a stiff sentence and make an example of him. Flummoxed by Johnson's unwillingness to do him a political favor, Wallace, who had some hesitation about spending time in Alabama's medieval penal system anyway, changed course and found a way to avoid a lengthy sentence while still claiming credit for refusing to turn over the records. According to a plan devised by Wallace, Seymore Trammell, and Glenn Curlee, Wallace would officially turn the records over to a grand jury, regale the public about the sanctity of standing up to the social engineers in Washington, and then privately encourage the grand jury to turn over the material.[50]

[handwritten margin note: *Wanted to go to jail.*]

The plan came off well enough even though Wallace had to appear before Judge Johnson on the contempt charge. Though Wallace pled guilty to the charge of failing to turn the records over to the commission, Johnson was well aware that the records had already passed from Wallace to the grand jury and on to the Civil Rights Commission. After scolding Wallace for his "devious" schemes, Johnson pronounced Wallace not guilty of contempt and announced to the world that he had in fact personally facilitated the transfer of the voter rolls. Wallace, claiming victory despite doing what he vowed he would not, would have none of Johnson's lecture and exaggerated the issue until it had become a mini War between the States. "I plead guilty to failing to deliver the voter registration records to the Civil Rights Commission. . . . I was willing to risk my freedom. . . . This 1959 attempt to have a second Sherman's March to the Sea has been stopped in the Cradle of the Confederacy." Not content with the favorable press coverage, including editorials from several of the state's most important dailies, Wallace wrote the official grand jury report of the entire proceeding, doling out high praise for his own courage. Politically savvy Alabamians understood that Wallace's grandstanding was his opening salvo in the 1962 campaign. Congressman Carl Elliott began keeping a clipping file on Wallace in case they crossed paths.[51]

By inventing a crisis, falling on the sword for southern honor and Alabama tradition, and flailing away at the federal dragon named Frank Johnson, Wallace wrote the road map for his 1962 campaign. For the next three years, Wallace crisscrossed the state, demonizing the federal government, backing segregation in the most unabashed manner possible, and extirpating Frank Johnson as a "carpet-baggin', scalawaggin', integratin' bald-faced liar." Clearly, it was good politics to blame blacks and the federal government for state and regional problems. "He always had the right enemies," reporter Bob Ingram noted of Wallace. With the occasional exception of the Kennedys, John and Robert, Wallace never mentioned any name on the stump except Frank Johnson. Press reports were incredulous that "Wallace refrained from attacking any of his opponents. Even when attacked by others, Wallace continued to mind his own business." What the state's news hounds did not grasp was that after 1958 Wallace was never running against any particular opponent; he was running against the federal government and its encroachment on southern tradition.[52]

The 1962 campaign featured a noticeably harder edge from Wallace on racial matters. He termed the NAACP "the same people who had us eating acorns and walking barefoot," called the supporters of his runoff opponent Ryan deGraffenreid "softies, sissy-britches, moderates, liberals, and NAACP members," and lashed out at the media. "I'll bet [*Birmingham News* publisher Robert] Newhouse hasn't been to Alabama more than once since he bought the paper, yet he is trying to dictate state policies. Well let me tell you, nobody from New York is going to have anything to do with the policies of this state when I'm your governor." Though he had already campaigned for the state house twice, the bench once, and the governor's mansion once, Wallace hit his stride as a campaign force in 1962. Mixing elements from his youth, his experiences in the military and driving trucks, his impeccable memory for names and places, and his clever oversimplifications about segregation and the federal government, Wallace took Alabama by storm. Emboldened by his growing fame and fully able to paint class, race, and century-old concepts about white southern morality into a black-and-white mural of right or wrong, honor or corruption, victory or pain, Wallace was now able to take a disparate set of white Alabamians on a lazy summer afternoon and mold them into an inferno of righteous indignation. His performance, *Montgomery Advertiser* editor Grover Hall summarized, was "one of the most brilliant runs in modern Alabama history."[53]

Despite Wallace's allegations of black bloc voting for deGraffenreid, the challenger was campaigning just as hard to forestall integration as the front-runner. "I believe in segregation," deGraffenreid promised voters. "I believe in it as strong as a man can believe in anything." In fact, deGraffenreid was no moderate on the issue. He helped write several segregation laws, including school placement laws, school district laws, and freedom of choice laws. Frustrated by having to prove his white supremacy credentials, deGraffenreid blurted out at one campaign appearance that "there's not a man in Alabama who wants to preserve segregation more than I do. I'm southern and I'm Alabamian from the tips of my toes to the roots of my hair." When Bull Connor endorsed Wallace as the only choice who could keep "those get-rich-quick so-called Negro preachers, Martin Luther King and [Fred] Shuttlesworth" out of Alabama, an exasperated deGraffenreid could only respond that he "was a better segregationist than either Connor or Wallace." DeGraffenreid's campaign literature included the charge that Wallace had received the bloc vote in 1958, that as a state representative he had voted against a state plan to withhold funding from integrated schools, and that he had no "workable program to keep segregation in our schools, colleges, parks, and playgrounds."[54]

The only difference between the candidates on the issue of segregation was the method of preserving it. Wallace used evocative physical imagery to describe the actions he would take to thwart integration. In stump speeches where Wallace often broke away from his notes whenever he saw the crowd lilting, segregation became a jihad, a noble effort to honor the vision of keen ancestors who wrested the South from its sworn enemies. In contrast, deGraffenreid vowed to create an Alabama Department of Human Rights to lead litigation efforts aimed at preserving segregation in the courts, not in the streets. "I don't want anybody deliberately creating chaos and turmoil," deGraffenreid declared at a May 15 rally, "at the front door of the schools where my children are going. I'm not looking for a fight by stirring up trouble." DeGraffenreid termed his legal strategy a "positive approach to segregation" and warned that Wallace's threats would lead to violence and immediate integration. Because Wallace's defense of segregation seemed to be more overtly masculine, deGraffenreid's rhetoric about the issue and his bleats that the Wallace campaign was spreading unfounded rumors about his wife fell on deaf ears. Forty years after the election, George Wallace Jr. noted that his father had run a conservative race in 1962 while deGraffenreid campaigned as Wallace had in 1958.[55]

Alabama voters grasped the differences between the two on the only issue that mattered in 1962. In a letter to the editor of the *Montgomery Advertiser,* Kay Dickens expressed a sentiment many came to believe about the 1962 race. "Who would Bobby Kennedy like least to be our governor," Dickens wrote. "In the final analysis, we do not have a choice—we can and must elect Mr. Wallace as our next governor." Mrs. Rillar Bowden was convinced deGraffenreid could not be trusted because Jim Folsom, who finished a close third to deGraffenreid, was supporting him. "Now that Big Jim and deGraff have joined hands in the run-off," Bowden declared, "I'm again for Wallace." The historian of antebellum Alabama politics Lewy Dorman was convinced that a deGraffenreid victory would make Folsom a "kingmaker" and give him undue influence in the new administration. In fact, Folsom became a significant issue because of his racial moderation. "If we are willing for Adam Clayton Powell to be entertained in the governor's mansion," H. P. Cowling wrote, "then vote against

George Wallace. If we are willing to keep Powell, Folsom, and liquors from the governor's mansion, then cast your vote for George Wallace, who is a God-fearing, Christian gentleman."[56]

As Wallace himself stated many times on the campaign trail, the issue of segregation left no room for middle ground. When Jim Dinsmore, editor of the Auburn University *Plainsman,* wrote that "integration is the only answer to the Negro problem in this country," he was twice hung in effigy. Auburn president Ralph Draughon responded that Dinsmore "has no limitation on extremism. He doesn't represent the thinking of the institution." Dean of Students James Foy called him "highly confused." The charged atmosphere rendered deGraffenreid's legal strategies for blocking integration a weak alternative compared to Wallace's calls for physical defiance.[57]

Some Alabamians viewed the differences in the candidates through the lens of religion. In Alabama, Sunday and Wednesday services, dinner on the grounds, and biannual revivals were as much a part of the fabric of life as Roy Acuff on the radio and the aroma of sweet potato pie in the oven. No less an authority than Billy Graham described Alabama as a place where "more people go to church . . . than any other place in the world." Though Dinsmore called integration "Christian and moral," only a small minority of white Alabamians sought to distance themselves from traditional Baptist and Methodist imperatives against social activism and integration. More often than not, theological liberals and social gospelers were quietly asked to find another church. The vast majority of white churches and pastors viewed integration as a moral question decided by their Creator and enforced by their ancestors. Leon Macon, editor of the *Alabama Baptist*—the popular publication of the state's leading denomination—wrote forcefully of the danger to the flock from social engineering. "We live in times," Macon asserted, "when minority groups are very aggressive. . . . Minority groups have no right to superimpose their positions upon the majority." For Macon, as well as many others in the pulpits and pews across the state, the social gospel was "one of the greatest scourges upon the church," and he warned repeatedly that "do-gooders" were "forcing situations on people they are not ready to handle."[58]

Wallace's segregation rhetoric, nonstop campaigning, and raw political skills were in perfect lockstep with Alabamians. He carried almost 56 percent of the vote and beat deGraffenreid by more than seventy thousand votes. The thoughts and words sown in 1962 were about to reap actions that would catapult George Wallace to heights he never imagined. Over the course of the next four years he would become the most powerful governor in Alabama history, the most recognized governor in the country, a regional spokesman, a national candidate for president, and one of the most important figures in southern political history. In endorsing deGraffenreid, the *Huntsville Times* concluded that

"Alabama must present a better image to the nation if we are to gain needed new industry, attract highly skilled and qualified men from other states and keep within our borders those we develop here." George Wallace was about to create several images of Alabama that would last throughout his lifetime and create an enduring legacy for Alabama well into the twenty-first century.[59]

2

Reconstruction Redux / 1963

In 1963, George Wallace found Alabama ripe for harvest.

Beset by staggering poverty, a prevailing sentiment of anti-intellectualism, and decades of ineffective, inattentive, or just plain incompetent governance, Alabamians had come to accept comparative inferiority and underdog status as a byproduct of their culture. Even within the relatively underdeveloped community of the eleven states of the old Confederacy, Alabama, along with its western neighbor, Mississippi, had developed a unique cultural and social stigma to match its economic malaise. In some respects, both Alabama's white and black populace had been waiting for decades for one of their own to bring them out into the sunshine and into a place of comparative equality with the rest of the fifty states.

Despite possessing roughly 10 percent of the nation's natural resources; climatic and meteorological blessings that make agriculture bountiful; a bustling industrial epicenter, Birmingham; and a commercial seaport, Mobile, the state had never developed a fully mixed economy capable of sustaining and elevating its own. In 1962—when George Wallace was campaigning to reach the office he had spent a lifetime waiting for and vowing to "face our enemies face to face, hip to hip, and toe to toe, and never surrender your governor's office to these carpetbaggers, scalawags, and pollywogs"—the average Alabamian had a per capita income of $1,401. The average American was earning some $800 more per year. As baby boomers across other parts of the nation contemplated college, a white collar job, and a ticket to suburbia, many Alabamians, ill equipped by a profoundly stultified education system, were facing a future in the mines, mills, or dirt. The etiology of poverty in Alabama is a complex tale characterized by a frightening cocktail of educational inadequacy, medieval public health services, paternalistic elites, an underdeveloped middle class, regressive taxation, unusually powerful interest groups such as the Farm Bureau and Alabama Power, generations of agricultural work cast against the recent backdrop of mechanization and corporate farming, and ineffectual state government.[1]

Alabamians had some portent of the contentious era they were entering. Wallace's predecessor, John Patterson, had been swept into office largely on the strength of his presumed fitness as an ardent defender of segregation and the enthusiasm of extreme racial conservatives who supported him. Patterson did little personally to court the Klan, although he did speak at some of their rallies, but his campaign staff, led by the highly organized Charles Meriwether, did nothing to discourage a closer relationship either. On more than a few occasions, prominent Klansmen, including Robert Shelton, were found on the premises of Patterson campaign headquarters in Tuscaloosa or Birmingham, sometimes necessitating the cartoonlike hiding of Klansmen in broom closets until they could be sneaked out through basements or back doors.[2]

Even public disclosure of Klan ties to the campaign did little to derail the Patterson express. His own campaign personnel concocted a letter on official campaign stationery with a forged Patterson signature documenting the close relationship between the candidate and "my good friend Robert Shelton." Patterson, who had no knowledge of the letter and had not yet officially met the Klan leader, was found on the Los Angeles television sound stage of *This Is Your Life* by *Montgomery Advertiser* reporter Bob Ingram. The scribe had procured a copy of the letter, which was being widely disseminated to Klansmen and Klan-friendly voters, and coyly asked Patterson, the current attorney general of the state, if he knew Shelton. The next day, the *Advertiser* ran the story of Patterson's denial next to a copy of the letter, purportedly signed by him. Patterson never rebuked the Klan.[3]

As governor, Patterson faced a multitude of issues including proration, an all too frequent aspect of state economic life when revenue projections exceed actual revenue and force the state to make sharp cuts in existing budgets. Yet his administration, which was on the watch while sit-ins and freedom rider activity escalated often with violent repercussions, remained popular primarily because of his anti-integration sentiment and rhetoric.

Though segregation and white supremacy had been pillars of Alabama political life, not all the state's key politicians were monolithically conservative. Lister Hill and John Sparkman were longtime U.S. senators, and both used their access, influence, and clout to bring home the bacon. Hill, along with George Norris, was responsible for the massive New Deal–era Tennessee Valley Authority and worked steadfastly to prevent privatization activists from wresting control. Sparkman, who in contrast to Hill rose to greatness from poverty, contributed significantly to the changing landscape of Huntsville with Redstone Arsenal and eventually the George C. Marshall Space Flight Center. Representative Carl Elliot, the son of a sharecropper, was instrumental in passing the National Defense Education Act, which provided loans for students in math and science education. The most significant aspect of all this relative liberalism is the amicable relationship between the state and the federal government, which was viewed as an economic facilitator, not an incipient instrument for social engineering.[4]

In the wake of the *Brown v. Board of Education* decision, the working relationship between Alabama and the federal government began to change. In 1958, the issue of race was dominant; in 1950 and even 1954, when Jim Folsom wrapped up the Democratic gubernatorial nomination just weeks before the *Brown* decision, Alabamians were substantially less myopic. Governor Patterson, who vocally supported his friend John F. Kennedy for the presidency in 1960, began to suffer from what he today calls "trying to carry water on both shoulders." That is, Patterson had to talk and act one way to curry favor with Washington and another way to win support at home. The weight on one of the shoulders was removed in the wake of the brutal beating of freedom riders and the burning of their bus in Anniston; after this, Patterson's calls were no longer welcome at the White House. The Kennedys collectively blamed Patterson for much of the carnage and doubted his ability to control the state's anti-integration zealots. Although the end of the Kennedy-Patterson relationship may have cost the Alabama governor the chance for an appointed Washington post after his term ended in early 1963, it may actually have helped him politically at home, especially in the wake of violence and federalized troops at the University of Mississippi during James Meredith's enrollment. One Alabamian, Virginia Congelton, summed up the sentiment of many in the state concerning the president. "The thing he and his brother Bobby did in Oxford was disgraceful. They did it just for the votes of the colored people."[5]

The increased civil rights activities across the South brought a heightened awareness not only of the present, but of the past. Stories of the Civil War and the perceived horrors of Reconstruction begin in Alabama on the front porch and at grandparents' knees. To many Alabamians, the Dunning school—the shorthand name for the school of thought that Reconstruction was excessively punitive on the white South—was not just an interpretation of history, it was a time-tested fact passed down by generations from a time when blacks and the federal government combined to shackle the South with social experimentation, rampant debt and corruption, and sexual license, all at the point of a bayonet. The definitive history of the state when Wallace entered the governor's office was still Albert Burton Moore's 1934 *History of Alabama*, which characterized slaves as "contented and carefree and sentimentally attached to their masters," slave owners as "elegant knights," and the wives of masters as "veritable Samaritans." Moore, who expressed admiration for Wallace in correspondence to the governor, and Reconstruction scholar Walter Fleming kept alive the myth of unchecked postbellum chaos. According to this interpretation, only the justified actions of southern patriots threw off the yoke of the Reconstruction burden and allowed the South to restore home rule. Moore supervised Alabama's Civil War Commemoration activities and, like Wallace, connected the civil rights movement with the looming specter of international communism. "If we do not understand and respect our tradition, we shall be easy prey for communist brain-washers. Communist propagandists first seek to ridicule the traditions—economic, social, religious, and political—of a people. . . . The attack of communism upon freedom is unrelenting and uncompromising." Even the state's official coloring book for children decried Reconstruction as "a sad time for the South" when "groups of northerners seeking riches and power streamed into the South." Wallace stoked these flames with repeated references to the old "Pittsburgh Plus" discriminatory freight rates and the coming storm of a second Reconstruction. "We were the most oppressed people and now that we have shaken off those economic shackles, they are trying to get at us by unsettling our social relationships." Wallace's infamous inaugural address included a reference to the evils of Reconstruction and well into his first term he was regularly complaining that Alabama was still recovering from the burdens of "plundering Reconstruction governments." For Wallace, as for many other Alabamians, Reconstruction, not the Civil War, was the lingering stigma of southern history.[6]

As a social and political philosophy, white supremacy had been around since before Alabama reached statehood, but in the years after Reconstruction, it became thoroughly institutionalized at nearly every level of social and political thought. In 1904 the state ballot added the Democratic rooster as its symbol with the motto "white supremacy for the right." Section 1 of the State Democratic Party bylaws mandated the "white supremacy" label as the official emblem of the party. White supremacy was not so much a mantra of the fringe Right as it was standard operating procedure for mainstream white Alabamians.[7]

These antiblack and anti–federal government lessons were strongly reinforced from the pulpits of Alabama's predominately Baptist and Methodist churches. Conversely, in black Baptist churches, the gospel was being used as a springboard for equality and a scriptural guarantee of ultimate triumph and deliverance. Indeed black ministers in the years since Reconstruction had assumed prominent community roles, were responsible for organizing almost every successful black protest movement, and remained economically self-reliant and virtually independent of white control. Meanwhile across town, the rafters of white Baptist churches were resonating with biblical imperatives to maintain the status quo and limit the prerogative of the local church to evangelism, not community consciousness or social justice. In those same churches, one might from time to time hear a sermon on the Good Samaritan with the emphasis on the wise decision of the hero to take the injured Jew to a local inn, not to his own home. Leon Macon, the editor of the state's largest religious publication, the *Alabama Baptist*, was a religious and cultural conservative who encouraged his flock to hold fast to their traditions and avoid social engineering. All this pulpit rattling did reach the pews. Alabamian Mrs. Catherine Patrick, in a letter to the editor to the *Mobile Register*, summed up the feelings many whites had for the religious ties to the civil rights movement. "Since so many outsiders have come into our state with all this freedom talk and use of the Bible for a cover-up, I really don't know" if Alabama is still a good place to raise children.[8]

Political elites coopted the social conservatism inherent in Protestant, evangelical ideology to rationalize their own racism. Bruce Henderson, who played a prominent role in the state's Citizens' Councils and the rock-ribbed Alabama Foundation and was a prominent legislator and gubernatorial candidate, was unequivocal in correspondence: "I am a segregationist because I believe separation to be according to the pattern of our creator and is one of our creator's ways of separating the different levels of civilization morally and spiritually for his own purpose." In the early 1960s, Alabama religious officials and politicians were openly critical of Billy Graham for his perceived moderation on segregation. During the 1960 presidential race, more than a few Baptists shared the sentiment of Mary Hawkins, secretary of the Young People's Department at the First Baptist Church in Foley, Alabama: "The Catholic Church has shown it does not plan to let Kennedy be independent of it! . . . A Catholic president would cause our nation to lose its religious liberty and the separation of church and state." Governor John Patterson found it almost impossible to hold together a fragile coalition of Alabama delegates at the 1960 Democratic Convention for John Kennedy, partly over the issue of the Massachusetts senator's Catholicism.[9]

Baptists and Methodists hardly had a monopoly on fundamentalism. Even denominations or sects with comparatively less strident superstructures tended to adopt segregationist interpretations of their faith. Cleveland Avenue Church of Christ minister O. B. Porterfield urged out-of-state preachers to stay away from Alabama, castigated them for "parading up and down the street with outside agitators, law breakers, beatniks, fornicators, nasty people, long bearded men, harlots and every other type person to stir up racial discord in Montgomery and Selma and in Alabama. . . . Men like Martin Luther King and Ralph Abernathy, that have brought so much strife and trouble to this area, to call them reverend, or any man is sacrilegious, a down right sin and a disgrace in the eyes of Almighty God, and I am opposed to calling them or anyone else by any such titles." Even in more moderate Presbyterian circles, anti-integration preaching was commonplace. Robert Strong cautioned his Trinity Presbyterian Church: "I do maintain that the religious overtones of the civil rights demonstrations should never deceive Bible-believing people. To join in with these demonstrations that are under the guidance of Martin Luther King is to be engaged in the most serious kind of religious compromise.... I cannot be persuaded that it is right to cooperate with him or with the organization which he heads." This religious paradox between white and black churches was really nothing new and dates as far back as the antebellum period where slaves were inundated with biblical admonitions to "obey your masters," but processed the Gospel themselves in terms of liberation from bondage.[10]

Equally as traditional in Alabama history was a preoccupation with public integration as a gateway to open sexual relations between the races. Depictions of lusty blacks as marauding sexual predators date to antebellum years but escalated significantly in the years after the Civil War and peaked with specific events such as the Scottsboro Boys case. Both elite and common Alabamians thought miscegenation, often referred to with the code phrase race mixing, was plausible if not predictable as soon as schools, water fountains, and movie theaters were desegregated. Alabamian Thomas Greaves observed that "one objective of having separate schools is to prevent inter-racial marriage and amalgamation of the races such as has already started in a large part of the Western Hemisphere." Black Belt state senator Walter Givhan warned a Citizens' Council crowd that the ultimate objective of the NAACP was really to "open the bedroom door of our white women to the Negro." Even blacks felt the palpable fears of their supposed demonic penchants according to this sexual mythology. In an oral history, S. Q. Bryant from Alabama A&M University admitted as much. "When I first came [to Alabama A&M] you couldn't hardly have drug a white woman coming across this campus alone. She would have been afraid. She was so drenched so much in this propaganda the white man has set up that she would have believed some black boy over here would have eaten her up."[11]

All these collective influences shaped Alabama history and created a platform from which Wallace could package himself as a defender of the traditions first learned on the front porch, a protector of pure white womanhood, God, and the heritage of the Confederacy; an advocate for the downtrodden, under-appreciated, and impoverished; and a public spokesman for the virtue, intelligence, and refinement of white Alabama. Wallace might be crude and transparent to outsiders, but within white Alabama he was reasoned, rational, and respected. Outside the South, Wallace was just another segregationist, albeit one with better raw political skills. But at home in the Heart of Dixie, Wallace was a gallant knight trudging off to battle the dragons of a prophesied Second Reconstruction. Only the slow burn of racial change, begun in the aftermath of World War II, fanned by the perceived activism of the Warren court and its monumental decisions, stoked by civil rights marchers, demonstrators, and protestors, and unleashed with the looming reality of mandated change in the highways and byways of Alabama could create the environment where Wallace could accumulate power heretofore unmatched in state history.

But with his uncanny ability to remember a name, punctuate an applause line, and subconsciously gauge the tenor of an audience, Wallace could surely have been successful in another era. John P. Kohn, a Montgomery lawyer, judge, sometime author, and Wallace confidant (who once proclaimed in a public speech "I am an unreconstructed Confederate, I am one hundred percent seg-regationist, I am one hundred percent racist. . . . I will never believe and never have believed that all people are born equal") understood Wallace's ambition and rare skills. "If George had parachuted into the Albanian countryside in the spring of 1962, he would have been the head of a collective farm by the fall, a member of the Communist party by mid-winter, on his way to the district party meeting as a delegate by the following year, and a member of the Com-intern in two or three years. Hell, George could believe whatever he needed to believe." Kohn's statement is an exaggeration, but it conveys a point about George Wallace's essence as an unmatched political campaigner and oppor-tunist. Nevertheless, only in the chaotic environment of regional, national, and international flux that characterized the early 1960s, only in the Deep South where the people can feel the ghosts of their history and hold dear such a pro-found sense of place, only in a state like Alabama with a clear inferiority com-plex and a myriad of social, economic, and political constraints, and only in an environment where faith, family, and honor are woven together into a fisted knot too strong to untangle, could George Wallace become so thoroughly in command of a people who decided for a time that they would rather break than bend.[12]

Decades after Wallace took office, his rhetoric seems ridiculous and his ac-tions seem radical if not reprehensible. Yet to many Alabamians living in a world of apocalyptic prophecy being fulfilled before their very eyes, Wallace seemed as reasonable as spring planting and fall harvest. Thus, the true chal-lenge of understanding the how and why of George Wallace is found not in staged stands in the schoolhouse door, but in the bones and sinew of Alabama history. It is, therefore, not just the actor but also the stage that is critical to un-raveling the tale of Wallaceism.

Taking Charge

Before assuming the office, Wallace and his team went about the business of or-ganizing the government. Albert Brewer, Rankin Fite, and Hugh Merrill were interested in the speakership, an office awarded almost exclusively by the governor during this era. Merrill's father had been both speaker and lieutenant governor, and obtaining the speakership for himself had been a lifelong dream. Merrill, however, was never more than a courtesy consideration to the administration, though he did later receive some road work on Highway 77 through the town of Ohatchee as a political payoff. Fite, as shrewd and wily a power broker as the Alabama legislature has ever seen, had been a key figure in the Folsom administration. Wallace, unwilling to be identified with Folsom's perpetual battles with corruption and acts of personal indiscretion, wanted to steer clear of any connection to the Cullman giant, and that made Fite an unnecessary risk. That left Brewer, a personable representative from North Alabama's Morgan County.[13]

Fite was too powerful to completely snub, and Wallace, who contrary to his boisterous and combative public persona, strenuously sought to avoid conflict in personal dealings, wanted to make sure Fite would not be a thorn in his side down the line. He called both Brewer and Fite into his temporary headquarters at the Bell Building in Montgomery. At that meeting, Wallace informed Brewer that he would be speaker, made it clear that Fite would be head of the powerful Ways and Means Committee, and also promised Fite that he would get a trade school for his district in the city of Hamilton. Wallace left the committee assignments completely to Brewer, although the incoming governor was concerned that state labor officials be properly consulted on labor committee posts.[14]

This inattention to the daily issues of governance was a foreshadowing of Wallace's intentions for dealing with the legislature. Wallace had very little practical interest in the details of running the state. As long as the legislators did not detract from the governor or attempt to overshadow him, as long as they would sign off on the few issues that Wallace genuinely cared about, as long as they would play ball on the litany of "nigger resolutions" he or his inner circle would insist be passed, Wallace allowed that body to function relatively unchecked. Nevertheless, Wallace would seek to accumulate maximum power through near total control of state patronage so that the legislature could be overpowered on any given issue.

Wallace assumed the governor's office on a frigid January 14 Alabama morning, just two weeks after Joe Namath led the University of Alabama Crimson Tide to a 17-0 Orange Bowl victory over the University of Oklahoma Sooners, and delivered an inaugural speech that would set the tone for the next several years of his political life. The speech—chock-full of rambling diatribes against the federal government, reminders of the horrors of Reconstruction, and pledges to keep Montgomery free of corruption—was written by Klansman and Wallace advisor Asa "Ace" Carter and archsegregationist Montgomery attorney John Kohn, though the new governor made minor editorial changes. Carter, who later gained literary fame for works such as *Education of Little Tree* and *The Vengeance Trail of Josey Wales,* was an unabashed racist and had participated in, sanctioned, and ordered various acts of violence including beatings, stabbings, shootings, and castrations. Kohn became, for a time, part of Wallace's circle of advisors on race. The speech was written largely to kick-start Wallace's regional and national aspirations, and the assembled reporters from national newspapers and magazines noted the speech's infamous tag line: "In the name of the greatest people that have ever trod this earth, I draw the line in the dust and toss the gauntlet before the feet of tyranny and I say segregation now, segregation tomorrow, segregation forever."[15]

Press Secretary Bill Jones's efforts to get national reporters to attend what would otherwise be a fairly nondescript gubernatorial inauguration was but the first salvo in what would become a systematic attempt to manage the media, control the flow of negative information, release positive information only through the governor, not allow cabinet officials or low-level staffers to become publicity hounds, and promulgate a singular message about the governor. This campaign began with behind-the-scenes maneuvering to get some 351 free billboard panels from the Outdoor Advertising Association of Alabama announcing the inaugural festivities. In all things public, Wallace was to be presented as constitutional, thrifty, effective, and above all, proud to be a southerner and an Alabamian. To that end, press releases about new industry almost always came from the governor or his office. Cabinet members who leaked news about accomplishments of their departments were scolded for circumventing the governor. Jones, for example, rebuked Assistant Highway Department director Bob Kendall for releasing information that did not give Wallace "maximum coverage . . . particularly in view of the value it may be to the Administration at the particular time." On at least two occasions within the first two months of the administration, Jones lectured highway department chief engineer Jack Ward in writing about releasing information to the press that had either no references to the governor or had not been preapproved by the palace guard. Jones kept his pulse on breaking stories and the state's news cycle, and became a master at finding ways to time the flow of announcements and statements in order to keep Wallace in the headlines or at least on the front page. Early in the administration's first year, Wallace himself issued a memo to all department heads demanding they "submit all statements regarding policy to this office prior to releasing to press, radio, or TV." Legislators could appear at public announcements and press conferences with Wallace only if they were in the good graces of the governor. The administration even removed the picture of highway director Ed Rodgers from the official state map because it was felt that all administration credit and recognition should go to Wallace, and

Wallace only. The governor was thrilled with assistant director of labor T. B. Britt's creed for cabinet members, which included the provision to "utilize all of the time and talent that I can spare toward good will and public relations for the Wallace Administration."[16]

Of course, not all the media manipulation was successful. Despite an October 1962 letter from Wallace to CBS anchor Howard K. Smith complaining of bias, prejudice, and intellectual dishonesty, the national coverage by that network of Alabama and southern civil rights opposition in general only increased in intensity. Ironically, Wallace complained in the letter that Smith was weak and "will say what is necessary to conform to what you consider the prevailing public and political opinion." Wallace spent a career doing just that: identifying the pulse of his constituents and tailoring his rhetoric and policies to fit. During the April and May Birmingham demonstrations, Wallace sent telegrams to the state congressional delegation urging hearings by the House Un-American Activities Committee. This investigation, which Wallace wanted held in Birmingham, was to include a thorough examination of the Huntley-Brinkley NBC news team.[17]

Early in his first term, Wallace tried to establish clear images of his leadership style and his administration's efficiency. Part of this objective could be met by quietly increasing the size of the executive department. Staff were imported from other departments to help with correspondence and other matters. These new employees remained on the books of other state government departments to facilitate the image that everything directly connected to the governor was as streamlined and free of frills as possible. Another way to craft a specific image of the governor involved the matter of alcohol. As soon as he took office, Wallace issued executive order number one, which eliminated the use of liquor agents by manufacturers, distillers, or distributors of alcohol in any dealings with the state ABC (Alcoholic Beverage Control) board. Throughout state history, these agents, political cronies of the sitting governor, received direct payments from wholesalers in exchange for essentially performing no work whatsoever. Doubtless, the abolition of the agents was a move in the right direction in terms of ethical practice of state government. But the move was pure politics and hardly removed the corruption, patronage, and cronyism from the state liquor business.[18]

The politics of Wallace and the liquor issue date to the downfall of one his mentors. Politically, Big Jim Folsom suffered tremendous public embarrassment while governor because of his alcohol-induced antics. During his second term, Folsom had a much-publicized cocktail in the governor's mansion with Harlem, New York, congressman Adam Clayton Powell. Folsom, in effect, had committed two sins: inviting a Negro into the mansion in clear violation of accepted de facto segregation and deigning to drink with him. Powell himself publicized the drink by referring to it during a speech at Alabama State University in Montgomery. Folsom had acquired a well-deserved reputation for his drinking, even at public functions and at times when he was expected to be tending to state business. Sometimes the alcoholism surfaced in hilarious ways, such as when a drunken Folsom cut a birthday cake with a samurai sword. Other times were more lamentable. According to his biographers, Folsom was at a party in the Gulf of Mexico and unable to be reached at one point during the Autherine Lucy crisis at the University of Alabama. During the 1962 primary campaign, Folsom slurred his speech while on television and could not seem to remember the names of his own children.[19]

Wallace sensed the unpopularity of Folsom's sloppiness and moved to take advantage of it by pledging to keep alcohol out of the mansion and abolish the agent system. Wallace himself had been a social drinker in previous years and occasionally drank to excess. Early in his political career as a legislator, Wallace developed a reputation for knowing the places where state politicos took their wives and the places where they took their mistresses while the legislature was in session. Ever the political animal, Wallace would sidle from table to table at these establishments, sharing a drink or two and networking with colleagues and interest group barons. Politically, the stand on liquor issues was quite popular. When he took office, some thirty years after the repeal of prohibition, only twenty-two of the state's sixty-seven counties were wet. Temperance societies were still meeting regularly, and Baptist preachers were counseling church members to abstain at all times. The no-liquor-in-the-mansion pledge came during an inadvertent campaign promise to be a "sober governor," which wrought an unexpected thunder of applause. From that point on, it was a regular component of his stump speeches. In response to his abolition of liquor in the mansion, Wallace received an outpouring of support from groups such as the Women's Christian Temperance Union of Birmingham and the Albertville First Methodist Church Women's Prayer Group. Return correspondence from the governor often included a pledge to do "my Christian duty to God and to the people." The response was so potent that Wallace would occasionally work an antiliquor bit into speeches well after he took office. Wallace's graduation speeches would frequently include the comment that "social drinking is a farce. Non-drinkers have a better chance in everything."[20]

While all indications are that Wallace kept his pledge to keep liquor out of the mansion, the matter of the liquor agents is more complicated. As early as April 1963, ABC attorneys were communicating with the Internal Revenue Service in Washington to gain a special tax exempt status to continue the practice of using agents. The administration was committed to continuing the practice of receiving the agent commissions, but with the proceeds going tax free to the state where officials could allocate the funds for other purposes. Theoretically, if not always practically, these tax exempt funds were to go to education, public relief, or various other funds. But these funds were not specifically earmarked and once in the system could be directed to any number of ultimate destinations. The revenue streams from these agent commissions—which ran between $500,000 and $1 million—were significant.[21]

Liquor agents never completely vanished, nor did the political machinations surrounding the state liquor business. Throughout 1963, Wallace and the palace guard shifted ABC liquor money in and out of different state banks—not over fiduciary management issues, but simply to steer the accounts into the hands of those who donated money to his campaign. In some cases, Wallace personally intervened to reallocate state funds with explicit directives to subordinates. For example, Wallace ordered ABC assistant administrator Herman Whisenant to "take [the] ABC account out of Alabama Exchange Bank and transfer it to the City Bank of Tuskegee. I want this done immediately." As freely as the administration moved liquor money in and out of banks for political rewards, it also attempted to moderate editorial coverage by withholding ABC liquor advertising. As with the banks, Wallace was wont to intervene personally when coverage became critical. Even the *Montgomery Advertiser,* edited by longtime Wallace confidant and ex officio campaign manager Grover Hall Jr., saw its state advertising dry up from time to time.[22]

If the liquor business was one way to mold a specific image of propriety for the new administration, the docking of the state yachts was another. These vessels, more party boats for state legislators and prospective industrial clients than anything else, carried a scandalous reputation in the hinterlands as floating dens of iniquity where too many drinks were served and too many elites were serviced by willing party girls. Executive order number two, issued the same day as the liquor agent directive, charged incoming State Docks director Houston Feaster with securing the "pleasure yachts" and taking them out of service. Shortly thereafter, Wallace ordered the two yachts, the *Jamelle* and the *Alice,* sold. Mobile's state senator, John Tyson, lobbied Wallace to keep the vessels, but the political capital, not revenue from the sale, was all that interested Wallace. In reality, the yachts were funded by state docks revenue, not taxes, but that nuance was never really explained to the public. The *Alice* fetched $41,101, somewhat less than full market value, and the *Jamelle* was later stripped of its more lavish accouterments and put back into service as a port authority boat, after Feaster appealed to Wallace to keep it for use at the docks.[23]

The sale of the state yachts, the pledge to keep liquor out of the mansion, and the public declaration to abolish the traditional liquor agent system were all small measures that actually saved the state very little money. They were, however, invaluable in shaping Wallace's public image. Though Wallace is remembered best for his ability to exploit the race issue—which he most certainly did—his ability to find these smaller issues and mine all the political gold out of them was almost as important in achieving a phenomenal level of adoration and popularity during his first term. By publicly demanding that all state employees stop using their state cars for personal travel to hunting lands or University of Alabama football games in Tuscaloosa or Birmingham, Wallace appeared to be reining in the elites and forcing them to live like the common Alabamian. By cutting the executive mansion fund and having Lurleen take a major role in the buying of groceries and planning of all receptions and state dinners, Wallace was showing the hard-working people of Section and Centre and Possum Trot that he was one of them. By vowing to cut the size of government and immediately dismissing three hundred workers from the Highway Department, Wallace was connecting with the folks in Opp and Billingsley and Jasper and telling them that he was watching their money like a hawk. By announcing a plan to sell one thousand state automobiles, Wallace was showing the farmers and truck drivers and millworkers that he knew exactly what the state needed to conduct its business and he was not going to ask for one iota more. No matter that the size of government actually grew during the first term; no matter that selling the cars allowed him to buy more and distribute more patronage; no matter that the tax burden fell increasingly on the working classes, Wallace had created a *populist* image even if he was closer to being a *popularist*. Though he stressed his hardscrabble roots in rural Barbour county, Wallace had very little interest in any detailed agenda if it had no immediate political payoff for him. He never launched a full frontal assault on economic issues in favor of the lower socioeconomic classes. As a *popularist,* he was able to understand the needs and lives of ordinary Alabamians and align his rhetoric accordingly, even if his actions did not follow suit. He confided on one occasion to Seymour Trammell that "my philosophy is going to be that people are not capable of governing themselves, and therefore, I'm going to tell them what they want to hear. And then just before the election, kick a nigger's ass and get elected."[24]

While these various and sundry token measures were popular with the masses, Wallace knew he needed something more substantive to whipsaw the legislature and increase his own base of power. In fact, if there is any constant in the programs, policies, actions, and rhetoric of Wallace throughout his first year in office, it was the acquisition of power. Wallace had direct and indirect methods for creating and consolidating power. The direct method was to convince the legislature to give him unprecedented power to deal with civil rights issues and then expand that power into other domains. In nearly every preceding gubernatorial administration, Alabama governors had considerable leeway with the legislature for the first two years of their term. In that period, legislators knew they had to cooperate with the administration in order to get roads, bridges, and other necessary appropriations to improve their districts and their own hopes for reelection. The last two years were usually characterized by a marked loss of gubernatorial prestige as legislators, interest groups, and other stakeholders began to line up behind potential candidates for the coming governor's race. Even more than in previous terms, Wallace knew that before he was inaugurated in 1963, candidates for the 1966 race such as John Patterson, Ryan deGraffenreid, and Richmond Flowers were already plotting strategy. He had to secure as much power as possible before they convinced their legislative subordinates to delay all action until they could get in office and claim credit. Fortunately for Wallace, he had entered office at a time when Martin Luther King, Fred Shuttlesworth, and others would give him all the ammunition he needed to take power for himself. In addition, numerous programmatic initiatives including road bonds, attorneys' bills, and junior college and trade school construction were designed to provide the administration with political hammers Wallace could use to threaten legislators. Wallace preferred to offer the carrot, but he always had at his disposal his brusque finance director and self-described "son-of-a-bitch," Seymour Trammell, who relished wielding the stick.[25]

The indirect method was more complicated but tailored better to Wallace's rare skills and interests. The only way to avoid the limiting effects of the legislature was to accumulate such a mandate with the people that they would not tolerate anything less than complete obedience from the legislature. Popularity of this magnitude had never been achieved in state history. Since policy and the details of governance bored him anyway, Wallace endeavored to make his entire term a nonstop, twenty-four-hour-a-day, three-hundred-sixty-five-day-a-year, four-year campaign. Wallace had countless campaign style opportunities at his disposal. The governor could call special sessions of the legislature at any time he wanted. He could make out-of-state trips for speaking tours, visit neighboring states for fact-finding missions, go on industry-seeking junkets, rally local Citizens' Councils, and campaign for other candidates. He could appear on statewide television almost at will. There were airport dedications, bridge openings, interest group conventions, Masons' meetings, graduations, reunions, company barbeques, Governor's Day rallies, college football bowl trips, Civil War Centennial commemorations, new industry announcements, and other opportunities to speak in front of an Alabama audience. If no audience was available, Wallace would invade a local diner to order a hamburger steak, immerse it in a sea of catsup, and trade political banter with whoever was on the premises, white or black. Though it was not evident at the time, future opportunities would present themselves as Wallace spoke out against the Civil Rights Act, campaigned for president and for independent electors, talked at colleges and universities, and appeared on national television programs such as the *Today Show, Meet the Press,* and *Face the Nation.*[26]

Politics and Policies

With the general objectives of maximizing both real power in the office of the governor and functional popularity in the state, the administration embarked on a program to pass its first legislative agenda and increase the governor's stature. After having to declare forced proration in February due to a $2 million revenue shortfall, Wallace concentrated on planning a special legislative session for road construction and education. Comparatively speaking, road legislation was an easy test for the new administration. Roads were necessary to service an expanding economy, brought easy recognition to local senators and representatives that they could use in reelection bids, and provided ample opportunities for the administration to repay its supporters with paving or plant mix contracts.[27]

The preferred method for major expenditures in the Wallace administration was deficit financing via bond sales. Within little over a week of the special session being called, a $100 million road bond issue passed with only token resistance in the senate. In a foreshadowing of future dealings in the first Wallace term, the house of representatives, under the control of speaker Albert Brewer, was in near lockstep with the administration. The senate, with its malleable filibuster and cloture provisions, was where the administration faced its battles.[28]

The bond issue was the single highest road expenditure in state history to date and all amendments earmarking or dictating the specific allocation of the funds were defeated. Wallace, in his first legislative session, had created what some called "the most potent political weapon ever handed an Alabama Governor." Theoretically, the money was to be spent by the collective decisions of a Highway Authority, but operationally, Wallace had control of three of the five positions on the authority board, his own, the appointed director of finance, Seymour Trammell, and the appointed highway director, Ed Rodgers. Essentially, the money had no real strings attached to it, and despite Wallace's public promise to spend it wisely, its dispersal became a political football with eleven counties losing projects and recalcitrant senators such as John Tyson of Mobile County, Larry Dumas of Jefferson County, Robert Wilson of Walker County, and E. C. Hornsby of Tallapoosa County being specifically targeted for road or bridge cuts within a month of the passage of the road bond bill. At the same time, all highway projects in the home counties of senate judiciary committee members who opposed a ten-point administration tax plan were axed.[29]

The most contentious of the road projects eliminated in 1963 was in Mobile. Within that area's delegation, Mylan Engel had towed the Wallace line, but John Tyson, Robert Eddington, and Clara Fields were more independent than the administration would have liked. In order to gain votes on his education package, Wallace stopped a $7.1 million interstate project in Mobile, even though the matching funds for federal dollars were actually supplied by Mobile city and county at a time when the state Highway Department was practically broke. In a naked example of realpolitik, Wallace publicly admitted that the "Mobile road program depends on how your senator votes." Tyson, the senator in question, attempted to rally his constituents and even accused the governor of adopting "Castro-type tactics." For his part, Wallace later tried to blame the delay of the Mobile project on the failure of the state to condemn the land needed to complete the project. The reality was that the Mobile project had already passed the condemnation stage. Eventually, the Mobile project was reinstated, but only after a public appeal from the AFL-CIO of Mobile, a face-to-face meeting between Mobile mayor Charles Trimmier and Wallace, and some progress on passing the education package was made. Before the resolution, Wallace received a number of disparaging telegrams from Mobile residents, including E. C. Kantrell: "Have you already forgotten your supporters in Mobile? You were elected to represent the people, not be a dictator. Put the I-10 road project through or thousands of voters will be former supporters." Birmingham resident Joe Russell understood that if Wallace could do this to Mobile, his own city and its projects might be next: "You are not the man I thought you were and surely not man enough to hold a responsible position as governor of the state of Alabama."[30]

Montgomery senator and Wallace critic Vaughn Hill Robison tried to link Wallace's road cancellations with President Kennedy's arm-twisting on behalf of the civil rights bill. Kennedy, according to many in the Deep South, regularly threatened to withhold federal funds from any southern states whose congressmen opposed the president's legislation. Referring to a published report, Robison wondered "whether I was reading national news or whether I was reading local news. On what meat does this our little Caesar feed?"[31]

The entire road building operation under the Wallace administration was almost completely political. In a limousine ride to Columbus, Georgia, after the November 1962 general election but before the January 1963 inauguration, Wallace and former legislator and Folsom finance director Fuller Kimbrell discussed the incoming governor's road plans. Kimbrell, Wallace said, would be an unofficial highway czar who would handle the road requests of legislators, supporters, interest groups, and contractors. The official highway director, Wallace explained, would be Ed Rodgers, but only for a limited period of time. Eventually, Herman Nelson, longtime highway department employee, would take over. Nelson had been the 1962 campaign manager for Jim Folsom, and Wallace had promised him the post in exchange for his support during the 1962 runoff against deGraffenreid. Kimbrell, Gerald Wallace, and Seymour Trammell comprised the inner circle on road matters and each could get a road built for any friend of the administration.[32]

Though he preferred to know as little as possible about the wheeling and dealing of Fuller, Gerald, and Seymour, Wallace himself occasionally intervened to get a road built or speed up a project that was farther down the priority list. One road that was particularly important to the governor was a stretch of Highway 231 from Montgomery to Dothan, the heart of Wallace support in South Alabama. When Highway Director Ed Rodgers made a speech in Dothan that indicated that the four-lane project might not be finished, Wallace caught immediate flak from a group of South Alabama legislators. He quickly fired off a directive to Rodgers demanding a "crash effort" and revealing "I am as interested in this as I am in any road in Alabama." Wallace also supervised the direction of funds for patching existing roads in the municipal aid program and instructed subordinates to purchase limestone, sandrock, and chert from specific contractors.[33]

Wallace's personal forays into the sea of political patronage were not confined to road issues. He personally directed Trammell, assistant finance department director Richard Stone, and other subordinates on matters as varied as prescription drug purchases, dry goods, batteries, and towing and wrecker service. A preferred method of the governor for directing state contracts was to issue a memo to one of his subordinates with the legally obtuse enjoinder "is there anyway that we can give any business to." When Bibb County campaign manager Belcher Hobson called on the governor to get some battery business, Wallace directed Stone to "do some business with him if we can." One day later, Hobson had a contract. In addition, the governor regularly recommended people for hire in all departments, and legions of Wallace friends and political supporters got highway courtesy cards. These cards effectively served as traffic citation mulligans. In some places within the state, it was nigh unto impossible to get a traffic ticket anyway: Wilcox County had a grand total of one highway patrolman assigned to road duty.[34]

Clearly, personal gubernatorial patronage was not endemic to the Wallace administration. But the governor and his staff worked fastidiously to create a reputation of unquestioned fiscal discipline, maniacal observance of the state bid law, and an end to business-as-usual in Montgomery. Ideally, Wallace wanted to be seen as a southern-style statesman, too concerned with attracting industry, rescuing education, and returning the country to a strict constructionist interpretation of the constitution to be bothered with the mundane world of political payoffs. The reality is that Wallace was right in the middle of much of the traditional spoils system.

Standard operating procedure for securing a road contract was a 10 percent, off-the-books fee to the Wallace administration. Kimbrell often smoothed relations between contractors and attempted to spread the paving and plant mix contracts. Kimbrell, one of the so-called James Boys with compatriot Rankin Fite, once secured $178,000 in paving for the town of Fayette, which had a population of some thirty-seven hundred at the time. One complication was the Alabama Bid Law—something Kimbrell had publicly campaigned against in 1955—which mandated a specific process for letting bids and granting contracts. In some cases, low bids were won by firms not friendly to the administration, and although the contracts were awarded, the palace guard elected not to actually buy anything on that contract. In other cases, firms were told not to bid on a specific project but that it would be made up to them later. In certain instances, low bids could be thrown out if another firm agreed to a price at 5 percent below the low bid price. Kimbrell himself could not resist the temptation to get in on the action and in fact had "won" two asphalt contracts before he even had an asphalt company. Finance department staffers recall a steady stream of contractors going in and out of the office to meet with Trammell, as well as with Gerald Wallace and Kimbrell neither of whom held formal positions in the government. The word about Gerald's being the man to see to get something done was so well known that the governor's brother actually received mail at the capitol concerning highway matters and memoranda from highway department officials. Wallace friend Oscar Harper, who had been primarily involved in the printing business, acquired an asphalt company of his own, Wiregrass Construction, and quickly earned multiple lucrative contracts. Harper himself became an influence peddler, receiving mail at the capitol, recommending people for employment, and funneling requests from throughout the state to various cabinet level departments. It was hardly a coincidence that Harper, one of George Wallace's few close friends, also received regular state business for envelopes, paper, letterhead stationery, identification tags, mail openers, desk trays, guest books, card files, scrapbooks, memo pads, miscellaneous printing, copies of speeches and resolutions, photo supplies, light bulbs, honorarium certificates, proclamations, film, photocopying processing cleaners and liquids, and even copies of legal briefs. The easiest method for keeping business outside the realm of the state bid law was to write proprietary specifications that only Harper's product line could match, or write multiple purchase requests to keep individual expenses below the five hundred to eight hundred dollar bid regulation requirements.[35]

The administration was active on the industrial development front as well.

One factor leading to the influx of new and expanded business was the Alabama aviation program of small city airport development, led by Asa Rountree. Wallace himself had practically no interest or involvement in airport construction or development. Rountree had led the initiative for years, had developed a strong set of contacts in the legislature and among the state's powerful interest groups, and was content to function independently.[36]

One of the few times that Wallace interacted with Rountree, other than to attend an airport ribbon-cutting ceremony, was when the governor was unable to land in Florala for a speech. Upset at the delay caused by landing elsewhere, Wallace inquired about Florala's lack of facilities, only to be informed that Rountree had already allocated funding for a new municipal airport. Rountree's small cities program was a double-edged sword. Funded entirely by a large aviation gas tax, the program allowed Alabama to create more airports than almost any other state in the union, even if many of them had little or no regular traffic. In 1963, Alabama enjoyed its third straight year of leading the nation in small city airport construction. The state had more than 140 fields and strips, an average of 2 for every county in the state. In some cases, Rountree could act on almost a moment's notice to help entice new industry. While the administration was negotiating to attract an Allied Paper Plant to Jackson, Rountree had already cleared the way for the paving and grading of a new airport. Unfortunately, the seven cents per gallon aviation fuel tax that built the airports also discouraged major airlines from locating in the state or making Birmingham a major hub. At the same time Atlanta was becoming the air capital of the South, Birmingham's airport was comparatively desolate. Because of the tax, which was as much as six cents higher than neighboring states, airlines rarely bought fuel in the state unless it was absolutely necessary.[37]

The quest to attract new industry became a way for Wallace to prove to Alabamians that they could have it all: that it was possible to fight for segregation, blame the federal government for everything, and still progress as a state. Education and road construction were important because they told Alabamians he had an agenda. But industrial development meant respect from outside the state and validated Wallace's self-appointed credentials as a champion of free enterprise. It made absolutely no difference what type of industry could be lured. It was simply a matter of numbers.

A significant part of Alabama's arsenal for wooing an industrial prospect consisted of two separate pieces of legislation that date to the governor's time in the legislature, the Wallace Act and the Cater Act. Both measures were written and supported by the powerful League of Municipalities, whose head, Ed Reid, was a political mentor for Wallace. The league was powerful enough to have its own floor leaders, and Wallace had held that position in the house. The relationship had other perquisites as well: Wallace frequently used the couch in Ed Reid's office for entertaining lady friends.[38]

The Wallace Act allowed municipal governing bodies to enter into contracts with prospective lessees, finance projects, construct or equip buildings, collect rent, and disburse payments to bondholders. Under its provisions, a municipality would enter into a lease contract with an industrial firm and agree to build a new facility financed through the sale of tax exempt bonds. Once the new plant was built, the municipality would collect rent from the firm that would be used to pay off the bond debt. Lease lengths were unlimited, although Supreme Court precedent in *Newberry v. Andalusia* suggested terms not exceed thirty years. In short, the Wallace Act was a way to allow corporations to get new facilities without tapping into their own lines of credit. The Cater Act was slightly different in that it called for the formation of a municipal industrial development corporation, a separate entity from the municipality, to finance and build new industrial facilities. The corporation was limited in its scope to promoting industry, constructing new facilities for industrial clients, and financing its activities through the sale of bonds. The Cater Act did not require a prebond issue lease agreement as the Wallace Act did, but for all practical purposes, both laws provided the ability to do the same thing.[39]

Taken together, the laws allowed for creative financing of industrial development. Unfortunately, the application of the Wallace and Cater Acts along with the sweetheart deals sanctioned by the Wallace administration, created a climate that attracted low-skill, low-wage industry without allowing the state to reap many benefits. Since the Wallace and Cater Acts provided for property rental, not ownership, the state never received any property tax from the new corporation. Once the thirty-year lease expired, the firm could sign a new lease for as long as ninety-nine years with payments of as little as one dollar. In order to entice the Woodward Iron Company to develop a new corporation, Cement Asbestos Products Company, in Ragland, Alabama, the administration agreed to a ten-year property tax exemption. Wallace granted the same exemption to Container Corporation of America and countless others.[40]

The net result of the administration's shotgun approach to offering concession after concession to any firm that would relocate to Alabama or expand its current facilities was that the state obtained short-term industries that drained public services without providing much to local communities. Schools were expected to educate additional students but received too few additional funds. Roads had to be built, but the new corporations paid little in property or income tax. Within the next decade or so, many of these firms shuffled off overseas or ceased operations entirely as changes in the economy slowly swept away the low-wage, low-skill era. As a result, Alabama was ill equipped to offer the financial services, government assistance, and skilled workers necessary to attract permanent industry. George Wallace was building an impressive treasure chest of new industry, but over the coming years it would prove to be little more than smoke and mirrors.

Education

With the road bond session an easy victory and other policies taking shape, the administration turned its attention to an education plan through which the governor promised a "dramatic breakthrough" for the state. But while road projects were fairly easy politics, education issues involved a litany of special interest groups, universities, teachers' unions, racial considerations, and local school systems. This complicated negotiating process has largely characterized the legislative process in Alabama since the passage of the 1901 state constitution. The condition of Alabama schools, in comparison to the rest of the nation, was dreadful. In objective categories such as per pupil expenditures, student-teacher ratio, and teacher pay, as well as subjective categories such as building safety, quality and availability of transportation, and employee morale, Alabama was at or near the bottom of the nation. And not all school systems within the state were functioning at even the Alabama average; sixteen county school systems were paying their teachers at rates below the state allotment schedule. Amendments to Alabama's 1901 constitution provided for funding through a variety of sales and use taxes that inevitably fluctuated wildly from year to year as the economy expanded or contracted. When forecasts proved too optimistic, school systems and other aspects of state government would be cast into fiscal austerity through mandatory proration, a condition that had occurred in four of the five years prior to 1963. Compounding the inadequacy of funding, were the state's attempts to operate two separate educational systems, white and black, based on such miserly funding.[41]

How ridiculous were the inequalities in the two separate systems? Most of the Negro schools were in deplorable physical condition with leaky roofs, broken windows, and little or no functioning equipment. Many students had long daily walks to reach school because convoluted districting took them far from their homes each day, and transportation was either substandard or nonexistent. In 1963 the state spent $8,641,494 in school plant operations and maintenance for its 587,000 white students: an average of $14.72 per student. For the state's 313,805 black students, Alabama spent $2,957,034: an average of $9.72 per student. Furthermore, according to the state's official documents, 38 percent of the state's 905 Negro schools had three teachers or fewer. The state had a grand total of three Negro senior high schools that had only the traditional tenth through twelfth grades. Student-teacher ratios were higher in Negro elementary and junior highs than in white schools. Numerous other disparities also existed.[42]

Alabama students, according to a report completed by Auburn University dean of education Truman Pierce, were competitive nationally until they reached the eleventh grade. In 1960, statewide testing indicated that eighth graders in the state exceeded national averages in arithmetic reasoning, arithmetic fundamentals, and basic English. Scores in vocabulary and reading comprehension were only one-tenth of a grade lower than national averages. Only in the category of spelling did state students fall nearly one full grade level below the national level. But by the eleventh grade, Alabamians equaled national averages only in arithmetic reasoning.[43]

By 1960, Alabama males had completed an average of 8.9 years of school, while females had finished an average of 9.3. Nationally, males had finished 10.5 years of school and females 11.0. In that same year, some 41.5 percent of Alabamians registering with the selective service were rejected for insufficient basic test scores; only four states had a higher percentage of rejections. The national average was 21.7 percent. Only 55 percent of Alabama eighth graders in 1955 finished high school compared to 98.5 percent of Wisconsin students. Alabama ranked 41st in literacy.[44]

The relationship between education and wealth in Alabama indicated a gross disparity between the haves and the have-nots. Four of the top five counties in terms of grade completed also ranked in the top five in median family income. The six counties lowest in completed grades were also lowest in median family income. Without question, the insufficient attention to both quality and quantity of education was a major factor in the state's poverty and inability to attract high-wage, high-skill industry.[45]

The AEA (Alabama Education Association), with the support of State School Superintendent Austin Meadows, released the results of its funding survey, which asked for $51.6 million in new money. The administration's review, completed by a Wallace-friendly legislative committee, recommended $25 million, primarily because the legislators believed that was all that could be raised in new taxes. Wallace had few concrete ideas of his own about necessary changes in education but was open to anything that would help Alabamians—and give him political capital. Representative Rankin Fite suggested to Wallace that five trade schools and five junior colleges might be built with little more than a two-cent-per-bottle beer tax. "Governor," Fite declared one day when he and Speaker Brewer came to the executive offices, "I'm going to make you famous." As a representative, Wallace had, with Fite's assistance, sponsored legislation creating five trade schools. He thought the idea was sound and gave it his full support. Postsecondary education could be easily packaged with another key need of the administration: the quest for industrial development.[46]

Unfortunately for the administration, not all the interests groups were ready to sign off on the idea. The state's universities wanted their own funding improved before any new drains on the revenue spigot were added. Business and industry groups were in favor of the new schools as sources of trained employees, but were hesitant to embrace any new idea that might lead to higher taxation. Wallace avoided public comment on education taxation issues, but did begin to enter the public relations fray: "Alabama is never going to reach its zenith in industrial growth until something is done about education."[47]

Wallace's failure to discuss his taxation plan for education in public did not mean he had no input in the process. The Ways and Means Committee, in charge of finding the necessary revenue, was led by Rankin Fite and dominated by proadministration forces, and nothing was going to come out of that group without Wallace's blessing. Part of the reason for Wallace's public silence on the source for new education funding was his past history on tax issues. In 1951, while in the legislature, Wallace led a three-day filibuster against a bill that raised the state sales tax to three cents. And in order to woo labor votes during the 1962 campaign, Wallace had repeatedly promised to veto any increase in the state sales tax. Consequently, he could not quickly endorse a plan to raise the tax to four cents without explaining his apparent ideological change. Pressed on the need to get some revenue stream written into law, Wallace responded, "They want a program, I'll give them a program." On April 6, the Ways and Means Committee, with Wallace's heavy input, announced a $51.5 million package based on a multitude of small tax increases, including an income tax on corporations from 3 to 5 percent that required a constitutional amendment; removal of federal income tax payments as a deduction for state income taxes; a 3 percent sales tax on utility services that predictably allowed exemptions for industry and farms; a 3 percent tax on telephone service; a 10 percent tax on road construction contracts; a 0.5 percent tax on certain construction; an increase in state insurance premiums; and a handful of other miscellaneous measures. The entire package was gaveled through without giving legislators a chance to vote on the bills individually. The 855-member Associated Industries of Alabama responded by calling the tax package a "deterrent to the industrial development of our state."[48]

While the house was able to pass a multifaceted education tax plan, the senate was in chaos. Since only twenty-two of Alabama's counties allowed alcohol consumption, the bottle beer tax for junior colleges and trade schools would be unfairly weighted toward them. Quickly, opposition forces began a filibuster to prevent passage of the beer tax. Despite their pleas to continue the delay, the filibuster broke apart on the third day after an agreement was reached to table the beer tax vote until the general education revenue package was finalized. Some five days later, a compromise was reached on a plan to increase the sales tax from three cents to four, but another filibuster broke out over the beer tax for the new trade schools and junior colleges.[49]

Speaker Brewer, who understood the political ramifications of Wallace's campaign pledges to veto any increase in the sales tax, went to the governor to plot strategy. Assuming that Wallace was actually going to veto the bill, Brewer wanted to know when the bill would be sent back so he could plan further action. Wallace, flummoxed that the speaker considered even for a moment the possibility of a veto, informed Brewer that he had no intention of killing the legislation, campaign promises notwithstanding. "I'll just yell nigger," the governor suggested, and everything will be all right. For Brewer, this was the first in a series of disillusionments that would ultimately end with Wallace snuffing out his political career in a contentious 1970 gubernatorial race.

Enraged by the senate's intransigence, Wallace went public to try to rally support. "I am concerned because we are tinkering with the future welfare of our most cherished possessions, our children." Wallace met with the senate opposition and even pledged to keep the site selection of the junior colleges and trade schools out of politics, a hollow promise to be sure. After the well-respected lieutenant governor Jim Allen brokered an end to the filibuster and the senate passed the beer tax by a 22 to 6 vote and a bill creating the University of South Alabama in Mobile, a new filibuster over the previously agreed upon sales tax erupted. All of this was too much for University of Alabama president Frank Rose to handle. The state of education in Alabama, Rose concluded, was "pathetic and 1,000 die every year who should live because of lack of facilities at the University Medical Center. I would not go to bed tonight before I reached my senator or representative to tell him to stop spending his time foolishly and denying the children of Alabama their birthright."[50]

The next day, while Birmingham witnessed the arrest of some eight hundred people in the wake of the Children's Crusade, the filibuster finally collapsed for good and the senate passed the sales tax bill. Wallace was monitoring events in Birmingham through Al Lingo, director of the State Highway Patrol, but the Children's Crusade was not his top priority. Some of the state's major newspapers did not even put events in Birmingham on the front page. Wallace's interest level picked up slightly with the bombing of A. D. King's home in nearby Ensley, but even then he generally let Lingo and Bull Connor handle the unrest.[51]

The education session, as fraught with politics as it was, produced the greatest single one-time increase in education funds to that point in state history. Even though the administration passed some major education appropriations, the trade schools and junior colleges were systemically awash in a sea of political expediency. In order to break the filibuster stalemate, the administration agreed to abandon the initial barriers that kept the allotment of new schools at ten. Soon enough, every board of education, every major legislator, and most of the friends of the governor had competed for a school of their own. What had started with Rankin Fite trying to secure a trade school for himself in exchange for not bucking the decision to make Albert Brewer speaker of the house, eventually became a statewide network of political patronage and pork typified more by a stream of concessions and compromises to get new buildings built and new administrators hired than any well-thought-out plan to attract new industry or prepare Alabamians to matriculate at a state university. The end result was that the schools mushroomed from ten to twenty, then twenty-four, then twenty-seven, including expansions of existing facilities, eventually reaching some forty-two different facilities. Even the naming of the schools reflects the appalling lack of planning inherent in the junior college and trade school expansion. Wallace, a handful of his minions and cronies, and a small group of state capitol reporters informally named the schools one afternoon while eating lunch in the state cafeteria.[52]

Apparently the new schools became more than a place for studying metallurgy or college algebra. In a confidential memoranda just a few years after the schools opened, State Superintendent of Education Austin Meadows cited the inability of school presidents to stay in close touch with the students and activities on campus. Meadows, according to the memo, had been receiving reports about the prevalence of "booze drinking," "sex relationships out in cars parked on the campus," and "gambling, especially with the use of cards." In keeping with administration guidelines on image and media, Meadows cautioned the collective presidents to "give no publicity to this report."[53]

In the regular session of the legislature, the administration made education an even greater priority. Reflecting general improvements in the state economy, the legislature appropriated a record $186 million for fiscal year 1963–64 and $191 million for 1964–65, nearly $40 million more than for the current year. The state's four-year colleges and universities received total appropriations of nearly $30 million, several million more than the current year. During the legislative year, state teacher salaries were increased by 17.64 percent to an average of $4,393. The limited free textbook program was expanded to include fourth and fifth graders. Politics aside, the Wallace administration had made an impressive start. But not even significant improvements in state education funding could obscure the issue of race. For example, educational television received a 110 percent increase in funding, but the new money came with a price. Administration legal advisor Cecil Jackson told the Alabama Educational Television Commission general manager Raymond Hurlburt to accept federal matching funds for programming only if there were "no integrated programs."[54]

Much of the other education legislation that came from the governor's office and the resolutions of the state Board of Education meetings were substantially less progressive than the size of the revenue enhancements. Seeking to squeeze out any dollar possible, the administration backed a plan to extend textbooks to six-year adoptions. Textbooks during this era were lucky to be usable after three years, let alone six. Though he frequently skipped cabinet, department, and agency meetings of all types, Wallace presided over the August 5, 1963, Board of Education meeting, which met largely in response to Supreme Court decisions barring regular Bible readings. Publicly, Wallace declared that every state including his own should defy the rulings: "I want the Supreme Court to know that we in Alabama are not going to conform to their ruling." Within the confines of the board, Wallace encouraged the adoption of a resolution on the same topic: "The Board of Education on the recommendation of the governor of the state of Alabama and the state Superintendent of Education does hereby instruct all public school systems in the state of Alabama to see that the Holy Bible is read in each and every public school at least once each day; and . . . is now part of the courses of study of said school." A separate resolution requested monthly reports documenting the required Bible reading.[55]

While the road bond bill and the junior colleges and trade schools provided Wallace an amazing amount of patronage power that could be used as a political hammer to force compliance with his agenda, the governor wanted even more personal control over state government and he used the special sessions to strive for it. Wallace wanted the power to assign all Alabama students to schools; he wanted a war chest for attracting new industry and defending segregation; he wanted legislative approval to use revenue promised to any state government department to hire outside lawyers to represent that agency. Attorney General Richmond Flowers, Wallace's nemesis and sometime foil, blasted the so-called attorney's bill as "the most dangerous bill I have ever seen introduced into the legislature" and "a centralization of power" that "Alabama will long regret." Wallace wanted to hire his own legal team, at state expense, for highway condemnation and civil rights issues. Senator Bob Gilchrist, a vocal Wallace critic, called the attorney's bill a "blank check to let the governor invade the educational trust fund, even at the expense of teacher salaries." Flowers, who could offer a rhetorical flourish to dramatize a point as well as anyone, assessed the totality of Wallace's power plays: "The Kennedy's themselves have never asked for power like this." It was no accident that Wallace's friends and supporters received regular highway condemnation work that paid into the thousands. Meanwhile, Flowers and his staff of lawyers, theoretically charged with performing this very same work, sat idly by as the governor sought to make the attorney general as impotent as possible.[56]

The Politics of Race

Policy battles may have provided legal power for Wallace to distribute patronage, but nothing increased the governor's popularity with white voters like his handling of racial issues. The Deep South civil rights battleground was a complex theater of engagement, and labels such as "racist," "segregationist," and "moderate" carried complex definitions whose distinctions have faded over time. While it is true that the governor would have adopted any cause and targeted any scapegoat necessary to increase his power and popularity, at times he seemed to relish playing the race card. Even so, polarized caricatures of Wallace as an unmitigated racist belie the governor's occasional acts of fundamental human decency and his remarkable ability to convince some African Americans in Alabama that his faux-Populist policies were worth suffering the concomitant racial oppression. In short, the Wallace phenomenon defies the stereotypical portraits of the governor because those descriptions too often suggest that he was a static figure, too ignorant to be proactive and too hardened to make adjustments. Actually, George Wallace almost always had the quickest, if not necessarily the most developed, mind in the room.

Wallace, on a few occasions, actually held back some of his inner circle who wanted the governor to take a harder line. Al Lingo, public safety director, was notorious for allowing troopers, directly or indirectly, to crack skulls first and ask questions later. Lingo, like Dallas County sheriff Jim Clark, was fond of using electric cattle prods to encourage demonstrators to move along. Seymore Trammell was a contact point for many strident white supremacists who had voted for Wallace and hoped he would carry their ideology to its ultimate conclusion. When the fringe elements approached Wallace about something specific, he was not opposed to picking up the phone and calling Albert Brewer or one of his floor leaders and recommending they look seriously at a wonderful new idea he had come across. More often than not, these administration folk knew the phone call meant Wallace had somebody in his office whom he was trying to appease.[57]

But if Wallace was often more deliberate and in fact more intelligent than he has been depicted, he was prone to fits of unscripted exuberance that led to dangerous reactions. Wallace's rhetorical excesses gave aid and comfort to fringe groups plotting violence who, even if caught, arrested, and brought to trial, stood a better-than-average chance of acquittal with Alabama's predominately white juries. In January 1962, at Birmingham's Tutwiler Hotel, Wallace, responding to questions and trying to validate his states' rights credentials, warned the assembled about the dangers of "appeasing niggers." In May 1963, Wallace, in a spastic fit over the truce in Birmingham between civil rights leaders and white business leaders, crudely demanded more money for highway patrolmen because "lawless Negro mobs" were rioting with the full protection of the federal government. In July 1963, while testifying before the Senate Commerce Committee, Wallace actually said, "Negroes are among my best and closest friends." But in that same session, he misquoted John Kennedy, saying that the president encouraged civil rights activists to engage in extralegal tactics: "If you don't get what you want, you should continue rioting in the streets."[58]

But even though Wallace and the issue of race is more complicated than simple stereotypes reveal and even though the governor was occasionally a moderating influence on his extreme supporters, he nonetheless consistently played the race card for political purposes. Perhaps if Wallace had used what historian Dan Carter calls "the politics of rage" only during major civil rights demonstrations or his campaigns, his bleats about maintaining segregation but not promoting racism would be more plausible. But the reality is that during his entire first term, race was a staple of the Wallace administration, connected to almost everyone and everything coming out of Montgomery. Race was used to pass legislation, to create and maintain popularity, to build a war chest for future campaigns, to instill in white Alabamians a pathological fear of blacks and the federal government, and quite simply for its own sake. Wallace may have thought he was something other than a racist, and his supporters then and now may have rationalized his ideology, but his actions, rhetoric, and correspondence stain his record far beyond merely a staged promise to stand in the schoolhouse door.

Privately, Wallace was fond of using the word "nigger" and telling off-color jokes. In the wake of the successful enrollment of Vivian Malone at the University of Alabama, Wallace asked administrator Jeff Bennett, in front of his nine-year-old son, how long it would take "to get the nigger bitch out of the dormitory." Now and again, Wallace would assemble a group of legislators to discuss pending legislation, then allow the meeting to disintegrate as he began an endless stream of racial rants and southern mythology about blacks. When he really got rolling, Wallace would talk out of the side of his mouth and roll his head back and forth in emotional bursts, stopping only when Seymore Trammell jumped in with an antiphonal burst of congratulations. The Citizens' Council had extensive access to the administration, as many legislators were members and the governor himself encouraged membership. The Klan also had the administration's ear, though more through access to Gerald Wallace and Trammell. Behind the scenes, Wallace would respond to criticism from the Left by telling his friends he would listen when "those people quit eating each other" or "stop throwing spears at each other," obvious basal references to grotesque presuppositions about Africa.[59]

One springboard for increasing Wallace's state and regional profile came a little over two months after the inauguration. At a meeting to encourage voter registration in Mobile attended by some one thousand black Alabamians, one of the speakers, U.S. District Attorney Vernol R. Jansen Jr., had the temerity to suggest that blacks ought to be able to register and vote. This was just the type of opportunity Wallace wanted. It allowed him to link the South's two arch villains since the time of the first Reconstruction, blacks and the federal government, to a national conspiracy to foment social experimentation. According to Wallace, the meeting was held "for the apparent purpose of instituting additional efforts to break down our heritage of segregation." In addition to Jansen, Leroy Johnson, an African American state legislator from Georgia, appeared on the dais. Not content with just blasting Jansen and calling for his immediate dismissal, Wallace sent telegrams to Senators Lister Hill and John Sparkman, hoping to apply pressure from both Montgomery and Washington. Ironically, Wallace seemed quite upset that Jansen was using race to further his career, speculating that he was seeking a federal judgeship. "In the event Mr. Jansen does attempt to obtain an appointment to fill any federal judgeship vacancy, I strongly urge you to do everything in your power to see that his efforts are blocked." The governor then added the trademark exaggeration that characterized his use of the race card: "We have reached the dictatorship level when it is possible for an attorney of the federal government to take actions such as those of Mr Jansen."[60]

Not content to exploit the issue for a day or so and then let it go, Wallace set out to gain as much information as possible about Jansen and the meeting. Jansen, according to Wallace, had done more than just speak at the rally; he actually made a "financial contribution." Reiterating his demand that Jansen be ousted, Wallace counseled Hill and Sparkman that "if he made a contribution to an organization whose avowed purpose is the breakdown of peace and order in our system . . . this constitutes an additional breach of the requirements of his office." Wallace also accused Mobile city commissioner Joseph Langan, a racial moderate, of sponsoring the event. For his own part, Wallace made public appeals for state and local lawmakers to use everything at their disposal to prevent integration. In other words, Wallace was telling state lawmakers to violate the law—the same charge he leveled against Jansen. Compounding the absurdity of the entire situation, Wallace had nothing but contempt for both Sparkman and Hill: he considered them soft on race. The furor reached its end with the state house considering a resolution censuring Jansen for "a shameless failure of some white men to stand up and fight for what counts most to us all."[61]

Wallace also perpetuated the color demarcations of white supremacy and black inferiority that had for decades prevented separate from being anywhere close to equal. During the Patterson administration, a report had been commissioned to document intellectual differences between blacks and whites. The goal was to create a scientific document that could serve as a legal bulwark in appeals against court-ordered desegregation. The author, University of North Carolina professor of histology and embryology W. C. George, had developed such an ardent reputation on race that University of Alabama president Frank

Rose refused to hire him. Not surprisingly, George's research reached the conclusions Governor Patterson expected.[62]

George documented a number of "important differences between whites and Negroes in intelligence, in personality, and in behavior," supposedly based on solid scientific evidence. According to George, among the most obvious variances between the races were that Negro bones are denser; the races have different protein components in their blood serum; Negroes are prone to "indolence, improvidence, and consequent pauperism" at much higher rates than whites; whites have intelligence quotients fifteen to twenty points higher than blacks; whites are six times more likely to be gifted and blacks are six times more likely to be "feeble-minded"; and blacks are more likely to be undisciplined, overly emotional, and incapable of regulating their own behavior. The end result of integration was intermarriage, which, according to George, led directly to decline. Assuming that the goal of any society was to achieve national greatness, George's prescription called for maximizing the quality of the gene pool and avoiding the deterioration that came from sexual relationships between whites and blacks. Apparently ignorant of African and world history, George concluded by suggesting that "nowhere in the world have they [blacks] demonstrated that they have the creative capacities to make a civilization." A review of the George report written by Vanderbilt University philosophy and psychology professor Herbert C. Sanborn read more like an endorsement than a thorough academic dissection. Hardly an objective scholar on racial matters, Sanborn himself had been extremely critical of integration at Ole Miss, calling it "the combined application of the tools of Communist, Fabian, and Zionist Socialism."[63]

While Patterson made little use of the document—he found it too crass to publicly position it as a conservative response to Gunnar Myrdal's *American Dilemma*—Wallace had the governor's office filling orders when interested outsiders wrote for more information or wanted the governor's input on the subject. Eventually, Wallace granted the University of Alabama permission to sell the report in book form. In addition to recommending George's *Biology of the Race Problem*, Wallace was also fond of Carleton Putnam's *Race and Reason* and Carleton Coon's *Origin of Races*.[64]

Beyond the vituperative literature of fringe science and the feeble rationalizations of lunatic supremacists, Wallace was constantly searching for instances of blacks and the federal government overstepping their bounds. Any link to criminal behavior or special perquisites coming from Washington, past, present, future, or imagined, was a public relations gold mine. By finding such cases, exaggerated or not, Wallace could charge out in front carrying the lance of racial purity and the shield of southern tradition, like some gallant neo-Klansman rescuing his homeland in a Thomas Dixon book. Whether it was encouraging Press Secretary Bill Jones to get as much information as possible about any of the individual federal troops brought into Birmingham or asking Attorney General Richmond Flowers to secure an injunction against unauthorized freedom walking in DeKalb or Etowah counties, Wallace knew how to turn the slightest infraction into an egregious offense against the South. In light of the civil rights demonstrations in the state and the atmosphere of the times, Wallace's popularity, derived in 1963 from regular exploitation of race, cannot be overestimated.[65]

Indeed, it was the seemingly little things that Wallace realized were most important to ordinary Alabamians in Flomaton or Hurtsboro or Woodville. Millions might be stolen during any administration in the highway or finance department, but unnecessary expenses in the executive mansion fund or wanton fluctuations in catering costs were the offenses that truck drivers and pipefitters and waitresses and hairdressers talked about. Seymore Trammell, Gerald Wallace, and Fuller Kimbrell might be playing fast and loose with state contracts and bid laws, but what killed a governor's credibility among the quilters and self-taught artists and hunters and fishermen and recreational softball players was spending more on groceries than the previous administration. The federal government might be contributing millions of dollars to Alabama for welfare, education, and road construction in matching funds, but if one Justice Department vehicle was used to transport a civil rights worker, then the entire Washington bureaucracy was immoral, unethical, and untrustworthy. In spite of Wallace's inability to stop the integration of school systems in Tuskegee and Mobile, in the midst of his setback when Vivian Malone and James Hood enrolled at the University of Alabama, and despite his failure to hold back the desegregation of public accommodations in Birmingham, Wallace always found just enough of these little things to augment his popularity at a time when he was seemingly losing all his major battles.

One immediate repercussion of Wallace's ability to find all manner of ways to use race was his siege against Richmond Flowers. Though Flowers, who was as ambitious as Wallace if not quite as politically savvy, ran for attorney general as a traditional Alabama segregationist, he almost immediately distanced himself from the new administration, particularly on matters of race. Though it is at least possible that Flowers made this sharp transition based on personal convictions, it seems much more likely that he understood the prevailing national winds concerning the inevitability of sweeping civil rights change and wanted to be out in front. This was not unlike Wallace's tactical decision a decade or so earlier to angle for a post on the Tuskegee Institute Board of Trustees. Flowers would run for governor in 1966 and be the first candidate in a century to court African American voters. But his public moderation went too far, too soon for most white Alabamians. Wallace minimized the office of attorney general whenever possible, and gladly made Flowers a co-scapegoat for Alabama's racial changes along with Judge Frank Johnson.[66]

One of the inevitable repercussions of publicly taunting Flowers was the trail it left for even less diplomatic folks from the hinterlands to follow. Birmingham resident Susanetta Harris's sentiments are representative of many Alabamians in 1963 who spared no opportunity to vent about the attorney general: "You, the attorney general . . . spew out with such spitefulness your baleful, perverted ideas of loyalty. You are the one bringing disgrace to the sovereign state of Alabama, and I know numerous people who dispair [sic] of what you are doing." Other Alabamians were even more truculent.[67]

Harris's correspondence is representative of another seemingly curious aspect of the Wallace phenomenon: his high level of support among Alabama women. Though historians have generally assumed that Wallace's support came primarily from lower-class, blue-collar, rural males, women were among the governor's most devoted admirers. A thorough examination of letters to the editor, correspondence to the governor, attendance at rallies, and interviews with campaign staff and reporters reveals that many white women were in virtual lockstep with the governor, especially during the contentious events of 1963. Any number of conservative influences in the state may have contributed to this phenomenon, but Wallace, with his ability to transform a crowd through language and animated gestures, and his ability to match the energy of a crowd, wooed many women into his camp with sheer magnetism. As long-time observer of Alabama politics Bob Ingram noted, "like it or not, people, your mothers and grandmothers had the hots for George Wallace."[68]

Once Wallace began to achieve some national renown as a states' rights man, the inner circle of the massive resistance crowd began to welcome him into their old boys network. Wallace had been a loyalist while attending the 1948 Democratic National Convention when the states' rights stalwarts fled the party and created the brief Dixiecrat movement. Fifteen years later, Wallace had abandoned all vestiges of affinity for the national Democratic party and was moving with ease in old Dixiecrat circles. Ross Barnett was a kindred spirit from the beginning and attended the 1963 inauguration. Even before the inauguration, Wallace dispatched Al Lingo to observe the Ole Miss crisis and issued his own statement praising Barnett and saying they were both "tired of being pushed around by the Justice Department and the irresponsible, lousy federal courts." Strom Thurmond became a regular correspondent, relying on the governor to provide him with "any supporting data that I might be able to use against [Martin Luther] King." Even Jessie Helms, not yet a professional politician, relied on Wallace for advice and offered encouragement. Lester Maddox, suddenly famous for his ax-handle resistance and refusal to desegregate his Pickrick cafeteria in Atlanta, received a congratulatory letter from

Wallace for his stand against a handful of black preachers who wanted to eat in the restaurant. Maddox, according to Wallace, had been a victim of the insidious antiprivate enterprise machinations of the federal government.[69]

Within the state, two organizations served as the focus for administration race battles: the State Sovereignty Commission headed by Eli Howell and the Citizens' Councils, a private organization with multiple chapters across the South. The Citizens' Councils offered an outlet for Klan-style sympathies but with comparatively more respectable members. More middle class in membership and less outwardly committed to violence, the Alabama Citizens' Councils emanated from a 150-mile radius of Selma and were "dedicated to maintenance of peace, good order and domestic tranquility in our communities and in our state and to the preservation of out state's rights." Local chapters elected local officers and belonged to a larger Association of Citizens' Councils based in Greenwood, Mississippi.[70]

Despite their noble-sounding mission statement, the Citizens' Councils were formed completely around the twin cornerstones of white supremacy and segregation. The Dunning myth was alive and well in the councils—promotional material chronicled the "poverty and degradation" of the defeated men in gray who were "unable to vote and [were] under the heel of Negro occupation troops. All they had was their undying courage and faith that the Almighty helps those who help themselves. . . . We are the same blood." Comparisons between the horrors of the first Reconstruction and its looming redux were palpable: "Our situation is not as hopeless as theirs, but just as insidious and deadly to our posterity if you and I do nothing. What decisions are you going to make for those baby children at home?"[71]

At the time Wallace took office, the state Citizens' Councils were in need of a jolt to revive the cause, and Wallace became a leading factor in the membership drive. According to a February 1961 memorandum, the prestige of the state's various councils had dwindled over the last five years and was at a "low ebb financially and in total membership." Leonard Wilson, the only white student to be expelled from the University of Alabama in the aftermath of the Autherine Lucy case, was named executive secretary of the statewide organization. Wilson began a program to reinvigorate the councils, start a chapter in every county that had none, promote essay contests in high schools, begin a letter-writing campaign explaining the councils' positions, and solicit contributions and membership from "ministers, doctors, attorneys, public officials, school teachers, businessmen, and northerners."[72]

New Citizens' Council members throughout the South received form letters from Wallace congratulating them on their decision to join and urging diligence in the fight for maintaining "racial integrity and our constitutional form of government." Wallace spoke frequently at Citizens' Council meetings throughout the state and region, expected his subordinates to do so as well, and in both speeches and correspondence, constantly encouraged people to consider joining the organization. As early as October 1963, Wallace was riding to council events in a Cadillac adorned with "Wallace for President" signs. Since the council meetings were a great focus group for trying new applause lines and floating trial balloons, Wallace kept a clipping file of anti–civil rights movement material from newspapers, magazines, and conservative newsletters and regaled the audience with the latest information about Martin Luther King, the Kennedys, Judge Frank Johnson, or the impetuous Supreme Court. Most of this was easy to accumulate from the flood of mail that came to Montgomery on a daily basis, which often included snippets from local papers all over the country. The governor was particularly interested in any published reports that documented connections between communism and Martin Luther King, Fred Shuttlesworth, the freedom riders, or any of the various organizations involved in the movement.[73]

Linking social activism to communism was nothing new in Alabama or the South in general, but in the eyes of many, Wallace's vehemence and burgeoning reputation across the region added credibility to his charges. The governor made the media a frequent whipping boy, focusing his wrath on newspapers. Yet even the most cursory search of letters to the editor in the state's newspapers reveals how little moderate editorials influenced rank-and-file readers and how thoroughly Alabamians were mimicking Wallace's rhetoric about the marriage of the Red Menace and black agitation. Mrs. Carroll Smith of Mobile's Tristan de Luna Chapter of the Daughters of the American Revolution connected communism with her interpretation of recent trends in Washington: "It does not take a super patriot to observe today a tremendous drive to increased centralization of power in the hands of the executive. To win the Cold War of ideas against the commusocialists [sic], the people of the US must know what our system is, have passionate faith in it, and be prepared to defend it." Even Parent-Teacher Association groups got involved in identifying the presence of communism in Alabama. An April 1963 meeting featured a presentation titled "Communism's Invisible Weapon: Brainwashing."[74]

Cast against the unfolding drama of the civil rights movement, the domestic cold war is too often minimized as a factor in the ideology of massive resistance. To be sure, the threat of communism was drastically overstated, and demagogues in the North and South seized the issue for their own political purposes. But in a state and region that placed a premium on national defense and patriotism, and at a time when Sputnik, the Bay of Pigs, and the Cuban Missile Crisis were closer to current events than to history, virulent anticommunism in the minds of a generation that came of age during World War II seemed reasonable. The actual relationship between communism and the civil rights movement may have been minimal, but the fear in the minds of many was real. Communists living in Birmingham during the 1930s actively espoused racial justice. Consequently, when that city's white supremacists like Art Hanes called protests in the streets "pure communism," many Alabamians believed him. And when George Wallace testified in Senate Commerce Committee meetings that the racial strife of the past few years was the product of communist insurgency, many Alabamians, with their memories of the 1930s combined with the complex intersection of cold war ideology and institutionalized racial presuppositions, thought the charge was reasonable.[75]

In addition to branding the civil rights movement a communist front, Wallace sought to indict the movement as a money-making scheme. Warming up at a press conference for a council meeting later that night, Wallace charged that "this so-called civil rights movement has been very profitable to some Negro leaders and it looks like some other folks are trying to get in on the act." Martin Luther King's principal interests, according to the Alabama governor, were making money and preaching. To a dedicated Marxist or even a citizen with a passing knowledge of economic history, these two charges would seem to be at odds with each other. Yet many Alabamians, had no difficulty accepting Wallace's assertions.[76]

If the Citizens' Council was the vehicle for the popular defense of segregation, the Committee on Constitutional Law and State Sovereignty led by Eli Howell was the official state organization for legal action. The legal and political measures considered by the administration, often through the auspices of the Sovereignty Commission, bordered on the absurd. State banking charters were held in abeyance until links with "Negro racial agitators" could be explored. Federally funded programs to develop conservation work for Alabamians age sixteen to twenty-one, such as HR 5131, were ignored for fear of mandatory integration. Wallace wired Representative Carl Elliot asking him to prevent passage of HR 5131 because the bill would lead to "flooding of Alabama and other southern states with disciplinary camps to take care of delinquents of all races from other areas." Letters were sent asking for federal aid without any controlling restrictions "which will affect our social systems and heritage." Legislation was offered with the administration's backing to mandate a five thousand dollar fine and five-year prison term for any state, county, or city employees who participated in civil rights demonstrations. Wallace asked Charlie Cooper, the head of the Legislative Reference Service, to draft a bill to "make it against the law for any person [to enter] the state upon the purpose of instigating or advocating the violation of State laws or city ordinances."[77]

Yet another seemingly small issue that Wallace exploited for his own political benefit was an automobile ride that Martin Luther King received in a

Justice Department vehicle. Tipped off that King had received a ride from Birmingham to Selma and unable to resist any opportunity to assail his two favorite targets, Wallace went public immediately and exaggerated the entire issue. "He has been traveling throughout the state in vehicles rented by the Justice Department. This is not surprising to me—but it is a matter which should be called to the attention of the people of this country. . . . A racial agitator and troublemaker who has caused demonstrations to occur throughout the US can now apparently travel at the expense of the US government." While Wallace was blasting King for misusing government transportation, Press Secretary Bill Jones was lining up a New England speaking tour for the governor using official state airplanes.[78]

The King–Justice Department car fiasco was one of the few times that Wallace took on the federal government and won. Wallace kept the eager media engaged with almost daily sound bites and charges. Forced to respond, the Justice Department admitted it gave King a ride but suggested it was only a five-minute trip and done purely for the purposes of facilitating an interview. Wallace, relying on surveillance information from police and others, knew that King had actually been driven from Birmingham to Selma. At a Citizens' Council meeting in Durham, North Carolina, the governor announced, to the uproarious approval of the assembled masses, that he would ask for a federal grand jury to investigate the King ride. A few days later, Wallace intensified his remarks. The federal government, Wallace said, was "eager to investigate and enjoin white people in Alabama but reluctant to give similar treatment to Negroes. . . . The people of Alabama have been intimidated too long by the federal courts and the Justice Department. We have some civil rights too." Wallace attempted to transport a Dallas County grand jury to Washington in an effort to boost his own image while further embarrassing Robert Kennedy. The Justice Department was forced to obtain a restraining order preventing the Alabama grand jury from subpoenaing agents for questioning on the matter. Eventually, the Justice Department admitted to loaning a car to the Reverend Nelson Smith to drive King to Selma. The Justice Department attorney who authorized the trip, Thomas Henderson, resigned his position. A day later Wallace demanded the resignation of Robert Kennedy in order to restore confidence in the federal government.[79]

Taken together, these incidents exploiting race for purely political purposes created an atmosphere of violence in Alabama. The combination of physical defiance, dangerous rhetoric, and constant manipulation created the illusion that any person acting for the purpose of maintaining white supremacy would be given safe harbor. Undeniably, Wallace stoked the flames that led to beatings, bombings, terror, and death. When the president of the United States was depicted as a dictator who sanctioned rioting, when the Supreme Court was described as an institution peopled by unqualified political hacks intent on eradicating God from American schools and society, when the state was portrayed as being inundated by hordes of communist outside agitators, beatniks, criminals, and sexual perverts, and when fundamental principles of free enterprise and private property were pictured as being ripped away from law-abiding taxpayers, violence looked less like a ridiculous and illegal option and more like a reasonable alternative. In short, Wallace created a siege mentality for his own purposes, with dangerous consequences.

Without question, Wallace knew exactly what was happening. Caught between a pathological desire to hear the roar of the crowd and a rationalized belief that he could take white Alabamians to the brink of explosion without actually detonating them, Wallace rarely felt a sense of personal responsibility for anything. He bragged to anyone within earshot that he singlehandedly prevented violence in Tuscaloosa with his stand in the schoolhouse door. Wallace later claimed, and his apologists accepted, that the governor devised something akin to a master strategy that placed him front and center in order to keep the Klan distanced and violence minimized. According to this interpretation, Wallace knew he could not forestall desegregation, but he wanted to ease the sense of defeat of the traditionalists. Further, Wallace, according to this view, only used race for political expediency—as if this somehow made it more forgivable—and, somehow, he always knew just when to quit.[80]

It is not the more celebrated instances of racial exploitation by the governor—the Birmingham crisis, the stand in the schoolhouse door, or the Sixteenth Street bombing—that transformed the state, but rather the daily diet of animus and demagoguery. The more publicized events served to create a regional and national reputation, but by then, Wallace was already powerful and popular within the state. The stand in the schoolhouse door was a staged surrender designed to reinforce an off-the-cuff campaign promise and generate national publicity. It worked. Wallace survived a bout with nervous jitters and refused to obey Deputy Attorney General Nicholas Katzenbach's request to leave the doorway to Foster Auditorium until he had read what historian Culpepper Clark has called a "five-minute denunciation of the federal government." The actions of the federal government, Wallace declared, were an "unwelcomed, unwanted, unwarranted and forced intrusion upon the campus of the University of Alabama." A few hours later, when asked to stand down by Brigadier General Henry V. Graham of the Alabama contingent of the 31st Dixie Division, Wallace spoke briefly again: "This is a bitter pill for members of the Alabama National Guard to swallow. . . . Alabama is winning this fight against Federal interference because we are awakening the people to the trend toward military dictatorship in this country. I am returning to Montgomery to continue working for constitutional government to benefit Alabamians—black and white." Rather than go through the entire charade again at the University of Alabama at Huntsville, Wallace wired university president Frank Rose: "Due to this illegal and unwarranted military occupation, I will not be present on the Huntsville campus tomorrow. However, we will continue relentlessly our fight against forced integration of the University of Alabama." Dave McGlathery enrolled at Huntsville without incident.[81]

From every objective viewpoint, Wallace lost at the University of Alabama. James Hood and Vivian Malone enrolled in school. John Kennedy and his brother Robert, once reticent to fully embrace the political realities of attacking segregation, grew increasingly bold and allowed themselves to be fully linked with civil rights as a "moral issue." Despite his blustering, Wallace was unable to remove the students in subsequent days, although Hood later withdrew. But from a subjective perspective, Wallace won in every way he *hoped* he might win. Large-scale violence was prevented, which added to his regional credibility. He became a recognized national spokesman for massive resistance and began to appear regularly on programs such as *Meet the Press*. Thousands of letters from across the country poured into Montgomery hailing the governor for his stand and giving him a platform from which to fight the Civil Rights Act and launch a brief presidential bid the following year. Within the state, he had honored his covenant and his overwhelming popularity increased. Most importantly, nobody in Alabama had expected him to actually prevent integration; they just expected him to postpone it. Wallace won in Alabama despite losing, because he changed the way the game was scored.

3
Sins of Omission, Sins of Commission / 1964

George Wallace welcomed the new year with a tremendous amount of confidence. Buoyed by a thriving national economy, the administration attracted $336.8 million in new and expanded industry during its maiden year. State docks profits topped the $1 million mark for the first time since 1956. Total freight entering the state shipping facilities reached an all-time high of more than 16 million tons. State tourism increased some 8 percent, significantly higher than the 2 percent national average. Alabama farmers enjoyed especially strong years in corn, cotton, pecans, peanuts, and poultry production. Even the state's flagship college football teams, Auburn and the University of Alabama, played in coveted New Year's Day bowl games. Wallace's Ivy League speaking tour was extremely successful in generating publicity and increasing his regional and state image as an unabashed defender of southern conservatism. A western tour to Colorado, Arizona, California, Oregon, and Washington was just days away. Over the past year, Wallace had done nothing less than transform himself from a Barbour County, Alabama, penny-ante politician and judge to the most recognized governor in the United States.[1]

National Vistas

The governor was so giddy that he was able to tell reporters that he did not want a second term in 1970, that he would probably retire from politics and become a country lawyer, and that he was generally tired of the unpleasantries of campaigning for office. Presumably, the governor offered these declarations with a straight face, but in reality, nothing could have been farther from the truth. Wallace was about to embark on the first of the national political campaigns that would result in chronic disregard for his duties as governor. The net result was a cycle of neglect that prevented meaningful progress on a variety of pressing issues.[2]

In January, Wallace was approached by John Carnett, a Baptist minister from Henderson, Texas, about running for president under the banner of the Major Political Party of America. Carnett's staunchly conservative group was small, though it did promise some one hundred thousand dollars for a campaign war chest. Wallace declined the offer, but he told Carnett their views were "virtually the same" and dispatched Bill Jones to meet with him. This was but the first of many fringe groups that would seek out the Alabama governor and offer money and support. The contrast between Alabama and national campaigns was significant. Wallace's national supporters were often well outside the political mainstream, disaffected by a changing economy, the clash of cultures, and a general belief in their growing powerlessness. Within the state, Wallace's supporters, though often exhibiting many of these same socioeconomic characteristics, were more comfortably within the mainstream of state politics.[3]

The 1964 national campaign resulted in Wallace's running in three presidential primaries, but the real focus of his foray north was to increase his popularity across the South by bashing the civil rights bill, later enacted as the Civil Rights Act of 1964. Wallace had no real belief that he could win even one primary, let alone an election. But he knew that there was a base of discontented Americans that he could tap into for future use. Even if that failed, Wallace's tours outside the state were remarkably popular within Alabama at a time when the citizenry should have expected greater attention to matters at home. When Wallace canvassed Ohio, Wisconsin, and Indiana and called the civil rights bill "the most far-reaching package of dictatorial rules, regulations, and restrictions ever proposed in the United States," people like Mrs. Bruce Holding Jr., Mrs. James Melton, and Miss Jonnie Murchison of Elmore County responded by holding fund-raising dinners, instead of suggesting their governor ought to be working in Montgomery. The Montgomery Speedway held an auto race with the proceeds going to the Wallace for President Fund and the winner receiving the George C. Wallace trophy. The state legislature gleefully paid more than twenty thousand dollars in transportation costs for Wallace's speaking tours and passed a salutary resolution: "We appreciate and endorse his use of the state airplane in his efforts and urge its continued use by him for these purposes."[4]

Wallace's excursions outside the state typically revolved around personal speaking tours and vocal denunciations of the civil rights bill. It was in the anti–civil rights bill speeches that Wallace first approached the tenor that would propel him to a status as a more viable presidential candidate in 1968 and help usher in a conservative transformation of American politics. In a signature July 4, 1964, speech in Atlanta, Georgia, Wallace lashed out with an entire laundry list of charges, countercharges, and woeful jeremiads against civil rights, the people who favored them, and government run amok. The Civil Rights Act of 1964 was a "fraud, a sham, and a hoax . . . an act of tyranny. It is the assassin's knife stuck in the back of liberty. . . . With this assassin's knife and a blackjack in the hand of the federal force-cult, the left-wing liberals will try to force us back into bondage." The law's proponents were "left-wing radical apologists," "vultures of the liberal left-wing press," "pinknik social engineers in Washington," and "communist front organizations with high sounding names." The federal judiciary, which was hell-bent on enforcing the law, was "the greatest single threat to individual freedom and liberty in the United States today." The ultimate intent of the laws was to "destroy the rights of private property, to destroy the freedom and liberty of you and me . . . where there are no property rights, there are no human rights." Wallace unequivocally asserted that neither he nor his state would enforce the law.[5]

Many of these speaking tours were packaged for mass consumption as industrial development excursions with a small dose of campaigning thrown in for good measure. Yet a confidential industrial prospects report prepared by Wallace staffer Leonard Beard indicates that very little hunting for economic development actually occurred. On an eight-day midwestern trip in February 1964, the administration saw no prospects on three of the days and only one prospect on two other occasions. One appointment, with Charles Taylor and Sons, had to be moved to the governor's hotel room because the firm wished that "no publicity be given out linking the company's name with the governor's visit." Another corporation, Columbus Plastic Products, agreed to receive the governor but Beard admitted that "this visit is to fill [the] schedule after many Columbus firms refused to see us. The company states they have no current need for a new plant anywhere." All of this scheduling of prospects was arranged primarily through the work of Cooper Green at Alabama Power. Wallace was quick to brag to prospects that other states could never supply energy as cheaply as Alabama Power.[6]

In early 1964, Wallace's Committee of 100 for Industrial Development began to meet, presumably to brainstorm ideas for economic growth and ways to attract new industry. In announcing appointments to the committee, Wallace was quick to lapse into the Alabama-against-the-world mentality for political mileage. "Our image among industrialists is not what those left-wing publications would lead you to believe. They are impressed favorably with our attitude—our belief in free enterprise and the profit system." The 100, led by their governor as chairman, were actually 111, or more, with a constantly fluctuating membership list when political considerations demanded someone be given a perquisite from the administration. The key members of the group were Alabama Power's Cooper Green and Fletcher Farrington of the Alabama Farm Bureau, members of two of the state's biggest and most powerful interest groups. Typically, the Farm Bureau demanded representation on all state agencies and boards however remote agriculture might be from the committee's purview. Lest the committee become convinced it had been chartered to accomplish something, the chairman gaveled through a resolution at the first meeting clarifying its purpose: "No information shall be released to the press by any member of the Advisory Board or by the committee. All press releases are to be given by the governor."[7]

Alabamians in Need

Perhaps Wallace should have been more interested in state affairs because many of the most vulnerable Alabamians obtained very little in the way of assistance from the state. Old age pensioners received monthly payments of $67.85, 88 percent of the national average. To make matters worse, the Alabama State Committee on Aging identified a monthly figure of $118 per month as a minimum standard of living for one person. Rubin Hanna, state chairman of the committee, described the situation as desperate: "This is real poverty in the midst of plenty. Poverty among the aged differs from that among others in the population because there is less possibility of recovery." Aid for blind people in Alabama averaged $47.93 per month, 59 percent of the national average. The permanently disabled received $45.92 per month, 60 percent of the national average. Allocations for aid to dependent children per household were $47.33, 37 percent of the national average. The average aid for dependent children per recipient totaled $11.64 per month, 38 percent of the national average. Alabama was second worst among southern states in unemployment compensation. Even the tuberculosis rate was disproportionately high at nearly twice the national average.[8]

The state was contributing approximately $27.84 million for state welfare programs; the federal government was providing nearly $88 million to Alabama. Of the state's total allocation, only about one-third was appropriated from the general fund, with the rest being collected from a variety of whiskey, beer, and cigarette taxes. Federal guidelines mandated a maximum of 60 cases per welfare worker; Alabama averaged nearly 120 cases per worker. The total number of old age pension recipients increased from 140,528 in 1962 to 147,880 in 1963 to 149,837 in 1965. In the midst of all this overwhelming need, the administration did almost nothing. A law was passed changing the Committee on the Aging of the State of Alabama to a full-fledged commission complete with a staff, but, predictably, the state refused to appropriate money for the new agency. When the 1965 budget called for an additional appropriation of $4.3 million, the administration favored a plan that relied on $4.6 million in new federal funds and $300,000 less in state money. Despite Wallace's regular carping about the unwanted and forced intrusions of the federal government into Alabama, it was clear that Washington was spending considerably more money in Alabama than the state was supplying in taxes.[9]

Situated against this backdrop of overwhelming need, Wallace actually favored a reduction in the state Department of Pensions and Security funds for the following biennial fiscal budget. As early as April 1963, the department's commissioner, Ruben King, complained that Wallace was crippling the agency with budget cutbacks. Wallace was prepared to allocate roughly $2.9 million less per year than King had requested. From the broadest perspective, the reduction of funding was ridiculous since federal money, some 75 percent of the annual state welfare coffers, was directly tied to the state's meeting certain requirements. King had requested the additional funds for several reasons. The state had only $105,000 as available balance from which to begin annual operations, a reduction of over $1 million from the previous year. Even more threatening was the expected increase in patient loads for an already overworked and underpaid cadre of welfare caseworkers. King cautioned Wallace, "Our caseworkers are carrying an average work load of 300 cases which is the highest . . . of any state with the same kind of program." By comparison, South Carolina had 198 cases per worker, Georgia 208, North Carolina 180, and New York 64.[10]

Smaller caseloads would have had positive effects across many fronts. Caseworkers could have spent more time with welfare recipients, counseling them and helping them find economic opportunity. Caseworkers could have spent time doing more investigative research on recipients and trimming the fraudulent from the state rolls. King assured the governor, who normally loved the chance to take any morsel of financial savings to the public, this would be the case: "Many demonstrations have proven that smaller case loads with frequent contacts will result in reducing dependency and over a period of time lowering assistance costs."[11]

Though King ended his April correspondence with an urgent handwritten plea in the margin, "Governor, I think that it [is] most urgent that we discuss this matter as soon as possible," four months later he was again pleading with Wallace to restore lost funds so that basic services could be provided. King, through his own legwork, had already shepherded a panoply of potential taxes to Ways and Means, but needed the governor's blessings to get them passed. To be sure, the proposed taxes were regressive—liquor agents tax, cigarette tax, and contracts tax—and certain to be passed on directly or indirectly to many of the people least able to pay them. Yet, as King insisted, "any increase in the old age pension or other assistance program above our biennial budget would require still additional funds." Wallace campaigned in 1962 on increasing old age pensions but had to be cajoled into not actually cutting them through Pensions and Security cutbacks.[12]

Despite his inimitable essence as a political animal, Wallace—for all the pain and heartache he caused myriads of Alabamians, for all the indifference he exhibited toward his wife and children, for all the prevailing apathy about the mundane machinations of governance he wore like a badge of honor— was prone to occasional bursts of sincere humanity. When Ada Scott from Fort Payne phoned the governor to report she had yet to receive her monthly pension check, Wallace ordered his secretary to call the Pensions Department and get the problem solved. When Josie Mae Randolph of Gadsden called Wallace during the Christmas season to tell him she was no longer receiving her state check for aid to the blind because she had begun receiving Social Security allotments, the governor asked Ruben King "to check into this because this did sound like a bad situation . . . and a needy case." Such incidents happened often enough to reveal the subtle complexities of Wallace's personality and character. Perhaps more importantly for Wallace, rumors of these acts of kindness swept through the state and, combined with the governor's amazing memory for names and faces, further endeared him to ordinary folk.[13]

Greeting the Winds of Change

While the most impoverished and vulnerable Alabamians were floundering in a sea of economic misery, their *popularist* Alabama governor was continuing his strategy of governance by perpetual campaign. In regional or national issues, the hot issue for exploitation was the looming civil rights bill, which was gathering momentum from a martyred president and his deal-making southern successor. Wallace would take this issue into Indiana, Wisconsin, and Ohio, declaring he was an advocate not of racism but of private property rights. Within the state, the hot issue was the move toward private schools as yet another strategy for circumventing or at least forestalling further integration.

The local school integration issue reached a flashpoint in September 1963 when a total of twenty-four black students in Tuskegee, Birmingham, Mobile, and Huntsville were admitted to previously all-white public schools. In his second "stand" of sorts, Wallace sent armed state troopers to Macon County to prevent thirteen black children from entering Tuskegee High. Claiming he was acting only to prevent violence, Wallace quickly closed the school for a week saying, "it is the obligation and duty of the governor to maintain peace and order." In reality, Wallace had invoked his own police powers to take control of the school away from local administrators, teachers, and law enforcement. The man who claimed to speak for states' rights and local government had superceded local authorities in the same style he was wont to accuse John Kennedy or Lyndon Johnson of practicing. School desegregation, the governor proclaimed, denied the majority their civil rights.[14]

Alabamians fully understood that school integration was coming to state high schools in the fall of 1963 and wrote the governor with their suggestions. Mrs. Louis Anderson of Safford, Alabama, urged the governor to take action: "I can't bear the thoughts of a Negro in our schools here in Orrville. All of our social activities are a necessary part of a small school. I am not just thinking of my son. I am thinking of all the children to come. . . . This country is now being ruled by a minority." Mrs. Fletcher King wrote to inform the governor that she preferred to close all the schools rather than face integration: "It is best for all that the races remain separate, and it is my hope that they will be kept apart in every way." Both women had high hopes that the success of Virginia's Prince Edward County could be adopted in Alabama and that private schools would flourish.[15]

M. H. Woodard of Cullman briefed the governor on another possibility: the repeal of the state compulsory school law. Woodard, who owned a clothes, shoes, and ready-to-wear shop, advised Wallace to call a special session of the legislature for the express purposes of rescinding the law that forced "white people to send their own children to integrated schools against their will." Woodard, and scores of other Alabamians, viewed closing schools or removing their children from the education process as preferable to integration. Privately, Wallace knew such an option was not viable, but Woodard and others believed Wallace's public rhetoric about keeping whites and blacks separate no matter the cost.[16]

More than anything, Wallace knew how to gauge the totality of public opinion. And he was on safe ground with Alabama parents if he blustered about the federal government ruining education even if he did not actually take steps to end it in the state. Of no small consideration was the growing political power of the state teachers' union, a force that Wallace would butt heads with in coming years. Finally, it was difficult politically to allow for the wholesale destruction of the entire public school system when Wallace was touting his education policies as the linchpin to making Alabama the "Athens of the South" and claiming education was the "primary function of state government."[17]

Wallace codified his stance toward closing certain schools with executive order number nine. The order was a simple two-page draft stating that conditions existed that were "calculated to result in a disruption of the peace and tranquility of this State and to occasion peril to the lives and property of the citizens" by this "threat of forced and unwarranted integration of the public schools." The order, which applied only to Tuskegee High, closed the school for a week, from September 2 until September 9, 1963. But it also served as a microcosm of Wallace's intent to fight desegregation and keep himself in the headlines whenever possible.[18]

The combination of closing the schools and sending armed troopers to the ones that remained open wrought a more complex reaction than Wallace anticipated. In Birmingham, fresh-faced white cheerleaders from West End High School greeted two Negro girls with melodic chants of "two, four, six, eight, who do we appreciate? Wallace, Wallace, Wallace," and "two, four, six, eight, we don't wanna integrate." Another girl walked out of school declaring, "I'm sorry this happened but I'm not going to school with niggers." A group of women from the West End area presented a petition to the school board asking it to close the schools rather than allow them to be integrated. But, evincing a growing sense of realism about the issue, the Birmingham Young Men's Business Club issued a resolution demanding that the governor stop "gambling with the lives and futures of the school children of this state to further your own political career." Even the Birmingham City Council applied light pressure to keep the schools open even if they were integrated.[19]

In Huntsville, twenty-five white women bulled through trooper lines to register their children with the full knowledge that their schools would be integrated. The city council, turning a bit of the governor's logic against him, warned him to keep Montgomery out of Huntsville's affairs. The presence of armed troopers caused a few to question what country they were living in. Thirteen-year-old Tricia Miree wrote the governor to tell him that "we have four Negroes going to our schools. No one in Huntsville minds. . . . Children all over the world want to go to school. . . . Public schools are for the public and the public is everyone. America is a free country. Leave it that way." Yet even in Huntsville, arguably Alabama's least classically southern city, assemblages of parents shouted out at black students that they were not wanted. Some openly sobbed at the specter of desegregation; others vowed to withdraw their children as soon as possible and send them to a private academy.[20]

Events in Birmingham, Huntsville, and Mobile played out over the course of a few weeks with attendance gradually returning to normal after several days of boycotting by whites. In Tuskegee, however, the scene was more contentious. On the same night that Wallace issued executive order number nine, Mayor James M. Rea of Notasulga, a tiny hamlet in Macon County, wired Wallace pledging his complete support: "The Notasulga Police Department is at your command for any service you may deem necessary in Macon County." Notasulga's finest were not needed since Wallace relied on Al Lingo's troopers to control the situation. Robert Kennedy responded to Wallace's use of troopers by dispatching Justice Department deputy director John Doar to the scene to gather information and provide a federal presence.[21]

With the September 9 deadline rapidly approaching, Wallace grew even more tense than normal. The governor lived for full contact campaign politics on the stump, but behind the scenes and in private dealings, he detested conflict and sought to avoid it whenever possible. When questioned by reporters about continuing to lock down Tuskegee High, the governor curtly snapped at the scribes and told them to read his executive orders. The entire issue was settled when President Kennedy federalized some seventeen thousand Alabama national guard troops and Wallace withdrew the troopers just as he had done in Tuscaloosa. The governor, of course, claimed victory and took political cover by discrediting the motivations of the president: "Is this being done because it has been announced that I may participate in some of the presidential primaries? When we get around to jailing our political opponents, we will have taken another long step toward a military dictatorship. The Kennedys have now taken personal command of their Alabama garrison."[22]

Defeated again, Wallace shifted gears to support the possibility of permanently closed public schools and state-supported private schools. The governor wired John Segrest, the head of the Macon County Private School Foundation, to commend him for his "splendid and dedicated efforts" and not so subtly interjected the implication that he could count on receiving resources from the state. Within days, Wallace was on television and in print calling for Alabamians to send their money and offer their prayers for the private schools. In early October, Wallace began referring to state assistance for the segregated private schools in terms of tuition grants, officially asked all state employees to donate money for private schools across the state, and spoke at numerous rallies. At one such rally, Wallace effusively praised private school parents. "You are made of the right kind of stuff. . . . Your forebearers [sic] and mine are the ones who brought individual liberty and freedom to the world, the people who brought this country into being." Less than one month after executive order number nine expired, Macon Academy opened with 128 white students in grades 7 through 12. Within two years, the school had grown to 338 students and offered instruction for kindergarten through twelfth grade.[23]

Conditions at the new school, however, were far from ideal. The students met in two hastily renovated homes, and space, lighting, personnel, and equipment were substandard. The school had no lunchroom and offered no transportation for students. Tuition was twenty to twenty-two dollars per month per student, but parents were assured that within the next year, the state would be supplementing if not fully funding the school. In promotional literature, Jefferson Academy near Birmingham stated that "after the first year, sustained financial support through state grants-in-aid to students is anticipated." Macon Academy met its first payroll on November 1, but not without some anxious moments.[24]

One indirect consequence of moving toward segregated academies was the potential disruption of Alabama's fall obsession, football. Wallace wired Wayne McLendon, the captain of the Tuskegee High football team to assure his full and complete support if the squad reassembled under the banner of a private school: "Your willingness to sacrifice for the principles in which we all believe is gratifying to me and the people of the State of Alabama. I wish to give my personal pledge, that should you wish to reactivate your team in conjunction with the efforts of the Macon County School Foundation, I will see to it that you are provided the necessary equipment."[25]

The governor's support for private schools was not just limited to speeches, pledges to find sports equipment, and public exhortations for others to contribute money. Wallace himself donated money from his own funds, allocated $6,000 from his 1964 presidential campaign chest to the private school campaign, and arranged for well-heeled social conservatives from outside the state to kick in handsomely. One such donor was W. P. Draper of New York City who funneled some $10,000 to Macon Academy on the recommendation of Wallace and National Citizens' Council president W. J. Simmons of Jackson, Mississippi. In 1966, Draper contributed another $10,000 to Macon Academy and $20,000 to Lowndes Academy. As he did with new members of the Citizens' Council, Wallace used the resources of his office to make sure every donor to Macon Academy got a signed letter of thanks. The Legislative Reference Division researched private school issues, including tuition grants in other states. Highway patrol officers were used to ferry students, checks, and packages back and forth from Montgomery to Tuskegee. Wallace even sent a special Christmas greeting to Macon Academy. In short, the governor's office served as a command center for private education where packages, contributions, equipment, and correspondence might be accumulated before being dispersed to Macon Academy, Hoover Academy, West End Academy, or some other embryonic segregated facility.[26]

Wallace's public defiance on school integration emboldened some who perpetuated violence on black Alabamians. Within one month of Wallace's issuance of executive order number nine, civil rights lawyer Arthur Shores's house in Birmingham was bombed for the second time in three weeks, leading to riots, one death, and eight serious injuries; as many as twenty other black residents of the Magic City were injured by gunfire. Businessman A. G. Gaston and his wife returned to Birmingham from a state dinner at the White House just in time for their house to be bombed. Cynthia Wesley, Carol Robertson, Addie Mae Collins, and Denise McNair were murdered by Klansmen while they attended Sunday school at the Sixteenth Street Baptist Church. Twenty-three others were seriously injured. Hours later Johnnie Robinson was shot to death by police for throwing rocks at passing cars. A group of whites in Anniston beat up two Negro ministers.[27]

While Wallace never publicly admitted to creating a climate that was conducive for violence, and many of his closest associates still credit the governor with actually preventing violence, more than a few contemporary observers felt otherwise. Martin Luther King laid the blame for the church bombing at Wallace's feet: "Governor Wallace is largely responsible for these vicious murders, for his irresponsible words and actions have created the atmosphere for violence and murder all over the state of Alabama." Richmond Flowers cited a correlation between the Birmingham bombing and Tuscaloosa: "The individuals who bombed the Sixteenth [Street Baptist] Church in their way were standing in the schoolhouse door." Many state newspapers, including those in Tuscaloosa and Birmingham, warned that Wallace's words and deeds made violence more likely. But Wallace told a Citizens' Council audience in Atlanta, "I don't apologize for anything I have done and if I had to do it all over again, I would do the same thing again."[28]

The climate of intransigence by the governor continued throughout 1964. In January, Tuskegee High had been resegregated: only black students attended. Whites had either enrolled at Macon Academy or were being shuttled by state troopers to school in nearby Notasulga or Shorter. When trooper-pooling became untenable, Wallace authorized the transfer of two buses from a Decatur trade school to Macon County so that free state transportation of white students whose parents objected to integration at Tuskegee High might continue. Wallace's actions were a thinly veiled attempt to circumvent Judge Frank Johnson's prohibition of using county transportation for the express purposes of maintaining segregated schools.[29]

When constitutional experts informed the governor's floor leaders in the legislature that it would be impossible to fund private schools in a way that would pass federal muster, Wallace, undeterred, responded by touring Macon Academy and announcing his full endorsement of legislation authorizing state grants-in-aid. The governor boasted that the entire state was proud of the students and he painstakingly shook the hand of every single one of them. An autographed picture of Wallace was hung prominently in the main hallway of the school. Wallace credited everyone affiliated with the school with "meeting the challenge with dignity and without malice."[30]

Wallace also continued to couch defiance and obfuscation as acceptable behavior for all white Alabamians with school-age children. Specifically, he urged the citizens of Huntsville to resist the enrollment of ten new black students in previously white schools. These new students—the sons and daughters of U.S. military personnel—were, according to the normally hawkish Wallace, something akin to nonresident aliens with a federal license to invade the South. "I am informed that each and every student ordered to be admitted is the child of Armed Forces and federal government personnel. Nonresidents who, with the active support and encouragement of the federal government, seek to destroy the policies, customs, and traditions of the state. Responsible Negro citizens seek to maintain the harmony which has always existed in this state and to enjoy the opportunities to grow with Alabama." The irony of taking so disproportionate a share of federal money while rejecting the children of federal employees was obviously lost on the governor.[31]

On the larger level, Wallace was shifting tactics. In addition to discouraging attendance at integrated schools, the governor planned to close the schools based on a rubric of economic hardship. Schools such as Tuskegee, the governor reasoned, could be closed if they could be rendered inefficient. If white students boycotted or attended private schools, Wallace could justify closing a school that had fewer than twenty students. Just days after his Huntsville declaration, Wallace, through the rubber stamp State Board of Education, ordered the immediate closing of Tuskegee High and the resumption of county school bus operations for the purpose of transporting white students to other schools. By now, Tuskegee High was vacant, save for the twelve black students who had integrated it earlier in the school year and the thirteen teachers still on staff. In response to the closing of Tuskegee High, Judge Johnson sent six of the twelve pupils to Shorter and the other six to Notasulga, foiling Wallace's end run. Judge Johnson's decision went further than just redirecting the twelve. He enjoined the Board of Education from altering the transfer of the students, interfering with the arrival or departure of children from the school, harassing or punishing the twelve in any fashion, or obstructing their transportation. Johnson's action placed the federal government firmly in the position of desegregation guarantor. Incensed, Wallace blasted Johnson, his old 1962 campaign whipping boy, and the ruling: "The action of this Federal judge is rash, head-strong, and vindictive. . . . This order was based on no evidence, only the sworn affidavit of a Negro attorney, which is the same as the NAACP. This act is a judicial tantrum. . . . The federal judge is attempting to run this state by usurpation of authority and the threat of bayonets. . . . In my judgment, this judge ought to be impeached." In the aftermath of Johnson's decision, parents withheld their children from Shorter and Notasulga. Almost as if on cue, Wallace cited the possibility of closing them permanently. "We've got those two schools down there with ten teachers in each and only six students. That's pretty uneconomical." The next day, the State Board of Education formally approved financial aid packages for the parents of former Tuskegee High students.[32]

Buoyed by the rebelliousness of their governor, many Macon County white folk were not ready to accede to Judge Johnson's dictum just yet. The stars and stripes came down the high school flag pole to be replaced by the stars and bars of the Confederate battle flag. Notasulga mayor James Rea refused to allow the six black students to enter Notasulga High. Barring the students, according to Rea, had nothing to do with race, but resulted from fire damage that some called suspicious. The blaze, according to Mayor Rea, had rendered the water supply and filtration system incapable of handling the additional six students. Wallace held a press conference to keep the resistance energized and repeated his familiar plea for assistance for the fledgling Macon Academy. The governor continued to suggest that closing schools for economic hardship was a viable option. This entire episode fueled an already virulent belief, stoked by the governor, that focused on outsiders as the cause of Alabama's educational inequalities. A 1964 *Montgomery Advertiser* editorial provides a vivid example. "So as to say, New York citizens went to school longer than our average 9.163 years and they have a higher per capita income. But is the income higher because they went to school longer or because they got up on us by destroying our economy in the Civil War and holding us down with freight rates differentials and the like thereafter."[33]

At the same press conference, Wallace was particularly adamant about the alleged beating of a news photographer named Vernol Merritt in Macon County during the contentious events of the preceding week. Merritt had reportedly been dragged off a school bus, clubbed about the head by various law enforcement personnel, forced to watch helplessly as his camera was smashed and film destroyed, and shocked with an electric cattle prod until he left the scene. The reality, according to the governor in a dose of revisionist history, was that Merritt was breaking the law by being on the bus. The troopers merely removed Merritt from the bus when he refused to leave, encouraged him to get off the ground when he chose not to, and helped him out of the area when swarthy local toughs threatened him. That his camera was inadvertently damaged was regrettable, and the governor was "certainly sorry that it happened and I hope that it never happens again." In other words, Wallace exclaimed, "the state troopers saved this photographer from harm." The governor did not speculate, however, on the presence of Dallas County sheriff Jim Clark, a notoriously brutal white supremacist, in a city some one hundred miles away from his legally constituted area of enforcement or the role of cattle prods in shaping media relations. Even Alabama reporters such as J. A Gordon, who sympathized with Clark's motives, admitted that he was wrong in abusing Merritt. According to Gordon, Merritt was hoping to "turn a fast buck by taking and selling inflammatory photographs to the *Black Star*, a pink publication aimed at Negro circulation. . . . It has long been my feeling that Alabama and the U.S. would be better off if these so called 'free lancers' were barred. . . . I don't say Sheriff Clark and the Macon County officer were right in roughing Merritt up—they were not." Some time later in a speech to the National Press Club in Washington, the governor proudly exclaimed, "No newsman was ever beaten to a pulp in Alabama, no newsman was ever even beaten in Alabama, but maybe for some of them it wouldn't be such a bad idea."[34]

Days later while Wallace was in Cincinnati as part of a speaking tour of the Midwest, staffers kept him abreast of Macon County developments, and the governor found a way to weave those events into his running diatribe against the federal government. Lyndon Johnson's government, the Alabama governor intoned, had fifty thousand troops "to march on little old Notasulga, but when Castro turned off the water at Guantanamo they ran under a rock like a bunch of scared rats." The old Reconstruction theme was always fresh red meat for Wallace's core constituents: link the actions of the federal government with discriminatory treatment of the South.[35]

But in the midst of all this inflammatory rhetoric, Wallace committed a massive blunder that nearly opened the door for immediate and complete integration of every school district in Alabama. By closing Tuskegee High under the aegis of the State Board of Education, Wallace had essentially declared that the board was a super agency capable of controlling each of the state's numerous county and city school boards. Thus, a single lawsuit in one court, not a litany of individual ones, could force a blanket integration injunction. Fortunately for Wallace, the state supreme court ruled that the board did not have the power to close schools. Since it had no legal power to close schools, the state board was therefore immune to a blanket injunction to desegregate. This had been the legal position of Richmond Flowers, who publicly gloated at this small victory and used it as a springboard to get back in the spotlight himself. In May, the U.S. Supreme Court ruled that Negroes cannot be deprived of a public education through the closing of a school as long as other facilities remain open in the state. The ruling effectively ended any chance that Wallace could close schools at his discretion.[36]

To the extent that Wallace had any victories during 1964 on the integration front, they were hollow and did not result from his actions. Macon County High burned in a fire that local authorities ruled was caused by arson. In the aftermath, the six black students who had been attending that integrated school were transferred to the all-Negro Tuskegee Institute High School. Other than this brief abeyance, court-ordered integration proceeded slowly, but was never close to being derailed by George Wallace. In May, William Wyatt, Anthony Lee, and Robert Judkins became the first black Alabamians to graduate from an integrated public school.[37]

When the 1964–65 academic year started across the state in late August and early September, numerous additional schools were integrated. The governor's response was to use this second wave of integration as yet another launching point for increasing his personal popularity and national name recognition. Wallace called a special session of the legislature designed to last only one day and result in only one piece of legislation: a resolution calling for a constitutional amendment giving individual states exclusive control over public schools. In his call for the session—broadcast statewide at taxpayer expense—Wallace called for a national crusade to get the amendment passed across the country: "The resolution I ask you to enact tonight will constitute a first step. The first shot in a battle to preserve the most democratic institutions on earth, local public schools. We are going to take this crusade across the country. . . . We shall use every resource and power at our command." The governor's speech was interrupted with rousing applause eighteen times in thirty-three minutes. A similar resolution, utterly ineffective as it turned out, had been passed just five years earlier. That measure, sponsored and shepherded through the legislature by Ryan deGraffenreid, was promptly ignored by every other state in the union.[38]

The 1964 resolution passed quickly and with unanimous votes in both the Alabama house and senate. The governor vowed to work for passage of the amendment even after he left office. The reality was that Wallace had already dropped out of the 1964 presidential race and was desperate to have a platform from which to get national headlines. The entire process was a state-sponsored public relations ploy and an attempt to secure additional speaking engagements around the country. Within the state, the entire sham further ingratiated the governor to militant white supremacy groups displeased with the mushrooming tide of integration.[39]

The Politics of Public Education

Even those aspects of Wallace's education policy that were not so transparent and political were not necessarily beneficial to Alabamians. Local schools were still left to provide free lunches for impoverished children without any meaningful assistance from the state. Per pupil expenses remained far below the national average. One report listed expenditures as low as $192.03 per black student and $216.91 per white student. Another report indicated that the state had fallen seven spots in that same category over the previous decade. Average teacher salaries were still some $1,300 below the national average. The federal government accounted for 23.5 percent of state education funding in Alabama; the national average was only 13.8 percent. Patronage irregularities continued. The State Board of Education issued proprietary specifications for duplicating machines strictly approving only Apeco Dial-a-Copy Electro-Stat Copymakers. Not coincidently, the only authorized dealer for these machines was Alton Dauphin Jr., the husband of Wallace's sister.[40]

Another education issue that the administration embraced was the fitness of textbooks and the patriotic credentials of their authors. Goaded by numerous groups of socially conservative allies such as the Daughters of the American Revolution, Wallace sought to censor any book written by a writer with Marxist associations, real or imagined. The board's textbook committee was designed to prevent the state from buying books by "people who advocate the overthrow of our government." The state board was so preoccupied with communism that members issued a resolution asking FBI director J. Edgar Hoover to "investigate all living authors of state-adopted textbooks to determine whether or not any of them are in any way connected with a communist organization." The DAR Textbook Study Committee completed reviews of its own and found each of the first fourteen books it checked to be unsatisfactory: "The 1964 Alabama official adoptions of textbooks includes some of the most blatant betrayals, deletions, and debunking of the United States history and ideology ever foisted on the Alabama public. Russia and China are presented as desirable and successful by authors ranging from identified communist members to individuals whose participation in communist fronts range through Russian, Chinese, Hungarian, Spanish, and others." Specific allegations brought by the DAR committee included an indictment against a tenth-grade history book that did not teach pupils to "despise and oppose communism." The DAR also suggested students should be prevented from reading any works by distinguished Harvard historian John Fairbank, a writer the DAR identified as a communist and a member of a group that was attempting to influence American foreign policy. Since Wallace was always quick to link the civil rights movement to procommunist influences, any public furor surrounding communism, no matter how seemingly insignificant, was welcome. Soon enough, national history textbooks were replaced by those written in Alabama, usually with a slant decisively sympathetic to conservative views. Liberal or moderate historians with revisionist interpretations need not apply.[41]

Ferreting out communism was not the only textbook issue to involve the administration. The state textbook adoption and depository system had been rife with corruption for years. The politically motivated Board of Education, Wallace's rubber stamp, was charged with the responsibility of selecting the winner of the state textbook depository contract who received a 3 percent rebate on all sales. In other states, the textbook publishers themselves had the prerogative of selecting the depository that operated on a percentage for warehousing and processing orders to the schools. These states purchased books wholesale through competitive bid laws. The books were then shipped to the depository, where they were processed and then sent on to the local school systems. In exchange for functioning as a middleman, the depository earned 8 percent of the net wholesale textbook price. A further complicating factor in Alabama was that the state still required parents to purchase textbooks for their children from local retail agents at a 15 percent markup. In every other state in the Union, textbooks were free for students.[42]

In Alabama, the publishing companies received 80 percent of the retail price of every textbook they sold. The remaining 20 percent was split between the local agents (8%), the state (3%), and the depository (9%). At the storefront level, most retailers were less than enthusiastic about selling textbooks for an 8 percent return but nevertheless benefited from the foot traffic that doubtless resulted in additional sales of complementary products. After transportation and other incidentals, the depository netted 4.34 percent of the retail price of each book. According to a six-year state audit, textbook depositor Paul Malone averaged annual pretax profits of $123,255.09 on annual adjusted net sales of about $2.52 million. Malone also profited from a separate contract for the State Mail Order Service for textbooks. According to a study by the *Birmingham News*, a neighboring state whose depository was remunerated at a flat rate of 8 percent of the wholesale price, netted only $22,000 in pretax profits on sales of about $2 million. Simplified further, Alabama school book depositories earned about 4.9 percent net profit on sales while similar enterprises in neighboring states were earning about 1.1 percent. The political patronage of textbooks in Alabama was considerably more lucrative than elsewhere across the South, even if the books were ultimately being purchased by Alabamians, not their state government.[43]

The holder of the depository contract at the start of the Wallace term was Paul Malone who won the contract on June 21, 1956, during the Folsom administration. In midsummer of 1963—just a few months after the governor assumed office—Wallace backer Elton B. Stephens made known his desire to wrest the contract away from Malone and secure the business for himself. Seizing on a technicality that required the depository to maintain at least three retail outlets in each county, Stephens urged Wallace to cancel the contract and assign it to his firm, EBSCO Investment Services. Stephens pledged that his firm could save the state some $50,000 per year that would "further your economic program." Presumably, Stephens's anticipated cost efficiency was so significant that it could survive his plan to increase the revenue percentage the textbook depository would receive from the state. Not content with the 3 percent Paul Malone's contract allowed, Stephens suggested a graduated scale that would pay EBSCO as much as 6 percent on certain levels of net sales. Aping an argument Wallace was already trying out in his private property sermons against the soon-to-be enacted civil rights bill, Stephens insisted, "as a taxpayer, I am against the state trying to operate the Book Depository. Unless private enterprise continues and pays taxes, the State cannot prosper."[44]

Just a few months after Stephens's initial written inquiry, Wallace authorized the Board of Education to cancel Malone's contract. A week or so later,
the board invited bids for the new textbook depository, understanding full
well that EBSCO was going to win. Soon enough, Wallace appointed Stephens
to his State Planning and Industrial Development Board as well.[45]

Malone's textbook service was not without operational snafus but hardly
deserved such an immediate and blatantly political firing. He responded by
gaining an injunction against Wallace, whom he personally blamed for the loss
of the contract. The administration, Malone alleged, had canceled the contract
after he refused, under pressure, to sell it directly to EBSCO. The state supreme
court later ruled that the injunction was actually a suit against the State of Alabama and voided it. Malone was not deterred. "This decision is not final and
within the time allowed by law, I will apply to that court for a rehearing of this
case. . . . The Supreme Court . . . did not hold that you were entitled to award
this contract to any other person or firm. I shall hold you personally responsible and shall seek redress against you and those with whom you participate
in an action for damages in a court having jurisdiction of such controversy."
Malone also raised the issue of how a summer disruption in textbook depository procedures would effect the necessity of delivering books to schools.
The entire system, after all, was supposed to ensure prompt delivery of school
books so that Alabama children might be educated.[46]

In June, Austin Meadows and the board officially awarded a five-year contract to Stephens and EBSCO after briefly considering another friend of the
administration, Grey Hodges of Dothan, for the sake of appearances. The administration also selected new subdepositories and transferred book hauling
to its friends. Subsequently, Meadows wired various publishers urging them to
send their new supply of textbooks directly to EBSCO facilities even though
the entire mess had yet to be resolved by the courts. Meadows assured vendors that if specific legal action was brought against them by Malone, the
state would appeal all the way to the state supreme court where "there is every reason to believe that no final action will be taken against you." The entire
matter was eventually settled, though the details were kept private at the time.
Malone received some $32,000 for selling his furniture and fixtures to Ste-
phens, agreed to a five-year noncompete clause in exchange for $92,000, and
leased his warehouse facilities to Stephens for $2,000 per month for a period
of at least two years.[47]

Textbook writing, buying, and warehousing were not the only political issues involving the books of Alabama schoolchildren. In October, Wallace publicly announced that he would use the Special Education Trust Fund to finance
free books for all Alabama schoolchildren and a 10 percent raise in teacher sala-

ries. At that time, Alabama was the only state where parents were required to purchase their children's books. The state did provide some books for grades one through five but offered virtually nothing for junior high and high school pupils. A flourishing national economy had trickled down to Alabama and led to an accumulation of more than $16 million in the Special Education Trust Fund. Never one to shy away from taking credit, Wallace remarked that the increase was the result of "sound financial management," the "low bid law," and an "overall strict economy." The fund had been growing throughout Wallace's term, though he had routinely resisted urgent pleas from school system superintendents throughout the state to use it to rebuild and repair old or damaged facilities, reduce student-teacher ratios, or otherwise address gaping holes in the quality of education. Wallace had a particular interest in education, but politics came first and that meant money could not be spent unless it came with tangible benefits for the governor. Wallace was fully aware of the lingering stigma that proration had on a governor. He also knew that providing textbooks that cost between ten and forty dollars per child would play well all across such a poor state.[48]

Shortly after Wallace's public announcement, the Board of Education endorsed the free textbook plan and then again two months later, endorsed it yet again. In November, Wallace reiterated his education plans, suggested the state should consider a $100 million bond issue for new schools, hinted at the possibility of a special session as early as January to pass such legislation, and privately plotted with Speaker Brewer and Senator Pete Matthews about exactly when to call the session. Early estimates indicated that the cost of the administration's textbook plan would total some $8 million in increased annual expenditures. But since the free books would not require any additional taxes, almost all reaction to the idea was positive. Reporter Rex Thomas summed up the general attitude about the textbook issue: "No matter how much a legislator may disagree with the governor, it's difficult to come out openly against something like free textbooks when it means money in dad's pocket."[49]

Dissent regarding the state's supplying books for its students was mainly limited to legislators already lining up for the 1966 gubernatorial election, the occasional fringe conservative who thought the idea was the genesis of a socialist explosion throughout American government, and those who thought free textbooks were a poor use of state funds. Among the few recognizable people to take a stand against the idea of free textbooks was Howard College dean of women Margaret Sizemore, a true social conservative. "I agree with practically everything you say. However, I am not sold on the question of free textbooks. . . . I would like to see the surplus used in more permanent ways. I realize that I am just one voice out of many, but many people I have talked with agree with me on this issue."[50]

Prison Politics

If Wallace anticipated the key political issues in education, he was completely unprepared for the furor over Alabama prisons and convict road crews. By 1964, the state was running multiple prisons, including the notorious Kilby Prison in Montgomery, an honor camp in Montgomery, Julia Tutwiler Prison for Women in Wetumpka, Draper Correctional Center in Elmore, Atmore State Prison in Atmore, the State Cattle Ranch in Greensboro, and the Shotgun Hill Youth Center in Speigner. All these facilities presumably operated under the auspices of the Alabama Board of Corrections. Some thirty-three road camps functioned separately and fell under the jurisdiction of the State Highway Department. Not surprisingly, the state's prison population ran about 55 percent black to 45 percent white despite the fact that only one in four Alabamians was African American. Of the eighteen inmates on death row in November 1964, twelve were black, and all but one of those was convicted of raping or killing a white woman.[51]

The conditions within these prisons were no less than medieval. According to a study by the *Tri-Cities Daily* of Atmore, drugs were rampant and fully condoned by staff guards; food was rancid; health care was practically nonexistent; and the entire facility was rife with corruption. More specifically, allegations charged that bugs and worms were commonly found in food and that inmates were charged twenty-five cents for any meal containing meat. Human waste was found on the floor. High percentages of inmates had contracted syphilis, presumably through nonconsensual homosexual intercourse. Many prisoners had fresh scars, emblematic of violent confrontations within Atmore. The habitually recalcitrant were forced into the Dog House, an eight-by-twelve box kept totally dark with a rudimentary hole punched into the floor for a toilet. Those who chronically complained of being sick were often sent to the Dog House where the one daily meal—cornbread—was sure to make them so within days. At Kilby, nineteen inmates were infected with hepatitis, which resulted in three deaths, because of rampant drug use.[52]

Wallace, generally uninterested in this type of policy issue anyway, was quick to remind the media that since he had no practical control of the state's prisons—it was the domain of the Board of Corrections—he could not be expected to solve whatever problems those facilities faced. While technically true, Wallace did have significant input into the composition of the board and clearly possessed enough power to pass any legislation necessary to address prison inadequacies. The Board of Corrections, in fact, was *directly* appointed by the governor, though the members served staggered terms so that no single governor could appoint every member. Nevertheless, the governor displayed no sense of powerlessness when he recalled all trusties from work on the capitol grounds and in various state and county facilities. The decision came after a sexual assault by a convict on a young girl on government property and was intended to "eliminate the use of convict labor during the daylight hours in the buildings composing the Capitol complex."[53]

Unfortunately, this was not the first nor the last sexual assault case involving an Alabama prisoner who received too little supervision. The most serious of many problems involving Alabama prison policy was the use of convict labor housed in road camps and monitored by Highway Department officials, who were not trained prison guards. In many ways, the entire road camp system was a microcosm of Alabama's regressive financial tradition, its inattention to meaningful capital improvement, and a pervading attitude in government that convicts deserved very little in the way of basic humanity. Alabama never built suitable facilities to house the number of prisoners the state incarcerated. The state rarely made any substantial modifications to existing facilities. Instead, officials viewed inmates as revenue streams and housed significant numbers of inmates near the public, including those convicted of violent crimes, while capitalizing on their labor to fund the Corrections Department. All these issues became public matters with the rape and murder of Martha Jane Chisenhall.

Chisenall was a twenty-one-year-old Jackson County woman when Johnny Beecher escaped from a road crew, raped her twice, and brutally murdered her. Beecher, a convicted rapist, hardly slipped through the cracks to get on a road crew; he was just one of 248 road crew inmates convicted of sexual offenses. None of the sexual offenders were assigned to road crews because of successful completion of a rehabilitation program. It was simply standard operating procedure to place them in camps. All told, some 1,900 Alabama convicts were serving their sentences on road crews. Board of Corrections commissioner Frank Lee publicly admitted, almost immediately, that the problem on the road gangs was severe: "The removal of those prisoners charged with sex crimes from road camps will not completely eliminate the possibility of such a recurrence in as much as many prisoners are assigned to road camps who would be more properly supervised if they remained under the direct supervision of the Board of Corrections, but on account of the lack of any other source of revenue for the operation of the department it has been the custom, and it has been necessary, to lease prisoners to the Highway Department in order to earn as much revenue as possible." Within days, Lee called for the complete elimination of the road camp system with an eye toward developing industrial employment within the walls of conventional prisons. The governor, instead of recommending changes, legislation, or alternative sources of funding that would close down the camps, looked for political cover: "As you know, the Prison Department is directed by a board appointed by the Governor and composed of members with staggered terms. I have made one appointment to the five man board—the other four appointments were made by Governors in previous administrations."[54]

Alabama was not the only southern state to use convict labor; Florida, Virginia, and North Carolina still had programs of some sort. A major difference, though, was that sister states used trained prison guards to supervise the convicts, not Highway Department personnel. Perhaps the Highway Department could be expected to monitor a small number of prisoners, but Alabama had 38 percent of the state's total prison population under the agency's watch. The state had no significant plan for screening escape risks, sexual predators, or inordinately violent offenders while at the same time making up lost revenue. When additional screening was done that resulted in the removal of the 248 convicted sex offenders, the Board of Corrections lost some $167,300 from a system already precariously funded.[55]

Compounding the inadequacy of the road crew system was the fact that it was colossally inefficient. Prisoners earned $2.60 per day for the Board of Corrections; but it cost the state $9.88 per convict every day they were in a road camp. Despite the dismal return on investment, Alabama relied on this system to supply one-third of the Board of Corrections budget. But the system could not be scrapped overnight. Simply put, Alabama did not have enough space to house road camp inmates in traditional facilities or replacement funds available to make up lost revenue. Kilby Prison, in particular, was ill equipped to provide much revenue as most of its machinery was substandard or makeshift. When questioned, the governor insisted the revenue was too important to lose and stated a preference for developing more sophisticated screening protocols instead of eliminating the system.[56]

On June 30, one day before Wallace met with Frank Lee and Highway Department commissioner Herman Nelson to discuss the road gang crisis, another road crew convict escaped. In fact, at least five convicts escaped in the weeks after Chisenhall was killed, and three remained at large. Even so, Wallace left the meeting believing the lost revenue was too important to end the program. He made no effort to find the additional revenue through liquidation of some of the twenty-two thousand acres owned by the Board of Corrections or through a tax increase. He made no attempt to call the legislature into special session and have them fix the problem. Prison reform was not a winning issue for building either popularity or power, and Wallace was uninterested in strapping such an albatross to his back. He preferred to sidestep the entire prison issue and try to keep it off the front pages whenever possible: "The problem must be solved; the people of Alabama are entitled to be protected. But it can't be solved in the twinkling of an eye." Lee and Nelson knew the issue could hurt them, however, and went on record favoring total elimination.[57]

Wallace established a special prison committee to look into the issue and come up with a solution, in part because he had received considerable mail from around the state calling for action. Colleen Bugler, for instance, noted the insufficient screening process for selecting work crew inmates and lax supervision: "It seems incredible to me that the State of Alabama should take such poor security measures with convicts whose criminal background is as infamous as that of Mrs. Chisenhall's alleged slayer. . . . Why are convicts with records of crimes of violence permitted the opportunities of escape which the work gangs easily provide, thus endangering the welfare of the citizens of Alabama." Another letter, signed only as "A Mother," suggested that Wallace was too soft on blacks: "Negroes are getting bolder and bolder as Washington takes up for them more and more, and our southern states can at least try to deal severely with criminals. I note that you continue to reprieve so many Negroes who have been sentenced to the electric chair by a fair trial by jury and [I] feel that Negroes now feel that they can get by with anything for whoever hears of one being electrocuted for a murder, rape, etc. . . . I have a daughter . . . and I think all others fear the ever increasing crimes against whites by Negroes in our state."[58]

Surely "Mother's" social commentary was grounded in something less than empirical research, but she nevertheless was on to something concerning the matter of early releases. In the period from September 15, 1939, through September 30, 1963, the Board of Pardons and Paroles had granted parole to 16,160 prisoners, a rate of 28.8 percent. In the first fiscal year of the Wallace administration, the parole rate had risen to 34.4 percent. The increased rate of paroles did not mean the Board of Pardons and Paroles had been given extra funding to thoroughly research their cases, reduce caseloads, or offer a program to combat recidivism. In fact, Wallace's first major budget resulted in the loss of eight parole officers in the first two years. Executive Director L. B. Stephens complained to Wallace that the cuts in funding, creatively listed as a $3,000 increase in "board salaries," a $20,000 decrease in "other salaries," and an $8,000 decrease in equipment purchases, would cripple his department: "This would greatly impair the services to the courts in probation matters and would have an adverse effect on law enforcement. It would, in fact, cost the state many times that amount in Welfare funds to feed the families of prisoners and would add additional costs to the Board of Corrections." Stephens made an end run around Wallace and convinced the legislative leadership on Ways and Means to reinstate the revenue; but the committee required Wallace's final authorization to get the funding back.[59]

The Prisons Committee came up with a variety of proposals: use the Board of Corrections' land as collateral for borrowing money to build a new prison; create a program of internal prison industry so that every inmate could have a revenue-producing job; tear down Kilby Prison and sell the land for profit. Their final report recommended eliminating the road camps but stopped short of suggesting anything specific and left all action to the legislature. Responding to Wallace's underwhelming interest in the problem, the legislature did little to remedy the situation. Within a few years, Judge Frank Johnson would be forced to take judicial action requiring Alabama to fix its multitude of prison problems.[60]

The Politics of Redistricting

Another issue that state government should have handled but did not was the matter of redistricting. The 1901 Constitution required the legislature to redistrict the state following each decennial census. But the state legislature was unable to redraw congressional lines even one time during the twentieth century. As early as November 1963, Democrats urged the governor to call a special session so that the state legislature could redistrict the state in time for the 1964 elections. When the House of Representatives was reconfigured after the 1960 census, Alabama lost one of its nine seats. Instead of redistricting the state into eight equivalent congressional regions, Alabama devised the 9–8 plan, where candidates from the nine old districts vied against each other for eight house seats in a statewide election. The plan was defective for any number of reasons: one of the old districts would effectively go two years without a representative; statewide campaigns for local seats were expensive and interjected regional Alabama politics, North Alabama versus South Alabama, into the equation; and a specific congressman could be targeted for defeat by playing the others off against him. Without a viable Republican party, this inconvenience could be tolerated despite the ineffectual representation it wrought. Frank Boykin, Mobile's longtime congressman, had been voted out in 1962, and though the city lost a military base a few years later, most of the state was relatively unconcerned about the lack of congressional representation for the state's second largest city. But to carry this ham-handed system into yet another election cycle was just another indication of the ineffectual nature of state government: schools could be closed on a moment's notice; conservation officers could be reassigned to work as civil rights demonstration police on a whim; demagogic speeches ushering in special sessions could be telecast all over the state; but the government was unable to rise to the challenge of meeting its daily responsibilities. To wit, within days of news leaking out that he planned to call a redistricting session, Wallace flatly denied any such intention.[61]

Nobody was as interested in redistricting as the eight incumbent Democratic congressmen who needed clear boundaries in which to campaign in an era when being a Democrat was suddenly no longer enough to assure reelection. Wallace understood the political realities shaping the 1964 congressional elections; he had singlehandedly reshaped the Alabama electorate during his first two years in office in his image and on his terms. Alabama's congressional delegation had long enjoyed a reputation for working well together, being fairly liberal on all matters not tied to segregation, and bringing home federal dollars in the form of programs as disparate as the Tennessee Valley Authority, Hill-Burton medical funds for the fast-rising medical school in Birmingham, Redstone Arsenal, and funding for Alabama's various military installations. That history was meaningless now as much of Alabama politics revolved around how best to mimic the governor, blast the civil rights movement, and attack the federal government for everything since Appomattox. This was a difficult field to navigate for the congressmen who, now more than ever, functioned in two different worlds: one where Washington, D.C., was evil incarnate; and one where they were part and parcel of the daily business of the federal government and their primary job responsibility was to draw down funds from the federal trough.

In January the eight traveled en masse to Montgomery to appeal to Wallace to call a special session for redistricting so that they might better control their political destinies. While it certainly would have been a better use of taxpayer dollars in this case for Wallace to travel to Washington for the meeting, he could not resist the temptation to force them to come groveling to him. Symbolically, the scene was no different from a medieval oath of fealty, an act of homage that a lesser noble might offer to a greater noble, and Wallace made sure there were plenty of photographs of the scene. Privately, Wallace chomped on his ever-present cigar, propped his feet on his desk, and gleefully described to his minions how the eight came calling on him for special favors. Personally, Wallace delighted in knowing that few of the eight had voted for him two years earlier but were now forced to recognize him as more powerful in Alabama than any of them dreamed of becoming. Publicly, Wallace received denunciations of the civil rights bill from the eight and continued to string them along with rationalizations about the excessive cost of calling a special session and how he could not trust the state senate to deal with the issue in a minimum number of days.[62]

Though the special session could have been easily called before the May primary, Wallace waited until late July to tell legislators he wanted them to redistrict the state beginning on August 4. Almost immediately, some legislators complained that it was too late for them to reach an agreement. The congressmen were relieved that Wallace called the session but understood nonetheless that their campaigns had been disrupted and were certain to remain in flux until the legislature concluded its work weeks or even months later. Republican Party congressional candidate Robert French boasted that the legislature would not be able to complete its work. The most crucial redistricting question was the apportionment of Jefferson County, which was seemingly too big for just one representative and too small for two. Even Wallace, by asking for the process to be finished in three weeks, admitted that formal campaigning would be restricted to the months of September and October. In previous elections, this would have been plenty of time, especially since the Democratic primary had already been conducted and historically the primary was the election in a one-party world. But Alabama was in the initial stages of tectonic shifts in its body politic. The Republican Party was viable for the first time in a hundred years, primarily because of the mounting antagonism toward Lyndon Johnson and the increasing popularity of Barry Goldwater across the Deep South.[63]

By not endorsing any particular redistricting plan, Wallace let the legislature bicker incessantly, and it bogged down in dozens of side issues and petty squabbles before it finished its business. In his session-opening keynote address, Wallace took ample time to tout his administration's accomplishments in tourism, fiscal responsibility, and industrial development. He later cautioned lawmakers to put aside local interests, be sensitive to the recommendations of the congressional delegation, and complete their work in a timely fashion. Later that same night, a bill was introduced by Senator Ollie Nabors of Etowah that led to the complete disruption of the legislature and what another legislator, Sonny Hornsby, threatened would be "the worst, longest, most blood-and-guts filibuster this senate has ever seen."[64]

Nabors's bill, commonly referred to simply as succession, proposed that the legal stipulation preventing the governor of Alabama from running for a second term be removed. Article 5, section 119 of the 1901 Alabama Constitution specified that the sitting governor "shall not be eligible to election or appointment to any office under this state, or to the Senate of the United States during his term and within one year after the expiration thereof." Anti-Wallace forces seized on the long delay and characterized the session as a conspiracy to get succession passed in exchange for redistricting the state in time for the election. Along with Vaughn Hill Robison, Bill McCain, and Hornsby, Senator Bob Gilchrist launched a filibuster, aiming the attack directly at Wallace: "If in disregard for fair play in the legislative process, you steamroll this bill, you're going to see a filibuster the like of which you have never seen, and it will be the death knell of this session." More than just these four opposed succession. Supporters of John Patterson and Ryan deGraffenreid knew Wallace could not be beaten in 1966, and they were intimately familiar with all the procedural rules that could be manipulated to prevent a vote on the issue, but for various reasons they elected to remain behind the scenes. Various redistricting measures were introduced, but they were completely overshadowed by the administration's end run on succession.[65]

Wallace, stung by the criticism and the obstinance of the four senators, and clearly wanting succession passed right away, lashed back with a state-wide speech broadcast at taxpayer expense. He identified the four senators as a "small group opposed to the Wallace administration." The filibusterers, according to the governor, were not actually damaging him, but they were inflicting great harm on the "old age people of Alabama. . . . Therefore any extended filibuster by those who oppose me is against the interests of the people of Alabama." He further identified the four senators as supporters of former governor John Patterson and former Wallace foe Ryan deGraffenreid, both surefire gubernatorial candidates in 1966, and asserted correctly that the succession bill was in fact supported by a majority of legislators in both houses.[66]

Reaction to the speech was almost universally hostile within the ranks of the legislature, as many viewed the tongue-lashing as a blistering of not just the recalcitrant four but also the legislature itself. After all, it was the legislature that had invited Wallace to make the speech in front of a joint session in the capitol. One unidentified legislator quickly developed his idea of an appropriate response: "The legislature should adopt a resolution pointing out to Wallace that the legislature is intended to represent the people back home, that they are not the lackey-boy to the governor." Bob Gilchrist was particularly unamused by the governor's remarks, and he noted the irony of Wallace's telecast: "I think it was his right to go on TV but not to use the taxpayer's money to intimidate and extort the legislative branch. What would be the reaction here if the President of the United States used national TV and the taxpayer's money to attack the senators who voted against the Civil Rights bill." But out in the hinterlands, the view of their popular governor was quite different. Talladega drugstore manager Virgil Chappell announced he would launch a campaign to raise the necessary funds to pay for Wallace's television time.[67]

Eventually, the legislature passed a redistricting bill (though it was immediately challenged in court), voted down succession, and passed another $15 million bond issue for junior colleges and trade schools. The school bond bill, which the governor called "the greatest enhancement of education in the history of the state," was patently political since the call for the funds did not come from any organized technical survey of needs and half of an earlier $15 million bill was still unspent. In order to minimize any damage from losing the succession fight, Wallace publicly disavowed any interest in it, though Trammell, Earl Morgan, and Cecil Jackson continued to fight for it behind the scenes.[68]

National Democratic Party Politics

Beyond the practicalities of providing real representation to all Alabamians in a representative democracy, redistricting, in the minds of most Alabama

Democrats, was important for keeping the state Democratic Party in firm control of Alabama politics. Clearly, George Wallace was not interested in doing anything to promote the national Democratic Party, and, surprisingly, he was increasingly hesitant to do much to help the state party either. Wallace's battle with the Kennedys and Lyndon Johnson had already shaped his outlook on the national party, and his battles within the state with Judge Roy Mayhall, chairman of the state party, did much the same. Mayhall was a liberal, a north Alabamian from Jasper, a supporter of the National Democratic Party, and a powerful influence in the state; Wallace was wary of him. Wallace friend Frank Mizell was a member of the Alabama Democratic Steering Committee and was in virtual lockstep with Wallace on the matter of Mayhall and his predilection for supporting the national party: "It will be my purpose to resist vigorously any efforts to affiliate Alabama Democrats with the so-called National Democratic Party so long as it is dominated by the power mad integration loving Kennedys."[69]

Wallace and Mayhall's disputes were both professional and personal. Mayhall spoke out frequently in the days after the assassination of John Kennedy, insinuating that Wallace's venomous diatribes against the president and the federal government had been a contributing factor. Mayhall also formed a special executive committee to devise a redistricting plan. This executive committee had no power to enact change, but it was sure to garner publicity for Mayhall and force the press to investigate Wallace's true reasons for not dealing with redistricting in a timely fashion. To make matters worse, Mayhall named Milton Cummings, a deGraffenreid supporter, to head the committee.[70]

All of this animosity between adherents to the national Democratic Party and the governor boiled over in the weeks preceding the 1964 Democratic National Convention in Atlantic City, New Jersey. The governor's national rebelliousness had been planned for some time. When Democratic National Committee Chair John Bailey wrote Wallace asking for his analysis of what "would help elect the president and help other Democrats in their campaigns," Wallace instructed his subordinates that no answer was required. Having dragged out his official withdrawal from the presidential race until July, Wallace (saying, "I feel that my mission has been accomplished") released his Alabama delegates from voting for him one month before the convention. In reality he had accomplished his goals. He knew, as did all political observers worth their salt, that he had no chance of winning the presidency in 1964. Wallace simply wanted to increase his national exposure, generate a suitable war chest for future purposes, and stoke the flames of his popularity both in Alabama and across the South. The accumulation of funds was not lost on Georgia governor Carl Sanders, a dashing and urbane antithesis to Wallace and a man who was closely connected to the national Democratic Party. "With all the money that

Wallace has collected on the pretense that he was serious in running for president," Sanders declared, "he could set up his own government and appoint his own ambassadors—provided he wouldn't quit that race too." Wallace responded by saying his biggest regret in not becoming president was that he could not name Sanders as ambassador to the Congo.[71]

Even though he released his delegates from voting for him, Wallace had no intention of relinquishing his control over them. In the state Democratic executive sessions, Wallace fought to tie the delegates into a "unit rule" system where a majority of the delegation could decide how all thirty-eight of the state's votes would be cast on each issue in Atlantic City. The administration also favored Bessemer mayor Jess Lanier, whom they correctly assumed they could control, as chairman. Convinced that some would buck the administration if they could do so secretly, antiadministration forces lobbied to have the vote on the chairman tallied by secret ballot; their motion carried 20 to 14. Minutes later, the governor arrived, asked for and received a five-minute recess and a revote on the secret ballot provision. After the recess was concluded and a fair amount of arm-twisting had been applied by the administration, the motion was overturned 28 to 6. Shortly thereafter, Lanier was elected. His first order of business was to call another recess "so we can go see the governor and find out who he wants for these other offices."[72]

At the convention, Wallace was intent on flexing some of his southern popularity in platform fights and generally being a burr in Lyndon Johnson's saddle. In his self-described "warning" to the platform committee in Atlantic City, Wallace threatened a mass revolt if the Democratic Party did not reverse course on the civil rights bill. His testimony began with a typical rambling indictment of the Reconstruction era when "a section of this country was reduced from the richest to the poorest overnight. The South was a conquered territory with carpetbaggers and scalawags protected by federal bayonets." Claiming he loved the Democratic Party, Wallace tried to minimize the necessity of civil rights legislation by claiming that any nation with such a strong economy, mighty military, and distinguished record in World War II could not be so "tainted and corrosive and filled with hate."[73]

In addition to hectoring the federal government for its century-old discriminatory practices and calling for repeal of the Civil Rights Act, Wallace peppered his remarks with a list of charges. While innocent Americans plowed their fields, worked with their hands, raised their children, and baked their bread, the federal government had become an unrecognizable monstrosity, foaming at the mouth, panting over its next victim, and usurping the constitutional boundaries imposed by the nation's God-fearing founding fathers. In reality, many of Wallace's accusations could have been more plausibly leveled at himself, for his actions in Montgomery.

Let me show you what our government, one branch or the other, has done through the auspices of individuals who claim membership in this party. It can and has compelled elected officials to violate the law and oath of office. It can and has enjoined the discretionary acts of a state governor, mayors, city officials, and law enforcement officers. It can and is controlling the entire local school systems of our states. It can and has supervised and passed upon and prescribed the adoption of curricula for our school systems. It can and has regulated many aspects of state, municipal, and county governments. It can and has been a vehicle for the destruction of neighborhood schools. It can and has destroyed the basic right of a state and its people to structure their own governments. It can and has taken an individual's private property and dedicated it to public use without consent or compensation to the owner. It can and has compelled one citizen to render personal services to another without his consent. The list goes on and on. . . . You have and are witnessing government marching with an almost wreckless [sic] vengeance—deaf to the entreaties of its most loyal and dedicated citizens. Heedless of the consequences. Engaging in a vindictive war of political retribution. Wielding its terrible swift sword of coercion.[74]

Packaging himself as a neo–Daniel Webster arguing constitutional issues before the moot court of Democratic public opinion, Wallace attacked. The American people, according to the governor, were "repelled by the callousness, the duplicity, the underhanded mealy-mouthed platitudes of politicians who would sell the birthright of our nation to be re-elected. The American people will insist upon a return to the virtues of honesty, integrity, efficiency, and economy in the operation of our federal government." Finally, Wallace noted these same American people were going to "demand an attitude of tolerance," apparently expecting treatment for the state of Alabama that he was not willing to extend to African Americans. Staunch social conservatives noted the impact Wallace was making. The anti-Semitic *Cross and the Flag* monthly saw real political possibilities for a soon-to-be described silent majority: "The slum vote is no longer the balance of power in American political life. The balance of power is made up of the following of Governor George C. Wallace and his compatriots, and their number is legion."[75]

Of course, Wallace's speech fell on deaf ears in Atlantic City, and the platform did not call for immediate repeal of the Civil Rights Act of 1964. But that did not mean Wallace was through orchestrating events. Though Wallace soon left the convention to attend a groundbreaking of a new inland dock at Demopolis, he remained in charge of all nonloyalist actions taken by the Alabama delegation. Relaying his strategy through Seymore Trammell, who was on site, Wallace urged the Alabama rank and file to refuse to sign loyalty oaths pledging to support the party nominee and the national platform. A day earlier, the Credentials Committee had announced that only those signing the loyalty oath would be seated on the floor during the convention. Jess Lanier, taking cues from the Wallace administration, also urged ignoring the loyalty oath, and a resolution binding members of the delegation not to sign it passed 33 to 4. A second resolution, praising Wallace for his platform committee testimony, passed unanimously.[76]

The resolutions and rhetoric coming out of the Alabama delegation were not enough to strike fear in the hearts of national party leaders. They removed Alabama from the temporary roll call of the convention, the first time such an action had occurred. After the Alabamians took their seats on the floor, Lanier received notice demanding that all credentials be returned except for those members who had signed a loyalty oath. Wallace wired Lanier urging him to continue urging committee members not to sign. Trammell, a bulldog if ever there was one, continued to whipsaw stragglers back into line. The next day, when the loyalty cards were delivered to Lanier, two delegates and four alternates had signed; the rest had refused.[77]

The next day, Democratic Party chairman John Bailey gave the Alabama delegation a simple ultimatum: "Either sign the pledge or go home." Almost immediately, all Alabama seats were removed from the convention floor, save those belonging to the few who had signed the loyalty oath. The nonsigners, led by Trammell who had received instruction from Wallace via telephone, met as a group and decided not to participate in the rest of the convention, an act of redundancy since their seats had already been removed. Selma native Earl Goodwin castigated the convention brass for its actions: "We have been rewarded by being ignored by the officials of our party and by being denied a part in the proceedings of this convention. . . . A final indignity has been visited on us in the removal of our chairs from the Convention hall. . . . We are unwilling to accept further insult and embarrassment to ourselves and to the good name of the great and sovereign State of Alabama." The state legislature responded by passing a resolution praising the delegation for its "forthright stand on principle." For its part, the loyalist delegation nominated Carl Sanders for vice president as a final swipe at Wallace. Bull Connor, white supremacist cum laude, was later forced to sign a loyalty oath in order to keep his post as Democratic national committeeman.[78]

The members who left knew their betrayal of the national party would eventually come home to roost. One member noted a project that was likely to lose federal backing right away: "If re-elected, Johnson won't forget Alabama. You can kiss the Tennessee-Tombigbee canal goodbye." Actually, the

Tennessee-Tombigbee project had been on tenuous political ground for some time. Glover Wilkins, administrator for the Tennessee-Tombigbee Waterway Development Authority, representing Mississippi, Kentucky, Tennessee, and Alabama, feared that Washington would cancel the project or continue to fund it only in tiny allotments. "If the four states who are members of the waterway compact didn't support certain presidential candidates," Wilkins predicted, "dire consequences would befall the project and [it] wouldn't be constructed." Another unidentified delegate reached similar conclusions: "If there is an air base or military installation to be closed you can be sure Johnson will be looking straight at those in Alabama. His record as a politician is about as easy to read as any—he takes care of his friends and guts his enemies. I feel sorry for Alabama and Mississippi." Other Democrats, like state Democratic committee member Joe Sanders of Dothan, blamed loyalists and called for Roy Mayhall to resign: "It appears that you are completely out of step with the Democrats of Alabama from the governor on down."[79]

Back home in Alabama, the preference of state voters in the 1964 presidential election was never in doubt: Wallace had no intention of allowing the increasingly liberal and civil rights–supporting Democratic Party to carry Alabama. Even before he took the oath of office as governor, Wallace was planning an independent elector campaign that would rob the party of the state's electoral votes. This was not a new idea. Similar campaigns had been waged in 1948 for a slate that supported Strom Thurmond and the Dixiecrats, and in 1960 for a slate that supported Virginia senator Harry F. Byrd.[80] Similar movements of varying strength were under way in other southern states including Florida, Georgia, and Louisiana, fueled in no small part by Wallace's regular statements that the South was the key to the outcome of the 1964 presidential election. Eli Howell and the State Sovereignty Commission formulated a two-thousand-word position paper on the South's crucial role in the election and disseminated it widely. The idea was to nominate presidential electors who would be pledged to no particular candidate and then bargain for platform positions on key issues at the convention. In effect, an unpledged slate of Wallace men would simply be another weapon at the governor's disposal to be used to intimidate opposition in the state and boost his popularity among the masses. Theoretically, if a large regional movement of unpledged electors could be created, the presidential election could be thrown into the electoral college. At this point, Wallace would negotiate with the candidates of the two major parties for southern concessions: "Party means nothing to me," he told Greenville attorney Calvin Poole; "the candidate who would espouse the states' rights–local government cause would get our votes." Obviously, race and the civil rights bill were intertwined with the unpledged elector movement. Campaign material claimed that national pledged electors would be forced to vote for "Bobby Kennedy, Hubert Humphrey, or Martin Luther King if they were nominated for President or Vice-President at the convention."[81]

Wallace campaigned vigorously for the slate of independent electors and kept familiar issues at the forefront of his appeal: state versus national government; social conservatism versus social change; constitutional government versus despotism. To be sure, Wallace and his administration were the organizers and sponsors of the entire effort. Strategically, the unpledged slate was brilliantly packaged by the administration as a referendum on who Alabamians should view as their favorite Democrat, Lyndon Johnson or George Wallace. This made the outcome a certainty even though the state's national Democrats—such as Lister Hill, John Sparkman, and Carl Elliot—had been extremely effective at bringing federal money into the state. A confidential elector campaign strategy memorandum asserted that any potential candidate must agree in advance to "withdraw his name" if the administration deemed it necessary. Electors also had to agree to contribute the fifty-dollar qualification fee and at least one hundred dollars toward the campaign, and run "under such conditions as will further the cause, rather than individual ambitions." Potential elector candidates could not even pick their opponents or place numbers on the ballot. They were expected to leave all that blank so that "some knowledgeable and responsible person ... will have authority to insert the place number for which each candidate is qualifying." Ultimately the administration selected key public figures and friends to serve as its candidates in the independent elector campaign.[82]

This unpledged elector campaign reflected how dominant racial presuppositions and political perceptions had become in Alabama. Wallace asked Alabamians to vote for the unpledged slate in order to "help defeat the so-called civil rights bill. These men will not yield to the Johnson and Kennedy crowd." The unpledged electors could have no impact on the civil rights bill, but promotional material exclaimed, "Governor Wallace is fighting heroically for our system of constitutional government. Unpledged electors [are] a weapon in that fight." On a campaign swing through North Carolina, Wallace assured the assembled Tarheels that the electoral college could be used "to get the liberals off the backs not only of the people of North Carolina, but people throughout the country." Wallace vowed that the independent electors will "help reverse the trend of centralization of power in Washington." The unpledged electors had nothing to do with congressional policy or judicial action in Washington, but a case could be made that they helped to further centralize power in Montgomery.[83]

In all campaign material, the link between voting for the unpledged slate of electors and supporting George Wallace was made crystal clear. Also clear was the connection to issues of race. Bull Connor was involved in the movement and wanted to be a candidate. But his position as national Democratic committeeman made him untenable as a candidate. The Citizens' Councils of Alabama were such public advocates of the idea that their executive committee issued a formal blessing: "We endorse the effective work done by Governor George Wallace to reincarnate the Solid South. We wholeheartedly endorse the Wallace free electoral ticket and movement." Independent elector Jud Scott dubbed the national Democratic Party devotees of a "vicious, South hating platform adopted to lock in the Negro vote." The support for independent electors went down to the company level where firms such as Hudson-Thompson circulated memoranda "giving you a list of the unpledged presidential electors to be voted for next Tuesday."[84]

The Wallace slate of independent electors won with more than 80 percent of the total vote in one of the largest landslides in Alabama history. In a demonstration of Wallace's awesome power, seven members of the state's congressional delegation accompanied him on a campaign trip to Maryland the next week and served as glorified stage props posing as the Alabama "truth squad." Those same candidates began to include photographs of the governor in their campaign material and echo Wallaceisms on the hustings. The administration took great joy in making its own clipping file of candidates who referred to Wallace in their political advertisements. Because Wallace had not yet called the special session for redistricting, they were unable to campaign locally for reelection and were still operating under the old 9–8 plan. Consequently, none of them, and almost no other political candidate in Alabama, could afford to run the risk of alienating the governor; otherwise, defeat was certain. Not coincidently, Carl Elliot, who had been in Congress since 1948 and was commonly viewed as the most progressive of any Alabama congressmen, was targeted by the administration and eliminated. If Wallace never said explicitly that Elliot should be taken out, his supporters received the message nonetheless. Mary G. Allen of Muscle Shoals clearly understood Wallace's plan to oust national Democrats from Congress. "We got Carl Elliot which is exactly what we wanted to do. He does not represent decent, Conservative Alabama voters. . . . He had to go." Others with progressive economic voting records, such as Bob Jones, attracted the ire of the administration, but Elliot was the only one singled out for removal in the 9–8 primary. Wallace's power had reached such a level that previous accomplishments of national Democrats were meaningless and Alabama was fast becoming bipolar: pro-Wallace or anti-Wallace, with very little gray area in between.[85]

Once redistricting was completed in late August, the state had a November congressional ballot that pitted eight Democrats against six Republicans. The entire administration fiasco of delayed redistricting, independent electors, contempt for the congressional delegation, mocking the loyalist state Democratic Party officials, rebellion at the National Convention, Wallace's aborted primary forays, and the incessant carping at President Johnson for the Civil Rights Act created a climate where the Republican Party could step in and flourish. Wallace was more than just a casual observer in the spread of the GOP in the state. Within weeks of his inauguration the governor was meeting privately in his office with state Republican Party chair John Grenier and Jim Martin, a Gadsden businessman who had come from nowhere to give Lister Hill quite an electoral scare in 1962. Grenier encouraged Wallace to get involved in unpledged elector campaigns, knowing that contempt for the national Democratic Party could help nascent state Republican organizations across the South. Martin and Grenier also encouraged Wallace and other white supremacist Democrats to consider actually joining the Republican ranks: "The Republican party doors are open to Alabamians who believe in states' rights and constitutional government and more expressly you, governor, who we all know have done a distinguished service to the cause of returning political power [to] Alabama and the South." In this environment and under these circumstances, the right kind of Republican presidential candidate in 1964 could be supported by southern Democrats, who were already upset at integration, indignant at the civil rights stance of John Kennedy and Lyndon Johnson, and warming to the ferocity of Wallace's states' rights, anticommunism attacks on Washington. Barry Goldwater was just the candidate to put Alabama in play for the GOP.[86]

With the exception of Goldwater's public opposition to the Tennessee Valley Authority, the Arizona senator's platform appealed to much of conservative Alabama. Some twenty-five hundred Alabamians cheered Goldwater at a September speech at Montgomery's Cramton Bowl. Applause lines like "we must say no to further encroachments on states' rights" earned the candidate sixty-seven interruptions and ovations. Attacks on President Johnson and the U.S. Supreme Court along with policy proposals to reduce the income tax brought similar shrieks of glee from the throng. After the speech, Public Safety Director Al Lingo drove Goldwater to a reception at the Montgomery Holiday Inn for donors who had contributed five thousand dollars or more to his campaign and stationed state personnel outside to prevent the uninvited from gate-crashing the event. Many prominent Alabama Democrats attended the Goldwater rally, including state representative Sam Nettles, an unofficial spokesman for the Black Belt faction in the house and former Birmingham mayor and Wallace unpledged elector Art Hanes. For his part, the governor never formally endorsed either Goldwater or Johnson, though the persistence of near daily aspersions against the federal government, the campaigning in three state primaries, and the unpledged elector movement left little doubt about whom Wallace preferred.[87]

With Goldwater stridently in opposition to the Civil Rights Act and blazing a trail of support across Alabama and the Deep South, Wallace lost interest in the unpledged elector slate. He briefly toyed with the idea of asking them to resign, since Goldwater clearly represented the socially conservative positions the governor favored. But leaving the slate on the ballot provided one more not so subtle reminder of whom Wallace wanted Alabamians to choose. Essentially, Alabamians could not vote for Lyndon Johnson in the election of 1964. They had the option of selecting electors committed to Goldwater or choosing the unpledged group. Frank Mizell even encouraged the administration to go public with a statement declaring that the electors would not cast their votes for Johnson if they were elected. The administration declined. In the days immediately before the election, Wallace moved closer to an unequivocal public declaration for Goldwater. He told journalists that polls predicting a "Lyndon Landslide" were not accurate and predicted that "there may be some surprised people next Wednesday morning." With congressional and local candidates nervous about Republican coattails dragging the bottom of the ticket along with Goldwater, Wallace made a handful of belated endorsements, appeared at a few rallies, and issued a statement asking voters to support the "nominees of the Alabama Democratic Party for all local and district races, as well as the nominees for Congress." Reporter Bob Ingram described the governor's efforts on behalf of Democratic congressmen as less "than a back-straining effort."[88]

On election day, Alabamians overwhelmingly voted for Barry Goldwater, elected five of the six GOP congressional candidates, and elected numerous Republicans in local races in the most smashing electoral turnabout since Reconstruction. Simply put, many white Alabamians voted straight-ticket Republican. Goldwater carried sixty-three of sixty-seven counties, with the only exceptions being three TVA counties, Lauderdale, Limestone, and Colbert, and predominately black Macon county. Many of the congressional races were routs, and only staunch conservative Armistead Selden went head-to-head with a Republican and won. State Democratic officials like J. E. "Dog" Brantley were outraged: "I said last January that Governor Wallace was gutting the Democratic party. The catastrophe that befell the Democrats Tuesday must be placed on the shoulders of the governor." Defeated congressmen George Grant and Kenneth Roberts blamed their losses at least partially on the Democratic slate of unpledged electors. Acting state GOP chairmen Tom Brigham (Grenier had since left to work on Goldwater's national campaign) noted that Wallace's bashing of the national Democratic Party led many voters directly to the GOP. Wallace remained curiously silent about the election results except to proclaim that the Tennessee-Tombigbee project was not jeopardized in the least by GOP victories.[89]

George Wallace's words and deeds cost the State of Alabama incalculable sums of federal dollars. Within days of the election, it was announced that Mobile was losing Brookley Air Force Base, South Alabama's largest single employer. NASA threatened to shut down Huntsville operations because of fear that the agency could no longer attract qualified engineers to come to Alabama. The state's new congressional delegation was not nearly as cohesive, as favored by the Democratic leadership or the president, as influential on ranking committees, or as effective in bringing home federal money. In the end, for all their devotion and loyalty to their governor, Alabamians received very little in return.[90]

4
Checks and Balances / 1965

On the third day of the new year, Martin Luther King traveled to Selma to launch a drive to register black Alabamians to vote. King, who had just been awarded the Nobel Peace Prize, was typically confident in his remarks: "Today marks the beginning of a determined, organized, mobilized, campaign to get the right to vote everywhere in Alabama. If we are refused, we will appeal to Governor Wallace. If he refuses to listen we will appeal to the legislature. If they don't listen, we will march by the thousands on the ballot boxes." One month later at Tuskegee Institute, Malcom X, predicted "the longest and hottest, and bloodiest [year] in the history of the Race Revolution." The images from the brutal beating of marchers at the Edmund Pettus Bridge mesmerized the nation and led to the landmark Voting Rights Act of 1965. But beyond the senseless savagery and indignity of Selma, a slow evolution in Wallace's awesome power within Alabama was emerging.[1]

George Wallace had operated virtually free of significant restraint within Alabama over the previous two years. To be sure, Judge Frank Johnson, President John Kennedy, President Lyndon Johnson, the Justice Department, King, and a grass-roots movement of personal empowerment demanding full equality had constantly nipped at his heels. Yet for all their ability to defeat Wallace on individual issues nationally, Wallace had used those same issues, individually and collectively, to increase his own power and popularity within the state. With every defeat at the hands of the federal government or judiciary, Wallace was winning and winning big with white Alabamians. But looming on the horizon were battles that would demonstrate the surprising strength of Wallace's opposition within the state and begin to reveal the limits of Wallace's command and control. Though much of the anti-Wallace dissent was purely political— an election year was fast approaching—some of the opposition had begun a closer examination of administration policy and expressed a growing concern about whether the governor was neglecting the real issues of the state.[2]

Public Safety

One aspect of Wallace's first two years that deserved closer inspection was the Department of Public Safety led by Colonel Albert J. Lingo. To be sure, the position of director of public safety was not an easy job nor was it especially well defined. In theory, though Alabama law decreed that members of the highway patrol "shall have the powers of peace officers in this state and may exercise such powers anywhere within the state," the department was traditionally charged with enforcing traffic laws, conducting accident investigations, and ensuring that state highways were safe and secure. Even this limited scope was difficult to achieve. According to the 1963–64 annual report of the Department of Public Safety, the state had 436 uniformed patrol officers operating out of eleven separate districts. Lingo not only was responsible for the troopers but also was charged with supervising driver's license bureaus, general administration, and general service branches. Allowing for scheduling, graduated manpower deployment, vacation and sick leave, administrative and noninvestigatory personnel, clearly, Alabama's sixty-seven counties had precious few patrolmen on duty, especially during graveyard shifts. For example, Wilcox County, tucked deep in the state's Black Belt, had one highway patrolman assigned to the entire county. As a result, throughout the 1960s the state regularly tallied gruesome numbers of fatalities on its roads. From 1963 to 1964 alone, more than fifteen thousand traffic accidents were investigated by troopers, with nearly seven hundred traffic deaths. A variety of factors were responsible for the high number of highway deaths: poorly constructed roads, unsafe speeds, insufficient lighting, mechanical failure, alcohol, operator error, and lax and insufficient enforcement. At one point, the administration even sponsored a bill that claimed the state could no longer afford to protect any civil rights workers and asked the federal government to provide manpower. The use of Alabama state troopers to observe demonstrators, Wallace argued, had led to "an alarming increase" in traffic deaths. Ironically, Department of Public Safety letterhead included the admonition, "Drive Carefully—Save a Life."[3]

The bifurcated mission of public safety—traffic enforcement and state police duties—was surely a contributing factor to the huge traffic enforcement problem plaguing the state. In addition to having troopers write speeding tickets and accident reports, Lingo and Wallace insisted on using them as state policemen, civil rights demonstration watchdogs, and in various other roles. The troopers, according to their director, suffered from an esteem problem because too many citizens denigrated them as mere "traffic cops" when they tried to perform the additional duties sanctioned by the administration. Lingo's proposed solution included adding the term "state police" to all badges, patches, and patrol cars so that Alabamians would feel more comfortable with their troopers taking on additional responsibilities.[4]

Some of those additional responsibilities included keeping Lingo, an ardent white supremacist, apprised of any potential civil rights demonstrations or integrated meetings. Just three weeks into his service, Lingo received a detailed report about the prospect of Robert Kennedy's venturing down to Mobile to take part in an integrated event at the Gold Room of the Battle House Hotel. The proposed audience was to include black attorneys Vernon Crawford and Clarence E. Moses, six black members of the Mobile County Democratic Executive Committee, local NAACP officials, and local civil rights activist John Leflore. Perhaps most distressing to Lingo's trooper informants was the possibility that "there would be a dinner and street dance after the meeting." Not too subtly included in the report was the fact that wives were also expected to attend, invoking the time-tested sexual mythology of insatiable black men and vulnerable white women.[5]

Lingo and Wallace were maniacal about gathering intelligence concerning civil rights demonstrators. Wallace wanted the information handy so he could document communist connections, criminal records, and various nefarious relationships in his speeches. Within Alabama and across the Deep South, obfuscation and distraction were the principle weapons for countering the logic of the civil rights movement, and smearing some demonstrator with multiple charges was Wallace's preferred expedient. Lingo, perhaps the only cabinet level appointee whom the governor felt he could not completely control, kept pertinent data in a file he labeled "Individuals Active in Civil Disturbances." This information was periodically published complete with pictures, brief descriptions of past arrests and incarcerations, and alleged organizational ties. The book was bizarrely detailed and included entries for citizens who were guilty of nothing more than practicing their constitutional rights of assembly and free speech. One citation warned that one supposedly subversive civil rights worker was guilty of "parading without a permit."[6]

Lingo often acted independently, and Wallace demanded not only complete loyalty but also deference on any of the issues that he genuinely cared about. The departments of banking, conservation, pensions and security, as well as numerous others could function in relative isolation, but key departments and key personnel—those that would attract media attention—were expected to take their marching orders directly from the administration. When word leaked out in early January 1965 that several aides and cabinet members were planning to seek elective office the following year, Wallace was furious. As soon as the governor returned from an Orange Bowl trip to watch his alma mater lose to the University of Texas (yet still claim its second national championship in four years), he demanded that all associates give a verbal and sometimes tape-recorded oath testifying that they would not enter any campaign while still serving their governor. Lingo, who would eventually make an ill-fated 1966 run for the Jefferson County sheriff's office, was among those unwilling to sign the pledge. Even so, Wallace did not demand his resignation as earlier promised. As late as June 1965, after Lingo had purchased a home in Jefferson County in order to establish residence, Wallace was still publicly telling the media that Lingo would not run.[7]

Lingo, who once served on a jury that convicted a white man of murdering a black man in a case prosecuted by Seymore Trammell and presided over by Judge George Wallace, was involved in more than a few instances of state-sponsored violence. FBI informant Gary Thomas Rowe testified that Lingo was involved with the Klan and the Birmingham Police Department in coordinating attacks on freedom rider buses. During the 1963 civil rights drama in Birmingham, Lingo, with the blessings of the governor, authorized the deployment of up to six hundred personnel—many of whom were conservation officers or otherwise ill prepared for such duty—and equipped them with tear gas, submachine guns, and sawed-off shotguns. Historian Glenn Eskew has described the trooper's irresponsible actions as "beating . . . with impunity. Some officers ran up on front porches and into tenement houses, attacking innocent occupants." When counseled by Birmingham police chief Jamie Moore that the presence of so many troopers with loaded weapons and itchy trigger fingers could lead to killings, Lingo responded forcefully. "You're damn right it'll kill somebody." Eskew has also suggested that, in the days before the Ku Klux Klan bombing of the A.G. Gaston Motel, Lingo was informed of the impending attack and asked to make state troopers available. Lingo, stating that he could handle the Klan, pulled the troopers; curiously, they were back on the scene within mere moments of the blast, indicating either state complicity or world-class response time. The Birmingham City Council later praised Lingo for meeting "every expectation as to firmness, restraints, and alertness. All of us appreciate the fine services and protection of your Troopers."[8]

In September 1963, Lingo, operating on Wallace's orders, staged his own "stand in the schoolhouse door" by preventing young Dwight and Floyd Armstrong from entering Birmingham's Graymont Elementary School. Wallace, through Lingo, sent out a request for Alabama cities to file a blanket letter asking for state government help in quelling any upcoming racial violence. The letters would accomplish several goals: Lingo would get carte blanche to intervene wherever and whenever he wanted; Wallace could boost his law and order image as the one person every Alabamian turned to for results; and, Wallace could tell the world that Alabama cities lived in fear of violent outside agitators wreaking havoc. Few cities actually complied. Ultimately, Lingo's actions in Selma during 1965, partially staged through the governor's office, would cause national outrage and speed passage of the landmark 1965 Voting Rights Act. From any objective perspective, the actions of Lingo's troopers were consistently violent; they often used force far in excess of necessity; and they operated with clear links to white supremacist organizations.[9]

In the aftermath of the debacle at the Edmund Pettus Bridge, unquestionably the singular event most responsible for passage of the Voting Rights Act of 1965, Wallace was furious with Lingo and nearly fired him. Two factors complicated the issue for Wallace and led to his retaining the embarrassing Lingo. Lingo was exceedingly popular with many Alabamians, including Citizens' Council and Klan folk. Wallace was already buying mailing lists from the Citizens' Councils and was counting on that organization to help him register numerous whites in an electoral counterattack against soon-to-be imposed federal voting requirements. White Alabamians by the thousands sent Wallace petitions and letters in support of Lingo and his actions in Selma. A second reason for not dismissing Lingo was that he was well equipped to hurt Wallace politically: simply put, Lingo knew too much. With the exception of the aftermath at the Edmund Pettus Bridge, there is no evidence that Wallace ever tried to restrain Lingo.[10]

Though the entire nation and much of the rest of the world was aghast at the brutality meted out on the Edmund Pettus Bridge, Wallace underplayed the entire incident. Lester Wingard, a citizen of Washington State, wrote the governor days after the beatings on the bridge to inquire about conditions in Alabama. Wingard and his wife were planning a trip across the country in the summer and he was concerned for their safety. "I am white, American born of French-German extraction and tan easily in the summer. . . . I do not have a southern accent. . . . Would it be best for us to by-pass your state as we have no Confederate flag to display?" Wallace's response was to disavow that anything significant had happened: "Regardless of what you have seen in the national press and on national television, law and order have been and will continue to be maintained in the State." The governor also reassured Wingard that it was comparatively safer to be in the Heart of Dixie where "one can travel thorough any city . . . at any time of day or night and have no fear," than to be in New York City or Washington D.C.[11]

In addition to condoning excessive force and violence, Lingo was also quite ambitious and seemed to know when the cameras were pointed his way. In January 1964, during the integration of Auburn University by Harold Franklin, Lingo developed a bizarre set of rules regulating all use of sound and photographic equipment. In 1965, he became vice president of the Alabama Peace Officers Association, an office that virtually assured ascendancy to the presidency the following year. In order to insure his election, Lingo ordered 150 state troopers to travel to the annual meeting in Tuscaloosa at state expense to vote. The strategy may have been successful, but it embittered other members of the law enforcement community. In the aftermath of Selma, with Lingo slowly edging out of the spotlight, he conducted a much ballyhooed moonshine raid on a still within Mobile's city limits. The destruction of the still, which was not yet fully operational, could have been easily completed by ABC investigators, county sheriffs, city policemen, or any number of qualified law enforcement personnel headquartered in South Alabama. Whether or not he made the residents of Mobile any safer from the hazards of rotgut white lightning by destroying the still, Lingo did manage to get himself in the headlines.[12]

Conservation

The overuse of troopers and other state personnel in civil rights matters also contributed to environmental mismanagement. From his first year, Wallace used Conservation Department personnel for assisting troopers in peace-keeping operations during civil rights demonstrations. Legally, the governor covered his bases by having the conservation officers en masse sign a make-shift contract that assigned them to police work because of the possibility of the "outbreak of a riot mob." Unfortunately for the conservation officers, they received no additional training or compensation for their new responsibilities. By 1965, Claude Kelley's game, fish, and water safety personnel had spent so much time performing additional duties that Kelley was forced to write Wallace to ask for additional monies. Kelley had already allocated his entire two-year travel budget through the first ten months just moving personnel to accommodate Wallace's wishes.[13]

Kelley was not the only one who wanted the game and fish officers back at their regular posts. The Alabama Wildlife Federation, numerous hunting clubs, and individual sportsmen wrote the governor complaining of poaching and other unauthorized activities because conservation department officials were out of the woods. This was not the first time hunters had been upset with the governor. In 1963, in the wake of a series of devastating forest fires that the state could not extinguish, Wallace was forced to ban hunting in the state for a two-week period.[14]

Perhaps nothing demonstrates the wide range of state governmental incompetence in this era quite like the issue of forest firefighting and prevention. Clearly, Wallace should have taken forestry issues seriously; one out of every five Alabama wage earners made a living in some phase of state timber industries. Alabama was second in the nation in pulpwood production. The state, which had some 19.9 million acres of forest land or roughly two-thirds of the state, suffered from too few rangers for fighting fires; dilapidated, unsafe, and ineffective equipment; and insufficient funding. Five months before a series of fires swept across the state, State Forester J. M. Stauffer warned Kelley that "the division of forestry does not have the resources or the reserve strength" to meet the critical demands of the summer. Kelley briefed forest industry insiders on the lack of adequate trained personnel in his department and assured them that the governor was "interested in working with leaders of the forest industry to bring about a well financed fire protection program." Two months before the fires erupted, Claude Kelley again urged Wallace, who had already cut the department's car allotment from twenty-three to eleven, to increase his funding in anticipation of the fall, the time when "our personnel should be working at a maximum."[15]

Despite the warnings of imminent danger from staffers, experts, and interest groups, the administration did nothing. In fact, financial constraints on the Conservation Department, including those related to additional duties assigned during civil rights demonstrations, actually led the administration to reduce the workforce. Several employees were furloughed, or more simply put, laid off, because the administration refused to provide the essential funds. When queried on the subject, Claude Kelley admitted that the extended unpaid vacations were made "in the interest of economy," though clearly the decision was not his. Salary increases for deserving personnel were postponed. The situation became so ridiculous that local contributions were solicited to put employees back on the job. All told, Conservation lost a total of 20 percent of its funds.[16]

The 1963 fires, which came on the heels of twenty-three consecutive October days without rainfall, were left to be contained by only 57 rangers and 150 other department employees. Consequently, untrained prisoners, lumber company workers, and other rank amateurs were the principal relief squads for assisting exhausted conservation personnel. The Auburn University Cooperative Extension Service advised all county agents to name emergency forest fire leaders in each county and begin recruiting volunteers. The state offered this new firefighting labor the absurdly low compensation of seventy-two cents per hour. As a result of insufficient staffing, small fires grew into larger ones when they might otherwise have been extinguished.[17]

In addition to having too few firefighters, the state was relying on outdated and shoddy equipment. L. W. Parker, the president of the Jefferson County Sportsmen's Club, wrote Kelley before the fires broke out to advise him that state firefighting equipment was "woefully inadequate both as regards quantity and condition." Julian McGowin, chairman of the Advisory Board on Conservation concurred: "Our Division of Forestry is not sufficient to do an adequate job in an emergency." McGowin and the board cited the need for an equipment reserve. For extinguishing dangerous fires that threatened one of the state's largest industries, Alabama had the sum total of one plane; State Forester J. M. Stauffer suggested the state needed at least ten. Neighboring states had vastly superior equipment in quality and quantity: Mississippi owned seven planes and had private contracts for twenty-five more; Florida had ten planes and private contracts with sixteen others; Georgia had thirty planes and access to three additional aircraft. To augment its pitifully small fleet, Alabama bought a used surplus plane from the U.S. Border Patrol at a General Services Administration heavy equipment sale in Atlanta. This second plane needed to be inspected, licensed, and modified with a radio before it could be put into service.[18]

While the personnel and equipment issues were unsettling, especially in light of repeated warnings from conservation officials and others, the paucity of government funding for an industry that had macroeconomic ramifications for tourism, logging, paper milling, and a dozen or more other business sectors, was almost beyond belief. To finance its Conservation Department, Alabama allocated $400,000 from the general fund, and relied on a variety of other taxes, duties, fees, and assessments to finance the remaining 75 percent of its annual budget. Included in that smattering of revenue sources were severance taxes, seedling sales, voluntary county appropriations, voluntary landowner receipts, and federal allocations. J. M. Stauffer estimated that the state needed around $4.3 million annually to provide adequate fire protection; at the time Alabama's fire appropriation was just under $1.5 million.[19]

Alabama languished far below the nation and even fared poorly when compared to other southern states in conservation funding. Alabama funded its fire protection expenditures at a rate of 7.5 cents per acre, substantially less than Florida, 22.7 cents; Georgia, 16; Louisiana, 20.3; Mississippi, 11; North Carolina, 13; South Carolina, 14.8; or Tennessee, 12.1. Of those same states, only Tennessee spent less in total dollars on fire prevention. Alabama received 26.3 percent of its annual appropriation from its general fund; no other southern state allocated less than 66.7 percent of its fire protection funding from its regular budget. Put another way, only Alabama was willing to put its forests at risk by relying so heavily on fluctuating sin taxes and miscellaneous sources to keep its rangers trained and properly equipped. The administration clearly understood the gravity of the problem: Wallace's chief of staff, Earl Morgan termed the situation "grave." Yet, the administration ignored Kelley's constant requests for more funding and the Advisory Board's finding that at least $1 million in new monies and permanent changes in financing were essential.[20]

A year later, in 1964, the conservation department was still woefully underfunded and Stauffer had little optimism that help was on the way: "It appears to me the possibility of getting additional money out of the general fund is dim." To be sure, Stauffer knew where the political power lay in the state: "If we have the governor's support, then we have fairly good assurance that any proposal will be passed." Thirty-five percent of Alabama's forest fire equipment was U.S. Army surplus received at no cost. Another 40 percent was so archaic that it was virtually unusable. Unfortunately, Wallace either was uninterested or was unwilling to get involved. The Alabama Forest Products Association formed a joint committee to study revenue possibilities but was unable to make much headway with the legislature. At a meeting that Wallace characteristically did not attend, board member William Stimpson summed up the reality of conservation and environmental affairs: "The financing of the forestry division is not adequate and the division is not in a position to provide fire control for the state." In the 1965 regular session, the legislature finally considered a five cent per acre tax on forest and timber land for fire control, though the governor never identified it as a priority.[21]

In the midst of this financial crisis, Wallace was presented with a serious proposal to establish a Mobile Bay Wildlife Refuge, primarily for ducks. Kelley, the U.S. Department of Interior, and the Migratory Bird Conservation Commission all recommended the preserve as sound environmental policy. After being vigorously lobbied by influential Mobile sportsmen such as Walter Cook to block the refuge, Wallace caved in and forced Kelley to write a letter to the Department of Interior in Washington opposing the idea. Political favors influenced other conservation matters as well. Administration friends received contracts to run park concessions such as boat rentals, fishing supplies, food, fuel and oil, and camping equipment rentals. As with other financial agreements, the state received its 10 percent of gross income based solely on the accounting of the private firms, not state auditors.[22]

As with most everything in Wallace's first term, racial considerations permeated conservation issues. After a group of African Americans attempted to integrate the Monte Sano State Park in Huntsville in May 1964, the administration sent a memorandum statewide reaffirming its policy regarding the use of facilities in the parks. The parks, according to the directive, were to remain segregated and were to be closed if any attempt to integrate them occurred. A few months later, after the Civil Rights Act of 1964 had supposedly answered the question once and for all, Mr. and Mrs. James Street filed a complaint with the Civil Rights Commission after being asked to leave Monte Santo.[23]

By 1965 the state had acquired three additional surplus aircraft for firefighting, but manpower, funding, and financing were no better than in the previous two years. Conservation officers were still being routed to deal with civil rights demonstrations; firefighting funds were still sadly lacking; and general fund revenues were still only a small fraction of the total budget. The Conservation Board, in another meeting Wallace missed, passed a resolution demanding that the legislature not use game and fish funds for any other purpose, as it had done in a recent legislative session. Not only did the department lack the funds to protect state forest land, it could not even afford to survey state land to mark permanent boundaries. State parks were in near total disrepair. Many of the buildings were twenty-five to thirty years old; seasonal employee hiring was delayed; and then those workers were let go early. All new equipment purchases were postponed. The situation was clearly beginning to wear on Stauffer: "To try to administer a two million dollar program on one factual item of money—general fund money—with all other sources of income dependent on contributions, etc., is a very touchy job and unless the division is able to get additional funds from some other source, it will have to shrink."[24]

Sometimes Conservation Department issues took on a comical tone. When the editor of *Outdoor Life* magazine called to arrange some photo opportunities, Ed Ewing and Bill Jones arranged for him to visit the farm of Brooks Holleman, an administration friend, and be feted by fellow cabinet members. Unfortunately, game wardens had already cited hunters at the farm for shooting at turkeys over baited fields, a fineable offense and a serious breech of fair chase sportsmanship. Needless to say, other arrangements had to be made in order to prevent a potential public relations gaffe.[25]

Working Men and Women

If conservation matters seemed to stagnate or even deteriorate during Wallace's first term, labor issues did improve, if only slightly. Wallace had campaigned in 1962 with a pledge to reduce the workweek of state employees, including prison guards, to forty hours, increase pay and offer extra pay for overtime, allocate more money for the employee retirement system, and provide a better medical and group life insurance plan. State employees frequently sent anonymous letters to the governor to remind him of campaign promises to reduce work hours or increase pay. One writer expected the governor to adjust state salaries to approach levels enjoyed by workers in the private sector: "You promised that state employees would be paid every two weeks instead of twice monthly as the pay schedule is now, which would mean a raise in salary. We have not heard anything about this since you became Governor." Prison guards, in particular, were quick to hold Wallace to his pledge and wrote him regularly in the first few months of 1963. The guards had good reason to want to spend less time on the job: conditions were brutal; prisons were overloaded and in desperate need of repairs; the prison board was riven with conflict; at least one warden was accused of using prisoners for his own sexual pleasures; inmate informants were secretly working for various Board of Corrections members; and even chaplains were solicited to take sides. One guard wrote

Wallace demanding the ouster of Director Frank Lee: "I suggest you get yourself another boy that can do the job or will at least give it the best he can and let Mr. Lee go." Eventually, in August, Wallace and Lee trimmed the workweek to forty hours, but not until numerous threats were made to take the situation public and damage the governor's credibility.[26]

In addition to getting the forty-hour workweek put into practice, the administration worked with the legislature to get an additional $5 per week in workmen's compensation benefits for all state employees. Other legislation that the administration supported raised the pay ceiling for classified state employees from $10,000 to $11,000 and from $9,000 to $10,000 for unclassified workers. The top rates for state government department heads increased $3,500 to $14,000. Though he blasted big government on the stump, Wallace increased the number of state employees 45 percent and the size of the state payroll 76 percent. For the private sector, Wallace—understanding that Alabama ranked second from the bottom in the South in unemployment compensation—endorsed a plan to increase benefits and in 1964 assembled various labor leaders to discuss the crafting of such legislation. The meeting included union representatives from steel, communications, construction, and transportation industries as well as government workers. Wallace used the forum to demonstrate to labor his "desire to improve the standards and working conditions" of all Alabamians. When speaking to union members, Wallace was wont to credit the AFL-CIO for helping create administration labor policy. The governor directed Department of Labor administrators to make sure Austin Meadows was paying prevailing wages on the flurry of new junior college and trade school buildings under construction and later issued an executive order requiring minimum wages to be paid on all state contracts.[27]

Not every administration labor policy was crafted for the working man. The state had no minimum wage or maximum hour provisions, which left the salaries and hours of certain workers completely to the discretion of private employers. Wallace did not actively pursue such legislation, even though Assistant Director of Labor T. B. Britt practically begged for such a law: "Alabama . . . has long needed a minimum wage law. We can boast that only two states in the union have lower wages. Can anyone be proud that the median per capita income in Alabama in 1960 was only $1462 as compared with $3013 in Delaware." The state also announced plans to purchase a $3.2 million insurance package, purportedly for state employees. This plan, however, was pure politics as it generated $320,000 in insurance commissions that could be redirected to friends of the administration. Wallace backed an Alabama Education Association program to increase the minimum teacher retirement compensation 10 percent, but even that adjustment only raised the benefit from

$4.00 to $4.40 per month. Though Alabama did pay prevailing wages on state construction projects, it was necessary to do so in order to qualify for federal grant money under the terms of the Higher Education Facilities Act of 1963. Wallace, as was his custom, rarely attended meetings of the Board of Control of the Employees Retirement System. And Wallace stridently worked to ensure Alabama remained a "right to work" state, despite the opinion of T. B. Britt who declared: "A workman is worthy of his hire, according to the scripture. . . . Alabama should repeal the Right-to-work law."[28]

The policy of governance by perpetual campaign also applied to the Labor Department. The department's director Arlis Fant, a member of the International Association of Machinists Local 291 himself, and T. B. Britt worked diligently to tout the administration's record. Fant's first annual report was sickeningly sweet: "This has been an outstanding year. . . . In accordance with Governor Wallace's instructions thrift and economy is being practiced and maintained at all times. Honesty and integrity has been the policy of the Department and nothing of a dishonest nature has occurred to my knowledge during the first year of this administration." Britt developed, much to Wallace's delight, a "creed for Wallace cabinet members," a stylized faux–Ten Commandments pledge to adhere to Wallace fundamentalism. Along with pledges to be honest, thrifty, and upbeat, Britt's creed stressed the need to "utilize all of the time and talent I can spare toward good will and public relations for the Wallace administration" and that "in legislative matters, the Wallace program shall always be my program, and the unison of staff members shall be apparent to everyone."[29]

In keeping with his general policy of governing through perpetual campaigning, Wallace was personally involved in the effort to trumpet his labor record. He ordered Fant, after the 1964 election and a full two years before the next one, to "write a letter to the presidents, the secretaries, and the folks in every local union in Alabama listing what we have done for labor. . . . Let's get this circularized if we have to send out several thousand of these letters." Fant's letter boasted that Wallace "is now and had been a friend to labor throughout his political career" and enumerated the administration's accomplishments: an increase in workmen's compensation benefits, the fifty-six-hour workweek for firemen and eight-hour workday for prison guards, the junior colleges and trade schools, free textbooks, and the directive authorizing payment of prevailing wages.[30]

The administration was rarely involved in any work stoppages, and Alabama faced few serious strikes anyway. In Wallace's first year, only sixteen strikes broke out, affecting fewer than five thousand employees; even fewer workers were sidelined by work stoppages during the governor's second year in office. Wallace typically responded to strikes by touting his prolabor record but staying as clear of the disputes as possible. While it is unclear that the administration took active steps against labor in strike situations, it is clear that it did almost nothing to solve such disputes. In an interoffice memorandum about one strike, Cecil Jackson summarized the administration's general labor policy concerning work stoppages: "We did not want to get involved." Eventually, the administration did get involved in the messy IBEW and Alabama Power dispute, inviting both sides to meet in the governor's office. Within days, a settlement was reached. Both sides praised the governor for his mediation efforts.[31]

Martin Luther King's announcement of a plan to boycott Alabama products was an issue with both racial and labor ramifications. King's plan, announced in the middle of the Selma voting rights campaign, was intended to crimp the Alabama economy by encouraging all Americans to stop buying products made in Alabama. Initially, the administration had some apprehension about the effectiveness of such a campaign. Childs Securities Corporation publicly announced it would no longer buy Alabama bonds. Harry Bridges of the International Longshoreman's and Warehouseman's Union agreed not to handle Alabama merchandise. King bragged to reporters he would not call off the boycott even if asked to do so by President Johnson.[32]

Despite the administration's fears, the boycott never became much of a factor. In fact, during the first month of the campaign, Alabama sales actually increased 8.4 percent from the previous month and 10.9 percent from the same month in 1964. Lodging receipts for February 1965 grew 3.75 percent from the previous year. The administration estimated that traffic at state tourist attractions increased 26 percent. Of the fourteen tourist or vacation attractions that the state tracked, most experienced increased attendance. In May, the state easily sold $15 million in road bonds despite the public opposition of King and Roy Wilkins. A "Buy Alabama" movement countered the attempted boycott and came complete with bumper stickers. An obvious factor, echoed unintentionally by T. B. Britt in his assessment of the state's economy, was that Alabama simply did not manufacture many consumer products. Wallace did receive considerable mail from the Alabama faithful concerned that food items in their grocery store marked with a giant "K," were labeled in honor of King. Correspondents like Mrs. A. J. Helton and Mrs. H. E. Thornton of Sylacauga, wondered "if we purchase these products are we supporting the demonstrations?" Wallace, to his credit, politely responded that those items were kosher products, were not linked to King or the civil rights movement at all, and should be purchased by all who wanted them. Oddly enough, Wallace, the indifferent Methodist, had strong support among many in the Montgomery Jewish community, which included some of his most generous financial contributors.[33]

Education

Though public safety, conservation, and labor issues were important, education took precedence in the regularly scheduled biennial legislative session and special sessions, and racial considerations were front and center. Early in 1965, the state was threatened with the loss of federal dollars if it failed to comply with terms of the Civil Rights Act of 1964. The potentially lost funds, estimated at the time at around $32 million, would have severely crimped Wallace's stated intentions of making Alabama the intellectual "Athens of the South." Though the governor remained mute, at least initially, on the matter, Austin Meadows suggested it would have a "crippling effect on education in Alabama." Others were ready to fight rather than switch. State senator Ed Eddins suggested the state should not go into any special sessions so that it could save as much money as possible to compensate for the loss of federal funds. Eddins's resolve was an indication that education, in the minds of many white Alabamians, would continue to take a backseat to white supremacy.[34]

Alabama's college and university presidents wanted Wallace to call a special session for education early in 1965. Wallace met with several of the presidents to discuss the proposed education budget for the next biennium and to sell his proposals. Most of Wallace's package was in lockstep with the Alabama Education Association, led by Annie Mae Turner, though the AEA hoped for an even larger budget. Less than a month before Wallace called the special session, both Frank Rose, president of the University of Alabama, and Turner were brought to a press conference of 125 reporters to publicize the administration's program. Neither disappointed their governor. Rose called Wallace's ideas for education the "finest, most promising program of education you can find anywhere in the country." Turner termed it a "giant step toward meeting the total needs." Wallace's strategy of getting significant involvement from education interest groups and stakeholders was good politics. Further, by leaking so many details to the press, he fully expected his popularity in the hinterlands and the strong support for his ideas to minimize any meaningful dissent in the senate.[35]

When Wallace called the special session, the fifth of his first term, he announced it would probably take only four weeks to pass the essential education legislation. Immediately, several legislators, almost exclusively senators, balked. Even Pete Matthews, an administration stalwart, responded, "Oh Lord," when asked to consider how long the session could last. The political reality by early 1965 was that legislators were already beginning to choose sides for the 1966 gubernatorial election.[36]

Wallace identified specific priorities in calling the session: a free textbook plan; a 10 percent pay raise for teachers; a 13 percent boost in other school funds; a 20 percent boost for state colleges and universities; general operating monies for the junior college and trade school system; and a $110 million construction bond. Some $50 million of the bond funds were to be allocated for university purposes, with $10 million earmarked for the fledgling University of South Alabama in Mobile and another $10 million for the University of Alabama's medical school in Birmingham, later known simply as UAB. Driving the session was the chance to spend up to $35 million in surplus funds, much of which had accumulated from the sales tax increase passed in 1963. Taken together, the chance to spend money without raising taxes, the political tradition of choosing sides early for the next gubernatorial race, the looming specter of another succession fight, and the power of George Wallace made this session the opening salvo of the 1966 governor's race.[37]

A dizzying array of events surrounded the calling of the education special session: Dallas County sheriff Jim Clark punched protestors such as Martin Luther King aide Reverend C. T. Vivian and then arrested them for criminal provocation; reporters and photographers were beaten during a four-hundred-person march in Marion while troopers and local law enforcement watched; Raymond Chisenall received $11,800 in compensation from the state for the rape and killing of his wife by an escaped road crew convict; Malcolm X was assassinated in New York City; Jimmie Lee Jackson was shot dead by a trooper during another Marion march. Inundated by a flood of telegrams from ABC, CBS, NBC, and the Associated Press in the wake of the press beatings, Wallace and his staff ruminated over several proposed responses, then agreed to "acknowledge these telegrams with [a] letter from Gov. saying nothing." Perhaps distracted by all that had occurred and cognizant of what was to come, Wallace gave an uncharacteristically poor speech at the opening of the session, junking much of his prepared remarks and trying to ad-lib the rest.[38]

Some aspects of the Wallace education agenda met immediate resistance. Jefferson County senator Larry Dumas publicly suggested that at least $20 million of the surplus should be saved in lieu of any future proration. Senator Bob Gilchrist called the textbook plan a "political program" and voiced a preference for using the surplus on new teachers. Free textbooks were decried as communist plots, "un-American," and a slippery slope toward socialism by zealots including members of the Daughters of the American Revolution and retired admiral John Crommelin. Even Austin Meadows, wary that administration austerity would negatively effect the classroom, declared that six-year textbook adoptions were unrealistic, and moved for book replacement every four years. The superintendent also said the state should not purchase two-year-old textbooks and expect them to last from year to year. Eventually, in a setback for the administration, the senate Finance Committee delayed the textbook bill and considered a panoply of possible amendments that would have done everything from forcing gradual grade-level implementation to eliminating any possible financial gain for Board of Education members in textbook deals. Montgomery was already murmuring about members of the state textbook adoption committee selling their sample books for big personal profits. Each member of the adoption committee received three copies of every book under consideration, and Meadows got six copies. These volumes could be easily sold for eight hundred to twelve hundred dollars of unreported income. Predictably, administration stalwarts such as Walter Givhan wanted amendments preventing authors who were members of subversive organizations.[39]

Emblematic of the political nature of the special session, the senate temporarily attached an amendment to the textbook bill calling for the creation of a Legislative Textbook Supervisory Committee. Composed of six house and three senate members, this committee was to function as a virtual appeals court, rejecting any publication found to be "indecent, immoral, anti-religious, subversive, communistic, unpatriotic or inaccurate according to the Constitution of the U.S. or to known and proven historical fact." The senate eventually killed the book police idea when George Hawkins and other senators noted that elected officials lacked the qualifications to evaluate textbooks. A final version of the textbook bill was passed with three additional provisions: an escalator clause that required purchase of books on a grade by grade basis starting with lower grades first, the elimination of the state textbook depository system, and a nebulous plank calling for an official announcement of the final cost of the free textbook program before any of the books were actually purchased.[40]

While the senate was bickering and delaying, the administration's package sailed through the house, which passed the textbook bill 81 to 13 and approved a record two-year, $459 million budget, including teacher raises, 89 to 0. The administration received some other good news from Auburn University. Dean Truman Pierce and Assistant Dean Robert Saunders compiled a report ("Alabama Schools in 1965") that cited many of the general improvements in education achieved during the first two years of the Wallace era. The report identified increased appropriations, improvements in the retired teacher pension plan, increases in per pupil expenditures, and higher teacher salaries. These and other changes led to what Pierce and Saunders termed an improvement in teacher morale, lower turnover, a return of some teachers who had earlier abandoned the system, and an increase in the number of teachers who had higher classification certificates.[41]

Those who dug deeper learned that not everything in Pierce's report was so rosy. While per pupil expenditures were increasing at a rate higher than the national average, Alabama remained forty-eighth among the fifty states in that category, ahead of only Mississippi and South Carolina. Though Alabama teachers were making more money than ever before, they had improved only three spots to forty-fourth place, and at $4,775 per year were still well below the national average of $6,592. In fact, only 1 percent of all Alabama teachers were paid at the national average. Furthermore, the pupil-to-teacher ratio in Alabama remained the worst in the nation, and some six thousand new teachers were needed just to lower the ratio to the national average. More subjectively, Pierce labeled the state's classrooms as among the worst in the nation and estimated an additional five thousand new rooms were needed immediately. Many of the state's school buses were significantly overloaded, and some 30 percent had been in service for ten years or more. Pierce estimated that the state needed some $300 million for capital improvements. Alabama's problems in education, Pierce summarized, were more a case of insufficient support than purely a lack of wealth: "The basic question is not one of whether or not the state is able to afford good education but rather to what extent does the state really wish to do so." The end result for Alabamians, when the state elected to do less than what was required, was a cycle of low achievement and therefore, a set of self-perpetuating problems with societal and economic ramifications: "When the level of educational advancement in Alabama is compared with that of other states," Pierce concluded, "it is obvious that much remains to be done if Alabama is to hold her own, to say nothing of advancing her rank among the states."[42]

Though Wallace realized the political capital that could be generated from improvements in education, he also knew where powerful Alabamians had traditionally drawn the line in the sand: increased taxation. The powerful Big Mules—banking, utilities, and industrial concerns, as well as other assorted special interest groups including the Farm Bureau—worked diligently to keep property taxes as low as possible and loopholes as wide as possible. During the prosperous 1950s, per capita income rose 68 percent, yet school expenditures increased at a far lower rate. From 1953 to 1960, average annual tax rates increased $16.70 per taxpayer nationally; within Alabama they increased only $11.76. For decades, state ad valorem taxes had been the lowest in the country. In fact, property taxes were not even being assessed at the rate the law allowed. Loopholes aside, in 1965 an additional $45 million could have been generated if property taxes were equalized to a rate only one half of what the law *actually required*. Municipalities, under the austere provisions of the 1901 state constitution, lacked home rule and needed an act of the state legislature to levy any ad valorem tax and an election to raise the tax over five mills. Compounding the state's regressive taxation policies were municipal levies, usually passed by the state legislature due to the constitutional provision preventing home rule. By 1964, 90 different cities had local sales taxes; 120 had gas taxes; and more than 100 had tobacco taxes. Municipal beer and liquor taxes, privilege licenses, lodging taxes, amusement taxes, and telephone and telegraph assessments made it next to impossible for working-class Alabamians to save money. Content to avoid sieges against entrenched economic interest groups whenever possible, Wallace (despite the improvements made during his first term) never threatened the education status quo because it would have required a fundamental reorganization of the state tax code, a restriction of Big Mule financial perquisites, and true populist convictions. Wallace, at this point in his first term, had both the power and popularity to challenge those elites who held the sons and daughters of pipefitters and carpenters and mechanics locked into a low-skill, low-wage economy courtesy of a substandard education. Wallace could have made Alabama a completely different place. At least he could have tried. He did not. As a result, the state never seriously contemplated the profound sea change necessary to make an Alabama education at least as good as the regional average. The echoes of that decision continued to rumble more than forty years later.[43]

The legislature eventually passed a $459 million biennial budget that included a 10 percent raise for teachers, a 10 percent increase in basic school operating funds, and a 20 percent increase in operational appropriations for higher education. This was virtually in lockstep with the plan initially outlined by the Alabama Education Association, though the governor neglected AEA calls for property tax reform and its disavowal of public funds for private schools. Based on every other education budget in state history, this was a dramatic and sweeping improvement. Yet indicative of the racial baggage concomitant to administration-backed legislation, it included the proviso that any teacher who participated in a demonstration or encouraged a student to do so would not be eligible for a pay raise. The remaining administration goal for the session, a school construction bond bill, was more problematic. The House passed a $126 million plan early in the session; the senate favored a $111 million bill and chose to filibuster rather than compromise in a conference committee. Because the fighting in the senate was so contentious and numerous pet amendments were attached, Lieutenant Governor Jim Allen had to vigorously gavel the bill through just to get it passed. Several antiadministration senators—including Dumas, Gilchrist, and Vaughn Hill Robison—wanted bond funding allocated on a teacher unit basis. The net result of this formula would be to divide the money based on population and would have clearly benefited Alabama's urban areas, typically anti-Wallace in temperament. The administration preferred a flat-rate allocation to every county that would unfairly reward rural counties, which were, not coincidently, overwhelmingly pro-Wallace.[44]

After vowing not to meet in conference with the administration-friendly house and filibustering for two days, the anti-Wallace senators reluctantly caved in, primarily because the political winds shifted as the session dragged on day after day. With the end of the session at hand and an election a year away, the six major opponents faced the prospect of earning the full brunt of public scorn for not adding millions of dollars for new schools. Furthermore, since the school construction bill was bond based, it meant, at least in the minds of the general public, that all the new buildings came at no additional cost to the average Alabamian. Wallace kept the heat on the legislature by trumpeting the education theme at a Governor's Day speech at Auburn. The legislature then compromised on a $116 million bill with $60 million allocated for public schools and $56 million for higher education.[45]

The Centrality of Race

Though the special session was called for education, the unrest that was swirling through Selma caused other issues to rise to the fore. At the same time legislators were haggling over free textbooks and bond bills, reporters were being trampled by state troopers in Dallas and Perry counties. Selma mayor Joe Smitherman was calling criticism of Wallace's handling of the situation "unwarranted and irresponsible." Jim Clark was denying that forcing children to march six miles was cruel and reassuring all who would listen that every Negro who wanted to register to vote in his county could do so without incident. State troopers were cracking skulls on the Edmund Pettus Bridge. The Reverend James Reeb was beaten to death in Selma; Detroit, Michigan, housewife and mother of five Viola Liuzzo was gunned down in her car after participating in the Selma march, the eleventh civil rights–related death in Alabama since Wallace took office. The crux of the Selma campaign was the quest for voting rights, and these issues played out in the state capital at the same time they were unfolding in Selma and Marion and Hayneville.[46]

The politics of the voting rights campaign began to heat up when Adam Clayton Powell, who knew a little something about grandstanding himself, led a delegation to investigate voter registration impediments in Dallas County. Wallace, William Dickinson (one of Alabama's new Republican congressmen elected in the 1964 Goldwater sweep), and others lashed out at the idea of black northerners intruding into Alabama business. "No self-appointed, self-serving group from this august body," Dickinson bellowed, "has any more moral or legal right to inject themselves into this situation than the eight congressmen from Alabama would have in going to Harlem to investigate the moral degeneration in Mr. Powell's district." Dickinson's remarks were obfuscatory and indicate how far Wallace's forensic tactics and style had seeped into the culture. Historian Wayne Flynt has described Wallace's oratory as "unethical and undemocratic" and credited the governor with bypassing rational thought and argument in favor of fear and emotion. Rather than defend his hallowed traditions rationally by publicly arguing that exclusionary voting practices had some intrinsic philosophical merit, Wallace charged the issue with emotion by attacking the credibility and morality of the protestors, demonstrators, and marchers. By blasting activists as outside agitators, communists, pinkniks, sexual deviants, or sandal-wearing freaks, Wallace aroused emotions in his disciples that he could not always control. When Dickinson railed against Powell or when fellow Republican congressman Jim Martin blamed the failure of registration on "singing, dancing, stomping mobs," they were aping Wallace in technique if not always in tenacity.[47]

Of course students rarely prove as facile as their teachers. Wallace, in typical fashion, wired President Johnson just days before the Selma to Montgomery march to blame the messengers, not the message: "Voter registration and voting rights are not the issues involved in these street demonstrations. The activities of the civil rights leaders are directed toward a defiance of lawful state and federal authority." These actions, the governor suggested, posed a threat to "the preservation of a lawful society."[48]

In the wake of increasingly strong prospects of federally guaranteed voting rights, the administration and the legislature were faced with three options: they could continue to prop up existing exclusionary registration practices; they could move to expand registration slightly in hopes of preventing a full-scale federal intervention; or they could fully embrace the winds of change and work to make the state a place where constitutional rights were fully assured and a person's race, class, or creed had no bearing on the exercise of the franchise. The administration chose the first option, electing again to break before bending. With nearly 1 million blacks living in Alabama and with at least half of them potential voters, Wallace was in no hurry to increase the number of registered African Americans beyond the 115,000 or so registered by March 1965.[49]

One tool for registration proscription, the use of "vouchers," had been legal since 1901 but only mandatory in Alabama since February 1964, thirteen months after Wallace assumed office. A "voucher" was a registered voter who agreed to vouch that a prospective registrant had lived in the state for at least one year, in the county for at least six months, and in the precinct for at least three months. Martha Witt Smith, Wallace's state voter registration consultant and, not coincidently, an employee of the State Sovereignty Commission, considered the vouchers an essential aspect of the voting process. Smith, who received official permission from the administration to carry a gun at all times, was appointed to the commission in December 1963. From her appointment until August 1965, the Alabama voter registration system changed four times, ultimately developing more than 100 different tests that could be used at the discretion of the individual county registrar. Individual county voting registrars, therefore, had all the flexibility they needed to adjust testing protocols whenever they felt undesirables had memorized test answers.[50]

If Wallace preferred obstinance to obeisance on the issue of expanding voting rights, others, such as state senator George Hawkins, were prepared to consider a slightly more conciliatory tact. Hawkins introduced a bill in the senate that would have reduced Alabama's stringent literacy requirements and repealed the state poll tax, still in operation despite the 1964 passage of the Twenty-fourth Amendment. Hawkins was no rabble-rousing liberal; he simply wanted to meet minimum federal registration levels in order to prevent an influx of federal registrars. "What I feel Alabama must do," the senator explained, "is get out from under the 50 percent stipulation outlined in the President's speech. As I understand it, once a state has registered 50 percent of its adult population it then no longer comes under the provisions of the proposed federal law."[51]

Hawkins's strategy appealed to moderates and should have made sense to white supremacists concerned about continuing the restriction of black access to the franchise and dedicated to keeping Washington out of Alabama. His bill made it out of the senate Constitutions Committee without much delay. Wallace, through an executive order, even granted ten additional days of voter registration in Dallas, Marengo, Perry, Autauga, and Wilcox counties. As the march from Selma to Montgomery approached, the attitude of the administration seemed to soften. Wallace wired President Johnson asking for federal support in keeping the marchers safe, though Wallace was later quick to tell insiders he did not want the responsibility or the expense of guaranteeing safety. In a sixteen-minute speech to a joint session of the legislature broadcast statewide, Wallace counseled against violence and urged Alabamians to "stay at your work bench, stay at your home, during the crisis. We will obey the court order, we will do our duty. We must obey even though it provokes our very insides." Rumors swept through the civil rights community that the governor might hold a meeting with some of the movement's key leaders when the march was completed.[52]

But the spirit of cooperation was short lived. With the prospect of the march increasing and a voting rights bill looking more and more likely, Lieutenant Governor Jim Allen and Speaker Brewer predicted another "tragic era of Reconstruction." Wallace ordered legal appeals to stop the march, though they were denied twice by Judge Frank Johnson in Montgomery and once in federal court in New Orleans. Saying Wallace was shirking a "solemn responsibility," President Johnson dispatched three thousand riot-trained troops to Selma. The state legislature passed a resolution alleging that the purpose of the march was to "foment local disorder and strife among our citizens" and even denied Billy Graham an opportunity to appear before a joint session. As the march of mostly black men neared Montgomery, Wallace sent all female state employees home in a macabre redux of a centuries-old sexual myth. The State Sovereignty Commission hired camera crews to film aspects of the march for future use. Five bombs were found in predominately black neighborhoods in Birmingham. Viola Liuzzo was shot to death. Wallace, who feasted on roast beef and catsup as the march approached the capitol, told reporters many of the marchers were communists and, on network television, decreed that the Liuzzo shooting notwithstanding, it was still safer to travel on Highway 80 in Alabama than ride on a subway in New York City. Congressman Dickinson announced he had it on good authority that the marchers were paid ten dollars per day and promised "all the sex they want from opposite members of either race. Free love among this group is not only condoned; it is encouraged. It is a fact and their way of life. Only by the ultimate sex act with one of another color can they demonstrate they have no prejudice." In addition, Dickinson regularly charged that much of the interracial sex actually occurred in churches and that priests and nuns were in a near constant state of drunkenness during the march.[53]

Faced with the inevitability of social change, Alabama, under the leadership of a sworn opponent of the Second Reconstruction, chose to continue its mission of tilting at black windmills. Though Wallace continued to lead the fight, the number of voices in opposition to him was growing as was the volume of their dissent. Senator Ed Horton of Limestone County recognized what was becoming increasingly obvious to those outside of Alabama: "Change is here. Somehow, some way, we are going to have to tackle this problem, face it, and solve it." Wallace foil Richmond Flowers recognized the winds of change as well. "Segregation as we know it," the attorney general declared, "is gone. Somehow, someway we have got to face it and adjust to it." State Chamber of Commerce president Winton Blount laid the blame at the feet of the governor: "Our political leaders were a symbol of defiance, and many of our officials were just dumb enough to be outsmarted by the agitators."[54]

But if these voices were rising, they were still not strong enough to overpower the governor. Doubtless, Wallace knew the eventual outcome, just as Horton and Flowers and Blount did. Nevertheless, at this crossroads (as in 1963 and 1964) with the destiny of the state more firmly in the hands of one man than ever before, Wallace would not reverse course. The allure of popularity and political power was simply too great. Senator Bob Gilchrist summed up the personal and political needs that consumed the governor: "He chose the cheers of the crowd rather than accomplishment. I have never met a man who craves the adulation of the people more than he. All politicians like it, but he craves it, he has to have it. Without it he becomes despondent. Rather than provide leadership, he did what he thought would be most pleasing to the people of Alabama and the state has suffered because of it." Consequently, the governor had Hawkins's voter registration bill killed in the house, assuring the eventual presence of federal registrars in Alabama. Part of Wallace's objection to the bill was that Hawkins, who was not one of the palace guard in the senate, was the chief sponsor. But beyond the personal issues, the governor was not prepared to move toward federal standards on voter registration. Administration opponents like Ed Horton attacked the governor for killing the bill: "The defeat is the governor's. He has talked a great deal about federal intrusion, yet by this action he is asking the federals to come in. Does he want federal registrars?" A separate bill requiring proof of literacy at an eighth-grade level as a prerequisite for voter registration passed both houses and went to the people in the form of a constitutional amendment even as Judge Johnson was issuing separate rulings banning literacy tests in Elmore, Macon, and Bullock counties. Wallace filmed a promotional clip raising money for the Sovereignty Commission's outrageous Selma film. The film, which some staffers referred to as the "Orgy Film," was shown on scheduled occasions in front of select audiences across the state, primarily because Earl Morgan thought that was the best venue for fund-raising. Not everybody considered the film reliable or appropriate. A Montgomery television station refused to air it for fear of starting a riot.[55]

Wallace supported the Sovereignty Commission's work, made frequent use of its research, and was kept apprised of its surveillance activities. These activities often climaxed in the form of an annual report that detailed some racial abomination or presaged some looming affront to white folks. The 1964 report focused on the National Council of Churches (NCC) and pronounced it as supportive of integration, racial demonstrations, providing bail funds to arrested demonstrators, and promoting premarital sex. The NCC, the report concluded, viewed white resisters as Nazis and was "active in support of abolishing public prayer in schools." The 1965 report cited the previous year's most important accomplishments as developing a close working relationship with Al Lingo and ferreting out communist sympathizers in the Student Non-Violent Coordinating Committee (SNCC), Southern Christian Education Fund, and Southern Conference for Human Welfare. The report further concluded that the Southern Christian Leadership Fund's principle of nonviolence was a "farce" and that SNCC's John Lewis was "closely advised by communists if not controlled by them." State Sovereignty Commission funds were used for paying attorney's fees in legal cases against the U.S. Department of Health Education and Welfare.[56]

While the Sovereignty Commission was busy identifying Reds running rampant through Alabama, the Citizens' Councils were equally active in pumping up their membership. Not surprisingly, a significant amount of overlap existed between the two white supremacist organizations. Herbert Lancaster, a Montgomery architect, and Senator Walter Givhan served on the State Sovereignty Commission and were ranking members of the state Citizens' Council hierarchy. Jack Giles, Wallace's director of the Department of Industrial Relations, was also a member of the commission, and the governor himself served as chairman. The 1965 National Citizens' Council Leadership Conference was held in Montgomery with representatives from twenty-four states journeying to the Cradle of the Confederacy. Wallace was active at the conference, meeting and greeting the arrivals, receiving members at his office in the capitol, appointing members of the Citizens' Council hierarchy such as director of public relations Richard Morphew to honorary Alabama colonel status, introducing former Mississippi governor Ross Barnett at the Saturday luncheon, and speaking to the assembled throng. Wallace continued to encourage folks to join the Council, send new members a welcome letter and an eight-by-ten glossy photograph suitable for framing, and buy new mailing lists when they became available. The Citizens' Council stayed active in a variety of affairs, once castigating the legislature for failing to take seriously its idea of imposing a ten thousand dollar fine and a mandatory five-year jail term for anyone caught *enforcing* the Civil Rights Act of 1964.[57]

Over time, the Citizens' Council has developed a historical reputation as the respectable white supremacy club, somehow preferable and more principled than the Klan. That characterization may be an oversimplification. Citizens' Council members sat on the jury that refused to convict Klansman Collie Leroy Wilkins of murdering Viola Liuzzo despite eyewitness testimony to the contrary. Perhaps they were convinced by closing remarks from Matt Murphy, Wilkins's Klan-sponsored attorney: "The FBI took this case away from your own white sheriff. I urge you as patriotic Americans to find this defendant not guilty." Earlier in the trial, Murphy had been allowed to offer his interpretation of the eyewitness, Gary Thomas Rowe. "He's worse than a nigger," Murphy asserted: "I stand here as a white man and I say we're never going to mongrelize the race with nigger blood and the Martin Luther Kings, the white niggers, the Jews, the Zionists who run that bunch of niggers. . . . God damned them and they went to Africa and the only thing they ever built was grass huts." Wilkins, who according to testimony gleefully exclaimed "that bitch and bastard are both dead and in Hell," after unloading a revolver at them, later received a standing ovation and signed autographs for a crowd of some six thousand at a Klan rally in Dunn, North Carolina. After the Liuzzo trial was over, white liberal Virginia Durr summed up the verdict's meaning: "I realized that murder had become not only condoned but honored if it was against the enemy."[58]

In addition to providing funds for the Sovereignty Commission and general support for the Citizens' Council, Wallace and his administration continued to govern in such a way as to make race a preeminent concern. The Pensions and Security Department was threatened with a loss of federal funds for its failure to comply with the terms of the Civil Rights Act of 1964. Director Ruben King filed suit against HEW over mandatory desegregation procedures relating to nursing homes and hospitals, thereby risking the $97 million in annual federal funds Alabama had been receiving. The lawsuit was even more unbelievable when situated against the context of the annual federal largesse Alabama was sopping up. All told, the state was given some $312 million from Washington in 1965; only seventeen states received higher amounts. With Wallace presiding over a State Board of Education meeting, a policy was passed preventing payment of Negro teachers and principals on days where school attendance was less than 63 percent. The administration also sponsored a bill authorizing $185 private tuition school grants for any Alabama student unwilling to attend an integrated school. State Sovereignty Commission Director Eli Howell told the legislature that the bill was "perhaps the most important piece of legislation you have ever considered." The total two-year appropriation for this program was nearly $4 million. Wallace also called a meeting of two hundred or so county and municipal school superintendents, urging deliberately slow or minimal compliance with federal desegregation guidelines. The governor also pressured local school boards to refuse to sign mandatory guideline compliance forms, claiming those that had voluntarily complied did so because they had been "badgered and brow-beaten." In fact, every local school system in Alabama depended on federal dollars that the state had shown no inclination to replace with additional taxation. Wallace had a Joan Baez television special canceled in Alabama because the activist singer had participated in the Selma to Montgomery March. Wallace also announced his intention to file a federal suit limiting the size of civil demonstrations and his firm opposition to the movement to abolish the state poll tax.[59]

In the midst of the 1965 demonstrations, the governor found himself the victim of a practical joke by an anonymous civil rights worker with a few extra dollars and a finely developed sense of humor. In July 1965, Wallace received a membership card in the mail from the National Association for the Advancement of Colored People. The governor was not amused. He wrote the NAACP complaining that "I did not make nor did I authorize anyone to make a donation to your organization in my name." Going further, Wallace threatened legal action: "Failure to confirm that my name has been removed from your list could subject your organization to a suit at law for damages." Executive Director Roy Wilkins, no doubt with a wonderful sense of irony, returned the correspondence with an apology for "any embarrassment you may have been caused."[60]

Industrial Development

Surprisingly, the continued racial animus, violence, and chaos had little short-term effect on the state's ability to attract industry. In 1963, during the Birmingham campaign, Wallace had declared that racial disturbances would have no effect on the state "in any business way." And from a strictly cliometric perspective, the governor appeared to be right. In fact, Alabama attracted $623 million in new and expanded capital investment in 1965, an incredible increase from the previous one-year record of $406 million set in the previous year. Unbelievably, the Wallace administration reached the $1 billion mark in new and expanded industrial development in only two and a half years. No administration in state history had attracted as much over four years, let alone thirty months. New plants and facilities comprised $279 million of the total industrial development bonanza and included 136 new businesses in forty-seven counties. Alabama's favorable corporate tax rates, the lowest in the South, and enticing property tax rates, the lowest in the nation, continued to be powerful drawing cards. To publicize such incentives, the administration planned a Red Carpet Industrial Tour for 1966, the brainchild of State Planning and Industrial Development Board director Leonard Beard. Wallace invited seventeen hundred newspaper editors to a state-sponsored tour of Montgomery, Selma, Huntsville, Birmingham, and Mobile to generate favorable publicity. The administration paid over $12,000 for a special section to be printed by the *Birmingham News* trumpeting Alabama as a "Young Giant of Industry." The governor continued to intercede when necessary to woo prospects and used state resources for site preparation, grading, and road building.[61]

Successes aside, the industrial development process in this racially charged climate was not easy and occasionally became almost comical. Former congressmen Frank Boykin took the liberty of writing Hammermill Paper Company chairman D. S. Leslie to warn him not to listen to the "so-called Dr. Martin Luther King" who was promoting a boycott of Alabama products. In the same letter, Boykin referred to Jim Clark as "that wonderful Sheriff who has done such an outstanding job in Selma." Almost frantic, Boykin wrote Wallace that King might be a "devil" and predicted that "sooner or later we will have to take some drastic action and maybe put it up to the people to either stand with the white people or colored people, one or the other." Despite some tense moments, Hammermill kept its commitment and built its new plant in Selma.[62]

Though the amount of industry flowing into the state kept increasing, the type of work it provided remained unchanged. Nearly 30 percent of the new and expanded industry, approximately $184 million, was in pulp and paper. The net result was that most of this new industry created a limited number of jobs in low-wage, low-skill careers. The list of new industries in 1965 included too many firms like Whatley Sand and Gravel, Jigg's Sausage Company, Mack Hooper Hosiery, and Kerr-McGee Fertilizer that relied on unskilled labor and not enough high-skill technology companies like Stanford Research

Institute, Astro Space Laboratories, and Sperry-Rand Corporation. Alabama's poultry industry grew rapidly throughout the 1960s, an essential replacement for gradually waning cotton production, but it became increasingly difficult to feed a family based on wages earned from a broiler or egg operation. Even administration estimates, overly optimistic by nature, predicted the 360 new or expanded industries would bring only 27,892 new jobs. Using Wallace and Cater Act incentives, the state gained comparatively little from the industrial growth in the short term, and in the long term saw those jobs leave for Mexico or Central America. Perhaps as significant, no long-term assessment was made as to how to translate the new network of trade schools into better relationships with "cutting edge" industry. In fact, no serious attempts were made at strategic industrial development planning for the trade schools until Jere Beasley became lieutenant governor in 1971. Former congressman Carl Elliot knew even then that the type of new industry coming to the state made the impressive figures being released by the administration misleading: "I personally think the time has come when we give attention to the quality of jobs we get before we go all-out with free industrial sites, free grading of these sites, free roads to these sites, free taxes, and partially free financing of the plants themselves." That industry continued to locate in Alabama during the Wallace years suggests that much of corporate America was more interested in tax incentives and probusiness attitudes than racial turmoil or issues of social justice.[63]

Shifting Sands

Industrial development was important to Wallace, but opposition to federal voter registration, white counterregistration efforts, legislative reapportionment, and congressional redistricting preoccupied the administration. In April, a three-judge panel nullified the hasty redistricting drawn in the special session before the 1964 election. The court cited "serious population disparities" in the legislature's plan. "The vote of an elector in the Sixth District," the judges ruled, "is worth only approximately 69 percent as much as the vote of an elector in the Fourth District." It hardly took a trained political scientist to understand the electoral realities of an expanded black voting base. By the 1966 election, several senate seats would be in black majority areas, and since each county had at least one representative in the state house, the ten majority black counties would be likely to select one of their own as well. Beyond the scope of geographic considerations, the pending inclusion of thousands of black voters was sure to have monumental ramifications on the party system in Alabama. Properly aligned and united, the "black voting bloc," feared since the days of Reconstruction, could hold the balance of power in close elections and force social and economic concessions considered anathema by traditionalists. With the astonishing gains by the state GOP in the 1964 congressional elections and the massive unpopularity of President Johnson in the Deep South, two-party politics was seemingly on Alabama's doorstep anyway.[64]

From the administration's standpoint, some action had to be taken on each of these issues, but 1965 was a different year, with different constituencies, and far more political resolve by Wallace's political opponents. One of the first indications of these changes came with the opening of the regular legislative session and the administration's predictable call to the house and senate floor leaders to pass another in the steady stream of "nigger resolutions." This one, less hyperbolic than some in the past, called for all government agencies to refrain from signing agreements to comply with the Civil Rights Act of 1964. Senator Horton had seen enough: "We are getting tired of these so-called nigger resolutions being thrown at us. You throw them at us and say we've got to pass them." Bob Gilchrist joined in the attack: "George Corley Wallace integrated Alabama. He didn't do it intentionally I hope. How many Negroes were in white schools in Alabama when John Patterson was governor. Not one." Kenneth Hammond, formerly a Wallace supporter, began to peck away at the administration also. Hammond, a 240-pound former football player and coach who once told a colleague in the middle of a heated debate to "step outside and I'll chastise your ass," was upset at Wallace's indifference to the Democratic Party in the 1964 election. Hammond's uncle lost a local race in Decatur and the senator blamed Wallace for the defeat. Sonny Hornsby got in on the action too: "We've passed our last grandstand nigger resolution in this senate. What we need is a real stand, not a grandstand. The strategy employed by the governor has set our state back 100 years." The senate promptly went into fullblown filibuster mode with at least eight senators, none of them racial liberals, refusing to pass the anticompliance resolution. The filibuster had little to do with the resolution; it was more the case of John Patterson supporters letting the administration know the free ride was over.[65]

Six days later, the filibuster collapsed and the resolution passed, but the criticism of Wallace never slowed. Horton blasted the governor for spending five minutes in his Farm Day address on agriculture and the rest of the time on race: "I ask the governor to quit appealing to the worst in the people and appeal to the best. I ask him to quit continually rubbing these sores." Gilchrist blasted Wallace for proposing more bond funding for road construction. In fact, the Wallace administration accumulated more long-term debt through deficit financing in its first twenty-eight months than all other administrations in state history combined. During the first Wallace term, state debt increased twelve times as fast as the national debt. The state Chamber of Commerce referred to the Wallace administration as a "Great Society at the State Level" because of all the bond financing. Gilchrist publicly challenged the governor to stop charging admission at state parks. He proposed bills to water down the governor's office by stripping away state funds for television broadcasts, eliminating the use of state aircraft and automobiles for personal use, as well as a provision to make all gubernatorial appointments subject to senate confirmation. Kenneth Hammond accused Wallace of deliberately discriminating against North Alabama, trying to destroy the state Democratic Party, and turning Alabama into a "haven for hate-mongers." Larry Dumas complained about administration-backed plans to chop up Jefferson County, the state's largest, in redistricting. If passed, this plan would have weakened the powerful urban county by splitting it into three separate congressional districts.[66]

Dumas had good reason to fear a chop-up bill; administration leaders in the senate passed such a bill in the middle of the night. Dumas, who had been assured by the senate leadership that the bill would not come up for a vote, had retired for the evening to his Montgomery hotel room. When the smoke cleared the next morning, Wallace denied any involvement. Dumas and others were not convinced. Senator A. C. Shelton called the entire fiasco a "damnable disgrace by jellyfish followers of the governor who came together at a midnight rump session." The house passed a similar bill less than three weeks later, despite the fact that the actual bill mysteriously disappeared from the lower chamber for a time. Wallace signed it, and the districts were officially redrawn.[67]

Another controversial piece of legislation connected to the issue of race was the administration-backed ban on communist speakers at state-supported schools, colleges, and universities. The bill would have blocked public speaking by anyone who had invoked their Fifth Amendment rights when questioned about membership in certain organizations or previous activities. Wallace had personally decreed the bill to be an administration priority on at least two occasions: during the brouhaha over the Jefferson County chop-up bill and in another statement outlining his priorities for racial legislation. Theoretically, Wallace could use such a law to prevent certain civil rights leaders from speaking in the state as long as he could draw a Red line from the speaker to someone with communist sympathies. Despite the protests of university presidents concerned that such a bill could hurt their accreditation, the administration pushed the bill through the senate education committee. Senator Hammond was threatened with loss of funding for DeKalb County projects if he opposed the bill. "Anything Wallace wants, he gets," the senator A. C. Shelton complained, "but that doesn't make it a wise bill." Senator Joe Smith, who represented Russell and Lee counties, supported the bill even though one of his most powerful constituents, former Auburn University president Ralph

Brown Draughon, testified emphatically against it. Despite all the administration arm-twisting, the senate, indicative of a small but noticeable reduction in
Wallace's power, killed the bill.[68]

The administration used yet another special session, Wallace's sixth, to reapportion the legislature. Even if federal courts had not forced it, Wallace may
have wanted a shuffling of the geographic lines anyway. The changes to the
political landscape since the passage of the Voting Rights Act were that significant. In August, federal registrars were dispatched to Autauga, Dallas, Elmore, Greene, Hale, Lowndes, Marengo, Montgomery, Perry, and Wilcox counties. The arrival of registrars was a bitter blow to the administration. Just two
years earlier, Wallace had sought to repel black registration by making himself solely responsible for naming county registrars. The reaction in white Alabama to federal registration was predictable. A *Montgomery Advertiser* editorial sounded as if it could have been written a century before: "This morning,
in some counties, federal agents, lineal descendants of the Reconstruction cor-
rupters, will be at work showing illiterates where to make their marks." Another *Advertiser* editorial described the presence of the registrars as a "federal
occupation" and their work as "orgiastic." Wallace identified the Voting Rights
Act as the intellectual work product of the Communist Party and termed it
"punitive, unreasonable, and destructive of constitutionally guaranteed free-
doms." By December, more than thirty-six thousand Alabamians, mostly black,
had registered to vote for the first time.[69]

Calling a reapportionment session was only half of Wallace's strategy for
nullifying the new black voters. Though conservative ideologues such as
William F. Buckley were calling for wholesale restriction of the franchise to
only those with at least a high school diploma, Wallace was a more practical
man and sought to counter new black voters with an equal or greater stream
of new white voters. Initially, Wallace also sought a court injunction to prevent
the addition of federally registered voters on county voting rolls and leaked to
reporters his fears of blacks, through chicanery or ignorance, casting multiple
ballots and voting in several different polling places. The legislature openly
discussed putting an invisible brand on some voters to keep multiple voting
at bay. Not surprisingly, this measure had not been considered throughout the
previous half century or so when electioneering shenanigans by white Alabamians had been the rule in some counties, not the exception. Wallace also
considered a plan from the State Sovereignty Commission to create a separate committee with subpoena power to aggressively question the leadership
of the civil rights movement. Part of the mission of the committee would be
to "clarify national misconceptions of Negro voting rights in Alabama with
evidence that a majority of literate Negroes are already registered." Another
Wallace friend suggested the purchase of a 50,000-watt radio station that could

broadcast the Wallace interpretation of national events into living rooms and automobiles in a Radio–Free South style. Since these tactics had no real chance at success, Wallace turned to a more aggressive approach: he enlisted his Citizens' Council brethren to launch their own voter registration drives. He also made use of the myriad letters and telegrams he had received over the years by instructing the State Sovereignty Commission to "write the people who have written me and signed petitions offering their support and ask them to get all their family and their friends registered to vote."[70]

Wallace kicked off the reapportionment session with a rousing speech in which he excoriated the usual suspects. A number of ideas generated discussion in the opening days of the session, but one in particular, known as the "white supremacy plan," emerged as the front-runner. This arrangement was predicated on merging the twelve majority black counties and breaking them into districts with larger white counties. The net result was classic gerrymandering: nullification of the new black voters by making their votes numerically insignificant when compared to the white voters in the new geographically convoluted districts. Senator Roland Cooper of Wilcox County claimed the intention was not to stifle black voters at all. The real goal, Cooper contended, was to "see that we do not create districts where illiterates outnumber literates." Perhaps Cooper spoke with his tongue in cheek since he later sarcastically remarked that the only qualities necessary to register for voting were to be "black and breathing," and that he was proud of the bill's none too subtle moniker. The state supreme court paved the way for passage of the bill by ruling that multicounty districts were constitutional and that any reapportionment could be approved by the legislature and need not require the consent of a state vote. The final plan for senate reapportionment included only one district that had more blacks over the age of twenty-one than whites.[71]

Though on the surface the reapportioned districts seemed to be nothing more than business as usual for the deepest of Deep South states, a major change was under way. In order to create boundaries that limited the possibility of blacks being elected to office, the legislature had to strip away the centuries-old tradition of rural supremacy and urban inferiority. The era of Black Belt dominance was over as urban Alabama received more representative power than at any time in state history. The four most populous counties went from sixteen representatives to forty in the house, and they would now hold thirteen of the thirty-five senate seats. The administration was reluctant to see its rural power base evaporate, but the alternative of doing business with substantial numbers of black legislators was even less appealing.[72]

Within two days of the reapportionment bill's passing, the Justice Department announced plans for legal action to overturn the plan. A three-judge panel accepted the senate plan, but voided the house version and then reshaped that body itself. "The conclusion is inescapable," the ruling declared, "that Elmore, Tallapoosa, and Macon were combined needlessly into a single house district for the sole purpose of preventing the election of a Negro house member." The court's plan created four districts with a total of eight representatives where the number of blacks was greater than whites. The era of white exclusivity and unlimited rural power in Alabama was over.[73]

Succession

The legislative and judicial checks and balances that caught up to George Wallace in 1965 revealed, for the first time, some limits to his awesome power. To be sure, Wallace was as popular as ever with white Alabamians; he still knew metaphorically exactly where they lived, what they cared about, and how to reach them. But in 1965, political factions led by national Democrats, the nascent Alabama Republican Party, prospective gubernatorial candidates, and rival politicians simply fed up with being dominated by Wallace began to push back. These anti-Wallace forces won several minor skirmishes and one very important battle near the end of the year: the fight over gubernatorial succession.

The 1901 Alabama Constitution prevented governors from running for consecutive terms, a provision shared by at least ten other states, including Georgia. Amending the state constitution was not difficult, and in fact had become something of an annual event; by 1963, Alabama voters had already changed their constitution 212 times and rejected another 142 amendments. As a result, the constitution was on its way to becoming the longest of any state in the Union and much closer in physical appearance to a New York City telephone book than a readable, understandable, document of state governance. While others had earlier pondered removing the restriction on consecutive terms, quite likely, no governor in recent state history could have won an immediate second term anyway. Few doubted that Wallace would win comfortably in 1966 if the law could be changed. On principle, plenty of legislators supported the idea of succession; but by the fall of 1965, nearly every politician, interest group, or influence peddler had already chosen sides for the 1966 election. As a result, this battle would singularly crystallize all anti-Wallace factions against the administration.[74]

Wallace had given his blessing to earlier attempts to modify the law. In August 1963, with the governor already tremendously popular in the state after his stand at the University of Alabama, the house passed a bill allowing Wallace to succeed himself. Though publicly avoiding comment, Wallace made it clear privately that he wanted the bill to become law. Nevertheless, the senate, already jousting with the administration over various bills centralizing power in the hands of the governor, killed the bill in committee. Had the state been at peace, Wallace might have applied the full weight of his office to the fight. But Wallace was already in the middle of a fracas over closing state schools to prevent integration and was preoccupied with planning a national speaking tour and a potential primary run the following year. Nationally, Wallace was taking hits from Oregon senator Wayne Morse, who was assailing the governor's war record and job performance. Instead of launching a bloody campaign to get succession passed, Wallace used the prospective bill to create leverage and ensure the passage of his other pet bills. The end result was that the fight for succession was postponed.[75]

Half a year later, in April 1964, rumors began to surface that Wallace would call a special session for the purpose of getting a succession bill passed. A month later in the aftermath of the governor's impressive performance in the Maryland primary, capitol beat reporter Bob Ingram was still reporting that Wallace was planning to call a special session. When the redistricting session was finally called in August 1964, Senators Ollie Nabors and Jimmy Clark introduced a succession bill on the first day. Nabors laughed at the idea that an Alabama empire could be created if the bill became law: "I have too much faith in the people to believe that would happen. It would be impossible for a bad governor [to build] up an organization." Wallace opponent Bob Gilchrist immediately called the entire redistricting session a smokescreen for getting succession passed, promised to filibuster it to death, and predicted if it passed Alabama would turn into a "wasteland of liberalism." Senators Bill McCain and Sonny Hornsby quickly announced their committed opposition. With the entire redistricting issue completely overshadowed and four senators filibustering to prevent passage, Wallace asked for the bill to be sent back to committee and feigned indifference. But in a televised joint session speech attacking the four, the governor referred to succession as something "supported by an overwhelming majority in both houses" and reiterated that the matter should go to the people for a vote. The reality in the legislature was that more than four were opposed to the bill, and former governor John Patterson was already in Montgomery directing an antisuccession strategy of his own. Two weeks after the redistricting session started and two weeks before it would end, Bob Ingram had already pronounced the bill dead. Even so, while the governor was publicly claiming to be uninterested in the entire matter, Trammell, Morgan, and Jackson kept pushing and applying pressure.[76]

When Wallace called the special session for reapportionment of the state legislature in September 1965, most legislators viewed his opening speech as a veiled call for succession. By law, any amendment to the constitution required a ninety-day period between its passage in the legislature and the special election required to make it official. Complicating the matter on the other end of the calendar was March 1, official filing date for entering the 1966 race. As a result, the legislative work needed to be completed before December so that the election, which would have been nothing more than a formality due to Wallace's staggering popularity, could be held. By now, every Alabamian with a political pulse knew the fight was coming, if not in this session, then in another one to be called shortly.[77]

Wallace wanted to run again for a number of reasons. His appetite whetted by the three 1964 primaries, the governor was unquestionably committed to running for president in 1968. Even if he knew he could not win, the chance to compete on the national stage and lock horns with the big boys was irresistible. The office of governor came with perquisites no other post could match. As governor, Wallace had unlimited access to the state plane, the ability to whip-saw state contractors into mandatory campaign donations, and a large staff of paid employees to assist him. Simply put, Wallace needed the office, the platform, and the flexibility of the governor's office in order to be a viable candidate for the White House. He also relished the chance to take on John Patterson, the only person to beat him, and a certain candidate in the 1966 race. Wallace also had spent a lifetime wanting to be governor, a factor not to be discounted when evaluating his thirst to be governor again. And even if he was generally disinterested in the machinations of daily governance, Wallace, in the minds of most white Alabamians, had been a fabulous governor. In a world that told them they were too poor, too stupid, too lazy, and too racist to matter, millworkers and miners and truck drivers and hog farmers in Alabama appreciated the way Wallace made them feel about themselves. If the issue was left to the voters, everyone in Alabama knew when it got right down to the lick log, Wallace would easily win another term.[78]

The governor did have other options. John Sparkman, Alabama's junior senator even though he had served since 1946, was up for reelection in 1966. The senator was well respected in Washington, having served on the Small Business and Banking committees, and had been Adlai Stevenson's vice presidential candidate in the 1952 election, but, back home, he was being regularly tarred by the Wallace crowd, fairly or not, with the sins of the national Democratic Party. Technically, Wallace was also forbidden by the state constitution from running for the U.S. Senate, but that issue was a good deal cloudier than the question of gubernatorial succession. The state senate was far less inclined to wage a protracted cloture fight on Sparkman's behalf, and B. G. Robison had already offered a bill that would have allowed Wallace to run against Sparkman, a race the governor would be clearly favored to win. The senator, keenly aware of the governor's power and popularity, made a habit of telling Alabama reporters that Wallace had told him "several times" he would not run for the senate. Furthermore, Attorney General Richmond Flowers, already planning his own quest for the governor's office in 1966, had, not coincidentally, ruled that the Alabama provision preventing Wallace from running for senate was unconstitutional since a state could not stipulate qualifications for a federal position. In the end, Wallace's general disinterest in policy and governance, unwillingness to live in Washington D.C., and ambivalence toward the senatorial system of party loyalty, made the office unattractive.[79]

The special session for succession began with a September 30 speech in which Wallace announced he was ready to "accept the judgement of the people" whether he should be permitted to run for governor. The actual bill was introduced in the senate by administration friend Jimmy McDow, though the administration sought to get it passed first in the house before turning its full attention to the more recalcitrant upper house. From the beginning, the administration's public spin was that the people of the state should have the right to vote on important issues themselves and that any truculence by the senate to remove the huddled masses from the democratic process should not be tolerated in any way, shape, or form; never mind that the administration had already passed at least nine separate bond issues worth some $300 million through legislative channels and killed amendments requiring referenda to pass them. Representative Granville Turner immediately sponsored two resolutions attempting to kill succession and also demanded equal time on state television for succession opponents. That Turner's resolutions failed was no surprise, especially in the malleable lower chamber, but his efforts did indicate that resistance was ready and waiting for the governor. John Patterson, with help from his former finance director Charles Meriwether and Ryan deGraffenreid set up war rooms to rally opposition forces. Media pressure forced Wallace to pay for the broadcast of the session's opening speech out of his own war chest.[80]

Some of that pressure came from formerly friendly camps such as the *Montgomery Advertiser,* run by Wallace confidant Grover Hall. Hall had been almost universally supportive of Wallaceism in the past, keeping time with the governor's drumming on the horrors of the First and Second Reconstructions, the communist connections of activists in the civil rights movement, and the questionable ulterior motives of Judge Johnson, Martin Luther King Jr., and anybody drawing a paycheck from the Kennedy or Johnson administrations. Understanding Wallace's presidential motivations, Hall, although still pro-Wallace on most policy matters, opposed succession in print, predicting a divisive third-party campaign with plenty of additional unpledged elector shenanigans akin to the 1964 fiasco. *Advertiser* editorials also noted that future Alabama chief executives might not be as trustworthy as Wallace.[81]

The *Advertiser* was not alone in its dissent; most of the state's largest metropolitan newspapers (including the *Huntsville Times, Tuscaloosa News, Birmingham News,* and *Birmingham Post-Herald*) opposed succession. While Wallace was not pleased with this journalistic intransigence, he seized the opportunity to lump the wayward Alabama newspapers into his regular indictments of all "liberal" media. Invoking an unofficial boycott of his own, Wallace pulled state liquor advertisements from the newspapers opposing him, a tactic he had used in the past. Though some editors demurred or at least found other issues to write about, Hall responded to Wallace's financial strong-arming: "We have seen federal bureaucrats speak of 'managing the news.' Here we have a governor who seeks to manage the editorials as well."[82]

The state's nascent Republican Party, though neither the most organized nor vociferous of the administration's opponents, was among those with a dog in the fight. Having made such surprising gains in the congressional election of 1964 and sensing the party realignment coming with white resistance to the national Democratic Party, the Alabama GOP was convinced it could contend for the governor's office as long as it did not have to face Wallace. State GOP chairman Thomas Brigham accused Wallace of intimidating the legislature. The most charismatic leaders in the party, organizer John Grenier and Congressman Jim Martin, had their eyes on the mansion in Montgomery and Sparkman's senate seat and wanted to keep Wallace's potentially gigantic Democratic coattails as far from the ballot as possible. Martin, who won a House of Representative seat in 1964, had narrowly lost an earlier Senate race against Lister Hill, and, with his pronounced social conservatism, figured to give Sparkman fits in 1966. To that end, Republican representative Alfred Goldthwaite went on the offensive calling the idea of succession a "grab to extend power that has never before been seen in this state." Fellow Republican Tandy Little complained about administration persuasion tactics. "Eight days ago today," Little complained, "we had forty-five house members who said they were irrevocably opposed to the bill. We come back one week later, and twenty of them have changed their minds. Every house member knows something of the pressure brought to bear."[83]

Even as succession opponents came out of the woodwork at the opening gavel of the session, some unlikely supporters did as well. Carl Elliot, the former congressman targeted for political extinction by the administration in 1964, announced as a candidate for governor and declared that he supported succession. Elliot was not eager to campaign against Wallace, but thought he could prosper from drawing a clear distinction between Wallace's preoccupation with looking backward and his own intention to pilot a progressive course reconciling Alabama with the rest of the country. Elliot was banking on the idea that venomous racial politics were passing away and planned to run a campaign that stressed the need for high-tech, high-skill industrial development, a more focused approach to education, and peaceful, cooperative relations with the federal government. "I think the legislature might as well pass it," the Jasper native stated, "so as to give him and me a chance to draw the lines in the forthcoming campaign."[84]

Some influential Alabamians vowed to support succession *because* Wallace was likely to run for president. Bruce Henderson, political insider, Citizens' Council leader, and a man commonly referred to as the most qualified man never elected governor, understood Wallace's ambition and thought it would have positive effects: "I am convinced that as a candidate for president his impact on the ideology of this nation would be tremendous. I have therefore made up my mind to vote for his second term. . . . We could help the falling morale of this country in no more definite way than by voting for Wallace for president. His political ideology would save this nation."[85]

With the house an easy bet to pass the bill, the matter was left to be decided in the senate. Even there, the issue was more complicated than a cursory glance might suggest. The administration had twenty-one votes in the thirty-five-member body for the bill, more than enough to pass it. Nevertheless, twenty-four votes were required to invoke cloture and stop a filibuster. Though outwardly confident, the administration knew getting the cloture votes was going to be difficult. Bob Gilchrist, acting as a veritable minority whip for the anti-succession camp, had worked the math as well, even if he had exaggerated his conclusions. "We have at least twenty senators," Gilchrist calculated, "who will not vote cloture. We have seventeen who will not even vote for succession. Wallace is whipped and we know it."[86]

Early in the session, Wallace announced plans for a cloture vote. The governor knew the vote would fail, but it would also draw his opponents out into the open where he could apply public pressure to match the private coercion already being brandished by Seymore Trammell, among others. When, as predicted, the vote failed 18 to 12, Wallace went on the offensive. Succession's opponents, the governor professed, were a "small, hard core of senators [who have] fought every facet of my administration." Blending fact with convenience, Wallace continued: "They have opposed the road program, the free textbook program, the trade school and junior college program." The administration withheld new roads construction, bridges, plant mix, and everything else possible from the twelve. Trammell and his legal chief Taylor Hardin informed Walter Graham, president of Southern Union State Community College in Wadley, that the college had lost its five hundred thousand dollar appropriation because of Julian Lowe's opposition. When Lowe went public instead of changing his vote, the administration backpedaled on the junior college money, but not on the public campaign. Wallace wanted the second term so badly that he even briefly considered a deal in which he would return some patronage power to the legislature. One bill along these lines was introduced that would have created a nine-member Highway Commission responsible for allocating road and plant mix contracts, a power previously held by the governor. Ultimately, a compromise could not be reached.[87]

Wallace visited the district of every opposition senator, sometimes even appearing on the same dais. After whipping the crowd into a frenzy, Wallace would turn to the crowd, point at their senator, and blame him for his succession troubles. "There is only one issue," the governor shouted, "and that is, should the people be allowed to vote for this amendment. I can't understand why there is so much opposition to the bill. All we're asking is that you be given the right to vote on it." On more than a few occasions, the senators quickly found themselves surrounded by a frothing, swearing mob bent on exacting retribution on behalf of their beloved governor. Wallace's sometime speechwriter and link to the Klan, Asa Carter, became a special advisor on the succession fight, and Leonard Wilson rallied the Citizens' Council rank and file. Richmond Flowers complained that the Klan was threatening senators and issued a twenty-six-page white paper that addressed the subject. John Tyson accused the Wallace palace guard of spreading rumors that deGraffenreid had bought Tyson's succession vote.[88]

But public and private pressure campaigns were only part of the administration's strategy. Wallace was counting on the support of Lieutenant Governor Jim Allen to gavel the bill through the senate. Allen was supportive of succession, but needed the vote to be closer in order to minimize the certain outrage following his actions. With the opposition forces bending but not breaking under the force of the Wallace offensive, the governor sought to circumvent existing law and asked the Alabama Supreme Court to rule on the constitutionality of the cloture rules. A favorable ruling would certainly reduce the cloture number from an unattainable twenty-four to a more feasible twenty-one. But, taken to its ultimate conclusion, this decision would potentially strip the senate of its traditional filibuster provisions. Wallace's critics did not mind pointing out that the governor would be furious if President Johnson turned to the U.S. Supreme Court every time the Senate eschewed his wishes. In the end, the state Supreme Court refused to declare the cloture rules unconstitutional.[89]

Frustrated by the court, the governor turned to another tactic: changing the cloture rules through legislation to make a simple majority of eighteen necessary to end debate. This was even more problematic than judicial remedies since many who favored succession and were willing to look the other way if necessary to get it passed had no intention of permanently rewriting the rules of order. John Tyson sensed the desperation: "I am convinced he [Wallace] would stop at nothing." Rural county senators were especially apprehensive since they were facing a marked loss of prestige and power in the next legislature and would be dependent on filibustering and cloture rules as weapons of political obstruction. Finally, Lieutenant Governor Allen made it clear, much to the administration's chagrin, that he had no intention of gaveling through something as contentious and well chronicled as succession. In all, Allen laid down the law to the administration on multiple fronts: it was impossible to amend the cloture rules to eighteen; nobody was going to force him to stop extended debate on this issue; the governor had no chance to get the required twenty-four cloture votes; he would not set a prescribed time for voting on the bill.[90]

In the end, Wallace could not coerce the compliance of the senators and could not rewrite the rules. When the final vote was taken, the administration had lost, 18 to 14; three senators were absent. The entire special session had cost the taxpayers $150,000. In the aftermath, Wallace vowed vengeance on the senators and blamed John Patterson for the defeat more than anyone else, but he resisted the temptation to lash out on television. Privately and in correspondence, Wallace reminded supporters of the seventeen who voted against him or abstained from voting in what amounted to the first stage of a campaign to ruin their political careers. As for future plans, Wallace surprised his cabinet with a tantalizing remark that fueled much media speculation about Alabama politics in 1966: "We might just run Lurleen for governor."[91]

5
Means to an End / 1966

The first glimpses of a new social and political order were dawning in Alabama. A century of unchecked rural power was washed away in the court-ordered reapportionment of the state legislature. The next election would give urban-oriented counties and major municipalities commensurate representation for the first time in state history. Federal voting registrars were changing the electoral landscape of the state with every passing day as more African Americans and poor whites gained access to the franchise for the first time in their lives. Political reporters such as Gene Kovarik were predicting that in the November 1966 election as many as eight blacks could win seats in the Alabama house of representatives. Alabama school systems were under pressure to submit plans to comply with federal guidelines for desegregation. Seemingly every social and political institution in the entire state was in flux. If Bear Bryant's Alabama Crimson Tide had not won its third national championship in five years, countless Alabamians might have thought they were living in another state.[1]

Most of the changes in the state were not welcomed by white Alabamians, particularly since those changes were being imposed by Congress, the federal judiciary, and a supposedly southern president. One change originating inside the state was a push to remove the "White Supremacy for the Right" state Democratic Party motto and crowing rooster symbol from all official party uses. The motto, institutionalized by section 1 of the state Democratic Party bylaws, had appeared on official Alabama ballots since 1904. Sensing the changing times, black Alabamians and loyalist Democrats as supporters of the national party spearheaded the drive to change the emblems. The administration, backed by Citizens' Councils and the states' rights crowd, opposed the changes.[2]

Rifts between loyalist Democrats and states' rights fire-eaters were nothing new; they dated to the antebellum era and were as common in Alabama as biscuits and gravy. More recently, conflict between loyalist factions and conservative forces erupted during the 1964 national convention in Atlantic City. A year after the convention, Wallace friend Jud Scott resigned his seat on the executive committee because of philosophical differences with its national loyalist chairman, Judge Roy Mayhall. "There is no doubt in my mind," Scott wrote, "but that you and your liberal friends are running the Committee, after receiving orders and directions from the Great Society. . . . I oppose turning our State over to a bunch of illiterates." Wallace's outspoken bashing of the national Democratic Party, the passage of the Civil Rights Act of 1964 and the Voting Rights Act of 1965, and the registration of thousands of black Alabamians hardened the resolve of states' rights advocates like Scott. And having already dealt the state Democratic Party a powerful blow with the 1964 independent elector campaign that helped elect five Republican congressmen, Wallace had no tolerance for the woeful bleats of party loyalists preaching unity for the sake of the party. Though still a national Democrat by registration and an Alabama Democrat by rhetoric, Wallace was essentially a man without a political party. He functioned within Alabama on the strength of his name and sheer power and outside the state on his fame. When black leaders informed Mayhall that their support in 1966 was contingent upon removing the motto, the battle lines were drawn.[3]

At the January 1966 meeting of the executive committee, loyalist Charles McKay offered an amendment to keep the rooster but alter the motto to read "Democrats for the Right." McKay reasoned that the electoral landscape had changed and that the party could no longer afford to "take a stick and run off a hundred and fifty or a hundred and seventy-five thousand prospective voters who might vote in that election for our candidates." Knowing a voice vote would kill the resolution while a secret ballot tally would prove more supportive, Mayhall used the power of the chair to engineer such a procedure and limited debate to fifteen minutes. By this time, Wallace, who had planned to make a fire and brimstone speech denouncing the loyalists, sized up the strength of the loyalist forces and left without uttering a word.[4]

Wallace's pullout did not mean the administration would remain silent. Leonard Wilson, Citizens' Council executive secretary, and Frank Mizzell, attorney for Wallace's State Sovereignty Commission, fought fiercely to keep the white supremacy label on all official Democratic Party documents. Wilson, using procedural rules, fought unsuccessfully to get the secret vote tabled in favor of a voice vote and then suggested anyone asking for a secret vote should resign immediately. Mizzell attacked the motives of those who would remove the sixty-one-year-old motto. "I feel," Mizzell alleged, "what has made people change their mind today is the feel of the Negro vote. . . . What you are doing today in sacrificing this emblem is giving ground and doing it in the same way in the name of the Negro." Henry Sweet provided similar testimony and reflected the emotionally charged atmosphere in the room: "I consider everyone who voted no [in favor of removing the old motto] a political coward. ... I never thought that we would substitute white supremacy [with] black supremacy in Alabama. ... I am ashamed to see it and I just hope for God's sake that you will not let Flowers and Katzenbach and Mayhall and Johnson and that element control your lives." Mayhall bristled at the personal attack and admonished the emotional Sweet to refrain from further outbursts. Sweet controlled his contempt for Mayhall but not for the "radicals, anarchists, delinquents, and street walkers" agitating for social change. In the end, the motion passed; the white supremacy motto was dead and one more vestige of state political tradition was gone.[5]

Beaten back on the motto, the administration was left to take solace in the survival of the rooster and a resolution backing the Wallace canon. Introduced by Albert Brewer at the governor's request, the "Statement of Principles of the Alabama Democratic Party" read like an abstract of a Wallace stump speech: "The Alabama Democratic Party ... stands against centralized control of management, business, labor and education and shall continue the effort to restore ... the right of people of the States and of local government to determine matters. ... The Alabama Democratic Party believes that the state should have the right to determine the qualifications of people to vote and further believes that the State should have the right to determine who shall serve upon its juries and how the courts of this state should function." Reading the resolution into the record was a hollow victory; the administration was powerless to force state Democratic candidates to run on such a platform. Taken together, the result of the motto fight, only a few months after the succession battle, along with the governor's insistence on the resolution revealed that George Wallace, while still immensely popular with the mass of white Alabamians, was losing his power over his rivals.[6]

Cabinet Independence

Angered at Mayhall's leadership and frustrated by his failure to overturn the ban on succession, Wallace became even less interested in the daily machinations of state government and more consumed with how to hold onto his power base. As a result, cabinet members, who already enjoyed a tremendous amount of latitude, found themselves even freer. No department head took advantage of the situation quite like Russellville native A. W. Todd, commissioner of agriculture. Todd, a former state senator and commissioner of agriculture during the second Folsom administration, was a successful agribusinessman with a lucrative poultry farm and financial interests in a feed and seed store, a feed mill, and a lumber company.[7]

Todd was the sort of interesting political personality that Alabama has always seemed to produce. He lost his arm in a hunting accident as a youth and was later dubbed "Nub," a nickname he disliked. In the post–World War II political landscape, however, Todd was always willing to let the illusion linger that the arm was lost in service against the Germans or Japanese. During his first term, Todd aggressively backed high inspection fees for out-of-state eggs, a policy that pleased his fellow poultry farmers. Todd was less adamant about constructing standards and practices for Alabama poultry growers. A 1967 report by veterinarian J. G. Mulligan noted that more than half the state's poultry would fail federal inspection and was "unfit for human consumption." Over the ensuing decades, the broiler and egg business was one of the few aspects of state agriculture that was expanding. In April 1963, less than four months after assuming office, Todd was arrested for allegedly threatening to kill an Agriculture Department employee with an axe. Rather than attempt to constrain this political wild card, Wallace simply left him to his own devices.[8]

Early in Wallace's first term, the administration placed little emphasis on agriculture, and the governor rarely attended agricultural board meetings. One exception was Wallace's embrace of a system of markets to help state farmers sell their produce. Conditioned by the abject poverty he witnessed firsthand in Barbour County, Wallace was a strong backer of farmers' markets and communicated this priority to Todd. The principal intellectual factor fueling the market idea was a study written by Agriculture and Industries Department staffer John Curry. Curry's report concluded that "present marketing procedures and limited facilities for product preparation and product movement are major limiting factors in developing full potentials." Curry's task force suggested not only the construction of more markets but also extensive training so that state farmers were prepared to wash, sort, cool, grade, and package their crops more competitively. Wallace spoke occasionally of the importance of the farmers' market program and its importance for Alabama producers. In 1965, Wallace scheduled meetings with agriculture interest groups to solicit support for his farmers' market program and met with Todd, Curry, and Senator Neil Metcalf of Geneva County to write legislation amending the Wallace and Cater Acts to include farmers' markets. The legislature did pass a bill to create a Farmer's Market Authority that was charged with establishing a network throughout the state. Unfortunately, very few markets were created and just two years later, the governor proposed eliminating farm-to-market road funds as a way to pacify urban legislators who wanted a redistribution of gas taxes and highway monies.[9]

All across the South, the family farm was giving way to both the New South industrial creed and the faceless efficiency of corporate agribusiness. In the twenty-five years after 1950, the number of southern farmers would shrink by two-thirds. Large-scale operations were using technology and science to improve yields; small farmers were struggling to pay the bank; sharecroppers were simply disappearing. In 1963, Alabama had a bumper crop in cotton, corn, pecans, peanuts, and poultry even though less acreage was under cultivation than in previous years. Throughout the 1960s, Alabama small farmers saw their profits dwindle until most were forced to sell and enter either manufacturing or service sectors. King Cotton slowly gave way to beef, peanuts, soybeans, and broilers. Other than lip service, the administration did little to ease this economic transition. Trade school matriculation was rarely tied to specific industrial occupations or corporations. Most new industry attracted to the state paid subsistence wages. Vows to fight an influx of cheap foreign crops were often hollow. The administration hardly welcomed Johnson administration antipoverty programs and tried to veto at least two designed to aid blacks. Wallace thrilled Huntsville residents with calls for aggressive efforts to lure more science and research to the state, but then proposed nothing substantive for accomplishing such a goal.[10]

Not surprisingly, agricultural policy had political ramifications, and not just for the governor. Todd had aspirations of becoming governor himself in 1966 and took advantage of opportunities to elevate his profile. While Wallace and most of the palace guard were campaigning in the 1964 Maryland primary, Todd began impounding foreign meat. When pressed by curious scribes, Todd portrayed himself as a consumer advocate and declared the meat was likely laced with bacteria and included some inappropriate additives, namely horsemeat. With the seizures generating a minor buzz and Alabama cattleman and farmers offering written support, Todd began including the rationale that foreign beef was costing the state "at least 1,000 jobs," and announced he would begin inspecting restaurants and testing meat. Soon enough, Todd had confiscated more than 1 million pounds of beef, mostly from Australia, and over 150,000 pounds of mutton. Todd even had the cold storage plant at the state docks inspected for foreign meat, though none was found and the search was technically a violation of the Warehousemen's Act. Department employees fashioned signs for retailers that read "Only Domestic Beef is sold here." When pressured by wholesalers, Todd agreed to release some of the imported meat provided it was taken out of the state. A New York importer, Tupman Thurlow Company, claiming Todd had assumed "police powers," filed suit in Frank Johnson's federal court. In response, Todd promised to reveal the results of his tests.[11]

When Judge Johnson was unimpressed with his test results and ordered him to release the meat, Todd was elated because he could now claim federal persecution at the hands of Wallace's self-constructed enemy: "Another popular figure in our state has proven where the U.S. government is concerned and a party to a court action, no state official is going to win a case in federal court. And like that other prominent figure in our state government, I am going to continue to use every legal means at my disposal to protect our people and oppose centralized government in control over state affairs." Though Todd released the seized goods as required, he later confiscated forty-seven cases of meat packaged by Tupman Thurlow and continued to seize other foreign meat from time to time. With legal channels to ban foreign meat evaporating, Todd worked with his hometown senator Emmett Oden to introduce a bill giving the commissioner exclusive power to regulate meat-packing across the state.[12]

Todd found other ways to keep himself in the headlines while trying to slay the same dragons as the governor. In September 1964, he announced that the federal government's release of surplus cotton had cost Alabama farmers $1.6 million dollars through price deflation. The commissioner also called for Alabama to ban all milk produced in neighboring states. The *Alabama Farmers Bulletin,* the official publication of the Department of Agriculture and Industries, became Todd's state-sponsored propaganda tool. Historically, the *Bulletin* was mailed only to farmers or other interested Alabamians who personally requested the periodical. Since the newsletter usually contained nothing more than research articles and farm advertisements, the subscription list was understandably small. Todd, however, sensed the public relations boost to be gained from a wider readership and began sending the *Bulletin* to thousands of Alabamians. He reshaped the publication to include photographs of him and regular coverage of his activities. Ultimately, Todd nearly quadrupled printing of the *Bulletin* to more than 128,000, substantially more than subscriptions to either the *Montgomery Advertiser* or *Birmingham Post-Herald.*[13]

The independent Board of Agriculture grew tired of Todd's publicity quest but received little support from Wallace. Todd, who had already alienated board members with his rambling filibuster-styled harangues at meetings, paid little attention to formal resolutions that called for more professional use of his office and the *Bulletin.* The board also objected to the commissioner's hiring underlings who carried formal titles like "seed analyst," "egg inspector," or "market news analyst," but had no professional qualifications. In reality, these new hires were campaign workers on the state payroll, beating the bushes to drum up support for Todd's 1966 gubernatorial hopes. Wallace never reprimanded Todd, primarily because state employees had worked for his own campaigns in 1964 and 1966, and were already an integral part of the planning process for the 1968 presidential campaign.[14]

Todd was not the only cabinet member to operate without much control from the administration. The state docks department, located in Mobile, functioned autonomously under the direction of Houston Feaster. The docks were built in 1922 by General William Siebert, one of the first builders of the Panama Canal, but never reached their full potential as a revenue stream. Six separate divisions were administered by the state docks director, but only one—the public grain elevator—consistently turned a profit. The state also operated inland dock facilities along Alabama's extensive river network. First appointed to his post in 1963, Feaster had worked as a longshoreman, been in the navy, and managed his father-in-law's plumbing business. More importantly, he supported Wallace politically by managing the 1958 and 1962 campaigns in Mobile county.[15]

The Wallace administration inherited a department in disarray. Mobile politico Mylan Engel sent Wallace a confidential report in September 1962 detailing numerous charges made by docks employees about mismanagement, ineffective marketing, and lack of planning. Engel concluded that the port of Mobile was slipping behind its Gulf of Mexico rivals. On the surface, the docks prospered under Feaster and Wallace. In fiscal year 1963, the docks turned a record profit that Feaster credited to "applying sound business principles over the last three quarters, putting into effect rigid economy measures, and expanding the sales effort." Revenue was growing, and general cargo tonnage and net profit shattered previous records.[16]

Indeed the docks facilities expanded significantly over the course of Wallace's first term. Two separate general obligation bond measures passed totaling over $13 million; new inland dock facilities were constructed at Phenix City, Columbia, Cordova, Eufaula, Demopolis, and Jackson; and record after record was announced by Wallace and Feaster. The grain elevator doubled its capacity; pay raises were given to all docks employees; over $1 million was spent to replace or repair archaic equipment; and a sales force was created to market the docks across the country. Regional sales offices were established in New York, Chicago, St. Louis, and Birmingham. Feaster even journeyed to South America to hunt for business. He also fired a docks employee he determined was taking kickbacks in exchange for not charging demurrage. Wallace could not resist taking some of the credit for the docks' new prosperity. "When I appointed him to the directorship," the governor said of Feaster, "I told him to manage full-time. I told him to get rid of the luxury yachts; I told him to build an even greater port; I told him to follow the competitive bidding law to the letter. . . . He is succeeding handsomely."[17]

Beneath the veneer of expansion and record profits, not everything was quite so rosy. Feaster's plan to solicit private firms to take control of the public grain elevator met with immediate criticism from many circles. Small farmers, merchants, and cooperatives relied on an open market of numerous grain dealers who could broker storage at the elevator. The outcry from private concerns such as the Lapeyrouse Grain Corporation was immediate: "It was rather shocking to read . . . that you are carrying on 'secret' negotiations to lease the Public Grain Elevator. . . . We need the Public Elevator operated by the state in order to exist." Even A. W. Todd, alerted to the negotiations by state farmers, entered the fray, noting that the public grain elevator "has greatly increased the market value for locally produced grain which, in the end, has resulted in increased farm income in the Mobile area." Feaster eventually decided against selling the elevator rights to one private firm.[18]

Patronage at the docks wrought further conflict. Wallace friend H. L. Holman was named engineer-architect for dock expansions largely on the personal endorsement of the governor and Seymore Trammell. Representative Buddy Crawford lobbied Wallace to get an inland docks facility in Henry County so he could make good on a campaign promise. Feaster hired Wallace friend Bob Weller for the sole reason that "the governor's office called me and requested that I employ Mr. Weller." During the 1962 campaign, Wallace promised Riley Smith a line handling contract with the docks department after he was inaugurated. Smith also secured a right-of-first-refusal from Wallace on the naming of the docks director and gave his blessing to Feaster's nomination. Feaster refused to grant the contract to Smith, citing union and tariff complications. Another continuous critic of docks operations was Theodore Richter, a Mobile engineer and a former docks consultant for Jim Folsom. Richter complained that Wallace was ignoring him, that his promises regarding docks operations were nothing more than "campaign talk," and that Feaster was badly mismanaging the entire enterprise. Though both Smith and Richter might be accused of sour grapes, at least Richter backed up his charges with documentation. Citing U.S. Department of Agriculture publications such as *Grain Market News,* Richter warned that Pascagoula and other neighboring ports were handling up to seventy-five times the wheat of Mobile and that the state docks had captured only 1.1 percent of the total Gulf Coast grain market. Richter may have been angling for a job, but at least he knew his audience. He counseled the governor that even though his information was from federal sources, he should not consider it "negro inspired."[19]

The docks were a frequent site of labor disputes; the Brotherhood of Railroad Trainmen, the Mobile District Labor Council, the United Paper Makers and Paper Workers, the International Brotherhood of Pulp, Sulphate, and Paper Mill Workers, the International Longshoremen's Association, and the Brotherhood of Locomotive Firemen and Enginemen all filed grievances. Wallace usually stayed out of these labor disputes except to remind unhappy workers that

"I am the only governor who ever put the minimum wage provisions in every state contract." More often than not, the disputes did not hurt Wallace politically, though they did complicate the working environment at the docks.[20]

Sometimes life at the state docks bordered on the comical. When itinerant flocks of pigeons decided to make docks' warehouses their new home, management orchestrated a makeshift pigeon hunt to eliminate the fowl. Unfortunately, as many men as birds were shot. Other problems were more severe. Feaster played fast and loose with state bid laws, exacting high-dollar change orders to construction projects without the consent of the governor. On other occasions, Feaster made purchases without requesting bids, a violation of state bid laws, or termed projects "emergency" matters so as to circumvent the process entirely. Some bids were taken over the telephone, and supposedly sealed bids were left open. One particular company, Massengale Construction, received most of the dock's building work, curiously entering bids that habitually came in at 1 percent below other contractors. In 1965, Massengale was paid over $700,000 for a job it did not bid on and that was originally specified for $90,365. Massengale's plumbing subcontractor of choice was Donaghey Plumbing, owned by Feaster's father-in-law. Author Philip Crass concluded that Feaster was able to show such record-setting profits because of accounting irregularities such as identifying the value of ash trays at $95, trash cans at $40, and listing bad debts as assets.[21]

Promises to Keep

Throughout 1966, a number of problems persisted primarily because the governor had devoted the previous three-plus years to perpetual campaigning. One particularly vexing problem was the lack of textbooks in state schools. Reports indicated that some classrooms were forced to share as few as six books among thirty students. Compounding the problem was the lack of available books in EBSCO's warehouse that prevented some parents from buying books for their children that the state was supposed to provide for free. Some local school systems were forced to provide supplementary funds to purchase books in the middle of the school year to alleviate the instructional crisis. The administration preferred to turn these problems over to Austin Meadows or plead with critics that the trouble "will be ironed out." The problems were not resolved. By December 1968, state education superintendent Ernest Stone admitted that 30 to 35 of Alabama's 119 school systems were in "real trouble" because of a lack of textbooks. Over $2 million of the original allocation for the "free textbook" system was spent on used books. Some of the books had to be taped together just to be issued to students. In some cases, parents were then assessed book levies for alleged damage to new books even though their children had been given used ones. The administration was forced to go to court to prop up the agent system created on behalf of their new publisher's warehouse. The textbook system remained chronically underfunded and inefficient into 1969.[22]

The censoring unit was the only aspect of the textbook system functioning like a well-oiled machine. All publishers were forced to abide by section 8 of the Free Textbook Act that mandated "all contract[s] . . . stipulate that the author or authors of such book or books is not a member of the Communist party or of a communist front organization." The governor and his legal advisor, Hugh Maddox, asked the administration at Jefferson State Junior College in Birmingham to stop using *Catcher in the Rye* in literature classes because of its questionable themes and use of profanity.[23]

Wallace's two at-large nominations to the state textbook review committee were Birmingham pharmacist Jimmy Jones and Montgomery minister Henry Lyons. Jones, a regular contributor to the ultraconservative *Birmingham Independent,* was a vocal critic of the United Nations and had strong connections to the John Birch Society. Jones was particularly interested in history textbooks and found one proposed book, *Under Freedom's Banner,* to be objectionable because of references to Jane Addams and Langston Hughes. Addams, according to Jones, was a Communist and also "an important figure in the formation of the League for Industrial Democracy, the organization that directs all of the civil rights activities in the United States." Lyons, pastor at the Highland Avenue Baptist Church, was a frequent speaker at Citizens' Council rallies and wore the sobriquet "High Priest of Segregation" like a badge of honor. Indicative of the tremendous paradox between the liberation theology of the black Baptist Church and the status quo interpretation of most white Baptist churches, Lyon considered integration to be "un-Christian" and suggested that striking down social barriers between the races would lead to "the curse and fury of good God." Both Jones and Lyons earned reappointment during Lurleen Wallace's administration.[24]

Not all education problems were confined to textbooks. The trade school and junior college system continued to be characterized by inefficiency and patronage, not merit and comprehensive planning. Construction change orders were common occurrences, with cost overruns of $450,000 at the Jefferson County trade school, $294,000 at the Gadsden Junior College, $150,000 at the Walker County Junior College, and $380,000 at Jefferson State. At one meeting in May 1966, the Trade School and Junior College Authority (comprised of Wallace, Trammell, and Meadows) ordered additional expenditures of $1.9 million to "meet commitments made by the authority." They authorized one change order for the express purpose of paneling the offices of the president and secretary of the Alexander City Junior College. Much of the construction work was doled out to friends of the administration who, unfortunately for state taxpayers, made rookie mistakes. A trade school at Muscle Shoals received substandard hose bibs that froze in inclement weather. Workers at the Tuscaloosa vo-tech installed a gas meter in the wrong location and had to move it to another location. The Tennessee Valley Junior College had to lower the elevation of footings in three separate buildings because they were not built on firm soil.[25]

True to his actions over the preceding three years, the governor continued to lobby Alabamians to support private schools. In a July 1966 special session speech broadcast on statewide television at taxpayer expense, Wallace had the name and address of a Montgomery segregated academy revenue distribution foundation placed on the screen. "I hope you will join me," the governor suggested, "in helping those whose schools have been taken away from them." Not surprisingly, Wallace's habitual pleas for donations brought more lawsuits against him and the State Board of Education for supporting private schools with public funds. The legal work was then doled out to the governor's friends, not the attorney general's office, and the taxpayers continued to pay the bill.[26]

To his credit, the governor took action on several important pieces of legislation. The administration backed a bill that provided a ten thousand dollar death benefit to the families of police and firefighters killed in the line of duty. Yet even the death benefit legislation was wrapped in racial baggage; the governor implied the bill was necessary because of the Supreme Court's attitude toward civil rights: "Decisions have been rendered which have actually encouraged law breakers to take to the streets; court decisions have been rendered which have tied the hands of officers in enforcing the law." To boost the state's fishing industry, Wallace supported a bill exempting sales tax on fuel for all commercial vessels. Aware of the state's paucity of doctors, Wallace backed plans for a medical school at the fledgling University of South Alabama in Mobile. As always, some Wallace reforms came after the federal government mandated change. When a three-judge federal panel overturned an Alabama law preventing women from serving on juries, Wallace asked legislative reference chief Charles Cooper to draft a bill to modify Alabama's archaic jury service laws to conform with federal standards. Even after the juries bill passed, old beliefs lingered. State senator H. B. Taylor announced he did not want his wife to sit on a jury "with a bunch of colored bucks trying a rape case." Taylor later observed that the only women interested in serving on a jury were "old maids who have nothing else to do."[27]

Wallace also launched an intensive promotional campaign to lure more industry to the state. Part of the effort involved Red Carpet Industrial Tours of the state planned by Leonard Beard. Smartly staged at the end of April before the summer heat and humidity and while the state was awash in the resplendent hues and aromas of azaleas, dogwoods, and other blooming flora, the tours always made positive impressions on visiting entrepreneurs and corporate leaders. Another aspect of industrial development involved the governor more personally. Capitalizing on the governor's fame and name recognition, advertisements appeared in prestigious business publications such as the *Wall Street Journal* and *Business Week,* featuring large pictures of Wallace with clever captions including: "The number is 265-2341. Ask for George Wallace"; "We're the free enterprise state. We've got everything industry is looking for"; and "$47,564.69 per hour has been invested by American industry in new Alabama plants and plant expansions since 1963." The copy included a promise that the governor would get personally involved with any industrial prospect: "When my secretary answers, tell her you're the president of a company or corporation that wants to make bigger profits in a new location. She'll switch you quickly."[28]

Determined to stay in the limelight, Wallace began speaking out on the war in Vietnam. Among the governor's considerable skills was the ability to get out front on an issue before it became vogue. Wallace sensed, as only a consummate campaigner could, that the civil rights movement was splintering in the aftermath of Selma and with the emergence of the Black Power movement. Robert Kennedy became a frequent target of the governor's Vietnam rhetoric, especially after the New York senator made a speech in Tuscaloosa. "This is the man," Wallace exclaimed, "who wanted to give blood for the Viet Cong." The governor vowed that "if any students sign petitions, raise clothes, money or blood" for the enemy he would expel them. The administration encouraged the legislature to pass a benefits package providing education funds for families of soldiers who died in Southeast Asia and other benefits for Alabama Vietnam veterans. Wallace asked Charles Cooper to draft a legislative resolution supporting the bombing of Haiphong and Hanoi. The governor sent Christmas greetings to General William Westmoreland, commander of U.S. forces, assuring him that "the much publicized protest marches and draft card burnings do not reflect the feeling of the people of Alabama. . . . We in Alabama are particularly mindful of the fact that all of you are fighting to preserve the freedom that allows us to celebrate the birthday of Christ against an enemy that does not even believe in His existence." Over time, Wallace honed a simplistic philosophy on the war that resonated on the hustings but obscured the complex rules of engagement in America's longest military conflict: win the war or get out.[29]

Even the governor's elemental war ethos was not without complications. When nineteen-year-old private Jimmy Williams of Wetumpka lost his life in the service of his country, he was refused burial in his hometown's private cemetery because of the color of his skin. The *Los Angeles Times* captured the absurdity of the situation with a descriptive editorial cartoon. In the sketch, a military officer stood watch in front of a large grave marker bearing the inscription "Here rests in honored glory an American Soldier known but to God." Confronting the honor guard was a stylized Alabamian voicing his concern for the racial background of the entombed: "How do us folks from Alabama know he ain't colored?" Trapped in a vise grip of patriotism versus southern traditionalism, Wallace escaped by calling press reports "very misleading" and "completely distorted." The governor assured anyone who would listen that the Williams family was offered a resting place in the cemetery but that they refused. What he failed to mention was that the plot offered was in an isolated grave in a far corner of the grounds that had become a potter's field. After a Justice Department investigation, Williams was eventually buried with full military honors in Andersonville National Cemetery in Georgia.[30]

Wallace's entree into the foreign policy debate was clearly tied to his plans for a wire-to-wire presidential campaign in 1968. Already receiving periodic updates on the progress of the war from Washington, the governor was counseled by advisors close to veterans groups to take an active stand in support of the war. One advisor, Blue Barber, noted that "if the governor has not been writing to widows and parents, he might wish to do so. . . . Viet Nam is now the biggest single issue with veterans over the Country. Alabama is no exception. There are 325,000 war veterans now living in Alabama."[31]

The Road Still Taken

If Vietnam provided a new outlet for Wallace, racial politics proved as durable as ever. In some instances, Wallace continued to take familiar positions. When Tom Harris, owner of Tom's Dairy Freeze in Chickasaw, was investigated by the Department of Justice for forcing blacks to eat outside the restaurant's service window and denying them dining room service, the governor responded with sympathy for Harris's plight. "I think," the governor mused, "the Civil Rights Act of 1964 is unconstitutional . . . but the socializing, integrating, carpetbagging, Supreme Court Justices are not interested in private property rights." Harris later signed a compliance form promising to provide equal levels of service to all customers.[32]

With interracial dating increasing across the country, Wallace began receiving mail concerning his views on intermarriage. Alabama had three separate restrictions on the books preventing sexual relations, married or otherwise, between whites and blacks. Article 4, section 102, of the 1901 Constitution directed the legislature to "never pass any law to authorize or legalize any marriage between any white person and a Negro, or descendant of a Negro." The 1940 state law code included a provision proscribing "marriage, adultery, and fornication" between the races or descendants of the races and authorizing a prison term of up to seven years for infractions. The same code prescribed fines up to one thousand dollars and six months of hard labor for any person who performed a marriage ceremony uniting blacks and whites. Wallace cited these laws in response to queries and noted "in my judgement this law is completely valid and should remain on the books."[33]

Wallace continued to inspire confidence from fringe groups with frightening presuppositions about race. One correspondent had three suggestions for solving what had long been called "the Negro problem": offer one hundred dollars to any black person over the age of twenty-one who would voluntarily agree to sterilization; import contract labor from India to replace malingering black workers; and open the lower half of California for a permanent Negro state and provide tracts of land for these black pioneers. Alabama Klan leader Robert Shelton continued to be paid as a Highway Department agent and have regular access to the administration, though Wallace left standing orders for him to stay away from the capitol when the national press was in town. Reports surfaced that Ralph Roton, undercover investigator for the state legislative commission investigating civil rights, was a Klansman who reported directly to Shelton. Friends of the administration continued to be paid handsomely for performing civil rights–related legal work that theoretically should have been performed by the office of the attorney general.[34]

The most public of all the racial matters the administration confronted in 1966 was the furor over compliance with title 11 of the Civil Rights Act of 1964 and the related battle over Health Education and Welfare desegregation guidelines. The crux of title 11 was that no state was eligible to receive federal funds if its schools practiced discrimination. By January 1965, the public had learned what the administration already knew: Alabama was in real danger of losing federal funds. Scheduled to receive at least $32 million for education, the state could scarcely afford such a significant loss to already underfunded schools. Austin Meadows characterized the potential effects as "crippling" and speculated that vocational programs and lunchroom services would be immediately lost, with others to follow. On the eve of launching a special session designed to pass bills providing for the free textbook system, a 10 percent increase in teacher salaries, and a major capital outlay for school construction, Wallace offered no comment on the issue.[35]

By March 1965, some local school systems were signing pledges to comply with the Civil Rights Act, but Wallace went public to urge systems not to sign guarantees until the matter could be fully resolved in court. Nonetheless, city and county school boards were given a March 4 deadline to sign compliance forms, and 106 of the 118 systems consented to abide by federal guidelines. The Bessemer board agreed to serve as a test case and refused to sign. Just two days later, Georgia became the sixth state to ratify the Wallace Amendment calling for public school systems to be the exclusive domain of the states and preventing the president, Congress, or federal judiciary from regulating them in any way, shape, or form.[36]

Despite the governor's strategy of defiance, Meadows, burdened with the task of making the schools function, continued to encourage systems to comply. The legislature sided with the governor and mulled a resolution asking all state government agencies to refrain from any deals on compliance. With the senate in a filibuster over the statement, Wallace took the stage at Montgomery's Farm Day to pressure passage. "Under the Civil Rights Act of 1964," Wallace declared, "the federal government is trying to take complete control of every school in Alabama and Georgia and all over the country." The next day the senate passed the measure. Two weeks later in his annual State of the State address, Wallace, despite having endorsed a statement that risked losing federal education dollars, made an impassioned plea for more education funding.[37]

Taking his cues from the governor's stance on federal education guidelines, Pensions and Security Director Ruben King announced he would file suit against HEW over rules requiring the state to integrate in order to receive federal funds for hospitals and nursing homes. All told, the state received $97 million annually from HEW, three-quarters of its annual funding. Wallace confided to reporters that he would resist the federal guidelines as long as possible through the courts, but would not risk the welfare funds if legal avenues were blocked. Publicly, Wallace's popularity and the reality of an election brought continued attacks on HEW guidelines and the Civil Rights Act that echoed from the lips of other candidates and political stakeholders. Albert Brewer, a candidate for lieutenant governor, expressed his amazement at "how far the guidelines go." Sitting lieutenant governor Jim Allen declared that the guidelines were "arbitrary, illegal, burdensome, and go far beyond the law. If in ignoring them we have to give up federal funds, then I say let's make the sacrifice and do it."[38]

Wallace challenged the state congressional delegation to pick up the pace in the case against compliance. "All of those who represent us in Washington," the governor barked, "[should] use all the influence and prestige they've got to have these guidelines rescinded." When told that John Sparkman and Lister Hill had been speaking out, Wallace's sarcastic response indicated the utter contempt with which he viewed the Alabama senators: "Have they spoken out *too*?" No question could have existed in any Alabamian's mind about how the governor felt. The desegregation guidelines, according to the governor, were yet another way for the federal government to take over every aspect of the local school. The ultimate intention, Wallace mused, was to desegregate faculties and staffs and hasten the pace of universal integration.[39]

The day after Wallace, Allen, and Brewer issued their indictments of HEW guidelines, hearing examiner Robert Irwin offered a recommendation that all federal welfare funds be withheld from Alabama. In his report, Irwin cited the state's failure to comply with the desegregation guidelines of the Civil Rights Act, noted the ongoing practice of segregation in many state hospitals and nursing homes, and termed the state's record of providing services down to the doctor's office level as "poor." He gave the state forty-five days to respond. Wallace did not need the time to formulate his reply. The man who had conspicuously used the issue of federal intervention to fashion a political career blamed Irwin's findings on partisan politics. "It is significant," Wallace retorted, "that no action was taken until the middle of a political campaign [Lurleen's]—the idea of threatening elderly people because Washington doesn't like somebody's politics. We have always stated that we will obey the law. ... I repeat, neither the senior citizens of our state nor our children are going to lose anything, and in addition to this we are not going to change our position one bit." Later that day in a campaign appearance on behalf of his ill wife, Wallace took his rhetorical flourish one step farther: "I have never advocated disobedience of the law. That's the other crowd that says we disobey unjust laws."[40]

With the forty-five-day clock running down, Wallace wanted a meeting with the state's congressional delegation to discuss his options. As with the 1964 meeting to discuss congressional redistricting, Wallace made the entire delegation travel to Montgomery to meet in his office, despite the fact that the congressmen wanted the meeting to include federal officials. In Washington, the Alabama delegation functioned within the party and seniority system, but back home in Alabama, they played by Wallace's rules. The joint statement released by the congressmen was pure forensic Wallaceism: "We find it shocking that an agency of the federal government would undertake to disregard the law and flout the repeatedly reaffirmed public policy of this nation. It is even more shocking that an agency of government should employ totalitarian methods in the form of threats to deny benefits of educational programs from innocent parties in order to accomplish an illegal purpose." Wallace relished photo opportunities in his office with the congressmen; he especially enjoyed the fact that they needed to be seen with him much more than he needed to be pictured with them. Once again, he propped his feet up on his desk, chomped on his omnipresent cigar, and rehashed every moment of the meeting with his cronies like a little leaguer reliving his first home run.[41]

Despite the show of gubernatorial, legislative, and congressional unity emanating from Alabama, HEW Secretary John Gardner announced federal aid would be cut off from Bibb County and Tarrant City school systems for failure to comply with antidiscrimination guidelines. The governor kept the issue smoldering in campaign speeches and addresses to large groups such as the Alabama Broadcaster's Association. Going further, the administration launched a stealth campaign to get school systems to withdraw their compliance agreements. Every school district received a copy of the Wallace-backed resolution calling for resistance, and many complained of intense administration pressure to back Wallace's court fight. Meadows, previously on record for claiming the state could not survive any loss of education funds, sent a formal letter to each superintendent asking them to reconsider honoring signed federal agreements. A few systems, such as Florala, withdrew their promise to desegregate. Publicly, administration leaders implied that very few local school boards had actually signed, even though all but a few had consented.[42]

The antiguidelines campaign reached a crescendo when the governor announced plans to hold mass meetings in cities where superintendents had signed compliance agreements. Wallace imagined raucous crowds, enraged by his caustic denunciations of the federal government, forcing local education leaders to withdraw their intent to comply. School board folk, trapped between professional obligations to educate children and the fever pitch of George Wallace on the warpath, wanted no part of these town meetings. "I don't want any fight with the governor," one superintendent explained anonymously; "that's a fight you can't possibly win. . . . It smacks purely of intimidation. I would like to ask the governor a question. What good will such mass meetings do except perhaps arouse somebody to do something foolish." The governor tried to ease growing concern over the reality that Alabama's already woefully underfunded education and welfare agencies would lose money, but his message was confusing. No money would be lost, the governor explained over and over, though he reminded Alabamians it would be better to lose funds than to agree to let Washington run their lives.[43]

Wallace attempted to get local education officials on board with the antiguidelines strategy by calling a meeting in Montgomery to discuss the issue and the possibility of a special session to allocate $44 million in accumulated Special Education Trust Fund revenue. The atmosphere was bizarre: education leaders needed additional revenue as soon as possible; legislators were lame ducks as many had already lost races in the May primary, not sought reelection, or were completely uninterested in doing anything to support the governor. Wallace was in the midst of getting his wife elected and wanted to keep himself in the national newspapers in order to raise money for his planned 1968 presidential campaign. After the meeting, the educators walked a tightrope, issuing a statement critical of the guidelines, but stopping short of embracing the unmitigated resistance called for by the governor: "We feel that serious consideration should be given to all aspects of this problem in order that the education experience of all children in Alabama may move forward in the best manner possible."[44]

The pressure was being felt everywhere. When Wallace transferred mental health patients back to segregated facilities purportedly because of complaints from the families of the afflicted, the state Mental Health Board voted to take no further action toward complying with HEW regulations. Wallace arranged a hasty meeting with the governors of six other southern states to try to broker a united front. At a public appearance in Louisiana where "Wallace for President" bumper stickers, buttons, and posters filled the hall, the governor exclaimed that "millions of people are just waiting for someone to continue this fight in 1968" and called for the South to resist all school and hospital federal antidiscrimination guidelines. Alabama was in no position to risk federal health care dollars; only 50 state hospitals had been approved to handle Medicare patients and only 60 of the 146 licensed hospitals in the state had been accredited by the National Joint Committee on Accreditation of Hospitals. In addition to desegregating patient wards, each facility had to construct a plan for integrating staffs and adhere to basic Social Security regulations. Education and public health in Alabama were screeching to a complete halt, and Alabamians were told it was the federal government, not their governor, slamming on the brakes.[45]

Applying pressure to hospitals, nursing homes, and schools brought limited responses, and Wallace decided state resistance needed to be codified to achieve maximum effect. The legislature would not be in regular session until 1967, but the governor could not wait and called a special session to begin July 26. Wallace had two goals for the session: spend the Special Education Trust Funds in order to take the issue away from political rivals in November and pass legislation legalizing his calls for resistance to the HEW regulations. The July 26 start date would be just three days before the beginning of the state Republican convention and, since the governor could open any special session with a speech broadcast on statewide television, Wallace could effectively keep the GOP off the front pages. In his speech, Wallace compared the HEW guidelines battle to his 1963 stand in the schoolhouse door. That issue, the governor declared, was "for the purpose of opposing the enemies of freedom." His current battle was similarly noble: "If men in high places in Washington can break the law of our constitution, then every revolutionary, every thug who can assemble will feel that they too can break the law. Tonight we recall that warning with dismay and alarm as guerilla bands burn and loot and riot in Chicago, Cleveland, Los Angeles, New York, Jacksonville, and other cities across this nation."[46]

The education package sailed through the house and senate. Wallace had consulted with key legislators and educators well in advance of the session and had brokered near universal support for his bills. Some $44.1 million of the Special Education Trust Fund was allocated for a 10 percent teacher raise, the hiring of over thirteen hundred new teachers, and a $135 annual pay raise for bus drivers. Also included in the appropriation was an $11 million chunk for the junior college and trade school system, allotments of varying size for state colleges and universities, additional money for the beleaguered free textbook system, and expansion of the educational television network. When all the numbers were added up, George Wallace had effectively doubled the state education budget over the course of his first term.[47]

The antiguidelines legislation was not quite as easy to pass. Wallace had purposely kept his proposed antiguidelines bill under wraps until the education dollars were spent. Thinking he could launch a last-minute, full-court press backed by popular opinion and thankful educators who had just received a funding boost, Wallace announced his antiguidelines package six days before he expected the session to end. The particulars were leaked to the media two days before the governor publicly announced them. Wallace's proposed legislation would render HEW guidelines null and void in Alabama. More specifically, the antiguidelines bill had four major provisions: school boards that lost federal funds would receive replacement money from the state's Special Education Trust Fund; all legal authority to enter into compliance agreements would be transferred from local school boards to the governor; any local school system that refused to rescind its signed promise to abide by HEW antidiscrimination regulations would be abolished; and any system that refused to rescind a previous agreement would forfeit eligibility to receive state education funds. Taken together, the antiguidelines package represented an enormous accumulation of power that the governor would have never tolerated in the hands of the president, Congress, or federal judiciary.[48]

The scope of Wallace's antiguidelines bill surprised even the administration's most trusted legislative lieutenants, and the governor quickly backed off the idea of abolishing recalcitrant school boards and withholding state funds. He reiterated his intention to have HEW regulations declared null and void and replace lost federal money with Special Education Trust Fund dollars. But he softened the wording of the harsher provisions by noting the governor would agree to represent any school board that so desired before the federal government instead of seizing complete control. The governor noted he simply wanted legal authority to preserve peace and order at all Alabama schools even though violence had been virtually nonexistent in desegregated schools. Wallace then scheduled a televised speech before a joint audience of both legislative houses to smooth over the rough edges and promote popular support for his bill. The address was uncharacteristically short but nevertheless replete with classic Wallace federal bashing. "Tell the bureaucrats of power," the governor implored, "that they can take their federal money and they know what they can do with it.... We are here tonight as a point of honor—to stand up for

every man and every woman in the state of Alabama. We have stood before—
and say: We shall not submit our children quietly in the night. We shall not
have them bargained away at secret meetings and backroom talks by Health,
Education, and Welfare officials in Washington." The twenty-three-minute
speech was interrupted sixteen times with applause from the assembled legislators and brought stock political reactions. In the aftermath of the speech,
administration loyalists hailed Wallace for battling Washington on constitutional grounds. But the West Jefferson Coordinating Council, a civil rights
group, wired its thanks to the governor, saying the bill "will help us to achieve
our goal more than you will ever know." And Jim Martin, the state's most recognizable Republican, castigated the proposal as a "fraud. It simply won't be
able to replace federal money with state money. Local schools will be straining
to meet their needs."[49]

The reaction from the state's education community was not what Wallace
had hoped. Almost immediately, the Alabama Education Association distributed a seven-point rebuke of the antiguidelines bill. In addition to objections
over the concept of abrogating local control, the AEA pointed out that Wallace
himself had suggested that the state could not afford to allocate more than
$44 million from the Special Education Trust Fund. The inherent contradic-
tion of Wallace's antiguidelines bill, according to AEA, was that either the
state could afford to allocate additional money or else it could not rely on it as
a source for replacing lost federal funds. Representatives of Auburn University
and the University of Alabama were equally unsympathetic and argued that all
surplus funds should be used for current needs, not replacement monies.[50]

Some educational stakeholders were more compliant. Austin Meadows and
the State Board of Education announced their enthusiastic support. Wallace
friend Ralph Adams, the president of Troy State College, offered his approval,
as did all twenty-eight junior college and trade school presidents. Wallace assured reporters that most of the state's teachers were in full support of the antiguidelines initiatives. Guy Kelly, superintendent of the Wilcox County school
system, described HEW officials as uninterested in the damage they were causing: "I told them we had 1,000 white children whose parents were aristocrats
and immensely wealthy and that we had 6,500 colored children who would
suffer from the loss of funds. I never heard from HEW again."[51]

Back in the legislature, opponents and supporters of the bill squared off
on the ramifications of snubbing federal funds. Both sides played fast and
loose with their rhetoric. Wallace backers termed the antiguidelines bill one
of the most significant pieces of legislation since the Declaration of Independence and Ordinance of Secession. The bill's foes called it a death knell for
the South. Wallace handled the entire manner deftly. Before the bill was even
written, the governor met with his most outspoken critics to try to convince

them of two things. Wallace described the bill as vital for forcing a court case that could ultimately rid Alabama of the guidelines once and for all. Without a state antiguidelines law, Alabama's opposition might never be heard. In addition, Wallace promised that the state would not lose a single dollar of federal money. Either the court would decide the case, the governor assured, or he would withdraw his objection if resistance was futile. Just like the Tuscaloosa stand, the antiguidelines fight was a staged event, cloaked in private admittance of defeat and reflective of the administration's preference for style over substance. As a result of behind-the-scenes dealing, Wallace convinced Vaughn Hill Robison and Bob Gilchrist, two administration adversaries who led the fight against succession, to write the antiguidelines bill. Albert Brewer shepherded the bill out of the house, 76 to 9, and the senate reported the bill out of committee with a favorable recommendation.[52]

In the senate, Wallace supported two amendments to the original draft of the bills. One amendment proposed to nullify all present and future compliance agreements signed by local school systems; the other would have granted exclusive authority to allocate education funds to the governor. The senate passed the bill without the amendments, 28 to 7, and Alabama continued the Wallace tradition of tilting at federal windmills. White supremacists, such as Bruce Henderson, hailed their governor for a "matchless" job in the war against Washington. Within weeks, Wallace engineered a resolution from the Southern Governor's Conference supporting the themes of the antiguidelines law.[53]

With the echoes of a jubilant Wallace victory still resounding in corridors across the capitol, a new school year began with more desegregation, including the shattering of color barriers on school athletic teams. If anyone truly considered the attempted nullification of federal law a victory, then it was surely a hollow one. Days after Wallace signed the bill, the NAACP filed a suit challenging the constitutionality of the new law. A federal court in New Orleans upheld the HEW guidelines in a ruling that affected three Alabama cases and required systems to hire and assign teachers without regard to race. The court also ruled that all grades had to be desegregated beginning with the 1967–68 school year.[54]

Means to an End

The next school year would be a matter of concern for the next governor, and no issue, HEW guidelines included, consumed Wallace as much as determining who that next governor would be. Based on a quantitative analysis, Alabama had made substantial progress over the first three-plus years of the Wallace era. School funding had doubled. Teachers had received two pay raises. More than $1 billion in new and expanded industry had been attracted to the state. Balance sheets indicated the state docks were thriving. Mile after mile of roads had been built, patched, and repaved. "I knew I had to stay in office," Wallace later told a biographer. George Wallace was going to run for president, and being governor, whether he had the official title or not, was essential for mounting a third-party campaign.[55]

After the stinging defeat of the succession bid, Wallace considered a spate of alternatives. He had floated a trial balloon of running Lurleen as far back as August 1965, before the question of succession was even resolved. Insiders had heard enough rumors to take away the shock value, but few were convinced that the governor would actually attempt it. As soon as the succession bill died in late October, Albert Brewer called the mansion and playfully teased Lurleen to "get your running shoes on." In the days after the senate refused to budge, the governor brought the idea up with increasing frequency, surprising the cabinet by suggesting the idea with a straight face. But Wallace was too smart to jump into a hasty decision based on the rebuke of a handful of senators. He considered several options.[56]

One possibility was to run a more legitimate ghost candidate whom Wallace would control in the campaign and in office. No candidate seemed to be completely trustworthy. Those who would truly function as a rubber stamp—Seymore Trammell, Roland Cooper, or Phil Hamm—were likely unelectable even with the full Wallace blessing. The Alabama political grapevine was already buzzing with the names of strong Democratic candidates including Ryan deGraffenreid, Carl Elliot, and former governor John Patterson who would be too formidable to beat with a weak candidate. Thanks to the 1964 independent elector campaign, five Republican congressmen now represented the state and, for the first time since Reconstruction, a GOP candidate such as Jim Martin could be expected to be a factor in November. More attractive candidates, such as the governor's brother Jack or Albert Brewer, stood a better chance of winning but might not tolerate being George's pawn. One candidate who wanted to run, but demurred until Wallace made up his mind on a shadow candidate, was Lieutenant Governor Jim Allen. Allen grew frustrated because he wanted to get a jump on the campaign, but Wallace was slow to make up his mind. Allen would have been a strong candidate, but Wallace harbored a grudge after the lieutenant governor refused to gavel through the succession bill. After the 1966 elections were over, Allen made it clear to Wallace that he was going to run for the senate in 1968 rather than be trapped into waiting on another Wallace decision.[57]

Wallace strongly considered dropping gubernatorial plans for a run at John Sparkman's senate seat. Sparkman, a senator since 1946, had a progressive voting record on most matters and held several important committee posts. Most Wallaceites considered him too connected to the national Democratic Party and therefore soft on the "nigger question," despite his repeated opposition to civil rights legislation. Wallace had no fear of Sparkman; he had already worked behind the scenes to defeat Congressman Carl Elliot in 1964, a man with a similar reputation and voting record. Most students of Alabama history are unaware of how close Wallace was to abandoning the governorship in favor of a senate race. After the official filing date in March 1966 had passed, Wallace legal advisor Hugh Maddox drafted a lawsuit alleging that Wallace had legally filed to enter the senate race but State Democratic Party Chair Roy Mayhall "refuse[d] to certify his name to the Secretary of State" and "no rule of procedure which might be adopted by the Democratic Executive Committee of the State of Alabama can infringe upon his constitutional right to be a candidate for the office of United States senator." The lawsuit was never filed and, after much soul searching, Wallace passed on a certain senate win. The course of Alabama history was thus changed forever.[58]

Even as the decision to commit to the governor's race became clear to Wallace, not everyone in the palace guard was convinced Lurleen could pull it off. John Kohn, Cecil Jackson, and Seymore Trammell were not optimistic about her chances. According to Wallace friend Oscar Harper, Ralph Adams was the first to believe that Lurleen was a surefire winner. Like Nub Todd, Adams was one of the colorful characters of Alabama politics. A friend of Wallace's since their time together at the university, Adams had been the governor's director of the state selective service system before being named president of Troy State College, later granted university status. Adams was notoriously niggardly: he drove a car whose windows would not close, used soap rather than pay for shaving cream, and wore stained neckties backward rather than buy new ones. Ace Carter, according to historian Dan Carter, was another Lurleen proponent. "She can win," the white supremacist speechwriter reportedly told Wallace. The tactic of running a governor's wife as a stand-in had been successful in Texas more than forty years earlier when Ma Ferguson had been elected on the strength of her husband Pa Ferguson's popularity with voters. When Press Secretary Ed Ewing announced in early November that the governor would have a "startling announcement" the following week, speculation proliferated throughout political circles. One rumor suggested Wallace would resign from the governorship to artificially meet the constitutional provision requiring a one-year respite before running for the same office. The major announcement never materialized. Wallace used the week to sort out public reaction to the rumors surrounding a Lurleen candidacy and then planned to hold a press conference breaking the news that Wilcox County was about to land a new paper mill. In one of the few times that the state press got the best of him, the *Birmingham Post-Herald* scooped the governor. Wallace responded with indignation, suggesting that the newspaper had somehow jeopardized the possibility of Wilcox getting the factory.[59]

As Wallace staffers began assembling unscientific poll results that identified Lurleen as a more popular choice than first imagined, other considerations came to the fore. Lurleen Wallace was diagnosed with cancer. The news, gleaned from a biopsy performed on November 23 by her gynecologist, Joe Perry, may have surprised Lurleen, but George had known years earlier. After the 1961 birth of Janie Lee, a biopsy was performed on abdominal wall tissue, and one pathology report indicated the tissue was malignant or at least premalignant. Medical norms of the time indicated briefing the husband, not necessarily the patient, and George elected not to tell his wife. Four years later, when news of the 1961 tests inadvertently reached Lurleen, she was understandably furious and scared. Jack House, author of *Lady of Courage: The Story of Lurleen Burns Wallace,* describes the governor as telling his wife he withheld the information because "there was no point in you worrying about that."[60]

In early December, doctors prescribed a radiation regimen for Mrs. Wallace. At this point, the administration moved quickly to quash the public perception of the medical severity of Lurleen's condition. Two factors helped the administration minimize the speculation. For the better part of three years, Wallace's communications staff—Bill Jones, Ed Ewing, and others—had effectively prevented cabinet heads from making major announcements. A curt memo would periodically circulate to all departments heads identifying "instances of items appearing in print, on radio and television which have not been completely in line with administration policies. Therefore, you are requested to submit all statements regarding policy to this office prior to press, radio, or TV." With a handful of notable exceptions, this policy enabled Wallace to control the flow of information to the media, leaking enough to keep reporters content and agreeing to regular interviews even if he preferred them to be off the record. In fact, the governor loved speaking and interacting with reporters. He believed that few state scribes could challenge him and win, and he relished encounters with national media knowing full well they chronically underestimated him. Statements described Lurleen's procedure as "minor surgery" and left lingering the idea that the entire matter was gynecological in nature. This misinformation, coupled with extraordinary loyalty from most subordinates, prevented the media from understanding the full implications of Lurleen's condition.[61]

A second and equally important factor was the different way the Montgomery press corps operated in those days. Many reporters knew of Wallace's history of infidelity, yet the matter never hit the front pages. Reporters in the mid 1960s, a few years away from the investigative mania arising in the aftermath of the Vietnam War and Watergate, were more inclined to defer publication on personal matters. When Lurleen confided off the record to Bob Ingram that she had been diagnosed with a tumor, the veteran newshound did not even think to ask whether it was malignant. Less than a week after Lurleen underwent the biopsy, Wallace spoke at Howard College, not yet renamed for its major benefactor Frank Samford, and hinted that Lurleen might run. This confidence, combined with the factors curtailing inquiry and publication of the medical specifics, allowed the administration to minimize voter fears.[62]

Despite the radiation, Lurleen underwent a two-hour curettement procedure to remove a malignant tumor from her uterus on January 10. Doctors performed a complete hysterectomy, appendectomy, and a thorough abdominal exploration. A few days before the operation, Lurleen assured Bob Ingram that she was fine and that she was seriously considering running for governor. "If I was half as sick as some people think I've been all these years," the first lady cajoled, "I couldn't have set the pace that is required of the wife of a governor." In fact, Mrs. Wallace was probably more rested as first lady than she had ever been in private life since the mansion staff provided assistance with the children that her husband never did. "I think everybody understands," she admitted about her political future, "that George would be right there all the time. He would speak for me during the campaign; he would speak for me during my four years in office. Let me say it this way—if I am elected governor there would not be any change from what we have now." Lurleen may have talked openly of full demurral to her husband, but Ingram noted that she was not the same "forlorn" wife who sat in the car during her husband's 1958 campaign appearances. After the surgery at Emory University in Atlanta, doctors released an upbeat appraisal of her prognosis: "No evidence of any remaining malignancy or of any other disease was found at operation." What the doctors did not say was more revealing. No indication was given to the public that she had been diagnosed with cancer for the second time.[63]

Lurleen was not the only Wallace recovering from medical problems; the governor was laboring with a heavy cast after breaking two bones in his wrist. The fracture occurred while Wallace was pummeling a heavy bag in Miami during Orange Bowl festivities between his alma mater and the University of Nebraska. After two weeks of recovery time, Lurleen was released from the hospital and returned to the mansion still unsure whether she was about to be a gubernatorial candidate or a housewife. The next month was a frustrating time for the governor. His attempt to gain control of the state Democratic Executive Committee failed. His forces were unable to win the battle to keep the "white supremacy" party logo. Legal tussles over the state textbook system resurfaced. Media reports accused the administration of circumventing state bid procedures by repairing Wallace's Lockheed Lodestar aircraft at a Dallas, Texas, repair facility. Columnists such as Mary Hodl of the *Gadsden Times* blasted Wallace for even considering running Lurleen in her condition and with her general disinterest in politics. Frustrated and angry, Wallace told Lurleen the entire campaign was off and that they would return to Barbour County. Lurleen, who must have sensed the accumulated disgruntlement necessary for her husband to abandon his political aspirations and perhaps also reflecting her own unhappiness at being isolated when her husband resumed his political career, simply told him that they would run.[64]

A simple woman who loved to fish, drink coffee, smoke cigarettes, and sit in the sunshine, Lurleen Burns had graduated from her high school at fifteen and had wanted to become a nurse. When she first came to Montgomery, she joined the Pink Ladies at St. Margaret's hospital, unaware she would ultimately spend more time there as a patient than as a volunteer. At five feet two inches tall and weighing little more than one hundred pounds, she was a pretty woman who liked to wear conservative clothes purchased from a department store or made by her best friend, Mary Jo Ventress, and high-heeled shoes to compensate for her height. Too shy to be at ease at formal events or campaign appearances, Lurleen was always happiest at home with her children, her close circle of friends, out on the lake, or playing with the family dog, Warrior. As first lady, she continued to do most of the grocery shopping and planning for mansion social events. She learned quickly that no matter what she cooked, her husband would immerse it in a sea of catsup before eating it. Ask a thousand Alabamians what they thought of George Wallace and the reply will come back a thousand different ways. Not so with Lurleen. She was as universally liked as any person in state history.[65]

Lurleen agreed to run for several reasons. She clearly felt what historian Dan Carter has called a "sense of duty" to her husband and his political dreams. She undoubtedly felt a tremendous amount of pressure from the palace guard to comply with team goals. But any discussion of why she would agree to do something so far removed from her essential character has to focus on the essential fact that she had a deep and abiding love for her husband. Despite his extended absences, indifference to responsibilities as a father, and track record of straying from the marriage, Lurleen Wallace loved her husband and that was enough. Her circle of friends advised against it. Her doctors implied it was a bad idea. Her daughter Peggy did not understand it. But Lurleen, as Bill Jones recalled, "did it for George." For Mrs. Wallace, running for governor was an act of love; for her husband, it was a means to an end.[66]

One tragic event changed the course of the entire decision process and convinced the governor that Lurleen could win. Ryan deGraffenreid, Wallace's opponent in the 1962 runoff, died in early February when the plane he was using for campaign shuttles crashed into Lookout Mountain on a stormy Alabama night. DeGraffenreid's flight from Fort Payne to Gadsden was only a twenty-minute, thirty-eight-mile trip, and Joe Dahl, the local airport manager, suggested driving to avoid the windy conditions and approaching storm. "You aren't really going to fly are you?" asked Dahl's wife. Trusting his pilot and not wanting to be late for a speech, deGraffenreid elected to fly, but the twin-engine Cessna 310, bandied about by gusts, never cleared the mountain. Their bodies torn apart in the crash, pilot and passenger died instantly. Wallace attended the funeral services, noting his former opponent was "truly one of the outstanding young men of our state."[67]

The ruggedly handsome forty-year-old deGraffenreid was an ambitious and aggressive man who would have presented a formidable challenge in the May primary. Since losing the 1962 runoff, deGraffenreid had crisscrossed the state, making more than six hundred speeches during the previous four years. Already announced as a formal candidate, deGraffenreid had in reality never stopped campaigning and was a major part of the backroom resistance to Wallace's succession drive in 1965. A former football player who had acquired a bit of the middle age spread that characterizes athletic men who no longer have the time or the inclination to stay fit, deGraffenreid even took the unusual step of taking up smoking to lose a few extra pounds. Respected by the state's political community, he had been a vocal proponent of segregation during the 1962 race but advocated a more legalistic strategy than the confrontational Wallace. With deGraffenreid out of the picture, Wallace no longer feared the embarrassment that might have come with running Lurleen and losing.[68]

The administration had a copy of 1964 polling that showed deGraffenreid's strength among Alabama voters. The survey, done for deGraffenreid by John F. Kraft, was designed to track popular support for Wallace and assess preferences for the 1966 race. Kraft's study showed deGraffenreid to be the clear front-runner for 1966, earning 35 percent of the "first choice" vote and 20 percent of the "second choice" ballots. He lagged a bit in South Alabama congressional districts but did not have the high negatives associated with former governor Jim Folsom or the surprising apathy voters felt toward former governor John Patterson. Kraft assessed the meaning of his survey: "With eighteen months to go, deGraffenreid must keep a careful eye on the enormous popularity of the incumbent, while bearing in mind that the issues which voters identify so closely with the governor, may be on the wane by next November and in the months following the national election. If the governor does not run to succeed himself . . . deGraffenreid begins with a good, solid start."[69]

As illuminating as the 1966 projections were, the survey identified the massive popularity Wallace had marshaled. Ninety percent of Alabamians thought Wallace was doing an excellent or pretty good job and 82 percent approved of his junkets across the county. Kraft summarized the rationale behind the extraordinary support for Wallace: "The governor had put Alabama and Alabamans [*sic*] on the map; he had attracted attention to the State and to what Alabamans believed; he had also, at least indirectly, represented an argument against integration and against a Federal Government threat to State's [*sic*] Rights and 'self-determination.'" The governor had unbelievably high approval ratings in his handling of segregation, new industry, the independent elector campaign, road construction, and old-age pensions. His worst rating, though most elected officials would have relished such a number, was an 18 percent disapproval of his views on state liquor laws. Kraft noted the obvious. "It would be ill advised," the pollster quipped, "to attempt to launch any sort of attack on the governor at this time."[70]

Though 90 percent of those polled thought Wallace had acted appropriately to preserve segregation, 42 percent thought it was no longer possible to keep Alabama schools from federally mandated integration. Kraft identified these results as indicative of a "softening of attitudes regarding segregation." But in the eighteen months between the poll and the formal start of campaigning, it is unclear that white Alabama voters were ready to quit the game, even if they had accepted the inevitability of defeat. Wallace understood that while outsiders viewed him as a racist, white Alabamians saw him as a principled segregationist. This distinction may seem contrived forty years later, but it was an essential part of the guilt, denial, and institutional fabric of an earlier South. Respectable whites couched their traditions of exclusion and social separation in their own constructed language of constitutional, scientific, scriptural, and organic justifications for segregation in order to twist blatant inconsistencies into a patchwork of southern logic. Washington elites and the national press corps thought Wallace was just another Barnett or Faubus, someone to ridicule and then ignore. But over the past few years Wallace had become something more, at least in the state and region. He had become a champion of southern traditions and the leading spokesman for the veracity of lessons learned on granddaddy's knee, in barbers' chairs, during Sunday school, and at hunting camps across the state. The governor never said anything new; on the contrary, he said things white Alabamians had been whispering among themselves for a century. The only difference was that Wallace said them louder and with more conviction than anybody they had ever seen. His opponents understood his power; ten of the fourteen senators who voted against succession chose not to run for office in 1966. That his message resonated is an indictment of the insufficient education, abject poverty, and power of a collective historical memory that was for Alabamians second nature. That his power and popularity reached such epic proportions is a tribute to his rare political skills and the inability of his constituents to see past the thick veneer of institutionalized racism and into the possibility that they, and he, were wrong.[71]

In assessing the landscape in 1966, Wallace sought to capitalize on the same apprehensions and misgivings he exploited in 1962. This election was not going to be about bringing education funding and student performance up to the regional average. It was not about protecting Alabamians from water and air pollution or attracting high-skill, high-wage jobs. It was not even about judging the abilities of Lurleen's rivals and presenting an alternative. This election was to be a referendum on whether George Wallace should continue to give the liberals hell. In other words, if voters wanted George to run for president, then they should vote for Lurleen for governor. "We are going to show the people of our country," the governor shouted, "that this election shows that the people have not in this state repudiated the governor of Alabama in his trips throughout this country talking about these philosophies that made our country great that are under attack by the socialist-liberal-beatnik-communist conspiracy in these United States." This was going to be a national campaign, and so the first folks to be told about Lurleen's candidacy were the national media, not Alabama reporters. The state's newspapermen, many of whom had logged mile after mile with Wallace, were understandably miffed. In calculating this decision, Wallace was able to play both sides against each other. In Alabama, he could rip the *New York Times, Washington Post,* or *Los Angeles Times* by exclaiming "what business is it of the Yankee press who we run for governor!" Outside the state, he was building a personal rapport with the same national press corps he was about to castigate in high school gymnasiums, town squares, and Elks lodges all across Alabama.[72]

Lurleen Wallace's press conference to announce she was a candidate was an elaborately orchestrated affair. Supporters waved Wallace placards under the banner of their home county. All sixty-seven Alabama counties were represented. The announcement was held at the capitol in the house chamber, full to capacity and with more than five hundred Wallaceites left outside. Foreshadowing a campaign in which the candidate read a brief script and her spouse then spoke, often extemporaneously, about the abuses and intentions of the federal government, Lurleen was off the dais in mere moments and George, in full throat, was answering questions and swaggering to and fro. Clearly running for president, the governor had to be metaphorically brought back to Alabama by curious scribes who wanted to get the specifics of this gubernatorial arrangement in print. Wallace did not disappoint. "If my wife is elected," George Wallace admitted, "I shall be by her side and will make all policy decisions affecting her administration." Questioned by colorful Alabama perpetual candidate Shorty Price, Wallace inadvertently snapped back, revealing more than he wanted: "This is my day."[73]

In fact this was George Wallace's day. By running his wife, he was boldly declaring that his political goals were more important than the checks and balances of the state constitution, the legislative process, or the succession provision. The day was replete with irony. Wallace promised no state property or personnel would be used in the campaign; the announcement was held in the state house chamber, elaborately staged by state employees, and included an unadulterated endorsement by the sitting governor who was about to crisscross the state on behalf of his chosen candidate. Wallace claimed on a regular basis that the Supreme Court was violating the spirit and letter of the U.S. Constitution; Lurleen's stand-in candidacy flaunted a sixty-five-year-old restriction in the state's constitution. And Lurleen was not even the first female candidate to declare in 1966. Twenty-three-year-old Delores Price, Shorty's wife, was a candidate until reminded that the state constitution required a person to reach the age of thirty before assuming office. Lurleen was about to be the first serious female candidate for governor in state history, yet feminists were aghast. *McCalls* magazine called Lurleen's venture "petticoat bragging," and asserted that the governor had "set back the course of women's rights and dignity by a century." Wallace was about to become the pioneer law-and-order candidate, influencing the tenor of every national campaign for the next twenty years and ushering in what Dan Carter has called a conservative transformation in the American electorate. On the day of Lurleeen's announcement, twenty-two bombs had already exploded in the homes, businesses, and churches of black Birmingham residents since the start of the year. On the same day Lurleen declared her intention to carry on the legacy of the state's most famous white supremacist, four black candidates from Barbour County announced their candidacies for local races.[74]

The 1966 field of candidates was an eclectic lot, full of political warriors past their time, opportunists who were before their time, and the type of cartoon characters that made politics second only to college football in Alabama for pure entertainment and spectacle. All told, eleven Democratic candidates entered the race, and by the first of March the formal campaigning was already running at full throttle. Three of the candidates never had a chance. Decatur lawyer and cattleman Sherman "Hoss" Powell relied on the wiles of Jackie Whitley, a go-go dancer, to attract crowds and used the slogan "Go-Go for Powell." Leeds resident Eunice Gore, a Tennessee Coal and Iron office clerk, ran because of heavenly inspiration: "Christ will be my architect for building a better Alabama." If Gore was the chosen one, the voters of Leeds never got the message; Gore's five mayoral races had resulted in no fewer than one and no more than thirty-two votes from his friends, neighbors, and townsfolk. Rex Scott, a Cordova grocer, got cold feet and quit in mid-March. The gubernatorial field was not the only race full of gothic Deep South political humor. In Cullman County, a father and son ran for the same office, county coroner, and used the same candidate cards. One side extolled the virtues of the father and the flip side detailed the qualifications of the son. In Colbert County, a woman incumbent sheriff was being challenged by her brother-in-law.[75]

Other gubernatorial candidates were viewed as more credible, even if they had no better chance at winning. Charles Woods was a wealthy communications entrepreneur from Dothan and World War II hero who had suffered severe facial burns when his transport plane crashed with four thousand gallons of fuel in the Chinese-Burma theater. He served a term on the State Corrections Board and, frustrated with not being reappointed, became a frequent critic of the prison system in print and in correspondence with the governor. Woods, whose disfigured face was featured prominently in campaign billboards, advocated repealing the sales tax on medicine and food. Despite his attempts to engage the electorate on substantive issues, the Woods campaign never gained any traction.[76]

A. W. Todd continued to court the state's farmers through his aggressive use of the *Alabama Farmers Bulletin* and his hiring of campaign workers in full-time Department of Agriculture positions. He reached out to his base by scheduling campaign stops at greased pig contests. In terms of policy issues, Todd was literally all over the map. For blacks and progressive whites, Todd proposed the creation of a biracial commission to study racial matters. For urbanites, he advocated a modified Highway Department that would be managed by a board culled from each state congressional district and a director appointed by that body, not the governor. For the politically disaffected, Todd spoke out regularly on the smear tactics and negative campaigning of his opponents. "Nothing has been so devastating to the Democratic party," the agriculture commissioner boomed, "since Sherman's March to the Sea 100 years ago." In the end, all of Todd's angling for votes from Agriculture Department employees was futile. The department had more than five hundred employees in Montgomery but Todd tallied only forty-four votes in the entire county.[77]

Former governor Jim Folsom ran again but was a shadow of his former engaging and gregarious self. By this time, the fifty-seven-year-old Folsom, wracked by years of alcoholism and a host of medical problems, had lost his fastball. The six-foot-eight-inch giant of a man offered a handful of feeble explanations for his past drinking indiscretions and claimed, à la Wallace, to be a teetotaler. "It's true Old Jim did take a drink," the two-time governor admitted, "but I never took any dope. But not anymore—I wouldn't take a drop now for a million dollars—not for a million dollars." The claims of sobriety seemed implausible to the small crowds who heard Folsom slur his speech and mix his words. Folsom's campaign appearances still featured country warm-up acts like the Red Raiders and the folksy slogan "Y'all Come," even though the corn shuck mop from years past was gone and the suds bucket had been replaced by a "Branch Head Hope Chest." Echoing the politics of a bygone era, Big Jim would roll into the state's small towns, head for the diner, barbershop, and courthouse, and press the flesh. Before making a rally speech, Folsom would be just as likely to curl up for a long nap under a shady tree or on a vacant park bench as to study his speech.[78]

Folsom never did articulate a consistent message during the race. On one day, he would declare all Alabama schoolkids deserved a free, hot lunch or vow to appoint a black to the state Parole Board. He might ridicule his opponents for doing nothing more than "cussing Yankees" in order to woo voters. The next day he would claim credit for training George Wallace. "In times past," Folsom exclaimed, "I helped the present governor, the honorable George Wallace up the ladder. He can't run. I wish he could. . . . I would vote for him in the next administration."[79]

On paper, four candidates had the credentials, the track record with voters, and the guts to get down in the mud to beat the Wallaces: Bob Gilchrist, John Patterson, Carl Elliot, and Richmond Flowers. At one point a candidate to be a Wallace floor leader, Gilchrist was usually associated with the loyal opposition of senators who fought the governor and was a late entrant in the race. The senator from Hartselle had been a frequent Wallace critic throughout his first term, was a leader in the antisuccession battle, and was close politically and personally to Ryan deGraffenreid. After his friend's tragic death, Gilchrist assumed command of deGraffenreid's campaign, hoping to capitalize on whatever momentum was left. Gilchrist had earned a significant amount of press over the previous three years in his pitched battles with the administration. Unfortunately for him, that coverage was usually beneath the fold or buried deep in the analysis while the Wallace name sat atop the headline. In order to get voter recognition, Gilchrist, an unknown compared to deGraffenreid, waged the most defiant campaign of all Lurleen's opponents. On the day he formally entered the race, Gilchrist came out with both guns blazing: "I do not approve of any public official who manufactures crises and engages in demagoguery to further his own political ambitions. If any chief executive, by proxy or otherwise, can control the structure of government for eight years, you have not democracy, but monarchy."[80]

Over the course of the next two months, Gilchrist launched a torrent of charges against Wallace hoping to lure the governor into a counterattack and some free publicity. Gilchrist accused Wallace of encouraging beatings, church bombings, and murder by fanning "the flames of hatred." Wallace's ham-handed tactics and reactionary rhetoric, according to Gilchrist, were responsible for more integration than at any time in state history. He taunted the governor for "wrapping himself in a skirt and bonnet" to stay in the seat of power. When that failed to get a sufficient reaction, Gilchrist pondered aloud the reaction if Lyndon Johnson announced plans to run Lady Bird as a stand-in. More specifically, Gilchrist charged Wallace with using the Highway Department for political purposes, giving Klan leader Robert Shelton kickbacks through highway consultant fees, delaying certain bond issues until 1970 to artificially inflate his record, using the lucrative insurance slush fund to reward backers, and boondoggling the textbook system in order to give the contact to EBSCO. The senator pointed out the massive amount of deficit financing the administration had accumulated, a threat to future revenue streams. He cited poor relations with the federal government and too much strife within the state Democratic Party. All the charges were essentially true; none of them mattered to voters.[81]

Despite earning the endorsement of the *Huntsville Times* and *Birmingham Post-Herald,* Gilchrist was soon reduced to convincing voters that Lurleen could not win without a runoff and that they should vote in the primary for the candidate they thought could beat her in the second ballot. Publicly, Gilchrist put up a brave front. "This thing has caught on," he boasted. "I've never seen anything like it. We've got more money today than we had two weeks ago. The people who are going to vote for her have already made up their mind; the people who aren't going to vote for Wallace are still looking. When he carries his campaign into the Tennessee Valley he's going to run into a Gilchrist wall." Privately, Gilchrist must have understood the hopelessness of his campaign.[82]

Former governor John Patterson was the only candidate previously to have taken on Wallace and won, but 1966 was a vastly different year from 1958. Patterson had continued to engender loyalty in some circles; his orchestration, along with Ryan deGraffenreid, helped win the succession fight. Everybody in Alabama knew he was going to run again in 1966. Indeed, Patterson was a relatively popular chief executive. He was able to kick the NAACP out of the state and his cavalier attitude toward attacks on freedom riders was in line with the beliefs of many white Alabamians: "We can't act as nursemaid to agitators. They'll stay at home when they learn nobody is there to protect them. The state of Alabama can't guarantee the safety of fools, and that's what they are." Patterson had also led unsuccessful charges to bolster education funding and equalize property tax assessments. Unfortunately, many of the voters who had chosen him eight years earlier had since found a new prince to lead the resistance to integration. He announced his candidacy to the strains of "Dixie" and a giant banner that identified him as "a proven defender of our rights."[83]

Patterson, like Gilchrist, tried to start his campaign talking about programs and policies such as increasing old-age pensions from $72 per month to $150 and floating a $600 million road bond to create a modern transportation network. Patterson even lured longtime Wallace man Sim Thomas into his fold after a rift developed between the Barbour County man and the governor over issues at Auburn University. The former governor also offered a half-hearted apology to black Alabamians. "I sometimes grieve a little bit," Patterson admitted in an appeal for black votes, "that there wasn't more accomplished when I was governor." Most campaign observers were surprised that despite these actions, forceful campaigning on law and order, and a statewide television speech, Patterson attracted only small, disinterested crowds and a flat level of support. Sensing an uphill battle, Patterson switched to a statewide "hand-shaking" campaign designed to put him in closer proximity to voters no longer sure of who he was and increased the tenor and quantity of his attacks on Wallace.[84]

With a month to go in the campaign, Patterson began complaining to reporters that the administration was intimidating his supporters, wiretapping his phones, using state troopers to launch false investigations, threatening termination from state jobs, and generally abusing its power in order to win. "The people are afraid," Patterson opined, "to take part openly in behalf of the candidate of their choice for fear of economic pressure from the state." Patterson went toe-to-toe with the Wallace record on desegregation, hoping, like Gilchrist, to lure the governor into a personal showdown. "We have been told over and over," Patterson mocked, "that we have been registering victory after victory and that we are the envy of our southern neighbors. It's becoming obvious to the majority of Alabama folks that just the opposite is true. . . . You cannot cover up this record of failure with clever, loud boasting or a string of generalities." Wallace paid him no attention. Patterson also indicted Wallace for souring relations with Washington, hastening the pace of integration, dereliction of duty, and defying the Alabama constitution. In perhaps his best line of the entire campaign, Patterson used Wallace's most famous words to illustrate a point: "I draw the line in the dust and toss the gauntlet before the feet of tyranny and I say preservation of the Alabama constitution now, tomorrow, and forever." The tragic confrontation in Selma, Patterson explained, was caused by Wallace's lackadaisical attitude and his preference to govern by telephone, not executive decision. Patterson also hinted at Wallace's overwhelming concentration of power and his attempted takeovers of local schools, voter registration boards, and jury pools. The stream of attacks remained constant until the May 3 primary. None of the charges, despite a measure or more of truth in all of them, stuck.[85]

If Gilchrist and Patterson represented the moderate to conservative wing of the serious candidates, Elliot and Flowers were the progressive choices. Flowers, who cut his political teeth as a strong segregationist and was famous for his African dialect jokes, openly courted black votes and promised to provide jobs for them. "We must move from the attitude of defiance," the attorney general told supporters, "to one of reason and progress. I want the vote of all the people. I want the vote of the Negro people and the white people." In his campaign for black votes, Flowers spoke frequently in black churches, at black schools such as Stillman College and Alabama State University, met with representatives of the Southern Christian Leadership Conference, and promised to "do every-thing in my power" to eradicate the Ku Klux Klan. Flowers was one of the few candidates who could get a response from Wallace. The governor had grown to despise Flowers, particularly after the attorney general had taken such a promi-nent public position as the governor's foil. That resentment, however, did not preclude Wallace from respecting Flowers's considerable abilities on the stump or with reporters. *Montgomery Advertiser* editor Grover Hall, a Wallace confi-dante, wrote of a relationship gone sour: "Wallace has been heard to growl that if Flowers had been his partisan, rather than his adversary, nothing could have kept him out of the governor's chair this year."[86]

Flowers may have been making headway with black Alabamians, but most whites were aghast. It was not unusual for Flowers to be booed lustily, as when the Madison County Democratic Women's Rally in Huntsville, unimpressed with his promise to name a woman to his cabinet, nearly ran him off the stage. When Flowers asserted that "waves of moderation" were sweeping the state, Alabamians clamored for more Wallaceism. When Flowers announced he would remove the Confederate flag from the capitol, white Alabama howled. When he said he was leading the race and would win, Alabama scoffed. When he advocated kindergartens, more hospitals, vocational training, and an Ala-bama Action Commission to reform government and heal racial wounds, white Alabama could not have cared less. When he questioned Lurleen's high school graduation and fitness to govern, miners and peanut farmers and auto me-chanics just shook their heads. As long as George Wallace was in this race, Flowers had no chance to win white votes.[87]

Flowers received the endorsement of several black groups and the bless-ing of Martin Luther King. The civil rights leader considered backing Carl Elliot, but Flowers's public appeals were ultimately more enticing than Elliot's behind-the-scenes promises of a better day if the Wallaces could be swept away. In the end, King did more to encourage Alabamians to withhold their votes from Lurleen than to cast them in favor of any one candidate. "I certainly don't need to tell you," the civil rights leader bellowed, "who not to vote for. I don't think there is a Negro in the state of Alabama who is going to vote for Sister Wallace." King's support made no difference in the ultimate outcome of the election, but may have prevented Carl Elliot from forcing a runoff. Elliot, chair of the House Subcommittee on Education and Labor, was part and par-cel of the Alabama congressional mold of the 1940s and 1950s: progressive on economic issues; supportive of a liberal federal government that involved it-self in public health, education, and electricity; able to court voters through class-based, not race-based, appeals; and savvy enough to realize Alabama expected him to support segregation nonetheless. Elliot grew up in rural poverty in North Alabama and pulled himself up by his bootstraps through hard work and education. Bitter at Wallace's efforts to defeat him in 1964, Elliot had two years to plan the race, and announced his intentions before the succession fight was waged.[88]

Though Elliot wanted the black vote, spoke at Alabama State University, and clearly worked behind the scenes to get it, he publicly conceded it to Flowers in order to stay in the good graces of white Alabamians. In comparison to his rivals, the six-foot-four-inch Jasper native articulated the most consistent vision of what a progressive government in Montgomery could accomplish. Elliot spoke about a different education environment where teachers had smaller classes, students had better resources, and both had roofs without leaks and floors without holes. Elliot favored a spirit of cooperation, not confrontation, with the federal government, and had the personal relationship with Lyndon Johnson necessary to pull it off. He frequently pointed out that the state got back $2.75 for every dollar it contributed to Washington in taxes. Elliot promised Alabamians that a different sort of industry could be attracted to the state that would bring jobs that paid living wages. Elliot described a world where racial peace, not continuous antagonism, prevailed.[89]

For all his strengths, Elliot's lack of charisma stood in stark relief to the Wallace road show. Despite regular concert appearances by Hank Williams Jr., Elliot rallies were much smaller than the candidate had hoped. One newspaper account described Elliot as a man "with no personal appeal who walks among the people as if his feet hurt." The former congressman had trouble attracting crowds in central and South Alabama. Even in his hometown of Jasper, Elliot could not compete with Lurleen. He drew a crowd of twelve hundred; Lurleen attracted four thousand. Elliot had one consistent applause line in a fairly dry stump speech. He promised, if elected, not to run his wife in 1970. In the end, Elliot, desperate for any momentum, resorted to criticizing Wallace supporters for tearing down his signs, echoed the chorus that Wallace was circumventing the constitution, and tried to convince Jefferson County voters that he would finish their roads while the governor would continue to treat them like an "unwanted stepchild."[90]

While these various candidates were flailing about, Lurleen Wallace was enjoying the best reception afforded a gubernatorial candidate in state history. The show was the same all over the state. Warm-up acts like Sam Smith and the Alabamians, the Wilburn Brothers, George Morgan, or Hank Thompson would entertain the audience with country and western songs. George Wallace Jr., whose long hair reflected the style of the time if not necessarily the temperament, would join the bands on stage and bang a tambourine. As the crowd grew restless, Lurleen would be introduced and begin to read from a brief script: "My pledge to you is that I will continue, with my husband's help, to provide the same kind of state government you have experienced in the last three years. Our administration will continue to operate the governor's mansion as the people's property, and alcoholic beverages will be absent from that property for another four years." Then, the candidate would introduce her number one advisor who would proceed with forty-five minutes of red meat for those who chose to blame their problems on the president, the federal judiciary, big city newspapers, intellectuals, or liberals. Long after Lurleen had retired to the car, George was still shaking hands and exchanging pleasantries with the locals. In this particular brand of retail politics, Wallace had no peer. He could remember a face and a name from years earlier, and his recollection startled and amazed people. Alabamians were thrilled that the same man who was on the national news every night knew who they were, where they worked, and their kin. People watching television in Massachusetts or Oregon might have seen Wallace as a dangerous racist. People in Boaz or Demopolis saw something else, a person who was connected to their past and present and was proud of them. Wallace might not always have governed as if he cared about ordinary folks, but on the campaign trail he developed a sincere kinship with them that few politicians could match.[91]

Because of Wallace's deep connection to Alabama voters, attacks on his administration by Lurleen's rivals hurt the accusers more than the accused. Wallace, after all, had been a forceful spokesman for a generation of white Alabama who had felt the stinging opprobrium of northern writers, southern do-gooders, and liberal preachers, teachers, and meddlers for a lifetime. Kraft's poll had indicated Wallace had a 90 percent approval rating, and his national speaking tours at state expense had an 82 percent favorable mark. Eight out of ten thought Wallace had handled segregation matters appropriately. Thus, attacks on Wallace were really criticisms of white Alabama, even if the charges were true. And white Alabama, in an environment created and controlled by their governor, was in no mood for either introspection or retreat. In a real sense, Wallace really did stand up for Alabama.[92]

The Wallace caravan drew huge crowds, much bigger on some days than George drew by himself in either 1958 or 1962. On most days, four rallies would be scheduled with the first stop scheduled for ten in the morning and the last for seven or eight at night. With Lurleen resting and chain smoking between stops, the governor would visit the offices of the local newspaper and glad-hand local dignitaries. Days later, the local paper, often a weekly, would issue an endorsement of Lurleen and a glowing summary of the accomplishments of her husband.[93]

Once Lurleen acclimated to the three or four thousand people and the amount of sound they could make, she relaxed a little. In front of a group of sixty-five hundred in Northport at the end of May, she spoke a little longer than usual and even offered a few ad-lib remarks, joking that as governor she planned to relocate the capital to her hometown. At that rally, Robert Shelton and his minions walked among the throng distributing Klan literature and Wallace bumper stickers. When George became ill in mid-April, Lurleen carried on alone, though even then she never spoke for more than ten minutes. In one-on-one conversations, Lurleen learned to thrust out her hand and say, "Hello, I'm Lurleen Wallace, good to see you." Over the course of a two-month primary campaign, the words flowed more easily. It mattered little to white Alabama, who loved her as one of their own, whether she stumbled over a few words or not.[94]

With a couple of exceptions, Wallace resisted the baiting of Lurleen's opponents and kept the focus of the campaign on his national ambitions. Wallace was fond of poking fun at Richmond Flowers and blistered the attorney general for suggesting the stars and bars should be removed from the capitol. "They want to take the Confederate flag down," Wallace told campaign crowds. "Let me tell you about that flag. Anywhere you see the Confederate flag flying you will find people who will fight harder for the American flag than anywhere else." The other matter that got Wallace upset during the campaign was newspaper crowd estimates. The governor believed the Birmingham, Mobile, Montgomery, and Huntsville newspapers purposely underestimated the attendance at his campaign events. After some initial insecurity Wallace revealed only to this inner circle, the governor realized by the eve of the election that Lurleen was going to win comfortably. Even Bob Ingram, who had initially downplayed the possibility of a Lurleen landslide, predicted a win without a runoff. A final campaign ad indicated what Wallace viewed as the strength of Lurleen's appeal. "He [Wallace] made a mark as YOUR spokesman," the copy read, "that shook up the liberals and left wingers and communist sympathizers. With your help we will continue the fight."[95]

On election day, May 3, poll watchers trained by the U.S. Civil Service Commission in Atlanta observed precincts in thirty-one localities and eleven Alabama counties. The goal was to prevent voting irregularities and white intimidation of black voters. If any intimidation occurred it was completely unnecessary. Lurleen Wallace crushed the field and won without a runoff in what the *Montgomery Advertiser* called "perhaps the most astonishing political achievement in state history." Wallace called it an "endorsement of our efforts to return constitutional government to this country." Lurleen, equally exhausted and exhilarated, lapsed into her stump speech mode: "I think it was a vote of approval of the Wallace record, of honesty in government, and of the administration's fight against the dangerous trends in our nation."[96]

Small county newspapers were ebullient. The editors of the *Dothan Eagle* noted they were "happy to find ourselves in agreement with the majority of the voters of Alabama." The *Evergreen Courant* exclaimed that the "big city newspapers and a handful of state senators may not like it that way, but the voters of Alabama are sold on the George Wallace administration in a big way." The *Clayton Record,* Wallace's hometown paper beamed: "Lurleen Wallace did a magnificent job and we are proud of our first woman governor of Alabama." The *Lee County Bulletin* had the most insightful commentary: "A clear majority is sensitive to criticism of this state, and the stronger the governor turns the criticism away from Alabama toward other people and places the more popular he will be."[97]

The size of the victory was overwhelming. Lurleen carried sixty of the sixty-seven counties and humiliated Folsom, Elliot, Gilchrist, Patterson, Flowers, and Todd in their home counties. The succession foes who bothered to run were defeated. The only senatorial candidates who won without a runoff were strong Wallace floor leaders. Administration-backed candidates Albert Brewer and MacDonald Gallion easily won the lieutenant governor and attorney general races. Two days after the election, "Stand Up for America" signs featuring the governor had already replaced "Stand Up for Alabama" signs featuring the Democratic primary winner.[98]

The November election was nothing more than a rubber stamp formality for the Wallaces. After the primary, Lurleen took some time off to go fishing and recover. Wallace himself stayed in full campaign mode in order to get the antiguidelines bill passed in the lame duck legislature. Squabbling in the Republican ranks led to speculation that Jim Martin would bypass the gubernatorial race and declare for John Sparkman's senate seat. Summer GOP polls indicated that Martin was ahead of Sparkman by two points, and both Barry Goldwater and Strom Thurmond offered varying degrees of support. Boxed in by Republican rival and former close associate John Grenier and betrayed by his own bold statements before Lurleen's primary win, Martin, the state's most recognizable Republican, rejected overtures from most of his party's top brass and some socially conservative Democrats to switch to the senate race. The results were disastrous for Martin and Grenier.[99]

Though Martin had been campaigning throughout the summer, Lurleen waited until the end of September to kick off her fall campaign. A few slight changes were evident. Her speeches were now five minutes or more rather than the two- or three-minute versions of the primary campaign. Her husband was running for president on the same stage and speaking more openly about it than ever. Wallace worked critiques of prospective 1968 candidates Lyndon Johnson, Richard Nixon, Jacob Javits, Robert Kennedy, George Romney, Nelson Rockefeller, and Hubert Humphrey into every peroration. Martin was a sluggish campaigner and his assessments of the Wallace record and ambition seemed warmed over from the Democratic primary.[100]

Nothing could derail the Wallace express. When armed guards forced four black Catholic nuns to leave a tea at the governor's mansion because of the color of their skin, the voters could have cared less. When Hamner Cobbs, longtime Wallace supporter and influential editor of the *Greensboro Watchmen*, switched his endorsement from Wallace to Martin, nobody blinked. When Barry Goldwater, hailed throughout all quarters of the state two years earlier, came to the state to campaign for Martin it made no difference at all. When Martin visited forty-seven cities over four days in his seven-car Victory Special train, it had no effect. On November 8, Lurleen Wallace even won a majority of the black vote in sweeping to a landslide victory over Martin. Martin won only two counties and lost by a two-to-one margin.[101]

Over the course of more than three years, George Wallace had become the most popular and powerful governor in Alabama history. Capitalizing on a strong national economy and a host of incentives, his administration had attracted record levels of industrial development, raised teacher salaries, created a network of junior colleges, and built mile after mile of roads. The overwhelming endorsement of his wife indicated that white Alabama approved of the Wallace administration, welcome affirmation for a man who was strangely insecure. But more than that, the Lurleen landslide convinced George that Alabama was willing to support his presidential aspirations by giving him the keys to the state airplane and carte blanche with the state coffers. He laughed when Lurleen playfully presented him with an apron for a Christmas present. During the next two years, he had no intention of being in the state long enough to wear it.

6
One Governor, Two Governors, or No Governor? / 1967–1968

Lurleen Wallace prepared for her inauguration as Alabama's forty-seventh governor confident that the following four years would bring amazing changes. Daughter Peggy was sixteen and soon to be out of the house and on her own. Husband George was orchestrating a nationwide presidential run and chomping at the bit to get back on the campaign trail. Martha Brewer, wife of Lieutenant Governor-elect Albert Brewer, was planning to help serve as a hostess for social events so Lurleen could travel to speaking engagements and ribbon-cuttings. The sixth most admired woman in America, according to a Gallup poll, spoke of plans to use her new office to serve the handicapped and mentally retarded and support the arts. The *Birmingham News* cautiously predicted that the new governor would be "a more positive, individualistic personality than people expect."[1]

Though her number one advisor refused to permit a traditional inaugural ball, other plans quickly took shape. The parade would be the largest in state history. Lurleen picked out a black cashmere suit with matching hat and tasteful pearls. The outgoing governor gave his successor a pair of diamond earrings for the occasion. Inaugural planners plucked Jefferson Davis's Bible from storage for the ceremonial oath, scheduled prayer breakfasts, and printed inaugural programs. On inauguration day, 250,000 Alabamians bundled up for the thirty-degree morning weather. Lurleen Wallace assured reporters her cancer was in full remission. "My health is excellent," she promised. "I have never felt better in my life. I am grateful that early detection and treatment rid me of the malignancy I suffered last year."[2]

While Lurleen was optimistic about the next four years of her life, most candidates from the 1966 campaign were about to embark on hard times. A. W. Todd found himself out of political office until an unlikely victory in the twilight of his life gave him the distinction of being both the youngest and oldest Alabamian to serve as commissioner of agriculture. John Patterson was locked out of Alabama politics until a rapprochement with George Wallace years later led to a post in the state judiciary. Jim Folsom continued to tarnish his legacy by running for state office without leaving the comfort of his front porch. Folsom, who continually tried to reinvent himself with little success, sported a Fu Manchu moustache in 1970 and delighted in his new sobriquet, the "Foxy Grandpaw." Bob Gilchrist, Ryan deGraffenreid's de facto stand-in, switched parties a few years later, then died of a heart attack at age forty-five. Richmond Flowers faced criminal proceedings for financial chicanery, kickbacks, and tax evasion and spent time in federal prison. Carl Elliott, broke from borrowing his federal retirement money to finance his lagging campaign, fell on such hard times that he had to beg creditors to stay out of court and borrow money to bury his beloved wife.[3]

As difficult as the years proved to be for her opponents, the sixteen months after inauguration would be the last days of Lurleen Wallace's life. Though she was able to feel the full love and admiration that Alabamians—black and white, rich and poor, male and female—felt for her, she did not live long enough to realize the potential of the office she came to embrace. Nervous and unsettled in the opening days of the 1966 campaign, Lurleen Wallace gradually developed such grace and ease during her short term that her death provoked a statewide outpouring of grief rarely seen before and never since. It was a curious time, and Lurleen was neither her own governor nor simply a ceremonial figurehead; she was a mixture of both depending on the day and the issue. Her health, a changing legislative dynamic, and the ambitions of her husband prevented clear demarcations of role, responsibility, and job description. Yet in the midst of swirling activity, Lurleen seemed to sense the inevitable recurrence of the cancer that would devastate her body until death became a welcome relief. In June 1967, she calmly but assuredly told her secretary and friend Catherine Steineker, "I won't be here a year from now." Her prediction proved accurate.[4]

Though no doubt existed that George Wallace was still the most powerful person in Montgomery, the new governor was more involved than anyone imagined during the campaign. Lurleen Wallace, despite her patience with her husband's lack of family involvement, was no pushover. In addition to her well-deserved reputation for fishing, Lurleen loved to fly planes, water-ski, and ride horses. Devout in her Methodism, she was not skittish about disciplining the children and keeping them in line. Comfortable in her own skin, she was more likely to pull up a chair and enjoy a cup of coffee and a cigarette with new acquaintances than try to impress them with her status. Though George's palace guard would never attempt it, Lurleen was legendary for putting him in his place with a carefully worded joke or playful anecdote. Once when George, in typical white-knuckle fashion, was worried that poor weather would make flying dangerous, Lurleen responded aloud for all to hear: "Now If he doesn't stop that, I'm just going to leave him out here." Anytime Wallace burst into her office during meetings, she loved to tell him that she was busy and would have to get back to him later. And Lurleen would pull similar stunts on cabinet members, reporters, and friends, being sure to poke fun at herself along the way. She teased Ed Ewing mercilessly after the amiable press secretary unknowingly complimented what he believed was a stylish hair cut, but was actually a wig. Montgomery storytellers recount the fable that Lurleen entered a contestant in the annual Calaveras County, California, frog-jumping jubilee and named it "Number One Advisor." "I don't think I've ever known a person who enjoyed living any more than Lurleen," Steineker told writer Anita Smith. This zest for life helped make Lurleen Wallace the most beloved governor in Alabama history.[5]

More than anything, Lurleen Wallace was authentic, a real Alabamian who could relate to the hardships and the simple pleasures that characterized life in the Deep South. Even after being elected governor, she continued to collect S&H Green Stamps in order to purchase a vacuum cleaner. Her genuineness and empathy attracted letters like one from Annie Pipkin in January 1968: "I went to Murphy School and took the G.E.D. test and passed it but I still get told you are too old. I am not a bad looking woman either and in good health. [I] didn't have to go to the doctor in thirteen years. So couldn't there be something done for us grandmothers that have to work?" Mrs. Loy Logan, like many other Alabamians, felt confident that she could confide in Lurleen and ask for help. "My husband was in the hospital," Logan noted. "He had to have one of his kidneys removed. He had a tumor. I was on my way home for a few minutes and was going back to the hospital to him and I had an automobile accident. I was in the hospital almost five weeks." Wracked by debt, Logan wanted the governor to suggest a way to get a loan since the $275 monthly pay the family earned was insufficient for hospital bills, medicine, and other basic necessities.[6]

Some of the correspondence was more humorous than heartwarming. Little Johnny Jones mailed the governor a one hundred dollar bill in Confederate money in hopes of exchanging it for five dollars in legal tender to buy a new basketball. The governor returned the CSA note with the advice that she had "talked to several coin collectors who tell me your note is worth several dollars and I would advise you contact" them. Alabamians felt a connection to Lurleen Wallace that made her seem like part of the family.[7]

The nameplate on the governor's desk was not the only thing that changed in Montgomery. Wallace family dynamics also changed significantly in 1967 with George paying more attention to his wife. Though always an affectionate man quick to offer a hug or kiss to family members, Wallace was prone to leave a conversation with Lurleen or one of the kids in midsentence anytime it occurred to him that political interests might be served by a quick phone call. Because the family had come to accept the preeminent position politics played in the household, they were rarely surprised when these emotionally chilling events occurred. "That's just daddy," the kids would sigh, longing for more time and attention with their father but understanding his nature nonetheless. "My sisters and I laugh about trying to get his attention occasionally at dinner," George Jr. recalled, "and we'd say, 'Dad?. . . Dad?. . . Governor?' and he'd say 'Yes.'" After Lurleen's election, Wallace became more attentive to her, often twirling her around the room as the two danced to the radio or a scratchy 78. This was in stark contrast to previous years when Lurleen would be called to the capitol, then wait patiently in an anteroom for her husband to finish his business and receive her.[8]

Lurleen suddenly found herself busy with official duties and making some of the same choices her husband had made for the past two decades. When Lurleen secretly made arrangements for a high school honor group to come to the mansion to tap Peggy into membership, she told her daughter to meet her at home so they could go shopping. When the ebullient students burst into the mansion to bestow their coveted membership on Peggy, she was surprisingly crestfallen: "We're not going shopping are we?" Lurleen quickly understood that, while happy to be inducted into the honor society, Peggy would have much rather spent quality time with her mother.[9]

If Lurleen was stronger, smarter, and more interesting than outsiders imagined, George was more sensitive and emotional than a first glance might indicate. In reality, six dimensions of George Wallace—political, ideological, compassionate, emotional, family man, crude—competed for supremacy inside one personality. Doubtless, the political Wallace, hungry for the campaign trail and thirsty for the roar of the crowd, held sway most of the time. But the rest of his personality was less cocksure, less confrontational, more sympathetic, and more complex. At a moment's notice, Wallace would dispatch the state plane to whisk an injured Alabamian across the state or country to receive specialized medical attention. Wallace hated reviewing death penalty cases and struggled over those decisions. During one execution day when the governor was traveling the state on another matter, he had Press Secretary Bill Jones call back to Montgomery every twenty minutes or so to check on any appeals or court-ordered stays. Back in Montgomery, Wallace stayed on the phone until just before the fateful moment, agonizing over the impending duties of Yellow Mama, Alabama's electric chair.[10]

Wallace expressed his humanity in other ways as well. After speaking to disabled veteran Charles Mosley, Wallace fired off a memo to Director of Industrial Relations Rex Roach asking him to get Mosley some work. Wallace made a similar request concerning George Parker, a sixty-five-year-old man who no longer had the stamina to perform his difficult job. Sensing that these employment difficulties were becoming increasingly common for older Alabamians, Wallace asked Roach to work up a "special program of publicity through the employment service to hire people over 40 and 45. It seems that people of this age bracket . . . have such a hard time getting employment." When John Price was unable to get medical services for his young son, Wallace intervened to get little Johnny Caulson Price admitted to a Crippled Children's Service facility in the Wiregrass area. On many occasions, Wallace could be seen weeping after hearing the plight of the unfortunate. He read, reread, and personally answered the letter of a "little girl in Mexico whose brother was killed in Vietnam."[11]

At home, Wallace could be a curmudgeon, refusing to gather around the tree on Christmas morning because it was one of the rare days when he could stay in bed until noon. This was especially perplexing for the Wallace children. The Christmas season was their favorite time, and their mother had painstakingly adorned their living quarters with festive decorations and holiday cheer. "He'd say don't wake me up," Peggy Wallace Kennedy recalled of Christmas mornings in the Wallace house, "and he'd play with us, you know, and then he'd say, leave me alone." Lurleen was the family disciplinarian not only because of her daily involvement with the children but also because George never seemed able to fill the role. After one attempt at spanking daughter Peggy resulted in laughter instead of tears of repentance, Wallace washed his hands of the task and advised her to "get your mama to do this." The family relished long weekends and summer trips to Lake Martin, but Wallace rarely accompanied them. When he did go, he often lingered inside on the telephone until a frustrated Lurleen suggested he return to Montgomery. In later years, as chronic pain made reflection an unavoidable event, Wallace told his children he wished he had spent more time with them. But by this time, George Jr. and Peggy had put that part of their past behind them. "I always told him," George Jr. reminisced, "'Dad, we understood. We were proud of you and understood what it took for you to do what you were doing and we knew you loved us.'" Peggy was even more circumspect: "I said, 'You know, Daddy, that's the way you are. That's the way you were and that's the way we loved you, so I mean, there is no sense in going back.'" Son-in-law and former Alabama Supreme Court justice Mark Kennedy summed up the governor's family relations with a unique perspective from inside and outside the family: "He kind of always kept his family, I can't speak for others, but always kind of kept us at arm's length."[12]

The lack of communication in the Wallace household was ironic. After all, the family business was based on public speeches, persuasive oratory, and the quest to stay connected to Alabamians. Wallace never pulled his brood together to tell them how much their life would change after his election in 1962.

Family meetings were never called to announce presidential or gubernatorial campaigns before that news hit the press. Everyone realized the possibility that assassination attempts could occur, but the family never discussed them in public or in private. In late 1967 and early 1968, the Wallaces neither fully revealed nor completely hid the gravity of Lurleen's cancer from the rest of the family. In effect, the Wallace family functioned with a communication system based on code and assumption. Information was gleaned through observation and inference; full verbal disclosure was never an option. "That's just the way it was," Peggy Wallace Kennedy recalled, "things that had to be said were said, but if something didn't need to be said, it just wasn't said."[13]

Amid the reality of constant campaigning and the political priorities of their father, the children cherished moments when he took off the hat of governor or candidate and put on the sweater of a concerned father. As a result, small snippets in time when their father gave them his full attention became treasured memories. For Peggy Wallace, one memory was watching the *Friday Night Fights* on television with her father sitting on the edge of the sofa and commenting on every blow. Peggy and her father shared another special moment when they ventured out to a Montgomery eatery not long after Lurleen died. The next day, newspaper reports indicated that the governor was dating again; obviously the errant scribe did not realize the long blond hair of Wallace's dinner companion belonged to his daughter, not a new girlfriend. George Jr. recalled long car rides he took with his father in the days after the 1968 presidential campaign ended, his father's beaming pride after his son scored a touchdown in a Pop Warner game, and his father's attendance at the press conference announcing George Jr.'s recording contract.[14]

None of these actions mitigate the tinderbox Wallace created with his venomous depictions of civil rights workers as communists, the federal government as a dictatorial usurper, and his general defiance of federal court orders and legislation. But they do reveal the complexities that characterize George Wallace and helped bind him to the hearts and minds of Alabamians, black and white. Exploitation of race may explain his victory in 1962, many of his policies, and his ascension to regional prominence; but it does not entirely explain the devotion he inspired. As time passed and segregation shifted from the front to the back burner, mothers remembered Wallace for the free textbook system; fathers embraced his support for a strong national defense; and Alabamians of all ages remembered the attention he gave them in diners, at factory shift changes, in his office where he loved to spend hours with common folk, or on the campaign trail. Wallace connected to Alabamians by pulling up his shirtsleeves and helping a voter pull an engine out of his car or leaving the mansion in the middle of the night to sit on a stack of pallets and listen to third-shift workers spill their life stories between puffs on a Marlboro and sips of Coca-Cola. Governance by perpetual campaigning had disastrous effects on the ability of Alabama to solve structural problems, but it forged a loose partnership with Alabamians that kept Wallace close to the people and in power for a quarter of a century.[15]

Substance and Style

From January 1967 to May 1968, when Lurleen was governor, her administration became a mixture of the previous four years of Wallaceism with a sprinkling of some new ideas such as mental health reform and a broad program for increasing the quantity and quality of state parks. The subsuming of all policies and administration to the 1968 presidential campaign and the governor's declining health led to a bizarre reality. Alabama had one official governor, two acting governors, and for long stretches of time no working governor. When they worked together, Lurleen and George formed an effective combination akin to the comfort of cotton with the raw power and precision of steel. Pockets of dissent popped up in response to George's actions and antics, but few people publicly challenged Lurleen, even if some of the defiant words she spoke were no different from her husband's. When George was campaigning, raising money, or driving to get on all fifty state ballots for the 1968 election, the pace in Montgomery slowed to a crawl with official ceremonial duties being fulfilled but little else. Leaving no doubt about administration priorities, "Wallace for President" souvenirs were sold during Lurleen's inauguration festivities. On the night of the inauguration, campaign staff held a meeting at the Woodley Country Club with Asa Carter, former Dallas County sheriff Jim Clark, and representatives from four southern states. Though they had only met in organizational sessions by the inauguration, some legislators were already complaining that the administration's priorities were focused on the 1968 presidential campaign and not the welfare of the state. Within the first three months of the new administration Assistant Banking Superintendent John DeCarlo had set up an office in the Wallace campaign headquarters where he began researching state election laws.[16]

Lurleen's inaugural speech, written by Taylor Hardin with help from his assistant Julia Allen, foreshadowed her ability to use gender, thought by some to be a stumbling block during the campaign, to move the legislature toward enacting administration ideas. "It is plain to see," Lurleen declared, "that federal bureaucrats . . . are already a part of a force which tomorrow may well lay down even sterner guidelines to control our thought, and actions, and every aspect of our lives. Even now a federal agency attempts to tell us the schools our children shall attend, to regulate the content of our textbooks, who shall teach them, and with whom our children shall associate. . . . I resent it. As your governor and as a mother I shall resist it." Press Secretary Ed Ewing told Lurleen in late 1966 that she would be able to accomplish things her husband never could because she was a woman. And throughout her brief tenure, references to motherhood peppered her speeches. In a speech to a joint session of the legislature about resisting federal desegregation orders, Lurleen spoke more as a mother than as a governor: "As a mother, my heart is filled with compassion for all the children of our state. As a mother, I understand as do the other mothers of this state what they are attempting to do with our children. This is the final step toward a complete takeover of their hearts and minds—this is what Hitler did in Germany." Lurleen did not write her own speeches, but the references to her perspective as a mother were natural, not forced, and her tears were honest reflections of her personality, not contrived political dramatics. Caught up in the moment, capitol beat scribes reported that Lurleen might appoint a woman to her cabinet, though she did not, instead keeping nearly all of her husband's appointees for a second term.[17]

George Wallace had established a Commission on the Status of Women in 1963 to study pay inequalities, percentages of male and female state employees, and opportunities for improvement. The commission, largely conservative in political orientation, nonetheless made four recommendations: women should be encouraged to run for office at the county level; women should be encouraged to work in professional occupations; education and training should be made available for women; and all state government departments should be made aware of the pay disparity between men and women. At the time of the commission's final report, Alabama had 112 employees at the highest pay grade, only 1 of them a woman. Though he initiated the study, Wallace did little to enact its suggestions and was slow to appoint a female cabinet member to his administration even after promising to do so in the 1970 campaign.[18]

More than on any other issue, Lurleen Wallace used her experiences as a mother to enact public policy on mental health. Though she had mentioned mental health issues in her brief campaign speeches, those references were more stump speech filler than a recitation of administration goals. Intrigued by the idea of helping the vulnerable and wanting to establish her own gubernatorial credibility, Lurleen began referring to mental health as a top priority in interviews and made sure the topic was broached in her inaugural address. In her call for a special session a month after inauguration, the new governor asked for half a million dollars to increase mental health employees' salaries and power to place them under the umbrella of the state merit system. In correspondence, Lurleen promised to "press for additional legislation" and make mental health reform "one of the projects which we hope to accomplish during the next four years." Legal advisor Hugh Maddox promised Congressman Bill Nichols the governor would "do all we can to see that the needs [of Bryce and

Partlow, state mental health facilities] . . . are met." People noticed. Lois Mills, director of medical records at Bryce, wrote the governor to express her appreciation and confidence that "you will do everything in your power to bring about better conditions for the patients and for the employees in the Mental Health Department."[19]

The Alabama Mental Health Association (AMHA), long despairing because of its inability to increase funding, seemed buoyed by this newfound advocate and released its legislative recommendations to the press. The AMHA, an interest group and lobby, asked for $2 million to activate dormant federal money that could not be used until the state provided matching funds. Though the AMHA had the resolve to ask for additional funding each year, the state Mental Health Board, the official administrative agency of Alabama, rarely challenged the governor. When HEW threatened to cut off funding because of noncompliance with Civil Rights Act standards, the board resolved to refer the matter "to the governor's office "and follow whatever actions it recommended. As was its custom, the previous legislature had passed reform legislation but refused to provide any financial resources. In this case, it created a system of regional mental health centers for outpatient care but refused to provide operating funds to build and staff them. The AMHA asked for operating capital as well as a commitment to bring per patient expenditures up to national averages. Lurleen agreed to serve as honorary chair along with Bear Bryant and Auburn football coach Shug Jordan to raise $1 million for interdenominational chapels at Bryce and Partlow.[20]

For all this activity, the singular moment leading to Lurleen's status as a mental health advocate had yet to occur. Encouraged by Ed Ewing and others to visit Bryce and Partlow and see conditions for herself, Lurleen and a passel of physicians, administration personnel, and reporters toured the overcrowded and dilapidated Tuscaloosa hospital in late February. No Alabama governor had visited in decades. By any standard, these mental health facilities were in shambles. Bryce had a 250-bed building that was so bad the state board even admitted it needed to be replaced. Many if not most of the cottages at Partlow had no air conditioning, and bed-bound patients were forced to endure hour after hour in oppressive heat while lying on plastic sheets. It was common knowledge in the medical community that Partlow had at least 800 patients above capacity. Chaplains complained that no rehabilitation or consolation could be offered in an environment where attendants routinely beat patients and strapped them down for hours. Patients were expected to help care for other patients, and the end result was a vicious cycle where they were denied meaningful care and instead warehoused in row after row of beds. As was her nature, Lurleen eschewed plans for a question-and-answer session with top administrators and instead opted for a less formal tour where she could see conditions for herself. Visibly shaken by the stark reality of mentally retarded patients shrieking and screaming, Lurleen held back tears until a young patient ran up to her, hugged her neck, and called her "Mama." Not much of an ad-libber anyway, Lurleen was so startled by the experience she could hardly enunciate her feelings. "It was very depressing," she eventually told reporters. "It was certainly not a pleasure trip. We must do something to help."[21]

The response from Alabamians to her visit was overwhelmingly positive. Letters poured into the governor's office. "I feel that now that you have seen for yourself the great needs of these institutions," Mary Cox wrote, "you will certainly see that something is done for them. May God bless you as you carry out your grave responsibilities, and may future historians record that you were a great humanitarian and a great governor." Hundreds of Alabamians, such as Becky Jagoe, now knew that the governor understood the reality of conditions and would seek to improve the unfortunate plight of their institutionalized relatives. "I was really shocked to see the patients under such awful living conditions," Jagoe confided to the governor. "It broke my heart to see the inside of that building, the uncleanliness of my cousin and the rest of the children. My eyes have never opened any wider."[22]

Affected by the awful conditions and emboldened by the response to her visit, Lurleen Wallace took action. In a speech to the Georgia legislature just days after her tour, Lurleen outlined a plan to put mental health employees into the umbrella of the state merit system, provide them a raise, and use bond money to construct regional mental health centers. At an appearance at the Auburn Chamber of Commerce's annual banquet, Lurleen made sure a section on mental health was included in her standard speech: "As we devote an ever-increasing amount of money and energy to the conservation and wise use of natural resources, any less effort to conserve our human resources would be in my conscience an absolute sin." Historian Leah Rawls Atkins attended the event and witnessed a woman growing into her job: "At Auburn she was elegant and beautiful. She moved gracefully. . . . Her hair was a lovely ash blonde, cut beautifully and casually styled. She read her speech like a professional and was at ease. She was not the woman I had seen so many times before." Because she never wrote her own speeches and rarely deviated from prepared texts, her mental health speeches were often leavened with ideology supplied by her husband's speechwriters, including State Sovereignty Commission official Eli Howell. As a result, some reasons she espoused for improving metal health facilities included making patients "less dependent on our society," a clear appeal to fiscal conservatives who thought any increase in taxation required either an emergency or a silver lining.[23]

Social conservatives were not necessarily quick to support Lurleen's mental health program either. Karl Prussion, an FBI counterspy from 1947 to 1959, had become a minor celebrity to some Deep South conservatives because he seemed willing to confirm their worst fears that communism and world domination lurked behind every liberal cause and activist. In a 1965 affidavit, Prussion had concluded that a "mental health program for America is one of the many communist objectives that seeks to control the individual and the family. The establishment of mental health clinics throughout our state would create an atmosphere of suspicion, fear, and hate." Richard Cotten, a Wallace backer and popular conservative radio commentator and newsletter editor, declared in a June 1967 radio broadcast that the National Institute of Mental Health and the Internal Revenue Service were teaming up to develop a "single state-approved religion" for all Americans. Kenneth Goff, reportedly an expert on Soviet uses of psychology to attain political objectives, wrote of Russian mental health brainwashing techniques used to capture the hearts and minds of formerly God-fearing, red-blooded, American patriots.[24]

Even George Wallace's national campaign benefactor, Texan H. L. Hunt, viewed mental health as a communist plot. Hunt, who spoke regularly with Wallace, was concerned that the administration "did not understand the mental relief racket and might cause the legislature to pass a bad bill in attempting to afford relief to the emotionally disturbed and mental cases." Mental health, according to Hunt, was a "real effective procommunist racket" and could easily be used as a guise to indoctrinate unsuspecting Americans. Wallace responded quickly to ease the fears of one of his biggest single sources of campaign cash: "I know your concern about any measure which would authorize communist or procommunist sympathizers to use our laws and our institutions in a way which would be detrimental to liberty and freedom. I can assure you that we are not sponsoring and we would not sponsor any such measures."[25]

Suspicions of communist infiltration were not limited to mental health. Some administration supporters expressed concern about the touring musical group Up with People. The group, typically characterized by freshly scrubbed college students traveling throughout the country providing wholesome musical entertainment, was thought by some Wallaceites to be dangerous. "This outfit," Mrs. H. W. Gill wrote, "is going to be nurtured and cultivated here in your state where the students will be oriented towards making trouble for George Wallace in the coming campaign." Methodist minister Milton Cutchen of Mobile authored a tract that identified Up with People as a false religious cult, soft on communism, and unpatriotic.[26]

While these allegations seem so comical that they can scarcely be believed, the conservative political climate and actions of fringe groups attracted by Wallace conditioned some Alabamians to be wary of all outsiders and suspect that hulking Red behemoths were on every street corner. Mrs. Elsie Gill, secretary of the well-heeled Forum of the Republic, frantically contacted George

ONE, TWO, OR NO GOVERNORS / 191

Wallace to alert him to the misguided intentions of his wife. "Are you aware," Gill wrote, "that mental health can be a political weapon by setting up norms of behavior so as to declare emotionally ill, those who would disagree with the management." Throughout the process of crafting and passing mental health legislation, both Wallaces faced sustained criticism from a lunatic fringe.[27]

A Different Kind of Legislature

Before the administration could pass any legislation, it had to come to grips with a new legislature exploring its own identity. In the aftermath of reapportionment, this legislature was more urban and less dominated by the Black Belt than in previous years. On the eve of the first special session of 1967, pundits were already speculating on issues that would cause a senate filibuster. The new urban bloc, led by the Jefferson and Mobile county delegations, wanted a wholesale reshuffling of the gas tax formula that had favored rural counties for decades. Lurleen was touting an expanded bid law that invariably drew behind-the-scenes resistance from veteran legislators who had acquired the skills necessary to get a road built or some extra perquisites for their junior college or trade school without using formal channels. Some traditionalists were even planning to fight tooth and nail against the shift to daylight savings time. Those issues would surface in the session, but nothing was going to be accomplished until a pay raise for legislators was signed into law.[28]

Within hours of Lurleen's session-opening speech, the senate passed several mental health bills out of the Finance Committee, including a pay raise and matching funds for federal money that could be used for funding regional outpatient centers. But even before addressing the governor's new priority, the legislature voted itself a three hundred dollar per month pay raise on top of the thirty dollars per day members received while in session. As was customary with pay raises, the bill was passed with an unrecorded voice vote to ensure plausible deniability with the folks back home. The house read, considered, debated, and passed the bill in a total of thirty-seven seconds thanks to the quick gavel of the new speaker, Rankin Fite. Word was passed to the administration that nothing else would be considered until Lurleen signed the pay raise bill. To ratchet up the pressure, George Lewis Bailes introduced a bill to cut the salaries of cabinet members by 50 percent. Forced to sign, veto, or amend the bill, the administration sent the bill back to the legislature with the increase set at two hundred dollars per month. Unsure which way the political winds were blowing, George avoided drawing clear lines back to himself on the amendment: "You can't tell what a woman's gonna do," the former governor blushed. Though Lurleen stepped out of her husband's shadows on several issues, she never attempted anything he disagreed with, and Montgomery

insiders never doubted that the number one advisor, not the governor, was behind the amendment. The senate, rather than pass the twenty-four hundred
dollar annual pay raise, chose to kill the bill, showing an independent streak
seen only once during the previous four years. Reporter Ted Pearson noted
the newfound confidence: "These makers of the laws . . . are neither awed nor
cowed when they look at those massive vote totals piled up by Lurleen and
George Wallace last November. Power and patronage may catch up with them,
but for the moment they're having a time of it."[29]

Because the administration dominated the house, most members who
wanted the pay raise were furious at the senate for killing the governor's
amendment. In fact, senators were prepared to launch a full-scale revolt against
the administration until the legislators got their three hundred a month raise.
"Dammit," one legislator exclaimed, "we're not going to move until we get that
raise." The senate, making good on an earlier promise, shut down all movement on administration bills, while Wallace seethed. Rankin Fite, aware that
the most strident opponents in the senate were in the Jefferson County delegation, disposed of three Jefferson County road bills in the house by assigning them to committees he controlled. Rather than be intimidated by the long
arm of the administration, the senate took the lead and passed the thirty-
six hundred dollar annual hike. An unnamed administration official told the
Birmingham News that Wallace was having a fit over the defeat of Lurleen's
amendment. The administration leaked a story suggesting the state would be
forced into proration because of the pay raise and that a 5 percent merit raise
for all state employees could no longer be considered because of greedy lawmakers.[30]

In the end, the raise issue was indicative of a growing rift between the administration and the legislature. When Washington-based political reporters
Rowland Evans and Robert Novak described Alabama lawmakers as a "Wallace
rubberstamp legislature," they failed to understand the changing dynamics
that made 1967 a dramatically different legislative landscape than it had been
in the first term. Many of the twenty-three senators who voted to override
Lurleen's amendment soon found their pet projects being opposed by the administration. George Wallace's political skin was plenty thick when it came to
personal criticism. Wallace actually hoped he would be attacked by political rivals because he was a devastating counterpuncher and could think on his feet
better than reporters, academics, or politicians. But when it came to perceived
affronts to his wife, Wallace became bitter and had no tolerance for dissent.

The administration excelled at legislative relations during the first term but
its success rate declined during Lurleen's administration. Even after the pay
raise issue was settled, urban legislators demanded a wholesale change in the
distribution of funds derived from the seven cent per gallon gas tax. Histori-

cally, gas tax funds, the highest in the nation, had gone disproportionately to rural counties that had more clout in the state legislature: of the seven cents per gallon levy, three went to the state for general projects, three went on an equal percentage to each county, and the final cent was further divided, with a majority going to the farm-to-market road program. As a result, large counties like Jefferson and small counties like Lamar or Conecuh would receive the same $552,000. While larger counties were in a constant scramble to keep roads open and in good repair, smaller counties had more highway money than they could spend. Coosa County had nearly a million dollars in road funds invested in securities, had no bond debt of its own, and had $153,000 in cash on hand. The administration's plans for a large road bond bill compounded the necessity of resolving the dispute. Simply put, urban legislators were not going to give the administration another $160 million dollars in patronage plums for appeasing rural lawmakers. After a few behind-the-scenes meetings, Wallace announced a compromise had been reached. The small farm-to-market road program would be eliminated—the funds would be reallocated to pay for the new bond bill—and, coupled with a three dollar increase in the price of auto tags, municipalities would be awash in over $4 million in road funds.[31]

The administration, eager to get the highway bond bill passed, thought giving up the farm-to-market program would appease the urban bloc and get the ball moving on the new bonds. Sacrificing this program, a favorite of the Folsom and first Wallace administrations, did little to satisfy critics and alienated traditional rural backers. Reuben Jackson, a Coosa County engineer, fired off a missive to George Wallace complaining about the ramifications of ending the program. "I have been talking with many rural people in my county," Jackson warned, "and unless we see or hear some change in the very near future in regards to this matter, I am seriously afraid your popularity in the smaller counties (of which 43 were of great importance to you and Mrs. Wallace in your elections) will greatly diminish." Jackson reminded the former governor that the new governor had promised to maintain the farm-to-market program in an address to the legislature. Talladega County probate judge William Killough complained that the farm-to-market program could not possibly be eliminated because it had "meant more to the counties . . . than anything else in the history of the state." Wallace, who woke up each morning thinking about votes and went to bed each night thinking of votes, blamed the entire matter on the federal courts that "reapportioned the legislature, giving the larger counties more representation than they ever had" and promised to revive "one of the finest programs ever conceived."[32]

Unfortunately for Wallace, nobody else agreed with his previously announced compromise. John Watkins, head of the League of Municipalities, balked at Wallace's supposed deal. "We have not had a part of it," Watkins revealed. "Our people are feeling it was futile to come down here and take part in the discussions." Bessemer mayor Jess Lanier echoed Watkins's sentiments: "They think we have thrown in the towel. This is not so. There was no agreement reached so far as the municipalities are concerned." This dissent was unexpected because Watkins and Lanier had been ardent Wallace backers. Wallace had been a floor leader for the League of Municipalities, and Watkins's predecessor, Ed Reid, had been one of the former governor's mentors. Lanier was one of Wallace's biggest supporters on the state Democratic Executive Committee and had been his point man at the 1964 national convention. Expected dissent came from the Jefferson County delegation, long overlooked by the administration because of the county's aggregate electoral indifference to the governor. Senator Hugh Morrow told the *Birmingham News* that no deal had been made: "It looks like they are going to force us to take a stand and prove to them that we are serious about getting some of the gasoline tax money redistributed." Jefferson County senator George Lewis Bailes suggested that Wallace frequently announced compromises that were nothing more than administration ultimatums. "If you go any other way," Wallace warned the Jefferson County delegation, "you're on your own."[33]

In fact, the larger counties and municipalities did band together to force the administration to consider other options. A joint senate-house committee was formed to hear testimony on potential compromises. But hardened battle lines caused the chairman, Alton Turner, to confess "it looks like a long, dry summer," even though the rural lawmaker admitted urban areas had been given the short shrift for decades. Citing inadequate and illegal distribution of funds, city fathers in Mobile, the second most populous county in the state, filed suit to get the gas tax matter settled in front of a three-judge federal panel and asked for an injunction preventing any allocation until the matter was resolved in court. In fiscal year 1965–66, Mobile County residents had paid nearly $7 million in gasoline taxes, but received back only $676,670. Mobile legislator Robert Eddington broached the possibility of increasing the gas tax to make up for past inequities and to complete vital urban road projects. Particularly important to urban interests was matching funds for completion of interstate projects: only 438 of 878 miles of planned interstate highways were open for traffic by September 1967. Interstate projects originally slated for completion by 1971 were in danger of not being ready until 1974, and the delay was certain to have lingering economic effects. Seeking a quick resolution in order to get other administration legislation free of the gas tax logjam, Lurleen proposed a freeze on revenue distribution at the end of the current year with a promise to support a new formula based on population.[34]

Unfortunately for the administration, her proposal was no more successful than her husband's earlier pronouncement of a compromise. The combined pressure to get a larger share of new road bonds, the need to fund the annual interest costs from the bonds with additional taxes of some sort, and the redistribution of gas tax proceeds rendered the administration unable to use its popularity to rule by executive fiat. Wallace, unquestionably directing Lurleen's legislative efforts, was not prepared for such resistance and found himself working rural and urban legislators, consulting with interest groups, and burning up phone lines to prevent the embarrassment of being defeated in the first special session of his wife's term. The special session had started late— in early March instead of late January—primarily because the administration was more concerned about exploring presidential ballot issues and establishing campaign priorities than in governance. In addition, the formal call came after the administration waited for television and radio stations to clear time to broadcast Lurleen's opening speech. For a man who preferred the adulation of the campaign to the nuts and bolts of crafting policy, the necessity of getting into the trenches with a rebellious legislature was all the more unpalatable.[35]

With less than a month left before the special session ended, Wallace took charge and skillfully played both sides against each other until a compromise was reached on the gas tax redistribution and road bond bill. Reversing course, Wallace aligned with the urban bloc in the house to get a bill through committee and onto the house floor. At this point, Wallace did not even care what sort of bills passed. He knew he would gain momentum with anything that came out of the house and with a predictable senate filibuster looming, he could fix the bill in a conference committee by dangling carrots to anyone digging in his heels. The urban bloc favored a new formula for the gas tax that would allocate 45 percent of revenue to finance the new bonds and then provide the balance to all counties and cities on a population basis. Additional funds for road construction would be supplied by increasing the cost of car tags from $3 to $13. Exerting tremendous political pressure, Wallace got a slightly altered bill through Ways and Means despite the reluctance of his own hand-picked speaker, Rankin Fite, who sided with the rural coalition. Fite, who was a legendary dealmaker, offered only token opposition and allowed the bill to be passed by a simple majority even though he could have ruled it was not included in the call for the special session. Such a ruling would have necessitated a two-thirds vote for passage. The bill Fite allowed to pass ensured that forty-three rural counties would lose road funds.[36]

Part of Wallace's strategy included dispatching the governor to the League of Municipalities meeting to profess a deep commitment to providing a more equitable revenue formula. In the senate, Wallace's traditional rural allies balked at the administration's new urban alliance. "If the urban counties think they are going to rape the small counties," Barbour County senator Jimmy Clark protested, "they had better forget it." Capitol beat reporters predicted rural

forces could filibuster the session to its conclusion and kill the bill. On one legislative day with two weeks left in the session, the senate convened and adjourned within ten minutes, a vivid description of the lines in the sand drawn
by both urban and rural coalitions. Behind the scenes, the administration was
working toward a compromise on four fronts: the administration leaked to reporters that it was intervening on behalf of the people to prevent a minority of
senators from killing the bill; Lieutenant Governor Albert Brewer was trying to
play peacemaker in the senate; Wallace was meeting with rural leader Roland
Cooper and urban leader Hugh Morrow to find common ground; and Wallace
was preparing to shift sides once again, this time in favor of rural counties.
With his pledge to support rural county goals of receiving a minimum of
$590,000, Wallace made his second power play in less than a month, revealing
how desperate he was to acquire the $160 million in bond money and return to
his national campaigning. With customary Wallace persuasiveness and by reversing course, the number one advisor picked up a net of seven votes in the
senate and moved closer to getting a bill passed. Suddenly in the driver's seat,
the rural bloc took to sleeping on cots outside the floor of the senate while
urban forces switched to filibustering to prevent passage of the bill.[37]

Stung by Wallace's defection, urban forces took to the media to lash out
at Wallace and his Black Belt cohorts. The Jefferson County delegation took
center stage with a pledge to filibuster until a compromise was reached. Individually, the rhetoric was demonstrably sharper. Senator Richard Dominick
told the *Birmingham News* that if the choice lay between the rural package
and no package he was "willing to go home empty-handed." Senator George
Lewis Bailes declared that his constituents felt "that unless we can get a reasonable program they would park their cars at the foot of Red Mountain and
walk the Red Mountain Expressway." League of Municipalities official and
Gadsden mayor Les Gilliland filed suit in federal court asking for a new gasoline tax revenue formula. "We have been blocked by the Black Belt–controlled
legislative committees," Gilliland argued, "in receiving some fair and just allocation of funds. . . . Millions of dollars have wrongfully been taken away from
the people of Alabama and squandered in some small county which did not
have legitimate need for the funds." Rural forces responded by banning Gilliland from the senate floor. Once again, Wallace reentered the fray, hoping to
engineer a final solution as the session neared its end and he prepared to head
north for a college campus speaking tour.[38]

Knowing full well Wallace would blame them in the media and in their districts for refusing to pass his bill, some urban legislators collapsed under the
pressure and backed the administration. "In the interest of the highway program," Senator Aubrey Carr noted, "I decided that a little bit of a loaf was
better than no loaf." Since the administration was opposed to the filibuster-

ing senators, it ended the first term tradition of sending over late night meals for legislators. With one day left in the special session, Wallace, understanding the political environment he had spent the last three weeks creating, predicted the road bond bill and gas tax redistribution would be passed and signed by Lurleen before the day was over.[39]

In the end Wallace was right: the legislature passed the $160 million road bond bill, a new gas tax redistribution formula, and an increase in auto and truck tags. The increase in tag prices would prove to be tremendously unpopular. Working mother Carolyn Rayborn expressed the sentiments of many Alabamians: "I realize that Alabama needs good roads but if the costs of operating a vehicle keeps going up, I am going to be forced to sell my car and my husband's truck and buy a couple of bicycles and we won't need any four-lane highways for that, just a little ole path will do. With gasoline $.40 cents a gallon, insurance sky high and car tags $13.00 . . . we just can't afford to own or operate a vehicle." Even though the bill passed, it was not an easy process. The clocks in the senate chamber were stopped at 11:45 p.m.—fifteen minutes before the session was mandated by Alabama law to end—so that a compromise could be worked out over the next several hours. As Wallace predicted, many urban senators caved in to public pressure, and concessions, previously unacceptable to the urban bloc, came fast and furious at the end. The Jefferson County delegation accepted a deal for $6.4 million in annual gas tax proceeds and a commitment for $200 million in state and federal highway dollars over the next four years. The late-hour deal came at a physical price for some lawmakers. Senator Jimmy Branyon of Fayette County collapsed from exhaustion. Senator Ollie Nabors from Etowah County collapsed twice over the final three days. Roland Cooper, exhibiting the gamesmanship that was commonplace in the legislature, locked two urban colleagues out of the chamber.[40]

Wallace was the only person pleased with the new law. The farm-to-market road program was abolished, hurting rural areas where getting truck crops to market was already difficult enough. Urban legislators received more highways funds than at any time in state history but would have to wait several more years before the gas tax would be distributed entirely on a population basis. Even as Wallace promised Jefferson County $200 million, $53 million more than it had received during the first term, anxious folks in and around Birmingham were crossing their fingers that the administration would stand by its word. Less than two months after vowing to do all he could to get the interstate system in Jefferson County finished by 1971, Wallace was already backpedaling: "There are many engineering and other problems connected with a two hundred million dollar road program. For that reason, there might be some portion of the program not completed by 1971."[41]

As contentious as the pay raise, road bond, and gas tax redistribution were, the administration did manage to pass seven of its nine priority items in the special session: state employees received a 5 percent merit raise; mental health employees received a 5 percent raise; legislators provided $450,000 for mental health matching funds and $900,000 for regional mental health centers; a $4 million bond issue passed to improve the state docks; a statewide competitive bid law passed, ensuring a competitive process for all purchases by city and county school boards in excess of $500; legislation reduced the aviation gas tax in order to boost major carrier service in the state; and the $160 million road bond bill passed, providing the administration with a powerful patronage weapon. The only two items that did not pass were formal acceptance of daylight savings time—Rankin Fite tabled the matter, effectively putting Alabama on the new time system without formally passing a law—and a law requiring banks to pay interest on state deposits. This new legislature was independent, to be sure, but not yet organized or unified enough to defeat Wallace when he put the power of his wife's office on the line.[42]

Federal Battles

Lurleen's role during the special session was largely ceremonial. George handled legislative matters, although Lurleen was drawn into the fray on one matter: the ongoing fight between the administration and the federal government over compliance with HEW guidelines. This clash had been simmering since passage of the landmark 1964 Civil Rights Act. It boiled over after two pronouncements: HEW Secretary John Gardner's January warning that Alabama was in grave danger of losing welfare funds, and a three-judge panel's March order that the state take "affirmative action to disestablish all state enforced or encouraged public school segregation." Both matters were perfect campaign fodder for George—they combined issues of race, federal intervention, and white southern perceptions of morality—and both required the administration to make public policy to defend the state from the charges. This was the kind of public policy that intrigued Wallace because it led to media coverage, speaking tours, campaign events, Citizens' Council rallies, and votes from disaffected southerners.[43]

Predictably, initial administration responses came from George, though Lurleen, a product of white southern society herself, did not disagree with her husband's philosophies and seconded her husband's comments in public statements and speeches. Gardner had attempted to communicate his message as succinctly as possible. "In all this time," Gardner explained, "the Alabama welfare agency has made no perceptible movement towards compliance for any part of its welfare programs. . . . Only the Alabama agency, among the welfare agencies of all the states, has failed to file an adequate statement of compliance." In the wake of Gardner's report, Wallace, placing the blame on the messenger not on his administration, issued a statement blasting the federal government for depriving "the elderly and the poor little underprivileged children of the right to enjoy these benefits." It was a perfect issue for the former governor who could turn the tables and make the issue not compliance, but rather heartless Washington bureaucrats who would take food and medicine from impoverished Alabamians of all colors. "The public health service," Wallace blasted, "is not interested in the health of the public, but only in punishing the people of Alabama of every race—the senior citizens, the underprivileged children, and now the unfortunates who are mentally ill. It is just another instance of the federal government trying to take over and run everything."[44]

Losing federal funds for the Alabama Pensions and Security Department would have a devastating effect. More than 80 percent of state welfare funds came from the federal government, and the loss of funds would immediately reduce assistance payments to the elderly, poor, and infirm from seventy to fourteen dollars per month. Despite regular appeals for more money by Pensions and Securities Commissioner Ruben King, the administration never considered a substantial tax increase that would have put Alabama on par with its neighbors in caring for poor people. Though federal mandates required no more than sixty patients per case worker, Alabama social workers continued to handle twice that number. Because of the wholesale poverty in the state—Alabama ranked forty-eighth in per capita income—and the net outmigration of people below age thirty, the Heart of Dixie had a higher percentage of citizens who were eligible for benefits than other states. Welfare interest groups were so powerless that lawmakers seriously considered outlawing payments to children born out of wedlock. Despite the fact that many of her rivals were touting dramatically expanded monthly pensions, Lurleen received the endorsement of the Old Age Pension Association in the 1966 campaign. "In the Wallace administration," a campaign tract declared, "there has been no double-talk or cowardly action at any time or place on the important issues."[45]

Because contesting HEW guidelines was such a fertile issue for Wallace politically, the administration decided to resist compliance until the last possible moment. In fact, Wallace made a habit of telling reporters that no funds had ever been withheld from Alabama, and no matter the legal avenues considered, no money would be. The *Birmingham News* speculated that the administration might use King to "stand in the doorway" a la Tuscaloosa to force a physical confrontation. Behind the scenes, Wallace ordered new Attorney General MacDonald Gallion to forestall the inevitable as long as possible. Gallion filed a brief with the court alleging compliance would be detrimental for medical reasons. "Respondents allege," Gallion wrote, "that the placement of patients, in order to achieve balance of race, color, or national origin, without regard to social background, would not be sound medical procedure." The administration further suggested that noncompliance was not a matter of refusal to obey the law, but instead was a case of legal interpretation. Alabama, the administration argued, simply believed the application of the law had not yet been fully defined and that the state was within its rights to delay implementation until courts clarified the application of the law. Rhetorically, Alabama was arguing that *it was* complying, but HEW was refusing to allow the state to invoke its constitutional right to interpret the law and apply it as it saw fit.[46]

With Gallion spearheading legal efforts, Wallace focused on maximizing publicity. Several members of the state's congressional delegation offered supportive comments for Wallace's latest federal battle, and the governor was able to parlay these relationships into a late January appearance before a congressional committee investigating HEW's report. Mississippi governor Paul Johnson pledged his support for Alabama's resistance and indicated that James Eastland and John Stennis—the Magnolia State's senators—would join in the "just cause." Lurleen, enlisted in the first of several battles against the federals, made her own public statement. Citing her credentials as governor, mother, daughter, and granddaughter, Lurleen depicted HEW's decision as shortsighted and cruel: "It would tear my heart to see them [Alabamians] deprived of necessities because action is pending to determine the exact meaning of a disputed law and a controversial regulation. The aged and the children do not understand the technicalities of compliance with the Civil Rights Act of 1964. They would understand the pain of an empty stomach, the chill of an unheated stove, the darkness of an unlighted house, of the stark reality of eviction."[47]

Interestingly enough, administration opponents also attempted to use Lurleen's gender, but to reach a different conclusion about compliance. Southern Christian Leadership Conference vice president Ralph Abernathy wired Lurleen to ask her to rethink her position. "As the first woman governor in the history of Alabama," Abernathy wrote, "as a mother, and a member of a sex that has been denied equal rights, you are in a position to show leadership and compassion for all poor families in Alabama. I earnestly urge you to lead your state immediately into compliance with the law."[48]

Wallace's appearance before the Senate Finance Committee to argue the HEW case was a vintage exhibition of the former governor's charisma. When Tennessee senator Albert Gore Sr. opened his questions with the comment that the witness was "not one of my political heroes," Wallace leaped at the opportunity to disarm the entire committee: "Well, senator, I'm sorry about that, because you are one of my political heroes. If you'll remember, I voted for you for vice-president at the [1956] Democratic National Convention." The retort filled the chamber with laughter and made the rest of the testimony less confrontational and more conversational.[49]

In his comments before the committee, Wallace painted Alabama as the aggrieved party in an ongoing morality play where the federal government was continually grasping for more power: "Too much of our birthrights of freedom and liberty are sold for a bowl of porridge and sacrificed upon the altar of expediency." HEW, Wallace continued, was asking Alabama to go far beyond what the law required. By all accounts, the trip to Washington was successful from the administration's viewpoint. Wallace received favorable feedback from five of the six senators on the committee, and congratulatory telegrams and letters of support poured into the governor's office from across the country. More importantly, the state won an injunction preventing HEW from slashing funds until all legal avenues were exhausted. Wallace called Judge Clarence Allgood's decision a "victory for those who stood with using our fight for constitutional government and states' rights."[50]

If Gardner's report on noncompliance generated a flurry of administration activity, the three-judge panel's order to integrate ninety-nine school systems by the fall of 1967 created an absolute panic. In fact, the furor over the blanket desegregation order so enveloped Alabama that the state hardly paid attention when the Fifth Circuit Court of Appeals upheld HEW guidelines the administration had spent the past two months fighting. The integration mandate was the most sweeping demand for action in state history. Alabama was ordered to cease offering tuition grants for private schools, denying admission to junior college and trade schools on the basis of race, and maintaining segregation at any state college or university. On the local level, school systems were given twenty days to formulate desegregation plans for students and faculties. The court ordered state and local systems to develop methods for improving facilities of previously all-black schools to meet standards of previously all-white schools. Where previous orders had been purposefully vague to allow for gradual change, the March 1967 ruling offered less wiggle room, demanded specific action by Superintendent of Education Ernest Stone, and threatened swift intervention if Alabama paid only lip service to its ruling. George and Lurleen, who rarely attended Board of Education meetings, immediately called a closed-door session and canvassed legislative floor leaders to compile a list of options.[51]

For the past four years, the administration had been fomenting two incongruous education strategies. On the one hand, the administration trumpeted its progressive policies: a growing system of junior colleges with more than twelve thousand students, free bus transportation for all trade school and junior college students, free textbooks for all elementary and secondary students, creation of the University of South Alabama, numerous bond issues for school renovation and construction, and increased teacher salaries. The State Sovereignty Commission prepared its own report documenting the

Wallace administration's educational improvements. According to the report, Wallace was responsible for increasing the number of teachers by 16.5 percent, school expenditures by 73 percent, appropriations to education-related activities by 95 percent, and teacher salaries by 70 percent. On the other hand, the administration continued to forestall change by supporting the growing private school movement in every way possible, publicly and privately favoring segregated schools, making little effort to make dual school systems separate and equal, and even preventing Joe Reed, African American president of ASTA (Alabama State Teachers Association)—the all-black teachers union—from attending state Board of Education meetings. A January 1967 press release from the Alabama Department of Education called integration "a complete failure. The continued use of powerful Federal forces to force mass school integration will bring a repeat of the 'tragic era' of a hundred years ago and the children who need public schools most will suffer." The transparent dichotomy between these two goals, improving education and preserving segregation, reduced the effectiveness of the administration's howls of outrage over court orders.[52]

Even administration insiders had no comprehension of the inadequacy of the Alabama school system. Legal advisor Hugh Maddox expressed shock at learning that less than 50 percent of all students who entered grade one made it to grade twelve. Twenty-two percent of Alabama schools had four or fewer teachers in their buildings, despite responsibilities for pupils of all ages. In the years before mandatory school busing to achieve racial balance, more than half of all students rode buses to school each day. The average daily round-trip was forty-seven miles. Some local school systems, particularly those in the Black Belt, were notoriously inadequate and discriminatory. A 1967 study of the Wilcox County schools by the National Education Association painted a horrific picture of life in that area of the state. The annual per capita income in Wilcox County was $543 for blacks and whites combined; it was even lower, $350, for blacks. Less than 20 percent of all houses passed a minimum standard of sound construction and plumbing facilities. Less than 10 percent of African American families owned their own home, and some lived in dilapidated shacks where newspapers and rags served as caulking between weathered slats. Of the five physicians in the county, two were over eighty, and only two of the other three would take Negro patients. As a result, 77 percent of babies born in the county were delivered by midwives, a traditional practice to be sure, but one that had been largely replaced across the rest of the country in favor of trained physicians and sanitary hospitals.[53]

The hopeless environment of abject poverty and substandard medical treatment in Wilcox County was compounded by two separate, discriminatory, and inadequate school systems. Simply put, the improvements and programs of the Wallace administration had not seeped into the fabric of daily life in Wilcox, where 83 percent of the citizens were functionally illiterate. Black schools received $123 per student for instruction, $0.56 per student for maintenance, $10 per student for transportation, and $3 per student for new buildings. White schools received $192 per student for instruction, $18.07 per student for maintenance, $40 per student for transportation, and $18 per student for new buildings. Black students rode in buses that averaged 11.2 years of age; white students rode in buses that averaged 5.5 years of age. Some of the classrooms relied on wooden stoves for heat, and most of the Negro schools had no toilet or shower facilities. Enrollment studies of Wilcox County indicated class sizes of 64, 55, 83, 60, 53, and 60. The NEA study also concluded that in the first year of the free textbook program, "the present superintendent oversaw an operation that distributed two-thirds again as many textbooks to each white child as to each Negro child—textbooks that cost the county nothing."[54]

While Wilcox County's educational inadequacies were not the sole blame of the Wallace administration, they do offer an important context for the decision to fight school desegregation inch by inch, block by block, and county by county. If Alabama had been providing an adequate education for its citizens, the administration's castigation of integration as harmful to teachers and students might have been credible. If Alabama had been turning out students who were fully prepared to attend college or enter a high-skill, high-technology workforce, the administration's complaints that education was a state issue and the federal government was abrogating the Constitution might have been taken seriously. But in a world where a majority of students of both races were receiving an education that paled when compared to other states in the region, Wallace's hullabaloo about disrupting a school system that he designated "one of the best in the nation" had no impact on Washington and was not even credible to increasing numbers of informed Alabamians.

No matter the state of education in Alabama, the administration planned to blame the messenger, shift the focus to federal usurpation of power, and complain about the little man—in this case little boys and girls—being trampled. Within four days of receiving the court order, Wallace leaked to reporters his plan of defiance, essentially a combination of nineteenth century–style nullification and interposition. Lurleen, as the official governor of the state, would argue that the police power of the state was superior to the authority of the three-judge panel. She would then place all state school systems under her control, eliminating the traditional authority of local school boards. Legally, the state would argue that the federal government's order had violated state law, and was therefore null and void. The irony was palpable; as in Macon County in 1963, Wallace was seizing control of local government functions at the same time he was excoriating the federal government for seizing state power. In his testimony to the Senate Finance Committee on HEW guidelines, Wallace pledged to obey the law once all appeals had been exhausted. But on the matter of school integration, he was boldly suggesting complete and utter defiance of court orders. Speculation mounted that one of Wallace's goals was to get Lurleen arrested for contempt and create a martyr for the cause of states' rights. Foreshadowing a fight that was not as enthusiastically embraced by Alabamians as previous battles, Wallace asked for a resolution of support from state superintendents of education. He did not get it.[55]

The administration was not deterred by the superintendents. The initial torrent of letters to the governor's office supported continuing the fight. "Stand firm for our freedom," Mrs. A. Ben Conolly implored Lurleen; "according to God's word we are not to mix with other races." Pickens County superintendent of education Alan Burns apologized for the lack of support from his colleagues and urged the Wallaces to keep the faith. Robert and Nell Payne suggested an even more radical option: "Now is the time for action. Close all schools then wait and see. A million of us can't be wrong." Buoyed by this wave of affirmation, Wallace scheduled a meeting with the presidents of the state's colleges and universities to lobby for their support and announced that Lurleen would address the matter on statewide radio and televison.[56]

One week after the blanket desegregation order was announced, Lurleen Wallace strode to the podium in the capitol to give a speech that was pure Wallaceism. Sternly but with a cracking voice, Lurleen—introduced by Lieutenant Governor Albert Brewer as "her excellency Governor George Wallace"— repudiated judicial intrusion: "This order takes over every single aspect of the operation of every school system within the State of Alabama. It destroys the authority of local school boards, the state Board of Education, the superintendent of education, and the governor. It reduces the constitutionally elected officials of your state to mere agents of the district court who must execute the commands of three judges who would determine all matters of educational policy." Patiently and with tears welling in her eyes, Lurleen made the administration's case that integration would have disastrous effects on Alabamians. She identified threats to the "life and health and safety" of children who have to ride buses. She suggested that free speech and academic freedom were in jeopardy because "no person, including teachers and parents, is free to discuss the order of the court." True to her husband's comments before the speech, Lurleen asked the legislature to place total control of all education functions and processes in her hands. "I also ask you to issue," Lurleen added, "as an exercise of the police power of this state, a cease and desist order, to be delivered and served upon the three federal judges who have issued this unfounded decree, advising them that their actions are beyond the police power of the State of Alabama."[57]

As was their custom, the governor's speechwriters added a section where Lurleen spoke from the heart through the lens of motherhood: "As a mother, my heart is filled with compassion for all the children of our State. As a mother, I understand as do the other mothers of this state what they are attempting to do. . . . I have no power of action as a mother, but as Governor I have not only the power, but the duty. I will do my duty." Gaining momentum, Lurleen finished her speech with a flourish: "I am serving notice that whatever power I possess under the Constitution of Alabama as Governor of Alabama shall be used to prevent the destruction of our public school system and they better understand what the people of Alabama mean. . . . We shall never quit and we shall win for we do, indeed, dare defend our rights."[58]

The speech elicited a raucous response typified by at least twenty thundering ovations. The response from legislators was overwhelmingly positive. "It was the greatest speech I have heard in eight years of service in the legislature," Senator Alton Turner gushed. Representative Phil Smith announced the legislature was "ready to do whatever she wants." Even Jefferson County lawmaker Hugh Morrow, a frequent critic of the Wallace administration, was on board. "Governor Wallace is advocating the exhausting of all legal remedies," Morrow declared, "which is as it should be. Then we will see where we will have to go." In fact, not one legislator—in the midst of a growing movement toward legislative independence—went on record as opposing Lurleen's plan. As always, Wallace kept his eyes on the national prize. When asked by a legislator if he would move to secede from the Union over the issue, Wallace laughed and noted, "Oh, we couldn't do that. Then I couldn't run for president." After Mississippi governor Paul Johnson and his predecessor Ross Barnett offered hearty congratulations for standing up to the social engineers and bureaucrats in Washington, the administration cobbled together a plan for a regional conference with other southern politicians.[59]

Within the state, the first wave of response to the speech was positive. As with similar federal battles during Wallace's first term, the correspondents often couched their support in religious terms as if the Wallaces were waging a holy war against amoral and immoral charlatans. "We thank God for you both," Mrs. J. W. Battle wrote, "and for your courageous and dedicated stand against the enemy that indicates a power from on high inspires and directs you." The Reverend Albert Branscomb identified a subsequent wave of federal policy that was looming in the shadows of the integration order: "I have yet to hear anyone express objection to the stand you have taken relative to the school situation in Alabama. . . . Mixed marriage will be the next thing on the agenda of the federal government and the Supreme Court." The Reverend C. H. Clark was aghast that the ruling would require white kids to ride buses with colored kids. "This," Clark concluded, "is depriving us [of] the right of a freedom of choice."[60]

Even if some in the administration approached the order to desegregate strictly as a legal and constitutional issue, many patently racist groups saw the Wallaces as standing up for their beliefs. *Thunderbolt,* the official publication of the National States' Rights Party, pointed out that the secretary of HEW Harold Howe removed his son from a 47 percent black school and enrolled him in the exclusive Taft private school in Waterford, Connecticut. At Taft, only 2 percent of the students were black and the annual tuition was nearly twice the per capita income of the average Alabamian. Americans for the Preservation of the White Race also expressed support for administration defiance. Wallace was certainly a segregationist and a demagogic opportunist, but never a venomous racist along the lines of the rank-and-file members of hate groups such as the Ku Klux Klan. Nevertheless, it is unquestionably clear that groups like the Klan and the National States Rights Party felt emboldened by the administration in a time when rhetoric often led to unfortunate action. Alabama Klan imperial wizard Robert Shelton, a familiar sight in and around the capitol, praised Wallace and announced that his organization stood with the former governor because of "his principles and beliefs, his decency, morality, and integrity." A Rhode Islander wrote Wallace in hopes that he could pass a personal message along to Shelton. Another correspondent asked Wallace to provide an address for Shelton so he could communicate directly. Upset by the possible national political ramifications of this association, Bill Jones instructed a state trooper to seize an ABC camera operator's film showing Wallace and Shelton shaking hands. Klansmen at national meetings could be seen sporting "Wallace for President" buttons and lapel pins. One woman wrote Wallace asking him to put her in touch with the local chapter of the Klan in Franklin County. She had been advised by the Franklin County Sheriff's office that this was the most direct route of contacting that organization.[61]

Perhaps as important as Wallace's words and deeds is the perception of his sympathies by the ultraright fringe. Members of Klavern 59 of the United Klans of America wrote Lurleen to congratulate her for her stand against federal civil rights guidelines: "May we assure you that we are ready at your command to support you in your laudable effort to exercise your constitutional right to maintain a state school system which is reserved to the respectful states." Byron de la Beckwith, later convicted of murdering Medgar Evers, wrote Wallace to seek financial support for his Mississippi lieutenant governor campaign. "I have personally sold over 2500 Wallace tags myself," de la Beckwith bragged, while disparaging legal efforts to try him for Evers's death. "As you realize," de la Beckwith coldly noted, "it will take me a good while yet to get over the social and financial 'cost' of residing in the 'Bastille' for ten months—awaiting a 'speedy trial' as the accused slayer of Mississippis [*sic*] field Sec of the NAACP—a nigger named Medgar Evers—we haven't had any trouble with that nigger since they buried him." Huntsville resident Beth Ransdell wrote Wallace to chastise him for characterizing NAACP leader Roy Wilkins as a moderate in comparison to Stokely Carmichael: "What I am trying to say is that your platform seems so ideal that people may look for a flaw, and your endorsement of Roy Wilkins might just furnish that flaw to plant a little doubt or distrust and give the feeling that you'll 'say' one platform and support another." Letter writers asking for the governor's feelings on the Klan were either ignored or told to contact "Justice Hugo Black of the Supreme Court of the United States who is avowed to have been a former member of the Klan."[62]

In the days after Lurleen's speech, the administration moved to turn rhetoric into action. Wallace dispatched Hugh Maddox to investigate the terms under which Alaska entered the Union, hoping rumors of a special arrangement to prevent federal control of education in that state could be used as justification for Alabama's truculence. The house, on the recommendation of the Wallaces, passed a resolution turning the legislature into a committee of the whole—a joint session designed to function as a public hearing—chaired by Albert Brewer. As a litany of witnesses addressed the legislature, it was clear the power of the administration limited dissent. The majority of the witnesses suggested the state should not comply with the court order and should neglect deadlines that called for immediate action. Troy State president Ralph Adams, Wallace's close friend, predicted the court order "would completely disrupt our institution and cause chaos, and it is possible we would have to close down the institution." Others noted the likelihood of violence and speculated Alabama could not find a pool of black educators to fill teaching positions as required by the court. In an untypically bombastic outburst, Albert Brewer denounced the court order: "Our people are not going to sit still when someone comes into their homes and tells them, 'your child has got to be sent over yonder to school.' There are going to be riots, stabbings, and knifings in every public school system in this state."[63]

All the while, Lurleen was kept in the public spotlight to pound home the administration's talking points. Defiance, Lurleen reasoned, was not illegal; it was a duty: "It has been recognized from the beginning of our nation that the people have a right and a duty to resist tyranny. Any usurpation by local, state, or federal government must be resisted by the people. It does not matter the source or the method of usurpation." At her personal appearances, Lurleen did not take reporters' questions or elaborate on the specifics of her interposition and nullification plan.[64]

Concurrent to the testimony in the legislature and Lurleen's public remarks was the publication of the University of Alabama's *Emphasis 1967,* an annual journal financed by student fees, which presented varying viewpoints on controversial issues. As part of the journal's point-counterpoint theme, a series of speakers was invited to come to Tuscaloosa and explain their ideas. The university's decision to include articles written by Black Panther Stokely Carmichael and Communist ideologue Bettina Aptheker created a firestorm of protest in the legislature. Representative Ralph Slate lashed out at the university's administration, noting *Emphasis* contained contributions of people "who want to turn the University of Alabama over to students who want to run things like they do in Berkeley, California." Other legislators quickly followed suit. Two responses were almost immediate: a proposed law banning certain speakers from the state, and a public airing of a previously private fight between the administration and university president Frank Rose.[65]

Wallace had never fully trusted Rose; the administration viewed the affable educator as a maverick who did not embrace Wallace's political philosophies. When Rose refused to denounce the March 1967 court order requiring the desegregation of state schools, Wallace and Brewer both scolded him. In the aftermath of the *Emphasis 1967* controversy, the administration and its supporters turned up the heat. Senator Alton Turner announced that Rose had "served his usefulness" and should offer his resignation. Another legislator suggested he would be reluctant to fund the university at existing levels unless he had a detailed accounting of how the money would be spent. Though he did not share the philosophy of either Carmichael or Aptheker, Rose defended their right to their opinion and the university's right to free discourse and academic freedom: "The right to seek knowledge and to decide for one's self is indispensable to American democracy." Ironically, Wallace, strongly in favor of a ban on certain "un-American" speakers in Alabama, had himself been a victim of colleges and universities across the country that were unwilling to offer him a podium and a microphone.[66]

Wallace's disgust at Rose's refusal to knuckle under was the latest in an ongoing conflict between the two. Wallace preferred to use state funding to expand his system of trade schools and junior colleges; Rose wanted more money for the university to make it an institution of national standing. Ralph Adams, practicing a little censorship of his own, refused to allow an editorial in the Troy State student paper that supported both Rose and the principle of academic freedom. Gary Dickey's supportive piece, "Lament for Dr. Rose," was not printed, but a blank space was left in the *Tropolitan* headlined with the banner "censored." Dickey was later expelled from school and had to enlist an attorney, Morris Dees who later founded the Southern Poverty Law Center, to regain his standing. Some professors who sided with Dickey found their contract renewals delayed and later said Adams required them to provide a personal pledge of loyalty. Not coincidently, the administration in 1967 awarded university status to Troy State and Lurleen received an honorary doctorate.[67]

The support Rose received from all quarters of Alabama surprised the administration. Some sixteen hundred students at the university signed a petition backing Rose's stance on academic freedom. Rose received hundreds of letters, telegrams, and phone calls from supportive alumni and friends. University of Alabama at Birmingham scholar Al Siegal, president of that institution's chapter of the American Association of University Professors, rebuked the administration's plan to place sole authority for education functions in the governor's hands: "Centralized control of the public schools as requested by the governor would subvert the educational process, impede its growth, strangle academic freedom, and demoralize teachers and students." Political opponents took notice and tried to defuse the situation. The house failed to pass a resolution authorizing the creation of a committee to investigate subversive activities on university campuses. Influential Mobile representative Bob Eddington backed Rose: "I feel universities should be free from political control; the first group of victims in any totalitarian state is the universities." Senator George Lewis Bailes announced he would fight any attempt to slash funding at the Capstone. Attendance at the Committee of the Whole was so surprisingly low that roll calls were not even recorded. Brewer, stung by public criticism when press reports identified him as critical of Rose's independence, told reporters the entire rift between Wallace and Rose was overblown. "These two outstanding men," Brewer reminded the press, "have worked together for five years to enhance greatly public education in Alabama." The much ballyhooed speaker ban bill died quietly in the legislature.[68]

The administration had expected an unconditional endorsement of defiance from Alabamians and politicians across the Deep South. Surprisingly, only three of the nine southern governors that were invited to the massive resistance conference attended. And two of the attendees—Georgia governor Lester Maddox and Louisiana governor John McKeithen—offered less than lukewarm support for interposition and nullification. "We expect to obey the law over in Louisiana," McKeithen advised, "to the best of our ability. . . . This does not mean we will adopt the Alabama position; the governor of Louisiana doesn't plan to stand in the schoolhouse door." Florida governor Claude Kirk, who declined the invitation to attend, cautioned the Wallaces against the plan they were fomenting: "The spirit of sectionalism on this subject is divisive and unwise. We who are pursuing a war on crime in Florida cannot join attempts to subvert or delay the law of the land as interpreted by the Supreme Court."[69]

On the Alabama front, school superintendents were scrambling to comply with the court's order to develop desegregation plans by April 11. Despite the short deadline, only two of the ninety-nine systems enjoined by the order, Bibb and Walker, failed to prepare their plans on time. And neither was considering noncompliance. Walker County was only a few days late with its plan, and Bibb County was delayed by an unexpected surgical procedure that sidetracked its superintendent. While the state's superintendents were reluctant to speak out against the administration's nullification plan—one noted he lived in "Wallace Country"—it was becoming increasingly clear that they preferred to travel the road of keeping schools open and on task. The Alabama Education Association issued a statement critical of administration goals. All the while, the three-judge panel observed the administration's response. After refusing to grant a stay of the order, the panel commented on the administration's rhetoric. Citing factual errors in Lurleen's speech, the panel issued a statement—prompted by legal work by civil rights attorney Fred Gray—that denied many of the administration's predictions of gloom and doom for students and teachers.[70]

Alabama's major daily newspapers, best exemplified by the *Birmingham News*, were sharply critical of the administration's plans. Wallace, the *News* editorialized, was using Alabama school kids as "pawns in a power struggle . . . a confrontation involving the presidential ambitions of George C. Wallace." An ad in the *Mobile Register* took the case against the administration farther: "Though not surprised, we are nonetheless heartsick that once again our state run administration has led us down the dead-end path of resistance. Racism has crucified this state for many years. Racism and the thirst for power now paint a dim picture of our future in Alabama. . . . In the name of protecting our children, we are all being misled." In the wake of criticism from the education community, the three-judge panel, and the media, Wallace began to backpedal. "Nobody," Wallace clarified, "said anything about defiance in the sense of resisting unlawfully." Lurleen's speech at Governor's Day in Tuscaloosa contained a lengthy section supporting the principles of academic freedom and dissent.[71]

As the administration backed off, school systems moved ahead in preparation for the start of a new school year. By late April, plans for ninety-three of the ninety-nine school systems had been formally approved. In early May, many of the systems began sending letters to parents explaining the freedom of choice plan and collecting preference forms. Theoretically, any student in the ninth grade or higher had the right to make his or her own selection, while elementary and junior high school pupils were subject to parental choice. In reality, parents wary of the changing social and political climate were unwilling to make dramatic changes with their kids until others had proven the road not previously taken to be safe. Clarke County, hoping to avoid a steady stream of fluctuating decisions, cautioned parents that "a choice once made cannot be changed except for serious hardship." Four weeks after the freedom of choice letters went out, the three-judge panel quietly revealed that it had approved the plan for desegregating faculties submitted by Ernest Stone, the Alabama superintendent of education.[72]

Education Policy

As the administration regrouped and planned to revisit the desegregation matter in the fall, other education issues came to the fore. The governor was required to submit a biennial education budget to each regular session of the legislature. Predictably, the Alabama Education Association asked for an increase: $375.5 million, over $100 million more than the 1966–67 budget. Doubtless, the additional funding was needed. Most schools in the state continued to have too many students and not enough teachers. Auburn University faculty ranked in the bottom 20 percent of all land-grant schools in salary. The free textbook system continued to lag as the administration publicly blamed local school officials for failing to order enough books, and principals and textbook consultants cited a lack of state funds to purchase the needed allotments. Privately, the administration knew the program was strapped financially. "Let's not forget about handling the textbook matter," Hugh Maddox confided to State Budget Director Jake Jordan; "and furthermore I need to talk to you about the size of the appropriation for the textbooks. They keep telling me in education that there is not enough money in the budget for all of the books we are going to need."[73]

Despite these pressing needs and the administration's trumpeting of massive industrial expansion, Lurleen's education budget called for a 3.6 percent *cut* in funding. Every other southern state that had passed a new education budget had increased revenue between 6.4 and 69 percent. Conspicuously not included in Lurleen's budget was the traditional appropriation for Tuskegee Institute, even though predominantly white private schools such as Marion Institute and Lyman Ward Academy were slated to received state funds. The administration's stated reason for the budget cuts was a declining rate of tax returns. But in fact, tax proceeds were improving, not declining. Sales tax collections had increased 4.06 percent over the previous year when the administration released its budget. Other revenue streams were growing as well. Income tax revenue was up 12.15 percent; the use tax had increased 3.17 percent; and the lodgings tax was up 8.59 percent. The miserly budget was simply another way for the administration to whipsaw school systems into following its line on federal compliance issues. A revised administration plan called for a slight increase over the preceding budget with the extra funding lumped into a conditional appropriation. This designation would allow Lurleen to control the extra funds and, based upon her determination that the revenue was available, dole them out at her discretion.[74]

Finding themselves under an administration assault that would cut their funding and cripple their authority, state education leaders lashed back. Harry Philpott rallied Auburn's board of trustees to ask the governor to reconsider: "Alabama has a great decision to make. We have to decide whether we are going to keep the momentum going or whether we are going backwards." Frank Rose, aghast at the administration's allocation of only 68 percent of his budget request, was similarly incensed: "We can't make faculty salary increases, get additional faculty members, cannot move forward with the planned development of the Huntsville campus or Birmingham Medical Center or the development of the college of general studies." Rose and Philpott, usually rivals for funding and esteem in a university cold war that dated to the nineteenth century, banded together to ask for more funding, new sources of revenue, firm rather than conditional appropriations, and a ban on new tax exemptions. AEA president Alton Crews called for a legislative committee to hold a public hearing on education funding. Crews announced plans for a series of fourteen regional meetings, sponsored by AEA and designed to boost public attitudes about education spending.[75]

The entire regular session of the legislature degenerated into hand-wringing, delaying tactics, and inactivity. Lurleen left midsession for a four-hour surgical procedure at M. D. Anderson Hospital in Houston. Concerned about his wife's recurrent poor health and more focused on the looming presidential run than managing the legislature, Wallace did little to intercede in what reporter Dan Dowe called the "most monumental" logjam in legislative history. Wallace seemed oblivious to a budget authored by Pete Turnham, based on more liberal revenue projections calculated by University of Alabama economists. Turnham's budget began to pick up steam in both houses. As the session dragged into August, the administration perked up and found a priority. With court-ordered desegregation less than a month from becoming reality in classrooms across the state, Lurleen began backing a bill to allow parents to pick the race of their children's teachers. The contentious legislature had yet to pass an education budget or general fund budget, settle the embarrassing matter of quickie divorces, contend with the increasing hazardous pollution that made Birmingham and Mobile difficult places to breathe, or resolve a bitter fight over ad valorem taxes. With a daunting 159-page senate calendar to be addressed, Lurleen sent word that the teacher choice bill "transcends any other matter which you may be presently considering and requires your immediate attention." The bill, which gave the governor power to withhold funds from local schools boards that did not abide by its provisions, passed easily.[76]

Lurleen actually had no interest in this issue. By signing the teacher choice bill into law, she revealed what most had suspected all along: for all intents and purposes George Wallace was governor. "I am signing into law," Lurleen noted in a press release, "a bill which will allow every parent of schoolchildren in Alabama to make a choice of the race of the teacher they prefer. This is one of the most meaningful pieces of legislation ever passed by the Alabama legislature. Under this legislation, the local boards of education again have the right to determine the placement and assignment of teachers within their system." Over the course of 1967, the administration had been confronted with the reality of a new social order. To be sure, the blanket desegregation order came about because of past administration intransigence. The court, citing Wallace's efforts at constructing a state-supported private school system and a "wide range of activities to maintain segregated public education," left no doubt about the administration's actions. At every opportunity over the past five years, Wallace, first through his own actions and then over the signature of his wife, chose to fight instead of switch. The resulting negative impact on the social, cultural, and educational fabric of the state cannot be measured.[77]

Teacher choice necessitated immediate action by school boards because the new academic year was only days away. The Anniston board mailed a simple form asking parents and guardians to check a box indicating white or Negro preference and identifying the race of the student. The Birmingham system's packet was more detailed. "The Governor of Alabama," the form read, "has requested that we invite you as a parent to indicate the race of the teacher which you would prefer to have for your child. This is only an invitation to you and is to be considered as a poll or indication of your choice and not meant to construe that a choice is being offered since the recently passed law has been challenged in court." The Birmingham form provided the same basic check boxes as Anniston's but left ample room for comments. Nanette Burbage's guardian indicated that she was attending private school because the "Negro's [sic] took over [the] previous all white school." Mr. and Mrs. Bowman requested a white teacher for their daughter Margaret "because we got Negro teachers."[78]

Given the environment in Alabama, the results of the more than three hundred thousand forms that came back to the administration were predictable. "The results of the poll taken in many areas of the state," Hugh Maddox wrote to Alabamian W. T. Carey, "indicate that only one-twentieth of one percent of the students in predominately white schools" desired a black teacher. The administration received a plethora of supportive correspondence. Emblematic of most of the writers, Mrs. Ralph Kirkland hoped Lurleen would enforce the teacher choice law so that her children would not have to ride the bus with black children or learn music and reading from black teachers. In response to legal challenges, the administration dispatched telegrams over Lurleen's signature to the Alabama Congress of Parents and Teachers, Alabama Principals

Association, Alabama State Bar, and AEA asking for legal and emotional support.[79]

Surprisingly, a number of Alabamians were tired of the constant stream of battles over school desegregation and simply wanted their children and their schools left alone. "I am the mother of four," Mrs. Maymie Brennan wrote, "and a true segregationist, southerner, and Alabamian but I do not feel that we can gain anything by continuing to talk about this situation. I feel that we will be bringing Washington right down on us if we do not shut up and it seems to me that since school has opened and without incident we should consider ourselves fortunate for the present time and do the best we can to educate our children with the facilities we have." Perhaps the most telling comment from Brennan's letter to the governor was her realization that the days of blind resistance were over: "civil rights appears to be with us to stay. We have not gained anything in the past, as you will recall, by saying what we would not do and in my heart I do not feel we can do anything but hurt our children at this time."[80]

Other Alabamians were just as passionate as Brennan in their disavowal of teacher choice. "I cannot understand," Mrs. Steve Holliday wrote, "how intelligent, educated, and civilized adults can pass a law like the teacher choice law that has recently been approved. A teacher should teach if, and only if, he or she has the knowledge and training to be of value to the students. . . . With the shortage of qualified teachers and generally low-caliber of Alabama schools, you cannot afford to be choosey as to color." Laurence Gunnison rejected the whole notion of color as a societal determinant of worth: "My wife and I have made every effort to instruct our children that the color of an individual's face has no bearing on his fitness to teach school or do anything else."[81]

Protocols

As with the myriad of bills designed to allow the state to pay tuition for white students to attend segregated academies, the teacher choice bill, a single puff of wind lost in the swirling tides of change, was ruled unconstitutional. Tuskegee eventually received funding, though the Wallaces were able to wrangle a plan to make the funding conditional. But even then, faced with public pressure over the school that had received state monies since 1881, they relented and released the appropriation. On the whole, the regular session provided little assistance for education. In the midst of a thriving national economy, Alabama had made some improvements. But those changes in education, industrial development, and road construction that looked so significant when compared to previous Alabama efforts, usually paled when lined up against neighboring southeastern states. The 1969 legislature, the next scheduled meeting in Alabama's biennial system, would have serious issues in education, air pollution, and property tax reform to consider in order to prevent additional federal court orders directing Alabama to solve its problems.[82]

Even though the administration conducted state business based on a strategy of perpetual campaigning, it was cautioned about the accompanying detrimental effects. In a Finance Department study, S. Douglas Smith identified a paucity of comprehensive planning and outlined the case for making government more thoughtful and systematic: "The governor must control planning or planning will control the governor. ... Immediate steps are needed to prevent a deteriorated situation from becoming worse." In an environment where the federal government was making funds available for any number of projects, Alabama was slow to make choices, identify long-term goals, and take advantage of federal funds. Increasingly, the federal government required comprehensive planning as an accountability tool for making sure states were spending federal dollars wisely and ethically. "Since comprehensive planning requires the making of choices today," Smith continued, "it will necessarily diminish the governor's choice of how funds will be spent unless the governor's office is in on the creation of these comprehensive functional plans which must be produced by the state departments." The administration did not heed Smith's warning.[83]

The administration did welcome some federal economic opportunity grants, including Head Start programs for Huntsville, Little River, Tuscumbia, and Lowndes County. Yet other programs were targeted for extinction. Lurleen followed her husband's lead in opposing funding for the primarily black South West Alabama Farmer's Cooperative Association (SWAFCA), even though the organization would eventually add a few white members. SWAFCA was plagued by managerial inefficiency and the inability of some members to fully grasp the mission of a cooperative, but it did assist poor black farmers with marketing their vegetables, and it eventually adopted a plan to produce gasohol. For the Wallaces, Selma mayor Joe Smitherman, and a host of probate judges throughout the Black Belt, SWAFCA was a Black Panther front sopping at the federal trough. "You fund this," Smitherman predicted, "and you open the gate for every Negro extremist group in the nation to break down the doors of Washington, bypassing local community action committees as well as the duly elected officials." Despite the vocal objections of Senator Lister Hill and Congressman Armistead Selden, and Lurleen's fourteen-point veto, Office of Economic Opportunity director Sargent Shriver approved SWAFCA's request for additional funding.[84]

On most nonceremonial matters during Lurleen's term, George Wallace was the day-to-day governor. He continued to formulate administration policy, work the legislature, and make patronage decisions. All 16,312 honorary colonels appointed by George were reappointed by Lurleen. During lunch in the state cafeteria, Wallace inadvertently revealed the real dynamics of power in Montgomery. "Lurleen," the former governor told his successor, "I want you to meet Frank Spain. Mr. Spain has just been appointed chairman of your newest committee." Seymore Trammell and Gerald Wallace lost some functional political power, primarily because Lurleen did not like or trust Trammell and was wary of her brother-in-law. Nevertheless, the second Wallace administration did not function much differently from the first. The number of state employees grew 38 percent from 1963 to 1967. The state payroll increased 68 percent in the same term.[85]

Two matters that Lurleen personally shepherded from idea to bill to law were the funding and construction of new mental health facilities and a large increase in state parks. After visiting Kentucky's modern parks on a governor's conference tour, Lurleen pushed for Alabama to revitalize its system. Her support led to a $43 million bond issue. As a result of Lurleen's influence and passion, the state passed a $15 million general obligation bond for constructing regional mental health facilities in Decatur, Mobile, Birmingham, and Wetumpka, building a new school for mentally retarded children, and renovating dilapidated facilities in Tuscaloosa. Because the bonds were of the general obligation variety, they required a state referendum in December authorizing their sale. Amendment one, with Lurleen's promotion, passed easily. The bonds were financed through a two-cent cigarette tax, which for any other governor might have been difficult to enact. Lurleen's actions went beyond simply advocating additional funding. To increase awareness of the situation, she narrated a film made in Alabama about mental health. Administration insiders understood the importance of the issue to the governor and the fact that her involvement was grounded in compassion, not political lip service. "As you know," Hugh Maddox wrote to an inquiring minister, "the governor's number one priority has been mental health and public health." The Medical Association of Alabama presented her with its highest honor, the William Crawford Gorgas Award. When the Montgomery County Association for Mental Health noted Lurleen had accomplished "more for the mentally ill than any governor before her in all their full terms," its commendation reflected the severity of mental health conditions, the paucity of interest by previous governors, and the authenticity of Lurleen Wallace.[86]

Lurleen never lost the memory of her trip to Bryce and Partlow. "That night," she told a meeting of the state medical association, "I got down on my knees and thanked the Lord that my four children were healthy, physically and mentally. I also made a vow that whatever I could do I would do to improve the lot of the mentally ill." Perhaps anticipating her own death, Lurleen spoke of what has to be her undeniable legacy: "When historians of the future write of the Lurleen Wallace administration, I personally can think of no tribute more pleasing to me [than] for them to say my administration was concerned about the health needs of the people." Unfortunately, Lurleen's vision was too little, too late, and a federal court order was required in 1971 to force her husband and the state to begin systematically treating its mentally ill in a humane environment of rehabilitation and care.[87]

End of Days

Wracked by cancer, Lurleen Wallace did not live to finish her term. From midsummer 1967 until she found final rest in May 1968, Lurleen battled near constant pain, drawing strength from her position, her husband and children, a cadre of close friends, and the best wishes of Alabamians. The January 1966 operation to remove a tumor had not eliminated her cancer, and by June 1967 it was clear she would require another procedure. The new tumor, roughly the size of a lemon, was also in the abdominal area and was causing pressure on the governor's colon and digestive tract. After announcing to the state that her cancer had returned, Lurleen spent the rest of the day presiding over a clemency hearing, greeting tourists at the capitol, and presenting a winner's trophy at the Montgomery Speedway. But even as cancer was wresting control of her body and shortening her days, Lurleen grew stronger as a governor, gaining ease and confidence with every speech and handshake. Since becoming governor, Lurleen had kept a poem on her desk. The four-stanza lyric was short and to the point. "A woman may be small of frame with tiny feet that patter; But when she puts her small foot down, her shoe size doesn't matter." Having known how to put her foot down with the children, Lurleen learned how and when she could put it down at the office. She was, as reporter Ted Pearson concluded, a working governor even if the nexus of power remained in her husband's hands.[88]

Though her doctors categorically denied that work had any connection to the recurrence of cancer, Lurleen's schedule, coupled with George's extensive travel and contentious dealings with a suddenly independent legislature, certainly increased her exhaustion and aggravated her symptoms. In an era when cancer care was still being refined, M. D. Anderson was in the vanguard of new therapies and was arguably the best place in the world to obtain treatment. Withal, in 1968 cancer was a horrific disease that was more likely to run rampant through a patient than be eradicated through aggressive treatment. Anderson doctors cured—a designation signifying five years without a recurrence—only 37 percent of their patients with localized malignancies. With the tumor removed, Lurleen convalesced in Gulf Shores, her unofficial home away from home, knowing she would have to return to Houston in a few weeks for cobalt treatments. Even while resting, Lurleen made her presence known in Montgomery, requesting that legislation be passed requiring Alabama and Confederate flags to be flown and "Dixie," "Alabama," and "The Star Spangled Banner" to be played at all football games in the state.[89]

While in Houston, Lurleen was inundated with flowers and well-wishers, including Texas governor John Connally and his wife, Nellie. During cobalt and radiation treatments she stayed in an apartment across the street from Anderson. Whenever possible, she kept her spirits up by knitting and by needling her husband that for once she was getting all the attention, not him. The cobalt treatments, delivered by a machine known as Eldorado 8 on loan from the Canadian Atomic Energy Commission, were painless and noninvasive, but soon left the governor nauseated and suffering from stomach cramps. Even so, Lurleen made friends with five-year-old Philip Bauer, an Alabamian also at Anderson for cancer treatment, and kept tabs on his progress. By the last week of the four-week regimen, Lurleen spent most of her time in bed and was unable to keep food down. When Catherine Steineker, against Lurleen's wishes, notified the doctors of her friend's massive discomfort and weakness, the doctors discontinued the treatments and admitted her for constant supervision. The break in cobalt treatments was little more than a reprieve; Lurleen still had to complete the full regimen, which meant she would travel back and forth to Houston until Halloween. Showing her resolve, Lurleen continued to speak out when possible in favor of the teacher choice bill.[90]

In the wake of pain and suffering, Lurleen continued to find solace in coffee and Benson and Hedges cigarettes, doing all she could to continue living her life as she pleased. "Things haven't really changed much," she told reporters, "since I became governor. I didn't give up much when I took this job." She noted that she continued to greet Peggy's suitors, clean the mansion, and spank the children when necessary. Rather than take another plane ride, she opted to return to Montgomery in November by car, seeing parts of the country she had never visited. But the brave front lapsed along with her strength into periodic bouts of reflection and questioning of close friends who had lost loved ones to cancer. "Nita," she asked confidant Juanita Halstead, "your brother died of cancer, didn't he?" Anderson oncologist R. Lee Clark was upbeat: "I still say we've got a 50–50 chance of winning this thing with Governor Wallace."[91]

As Thanksgiving approached, the administration kept an optimistic tone about her health. Though she was still working out of the mansion while recuperating, Lurleen announced she would soon return to a partial schedule and hoped to attend the Iron Bowl, the annual gridiron epic between Auburn and Alabama. With Lurleen's strength sapped and her husband campaigning for president, official business slowed to a crawl or got pushed to Hugh Maddox, whom reporter Hugh Sparrow called "the acting governor." Vacancies on state boards and committees remained unfilled, correspondence went unanswered, and the governor's office—a hub of bustling activity over the previous five years—was eerily quiet and empty. Even so, Lurleen announced she would fly to California to support her husband's ballot drive and make a few public appearances. Back in Alabama, Lurleen kept up appearances by attacking the U.S. Supreme Court's affirmation of the *Lee v. Macon* desegregation ruling as a master plan of "the enemies of our constitution." Calling the ruling unfortunate, Lurleen grieved for the state's loss of the right to operate its own school system. Though her remarks were made at what was billed as a press conference, aides refused to allow reporters to ask questions.[92]

Facing some public pressure about state business, the administration appointed thirteen members to an education commission developed by Albert Brewer, though it is unclear if Lurleen had any involvement in the decision-making process. What is clear is that no blacks were named to the commission. Joe Reed, executive secretary of ASTA, decried the selections as continuing the "perpetuation of racism and bigotry in the State of Alabama." "We feel," Reed said of his organization's official position, "that any commission set up to study public education or any other public matter that excludes Negroes is illegally constituted." Though Lurleen announced the appointments in front of reporters, aides again refused to allow reporters to ask questions. Unaware of the full gravity of Lurleen's battle against cancer, some legislators spoke critically of her and the administration. "Lurleen said this [teacher choice] would be the most important product of the legislature, but it only lasted long enough to make it to court. The whole thing was just to stir up animosity and get the Wallaces publicity. Wallace himself is still governor whether he is still in California or wherever he happens to be at the moment." Others expressed dissatisfaction with the number of state employees traveling at state expense and earning state salaries while working on Wallace's presidential campaign.[93]

Just before New Year's, Lurleen returned to Houston for what was posited as a routine checkup but was actually a round of tests to determine why the governor's pain had reached excruciating levels in her spine and hip. "I just don't know why it keeps hurting so bad if it's cured," she confided to Juanita Halstead as she prepared to celebrate Christmas for the last time. The first round of tests were inconclusive, but a subsequent battery revealed an inoperable pecan-shaped nodule in her pelvic area. Joe Perry, one of Lurleen's Montgomery physicians, downplayed the severity: "The governor's condition suggests a small area of recurrence. It is reasonable that this recurrence will subside with further treatment." Lurleen was also publicly upbeat: "I'm not that sick anyway. In fact I plan to go with George on some of his trips." Two days later she made her last public appearance at a Wallace rally in Texas.[94]

The next round of treatments was more difficult and added to the considerable mental strain the governor was under. Her weight loss was more noticeable now, and her face revealed the toll that pain and restlessness had taken. "Oh, Catherine," she confided to Steineker in a rare moment of self-pity, "I don't want to die." Lurleen would lie flat on a table under a betatron machine that roared like a freight train for five minutes. Though George, a circle of friends, and a constant stream of encouraging cards and letters were nearby, the strain began to mount. Fearful of a potential drug addiction, Lurleen resisted pain medication until she could not bear it. When the veins in her arms no longer tolerated intravenous needles, insertions were made in her neck, a sight that brought George to immediate tears. Even in this condition, Lurleen Wallace continued to think of others. "Would you do me a favor," she asked Press Secretary Ed Ewing. "Would you tell [bodyguard] Larry Wright how much I appreciate him being over there every night. I never get to see him, but it's such a comfort to know that he's over there."[95]

Over the last four months of her life, doctors tried surgical procedures to improve her chances of survival and decrease her discomfort. None proved successful. A ten-inch section of bowel and the betatron-shrunken pelvic tumor were removed in hopes of lessening the severe abdominal pain. By this time Lurleen weighed only eighty pounds and was almost completely unable to eat solid food. Good days were measured by low fevers, minimal chest congestion, and brief walks. The intestinal procedure led to an infection and another thirty-minute operation to drain an abscess. Soon, a blood clot developed in her lungs, despite the fact that she had been on anticoagulant drugs since the pelvic tumor and intestinal section were removed. Lurleen's body was shutting down, and the end was a matter of time. Home at the mansion, Lurleen spent her last three and a half weeks summoning up enough strength for an occasional car ride, a few hours soaking up the sun on the back patio, and watching her husband and children for the last times.[96]

Reports from the administration bordered on misinformation. At various times, her condition was so optimistically described that reporters speculated on when she might return to the office. Years later, Ewing recalled the fine line between complete honesty and respecting the family's privacy: "We were dealing with a wife, a mother, a person who watched the news when she could on TV and so it was a very difficult thing . . . and I found as we went along, that if we gave out some encouraging news that the doctors agreed on and said this is the way it is, then the press would have her well and going home the next day." In receiving the Gorgas Award on her mother's behalf, daughter Bobby Jo told the assembled throng "mother said to tell you she hopes to be with you next year." Correspondence continued to be mailed over the governor's signature up to the day she died. It was generally believed on the street that her problems were simply complications from surgery and treatment, not a cancerous march toward death. Even Albert Brewer, the lieutenant governor and next in line of succession, did not have a complete understanding of how grave Lurleen's condition was until just a day or so before her death. Her weight, now less than seventy pounds, caused obvious consternation in the family. "Mother just eat it," George Jr. begged her at breakfast time. "Son, I would if I could," Lurleen replied despondently. Best friend Mary Jo Ventress launched Operation Obesity, a humorous attempt to cheer up the governor and increase her caloric intake. Wallace, sensing the inevitable, began to restrict his travel.[97]

With her family by her side, Lurleen Wallace drew her last breath at 12:34 a.m. on May 7, 1968, and slipped away from a world of pain into peace. Her husband sat on the edge of her bed, stroking her hair, and whispering all the words he had said too infrequently over the past quarter century: "Honey, you've been a great wife; you've been a good governor; you've been the greatest mother of anyone. Oh, how much we love you. Good-bye, sweetheart." Alabama lost its governor, someone who may have had the heart and soul to push for more help for the state's most vulnerable had she served out her term. Four children lost a mother who had loved them dearly and passed on to them a legacy of grace and authenticity that would help carry them through the rest of their lives. George Wallace lost the love of his life, someone who had grown in stature in his eyes, someone he would miss every day for as long as he lived.[98]

7
Crossroads / 1968–1970

On the night before Lurleen Wallace died, Press Secretary Ed Ewing received a call from one of the governor's physicians. "Ed," Hamilton Hutchinson confided, "you need to get a good night's rest tonight because you are going to be busy tomorrow." Ewing, conditioned to working in an environment where communication was based on assumption, knew exactly what Hutchinson was suggesting. Over the next four days, Ewing, Bill Jones, Cecil Jackson, and the Reverend John Vickers planned the funeral. The family was too devastated to offer much input.[1]

Lurleen had made a few simple requests for the occasion she knew was coming. She wanted two poems read: Elizabeth Barrett Browning's "How Do I Love Thee" and an anonymous work known to the governor as "I Love You." She asked to be dressed in a simple white satin gown and pink slippers. Most importantly, Lurleen wanted a closed casket to hide her deteriorated condition from the people who had come to love and admire her so much. All of her requests were met save one: the casket was left open, with the governor ensconced in a protective glass bubble. Thousands of Alabamians came through the capitol rotunda to pay their respects. The graceful and authentic governor they had come to respect and cherish was laid to rest in Montgomery's Greenwood Cemetery, in a section of plots that came to be known as Governor's Circle. The woman who paused in the middle of a campaign trip to ride a carousel and stooped down to greet schoolchildren whenever she saw them was memorialized by governors, senators, congressmen, a representative of President Lyndon Johnson, and other dignitaries from all over the country. The cemetery was so overwhelmed with floral arrangements that the grassy knoll where her gray steel casket was buried had fresh flowers for more than a year.[2]

George Wallace, realizing that he had lost the anchor he had relied on for years, was disconsolate. An emotional man, Wallace wept openly and frequently, allowing the family to recognize the depth of his love for the wife he too often took for granted. Campaign activities were temporarily suspended. Personal reflection replaced attacks on the federal government and appeals for law and order. "You people did a real good job of burying her," Wallace told Jones, Jackson, Ewing, Seymore Trammell, and Earl Morgan. "I had to get elected governor and you all got me elected governor. I've got to get on the ballot in California and you all got it done." That night, Jones told his wife that was the first time George Wallace had thanked him for anything.[3]

As the Wallaces picked up the pieces of their lives and struggled to move on, another family, the Brewers, were experiencing wholesale changes of their own. Closely connected to the administration since 1963, Albert Brewer took the oath of office in a brief, solemn ceremony attended by wife, Martha, daughters, Becky and Allison, his parents, and Wallace. The Brewers graciously allowed the Wallace family time to grieve on their own terms before they left the mansion for a house Wallace bought them on Farrar Street. The new governor, struck by the tragedy that had put him in a position he had thought about but never allowed himself to consider a possibility, made few public comments in the days after taking office except to note his appreciation "that my longtime personal friend George Wallace is with me on this occasion." Over the next three years, that friendship was tested, eroded, and eventually destroyed as Brewer, Wallace, and the State of Alabama faced a political crossroads that defined the next three decades of state history.[4]

In most every observable fashion, Brewer was a different political animal than Wallace. To be sure, both were ambitious and hungry to succeed in politics, a profession they had both envisioned since youth. But on the stump, Wallace was a torrent of emotion, a forensic cockleburr sticking and puncturing until the assembled throng was provoked to run through a brick wall and blame it for not getting out of the way. Brewer was less gifted, preferring to quietly woo his constituents through substance and sincerity. Sarah Long, a former teacher, recognized Brewer's classically southern mixture of drive and composure: "You couldn't be in the same room with Albert Brewer and not realize he was different. He had ideas of his own. He always had. He was a nonconformist, a challenger. But he never disrupted classes—he was always polite and well-mannered." Both enjoyed their time as governor but for dramatically different reasons. Wallace had little interest in the pedestrian machinations of grinding legislation in and out of committees and crafting policy; he loved to walk into a stuffy gymnasium or stomp across the back of a flatbed truck in front of a town square until the machinists and pea pickers and church secretaries had red hands from clapping and hoarse throats from yelling. Brewer, capable if rarely spectacular on the hustings, nevertheless relished making the cogs and levers and pulleys of Montgomery grind together until something resembling a solution was fashioned. Wallace preferred the power play in dealing with the legislature, publicly scolding his rivals, doling out patronage to get a concession, or using Trammell to hammer opponents into submission. Brewer was more likely to negotiate or compromise until reasonable common ground could be found. In no small way, they had depended on each other over the past few years: Brewer could not have become speaker of the house or lieutenant governor without Wallace's blessing; Wallace could not have passed his legislative agenda and campaign-issue resolutions without Brewer's shepherding the bills into laws.[5]

With Montgomery still shut down for the funeral and Brewer back home in Decatur, the palace guard had a long weekend to clean out records before the next administration arrived. The night before new finance director Bob Ingram took over his post, the lights at the Finance Department burned all night long, fueling speculation about a document purge. Ingram never confirmed that documents were destroyed, but soon confirmed that other practices— kickbacks, payoffs, and patronage slush—had been standard operating procedure at the Finance Department. "I called every asphalt dealer in the state," Ingram recalled about his first days on the job, "and we had a meeting in the State House and we made it plain that if anybody came to them and said 'you can get a contract if you pay me $.50 a ton or whatever,' you will not even get an invitation to bid if that happens. . . . I took the job with the understanding that I was not going to be that kind of Finance Director. I mean, I wasn't going to be involved with all these things that Trammell was. I didn't want it and I wasn't going to do it."[6]

Brewer was shocked at practices that had been going on in an administration that he was so close to and that had been roundly praised in the media for its honesty and stewardship. "I was astounded," Brewer remembered, "at the extent to which friends of the administration had been favored in state business." Gerald Wallace's wrecker retainers were typical of the sweetheart deals Brewer and Ingram uncovered in the early days of their administration. In every county, state troopers would have a list of preferred wreckers to call if a stranded motorist needed assistance. Not coincidently, the trooper's preferred list of companies shared a common attorney: Gerald Wallace, who was receiving a monthly fee for services. A hundred dollars "or whatever it was, doesn't sound like much," Brewer recalled, "but the multiplier on it was pretty impressive." Another Wallaceite, Felix Petrie, received a 15 percent commission on any tax stamps the state purchased for cigarettes and alcohol.[7]

The shenanigans the new administration discovered put Brewer in a difficult spot from which there appeared to be no easy way to extricate himself. If the Brewer administration revealed the corruption and unethical practices, it risked a backlash from Wallace supporters gearing up for a presidential run and grieving Lurleen's death. In the charged atmosphere of southern civility, any false step could change the public image of Brewer from loyal foot soldier to ungrateful usurper. Those ramifications would be fatal for Brewer, who intended to run for an elected term in 1970. With that campaign in mind, it would also be devastating to look the other way and allow the Wallaceites to continue to play fast and loose with state government. And that was a possibility that Brewer, a devout Baptist, never considered. As a result, the Brewer administration had to eliminate the practices but do so without drawing public attention.[8]

One way to clean up the improprieties was to surround the new administration with career employees who had a reputation for playing by the rules. One such man was Tom Brassell, whom Brewer named assistant finance director. Alerted to Brassell's credentials by state senator Alton Turner, Brewer was leaning toward naming him to the post at the same time Ingram identified Brassell's selection as his one condition for taking the directorship. Brassell was not always loved by his peers; some staff viewed him as too meticulous and even sneaky. But his knowledge and service were invaluable to Brewer and Ingram. "There is no man in the state government that I trusted more or trust now," Ingram declared thirty-one years after he left the Finance Department. "He knew all the ins and outs," Brewer remembered, "and he already knew a lot of the things that had gone on." At times, Brassell's fastidious penchant for following the letter of the law had to be reigned in. "Sometimes," Ingram opined, "I'd say 'come on Tom, we've got more important issues here to worry about than how much to pay for a bolt down here.'" Brewer had to remind Brassell that the administration had numerous priorities, not just ferreting out past sins of the Wallace administration: "I think Tom would have liked to have broadcast it to the world to show how corrupt some folks had been, but we made a decision and I think the right decision, to look forward and not back. I don't believe we could have accomplished all the things we got done in the legislative session, if we had been in a war."[9]

Brewer also had to navigate a minefield of personalities and holdovers from the Wallace administration. Cecil Jackson, in a show of class Brewer never forgot, instructed all of Lurleen's cabinet members to submit their resignations to the new governor, who would then accept or reject at his discretion. Brewer kept most of the cabinet, perhaps against his better judgment, reshuffled others to different positions, and soon fired public safety director William Russell and Conservation head Claude Kelley for their refusal to resign. Though Lurleen was loved and admired, many Montgomery insiders and career employees welcomed Brewer, confident his interest in policy would lead to greater attention to detail and a more comprehensive role for state government. Reporters viewed the carryover of cabinet heads from the Wallace era as an indication the former governor had no plans to run in 1970. Less than a month after Lurleen's funeral, Wallace called Brewer and Ingram over to his house to assure them he had no interest in being governor again. In June, Wallace surprised South Carolina scribes by issuing a blanket declaration against running for governor when his usual practice was to leave the door open with careful wording: "I will not seek public office in my state again, ever."[10]

For his part, Brewer supported Wallace's presidential aspirations. In October 1967, Gerald Wallace contacted Brewer to ask him to raise some money for the campaign from his Morgan County associates. Brewer solicited funds on Wallace's behalf and made a thousand dollar contribution of his own. The most significant campaign expense was the elaborate and costly effort to get on the ballot in California. "If we are successful in California," Brewer wrote to his friends, "indications are that this success will give significant impetus that the campaign expenses in other states can be realized by contributions very regularly." As governor, Brewer provided a security detail of state troopers for the campaign and family and made several speeches on Wallace's behalf. Brewer's speeches for Wallace's were red meat for Alabamians glad that their new governor was embracing their favorite son: "Whoever would have thought Hubert Humphrey would have been for law and order. . . . A year ago the Democratic presidential nominee said he could lead a demonstration himself. We know you are disturbed about the demonstrations back home, about the hippies and those who advocate a Communist victory. But those people don't represent the overwhelming majority of Americans." On one occasion, Brewer predicted Wallace was going to win sixteen states and predicted a major revolt from the Democrats in order to support Wallace. "Several governors in the South and elsewhere," Brewer quipped, "have indicated they could not support Vice President Hubert Humphrey unless he took a strong stand on law and order."[11]

Back in Montgomery, Brewer identified a number of priorities that were possible in the political climate: educational improvements, elimination of extraneous expenses, streamlining of procedures, increased accountability, and repairing the state's lagging image. More sweeping changes would have to wait until the next regular session. Brewer's first major initiatives were designed to tighten the fiscal belt. State troopers, burdened by the Department of Public Safety's poor financial situation, had been paying for their own meals while on patrol and been restricted in their mileage. The Wallaces had promised teachers a 4 percent raise but the Revenue Department's own estimates still indicated the possibility of proration. Brewer understood that his administration would get the blame if the raises were not granted. State auditor Melba Till Allen, who had ambitions for higher office herself, declared that Brewer should begin investigating the expense records of two state employees who had recently resigned.[12]

One place to start was with the creation of a state motor pool. Even though Wallace had initially restricted the use of state cars in 1963, the number of employees with cars had swelled to more than three thousand. While these vehicles were used by many in official capacities, Alabamians were suspicious when they saw marked cars at hunting camps, golf courses, and grocery stores on a daily basis. "If you can stop the misuse of state automobiles," B. G. Thornton of Coosada wrote to Brewer, "you will get my vote for a full four year term. It is amazing to see the number of state vehicles on the lake on weekends." By early June, Brewer told reporters at his weekly press conference, an exchange that neither Wallace regularly scheduled, that he would establish a motor pool by executive order and then encourage the legislature to codify the institution. State cars, under Brewer's system, had to be checked out and gasoline had to be purchased from the state, eliminating the cushy relationships some state employees had created with local service stations. A *Birmingham News* investigation revealed that one Wallace official purchased more than 50 gallons of gas on the same day. J. C. Fowler, a trooper assigned to Wallace's office, signed thirty-seven separate receipts for 588 gallons for ten separate cars on the same day. Each transaction was made at the same Boyett Brothers American Oil service station in Montgomery. "There is no reason," Brewer announced, "why government shouldn't be run like a business and get the most for its money."[13]

Brewer intended the motor pool to be more than just good publicity for his administration. All state cars soon bore a prominent insignia. At a cost of thirty-four cents each, the emblem was an inexpensive but powerful tool to prevent personal use of state vehicles. He issued a terse memorandum to state employees about the motor pool with an underlined imperative, "I intend for it to work." When Adjutant General Alfred Harrison was slow to respond to requests to turn in extraneous vehicles, Brewer demanded action: "Please give me a report on the number of vehicles which you presently have with a written justification for those which should be retained by the department rather than being placed in the car pool." The administration caught some flack from employees who had grown accustomed to having a state car and access to state gas for personal use. One of the governor's friends from his hometown of Decatur called for a special exception. The governor waited for a good reason why his friend and member of the same church needed to have the car. Hearing none, he affirmed his executive order. Soon enough, the state had collected enough cars to sell off more than a thousand of them, including the governor's Cadillac limousine. Some Alabamians thought selling "number one" was a bad idea. "How are we going to uphold Alabama's first place in greeting out of state . . . dignitaries," Mrs. Sim Wilbanks inquired: "A chief executive officer needs the trappings of his office to discharge his duties." In reality, the limo, and some of the other state cars, had been unusable for years but had remained on the state books. The net savings was not significant to the overall budget, but the motor pool established a precedent for future dealings by the Brewer administration.[14]

Brewer took other small steps that announced Montgomery was in different hands. Duplicate copy machines were rounded up and sold off. Expensive mainframe computers were consolidated in order to make departments share resources instead of competing to outmodernize each other. He cut twelve senior assistant positions in various departments for a savings of $150,000. Wallace used the positions as personal agents who could be assigned to any task, usually campaign matters. Lane Brislin, for example, had been an assistant to Houston Feaster in the docks department, but most days he could be found at the Finance Department in Montgomery. Lesser salaried employees—clerks, stenographers, secretaries—had been on the books of various departments as well but had been working in the governor's office. Brewer reassigned them to their former responsibilities and made sure they landed on their feet.[15]

All of this realignment did not mean Brewer was uninterested in the patronage and employment power that came with being chief executive. During Lurleen's bout with cancer, Brewer became acting governor by statute when Lurleen had been gone from the state for a period of twenty consecutive days. In his fifteen-hour term as acting governor, Brewer named twenty-five honorary colonels including his secretary, Mrs. Edna Harris. Sometimes naming friends and neighbors as honorary colonels could end up being more frustrating than helpful. Herman Ross asked Brewer to launch an investigation of a Mobile tavern after he was charged $1.43 for a highball: "Governor such prices are ridiculous and a hold-up especially [in] a meager joint. If these people can't sell drinks at a reasonable profit, they should not be able to run a cocktail lounge." As with most every democratic government since Cleisthenes, friends of the administration received special consideration. Brewer personally wrote docks director Houston Feaster in hopes of landing a job for friend Virgil Blake. Morgan County probate judge T. C. Almon informed Brewer that Blake was retiring from the Huntsville Arsenal and needed a position in state government: "He would be a great benefit to you during your campaign, not only in raising money, but in helping to secure votes and reporting back to headquarters. He has sense enough to understand the Hatch Act and would not get in any trouble by soliciting votes for you if he were an employee of the state." On balance, however, the Brewer administration was more subtle and less overtly political in its dispensation of favors. Morale among career employees improved. Brewer even allowed departments to hold Christmas parties, a practice banned during the Wallace years.[16]

Some of the cost-cutting initiatives elicited a verbal response from Wallace. After the motor pool had been announced, Wallace called Ingram to complain:

"I want you to stop the motor pool. . . . That's a reflection on Lurleen. . . . She didn't do it so the fact that you are doing it means that you think she should have done it." Wallace's criticisms were the first indication that he might be planning a return to the governor's office. "Anything we did," Ingram mused, "that had not been done by Lurleen was a reflection on Lurleen." The motor pool was *not* designed by Brassell, Ingram, and Brewer to be a reflection on Lurleen or her husband. Brewer, out of respect for Lurleen and the Wallace family, had been reluctant to propose substantive changes during his first few months in office. Wallace's criticisms ended any consideration Brewer gave to continued reticence. "Early on," Ingram later recalled, "Brewer moved slow on some things just not to rock any boats, but it wasn't long before he was as fed up with it. . . . I mean, it was getting ridiculous and so we just did our thing whether he liked it or didn't like it."[17]

If the motor pool frustrated Wallace, Brewer's abolition of liquor agents positively infuriated him. Theoretically, the liquor agents had been eliminated early in 1963 by legislation trumpeted by Wallace and cosponsored by Brewer. In reality, the agents, who were paid commissions by distilleries with every sale to the state's Alcoholic Beverage Control Board, continued to operate and earn up to 2 percent on every transaction, despite performing no work. Jack Anderson and Drew Pearson reported in late November that the agents were alive and well in Alabama and had been operating during both Wallace administrations. According to Anderson, one longtime Wallace backer—Robert Millsap— had received $138,000 in commissions from the sale of Ezra Brooks and Mar-Sale liquor. Wallace demanded a full investigation and denied any knowledge of the actions: "If Mr. Millsap received any commissions from Ezra Brooks as alleged he knows that this is without my knowledge or the knowledge of my wife, and was in violation of my policy, my wife's policy, and that of Governor Brewer."[18]

Brewer expressed disbelief at the allegations but promised an investigation to determine the truth. "Steps will be taken," he asserted, "to secure information from these distilleries about their operation and we intend to make it clear that if they don't want to do business on an open basis, we can do without their products." Behind the scenes, Brewer asked Spencer Robb—a former FBI agent and the newly named ABC administrator—to ferret out any agents and stop all distilleries from paying them. Less than a week later, the Internal Revenue Service announced its own investigation. Despite Brewer's actions, he remained firm in offering public support for Wallace. "I personally resented the implications and insinuations that this practice was carried on with knowledge and consent of former Governor George C. Wallace and the late Governor Lurleen Wallace. There's absolutely no evidence and I am personally convinced that neither had any knowledge whatsoever of this matter."

Even in private correspondence, Brewer remained ardent in his conviction that Wallace did not sanction the agents. "I am convinced," the governor wrote inquiring Alabamians, "that the Board as well as the companies doing business in Alabama had instructions from Governor Wallace, both in his administration and the administration of his wife, that they were not to pay anyone for the privilege of doing business." Pearson, convinced Brewer was in Wallace's hip pocket, did not forward any of the evidence he had uncovered to the new administration.[19]

Despite such public denials and the endorsement of Wallace, Brewer soon found himself at odds with the former governor. Brewer spent his first Thanksgiving as governor in the mansion with his wife and children, brothers and sister, and their families. During that afternoon, Wallace called Brewer to express his frustration with the liquor agent controversy. "That's a reflection on Lurleen," Wallace charged. "I don't appreciate it. It just sounds bad." Brewer affirmed his commitment to uncovering the truth, denied that the fiasco reflected on Lurleen, and reminded Wallace that they both had spoken out against the agents. The next day, Brewer, after a morning round of golf with friends and family, received another call from Wallace, who was obviously still angry. A few minutes later Wallace arrived at the mansion, and the two removed themselves to a private study Martha Brewer had created. Wallace reiterated his displeasure about the publicity the liquor agents had received: "I'm really upset about all this talk about these whiskey agents. It reflects on me and it reflects on Lurleen. . . . If you keep on talking about it, it's going to reflect on me and I may just have to run against you in 1970." Brewer did not shirk from the challenge, but reminded the former governor of his loyalty: "She never had a better friend, and you never had a better friend than I've been to you and to her, and you told me [so] yourself when she died."[20]

The two talked infrequently after the Thanksgiving weekend meeting in the mansion. Brewer grew in strength and confidence and began to transform his ideas into official policy. He announced publicly that he would be a candidate in 1970 and set about the business of improving the state while making his candidacy as formidable as possible. Wallace backed off the stage, resurfacing occasionally to keep his name from being forgotten and tease voters and pundits with the allure of a Wallace-Brewer showdown in 1970. In the months after the presidential campaign ended, Wallace turned down most speaking requests and granted few interviews. He interjected himself in a Tennessee congressional race when an American Independent Party candidate, William J. Davis, asked for the former governor's help in a March 1969 special election. Though reluctant to campaign for others, Wallace used the race as a gauge of whether his infant party had any of its own legs or whether the party was limited by his celebrity.[21]

Wallace had carried Tennessee's eighth congressional district easily in 1968 and nearly won the entire state, a fact not lost on either Richard Nixon or Hubert Humphrey. Had the Alabamian won in either Tennessee or North Carolina, and had Hubert Humphrey garnered an additional 1 percent of the vote in either Ohio or New Jersey, the presidential election would have been thrown into the House of Representatives for resolution. As a result, the special congressional race received some national attention. Arriving on the scene, Wallace declared the race "the most important political race between now and the next national election." In his first major political activity since November 1968, Wallace took to the streets to announce to Tennessee voters that a "Wallace man should be a Davis man." Davis was crushed by Democrat Ed Jones confirming that while Wallace may have started a movement, he had not launched a party.[22]

Reporter James Free called the Tennessee debacle a "near disaster for Wallace," but it did not keep him off the state or national stage. Appearing at a Washington Gridiron Club Banquet on the same dais as his 1968 campaign rivals, Wallace flashed his forensic skills yet again and brought down the house with some well placed comedic timing. Noting that President Nixon faced a rebellious Congress and echoing his own tagline about antiwar protestors never lying down in front of his motorcade, Wallace uttered the quip of the night: "If I were president and congress tried to roadblock my program, that would be the last roadblock they'd ever put up." Four months later, Wallace, out of government work but popular nonetheless, was a guest on both ABC's *Issues and Answers* and NBC's *Today.* Concerned that Brewer was becoming too strong, Wallace had a resolution introduced in the fall of 1969 legislative session calling for continued defiance against court-ordered integration. The resolution passed easily in both houses and even Brewer admitted "if I were a member of the legislature, I would probably vote for it."[23]

Despite a well-publicized rupture in November 1968 with many of his presidential campaign staff—Seymore Trammell, Cecil Jackson, Ed Ewing, and Bill Jones—Wallace persuaded Jones to run his skeleton campaign headquarters. Jones and the others had put together a modest proposal to keep a permanent Wallace office operating with a staff large enough to continue raising money and fielding speaking opportunities. Wallace turned him down cold, preferring to have only one person who could help ease the transition as smoothly, and cheaply, as possible. For most of the old palace guard—men who had worked long hard hours, been forced to keep their families at arm's length, and made less than market wages—this break was a welcome respite. "I was extremely tired," Ewing recalled. "My son had been born . . . and he was very young. My wife was here [in Montgomery] raising him and I was on the road all the time. You didn't feel like you had gotten into a town good until you got the first bomb threat and we were working, you know, day, night, weekend. . . . After that campaign, I was through." Jones stayed out of a sense of personal friendship and loyalty that dated to his days with Wallace at the University of Alabama. But even he left after less than six months. "It was obvious then to all of us," Jones admitted, "that they were going to run for governor and I still think that was a mistake for them to do." The signs were so apparent that Wallace would run in 1970 that nobody should have been surprised. "Wallace will run all right," conservative commentator John J. Synon predicted. "I am sure of it. I say I am sure because I know the man and I know the species of politician he is. As things stand, Wallace is without a vestige of power and sorely needs both a fulcrum and a forum to maintain himself as leader of the national resistance. The governor's office offers both." As the old crew was eased out to pasture, a new inner circle led by Taylor Hardin and including old standbys Gerald Wallace and Ralph Adams began to emerge.[24]

The rift between the staff and Wallace was caused by money and ambition. Jones was in Hawaii at one point during the 1968 campaign, setting up an organization and a state convention in order to comply with state ballot guidelines, when he was informed that his expenses would not be covered. Less than two months before the election, Ralph Adams and Gerald Wallace became convinced that the campaign could not win; they wanted to bank the remaining funds for future campaigns. Jones remains bitter about not spending the accumulated bankroll to grab every vote possible and finish strong, even if they had no chance of winning: "I think he [Wallace] was influenced by two factors. One, his desire to be governor of Alabama above anything else. Two, Gerald, Ralph and in my judgement, Jack [Wallace]. I have no doubt about the first two. Being governor of Alabama meant money in their pocketbooks. Running for president probably did not." In fact, Gerald, with the blessing of his brother, had taken over control of all campaign finances. Adams and Jack Wallace received the power to authorize disbursements. According to historian Dan Carter, Trammell complained to the candidate but to no avail: "Gerald only wants to steal. He wants to stop spending and start shoveling the money into bank vaults." Despite having enough money to advertise extensively, the campaign slowed to a crawl in the final six weeks. September polls suggested that Wallace had more than 20 percent of the national vote; on election day he actually received 13 percent. In hindsight, it appears the chaos of the 1968 Democratic National Convention was at least partially responsible for Wallace's brief polling spike. By late October, numerous polls were released showing Wallace's numbers dropping. Though publicly he complained that pollsters were trying to rig the election, privately he knew that his decision to stop spending money was responsible for the dip.[25]

The years out of office were difficult for Wallace, who loved being the nexus of power in Montgomery and the champion of white Alabama. Like a slow drip from a rusty spigot, bits of negative publicity dropped into the public's eye about past administration indiscretions. Seymore Trammell and Gerald Wallace faced mounting pressure from federal investigators over tax and bribery issues. National campaign "friend" Janeen Welch was arrested in Chicago for prostitution. Making matters worse, former friend and administration subordinate Albert Brewer was beginning to earn rave reviews for his leadership as governor. Some national observers characterized Wallace's newfound taciturnity as apathy or even fear. "Wallace doesn't even demonstrate much interest in Alabama state politics now," Jules Witcover surmised, "suggesting that he's risen above that and has no taste for a fight against Governor Albert Brewer." Witcover could not have been more wrong.[26]

Albert Brewer: Policy and Performance

Realizing Wallace was considering running in 1970, Brewer grew bolder in his approach to government. On several issues Brewer took a cue from his wife, Martha, a soul mate and unofficial advisor. When a Winston County mother called Mrs. Brewer to inform her that an unsafe bridge was in the middle of a school bus route, she asked her husband to look into the matter. Brewer called the Highway Department and asked that the bridge be repaired as soon as possible. When the work crew tarried, Martha Brewer received another call from Winston County, informing her that nothing was happening. When Brewer firmly informed Highway Director Marion Wilkins that the bridge was going to be fixed immediately, the work was quickly completed. The next day Martha Brewer received yet another call from the Winston County mother asking her to pave a road. "Al," Martha Brewer apologized," I will never ask you to do anything again."[27]

Her influence was also felt in less comical and more substantive ways. When a Bessemer woman telephoned Martha Brewer to inform her about pornographic movies being shown in her hometown, a complaint turned into a policy and a series of actions. Admitting he had no idea that such films were on public display in Alabama, Brewer agreed with his wife that the movies were inappropriate and authorized a series of raids on theaters across the state. "The trash and filth being shown on some motion picture screens in Alabama," Brewer railed, "is almost unbelievable. I am determined that the full weight of law enforcement authorities of this state will be applied to stop this wholesale spreading of obscenity." Alabamians, socially conservative by nature, hailed Brewer for his stand against pornography and similar efforts to curtail narcotics and alcohol abuse. "With the current concern over morals in the state of Alabama," Curtis Adams wrote to Brewer, "a strong stand against pornography, lewd movies, etc. is very popular. A very strong stand with proper publicity might be just the thing to insure your re-election, even against Mr. George Wallace." Ultimately, court decisions prevented Brewer's self-described "ill-fated swing into censorship" from much legal success, but his actions remained popular.[28]

Some Alabamians viewed legislative scandals as a moral issue as repugnant as dirty movies. For decades, Alabama lawmakers had operated in an environment where special interests camped out on the floor and did their bidding in full view. Behind the scenes, many solons were on retainer as legal counsel or otherwise financially linked to groups the public expected them to regulate. State senator W. G. McCarley was indicted and removed from the senate for asking for a thirty-five hundred dollar bribe from the Fraternal Order of Police to get a pension bill out of committee. McCarley's defense was that he was nothing more than a message boy for more powerful colleagues such as Roland Cooper and Ray Lolley. Lolley was under indictment himself for seeking five thousand dollars from BlueCross and BlueShield. Though both were ultimately acquitted, Alabamians saw enough smoke to suspect a fire was burning out of control in state government.[29]

Reflecting the antipathy some Alabamians were developing toward legislative corruption, Brewer established a code of ethics by executive order. "Confidence of the public has been shaken because of recent events," executive order fifteen declared. Reestablishing confidence, the governor assured the public, was "essential to the preservation of a free and democratic society." The order created a ten-member ethics commission charged with investigating improprieties and drafting general standards of conduct for future codification. Brewer's ten-point plan was the first real attempt at limiting legislative abuse in a generation. Included in his order were provisions eliminating gifts, establishing disclosure of confidential information to businesses or other for-profit agencies, and creating prohibitions against receiving fees or doing business with anyone the legislature was theoretically charged with regulating. Most legislators were pleased with the order since they had been under increasing scrutiny from constituents in light of the charges against Lolley and McCarley. Brewer kept the momentum going by providing secretarial help for the commission out of his executive funds and speaking out publicly against legislators performing legal work for interest groups. New University of Alabama president David Matthews provided faculty, free of charge, to the state as consultants and experts.[30]

Howell Heflin, a prominent North Alabama lawyer and former president of the State Bar Association, was tapped to chair the commission. Initially, Heflin, who would soon announce his candidacy for the state supreme court, moved a little too slowly for Brewer's tastes. "Some concern has been expressed by one or two members of the Ethics Commission," Brewer wrote to his legal advisor Richard Holmes, "about the fact that they have not met recently. I would like for you to call Howell Heflin . . . to determine if there are any plans for future meetings in the immediate future." This concern was in stark contrast to the previous two administrations' penchant for allowing committees to function on their own timetable. Brewer understood that the executive order provided him almost no power to intervene against an elected official who might have crossed ethical boundaries, and he wanted the commission to draft a bill with some teeth. "I can find no provision of law," attorney James Solomon concluded, "which authorizes the governor to take direct action. . . . If the conduct of such officer or official was simply unethical or not illegal, I am doubtful if any judicial action of a criminal nature can be taken against such official."[31]

In time, Heflin got the commission rolling. Subcommittees on lobbying, legislative ethics, executive branch ethics, judicial ethics, and state regulatory agencies were created, staffed, and charged with making full investigations and reports. The commission quickly resolved to amend Brewer's preference for full disclosure statements from all state employees to only those at the highest pay scales and with the most authority. Heflin viewed the modification as essential for garnering quick public approval of the commission's actions. "If we are able to present you with a list of approximately 1,000 names," the Tuscumbia giant surmised, "it would have quite an impact on the public and the press. We believe such a dramatic event would do much to improve the confidence of the public in the integrity of our state government and its officials." Disclosure statements soon trickled into the Ethics Commission offices.[32]

The final report of the Ethics Commission was a mixture of good ideas that would eventually be translated into law and polite refusals to make more sweeping recommendations. The commission found that a comprehensive code of conduct was needed for all executive branch employees and legislators. It also suggested a continuation of mandatory filing of full disclosure statements and asked that it be given a permanent charter with broad subpoena powers, authority to hold public hearings, and a membership appointed by the state supreme court, not the governor. Surprisingly, the commission took a hands-off position on lobbying abuses. Lobbyists, the final report noted, "provide an important service to legislators and others in government by supplying information, articulating the views of constituents." Most lobbyists, the report concluded, were assets, conducted their business in an ethical fashion, and "no improper conduct was revealed by the investigations of this committee." Even so, the commission recommended that all paid lobbyists be officially registered with the leadership of the legislature and that the practice of allowing paid agents on the floor during sessions be eliminated.[33]

The Brewer administration was equally proactive in addressing industrial development, repairing the state's contentious image in the financial community, and making government a more systematic process. Brewer traveled to New York to speak to a group of two hundred industry leaders at the request of Pepsi-Cola president James Somerall, a native Alabamian and former roommate of state highway director Bob Kendall. By all accounts, Brewer's appearance was a smashing success. "If you took a poll," General Foods president Clarence Francis noted, "and asked questions of the people in this room on what they knew about Alabama, you would be surprised at the ignorance about your state. This meeting is a wonderful way to get your story across." U.S. Steel president Robert Tyson was equally effusive in his praise: "Your governor is most personable and I'm very impressed with him. I attend many of these functions and this certainly is one of the finest."[34]

The administration was also active on other industrial development fronts. Brewer communicated regularly with Standard Oil, Schlage Lock, Fruehauf Trucking, Georgia Pacific, Chrysler, and other corporations with the potential to provide high-skill, high-wage employment. Brewer intervened in a rate dispute between Alabama Power and Olin-Mathieson Chemical Corporation in order to smooth the way for future plant expansions. Brewer painstakingly prepared for meetings and was particularly effective in one-on-one meetings with industrial contacts. State planning and industrial development director Ed Mitchell frequently tapped Brewer for face time with prospects. "We have concluded," Mitchell told Brewer on one occasion, "that your personal intervention is necessary if we are to stay in the ball game."[35]

Brewer's personal input extended beyond salesmanship into strategic planning. He spearheaded an effort to separate recruitment of industrial prospects from long-range planning efforts. With the assistance of Hugh Maddox, Brewer suggested merging attempts to obtain federal grants with local state planning efforts. Previously, federal grant applications had been the domain of various state departments. As a result, some opportunities were completely ignored while duplicate applications from several state agencies were filed for others. The Alabama Program Development Office was created to streamline these functions and though not a splashy venture, did improve government efficiency.[36]

Brewer's courting of industry was especially important in light of pollution abuses that energized many Alabamians to demand tighter regulation. Throughout 1968, numerous fish kills were reported along Alabama's industrial corridors: 50,000 fish were killed in the Tombigbee in early June; 53,000 were found dead further downstream ten days later. One month later, 29,000 fish were killed in the Black Warrior River. One day later, 135,000 fish were reported dead along or in the Dog River in Mobile. Three weeks later, estimates indicated nearly 400,000 fish were dead in the Dog River. By September, the official tally was over 1 million. Various other kills were reported on Lake Demopolis, Tar Creek, Cedar Creek, and the Cahaba River. Many of the estimates were conservative since they only included fish that could be observed floating dead on top of the water. Industrial pollution became so widespread that the *Montgomery Advertiser* printed a satirical cartoon hailing the great fishing in the state. "Fishing is great in Alabama," the caption read, "all you have to do is dip 'em up."[37]

Little doubt existed that the cause of the fish kills was industrial water pollution. A preliminary report concerning the Tombigbee kill asserted that Geigy Chemical Company was discharging effluent into the water in full view of the investigating conservation officer. Geigy, the report continued, had knowledge of the disastrous effects of its refuse, yet continued to discharge into the river for several hours. Geigy was dumping diazinon, an insecticide, into the river. Instead of processing the chemical to break it down, Geigy had simply relied on diffusion, hoping the river would water down the chemical until it was harmless. Thirty parts per billion was enough to kill half the fish in a given area; State of Alabama tests indicated up to 170 parts per billion on parts of the Tombigbee. Subsequent gas chromatography tests revealed 217 parts per billion. The conclusion of investigator Charles Kelley was obvious: "I feel it is past time for re-evaluation of the operating permit issued Geigy Chemical Company."[38]

Geigy expected the state to be concerned but hoped the tradition of looking the other way would continue. Fish kills, unfortunately, were nothing new on Alabama waterways. The state had the sixth highest loss of fish in industrial incidents in 1967, nearly 1 million of the total 9 million lost nationwide. The Lurleen Wallace administration had been warned by Max Edwards, assistant secretary of the U.S. Department of the Interior, to take preventative action. Though Edwards was responding to a disaster along the Clinch River between Tennessee and Virginia, his intention was to have each state tighten its own pollution controls. "It would be most helpful," Edwards urged, "if you could focus public attention in your state on this kind of potential pollution problem and obtain the cooperation of the state agencies, local governments, and industries . . . to prevent future ecological disasters." Geigy plant manager Bruce Trickey wrote Brewer to assure him of diazinon's harmlessness and the company's commitment to safe operating procedures. Tests on laboratory monkeys, Trickey asserted, indicated granular diazinon could be eaten in quantities up to 300 milligrams per day with "no fear of injury." He added that Geigy had spent $1.6 million over the previous two years on treatment and pollution controls and had a long-standing practice of allocating almost half a million dollars per year to maintain existing equipment. In an appearance before the Water Improvement Commission, Geigy officials reiterated the company's reputation as a good citizen and its commitment to taking all reasonable steps to make sure its effluent had no effects on the environment.[39]

Instead of heeding Edwards's warning, Alabama took little action to safeguard its waters, even after being informed that state standards did not pass federal muster. If anything, the Wallace administration seemed flummoxed that the federal government was intervening in state matters. "I am appalled," Leonard Beard—point man for industrial development and planning efforts—moaned, "over what I consider an attempt on the part of Secretary Udall to take over the rights of the state with respect to water pollution control and reduce the state's water pollution control agency to a puppet of the Department of the Interior."[40]

Despite the state's penchant for ignoring industrial pollution and blaming the federal government for interfering with states' rights, Brewer intended to make changes. When informed of the Tombigbee fish kills, Brewer called for an emergency meeting of the Water Improvement Commission. He attended the meeting, an indication to all state departments that the new chief executive was going to be involved in all aspects of governance, including oversight. Within weeks, the administration announced plans to sue Geigy for environmental damage and offer tougher pollution laws in the next legislative session. The Water Improvement Commission issued instructions to municipalities to refrain from dumping grass cuttings in state waterways, an unfortunate practice that had robbed some streams and rivers of oxygen. The Mobile City Commission was ordered to investigate chronic abuses at the Eslava Creek sewage treatment facility. Conservation director Claude Kelley, who had earlier refused to offer the customary resignation during the change of administration, was finally forced out after news of his fistfight with department employee Graham Hixon became public knowledge. Brewer's choice to replace Kelley was Joe Graham, a former state senator who had been working as a vice president for the Alabama Forest Products Association. Though Graham was well respected for his tenure in Montgomery, some in the conservation community questioned whether his close ties with industry would prevent a tougher water pollution enforcement policy from being implemented.[41]

Despite some reluctance over the hiring of Graham, most Alabamians were receptive to Brewer's leadership. "It was with a great deal of pleasure," Philip Green of Boaz wrote to Brewer, "[that I] read in the newspaper last night and this morning that you may intend to do something about the water pollution of our water streams in Alabama." Green, an attorney, noted that a lawsuit had been filed in Boaz a few years earlier because a cow died after drinking from a nearby creek. Nothing had been done to improve the water since that incident. Alabama sportsmen were equally supportive of Brewer's engagement on water pollution. "I congratulate you," Bass Angler Sportsmen president Ray Scott declared, "on your apparent active interest in our water pollution problem. . . . Your office has never before shown such interest and we therefore thank you and beg for your active and persistent interest in our future." Unaccustomed to gubernatorial efforts at restricting environmental damage, Scott encouraged his membership to send Brewer telegrams encouraging further endeavors.[42]

On the surface, the Alabama Water Improvement Commission had made some strides in the twenty years since its creation as the watchdog of Alabama waterways. In 1942, Alabama municipalities were dumping 82.7 percent of their sewage untreated; by 1966, only 6.4 percent of the discharge was raw. Nevertheless, industrial polluters were rarely sanctioned in a political climate where industry helped craft the rules designed to monitor their actions. Brewer hoped to make the Water Improvement Commission more independent and less influenced by industrial lobbying. "The time has come," he wrote state senator E. O. Eddins, "when we all must face up to our problem in this area because the public will no longer be satisfied with anything less than the proper protection of our natural resources."[43]

When the 1969 regular session of the legislature opened—364 days after the death of Lurleen Wallace—Brewer announced plans to seek pollution control legislation. Two senators, Bo Torbert and Jack Giles, offered bills. Both bills were relatively weak and reflected the influence of industry. In fact the Torbert bill, the one that emerged as the favorite and was eventually passed, was crafted in direct consultation with industry leaders, including Earl Mallick, United States Steel vice president. Birmingham's industrial giants, while providing thousands of jobs, had been choking off the oxygen supply in creeks and rivers, discharging hazardous waste, and blasting particulate matter into the air for years. Particulate counts, published daily by the state's major newspapers, were regularly in excess of safe levels. "I live and work in Birmingham," Tulah Davis told Brewer, "and all week I have literally not been able to see the city when I look out the window due to the heavy particulate count from the gook being spilled into the air."[44]

The entire legislative dynamic surrounding the air and water pollution bills was a microcosm of Alabama politics: federal agencies were threatening Alabama with a loss of funds; political leaders seemed more interested in blaming Washington than addressing the causative factors; Alabama power brokers talked about regulating industrial polluters while engaging in protracted negotiations with them; and interest groups, not experts, defined the parameters of what was possible and what was unacceptable. Jefferson County legislators, instead of championing the efforts to improve the health of their constituents, usually sided with industrial firms since single-member districts had not yet been implemented, and candidates relied on corporate money to get reelected.

Brewer, more concerned with education reform than pollution, was hesitant to risk his limited political capital over an issue that might please some voters, but would not necessarily secure their ballots on election day. In the end, a few zealots were unable to defeat the bunkered forces of the status quo, and Alabama's traditional conservative political machinery snuffed out the prospect of meaningful reform. While industry championed the Torbert bill as a solution to a minor problem, others knew better. "The Big Mules are in control," Giles sighed. Senator Aubrey Carr called the Torbert bill "completely worthless . . . a built-in umbrella for polluters." Years later, Albert Brewer recalled the futility of battling industry on pollution bills. "It [the Torbert bill] was probably the best we could get at the time. . . . I really doubted that any bill could pass at that time. And historically we'd been trying for pollution bills and could not get one passed or not anything that was significant passed."[45]

Experts agreed that the Torbert bill was too weak to offer any meaningful hope for curbing industrial pollution. "We feel this bill is a fraud," the University of Alabama Chemistry Department wrote en masse to Brewer. "It has been rejected by health officials, and it clearly will do nothing to change the almost unbearable conditions of air pollution in cities like Tuscaloosa and Birmingham. . . . It is well known that equipment is available to control these emissions, but industry seems more intent on saving their investment for other things. . . . Passage of the Torbert Bill is an action that we will all regret."[46]

Despite the suggestions by Torbert bill backers that it would keep Alabama in the good graces of the Department of the Interior and help it qualify for federal block grants, Washington was unimpressed. The Torbert bill gave existing industry seven years to curb pollution and further limited local municipal efforts by giving functional and fiscal authority for all pollution control programs to the state. "The draft submitted to us," William Megonnell, assistant HEW commissioner for standards and compliance, noted, "contains provisions unfortunately, which would make it extremely difficult if not impossible to prevent, abate, or control air pollution sufficiently to have any impact on air quality in Alabama. . . . The awarding of funds for support of any program so likely to be ineffectual would be most difficult to justify." Gene Welsh, regional air pollution control director for the Environmental Protection Agency called the bill "half-baked and ridiculous" and a "horrible example of ineffective legislation." Though he had promised to help the Brewer administration write the legislation to make sure it met federal compliance standards, Welsh was not consulted. Brewer later considered a special session to address the inadequacy of the state's pollution regulations, but by then he was a lame duck with no hopes of going toe-to-toe with Alabama's industrial interest groups and winning.[47]

As a result, the state continued to be plagued by industrial pollution. In 1970, a new round of fish kills and mercury poisoning caused Alabama health officials to warn against eating any fish caught in certain waters. Brewer admitted pollution had become an unmanageable problem: "It has now moved into the area where it is endangering human life and bringing tremendous economic damage to our state, particularly since commercial fishing on several rivers has been banned." The governor asked President Nixon to declare parts of the state a disaster area. Some four hundred commercial fishing operations were closed. "It looks like I've just lost my job," fish camp proprietor Charlie Roberts moaned. "No customers now. I guess I'll be living off poisoned fish and watermelon." Ray Scott's BASS Association filed suit asking the government to prosecute more than two hundred industries and municipalities for dumping refuse into state waterways. The state lost two hundred thousand dollars in federal funds because the new pollution law did not meet federal guidelines. To his credit, Torbert prepared a tougher law that met federal standards, and Brewer commissioned a survey of state waterways to determine the extent of damages. Unfortunately, Alabama had yet again waited for the federal government to demand action, despite its claims that it could solve its own problems. Birmingham resident Tulah Davis spoke for many frustrated Alabamians: "If something is not done, if plans are not made in the NEAR future, I and many others like me will be moving out of the state permanently. . . . Other states seem to have more progressive and concerned governments and I'd rather support such a state and its leaders with my tax money than my home state, if strong and firm laws aren't made."[48]

As with pollution, Brewer's attempts at property tax reform and constitutional revision reveal his administration's ability to force consideration of important issues but lack of the raw political power necessary to impose lasting change. Brewer included both items in his session-opening speech, and the legislature passed his bill creating a twenty-one-member Constitutional Revisions Commission. The study group met intermittently for two years and issued some recommendations to the 1971 legislature, but never generated enough momentum to change the state's antiquated document. Brewer, after speaking to fellow southern governors whose states were considering constitutional reform, surmised that a new document would be defeated at the polls easily with single-issue lobbying. "It appeared to me," he recalled, "that our best hope for success at that time was to let the legislature do it on an article by article basis and have a commission that would make recommendations and hopefully the legislature would follow up." Brewer planned to use his bully pulpit as governor in 1971, fresh off a November 1970 victory, to push the legislature to codify the commission's suggestions and usher the public to the polls to ratify the new articles.[49]

Brewer quickly came to the realization that the legislature had no stomach for addressing the property tax issue. Legally, the state constitution set the property tax at 60 percent of assessed value. In reality, that provision was never followed. Collections were based on varied property assessments, with some counties devising their own protocols for reducing their tax load. The rural-dominated legislature had been uninterested in any type of equalization code that would have shifted some of the burden off of urban backs. Lurleen Wallace's administration had backed a bill revising the measure to a collection rate of not more than 30 percent, a purposefully vague law that allowed counties to assess anywhere from 1 percent up to a maximum of 30 percent. Simply put, rural counties generally received more in ad valorem taxes back from the state than they contributed, while urban counties received as little as 40 percent of their contribution. Compounding the issue was the newfound independence of the urban legislative bloc that had begun under Lurleen's administration and continued to thrive after Brewer became governor. Ad valorem taxation pitted two of the state's most powerful interest groups, the Farm Bureau and utilities, against each other. The Farm Bureau favored a classification system that would tax agricultural land at the lowest rates while still allowing handsome sales tax exemptions on machinery and other farm purchases. Not surprisingly, the highest rates, according to the Farm Bureau plan, would be borne by utilities. Power and gas companies preferred a flat rate where each land owner, regardless of residential, commercial, or industrial use, would be assessed at the same percentage. Brewer never articulated a consistent position on the matter and likely could not have pushed the contentious legislature to any one position anyway. Despite federal, state, and local reasons to make change, the legislature did nothing, preferring to table the matter for another two years until the interest groups waged another titanic battle.[50]

At the end of the regular session, the Brewer administration had passed funding measures for a state Medicaid program, several highway safety laws, including chemical testing of suspected drunk drivers, two antipornography bills, a new securities commission, an 8.3 percent pay increase for all state employees, a meat inspection act, and a bill authorizing the payment of prevailing wages on all state construction contracts—a provision neither Wallace administration had been able to pass. In addition to the inability to pass property tax reform and the passage of a weak antipollution bill, the administration suffered other setbacks, including failure to address consumer credit protection or switch to annual instead of biennial legislative sessions.[51]

Education: Revenue and Accountability

The administration's biggest achievement came in the form of major education initiatives. Brewer's education strategy merged two competing interests:

improving the state's underfunded and underperforming schools and bridging the divide between federal mandates to hasten desegregation and white Alabama's preference for keeping white schools white. Neither proposition was easy given the state's history of regressive taxation, resistance to new levies, abysmal federal relations, robust distaste for federal intervention, and racial divisions. Yet Brewer, who was hesitant to stake his political capital against entrenched interests on other matters, provided an amazing degree of leadership and moxie in shepherding the most significant education reform in decades through the legislature and into the classroom.

Though he had been an education advocate throughout his tenure in public office and had pushed the creation of an education study commission through the legislature as lieutenant governor, Brewer needed time to formulate a specific revenue plan. A week after taking office, he received a briefing from Education Superintendent Ernest Stone about needs and current conditions. Stone apprised Brewer of teacher apprehension about whether a conditional appropriation for a 4 percent salary hike promised by Lurleen would be released. Brewer released the funding, which further convinced education leaders of his sincerity in helping them. Elsewhere, Brewer gathered as much information as possible about Alabama's schools. The news was not good. Reams of objective evidence indicated that the state, despite the Wallace initiatives of the past few years, had been merely treading water and not improving when compared to regional or national averages.[52]

Behind the scenes, Brewer had told Education Department officials that he intended to change the tone of the governor's office in regard to HEW and court-ordered desegregation: "I want to tell you now that I'm not going to be out haranguing and raising cane and everything about this. I want to try to do it in a way that will let us do the most palatable thing we can do for the people, the patrons of our system." Through an intermediary, Brewer notified President Johnson that he was amenable to resolving disputes quietly and diplomatically. Brewer offered no oath of fealty to the president, but indicated that if given the opportunity to solve its own problems, Alabama would provide a good faith effort and not be bound by previous patterns of blanket resistance. Word came back to Montgomery that Johnson was agreeable and that he wanted to stay out of the courtroom as well. A few weeks later, however, U.S. Attorney General Ramsey Clark filed suit in middle district court in Montgomery to eliminate freedom of choice in favor of faster methods of desegregation. No less a source than Spiro Agnew, governor of Maryland, offered Brewer insight into the sorry state of relations between Alabama and the federal government. "The problem is," Agnew declared, "that nobody believes you, nobody trusts you." Quickly, the State Board of Education authorized legal counsel to fight the lawsuit and issued its own self-serving resolution: "It is the considered opinion of this board that the freedom of choice plan even though involuntarily accepted by each board, had been implemented in good faith by each board and each school system." Soon enough, Brewer was engaging in Wallace-like rhetoric, blasting social engineering and heartless Washington bureaucrats. New governor or not, the battle against the Yankees would continue.[53]

Apart from the legal battles, education leaders were crying out for help and Brewer was listening. "Last year when the legislature met," Auburn University president Harry Philpott observed, "there was little or no support for additional educational advance. There was little or no support for the tax revenues and the tax reforms which would give to us a better system of education." The free textbook system was operating at typical peak inefficiency. "I know that this problem has existed since the inception of the free textbook system," Brewer wrote to Stone, "and I would like to work with you to alleviate this situation so that it will not reoccur." The textbook crisis was typical of other problems in education: inefficiency, waste, political patronage, inadequate resources, and limited follow through had become standard operating procedure. The average cost of books per student was $4.01, a figure based on aggregations of all twelve grades and an approximation of five books per student. Even this figure was inaccurate since it presupposed that no lost or stolen books would have to be replaced or judged to be too worn for use. The textbook budget, adopted under Lurleen's administration, called for $1.16 per pupil, roughly one-quarter the minimum amount to make sure each child had a book for each class. Meanwhile, Alabama's Deep South peer states—Mississippi, Louisiana, Arkansas, and Tennessee—were all budgeting in excess of $4.00 per student. Alabamians continued to debate the political orientation of the authors rather than concentrate on the availability of books for students. Brewer, like his two predecessors and despite his deep interest in correcting policy failures, was convinced that some of the books the state had purchased had an "undue emphasis placed on social problems . . . which I thought presented our state in an unfair light."[54]

Education in Alabama was an acute problem. State-educated teachers continued to opt for greener pastures across state lines. Newly hired teachers in Georgia received a higher annual salary than Alabama teachers with a master's degree and ten years of classroom experience. Only 55 percent of trained teachers who graduated from Alabama's twenty-one colleges and universities took teaching positions in state. Some teachers, disgusted at the lack of community interest, were leaving the profession altogether. "No legislature passing any amount of legislation," James Davis wrote of his wife's decision to quit teaching in Alabama public schools, "no tax bills; no amount of money appropriated for schools can improve the education system in Alabama at this time, because, frankly, the parents of the students just don't give a damn whether their children get an education or not." An AEA study indicated that Alabama would spend less per child than any state in the nation during the fiscal year, a full $81 per child less than the regional average and $216 per child under the U.S. mean. Schools were so notoriously underinsured that natural disasters or unfortunate acts of vandalism could not be overcome. Most school system superintendents were elected, making political connections at least as important as professional credentials.[55]

In nearly every identifiable category—teacher salaries, per pupil expenditures, literacy, local funding, transportation, and facilities—Alabama education, despite Wallace administration pay raises, bond issues, free textbooks, and trade schools, was in desperate condition. In broader assessments, Alabama was doing a poor job of managing scarce resources. The state was paying between thirteen and thirty-four cents per gallon for school bus gasoline and between eleven and sixty-five cents per quart for oil. One study by Jefferson County legislator Tom Gloor indicated that taxi cabs would be a more cost-effective mode of transportation than some bus routes. The trade school and junior college system was spiraling out of control. The latest junior college, Lurleen B. Wallace, was located in Andalusia despite the fact that three other schools already operated within forty-five miles of that South Alabama town; five schools were within fifty-eight miles; and six were within seventy-eight miles. Attendance in state public schools, a traditional measuring stick for the allocation of funding, was dwindling as private school growth mushroomed. Though the need for new revenue was apparent, Alabama also needed to cut the waste and inefficiency in the educational system. "For too long," Brewer admitted, "we have taken the available funds and let the educators divide them up as they chose—this is nothing more than a complete abdication of legislative responsibility and executive responsibility. If we are to assume the burden of providing the revenues . . . then we also have a high responsibility to appropriate the funds to the maximum utilization for the benefit of the school children of our state." While good work was being done by dedicated professionals at every level, success stories were difficult to find. "The greatest problem in gathering educational news throughout the state," Hugh Maddox grumbled, "appears to be a lack of a concern on the part of local boards of education of the value of a good public relations program."[56]

The Education Study Commission reached predictable conclusions about the state of education: "By most of the standards used nationally to judge our schools, Alabama ranks near or at the bottom in the listing of our states. Public elementary and secondary schools are overcrowded, suffer from shortages of teaching material, and do not have the teaching personnel to guarantee educational excellence." The commission called the retention of teachers in the face of mounting morale issues and competition from other states "one of our most serious problems." The commission's three-hundred-page final report issued forty-three separate recommendations for improving education, including a call for new revenue streams. This new funding, the report suggested, should be appropriated through an equalization of property taxes at 30 percent, an increase in income taxes or an adjustment of tax brackets, a 2 percent levy on all items previously exempt from sales tax, and an across-the-board sales tax hike of a half penny. Brewer had some disagreement with the funding initiatives; he preferred to stay out of the property tax quagmire and was ideologically opposed to more increases in the sales tax. Based on his own beliefs and the knowledge that election season was little more than a year away, Brewer steered clear of direct taxes on rank-and-file voters and opted for utility fees, insurance premium taxes, and raising the maximum rate on income taxes. Brewer hoped to kick-start additional revenue streams by forcing local systems to provide minimum funding levels in order to qualify for full state allotments.[57]

The report included substantive changes as well as plans for increased funding. "We looked at everything from teacher salaries to school supplies to building programs," Philpott, an influential commission member, later recalled. The suggestions included new kindergartens; changes in the selection process for State Board of Education members; salary hikes for teachers; a moratorium on new school systems, junior colleges, trade schools, and four-year colleges; a revised teacher-to-student ratio of 1 to 25; and an increase in special education and vocational curricula. The commission's final report, which included input from AEA, state parent-teacher organizations, and other education stakeholders, contained compromises, but was signed by all members without a minority report. The League of Municipalities was so pleased with Brewer's commitment to making change that it issued a glowing endorsement before the governor even released the program. When news of his program hit the streets, the *Birmingham News* was equally supportive: "For the time being, Governor Brewer's proposals to the legislature represent a serious, well-informed effort by a governor whose concern for the welfare of Alabama's schools—and its schoolchildren who represent its future—is exemplary."[58]

Taking the initiative, Brewer pushed the Education Study Commission to complete its work early so he could schedule a special session targeted exclusively for education. And the new governor was not afraid to consider taking on sacred cows; he investigated abolishing teacher tenure and restricting raises to cases of individual merit. Getting wind of Brewer's snooping on teacher tenure and merit pay, the Alabama Education Association released its own statement defending tenure as a right guaranteed by law and pledged to fight tooth and nail for its continuance. Brewer, wisely realizing that an assault on tenure was the legislative equivalent of launching a land war in Asia, retreated from his preferred position in order to keep teachers as allies during what he expected to be a contentious fight. Brewer might have been able to force concessions from AEA because the rest of his program was needed so badly. "If we had pushed the tenure thing as a part of our program," the governor recalled three decades later, "they would have had to swallow tenure to get the money and I think they would have at that time."[59]

Brewer's education revenue package was nothing short of revolutionary based on Alabama standards. Though he identified education as his number one priority, Brewer managed to keep most of his agenda, save tenure and merit pay, from hitting the press until he was ready to announce the entire package. Even supporters were kept at arm's length. "Our exact goals in education at this time are still somewhat indefinite," he admitted to a constituent. Taking much from the work product of the Education Study Commission, Brewer packaged thirty bills together to address the structural, political, revenue, accountability, and morale issues plaguing state schools. Before the session started, he held conferences with key legislative factions to curry support. At the start of the session he gave an impassioned speech that rallied his floor leaders and education advocates. His twin themes of improvement and accountability were apparent: "I am convinced that the people of Alabama are ready and willing to pay for a quality educational system. But I am not going to ask them to shoulder this burden unless and until we can assure them that they are going to get more for the education tax dollar. . . . I ask not only for better paychecks for our teachers, but better teachers for our paychecks." With the exception of a two and a half–week filibuster by urban legislators trying to wring more concessions from their rural colleagues, the session went smoothly, with Brewer skillfully compromising when necessary and holding his ground when possible. Brewer's leadership forced public pressure on filibusterers until their truculence was viewed not as a quest to equalize funding, but as an attempt to prevent schoolchildren from getting a better education. "We have reached the determination," state senator Hugh Morrow admitted, "that we can no longer be placed in the position of killing education for the school children of Alabama."[60]

The net result was a $702 million biennial budget, $132 million more than the previous allotment, and a dramatic first step toward making an Alabama education at least as good as elsewhere in the Deep South. Teachers were slated for a 21.2 percent raise over the next two years. Structurally, the Alabama state superintendent and all local superintendents became appointed, not elected, officials. The education study commission was codified into permanent status, though it never again functioned as effectively. The Alabama Commission on Higher Education (ACHE) was created, though it could not prevent Ralph Adams from establishing Troy State branch campuses across the state, and historically black colleges have consistently felt aggrieved by ACHE. The beleaguered textbook system was bolstered, though it remained underfunded and mismanaged. Some of Brewer's package was akin to placing a Band-Aid on a gunshot wound, but considering the realm of the possible it was an unprecedented achievement by an unelected governor in the lingering shadow of the most powerful politician in state history.[61]

Alabama educators and newspapers were enthusiastic in their support for Brewer's program and viewed him as a working governor more interested in state affairs than in increasing his regional or national popularity. A September 1969 survey by the Oliver Quayle Company revealed phenomenal approval ratings for Brewer, equal to Wallace's in his first administration. Seventy percent of Alabamians surveyed gave Brewer a favorable rating, and 29 percent rated their governor as excellent. Quayle's analysis indicated that many voters felt Brewer was "a hard-working governor who really gets things done." Surprisingly though, Brewer's approval ratings had declined slightly since March. "Last March," the Quayle analysts wrote, "we advised Governor Brewer and his staff to work on voters under thirty-five years old in an effort to correct his weakness among young voters. If such efforts were made, they met with scant success, for his standing among this group has increased only a single point in the past six months while Wallace has gained seven points in the same period." This was a troubling development and a portent of future trouble since voters under the age of thirty-five—an age when their young children were either in their school years or fast approaching them—were more likely than older voters to favor educational improvements. Forty-six percent of Brewer's support was actually coming from voters fifty and older. Only 4 percent of voters who intended to vote for him listed his education program as their principal reason. In other words, while Brewer was achieving the greatest success of his gubernatorial career—the passage of his educational program—many Alabama voters were apathetic.[62]

Even so, the Quayle polls indicated that many Alabamians were dissatisfied with George Wallace; Brewer had a ten-point lead in September 1969. Only half the voters who voted for Lurleen in 1966 planned to vote for her husband in 1970. "Over the past six months," Quayle analysts concluded, "George Wallace has faded somewhat (the feeling here is that a significant part of his sag can be attributed to his rather poorly received advice to parents at the beginning of this month) and Brewer has gained ground (despite some slippage in his job rating) but this is by no means to say that the incumbent is by any means home free." In the press, Brewer coyly claimed to have no idea whether Wallace would run: "I have announced my intention to seek election. I have no control over my opposition." Even so, the administration knew, Wallace's promises notwithstanding, that the former governor would run again.[63]

Quayle suggested Brewer "should make busy and dynamic noises for the next several months to keep his job rating up." This was Brewer's nature anyway, but federal matters involving the pace of desegregation kept the governor in the headlines. Thrown into the fire with federal suits designed to replace freedom of choice with integration by block assignments of students to specific schools, the Brewer administration found itself carrying water on both shoulders: pushing for a scientific management approach to education while juggling the imperatives of white Alabamians to make social change as slowly as possible. Brewer knew three months into his term and six months before he announced his education program that federal court decisions could have dramatic effects on his ability to convince the legislature to appropriate more funds. Simply put, another round of protracted white flight to private schools would erode the chances of convincing white Alabama to pay higher taxes for public schools. Taxpayers "are not going to provide sufficient support . . . to increase financing for public education or even to maintain the same level of support," the governor argued fruitlessly to a three-judge federal panel, if courts imposed additional requirements for school integration.[64]

Frank Johnson and the rest of the panel issued a stern decree directing faculty desegregation in 76 schools and the closing of up to 145 previously all-black schools. Nearly 220 teachers "crossed over" to teach in schools where their skin color was different from the majority of the student body. Several new Negro schools, including Lanier High School in Lanett, were closed. Ernest Stone estimated the total financial loss to the state at over $15 million. Despite the court's semantics about freedom of choice continuing under certain conditions, the practice as Alabamians had come to know it was effectively over. Curiously enough, white Alabama's embrace of freedom of choice was a new phenomenon. In the wake of the *Brown* decision and several subsequent cases, white Alabamians howled that black parents wanted their children to have the right to attend a school of their own choosing. In practice, however, freedom of choice led to few decisions in the black community to send their children to all-white schools and no decisions in white households to send their sons and daughters to all-black schools. Freedom of choice later became popular among whites *because* it effectively kept wholesale integration from occurring. Freedom of choice might as well have been renamed freedom to remain segregated. The court decision to end freedom of choice, then, was viewed as a final deadly assault on the concept of separate schools.[65]

Brewer lashed out at the ruling, blaming the federal government for "trying to achieve social objectives while we are trying to educate our young people." In correspondence, Brewer was no less restrained: "We have exhausted nearly every legal remedy at our command and will continue to resist the take-over of our schools in every way possible." The governor suggested that a massive letter-writing campaign expressing displeasure with the court ruling might effect change, but that movement never took shape. Some in the administration considered a wholesale resignation of all members of the state Board of Education. Brewer viewed the resignations as a way to "dramatically show the court the serious nature of this order and the impossibility of implementing the order and still maintaining a quality school system." A year later, an exasperated Brewer was even pushing private schools as a safety valve."My brother is a high school principal," he wrote to Mrs. Richard Knox, "and he told me last week he was faced with a decision whether to lower his academic standards to accommodate the level of the Negro students, or to maintain his present standards knowing they could not possibly meet them. . . . I see in the future the opening of private schools. The funds to support this effort must be supplied, at least in part, from state funds." On other occasions, Brewer championed private schools, but he never wavered in his commitment for Alabama to have a viable public school system.[66]

The education community mimicked Brewer's outrage at the court decision. "Innocent children who need the very best education we can give them," Vernon St. John, AEA president railed, "will be the unfortunate victims of this unjust order of the federal courts. . . . This court decision has struck a disastrous blow at quality education in Alabama when our teachers and school officials need full public support in their difficult and awesome task of educating Alabama's some 900,000 children now preparing to enter classes again for a new term." Some Alabamians repeated their calls from previous years to close the schools. Brewer called a special meeting of school superintendents to "document in detail cases of extreme hardship" as a result of the court's decisions. The merger of the Alabama Education Association (white) with the Alabama State Teachers Association (black) compounded the tension.[67]

Over the course of his term, Brewer consistently appealed federal court decisions and fought efforts to hasten the pace of desegregation. At one point the governor averred "much of my time is spent on trying to save our school system from the courts and the liberals who are trying to take them over and run them to accomplish social ends." The looming prospect of a 1970 battle against Wallace was a factor in Brewer's ongoing struggle against the combined efforts of HEW and the Justice Department. It was not necessary to out-Wallace the former governor since that was a game Brewer was ill equipped and unwilling to play. But Alabamians, even in their realization that integration was here to stay, expected their chief executive to continue to fight for their traditions regardless of whether the prospect for victory was promising or not. A reprise of Chancellorsville or Bull Run was too much to expect, but Alabamians had grown accustomed to Wallace assuming the role of George

Edward Pickett and charging headlong into a sea of Yankees. They expected no less of Albert Brewer.[68]

The 1970 Campaign

Wallace spent most of 1969 resting and charting the political winds. By fall he was ready to get off the bench and back in the game. As in 1962, Wallace came out firing not at his political opponents, but at the federal judiciary. While governor, Wallace had never enforced freedom of choice, but by September 1969 he viewed the principle as if it had come down from Mount Sinai with ten other commandments: "Freedom of choice is the law. Take your children to the school you want them to go to and tell the teacher, 'here they are and here they're going to stay!' Keep bringing them back day after day." Wallace urged parents to take to the street in peaceful marches that would illustrate their commitment. The rhetoric was clearly a trial balloon for the governor's race to see if the same appeals still resonated with the people. Challenged by reporters, Wallace rejected the notion that he might be plotting a foray in 1970: "I don't have to do this to run for governor of Alabama. I may never run for governor of Alabama again. I feel that I have the right [to speak out] since I would still be in an advisory capacity if my wife, Lurleen, had lived to serve out her term."[69]

Above and beyond generating headlines, Wallace interacted with the people and spoke at rallies sponsored by the Concerned Parents for Public Schools. With Wallace added to the roster of speakers, the crowds grew from a few hundred to a few thousand. Alabamians may have approved of Albert Brewer's roll-up-the-sleeves work ethic, but it was Wallace who made their hearts flutter. The events included all the trappings of a campaign stop: literature, buttons, bumper stickers, booklets, and a country and western opening act to warm up the crowd. The former governor was delighted when a Negro gentleman pumped his hand after the speech and declared "let me shake the hand of our next president." Brewer told reporters the Wallace appearance was not a stump speech, but all of Alabama understood that the old allies were about to wage the most contentious gubernatorial election in state history.[70]

Within weeks of his Concerned Parents appearance, Wallace staffers began lining up sound trucks for the following spring. An anonymous supporter realized exactly what that meant: "You don't need sound trucks to run for president." Wallace neither affirmed nor denied his intent to run for governor but parsed his words carefully to create enough wiggle room to make previous comments less damaging: "I have no plans to run for governor *now*. I have never said that I would not run." In reality, Wallace had told reporters during the 1968 campaign that he would not run, told Brewer and Ingram as many as a dozen times, and volunteered the information to several legislators. "You all go do a good job," Wallace told state senator Eddie Gilmore, "I'm not going to run again. You help Al. He's going to be a great governor."[71]

The Brewer campaign enlisted Bill Jones to find a film of a South Carolina appearance where Wallace told reporters that he would never run for governor again. Jones searched his extensive contacts but never found the film, which seemed to have been mysteriously misplaced. Gracious to a fault, Brewer sent two state troopers with Wallace when the former governor traveled to Vietnam for a fact-finding tour in November. On his return home, Wallace inched closer to declaring: "I have not made a definite decision but I am seriously considering the matter." He told reporters that if he decided to run, it would be because people wanted him to use that office for a presidential run.[72]

Over the next weeks and months, Wallace would name numerous opponents who he believed were conspiring to end his political career. He identified national Republicans such as Richard Nixon and his postmaster general, Alabamian Winton Blount; national Democrats such as state party chairman Robert Vance; militants and communists who had opposed him every step of the way since his first term; big city newspapers; and certain unnamed state officials, a veiled reference to Brewer. Though his stump speeches often featured aspersions that bordered on paranoia, on this matter, Wallace was correct. The Nixon administration, through the input of Blount and various cloak-and-dagger machinations, provided four hundred thousand dollars to the Brewer campaign in hopes that the new governor could defeat the former one and eliminate a rival in 1972. Nixon, relying on the political projections of Kevin Phillips and a "southern strategy" championed by South Carolina strategist Harry Dent, feared Wallace as a third-party candidate who could siphon off socially conservative votes. As the southern electorate slowly realigned in the wake of the civil rights movement, and the national Democratic party tilted leftward, Nixon knew traditional Democratic alliances were unraveling in the South and an anticipated liberal standard-bearer such as Hubert Humphrey, George McGovern, or Edmund Muskie could not beat him in the South. Wallace, if he ran as a Democrat, could win the South but would not stir the masses in the traditional Democratic strongholds in the Northeast or Midwest. As a result, Nixon only feared a three-horse race in which Wallace could hurt him in the South and a national Democrat could win in electoral-rich states like Illinois, Ohio, and New York. Defeating Wallace's bid for governor in 1970 was a sure way to mute the Alabamian's prospect of barnstorming the country in 1972 under the American Independent banner.[73]

Reporter Ted Pearson confirmed the GOP strategy, though the details of the cash transfer had yet to become public knowledge. "The public will see little, if any overt activity by the Republican strategy board in behalf of Brewer. But with . . . Winton Blount . . . calling the tactical shots, the behind-the-scenes blessing of Brewer will not only be warm but practical: in such ways as encouraging the legion of Republican conservatives in Alabama to back Brewer and encouraging the flow of campaign money . . . to the Brewer coffers." For his part, Brewer denied he was the adopted son of the Republican Party, noting any such arrangement could end up helping Wallace more than himself.[74]

From numerous sources and his own political instincts, Wallace knew this race would be difficult and he, not Brewer, was the underdog. Wallace staffers had commissioned a poll in January 1970 that revealed Brewer had a nineteen-point lead among likely Democratic primary voters. Brewer's own January polling was less optimistic, but still revealed the governor had an eight-point lead, a reduction of one point since the September 1969 survey. None of the handful of minor candidates—Charles Woods, Jim Folsom, John Cashin, or Asa Carter—had much individual support. But the high number of undecided voters indicated that a quarter of the electorate was not yet sold on either Brewer or Wallace. In other words, both Brewer and Wallace had considerable ground to make up if they wanted to avoid a two-man runoff.[75]

In the days before the campaign officially kicked off, both Brewer and Wallace sharpened their attacks on federal desegregation. "I will continue to support public education," Brewer promised, "but we have got to do what we can to assist parents who choose another course to educate their children." He reiterated on several occasions that he was studying ways to aid private schools since public schools "cannot continue to operate as they do now in the face of total integration." Calling busing the "most iniquitous thing that can happen to school children," the governor urged "total resistance" to any federally mandated plan to use busing in order to achieve racial balance. Citing separate standards for the South and the rest of the country, Brewer announced he would continue to appeal court decisions and lobby for a national freedom-of-choice law: "The question now is not integration or segregation, it is what kind of schools we are going to operate. The question is, are we going to stop herding teachers and children around like cattle to achieve a racial balance in the South." Both Wallace and Brewer spoke at a February Concerned Parents rally as both jockeyed to be seen as committed protectors of southern traditions.[76]

On the eve of Wallace's formal announcement for governor, Brewer scooped the headlines by calling the legislature into a special five-day session to pass a freedom-of-choice law. Though Brewer had been outspoken on the issue since he assumed office, it was clear that this session had political overtones: "I ask you—what is fair and equal treatment? Is it fair that the children of New York have freedom of choice and the children of Alabama can't have it? During the last four weeks, we have seen the first encouraging sign in many years in the school situation. For the first time, we're on the offensive. Finally we're getting something done." After three minutes of discussion, the house and senate passed Brewer's freedom-of-choice bill. Even Wallace admitted that Brewer was "not soft" on integration, though he stated that he himself was the only candidate who could apply meaningful pressure on Washington. "When I am elected governor of Alabama," Wallace predicted, "it will be un-necessary to run in 1972 because then Mr. Nixon is going to carry out commitments he made about public schools in 1968."[77]

With Brewer's fitness as a defender of freedom of choice firmly established, the battle lines of the campaign emerged on two fronts. The Wallace campaign advised Alabamians to vote for the former governor in order to keep his national movement alive. "I had no plans to run for state office again," Wallace declared, "but conditions now make it imperative that I run. This race for governor will have a terrific impact on government at the national level and I am serving a useful purpose by running." Alabamians who wanted a full-time governor dedicated to all their concerns were advised by the Brewer campaign to vote for the present governor. "I offer my record of progress and achievement and constructive gain," Brewer announced. "I hope that race will not enter into the issues."[78]

Quayle's January polling identified two potential Brewer slogans that resonated with Alabama voters: "Alabama First," and "Full Time for Alabama." The results also indicated another troublesome trend: Alabamians, though they preferred Brewer by eight points, expected that Wallace would eventually win. Surprisingly, Quayle advised Brewer not to confront Wallace directly: "Take the high road, make the election a Brewer referendum by running on the Brewer record and the opportunity voters have of continuing with this type of responsible, hard working leadership. Ignore Wallace as much as possible. . . . Wallace will find it very difficult to sustain his campaign if Brewer does not react." Armed with inside knowledge from various sources about past Wallace administration indiscretions and steamed that Wallace had broken a promise not to run, Brewer found it difficult to keep from attacking: "It was like tying our hands behind our back. After the campaign was over, [campaign manager] Alton Turner said with some profanity, that he wished he had never seen a poll because if you are going to lose anyway, you wish you could just take the gloves off." Even so, Brewer resisted opportunities to "take the hide off" Wallace and ran a vigorous issue-oriented race.[79]

Wallace, on the other hand, began his campaign with a stream of aggressive promises. Understanding that his national forays brought him fame but also caused some voters to long for a full-time governor in Montgomery, Wallace thought the promises would demonstrate a commitment to governance. He proposed continued expansion of highway, education, and industrial development programs begun in his first term, pledged no new taxes would be sponsored by his administration and any levies passed by the legislature would be subject to voter approval, vowed to slash utility rates and investigate unfair billing practices, and planned to provide tax credits for families with schoolchildren. Wallace announced he would expand the bus system for ferrying students to junior colleges and trade schools and create a Bureau of Consumers Affairs composed of five housewives to monitor deceptive advertising. As the campaign unfolded, Wallace made new promises, including pledges to cut insurance rates, build new medical schools, boost old age pensions to one hundred per month, provide health insurance for any Alabamian in need, construct four-lane highways between every major city, expand state parks and farmers markets, craft stronger ethics laws, and create a Governor's Youth Council. Even though the expanded programs were not consistent with a vow to veto any new taxes, Wallace continued to announce new initiatives on a weekly basis, and the promises came wrapped in a ribbon of white southern morality: "I will sit in the governor's office, preside over another four years of unequaled accomplishments by and for the people of Alabama, and at the same time keep my foot in the backs of those who now have their feet on our necks. We will get our schools and our children back and we will continue to demand tax relief for the working men and women of modest income." In contrast, Brewer made few promises except to remove merit qualifications from a teacher pay-raise plan, fix the free textbook system, and cut the cost of car tags back to three dollars.[80]

Only one of the handful of lesser known candidates, millionaire Dothan businessman Charles Woods, made any inroads. Buoyed by his surprising performance in 1966, Woods spent aggressively on print and electronic media ads and galvanized a small but loyal following convinced that neither Wallace nor Brewer, both political insiders, would make much of a difference in Montgomery. Woods focused his campaign on corruption in asphalt contracts and among liquor agents and on inefficient textbook operations, issues that occurred while both Wallace and Brewer were in prominent positions. Woods attracted some Alabama progressives with his appeals to shift the tax burden to big business, increase property taxes, and remove the sales tax from medicine and groceries. Ultimately, Woods's 149,887 votes in the May primary forced Wallace and Brewer into a runoff.[81]

Quayle's March 1970 polling indicated that Brewer had done nothing in the first two weeks of the campaign to hurt his chances of winning in May. Though he had lost 5 percentage points from 42 to 37, Brewer maintained the same 8-point lead he enjoyed in the January poll; Wallace had also lost 5 points, dropping from 34 to 29 percent of the vote. The poll revealed that the undecided vote, only 10 percent in January, had grown to 28 percent in March.

Alabamians, intrigued by the start of the political season, were contemplating their next move. The poll also indicated that Alabamians were less sure that Wallace would eventually pull ahead and win. Thirty-two percent identified Wallace as the man they expected to win, but 34 percent viewed Brewer as the eventual winner. An equal 34 percent was unsure who would win. Quayle summed up its latest survey with an ominous prediction: "The real problem now is that too many voters who are undecided in this contest feel that it may be in the bag for Governor Brewer, and therefore may stay home on May 5th and not vote for him."[82]

The opening weeks of the campaign featured little of the racial animus that would later characterize it as the gold standard for bitter races. Wallace uncharacteristically struggled to find his way on the stump; a University of Alabama crowd booed him off the stage. Throughout the campaign, Wallace faced heckling from crowds, something predictable outside the state but previously unthinkable within Alabama. Unable to strike a chord, Wallace alternately called for winning the war in Vietnam, leniency for accused war criminal William Calley of My Lai infamy, and turning out Richard Nixon for betraying the South on integration. He talked of "strange bedfellows" who were conspiring to destroy him and took to carrying a cot as a stage prop to demonstrate that his scheming rivals were all in bed together. Wallace claimed that his preference for national campaigning was the true role an Alabama governor should play: "The *Birmingham News* and the other big city newspapers say the governor of Alabama ought to sit in the kitchen and shell peas, and cut ribbons, and kiss beauty queens. Well I can do that too, but I also plan to continue to speak out on issues affecting our country and our state."[83]

Both Wallace and Brewer crisscrossed the state at breakneck pace. Generally, Brewer received more favorable coverage from the state's newspapers and soon began racking up endorsements from the media and labor unions. He continued to peck away at recent federal court decisions and claimed his governance was making a difference: "For the first time we are on the offensive. For the first time we have some hope of success. For the first time, instead of just talking, we are taking action." Brewer made no direct overtures for black votes but was counseled by Quayle to "prepare for last minute organizational efforts to get Negro voters." Brewer never roused the passions that Wallace did, but learned the art of counterpunching from years of watching Wallace. When Wallace told crowds not to elect him if all they needed was a ribbon cutter, Brewer told crowds he enjoyed the ceremonial duty since it meant local people were seeing state government accomplish something on their behalf. When Wallace told Alabamians that Brewer was carried by Lurleen's skirt-tails, Brewer announced record fund-raising amounts for the Lurleen Wallace Cancer Hospital. When Wallace announced a new series of promises, Brewer replied "the only promise I make is that when I'm elected I will never embarrass you or your state." When Wallace referred to sissies and liberals in state government who were afraid to stand up for Alabama, Brewer reminded his supporters that he had vetoed new funding for SWAFCA just as his two predecessors had done. Quayle's April 1970 poll revealed Brewer had widened his lead to 10 points and the undecided vote had been trimmed from 28 to 12 percent. Ralph Paul, a Geneva County lawyer, could not believe what he was witnessing: "You won't believe this and I wouldn't have myself until a few weeks ago, but Brewer is going to carry this county where Wallace has been getting 80 percent or better in the past." At the crossroads of their political careers, Brewer was on the precipice of sending Wallace to Buck's Pocket, mythical home of washed-up Alabama politicians.[84]

Two weeks before the May 5 primary, the Wallace campaign began to circulate a series of smear sheets designed to frighten Alabamians about the racial future of the state under a Brewer administration. One piece of literature, doctored from a photo of Brewer with country crooner Johnny Cash, depicted Elijah Muhammad and Cassius Clay with the governor under the headline "Governor Brewer and the Black Muslims." Another sheet questioned Brewer's patriotism and suggested he was not a member of the American Legion. An advertisement in state papers stated that "Blacks back Brewer against Wallace" and depicted a copy of an Alabama Democratic Conference memoranda pledging to defeat Wallace. While blacks were unlikely to support Wallace in the primary, it was unclear whether they would vote for Brewer. John Cashin, a rising leader in the African American political community, implored blacks to vote for neither candidate so they could hold valuable bargaining chips in the event of a runoff. The Alabama Democratic Conference never formally endorsed Brewer before the primary, and some blacks elected to vote for Woods. Though he effectively countered Wallace throughout the early campaign, Brewer never found a response to the smear sheets that would soothe voter concerns. Slowly but surely, allegations that Brewer would get the notorious "bloc vote" began to stem his momentum and allowed Wallace to hit his stride.[85]

In its last poll before the primary, Quayle cautioned Brewer to "run scared," because Wallace was capable of making up any lead once he connected to his base. More than anything, the smear sheets energized the old Wallace faithful and forced some tentative Brewer backers to switch to Charles Woods or stay home. On May 5, one day after the nation reacted in horror to the tragedy at Kent State University, Alabama voters provided Brewer a narrow lead over Wallace. Yet Brewer was not able to garner over 50 percent of the vote, necessitating a June 2 runoff. Brewer told his supporters he would continue to run a "clean campaign . . . that befits the office of governor." Wallace remained defiant, noting he had done "[remarkably] well with the opposition we faced, with the Washington interference and the bloc vote."[86]

Outwardly Wallace appeared optimistic as the election returns indicated he was running close enough to force a two-man race in June; inwardly he was devastated. Wallace retired to a Birmingham hotel room, turned out the lights, climbed into bed, and pulled the covers over his head convinced his political career was finished. Wallace understood Alabama political history; no gubernatorial candidate who finished second in the primary had won a runoff since 1914. Gerald Wallace massed the trusted inner circle and went to Birmingham to get him up, shaved, and back on the stump. Roused from his depression, Wallace pounded Brewer daily for receiving the bloc vote. He might lose the election, Wallace concluded, but he was going to pull out all the stops to make sure he did not go down without a fight.[87]

Wallace forces worked frenetically on numerous fronts to keep the momentum they created in the two weeks before the primary rolling. More than thirty thousand new voters were registered by Wallace backers in preparation for the runoff. In an effort to woo Woods's supporters, Wallace announced he had offered Charles Woods the plum job of finance director. Wallace intensified his attacks on the bloc vote and speculated that a Brewer victory would mean "control of the state will be turned over to them [militant blacks] for fifty years." Wallace spoke of a "spotted alliance" between rich whites and blacks and warned friends in Barbour County, "don't let them niggers beat us, you hear." The smear sheets proliferated with depictions of a young blond girl surrounded by several black boys on a beach. The implication was clear: Albert Brewer would preside over a new world order that would make such a scene a recurring nightmare for white Alabama. Vicious rumors circulated about Brewer's religious convictions and the sexual proclivities of the governor's wife and daughters. Placards asking "Do you want the Black Bloc Vote to elect and control the Governor's Office and Our State?" were stapled to telephone polls, and community billboards, placed under windshields, and published in newspapers. Klan contacts were mobilized to pepper the state with Wallace literature and anti-Brewer propaganda and to vandalize Brewer signs.[88]

Brewer supporters were not above a little unethical electioneering themselves. Brewer supporters spied on Wallace, and rumors were circulated that George Wallace Jr. was addicted to drugs. Press Secretary Bob Inman and his chopper pilot crashed on Gerald Wallace's farm while trying to uncover some dirt to use in the campaign. But the Brewer operatives were comparative novices at slash-and-burn campaigning, and they never slowed the Wallace momentum. Quayle's May poll revealed the changing tides: "Playing the gut race issue, Wallace has closed hard on Governor Brewer, and the movement is very definitely wrong; in our April study we reported that there was no need to hit the panic button, but we are hitting it now."[89]

In the end, Wallace beat Brewer for several reasons. More of Woods's supporters voted for Wallace than Brewer. His campaign registered thousands of new voters and Brewer's did not. He created enough racial uproar to make sure his base voted on election day. The notorious bloc vote did not turn out significantly enough for Brewer to rack up better numbers in Jefferson and Montgomery County. Eleven North and Central Alabama counties that Brewer had won in the primary switched their support to Wallace, a South Alabamian, in the runoff. Some Alabamians, confronted with a social and political crossroads, simply made a choice to pick the candidate who would keep them in the headlines and on the nightly news instead of the candidate who might help them improve from forty-eighth to forty-third place in some statistical ranking. Wallace would get another chance to stand up for Alabama.[90]

Wallace greets young women with their babies at a yard sale. He never passed up a chance to campaign with Alabama voters. (Courtesy Alabama Department of Archives and History.)

The charismatic Wallace had superior interpersonal communication skills. Here, he speaks to some Alabama women after church. (Courtesy Alabama Department of Archives and History).

Wallace's appeal spanned all age groups, and during his first term, he was as popular as any rock star. (Courtesy Alabama Department of Archives and History.)

Though Wallace's core supporters were blue-collar workers and the lower middle class, he also won support from some Alabama elites, including women. (Courtesy Alabama Department of Archives and History.)

Albert Brewer was sworn in as governor after Lurleen Wallace died in office. (Courtesy Alabama Department of Archives and History.)

A consummate campaigner, Wallace was at ease with people of every socio-economic class. (Courtesy Alabama Department of Archives and History.)

Reporters often under-estimated Wallace and were surprised by his skills and his intelligence. (Courtesy Alabama Department of Archives and History.)

After he was paralyzed, Wallace often reached out to children, the elderly, and the incapacitated. Here, he and his second wife, Cornelia, greet a young Alabama girl. (Courtesy Alabama Department of Archives and History.)

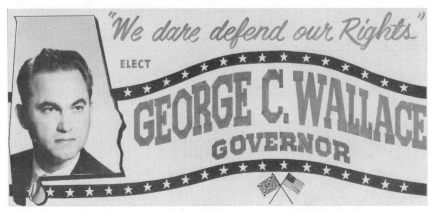

Early Wallace campaign material often included the Confederate flag. (Courtesy Alabama Department of Archives and History.)

Credit for administration successes was always directed toward the governor. (Courtesy Alabama Department of Archives and History.)

Wallace often spoke at Citizens' Council rallies. Lurleen can be seen just to the left of the Confederate flag, waiting patiently in the background. (Courtesy Alabama Department of Archives and History.)

Unlike Lurleen, Wallace's second wife, Cornelia, loved the limelight. (Courtesy Alabama Department of Archives and History.)

Over time, Lurleen Wallace grew more comfortable in her role as governor. Here, she poses with members of the Alabama National Guard. (Courtesy Alabama Department of Archives and History.)

Wallace hands a gift to an unidentified African American man. He loved dressing up and playing Santa Claus. (Courtesy Alabama Department of Archives and History.)

Wallace forged a connection with his constituents that survived after segregation fell, after he was confined to a wheelchair, and after presidential campaigns became distant memories. (Courtesy Alabama Department of Archives and History.)

8
Turning Point / 1970–1972

With Albert Brewer dispatched, Wallace moved quickly to distance himself from the bitter tenor of the campaign and to assure Alabamians that he intended to keep his numerous campaign promises. "We will have a progressive administration," Wallace told Associated Press reporter Rex Thomas, "that will attempt . . . to care for the needs of the people of our state. . . . And I'll be governor of all the people of the state. . . . We want to see Alabama prosper and more industrial jobs for people of all races. We want to see a better school system for people of all races. We want to see our people join together to work toward the future." Other observers were not convinced. The *Los Angeles Times* called Wallace's victory a "distinct setback for those who have wanted and worked for racial progress." The *Washington Post* concluded that "the Confederacy still lives and George Wallace remains its prophet." The *Washington Star,* a conservative paper, characterized the Wallace campaign as one based on fear.[1]

Inside the state, potential rivals scattered. State GOP chair Richard Bennett announced his party had no plans to enter a candidate against Wallace in November. Republican congressman William Dickinson wanted no part of a race against Wallace either: "If we try to storm that bastion again we may find[,] after the smoke clears, that we have lost the only three congressmen we have left." Brewer rebuffed the overtures of his most ardent supporters to enter the November race as a write-in candidate. In the aftermath of the runoff, Brewer, normally composed and gracious, was swept up in rage: "[That was] the dirtiest campaign I've ever seen in all my political career. It was nigger, nigger, nigger all over again. I hoped race wouldn't become an issue in this campaign, but it boiled down to a hate and smear issue. And if that's what it takes to win, the cost is too high." Wallace called Brewer his "personal friend" and congratulated his former ally for running an "excellent race." Wallace's rhetoric notwithstanding, the two did not speak on election night, and the wounds of 1970 never healed.[2]

In the years after the 1970 runoff, students of Alabama history debated the legacy of that campaign in coffee shops, watering holes, and courthouses, speculating whether Alabama would have turned a different page had Wallace lost. Wallace's strategy proved an excellent model for Georgia agribusinessman Jimmy Carter, who steered his own campaign hard to the right to defeat former governor Carl Sanders. Carter, nevertheless, governed as a moderate as did other New South governors such as Dale Bumpers in Arkansas, John West in South Carolina, and Reuben Askew in Florida. While little doubt exists that Brewer would have formulated different priorities, in the end, the fact that he came as close as he did may be the most remarkable aspect of the entire campaign. With a regional and national profile, a network of contacts and campaign workers who would stop at nothing, and a highly developed sense of the electorate, Wallace was simply too dynamic, too battle tested, and too entrenched in the hearts of many Alabamians to be beaten. That Brewer ran as well as he did is a testament to his leadership and accomplishments during his thirty-three-month tenure as governor. Alabama never elected a New South governor along the lines of a Carter or Askew.[3]

Wallace's narrow victory was hardly a mandate; he would never again possess the same power or popularity that he enjoyed from 1963 to 1966. A new legislature, dominated by urban districts, had no interest in serving as a rubber stamp. Two African Americans—Fred Gray and Thomas Reed—won house races in 1970, the first to serve since Reconstruction. The state's major newspapers, largely supportive of Brewer, were critical of Wallace's campaign tactics and showed no inclination to offer the traditional honeymoon period extended to a new administration. With the exception of Taylor Hardin, Wallace's new inner circle was less experienced than the group who had served him and Lurleen in the past. And a group of young Turks, including Attorney General Bill Baxley and Lieutenant Governor Jere Beasley, were intent on making their own mark. Circuit judge Richard Emmet wasted no time in declaring himself a candidate for the 1974 race and began to schedule speaking engagements across the state. Brewer took a partnership in a Montgomery law firm but kept his campaign files in order, anticipating that the racial climate would soften over the next four years.[4]

The November general election was little more than a formality, with Wallace trouncing John Cashin and A. C. Shelton en route to garnering nearly three-quarters of the total vote. Despite a June pledge that he had "no national political plans at this moment," Wallace tried out several national campaign talking points to see if they resonated in Alabama. At a September rally in Mobile, Wallace christened his supporters the "hard-hat movement" and announced that "being a southerner is no longer geographical, it's a state of mind." He urged parents to defy federal court orders and practice freedom of choice, foreshadowing later sustained attacks on busing. In his monthly news-letter, Wallace called for a renewed commitment to law and order that would stop "the assassination of policemen" and lead to an elimination of the "slob-bering tolerance of certain members of the judiciary." At a speech before the John Birch Society, Wallace took a swipe at Richard Nixon: "We cannot let this great land of freedom be destroyed. We cannot let 194 years of freedom and justice slip from our grasp . . . because some of our leaders either don't see the danger or don't care."[5]

Brewer had no intention of leaving surplus funds for Wallace. Over the last seven months of his term, he released another teacher raise from condi-tional appropriations and let contracts for roads, mental health facilities, and state park construction. Brewer mulled calling a special session for enacting tougher pollution regulations but ultimately rejected the idea, reasoning he had no power to get such a contentious bill passed. Wallace would have several major problems to address in 1971: ad valorem taxation, pollution, education and general fund budgets, medicaid funding, and mental health operations. And given his narrow victory and the new legislative climate, old fashioned power politics, perpetual campaigning, and patronage payoffs were no longer sure bets for success.[6]

In the 1967 inaugural motorcade, Wallace, Lurleen, and Brewer had rid-den together in a convertible Ford Mustang waving at the throng of applaud-ing Alabamians. During that parade, Wallace leaned over to Brewer and sug-gested that Brewer would be riding to the 1971 gala as the new governor. With that memory in mind, Brewer, the outgoing governor, Wallace, the incoming chief executive, and Jere Beasley, the incoming lieutenant governor, shared a tense ride in a closed car where even small talk was difficult. Finally, as the car turned up Dexter Avenue toward the capitol, Wallace broke the ice by remark-ing, "I hope nobody shoots us." Lieutenant Governor-elect Jere Beasley, under-standing that neither he nor Brewer would be targets, replied, "well if they do, I hope they don't miss." Minutes after Wallace took the oath of office, Brewer drifted off into the crowd and the torch had been passed.[7]

Wallace's second inaugural was noticeably different from the frigid morn-ing in 1963 when his rhetorical flourish, "segregation now, segregation to-morrow, segregation forever," foreshadowed four years of bitter race relations and emerging national ambitions. The 1971 speech focused on the theme of people power and indicated that his administration was dedicated to the in-terests of "black and white, young and old, rich and poor." Even so, he included a vintage attack on the federal government: "For too long the voice of the people has been silenced by their own disruptive government, by governmental bribery in quasi-governmental handouts such as HEW and others that exist in America today. An aroused people can save this nation from those evil forces who seek our destruction." Blacks, prevented from participating in 1963, were sprinkled throughout the 208 bands, 15,205 musicians, 94 floats, and 31 marching units. Though the formal ball was canceled during Lurleen's inauguration—purportedly because of the Vietnam War—the gala was back in 1971 even though American troops were still fighting in Southeast Asia.[8]

Wallace's new bride, the former Cornelia Ellis Snively, was the star of the inaugural ball. Cornelia, the daughter of Ruby Folsom Ellis and the niece of Big Jim Folsom, was no stranger to either politics or the public eye. Brash, energetic, and gorgeous, Cornelia—twenty years younger than her new husband—first met Wallace at age seven when her uncle was governor and George was in the legislature. The pair began dating in the summer of 1970, and the divorcee and the widower soon became virtually inseparable in private, even while they tried to squelch public gossip about their courtship. At a 1970 campaign rally, precocious Lee Wallace informed her candidate father, "I want you to marry that black-haired girl with the two children." By September, the *Birmingham News* was reporting rumors that marriage could be in the offing. George and Cornelia brought their families together for dinner and their host, Miss Ruby, gave the Wallace children plenty to laugh about with her ripped Hawaiian dress, lime green fishnet stockings, and obvious inebriation. Even so, they soon realized that their father was serious about Cornelia. After that night, the family giggled at their father who was giddy with love and the allure of the vivacious Cornelia. Characteristically, Wallace never told his children about the seriousness of the relationship or his plans for marriage.[9]

On Christmas Day 1970, Wallace and Cornelia announced their engagement. Nattily attired in a blue double-breasted suit with a canary yellow shirt and colorful tie, Wallace was clearly receiving an image makeover from his fiancée. Over the next few months, Cornelia diversified his wardrobe—the black and navy blue suits of the past disappeared—his sideburns grew, and the slicked-back hair of days gone by was replaced with a bouncy coiffure topped off with hair spray. Eventually, campaign staff would tout the newlyweds as a southern-fried version of John and Jacqueline Kennedy. Cornelia was no wallflower; she loved the stage and spotlight more than Lurleen and relished reporters' questions. On one occasion, Cornelia announced that the administration was considering a soft drink tax for increasing mental health revenue. Wallace, already on record as opposing any new levies, was forced to rebuff his wife. Wallace forbade Cornelia from testifying before the Ways and Means Committee about the governor's mansion budget, fearing what his wild-card wife might say. When Cornelia declined to offer comments at a Business Management and Government Conference, she admitted she was on a short lease: "Whenever I'm called on to talk, George nearly has heart failure." Family members noted Cornelia's occasional rhetorical excesses. "She said some things that angered him," George Wallace Jr. recalled, "but he had a tiger by the tail. She tended to want her own headlines and that wasn't the name of the game."[10]

Wallace was concerned for a time that Cornelia's status as a divorcee would cause some Alabamians to think negatively of the marriage. Wallace called Chriss Doss, a newly elected Jefferson County representative and an ordained minister, to see how the marriage would play across the state. "There are some pockets where that is still an issue," Doss replied, "but I don't think it amounts to that much." Doss was a Brewer supporter in 1970, though he avoided taking public stands that might have hurt him in his own race. Essentially, Wallace was reaching out to him to see if he could sway him into his camp for the next four years. "Wallace was a very sharp politician," Doss recalled years later, "and he looked for good people that were not in his camp and he would baby them or court them and try to bring them on board." Doss might have officiated had the wedding been in Birmingham, but the governor and Cornelia decided to hold the ceremony in Montgomery. The ceremony was held at Trinity Presbyterian, the same church where Cornelia had married John Snively years before.[11]

Administration staffers were often aghast at Cornelia's propensity to get in front of a camera. "There were those of us who would get a little nervous if she had an interview," aide Elvin Stanton admitted. During the 1972 presidential campaign, Cornelia occasionally strayed off property when the campaign motorcade was ready to head to the next stop. This resulted in arguments because senior staff would have to find her, make arrangements to pick her up later, or wait patiently until she was ready to leave. Some felt Cornelia wanted a strong voice in policy and strategy matters even though the inner circle did not view her as politically astute. Nevertheless, Cornelia was initially accepted by the family because she served as a surrogate mother for young Lee. Over time, the older children wanted Cornelia to focus more on motherhood and less on public matters. "She was very good to all of us," Peggy Wallace Kennedy recalled, "and we loved her. She had two boys of her own and she made sure that all three of the kids were taken care of and that there was somebody there. Her problem was that if she thought that if a nanny was there, then everything was a-okay, instead of her being there." George Jr. felt similarly: "I think some of us felt that Lee especially needed someone who was going to be . . . there and totally attentive to her more than maybe Cornelia was."[12]

Politics and Policy

New bride or not, Wallace got off to a rocky political start. Reluctant to turn over the speakership to Rankin Fite again, Wallace settled on Sage Lyons of Mobile. Fite was not pleased and had the connections to make life miserable for the administration: "I don't mind getting done in by my enemies, but it's pretty hard to take when your friends do it to you." Wallace aide Finus Gaston and Beasley spoke to a Klan rally in Tuscaloosa, provoking an outpouring of negative publicity. Wallace did not suggest Beasley attend the meeting—in fact he discouraged it—but others from the campaign staff thought it was important to pay off political debts. "They did such a hatchet job on Brewer," Beasley recalled, "they were directly responsible for Brewer failing." Brewer was not the only one who carried a grudge from the 1970 campaign. Beasley was directed by the administration to launch a probe of Brewer's administration. "It was pretty obvious," Beasley remembered, "that they wanted to embarrass Brewer any way they could." The new administration roundly criticized Brewer for ABC leases, tractor purchases, park construction, and general mismanagement. Seventy-eight Brewer appointments were returned by Wallace to the senate for reconsideration. Administration floor leaders developed a strategy of complaining that the state was broke because of Brewer's fiscal irresponsibility; in fact, revenue increased throughout 1971 and Brewer left small surpluses in both the general fund and the Special Education Trust Fund. Wallace's promise of an open-door administration never materialized as the governor called few press conferences in 1971 and granted only a handful of extended interviews.[13]

Some of the newly elected members of the Board of Education accused Wallace of engineering the appointment of Leroy Brown as superintendent and preventing them from interviewing other candidates. "There has been no analysis," Roscoe Roberts complained, "no comparisons. The only concern has been getting the matter to a vote." Wallace clearly backed the hiring of Brown, a personal friend, and made his feelings known to the five board members he counted as supporters. Brown was appointed in a bitter 5 to 3 vote; the minority favored Auburn University education expert Truman Pierce.[14]

In keeping with tradition from his first term and Lurleen's, Wallace decided the first order of business was to call a special session for a highway bond issue. Road funds were an easy way to pay off local campaign promises, strike a partnership with legislators who were measured by some constituents according to the total number of new and repaired miles of asphalt in their district, and arm the administration with patronage inducements. Initial Highway Department estimates ranged from $150 to $175 million for the new bond, but the administration preferred $200 million. Wallace expanded the amount of deficit financing he wanted, adding bonds for mental health, parks, construction of new medical school facilities at UAB and the University of South Alabama, creation of two-year medical schools at Tuscaloosa and Huntsville, and expansion of the Auburn pharmacy program.[15]

Earlier bond issues had easily passed in 1963 and with some wrangling in 1967. But in 1971, the bonds were a major source of contention in a legislature that decided it would fight Wallace every step of the way. Some legislators, aware of the ammunition that bonds provided the governor, wanted the Conservation and Highway Departments placed on a pay-as-you-go basis. Others pointed to the record amount of state debt accumulated under George and Lurleen's watch. Even the formerly reliable house slashed the bond bill to $160 million before extended debate began. On one occasion, the senate voted to adjourn rather than consider any of the Wallace bills. Wallace planned to pay the interest on the bonds through a combination of gas tax increases, inspection fees for gas distributors, and per axle use fees for common carriers. The distinction was subtle, but Wallace averred that the taxes were not direct levies on Alabamians, allowing him to technically keep his campaign promise of no new taxes. When the legislature debated alternative plans for financing the bonds, Wallace, surprised at the resistance, lashed back: "When I submitted this legislation, I felt we had the burden of paying placed upon big business and special interest groups but now those same groups apparently have some legislators representing them who would like to place the taxation upon the little man in Alabama."[16]

After surveying the landscape, Wallace scaled back the highway bond to $135 million, still confident he could pass the bill. Senator Joe Fine, a Wallace campaign operative in 1968, countered with a $50 million proposal, drawing the ire of Wallace, who called him and his peers "obstructionists." An anonymous senator who was a friend of the administration noted Wallace's apparent lack of appreciation for the independence of the legislature: "He's too imperialistic. He thinks he can send just about anything up here one minute and that we'll vote for it without question." Another senator declared that a lawmaker could find himself in the crosshairs by opposing administration projects: "In this legislature, you're either one hundred percent for the administration on every issue or you're some kind of son-of-a-bitch." The reality is that many legislators were Brewer supporters, represented districts that Wallace did not carry in 1970, or felt otherwise emboldened by reapportionment and Wallace's narrow victory. In addition, the new palace guard—Billy Joe Camp, Taylor Hardin, Harry Pennington, and Elvin Stanton—were not nearly as skilled in legislative relations as Trammell, Jackson, Maddox, Jones, and Ewing. Though a $53 million bond issue for mental health and medical education passed, the special session ended without enacting a highway bond bill, a bitter pill for the administration to swallow. Bowen Brassell, a Phenix City legislator and past Wallace supporter, sided with the independents. After being passed over by the administration for important committee assignments, Brassell "looked the governor in the eye and said 'what have you ever done for me.'" The senate, led by state senator Richard Shelby, even defeated a Wallace nomination for the Tuscaloosa Civil Service Board, the first such rejection of a gubernatorial appointment in years.[17]

Wallace was troubled by the legislative truculence but not deterred. He announced that all administration bills that did not pass in the special session would be reintroduced in the regular session: "There are some people up there that just don't like George Wallace," the governor declared, suggesting that the legislature was more interested in personalities than policy. "They're just using the budget bill as an excuse because they want me to look bad." Pierre Pelham, Wallace's floor leader in the senate, notified the opposition they would have to pay a price: "You whipped us this time. . . .But you're going to have to spend the entire summer down here." The special session was not a total waste. In addition to the mental health–medical educations bonds, the legislature passed a six-month utility rate freeze, a bill extending the life of the Constitutional Commission created under Brewer's watch, and a provision restructuring the Highway Department.[18]

Other than administration opponents in the legislature, Jere Beasley was the only clear winner in the special session. Traditionally, the lieutenant governor had functioned exclusively as the president of the senate and had no real ties to the executive branch. Beasley, however, wanted to expand the office to become something akin to a state vice president with an accompanying boost in prestige, pay, and resources. Specifically, he wanted an expanded staff, more office space, an increase in his monthly expense account from three hundred to fifteen hundred dollars, and higher visibility from which he could eventually launch his own campaign for governor. Despite his poor decision to speak to the Klan and the transparent purpose of his Fiscal Study Committee in investigating Albert Brewer, Beasley was able to gain some momentum with the legislature and the governor's office. In late February, he traveled to South Carolina to investigate ways to tailor trade school curricula to meet the needs of industrial prospects. "Every problem in this state," Beasley told reporters upon his return, "involves the economy. We're going to add a new dimension—a new scope—to our vocational education program. This will be a crash industry. If company XYZ wants to locate in a town, we will propose to train the people they want right there to do specifically what they want done." In the special session, Beasley told the administration he thought its highway bond bill was too much money and assigned it to a committee that was more likely to compromise on it than blindly pass it. Despite this brashness, Beasley faced no censure from Wallace. The governor was already preoccupied with running for president and was amenable, initially, to transferring more responsibility to Beasley. Various reporters and capitol insiders noted Wallace was giving Beasley a wide berth and speculated he intended to give the ambitious lawyer the keys to the store while he was off raising money and campaigning. "What George Wallace is doing," an anonymous senator speculated, "is setting Jere up in business so he can run the state while [Wallace] campaigns for president." By mid-year, Beasley had a large expense account, two executive assistants, and three secretaries.[19]

As the regular session heated up, the administration faced mounting pressure to recoup some respect from the legislature and get education and general fund budgets passed. In a unique three-part strategic ideology that combined Machiavellian and Deep South components, Wallace wanted his Alabama opponents to fear and respect him, his Washington enemies to underestimate and loathe him, and his base of blue-collar, socially conservative men and women to love him. Like any three-legged table, damage to any of the single supports could bring the other two crashing down. Had he lost to Albert Brewer, his Washington aspirations would have been irrelevant. Had the federal government ignored him, he would have lost a valuable tool for whipping the Alabama masses into a frenzy. And if he appeared powerless to discipline an independent legislature, he faced the eventual prospect of losing stature with the electorate in Alabama and across the fruited plain.

In his speech to the legislature kicking off the regular session, Wallace flashed his forensic creativity, chastising the senate for failing to pass the road bond bill. The senate's failure, Wallace alleged, was certain to lead to the firing of eighteen hundred Highway Department employees unless the bonds were passed immediately. The governor reminded voters who were watching on statewide television and listening on statewide radio that he intended to keep his campaign promises. Specifically, he announced plans to push for higher old-age pensions and workman's compensation benefits, and to lower insurance premiums, reopen closed schools, and eliminate the sales tax from prescription drugs. The *Montgomery Advertiser* concluded that Wallace had recovered the old magic: "There were certainly strong flashes of his old style, obviously calculated to prove he hasn't lost it. The speech . . . had something for everybody—except the price tags which are yet to be revealed. Our guess is his pitch for populist legislation had some Big Mules choking on their martinis at Mountain Brook Country Club."[20]

In the midst of the administration's defeat on the highway bond bill, the U.S. Supreme Court issued a ruling authorizing the use of busing to achieve racial balance in schools. Though Wallace blasted the decision as one "written in an insane asylum," he seized on a small opening the court left for voiding busing in certain circumstances: "An objection to transportation of students may have validity when the time or distance of travel is so great as to risk either the health of the children or significantly impinge on the educational process." Out of this court disclaimer, Wallace fashioned a pupil transfer protocol in which Alabama parents needed only to authenticate that the "time or distance of travel to another school is so great as to risk either the health or safety of the child." Convinced "the busing issue is not a southern issue, it is a national issue," Wallace crafted a three-point plan to oppose increased busing in Alabama and create an issue that would catapult him into the 1972 presidential campaign. Wallace planned to circumvent the court ruling with a pupil transfer law, minimize the need for busing by opening closed schools, and station troopers in schools as a show of the administration's muscle.[21]

Wallace knew that busing would be especially unpopular in Alabama and hoped to distract the legislature from opposing his agenda by interjecting the issue into another anti–federal government campaign. Before turning to the legislature for an antibusing bill, Wallace issued three executive orders, the crux of which was using state police powers to nullify the court order and reinstate freedom of choice. The response from white Alabama was immediate and positive. "Thank goodness we have a man like you," Karl Berger wrote to the governor, "fighting for us common people—against this treasonous school busing." Old fears about miscegenation still reigned in some quarters of the state. "I just pray," Charles Millican wrote, "that they can't force you to spend one dime to bus one single child. . . . If we do mix the blacks with the white girls, well the first thing to happen might be the white girl will be coming home with a black baby and also the Negro girl will have a half-white baby." State senator Walter Givhan was effusive in his praise for the governor: "I want to take this opportunity to thank you for the stand you took yesterday on the busing situation. . . . This move was one of the most important things to preserve the Anglo-Saxon race and to keep the schools segregated."[22]

As with earlier battles over integration during Wallace's first term, some Alabama preachers could be counted on to provide biblical justification for the South's cultural folkways and social restrictions. The Reverend J. M. Drummond was fully behind any attempt by the administration to keep whites and blacks apart: "Governor, the way I think about integration is that I do not ever intend to submit to it. We don't want it and we won't have it. I do not want a book or paper with a nigger picture in it. Governor, if the day ever comes that we give over to integration, that will cook the goose for all of us." Wallace replied to Drummond's letter, noting, "I find myself in agreement with almost everything you composed in your letter." Even so, other predominately white congregations began to bicker over scriptural justifications for social separation. First Baptist Church of Birmingham split when senior pastor

Herbert Gilmore and youth director Betty Brock resigned, following a contentious church vote to bar a black woman from membership.[23]

All the while, Wallace denounced busing as proof that President Nixon could not be trusted. "The president's latest remarks about school busing . . . are just another attempt . . . to confuse and bamboozle the American people as to where to put the blame for the destruction of their public school system. The president continues to tell us . . . how much he opposes the busing of your school children and yet departments under his direct control are forever going before the courts seeking even more drastic and far-reaching busing plans." Aware that his gubernatorial campaign had caught fire with charges of bloc voting and distributing racial smear sheets, Wallace understood that many Alabamians were not yet willing to turn the page on segregation. With attacks on busing and cries for law and order, the governor used these coded appeals to keep his base energized. The fringe right paid little attention to legislative defeats: "The forces behind busing," the conservative Liberty Lobby observed in its newsletter, "are the same left-wing radical planners who have already led this nation far down the road toward national destruction."[24]

The push to open schools closed by HEW and court orders began with a campaign promise to return freedom of choice. In early March—before the special session started and before the Supreme Court affirmed busing—Wallace asked Leroy Brown to compile a list of closed schools. Tired of playing defense, Wallace intended to use Brown's list to stir up emotions and breathe new life into his quest to pressure Nixon. Brown and his staff assembled documentation on school bus accidents across the South and other "hardships . . . on those who are bused." Ultimately, the administration planned to file a lawsuit, demonstrating the excessive hardships on Alabama pupils and demanding that the schools be reopened. Unfortunately, Wallace soon discovered that many of the closed schools had bigger problems than court orders. White Hill School was one of the facilities shut down by federal court order. According to Perry County superintendent L. G. Walker, "the building was sub-standard, a three-room frame building, heated with 'pot belly' stoves. The well on the grounds was unsafe, the children bringing their water for the day in glass bottles. . . . There were no indoor toilets and no lunchroom." Walker concluded that the best interests of the students were met by transferring them elsewhere and doubted "if we could get children to return to it." When it became clear that local school boards were closing unsafe schools and facilities with declining attendance, Wallace shifted strategy, hoping to use the buildings to start private schools.[25]

Undeterred by Brown's list and the reality that the courts had not done as much damage as he expected, the administration instructed each local superintendent to compile a new list complete with justification for reopening the school. Wallace used the information to blister U.S. Attorney General John Mitchell about the "critical problems of overcrowding of the schools, inconvenience to teachers, parents, and children in transportation, and . . . discipline." According to the governor, Alabama schools were so rife with criminal conduct that "student fights, beatings, knifings, shootings, and other acts of violence" necessitated regular law enforcement just to restore order.[26]

Though some violence had occurred, the administration exaggerated its severity and pushed for an appropriation for additional state troopers, who would be stationed at local schools. Parents across Alabama were alarmed by the plan, and the education community was united in its opposition. Their resolve hardened when it became clear that Wallace intended to finance the new troopers with education dollars. Paul Hubbert, new executive secretary of the Alabama Education Association, pronounced troopers to be a failure when tried elsewhere: "In other states where police officers have been assigned on a regular basis to schools, school officials and teachers have tended to turn over most of the supervision of school conduct and behavior to the police force. . . . Students have come to feel that school is some sort of prison." The Alabama Association of School Administrators announced its opposition. Even Leroy Brown, who usually backed administration proposals, thought the troopers were a bad idea and sponsored a Board of Education resolution opposing the bill. ACT Educational Program offered a unique perspective on the trooper bill. Though ACT officials made their objection to school troopers clear, they suggested that new troopers should be black. "If there is a necessity for state troopers to be hired," ACT project director Henry Rembert suggested, "then we propose that all of them be black, since there are no black state troopers in the entire state of Alabama. . . . This would be at least a beginning to integrating the state troopers and to make up for the huge total lack of blacks who could have long ago been employed." Few in the legislature thought that idea was sound; Fred Gray's efforts to require that any new trooper increases include blacks were not seriously considered.[27]

In the end, Wallace's three-part plan to battle federal education initiatives achieved little. The trooper bill was defeated in the senate. The campaign to open closed schools never made much headway. Wallace asked for exclusive control of school transportation funds, threatened to personally register any student who wanted to attend a different school, announced he would ignore *Lee v. Macon* guidelines banning freedom of choice, and issued executive orders mandating the transfer of students. Most of the rhetoric was hollow, and federal judge Sam Pointer struck down the executive orders: "The school board is not free to disobey the court. Even taking the plaintiff's assertion that the governor ordered the school board to violate the law, we would only have an exercise of free speech by the governor, to which he is entitled." Wallace responded by characterizing Pointer as a man who "doesn't have enough legal brains to try a chicken thief." Wallace later admitted the retort was "below the dignity of the governor," but nevertheless characterized his outburst as the result of reading "a stack of mail . . . that is ten feet high of little children being bused as high as forty-eight miles one way, parents who have children in three or four different schools, children who were in buses last year that had accidents, and [a] continual stream of people who come to my office who say their income is such that they cannot put their children in private schools."[28]

One fleeting administration success was the passage of act number 1418, Wallace's plan to prop up freedom of choice and reduce busing. Under 1418, any parent who determined "the time or distance of travel to any school is so great as to risk the health or safety" of their child could petition for admittance to another school. The language of the new law was taken directly from the *Swann v. Mecklenburg County (N.C.)* case in which the Supreme Court had affirmed busing but included the time and distance factor as a mitigating circumstance. The law passed easily, a product of racial attitudes about excessive desegregation and the already rampant amount of busing in Alabama necessitated by the rural nature of the state. Even before the court decisions, so many Alabama students were bused in the state that sixteen- and seventeen-year-old students served as paid bus drivers.[29]

Wallace lobbied Attorney General John Mitchell to support 1418, confident that both HEW and the federal courts would be quick to challenge the new law. Teasing his former and future rival, Wallace challenged Nixon to organize a national summit to discuss busing. In a scathing editorial, the *Birmingham News* characterized Wallace's poke at the president as "part of the governor's continuing effort to embarrass Mr. Nixon politically on the busing issue, by making it appear that he talks one way and acts another." A handful of parents in Jefferson County—backed by Concerned Parents for Public Education— applied for transfer authorization based on 1418. When the local schools refused to grant the requests, the Concerned Parents filed suit in state court asking for an injunction granting the children the right to attend the school of their choice. Sensing reluctance at the local school level to allow freedom-of-choice transfers, Wallace asked the house and senate to issue a joint resolution ordering local boards of education to admit the students. "The problem," Wallace informed his legal advisor John Harris, "is that many students have gone to these schools and now the superintendents tell them they are going to have them arrested for trespassing if they haven't left." The state courts affirmed the constitutionality of 1418.[30]

Less than one month after the state court's affirmation of 1418, Pointer responded to a petition asking him to take jurisdiction of the case. On December 3 he ruled 1418 unconstitutional. Wallace blasted Pointer's decision:

"Without a proper petition being filed by any real party in interest, Judge Pointer arrogated unto himself jurisdiction over a state statute" even though a "mature, intelligent, and experienced state circuit judge had previously upheld the constitutionality of this law." Once again, Wallace argued, the state had devised an appropriate solution to its own problems only to be trumped by devious federal forces intent on punishing the South. The governor wired the state's congressional delegation, asking it to pressure Mississippi senator James Eastland, head of the powerful Judicial Committee, to launch an investigation of Pointer. Wallace knew busing was a hot-button issue and the response to Pointer's decision cemented his intention to make it the centerpiece of his 1972 campaign. Even the Alabama Republican Party issued a statement defending Wallace's antibusing law and criticizing Pointer, a Nixon appointee.[31]

Elsewhere on the education front, Wallace watched in disbelief as the legislature and the AEA crushed his proposed budget. Both the AEA and the new Board of Education hoped to build on the success of Brewer's program and carry the momentum for another major breakthrough in funding. The Wallace-backed board issued a resolution asking the governor to recess the regular session after the opening day and call a special session, allowing legislators to focus exclusively on improving state schools. Wallace refused to heed the advice and instead asked cabinet officials to prepare to tighten their belts: "Alabamians are in no mood to impose taxes on themselves." At the AEA's annual March convention, Wallace pledged to raise teacher salaries, increase the appropriation for the free textbook program, and make sure teachers received the same contribution to their retirement plan as all other state employees. Even so, Wallace reiterated to the convention that the public was "simply turned off on education and educators as far as more taxes are concerned."[32]

By law, the governor was required to submit his proposed education budgets by the fifth day of the regular session. The administration, however, was not prepared to offer either an education or general fund appropriation request. A month after the session started Wallace asked the legislature for an extension. While the administration developed its budget, the Alabama Education Study Commission issued some frightening findings about the quality of state teachers: "The average scholastic capabilities of students graduating from Alabama's teacher colleges—many of whom enter the teaching profession—are alarmingly deficient for a profession in which proficiency is absolutely vital." In assessing the results of more than 11,500 National Teacher Examinations given to new Alabama teachers over a three-year period, the commission determined that the Alabama average was thirty points out of a possible one hundred. The national average was sixty, further indication that the state had serious issues to confront in order to make Alabama students competitive.[33]

By all accounts, the AEA had enjoyed only minimal influence with the legislature over the preceding decades. To be sure, politicians of every ilk spoke at AEA meetings, but the interest group's call for more funding rarely translated into action. Even Albert Brewer had relied on the Alabama Education Study Commission, not the AEA, to pass his education package. Though it made no formal endorsement in the 1970 race, AEA's rank-and-file membership clearly supported Brewer. "Not only was Brewer helpful in the sense that he lowered the rhetoric and made it possible to get on through the desegregation process," Paul Hubbert recalled, "but he actually was proactive in helping education. [He] endeared himself to the education community by doing so." This support was not lost on Wallace, who called Hubbert for a conference after the election but before he took office in January. Hubbert, already suspicious of Wallace's commitment to education, left the meeting convinced that "Wallace was pissed off at us and that we were going to have a rough time."[34]

A month after taking office, Wallace called Hubbert for another conference. At this meeting, the governor focused the discussion on the amount of money invested in the teacher's retirement system. "Paul," Wallace inquired, "you all have a lot of money in that retirement system, don't you? Well Frank Johnson has issued a ruling on mental health and I just don't believe people are willing to pay any new taxes and we've got to find a way to deal with that. What if we borrowed a little money and use that to take care of that problem?" Hubbert coyly suggested the teachers would be willing to loan some money at market rates if Wallace would "pledge the full faith of the state to pay them off." Hubbert understood that Wallace was not asking for a loan, he was making a declaration. By mid-June, Wallace went public with his plan for taking $30 million from the Teacher's Retirement Fund and redirecting it into operating capital for Lurleen's regional mental health centers.[35]

To be sure, the state had serious mental health problems that required attention and resources. In March 1971, Judge Johnson officially notified the state that it must implement a comprehensive program "so as to give each of the treatable patients . . . a reasonable opportunity to be cured, or to improve his or her mental condition." Patient per diem expenditures were increasing; by 1971, each patient was receiving $6.86 per day, a $3 improvement from six years earlier. Even so, that level of funding represented only 47 percent of the national average. The physician William Tarnower, a court-ordered monitor who toured Bryce Hospital to evaluate patient care, was mortified: "It impressed me as a depressing and dehumanizing environment reminding me of graveyard lots where the patients are essentially living out their lives without rights of privacy or ownership."[36]

Tarnower's report was based on a visit six months after Johnson's order and after the state claimed to have made substantial progress. He noted gross overcrowding, numerous patients without a medical reason to be at Bryce, a short-

age of aides, public shower and toilet facilities, and a disinterested staff leading a treatment program largely based on housekeeping. The sight and sound
of Bryce patients was considered disruptive to Sunday morning worship in
nearby Tuscaloosa churches; consequently, most were confined to the ward on
that day. Another court-appointed observer, Glenn Morris, documented in-
sects and rodents in open view, the presence of offensive odors, beds that had
been placed on the floor, uncovered food being delivered to the loading dock,
and the lack of a fire evacuation plan.[37]

As bad as the situation was, the most significant reason for the administration to advocate taking education money for mental health was that Wallace
had campaigned on a promise not to raise taxes. "We're not going to tax the
little man," the governor reiterated, "when there is $343 million laying there
drawing interest." After his meeting with Wallace, Hubbert informed teachers of the governor's plan and motivated them to prevent it. Hubbert charged
the editors and staff of the *Alabama School Journal,* the official magazine of
the AEA, with creating an issue that would catch the eye of teachers. Printed
in tabloid form, the July special edition was bold and to the point: "Alabama
teachers and all members of the teaching profession are urgently warned to
stand up and fight for their retirement program and to resist any effort by
Governor George Wallace and administration leaders to reduce state funding needed to keep it fiscally sound and healthy." Within days, AEA telephones
were ringing off the hook with angry teachers wanting to know what they
could do to help. State employees and the media sided with AEA. "Everybody
has a retirement program," Hubbert noted about the fight, "and they don't
want anybody messing with it.... Even rank and file people out there thought
that the government was betraying the employees if it took money from the
retirement program. We had an outpouring of public support. Wallace just
simply underestimated the volatility of that issue."[38]

With the battle lines formed, Wallace called Hubbert for a third meeting.
This time, the governor expected to pressure Hubbert, E. L. Bottoms—executive
director of the Retirement Systems of Alabama—and Hugh Gillespie—the retirement fund actuary—into admitting that borrowing the money was legal.
The members of the House Ways and Means Committee and the Senate Finance and Taxation Committee formed the peanut gallery. Wallace grilled
Gillespie about the legality of borrowing the mental health money from the
retirement fund and later paying it back. Gillespie refused to answer the question, offering only that such a practice was against his better judgment. Frustrated by Gillespie's evasiveness, Wallace refused to let him off the hook: "Now
Mr. Gillespie, the State of Alabama is paying you money and the Governor of
Alabama is asking you a question and I want a direct answer. If we borrow
money and pay it back and pay interest on it, will it be all right?" Grudgingly,

Gillespie admitted that such a practice was possible. "Now you have heard the actuary," Wallace wheeled and informed the legislators, "the budget is going to come up and I want it in committee and out of committee and we are going to have to go this route or you are going to have to raise taxes on the people. And if you try to raise taxes on the people, I'm going to tell on you."[39]

Even if the process was technically allowable, Hubbert did not trust that Wallace would pay back the money. Hubbert was wary of Wallace personally, but also knew that a handful of other states had borrowed money from retirement funds and never paid it back. The AEA rallied teachers, white and black, to come to the capitol, and thousands lobbied legislators to reject the governor's plan. As many as four hundred teachers could be seen on the floor at any given time, and they soon earned the sobriquet "Hubbert's Herd." Superintendents, by and large, supported AEA's position, though Wilcox superintendent Guy Kelley, a Wallaceite to the core, called Hubbert's group a "radical . . . civil rights activist organization." The eight-member state Board of Education, which usually sided with the administration in 5 to 3 votes, unanimously resolved to oppose "any diversion or withholding of state matching funds due to the Teacher's Retirement System of Alabama." Wallace countered by offering a 5 percent teacher raise if his bill was passed. He also stepped up his personal attacks on Hubbert: "[Education's] top leadership is . . . probably education's worst enemy." The governor also blamed Brewer for releasing conditional appropriations at the end of his term. "[Alabama is in] the worst financial condition in years," he told capitol beat reporters, "and I think you know how."[40]

Despite the attacks, the administration made little headway in getting its budget moved to the floor for a vote. Wallace called Hubbert for a fourth meeting, and this time the governor and Taylor Hardin tempted him with the prospect of his own position in state government. "That was kind of their style," Hubbert recalled three decades later, "they thought everybody had a price . . . and they wanted to know what mine was." Undeterred by Hubbert's refusal, Wallace scheduled a meeting with the AEA board, hoping to use his personal charisma to convince it to supercede Hubbert. Before the conference, Hubbert met with the board independently to check its pulse: "You are going to be in the governor's office and . . . he's very persuasive. Now you all can cut my throat or you can stand up to him and tell him AEA is not backing down. Now in my judgement, you need to tell him that we're not backing down, but if you want to slice my throat, you've got an opportunity right there in front of you." The board backed Hubbert.[41]

Aware that AEA would tell the press about his backroom dealing, Wallace preempted Hubbert, telling the press he had no intention of backing down, and calling reports that he had thrown in the towel "totally inaccurate." After several days of conference committee wrangling, the house was presented with a bill for a vote. Several house members—including Ben Cherner, Ronnie Flippo, David Cox, and John Baker—found Hubbert waiting in the capitol rotunda around midnight and asked him what he wanted done. "Kill it," Hubbert told the legislators, "we're not going to accept it the way it is." The house voted 89 to 12 against diverting the funds.[42]

After calling a few legislators to see if the bill could be reconsidered, Wallace gave up. "As governor I did my duty. I presented them a plan and they did not enact it. They'll just have to find the money it will take to operate the mental health facilities." Some in the administration played the guilt card. Mental Health director Stonewall Stickney suggested numerous patients at Bryce, Searcy, and Partlow would be sent home because of insufficient funds. Stickney announced that he asked each state hospital to draft plans for closing: "I want to make it very clear that this is not a bluff to impress the legislature." Wallace's floor leaders got into the act as well. "I'm surprised that the AEA," Wallace floor leader Bob Wilson charged, "well-fed after two Wallace administrations has taken the stand it has against mental health in Alabama. I hope when teachers go home tonight, well-fed, and in comfortable homes, that they will think about the people in mental institutions." At the last minute, Wallace switched strategies, asking that mental health money be diverted directly from the Special Education Trust Fund and leaving the retirement system alone. Wallace suggested that the federal government might even come to the rescue with extra assistance, allowing him to pay back any diverted funds ahead of schedule. The legislature and the suddenly emboldened AEA were not persuaded.[43]

The legislature did more than just kill the administration's education fund diversion, it killed the governor's general fund budget and education budget—the first time in state history that a regular session of the legislature failed to produce the appropriations—refused to pass important property tax and ethics legislation, and then adjourned the regular session. "This is the damndest bunch," a veteran Goat Hill doorkeeper noted of the legislature. "I've been here twenty years and there has never been a group like this. You don't tell these folks what to do." The failure to pass basic budgets was a devastating blow, and it revealed how unprepared the administration was to operate in an environment where the governor's hands were tied by campaign promises and an independent legislature was flexing its muscles. Even when Wallace navigated part of his package through the legislative labyrinth, he had to live with a gutted law; the road bond bill finally passed, but at $110 million, not $200 million. In the middle of the fiasco, the *Birmingham News* captured the new dynamic with a prescient editorial: "Wallace is simply slashing out in desperation at all who dare challenge his deity. Sensing, as he must, that he has lost his powers of intimidation and lost the ability to crush those who oppose him, Wallace is giving off the sounds of a wounded and cornered old lion, no longer monarch of all he surveys." As the house adjourned sine die, freshmen legislator Chriss Doss walked past house speaker Sage Lyons. "Chris," Lyons queried, "what's going on? You can't do this." Doss replied, "Sage, we've just done it."[44]

The clearest indication that Wallace no longer elicited the same fear and dread among Montgomery power brokers was the forceful challenge of Jere Beasley. With Wallace still determined to get the road bond bill passed, Beasley assigned the administration's highway package to Senator Crum Foshee's committee on transportation, commerce, and common carriers. Beasley knew Wallace was stung when the bill was killed in the special session and that the governor desperately wanted the bill passed in the regular session. Nevertheless, he sent the bill to Foshee, an independent, instead of assigning it to Bob Wilson's finance and taxation committee, which was packed with administration supporters. "I put it in a committee," Beasley later recalled, "that . . . would achieve a compromise on it and that was probably a dumb political move on my part." Wallace was disappointed, but tried to maneuver around Beasley's actions by threatening to prevent the construction of a new bridge that Foshee and Senator Obie Littleton needed between their districts.[45]

Wallace had already been rethinking his decision to allow Beasley additional staff and an increased operating budget. Some reporters speculated that Wallace and Beasley had run as a team in 1970, though Wallace never endorsed Beasley or made any efforts to help his campaign. In fact, Wallace rarely campaigned on behalf of other candidates or made public endorsements of any kind. He preferred to keep all options open, to keep the attention on himself, and not to be saddled with unnecessary associations that could come back to bite him later. This tactic led to some hard feelings when Wallace did little or nothing to help past associates, such as Bill Jones in a 1966 congressional race. The only real exception was his announcement that he would not vote for Seymore Trammell in the 1970 treasurer's race, a public acknowledgment of the bitter break between the two after the 1968 campaign. Wallace also had keen instincts for identifying future rivals and eliminating opponents who could challenge him. He had already successfully targeted and eliminated John Tyson, Carl Elliot, Bob Gilchrist, Richmond Flowers, and Albert Brewer. "George Wallace probably killed off more political careers than you can shake a stick at," Beasley opined. "But he really caused a political vacuum in the state insofar as leadership for several years . . . because he did kill off a lot of folks politically and enjoyed doing it. . . . He looked at anybody as a threat."[46]

The need to eliminate Jere Beasley became clear when the lieutenant governor defied the administration a second time. On his way to Idaho for a conference, Beasley appointed Junie Pierce, part of the independent faction, to preside over the senate rather than pass the gavel to Pierre Pelham, senate president pro tem and an ardent Wallaceite. Wallace immediately fired Wayne McMahan, Beasley's executive assistant, and Tommy Cooksey, a Beasley friend and director of publicity and tourism. The governor reassigned Beasley's secretaries, left him with one phone line, and took away his car and state trooper. Attorney General Bill Baxley ruled that the chair must be ceded to Pelham, and within minutes 170 bills were taken from independent committees and sent to proadministration forces. In the middle of the melee, Hugh Morrow—who had lost to Beasley in the 1970 runoff—teased the governor about his new adversary: "I understand . . . that you are requesting a recount in the lieutenant governor's race. . . . Janie and I told you all the time that I would be a better lieutenant governor than Jere." Wallace refused Beasley's calls, and the lieutenant governor was reduced to going through Taylor Hardin to get a message to Wallace. Beasley and Hardin had a bitter personality conflict, and the new channel of communication ensured that Beasley was completely cut off from the administration. Regrouping, Beasley held a press conference announcing he was a strong Wallace man but admitting he had some problems with the administration's new palace guard. Two months later, Beasley and Wallace patched up their differences, and the lieutenant governor agreed to get the administration's package moving through the senate in exchange for getting back McMahan and a secretary. Even so, Wallace never again trusted Beasley, and the two continued to spar now and again. The ambitious Beasley refused to back down, blocking some administration bills and assigning others to committees he controlled so that he could kill them.[47]

The failure to pass education and general fund budgets obscured a handful of administration successes in the regular session. Wallace created a consumer advisory council through executive order, fulfilling a campaign promise, and convinced the legislature to pass the minicode, a package of twenty-two consumer protection laws. Wallace signed the bill even though his brother Gerald had lobbied strenuously against it. To his credit, Wallace worked to lower the allowable interest rates in the minicode and brokered an agreement among state bankers not to charge the maximum rates.[48]

On other fronts, Wallace signed tough air and water pollution control laws. Federal pressure had as much to do with the passage of the new law as administration support. The Clean Air Act strengthened requirements (Alabama was not even in compliance with previous standards) for states to receive federal dollars for pollution control. In April, the Environmental Protection Agency conducted tests of the air quality in Birmingham, determining that the city had a disastrous particulate count of 607 micrograms per cubic meter of air. The average daily particulate count in Birmingham was 162, far in excess of the national urban average of 97. The thick, stale air caused some Alabamians to leave the state. "One day I would like to return to Alabama," Barbara Lampe wrote to Wallace, "but I feel this would be unwise until the time that pollution will be in the first stages of disappearance in Birmingham. . . . As governor of Alabama, it is your duty to investigate the pollution situation in Alabama." As a result of the tests, the EPA issued a finding that "the health of the citizens of Birmingham was in imminent danger," and dispatched a team of experts and spokesmen to Alabama.[49]

Rhetoric aside, all interested parties in Montgomery understood that something substantive needed to be accomplished. One analysis of the 1969 Air Pollution Control Act indicated that the commission charged with monitoring pollution had no "authority to either prevent air pollution before it occurs, or abate air pollution." The same review determined that the commission lacked the power to subpoena records from polluters, issue legal orders to cease hazardous practices, and establish emission control or fuel quality regulations. Any suspected polluter need only advise the commission that it was studying the problem to gain approval to continue operations. Even then, the company had seven years to implement a plan to fix the problem. "This degree of permissiveness," the study concluded, "is without precedent in the field of air pollution control." Wallace vowed to make changes: "We have known for some time that our present air pollution control law is inadequate to carry out a comprehensive control program. This was true at the time of its enactment in 1969 and is even more so now because of passage of the Clean Air Amendments of 1970." When the house and senate proposed different bills, Wallace pledged to sign whichever law offered the strongest protection from industrial abuses.[50]

The 1971 Alabama Air Pollution Control Law was substantially stronger than the 1969 bill. The 1969 law allowed for the creation of a pollution control commission that was heavily stacked in favor of industry and did not come close to passing federal muster. The new law created a Pollution Control Board without any industrial representation and gave it the power to take specific action to shut down polluters. Local municipalities and boards of health, under the new law, had authority to institute and enforce local standards, and the governor could invoke special powers by declaring an air-pollution emergency. "Overall, I believe this to be an excellent proposed air pollution control law," EPA official Robert Duprey said of the 1971 bill, "which should greatly strengthen air pollution control efforts in Alabama."[51]

The new water pollution control law was equally strong. The seven-member board created by the law was comprised of the state health officer, the director of the Department of Conservation, a physician, an engineer, an attorney, and two "residents of the state with special expertise." Industry, long the arbiter of its own vices, no longer had representation on the Water Improvement Commission. The attorney general was given power to investigate and prosecute any firm whose permit to discharge effluent into Alabama waters was revoked. Those convicted of polluting faced fines, as well as the cost of replenishing the wildlife, fish, and environment.[52]

After Wallace signed the water and air pollution bills, Ira Myers asked the governor to name the new members of both boards immediately. The new investigatory powers of the boards, Myers reasoned, should be put to use as quickly as possible. The publicized pollution problems in Birmingham were troublesome enough, but Mobile was experiencing increasing particulate counts, and fish kills proliferated across the state. Conditions in Mobile became so bad in early October that residents were warned to stay inside and avoid strenuous exercise. A *Birmingham News* study indicated that fifteen towns were dumping raw sewage directly into Alabama streams. Despite worsening conditions, Wallace was slow to name the pollution panel, perhaps punishing the urban bloc that had earlier dealt him such a crushing defeat.[53]

Alabamians grew impatient with Wallace's delay in naming the board. "As a resident of this state," Frances Luke wrote the governor, "I urge you to please prevent further delay and name the commissions on water and air pollution." Some Alabamians, such as Mrs. R. J. Smith were practically frantic: "Birmingham is so smokey today that I can hardly breathe. Please, please go ahead and appoint the members to the pollution control committee provided by the legislature. I know you must have good reasons for not having done this sooner, but it is difficult for me to know what they could possibly be while breathing this mess. It is horrible, and we need some help." In mid-November, Wallace relented and appointed the board, some forty-five days after the legal deadline to name it. The EPA gave the laws its blessing, and Alabama found itself in full compliance with minimum federal pollution guidelines for the first time in history.[54]

While pollution legislation came with uneven support from the administration, judicial reform was passed over its objection. New supreme court chief justice Howell Heflin campaigned in 1970 on a platform of judicial reform and intended to see his vision become law. Through his tenure leading the State Bar Association and Albert Brewer's Ethics Commission, Heflin had acquired some appreciation for the intricacies of grinding out legislation. Over a period of three years, Heflin spearheaded a drive to give the state supreme court license to draft its own rules of procedure and appeals, a system of court training for judges, a Department of Court Management, a permanent study commission for court proceedings, a retirement system for judges, and the abolition of Alabama's antiquated justice-of-the-peace courts. By the fall of 1972, the previously backlogged court had cleared its docket. The changes were hailed across the nation, and numerous other states came to Alabama to study its suddenly progressive judicial system.[55]

Hugh Maddox, appointed by Brewer to the court, played a major role in convincing the legislature to pass Heflin's package. "I think they tried to block it," Maddox recalled of the Wallace administration's stand on the judicial changes. "Probably one of the reasons was . . . the perception . . . of . . . where Heflin was going. Whether he was going to run for governor or run for the senate and I think some of the opposition came as a result of them trying to clip . . . Howell Heflin's wings." Jere Beasley, in another instance that caused friction with the administration, shepherded the package through the senate. In his authorized biography, Heflin concurred with Maddox's assessment of the governor's political concerns: "He didn't want to come out too vehemently against it because it wouldn't look good, but he wasn't for it. . . . One reason Wallace was opposed was that I had never supported him, and he didn't want me to gain any strength. Some of Wallace's opposition was based on 'Heflin's got a political name, and you better be careful about him. He'll be running for something one of these days, and you don't want him to get too much publicity.'"[56]

With the regular session adjourned, Wallace was in the surprising and unnerving position of rehabilitating himself in his own state. For starters, the governor had to devise a way to disburse funds: state employees needed paychecks; schools needed textbooks; troopers needed gasoline; and the government had to roll on with or without a budget. Wallace met with Baxley to assess his options, and the attorney general ruled out the prospect of using executive orders to authorize disbursement of funds. Wallace had no choice but to call a special session and convince the legislature to pass an appropriation. Publicly, he seemed unfazed. At a New York fund-raiser just days after the regular session ended, Wallace was in fine form, blasting the "permissive attitude of the bleeding hearts and the courts which tell the criminals that anything they do is all right." Back in Alabama, the governor assured state employees he was working on a plan to make sure they received their paychecks on time and in the correct amount.[57]

An October 1971 *Montgomery Advertiser–Alabama Journal* poll indicated how low the governor's status had shrunk: 47 percent of Alabamians thought Wallace should not run for president in 1972. The nay-sayers fell into two camps: a growing list of Alabamians who were opposed to Wallace on principle and a group who still supported Wallace but thought the state's serious problems necessitated a full-time governor. In the midst of a major fund-raising drive and with active campaigning in presidential primaries only months away, the governor understood that the mess in the legislature had to be cleared up as soon as possible. At the same time as the budget crisis was unfolding, former Wallace aides and campaign contributors Seymore Trammell, Houston Feaster, Earl Goodwin, Elton Stephens, and Robert Cottingham faced charges of income tax evasion, conspiracy to evade taxes, writing false invoices, and soliciting bribes. Two thousand union dockworkers in Mobile went on strike, leaving all but three of the state's thirty-three shipping berths dormant. Just when Wallace thought his week could not get any worse, a passenger in a speeding car fired a shot at the mansion.[58]

Behind the scenes, Wallace struck a deal with Harry Brock—a close friend, supporter, and president of Birmingham's Central Bank and Trust—to loan the state enough money to meet payroll and operating expenses. What began as a novelty to avoid the embarrassment of missing the October 1, 1971, payroll, soon evolved into a point of pride for Wallace: maybe he did not need the legislative branch after all. "We're doing fine," the governor promised. "We are traveling less and spending less, but we are continuing to operate. So far we have saved about $1 million." Pundits who predicted Wallace would call a special session immediately after the regular session adjourned saw their predictions go up in smoke. Wallace, forever thinking on his feet and wiggling out of tight spots, once again turned lemons into lemonade: "If we keep on running things this smoothly, I just may not call a special session. I just may run the state without the legislature. How about that?"[59]

Much as he liked to poke fun at the legislature, Wallace knew he had to call it back into session. George Beck, an attorney working in Baxley's office, summed up the inevitable: "We don't have any money for travel expenses so we're not going anywhere, and we are running out of stationery so we soon won't be able to write opinions." Even as the administration worked behind the scenes with floor leaders to plan the sessions, the governor reiterated his intent not to sign any bills that included new taxes. Wallace wanted three short sessions to address three separate problems: the budget, federal mandates to address ad valorem taxes, and elector changes that would allow Wallace to strip the state Democratic Party of its power to appoint presidential electors. The governor showed no interest in reapportioning the state legislature, and left that matter, yet again, to federal courts. Ever the optimist when the camera lights were on, Wallace sounded a chord of defiance when critics characterized him as too weak to topple the independents in the legislature: "You know, you people are always talking about how Wallace is grabbing the headlines. When I left the legislature alone, you said 'Wallace wasn't giving the legislature any leadership.' When I tried to give them leadership, you talked about how Wallace was twisting arms. I think that when they come back in session, they are going to get plenty of leadership."[60]

Despite the travel constraints in various departments, Wallace continued to travel across the country to raise money for his presidential campaign coffers. Wallace asked Press Secretary Billy Joe Camp to "rework the military speech . . . and also have the Red China and Nationalist China reworked with direct criticism of Nixon." Wallace also wanted to create an image as a tax cutter. "Get someone to draw up a resolution," he told Camp, "calling upon the president to recommend to the Congress to enact a $1200 . . . exemption for each dependent . . . [Draft] another resolution . . . calling for the repeal of the tax exempt foundations with the exception of the Red Cross etc." Over the course of 1971, Wallace used Alabama audiences to hone his three-part message for the presidential primaries: end busing, cut taxes, and bolster national defense. Ironically, while Wallace was touring the country bemoaning "inequality in the tax structure," interest groups in Alabama, often with the administration's assistance, were defeating attempts to reform the state's regressive tax codes.[61]

Across the South, Wallace faced criticism from other governors about his looming presidential bid. "Governor Wallace represents the mood of yesteryear in the South," Florida governor Reuben Askew declared. South Carolina governor John West predicted a "very definite change in the mood of the South. No longer will the South accept race as the overriding issue." North Carolina governor Robert Scott simply noted he would work against the Alabamian. Wallace was particularly upset that Georgia governor Jimmy Carter was hesitant to endorse him. Despite the reluctance of his peers to support his presidential aspirations, Wallace convinced them to pass four resolutions, including one against busing, at the Southern Governors' Conference. Though his appeal was waning with neighboring chief executives and with some in Alabama, Wallace found receptive audiences of working men and women across the South, and money continued to trickle into the campaign chest.[62]

As the special session for appropriations began, Wallace's plan for financing mental health still centered on diverting funds from education. This time, Wallace offered a few carrots to the teachers, while threatening recalcitrant legislators with a stick. The governor opened the special session with a rousing thirty-minute speech to the assembled solons. Leaving little doubt that his mind was drifting to the Florida primary, the governor spent five minutes addressing state business and the remaining twenty-five minutes on national issues. A hearty section of supporters festooned with "Wallace in '72" buttons roared with delight at every applause line. Wallace simplified his education fund diversion strategy to a two-sentence justification: "In some instances, we have one fund with plenty of money. . . . Why don't we appropriate some of that money to a fund without enough money?" Teachers were promised a 5 percent salary hike in year one of the proposed biennial budget and another 5 percent raise in year two. In addition, the governor pledged to increase teacher benefits 1.5 percent. Though Wallace still wanted the mental health funds diverted from education, the tactic changed slightly. Having seen his bid to use retirement and Special Education Trust Fund dollars turned back, this time Wallace asked that 5 percent of sales tax dollars earmarked for education, some $14 million, be released.[63]

The showdown on the diversion of funds occurred almost immediately. On the second day of the session, Leroy Brown—who had earlier endorsed the administration's plan—broke with the governor and announced his opposition. Wallace, Taylor Hardin, and fourteen other aides and cabinet members descended on the capitol to try what the *Birmingham News* called a "squeeze play." Two legislators, Horace Parker and Chriss Doss, characterized the administration's tactics as "harassment." Hubbert countered by sending in droves of teachers, who had turned their classes over to substitutes in order to come to Montgomery and fight for education. Hubbert realized that teachers might back off in hopes of earning the two promised raises: "[Teachers] have been made aware of [the administration's plan]. Teachers will be fighting just as hard to stop this raid on our funds as they fought to stop other proposed raids in the regular legislative session. But this time the hurt to education, if the bill proposing the cut is passed, will be worse because the diversion will be permanent." The administration responded by using armed troopers to eject lobbying teachers.[64]

The battle was over before Wallace fired the first shot. The house killed the administration package on the third day of the session and quickly passed its own education budget. Wallace returned to the floor to ask the house to reconsider the legislation but was told the administration had already lost three or four votes. "It was dead before it started," Doss recalled. "It was the best issue that Paul Hubbert could have had because it was an emotional issue . . . and Paul played it pretty good." Another legislator told Hubbert he was completely inundated by teachers expressing their opposition: "I couldn't go home; I couldn't go to church; I couldn't go to the grocery store. I was just flogged by teachers." Representative Ronnie Flippo, who was a certified public accountant, a handful of his colleagues, and Hubbert worked all night at the Albert Pick Hotel and the AEA office to craft the substitute budget. The independents passed an $828 million biennial education budget, including a 10 percent raise for teachers, a boost in teacher retirement funding, and $11.6 million in conditional appropriations for textbooks, special education, and junior colleges. Flummoxed by its resounding defeat, the administration offered little resistance to the revised budget. The legislature also passed a general fund budget that included funds for mental health. Even though Hubbert was on record as saying education would suffer unless $1.23 billion was allocated, he was pleased. "It was a victory to save the money from the retirement system and to keep the earmarking on the sales tax."[65]

As only Wallace could do, the governor claimed victory in the face of obvious defeat, and then flew to Texas to raise money for the presidential campaign: "You passed an appropriation's package without adding one red cent of new taxes. No other state's legislature can say that." With more than a hint of sarcasm, he heaped lavish praise on the group that just handed him what reporter Al Fox called his "worst legislative defeat": "You are certainly the most dedicated and most conscientious legislature I know. . . . I want to congratulate you for having solved these problems . . . I want to congratulate you and say 'I'm proud of you.' I know the people of Alabama are proud of you. I think you have done an excellent job." What Wallace failed to mention is that his failure had elevated Hubbert to a place of power heretofore unimaginable for an AEA leader. For the next fifteen years, Wallace would have to battle or ally with Hubbert in order to pass anything related to education.[66]

In the next special session, the administration was more successful and passed a property tax classification system advocated by the Farm Bureau. Under the classification plan, utilities paid 30 percent; homeowners and farm owners paid 15 percent; and all other properties were levied at 25 percent. Other agricultural interest groups, such as the Alabama Poultry Industry Association (APIA), supported attempts to limit tax rates on farm property. "Many acres of farm land produce little income," APIA president Morgan Edwards averred, "and should not have the same ad valorem tax rate as industrial land in cities. . . . Any unfair taxation in agriculture could result in many farmers being forced to leave their land and farms and move to the already crowded cities." Wallace and Beasley both supported the classification plan and appeared in television commercials on behalf of it. The commercials ran so often that one little girl who saw Wallace on a news broadcast echoed an advertising slogan for Farm Bureau insurance, exclaiming, "Mommy, Mommy, it's the Farm Bureau man." Urban groups, whose land was often assessed at a higher market value than rural property, opposed the classification system, setting up another confrontation between independents and the administration. "We have seen the governor and lieutenant governor," Jefferson County solon Tom Gloor moaned, "appear repeatedly on paid television commercials to huckster the classification plan like a cake of soap. . . . Tremendous amounts of money are being spent to try to stampede the legislature . . . to give legal sanction to the unequal treatment which has allowed large rural landowners to escape paying their fair share."[67]

Much of the effort to reform property tax rates and assessments in Alabama came from lawsuits filed by Martha Hornbeak. Her litigation begat court orders, primarily because existing laws were not being enforced uniformly throughout the state. Under the previous codes, all property was taxed at 60 percent of assessed value. Assessments, however, varied greatly from county to county, and federal courts required a clearer statute that would equalize rates and identify a more realistic market value. Rallied by the Farm Bureau, a previous legislature had written another purposefully vague law allowing counties and municipalities to levy any rate up to 30 percent. Hornbeak went back to court, winning a judgment that overturned the not-more-than-30-percent law and directed the state to address the issue once and for all. Frank Johnson gave the state until December 29 to solve the quandary and promised that he would fix the mess if no legislation was passed. On the eve of the special session, Baxley clarified the legislature's mission, noting that unless a new code was implemented all property would be taxed at the old rate of 60 percent. The only fact urban and rural forces could agree on was that the old 60 percent rule, if enforced, was intolerable.[68]

Hornbeak was a passionate advocate for a more equitable system, primarily because Alabama's rates were among the country's lowest and its schools were among the nation's worst. In the decades since mechanization, subsidies, and federal price supports swept across the agricultural South, the small farmer had become an increasingly mythical figure, cast aside as insurance companies, banks, and agribusinesses gobbled up huge parcels of land. Yet the sentiment among many on Goat Hill, thanks in large part to the effective lobbying of the Farm Bureau, was that property tax increases would lead to higher prices at the checkout line and break the back of the small farmer. In senate testimony, Hornbeak challenged the assertions that Alabama's family farms were sacred cows: "Gentlemen, the farmer's image as a more virtuous and more hard-working citizen than the . . . wicked city population just does not hold up—it is an emotional political appeal irrelevant to our serious discussion to-day. . . . There is much more help for the farmer already in the form of federal subsidies, low interest loans and special technical advice, than there is for the businessman, who cannot even get a small business loan without putting up substantial collateral."[69]

Wallace had good reason to support the Farm Bureau classification plan. He never enjoyed the same electoral or legislative support in urban counties as he did in rural areas. In the 1970 runoff, Brewer carried Jefferson, Madison, Montgomery, and Tuscaloosa counties. Though the governor beat Brewer in Mobile County, that result had more to do with traditional South Alabama cleavages than any urban-rural dialectic. Urban legislators traditionally balked at Wallace's legislative agenda, and it is no coincidence that Birmingham and Huntsville were the last places in the state to have interstate highways completed. Legislators from rural and suburban areas—growing rapidly due to white flight—sided more frequently with the administration. And since Wallace, according to John Cashin, "could smell a block of votes through ten feet of concrete," it made little sense to alienate his most ardent supporters.[70]

A second important factor was Wallace's campaign against Alabama utilities. In the 1970 campaign and throughout 1971, the governor wasted no opportunity to blame utilities for high rates, unchecked greed in continually asking for additional increases, and unlimited power with the legislature. "It is a crying shame that the utilities get everything they want," he complained to Mrs. H. L. Spenard. The governor made it crystal clear that he would not support any property tax plan that gave utility companies a break: "The ad valorem tax problem should be solved without decreasing the tax now paid by utility companies. ... This revenue supplies a substantial part of the income of our cities and counties."[71]

Wallace's positioning of himself as the slayer of high utility bills was well received in Bluff Springs and Clopton and Slocomb. "I was shocked," R. L. Faust confessed, "when I read that PSC [Public Service Commission] had granted the Alabama Power Company an increase in rates but very pleased that you are objecting and going to bat for the poor people." Jack Busby, a Brewer man in 1970, was equally impressed: "Two commendations are in order for your stand on the proposed power and telephone company rate increase. If the increases are granted, they will cause undue financial hardship to the working people and small businessmen of Alabama. Please keep fighting this." John Ripp, an economics professor at Birmingham Southern College and president of the Alabama Consumers Association, hailed Wallace's rate-fighting crusade: "Consumers of Alabama are indeed fortunate that you have taken such effective leadership on these important issues."[72]

Wallace put his utility rhetoric into action. He appealed PSC decisions to increase rates, hired law firms to mount legal challenges, and filed petitions in court claiming existing rates were "excessive, unreasonable, and unjust." Wallace sponsored bills to shift consumer taxes to utilities, delay the period of adjustment before rate increases could be implemented to six months, force utilities to disclose any change in fiscal policy, and change the base rate formula. The governor even lobbied to get South Central Bell Telephone to rescind authorized rate increases in the wake of Nixon's freezing of wages and prices. Wallace was rarely successful in challenging the utilities on rates, but he stoked his popularity at a time when legislative defeats were changing public perception. Throughout 1971, Wallace increased his attacks on the utilities, characterizing them as so powerful that even he could not beat them and reminding voters that they were his enemy: "The utilities fought me in the race for governor and one of the reasons I had a hard time getting elected was the fact that much money was raised by them to help defeat me."[73]

Even with the antiutility quest resonating in the hinterlands, the administration faced the daunting challenge of guiding the classification plan past the urban bloc. Despite the assistance of the Farm Bureau, the timber lobby, countless other agricultural interest groups, the rural bloc of the legislature, and Beasley, Wallace became exasperated with the slow pace of the session and the concerted efforts of his opposition: "We are witnessing in the state senate ... a situation which must be repulsive to the vast majority of Alabamians. A small obstructionist group which has been at work for a full year fighting this administration on any and every measure is again at work. . . . Their sole interest is in the political harassment and attempted embarrassment of George Wallace and his administration." Over the course of a month and a half, the administration and the urban bloc traded barbs in a war of words that strained the limits of rhetorical license. The urban forces called Wallace "King George," charged him with turning Alabama into a constitutional monarchy, and accused the Farm Bureau of paying legislators. Wallace claimed his opponents were clowns and indicated they were backers of Chinese communists Mao Tse-Tung and Chou En-Lai. In the end, Beasley gaveled through the bill, Alabama voters ratified the accompanying constitutional changes, and the administration savored one of its few victories of the year.[74]

Hoping to seize on the momentum of the ad valorem fight, Wallace instructed his floor leaders to flood the legislative hopper with bills in an effort to keep the legislature from adjourning. The governor was not punishing his rivals by keeping them from returning home to their families; he wanted the lawmakers to pass a bill stripping the state Democratic Party of its right to name convention delegates and effectively giving that power to him as the certain winner of the Alabama primary. The house passed the bill, but independents in the senate had no interest in helping the governor. The administration beat back several attempts to adjourn the senate, but ultimately was powerless to get the bill passed. After a year of squabbling, Wallace washed his hands of the legislature and focused his undivided attention on the presidential campaign.[75]

The Road to Maryland

Finally free of the time-consuming and humdrum responsibilities of running state government, Wallace prepared to launch his third bid for the White House—this time as a Democrat. He announced in mid-January that he would enter the Florida primary and geared up to spend the better part of two months pounding home the themes of busing, taxes, and a strong national defense. Cornelia confided to reporters that she was considering placing her children in Florida schools for the next two months. She ultimately decided against it, noting, "George does have to go back to Alabama every once in a while to be governor." Even before making his official announcement in Tallahassee, Wallace made a startling prediction: "If the people of Florida endorse George Wallace, the president himself will abolish the busing of school children." National campaign coordinator Charles Snider created a slew of slick publications to convince general, young, union, and female audiences that the Alabama governor deserved a closer look. Wallace's speeches were leavened with down-home oversimplifications of complex issues, jabs at the federal government, and castigation of the villain du jour. On the stump, Wallace loved to tell a story about New York governor Nelson Rockefeller that expressed how out of touch the Nixon administration had become. Rockefeller, Wallace recounted, went down to the pier to welcome in a shipment of men and equipment rolling back from Southeast Asia as part of the administration's Vietnamization policy. The first piece to roll off the truck was a bulldozer adorned with a "Wallace in '72" bumper sticker.[76]

Wallace's popularity and power was clearly waning in Alabama, but Floridians found the governor fascinating. At a time when films like *Dirty Harry* and *Billy Jack*—lone wolf figures taking on a corrupt system against all odds—were packing in moviegoers, Wallace captured audiences, especially in conservative north and central Florida, with his criticisms of nincompoop professors, pseudointellectuals, and limousine liberals. Wallace's outsider image was boosted when the Democratic Party announced in early January 1972 that it was not allocating any hotel space for Wallace and his supporters at the national convention. "I do not consider him to be a bona fide candidate," mocked committee convention manager Richard Murphy. Maine senator Edmund Muskie, soon to be drummed out of contention, received 550 rooms, and Arkansas congressman Wilbur Mills, not even an official candidate, was promised 200 rooms. With the convention scheduled for Miami, Wallace used the snub to his advantage as he stumped the state for primary votes: "Chairman [Lawrence] O'Brien and others cannot stand the fact that I represent and speak out for the average working citizen who continues to hold this country together with his tax dollar." Bill France, NASCAR president and Wallace's Florida campaign chair, arranged for Cornelia to drive the Daytona 500 pace car at the famed Florida speedway. Administration staff assembled a chart documenting the votes and statements of all his opponents on busing and civil rights legislation. At every rally, he would hold up his chart and remind Floridians that most of his rivals—Muskie, George McGovern, John Lindsay, Henry "Scoop" Jackson, Hubert Humphrey, and others—had supported a system for achieving racial balance that most Floridians opposed.[77]

Two weeks before the Florida primary, Frank Johnson documented the atrocious standard of care in the state's mental health institutions and ruled that Alabama must immediately correct its glaring deficiencies. Johnson cited everything from fire hazards and lighting systems to unsafe immunization policies and staff deficiencies: "There has never been a time when such a [special] session was more urgently required. If the legislature does not act promptly to appropriate the necessary funding for mental health, the court will be compelled to appropriate the necessary funding for mental health, the court will be compelled to grant plaintiff's motion to add various state officials and agencies as additional parties to this litigation." In a poignant editorial, the *Mont-gomery Advertiser* concurred with the finding: "When a state fails to do its duty by those trapped in the unending nightmare of mental retardation or dis-ease, federal courts should move with more than deliberate speed to guaran-tee these helpless souls that their world should be made as decent as possible." Wallace was strangely silent about Johnson's ruling, especially considering that Lurleen had invested so much energy to make a difference for mental health patients. As the Department of Mental Health scrambled to hire three hundred new aides as quickly as possible, news leaked that Oscar Harper's Topps Vend-ing Company, a firm that listed Gerald Wallace as a partner, had won the state cigarette vending contract. Other reports indicated the governor had used state employees and state postage to prepare and mail fund-raising correspondence. None of Wallace's ten Democratic campaign opponents made much headway with the reports, and the governor rolled to an easy victory in the March 15 Florida primary. "He knew that the people, the rank and file people . . . really weren't concerned about what's happening in state government in Alabama," Elvin Stanton recalled. "They were worried about their taxes and they were worried about the federal government taking over their lives and their schools and their labor unions." Two days after Wallace's Florida victory, Nixon an-nounced a ban on additional busing.[78]

Two weeks later, Highway Director Guerry Pruett quit his post, vowing that he did not want to be associated with the Wallace administration "in any capacity." The *Montgomery Advertiser* bemoaned the decision, noting Pru-ett's reputation for propriety and efficiency: "No man of integrity, who simply wanted to do a good job, could long exist in such an environment. . . . But he plainly had hopes—hopes that were dashed by his experience with a state government that is largely an arm of the lucrative Wallace campaign. Pru-ett's discrete silence on his reasons was a form of eloquence in itself." Pruett's lengthy letter of resignation, according to some published reports, included strong critiques of the administration's road policies. "I'm not going to discuss that stuff," Wallace snapped at reporters, "next question." It may well be that George Wallace was more popular outside of Alabama in 1972 than he was in-side its borders.[79]

Over the next two months, the Wallace campaign picked up momentum as it ventured north of the Mason-Dixon Line for primaries in Wisconsin, Indi-ana, Michigan, and Maryland. Wallace did especially well in states where bus-ing was a consideration. His calls for an improved national defense resonated with blue-collar workers and the "silent majority," which increasingly viewed the entire Vietnam War as a fiasco. Wallace made ample use of tax issues as well, especially when opponents bemoaned the Alabama codes. "The gover-nor," Stanton remembered, "would counter that very effectively. You know he'd say 'Mr. Lindsay is talking about how regressive the tax structure is in Alabama. Well let me ask you, in Alabama, if you have a home that is worth $85,000, let me tell you what the property tax is.' And then he would . . . and the people would go oooooh." When he noted the substantially higher tax on a similar house elsewhere in the country, the crowd would erupt again, believing that the Alabama governor had real credentials as a tax cutter. Wallace routinely followed up his tax rate comparison with a broad indictment of the federal government and changing cultural attitudes: "I'm sick and tired of giving up fifty percent of my income to the United States to waste half of it on nations that spit on us and half of it on welfare. I'm sick of permissiveness in this society."[80]

Despite his campaign skills, Wallace's second- and third-place finishes rarely came with comparable delegate counts, a product of an inexperienced campaign staff and state Democratic Party infrastructures that had little interest in the Alabamian as a national candidate. In Wisconsin, Wallace finished second, only 8 percentage points behind McGovern, yet earned no delegates. The campaign understood the simple math of the delegate deficiencies, but hoped to create enough momentum to engineer a convention fight. "There was some concern," Stanton admitted, "but I think the feeling was that if he continues to have great success, we can go and get some of those delegates. And . . . if this thing continues to mushroom to where he's the undecided favorite and we can make it work, then we'll be able to garner those from other people in other ways." At home in Alabama, department heads in Montgomery were told to bring a fifteen hundred dollar contribution and as many well-heeled guests as possible to a fund-raising dinner organized by Taylor Hardin and Gerald Wallace.[81]

Concerned about the long-term impact of losing big in Wisconsin, Wallace was late to start his campaign there. Historian Dan Carter has documented that Cornelia was responsible for ultimately convincing Wallace that he could compete in Wisconsin. On the ground in a state famous for producing both Robert LaFollette and Joe McCarthy, Wallace blamed his gubernatorial duties for his delay. "A governor is not like a senator, who can miss roll calls. A governor has to sign papers and has other duties which require his attention." Actually, Wallace's preference was to make the occasional phone call from the road to check on the store and rely on subordinates to keep the levers and pulleys of state government operating. He rarely deviated from the campaign schedule just to interject himself in state business. "He stayed on the phone and he would call people at midnight," Stanton recalled, "sometimes later than that. . . . He stayed in touch a lot more with state government than people gave him credit for, and he did it person-to-person. But it's true, he had some pretty good staff people who were keeping things going."[82]

As late as December 1971, Wallace was noncommittal about the Maryland primary: "I have thought about the Maryland Primary. I have just thought about it. I don't have any firm feeling in my mind about whether to become involved or not." On the morning of May 15, 1972, Wallace debated canceling the scheduled appearances for that day in Maryland, ultimately deferring to senior advisors who wanted to avoid the perception they were taking Maryland for granted. Poor communication and scheduling snafus caused the entire entourage to be late, and Wallace was irritable. The first speech on that day was in Wheaton, Maryland, and the governor endured some heckling and profanity. The next appearance, in Laurel, was less confrontational, though because of the constant campaigning Wallace was in poor voice and uncharacteristically fumbled a few applause lines.[83]

Against the recommendations of his Secret Service detail, Wallace stepped down from the platform and toward the rope line to greet well-wishers and shake hands. A moment later, Arthur Bremer, a wandering malcontent whose only goal was to leap from obscurity into the national spotlight, stepped toward Wallace and fired five shots from his .38-caliber revolver. In an instant, Bremer wounded Wallace, Secret Service Agent Nick Zarvos, campaign worker Dora Thompson, and Alabama trooper E. C. Dothard. All would survive, but George Wallace, a pulsating dynamo of raw physical energy, would never walk again.[84]

9
A New Reality / 1972–1974

In the minutes and hours after Bremer's cowardly act, a flurry of activity commenced. Cornelia Wallace flung herself on top of her husband's supine body, shielding him from additional bullets that she anticipated being fired. Her fashionable bright yellow and white outfit and matching yellow shoes absorbed blotches of blood. "I'm shot," Wallace told his wife. "I've been shot." Bystanders tackled Bremer and began pummeling him wildly. Chaos reigned in Laurel as pushing and shoving between supporters and hecklers broke out across the panic-filled shopping center. The governor's broken body was lifted into an ambulance and transported to Silver Springs Holy Cross Hospital. The red hotline telephone in Montgomery rang and secretary Sara Crumpton ran across the hall to tell Elvin Stanton that the Secret Service had called: "Something bad has happened," she told Stanton, but she was not sure exactly what. The next call confirmed that Wallace had been shot, but indicated that E. C. Dothard was the most seriously injured and that the trooper might not live. United Press International, relying on inaccurate information that characterized Wallace's wounds as fatal, issued an obituary. The Nixon administration moved to plant McGovern campaign material in Bremer's apartment but were foiled when the FBI sealed the apartment before operatives could arrive. According to *Washington Post* reporter Bob Woodward, Nixon was so "agitated and worried" that he demanded updates on the Bremer investigation every thirty minutes from FBI official Mark Felt, later revealed as Watergate informant Deep Throat.[1]

Wallace received death threats regularly and reflected on the possibility in private moments, though he rarely discussed the eventuality with family or colleagues. Routinely accosted by hecklers and habitually ducking to avoid incoming bricks or streams of spittle, Wallace learned to simply pull his handkerchief out of his pocket and wipe off the expectoration. Each day, after the roar of the crowds subsided, the limousine had dropped the traveling party off at the hotel and room service had come and gone, the governor quietly pondered the taunts and threats. And each day he judged them to be a risk he was willing to take. The family steeled itself against the reality that one day a phone call would come, bringing the news that shots had hit their mark. "There was always this unspoken fear about it," Peggy Wallace Kennedy, who was at Troy State at the time of the shooting, admitted. "I was really relieved in a way that it was over and it had been done because it was going to be done and I knew it was going to be done and . . . now I didn't have to worry about it anymore." In the days before Laurel, George Jr. dreamed about assassination attempts, often waking up in a cold sweat after picturing his father being shot in the throat. "He was resigned to the fact," George Jr. said of his father, "that there probably would be an attempt on his life. . . . But he always felt as though it would be a head wound. . . . He actually carried a gun in his pocket for a couple of days in '68, and the Secret Service had him do that and he finally gave it back. And he wore a vest a couple of times in '72, but it was too cumbersome." The day before he left for Maryland, Wallace's mother, Mozelle, fearful of an attempt on her son's life, cautioned him: "I'm worried about you, be careful." Days before the shooting, Wallace told Birmingham legislator Tom Gloor that something was about to happen. "Tommy, somebody's gonna get killed before this things over and I hope it's not me."[2]

Within thirty minutes of arriving at Holy Cross Hospital in Silver Springs, Maryland, Wallace was wheeled into the operating room. "Oh my God, honey, honey," Cornelia moaned. The quick action by medical personnel and rapid transport doubtless saved his life. The governor's blue short-sleeve shirt and blue and white blood-soaked tie were quickly cut away in order to begin assessing the wounds. Wallace's charcoal gray and light check "flex" suit pants with expanding buckle were removed and the stick of cinnamon chewing gum, tube of ChapStick, and Howard Johnson's matchbook tucked in his front pockets were bagged and tagged. Twenty-five specialists and surgeons from across the country eventually consulted on the case, and within a day of the shooting, some of them began to delicately identify the looming prognosis: "The outlook cannot be predicted," James Galbraith, a UAB neurosurgeon noted, "but it is not favorable. . . . It would be unusual to get complete recovery under these circumstances."[3]

The official diagnosis in Wallace's medical chart noted "multiple gunshot wounds as follows: Thru and thru wound, right forearm with entry into right anterior lower chest perforating the stomach and abrasion of descending colon; thru and thru gunshot-wound of right arm and entering right pleural cavity and peritoneal cavity—entering through spinal canal. Superficial wound of right anterior shoulder; grazing wound of skin behind right shoulder; abdominal wall abscess." In order to control the bacterial infection caused by the leaking of the governor's undigested hamburger steak into his gastrointestinal system, the initial surgical procedures included an exploratory laparotomy to control the internal bleeding, and various procedures to "repair" and stabilize the abdominal area. Spinal procedures were deemed to be of secondary importance.[4]

As soon as he was cognizant, Wallace received the good news that he had won the Michigan and Maryland primaries. Though he had no chance to win the nomination in the year that the Democratic party coronated George McGovern, Wallace was comforted by the news that he was second in the overall delegate count. Over the next few weeks, numerous political dignitaries, including Richard Nixon, Spiro Agnew, George McGovern, Shirley Chisholm, and Ted Kennedy, stopped by to pay respects to the fallen Alabamian and wish him a quick and complete recovery. Chisholm's visit and prayers in the hospital room reduced her and the governor to tears. Former president Lyndon Johnson and Pope Paul VI sent telegrams. During these trying times, Wallace and Hubert Humphrey cemented one of the most curious friendships in recent political history. The Alabamian and the Minnesotan, each the victim of stereotyping in the other's state, became such strong friends that years later, Wallace was nearly inconsolable when Humphrey died.[5]

Back in Alabama, executive secretary Harry Pennington controlled daily operations—an easy transition given the preexisting realities of Wallace's presidential campaigning and the governor's general disinterest in state policy— with the assistance of legal advisor Bill Jackson, Press Secretary Billy Joe Camp and his assistant, Elvin Stanton, and finance director Taylor Hardin. During the campaign season, the daily governance of the State of Alabama was conducted via the telephone anyway. "We would just get some feedback from somebody that we would share with him from time to time," Stanton remembered. Camp and Stanton stayed in Maryland to coordinate the flurry of press inquiries at the hospital. Jackson authored a legal opinion on the suddenly important issue of gubernatorial succession. Given the feuding between Wallace and the lieutenant governor, the palace guard wanted to avoid handing over the reins of power to the ambitious Beasley. According to Jackson, article five, section 127 of the state constitution mandated that if the governor was absent from the state for a period of twenty days, the "power and authority of the office . . . devolves upon the Lieutenant Governor." Jackson pondered semantic issues of when to start counting the twenty days and which powers and duties could remain with Wallace, but such digressions were moot: it was clear that Wallace would be at Holy Cross for weeks and that Beasley would eventually be in charge.[6]

Beasley made little use of his new power other than to declare a Day of Prayer and issue an executive order blocking a utility rate increase. At his first cabinet meeting, Beasley broke the ice by announcing that Taylor Hardin and Billy Joe Camp, his outspoken rivals during his previous battles with the administration, would be fired. Beasley was kidding, but many in the administration were not amused. Though he was brazen, Beasley was smart enough to keep his office located in the lieutenant governor's suite and not make a symbolic move into the governor's permanent office space—a move that would have infuriated Alabamians. The acting governor did not travel outside of Alabama to campaign for Wallace, and some of the palace guard never forgave him. And Harry Pennington continued to coordinate the daily functions of the executive branch. "I want all appointments that are ready to go out to be brought to my desk," Pennington demanded in writing, "Please see to it that no appointments are sent out that have not been to my desk for approval."[7]

As would be expected, Wallace had a difficult time adjusting to his paralysis. "In the beginning," Peggy Wallace Kennedy recalled, "he was very bitter and he stayed very bitter and very angry for a long time. We all suffered from that bitterness and anger. . . . There was no way that my daddy, with that personality, couldn't have had the bitterness and anger." Daughter Bobbie Jo Parsons optimistically told reporters that her father was anxious to resume campaigning, but he was far weaker than friendly press reports averred. "There was a time that we didn't know if there would be a George Wallace," Stanton recalled of the tenuous moments in Maryland. Erroneous reports suggested that Charles Snider promised that Wallace would travel to Oregon for its late May primary. Doctors, however, quickly scuttled discussions of campaign appearances. "It's problematic," Galbraith told reporters, "that he will get any return of function at all. It's unlikely that he will get anything like normal use of his legs." Physical therapists manipulated Wallace's legs, sometimes as often as every hour, in order to keep blood circulating and minimize muscle atrophy.[8]

Perhaps the most difficult aspect to paraplegia is the false hopes that are raised with every new physical anomaly. When tickling and other forms of stimulation led to movement of Wallace's toes, reflex foot action, and brief sensations in other parts of his legs, prospects momentarily brightened for the patient and his family even as doctors urged caution. Well-meaning supporters from across the country flooded the hospital with cards and letters and ideas about miracle cures and devices that supposedly regenerated damaged spinal cords. Some twenty thousand responses were mailed from the governor's office alone, with thousands being diverted to Faulkner Junior College and the University of Alabama at Huntsville for processing. Countless other letters of support to the governor went unanswered because the volume was so massive. Instead of regaining mobility, Wallace was faced with a stream of surgical procedures to drain pus from his infected abdomen. More than a week after the shooting, Wallace was still on a liquid diet. Two weeks after the shooting, he was barely able to be wheeled seventy-five feet down the hall to visit Cornelia in the room provided for her by the hospital. More than anything, Wallace was unprepared for the roller coaster of emotions he encountered, resulting in mental health as precarious as his physical condition. And in a world where the hospital was receiving death threats because they were caring for George Wallace, moments of solace were fleeting.[9]

The political realities were equally bleak. Commercials aired in several states and stand-in speakers were hastily assembled, but the momentum was lost. McGovern won handily in Rhode Island and Oregon, combining with the governor's incapacitation to make long-shot plans of a draft-Wallace movement at the convention even more remote. Though the campaign made overtures toward the vice presidency, serious discussions never materialized. Humphrey, still holding out the possibility that he could be drafted for the nomination, announced he could accept Wallace on the ticket assuming the Alabamian fully endorsed the national platform, both of which were highly unlikely. Wallace's last hope was to gain entrée to the convention dais and hope for a political miracle. When Democratic National Committee chair Larry O'Brien visited Wallace at Holy Cross and promised him the opportunity to make a speech at the convention, the entire focus was to get the governor physically capable of traveling to Miami.[10]

Politically, much work was left to be done. In order to satisfy the McGovern Commission's complicated new Democratic Party regulations for minority participation, Wallace's campaign staff had to recruit five black delegates, three of whom had to be female with at least two under the age of thirty-one. Given Wallace's reputation in the state, this task would have been difficult enough. However a series of legal challenges by John Cashin, African American leader of the National Democratic Party of Alabama, sought to bar any of Wallace's delegates from receiving official credentials at the convention. The landscape was further altered when a growing feud between Cashin and Joe Reed, leader of another mostly African American group—the Alabama Democratic Conference—went public. Alabama Democratic Party chief Robert Vance vowed not to certify the Alabama delegation unless it met the national party's racial and gender quotas, forcing Taylor Hardin and Harry Pennington to concentrate on finding five willing black Alabamians. When the five were finally selected, one Wallace supporter was fed up with grumbling that they were a collection of Uncle Toms: "Y'all wanted five blacks and we got you five blacks. Whadda ya want, all of 'em to be Angela Davis."[11]

Over the course of Wallace's fifty-four-day hospital stay, events in Alabama revealed that for all the sympathy the state had for its fallen governor, Alabama had numerous other crises to confront: an American Public Health Association study indicated that the maternal mortality rate in Alabama was 64 percent higher than the national average and the state had only about 25 percent of the physicians it needed to adequately address prenatal and postpartum care in rural locales; a *Montgomery Advertiser* report determined that some city policemen were using food stamps to buy groceries for their families; white Montgomery residents mounted a furious charge to beat back an attempt to change Jackson Street to Martin Luther King Avenue; the administration was discovered to have used federal antipoverty funds, supposedly targeted for veterans, to pay their own office staff; officials at the Partlow mental health facility were caught allocating ten thousand dollars for administrative office remodeling—drapes, credenzas, and armchairs—at the same time that the administration was appealing a federal court order citing mental health bathrooms that featured broken toilet seats and no toilet paper. In rejecting the administration's appeal of his order on mental health, Judge Johnson called the request "frivolous . . . no more than an attempt prompted by [Wallace's] own lack of diligence." At the time of the administration's appeal of the ruling, fifteen counties—more than 22 percent of the state—had no mental health facilities at all, and some municipalities, such as Gadsden, had a brand new building but no operating funds for equipment or staff. An anonymous Alabama attorney summarized a growing feeling in the state about Wallace: "The truth about George is that he has always been far too interested in running for president to take the time to do what Alabama needs. And now he's going across the country, just what he did in Alabama—telling us what the problems are and not offering any real solution to them."[12]

The larger issue is not that Alabamians were consumed with these unfortunate illustrations of inefficient governance while Wallace lay paralyzed in Silver Springs, Maryland. They were not. The cold reality in Alabama is that in practically any fifty-four-day period, similar examples of inattention to the basic functions of government were present. And Alabamians were no more interested then either. Prior to the elimination of the poll tax, it could be argued that poor whites—the typical Alabamian—had limited access to the franchise and therefore could not be held accountable for their mediocre state government. And prior to the passing of the Voting Rights Act of 1965, it could be argued that blacks—some 25 percent of Alabama—had no access to the ballot and therefore could not be held accountable for the dismal performance of their elected leaders. But by 1972, rank-and-file Alabamians had easy access to the polls and simply chose not to expect anything better from their political system.

As in previous terms, George Wallace was more interested in campaigning than governing. But Wallace deserves only half the blame for the litany of fundamental problems Alabama never addressed. No matter how powerful the interest groups were in Alabama, Alabamians had no stomach to do anything about them. And with their cultural hero, George Wallace, defender of front porch traditions, foe of the First and Second Reconstructions, rhetorical slayer of big government, intellectuals, federal courts, and all things Yankee, destined to spend the rest of his life paralyzed from the waist down, they had no plans to hold him accountable either.

Just weeks after the bullets ripped through his body, Wallace summoned amazing physical strength to appear at the Democratic National Convention in Miami. His ambulance plane landed first in Montgomery so that Wallace could satisfy constitutional requirements necessary to reclaim his office. As the Troy State marching band played before a reserved crowd of five thousand, Wallace restrained his weak voice and spoke for only a few minutes. During the flights to Montgomery and Miami, Wallace maintained his therapy regime by lifting himself from his chair periodically. Though still limited to a liquid diet, Wallace was now gaining strength on a daily basis. By the time he arrived in Miami, Wallace had learned to steady himself with braces, gained demonstrable upper body strength through his strenuous physical therapy sessions, and, remarkably, added four pounds of body weight. Cornelia, in a speech to the South Carolina legislature, revealed that her husband was performing 155 push-ups per day. He was now able to wheel himself for extended periods of time. "I am still an active and viable candidate," he told the sparse crowd of seventy-five people who greeted him at the airport in Miami, "even though I was sidelined for a few days. We're back in the fight." A day after settling in at the Four Ambassador's Hotel, Wallace sounded the charge again: "We're back in full swing. . . . I'm going to be as active as any candidate because I am able to be active and I will be." Nine-year-old Lee spoke to the same group: "When you cast your ballot, please cast it for George C. Wallace. I guess you heard about my daddy's accident. . . . I think myself he has come back fighting like the old George Wallace."[13]

For all the governor's optimism and the good wishes of his youngest daughter, the raw politics of the convention was one defeat after another. The platform committee crushed the Wallace planks in five minutes despite a brief impassioned appearance by a pale Wallace. "I am here because I want to help the Democratic party," he pleaded. "I want it to become again the party of the average citizen as it used to be and not the party of the pseudo-intellectual snobbery that it has come to be." The Wallace antibusing provision, the centerpiece of Wallace's entire big government–bashing stump speech, was rejected by a 78 to 16 committee vote. His plan to reshape the party included a call for Larry O'Brien to resign, a request that did little to help him get a minority platform report considered by the party apparatchiks. And Wallace refused to renounce all intentions to launch a belated third-party drive, a further insult to national Democrats, even though he had neither the interest nor the stamina to attend the American Independent Party convention in Louisville, Kentucky. Privately, Wallace told friends that McGovern was bound for an electoral beating in November.[14]

Wallace's twelve-minute address at the convention was his only respite from the cold reality of his wheeled world. Over the preceding fourteen years, Wallace had battled insecurity, marital conflict, self-doubt, an array of federal court orders, brief bouts of melancholy, the collective opprobrium of civil rights leaders, scathing editorials from northeastern newspapers, the emotional tugging guilty fathers feel for not being available to their children, and persistent criticism from Alabama's small but vocal set of social liberals and economic progressives. In the midst of being the eye of the storm, Wallace could always find sanctuary on the stage, where his frenetic energy could be released in front of throngs of kindred spirits desperate to blame life's woes and their own shortcomings on activist federal judges, long-haired, dope-smoking college professors, and agitating blacks. But Bremer's bullets changed this too. Wallace would never prowl the stage in quite the same way again. In the eyes of Alabamians, Wallace, almost instantaneously, ceased being the valiant knight beckoning the state and region to gird against the lurking danger of social change and became a tragic and sympathetic figure to be pitied if not loved.

As his father was wheeled up the ramp to the lectern to a standing ovation, George Jr. surveyed the crowd and noticed Jacqueline Kennedy Onassis turn and walk out of the convention, indicative of the outlaw status Wallace carried within the Democratic Party. Wallace's speech was mediocre, compared to the electric atmospheres he created in Madison Square Garden in 1968, at Milwaukee's Serb Hall in 1964 and 1968, or any of a thousand events on the back of a flatbed pickup truck along the highways and byways of rural Alabama. But in other ways, Wallace's convention speech was incredible. Lucky to be alive, no longer in control of his bladder or bowel functions, in physical pain that few in the packed arena could understand, and sweating profusely, the governor looked the Democratic Party delegates right in the eye and gave them his version of hell. No matter that his bleats for smaller government and tax reform went unheeded, that his calls to end busing and beef up the military gained no purchase, and that his demand to end foreign aid to nations "that spit in our faces," drew more yawns than cheers, Wallace made his case on a night a lesser man would have been in a hospital or the grave.[15]

Back in Alabama

With the speech finished, the sole focus of the previous eighteen months, the presidential campaign, was over and Wallace returned to his other job, governor. Campaigning had involved every level and nearly every person in the executive branch. The State Sovereignty Commission had been enlisted to provide opposition research, to assemble the voting records of Wallace's rivals, and to draft a litany of election bills to streamline the primary process in Alabama. Wallace, through an assistant, had asked Senator Jim Allen to provide inside information on Senator Henry "Scoop" Jackson. Taylor Hardin, Harry Pennington, Mickey Griffin, Billy Joe Camp, Elvin Stanton, Bobby Bowick, George Mangum, and many others had devoted a majority of their time to the vagaries of the primary season: logistics, fund-raising, responding to mail, scheduling, event-planning, and media relations. The research and planning for Florida alone had been extensive enough to involve most of the palace guard. With the convention over, each of them was forced to return to their workaday jobs: running the State of Alabama.[16]

Exhausted, Wallace returned to Alabama and was immediately admitted to Spain Rehabilitation Hospital in Birmingham. At the same time, contractors installed a chairlift in the mansion, widened door thresholds to accommodate the chair, and replaced entry and exit steps with ramps. Press reports continued to cite the governor's progress, including the recurrent tingling sensations in his upper legs. Wallace pressed seventy-pound dumbbells, transferred himself in and out of his chair, and learned to dress himself. Physical therapists Judith Cantey and Beverly Rich praised their patient: "He pushes himself to the maximum." Despite the optimism, Wallace found himself in surgery nine days after his convention speech. Yet another abdominal abscess had formed. A month later, Wallace was under the knife again, his fifth surgery in ninety-two days, to drain yet another persistent abscess.[17]

The dichotomy between the optimism of the press releases and the reality that Wallace was suffering physically, emotionally, and mentally was palpable, yet not surprising. The administration continued to aggressively manage the flow of information about the governor and his governance. Even before the 1972 campaign had been officially launched, Wallace and the administration were obsessed with keeping a strong connection with ordinary Alabamians. "Let's get a list of the football players and coaching staff," Wallace told Press Secretary Billy Joe Camp, "at Auburn, Alabama, Troy, Livingston, Florence, Jacksonville, Samford etc. and send them a Colonel Commission." All told, 499 college football players received an unexpected honorary title during the 1972 season. The governor also wanted his picture in every State of Alabama college or university football program. Just after Thanksgiving, Wallace fired off a terse missive to assistant Jesse Gann: "Are we getting any of our pictures out? We should have the coordinators get them out to some of the stores in the rural area etc. Let's make a move on this." Always conscious of image, votes, and voters, Wallace asked his staff to target certain voters: "Let's write a letter to the patients, staff, and administrators of the Veteran's Hospital, Masonic Homes, orphanages, and the nursing homes, wishing all of them a happy holiday season. You might send pictures to them." Based on a suggestion from friend Ralph Adams, Wallace made sure his name was imprinted on every diploma awarded at a state-sponsored junior college, college, or university.[18]

While the governor missed scads of state agency board meetings, he could be fastidious when it came to voter correspondence. "I have several letters where people have talked with you and others and you promised to call them back," Wallace scolded Bobby Bowick in October, "but they never heard from you again. . . . Don't leave people dangling." Three months later, Wallace was still choleric over unanswered letters and unreturned phone calls. Because incoming mail was viewed as an opportunity to interact with a voter, specific procedures for handling it were established. In addition to identifying those authorized to open letters and prepare return correspondence over the governor's signature, Wallace and the administration ordered weekly reports listing the names of each Alabamian who had not yet received a response, and a daily report "showing any significant mail run on a particular subject, identifying the subject and the number of mailings received that day on the subject." Answering mail could be problematic if Alabamians deconstructed the date on the letter from the governor and his travel plans. Several letters, for example, were dated May 15, 1972—the date of the shooting—a day that the governor could not have possibly written a letter.[19]

While the governor routinely missed department meetings before, during, and after the shooting, the officials who ran those agencies were expected to instantly produce material for Wallace when he faced press scrutiny. "Governor Wallace," press aide Elvin Stanton wrote just before a Wallace appearance on national television, "wants us to contact Ruben King to get some info from him regarding our welfare program and how it is administered in the state as compared to the administration of other welfare programs in larger urban states so he can delineate the difference on the *Meet the Press* program." Considering he had been in office for nearly a decade, Wallace should have understood more of the daily machinations of the state's largest single government agency, especially since it had been threatened with federal court orders on numerous occasions.[20]

Despite the administration's attempts to manage the flow of information, the preoccupation with the presidential campaign was evident to most Alabamians. A list of constituent complaints assembled by assistant George Mangum identified unkept promises, unreturned mail and phone calls, and an office staff that was increasingly keeping the governor off-limits from his Alabama admirers. "People close to the governor," Mangum wrote, "are not looking after the Governor's interest. . . . If I believe what people hit me with, then I must believe our stock is down."[21]

After the shooting, Wallace—now unable to keep up a hectic public speaking schedule—was even more committed to reclaiming his close connection with Alabamians. Wallace was not afraid to encourage the press to embellish his personal accomplishments, an indication that the governor rarely separated the personal from the professional. "We should get some publicity out," the governor counseled Camp, "on the award given to me the other night by the National Rehabilitation Institute. Cornelia has the citation." The administration mailed 46,445 letters to high school seniors in private and public schools. Wallace asked assistant Johnny Goff to mail a personal letter from the governor to every teacher at the start of the 1973 academic year. "I have received a number of letters from school children, especially in Alabama, wishing me a recovery," the governor demanded of his correspondence team, "I want each one of these children written and an autographed picture sent to them." On other occasions, Wallace ordered autographed pictures of himself and Cornelia sent to every nursing home resident, orphan, and mental health inpatient in Alabama.[22]

The quest to mail photos across the state became absurd. On one day alone, 13,000 snapshots were mailed to state nursing homes. In a February 1973 photo order, the administration purchased 275,000 pictures, even though 104,000 had been on hand as recently as three months earlier. By August 1973, Johnny Goff had sent letters and pictures to 138,082 Alabamians and was briefing Wallace regularly with reports of his direct mail activities. The autographed pictures included individual poses of the governor as well as stills of Cornelia and George. Wallace believed the old adage that a picture was worth a thousand words: "The picture taken of me . . . shaking the old black man's hand who was 104 years old—see if we can get a copy of this."[23]

The press releases, photos, and publicity campaigns were designed not only to engender goodwill with Alabama voters but also to obscure the larger issue that Wallace was even less involved in the policy and practice of state government than ever before. By January 1973, reporters referred to Wallace appearances across the state as "ceremonial." That same month, Wallace underwent yet another surgical procedure, this one designed to relieve inflammation on a swollen prostate and prevent recurrent urinary tract infections. The operation was expected to hospitalize the governor for ten days to two weeks; Wallace checked out twenty-eight days later. Rumors swept Montgomery that Wallace was no longer capable of governing. Content that the governor was out of commission, crony Oscar Harper attempted to fire Pensions and Security Department director Ruben King, the man responsible for the state's $172 million welfare program. Rather than knuckle under, King went to the media, splashing the entire affair across the front pages and making Wallace appear to be all the more impotent. "No five-percenter hired me," King retorted, validating suspicions that Harper was continuing to profit from state government in imaginative ways, "and no five-percenter is going to fire me." A four-hour meeting with Wallace ended with King agreeing to retire in two months.[24]

In the midst of assimilating the new reality of a paralyzed Wallace, *Montgomery Advertiser* editor Harold Martin called on Wallace to retire: "It would be in the best interest of the state of Alabama and of the governor himself if he retired, or short of that, appoint a committee of outstanding businessmen to share the burden of state government for the duration of his term, looking forward to an orderly transition in 1974." Martin, in a series of exposés, identified that Harper, Gerald Wallace, and Frank Long were wielding tremendous power. "I can't even get to the governor to discuss my problems," one department head told Martin. While Gerald and his merry band had almost unfettered access during the first term, Wallace had explicitly promised the cabinet in 1971 that his brother would be kept on a tight leash. The bedlam of the presidential campaign, the shooting, and the protracted recovery gave good cover for Gerald, Harper, and Long to return to their underground seat of power. Martin's chief criticism was not only that the unofficial palace guard was enriching themselves but also that Wallace was too incapacitated to do anything about it: "Alabama citizens are crushed emotionally by the appearance of the once vivacious Wallace in a wheelchair, suffering constant pain. But more and more Alabamians are facing up to the reality that the state can't continue to function without leadership."[25]

The immediate response of many Alabamians was to rush to Wallace's defense, just as they had done in the face of attacks since 1963. "Governor Wallace has done more for the state," Clifford Wilkinson of Alberta, Alabama, wrote, "than any other governor during my time and I am seventy-four years old." Charles Cook of Chickasaw reduced Martin's charges to an attack on a helpless man: "I think Governor Wallace deserves a lot of credit for what he has done for the people of the state. I certainly wouldn't want to be guilty of trying to hurt an innocent man because he was shot by a criminal." And many Alabamians preferred to attack the messenger, Martin, rather than assess his message. "Mr. Martin," Notasulga resident Freddie Ware blasted, "you are a literary leech and people know it. First, your little speech stunk. Secondly, why don't you take your medical and investigation knowledge and leave Alabama? . . . So smarty Martin, why not clam up? I know all who read your speech felt it was absurd and shameful to say Governor Wallace should git [*sic*] out for being 'unfit.'"[26]

While the reaction of Wallace's supporters was predictable, a surprising number of Alabamians found Martin's characterization of Wallace's health compelling. Tuscaloosa state senator Richard Shelby praised Martin: "It took a lot of courage to say what Mr. Martin did relative to Governor Wallace's physical condition at this time. It has been obvious to thousands of people for quite some time that this state is leaderless, but no one, including myself, spoke out and said so. I want to commend you for your statements . . . and hope that your remarks will not be swept under the rug." According to the *Advertiser,* letter writers, by a margin of two to one, advocated Wallace's retirement or at least a trusteeship of the office. Others seemed downright ebullient at the prospect of turning Wallace out. "Hurray for Mr. Martin," Harvey Crumhorn cheered. "My wife and I were very pleased to hear that you and your paper are urging Governor Wallace to resign. . . . Governor Wallace was shot while on a campaign trip for his personal gain. It is unfair to the people of Alabama to be burdened with him." Vennie Watkins of Tarrant advocated retirement because Wallace had failed to live up to his bevy of campaign promises made in the tight race with Albert Brewer: "I do not believe Wallace should be given state retirement since he was not on state business and was indeed advising in no uncertain terms that everyone in this state was a liar. I heard him say that he would be a full-time governor."[27]

The Martin-resignation furor fueled a new set of rumors about Wallace's level of incapacitation, including speculation that Wallace was addicted to pain medication, that he was consulting psychics, and that he scheduled regular acupuncture sessions. A *Newsweek* report termed the governor "tormented by pain and depression," and suggested that the looming 1974 campaign could only be won by appealing to a sympathy vote. "They keep George so sedated," a Wallace staffer told the magazine, "that half the time he's in a haze. Every forty-five minutes they bring him some kind of medication, just like clockwork."[28]

The rumors were a combination of smoke and fire. Wallace was depressed, occasionally battled his therapists and nurses, and brooded, understandably, over his paralysis. He rarely went to his state capitol office, and when he did, he arrived late in the morning and often left early in the afternoon. Victories were small, but savored nonetheless: brace-walking between parallel bars, dressing and undressing, increasing the weight on the dumbbell and barbell exercises designed to make his upper body stronger. Wallace swallowed a variety of medications each day including pain pills of varying strength, as well as pharmacology designed to battle infection, help him sleep, and boost his vitamin intake. At one point, he used an electrical stimulation device that sent pulsed bursts of electric shock through his spinal nervous system. Wallace never admitted to visiting mystery healers, curtly telling inquisitors he had no comment. After Gerald Wallace watched a film about acupuncture, he encouraged his brother to try it. Ling Sun-Chu, a New York specialist raised in China and trained in Shanghai and at both the University of Hamburg and Harvard, flew into Montgomery each weekend and administered treatments. Both Sun-Chu and Wallace were wary of each other initially. The patient was leery of additional pain and was skeptical of Asian remedies. The healer found Wallace "sluggish and confused" during their initial sessions. Seven treatments later, Wallace credited acupuncture with reducing his pain, helping him sleep, and making his legs warmer and his skin color healthier. The improvements were ephemeral, however, and the governor was destined to spend his remaining days with phantom leg pain, chronic spinal pain, a host of other physical complications, and the perpetual gloom of waking each morning to discover his nightmare was as real as the wheelchair sitting beside his bed.[29]

One way for Wallace to cope with his paralysis was to use dark humor to set others at ease. "I don't go around jumping over many fences or running up the stairs," he frequently wisecracked to onlookers who asked about his condition. One prank Wallace enjoyed was yelping "ouch" whenever his chair was turned into a wall or his leg accidently came in contact with someone. He had no feeling, of course, but the joke caused others to relax around a figure who seemed less approachable in a wheelchair than he ever had while walking a rope line or chatting up factory workers during a shift change. Wallace developed a morbid response line for dealing with questions about his political plans: "I can't predict the future. If I could, I'd stay home occasionally instead of going off on campaign trips."[30]

Rather than allow the rumors to fester, the administration coordinated a counterattack to calm the fears. Wallace's personal physician, Ham Hutchinson, rejected the notion that Wallace was constantly sedated. "His spirits are good," Hutchinson announced; "he's as sharp as ever, and you know how sharp that is." Hutchinson told Associated Press reporter Rex Thomas that Wallace had actually gained close to ten pounds. House floor leader Joe McCorquodale was enlisted to assure that Wallace was "mentally sharp and fully aware." And the governor made a rare public appearance, traveling to the National Governors' Conference in Washington D.C. "I run the state executive branch as I always have," Wallace boasted, "and always will as long as I am governor." The message was clear if not especially accurate: do not believe everything you read or hear.[31]

Chomping on his trademark cigar, Wallace toyed with reporters covering the Governors' Conference who tried to pin him down on whether he would enter the 1974 gubernatorial race. Only once did he allow his electoral self-confidence to get the best of him. "I can win any election I run in," he bragged to the national press. Wallace delighted in a quadrennial waltz with reporters in which he would claim not to have any idea of whether he was interested in being governor, and then they would write story after story speculating on his plans. He danced on whether he would run in one campaign or another in 1962, 1964, 1968, 1970, 1972, and 1974. In the end, Wallace ran, as he always did, because running for office was *his chosen profession.* "If George didn't have either his legs or his politics," Cornelia assessed, "I don't think he'd have much reason to go on living." And national campaign director Charles Snider understood that a 1976 presidential campaign was unthinkable without Wallace in the governor's office.[32]

Conflict without Resolution

Feeling feisty enough to joust with the scribes, Wallace reluctantly turned his attention to state business. Throughout the almost quarter century of Wallace rule in Alabama, the state faced decree after decree from the federal government to address internal problems. From integration to mental health to prison reform, decrees from federal judges and Washington's threats to withhold funds did as much to change Alabama as the combined actions of executive and legislative branches of state government. As the 1973 regular session approached, Alabama was faced with yet another mandate to reapportion the legislature. "One man, one vote" requirements—essentially creating roughly equal districts without regard to race or any other sociological factor—enacted by the federal court led to a three-judge panel electoral map that crossed county lines and abrogated traditional districts. The thought of this particular plan horrified incumbents: minorities would be proportionately represented; fundraising would be more difficult; years of providing pork for districts would suddenly be meaningless with the obliteration of old lines; probate judges, some more dedicated than others, would be required to enforce the court plan; and voters, in some cases, would be directed to new polling places. Publicly, the rhetoric focused on the difficulty of counting votes with districts that crossed municipal and county boundaries, and the question of whether one house member could adequately represent the citizens of several counties. And since the plan came from the federal government, the most common jeremiad wailed by solons was that this reapportionment scheme was sure to be the death of local government. Paradoxically, many of these same legislators had steadfastly resisted attempts to rescind the constitutional provision limiting home rule, thus keeping power in the state legislature at the expense of county and municipal governments. According to reporter Don Wasson, legislators predicted the court plan would make "the ensuing four years . . . the most chaotic in the history of the state." A legal challenge was defeated when the U.S. Supreme Court upheld the constitutionality of the three judge panel. The tumult surrounding the issue caused many legislators to beg Wallace to call a special session so that the legislature could craft a substitute blueprint.[33]

When Wallace proved reluctant to call a special session, a new round of rumors suggested he was physically incapable of tending to the recalcitrant legislature that had dealt him so many setbacks during the 1971 sessions. Though a special session could have been called as early as November 1972, Wallace waited six months before announcing that the court reapportionment plan was "atrocious" and leaking word that he would call the lawmakers back to work only if he was convinced that a new plan would pass in the senate. House speaker Sage Lyons began quietly signing up legislators who wished to sponsor a bill, an informal method of gauging support. The administration's biggest problem in the upper chamber was that they controlled only nine of the thirty-fives votes in that body. Despite the half year of inactivity, Wallace complained that the state needed a ninety-day reprieve from the federal courts in order to consider the issue. The chances of the federal court, Wallace's favorite whipping boy, extending any courtesy was remote. When the court issued its own reapportionment plan in a January 1972 decision, it cited Alabama's tradition of failing to meet its own responsibilities: "This court [acted] only when confronted with totally inadequate legislative response to, or complete disregard for, its constitutional mandate." Frustrated with its babysitting role in Alabama—the court had reapportioned Alabama three consecutive times when the legislature could not do it—the three-judge panel gave Wallace a firm May 17 deadline for producing a substitute. According to one report, many legislators refused to even read the court's rulings because they considered them insulting.[34]

Wallace, wearing thick glasses, opened the 1973 regular session with a thirty-minute speech he delivered while standing in a specially constructed box designed to support his weight. Though capitol speculation indicated that the governor might stride to the lectern with the aid of braces or crutches, he did not attempt such an exhausting maneuver. The "standing box" clasped the governor tightly inside a padded area, allowing him to stand and project his voice while also preventing him from falling. In order to become more familiar with the box, Wallace stood in it to read his morning newspapers at the mansion. Though his speech covered many topics and successfully countered the suspicion that he was unable to perform his job, Wallace rarely mentioned reapportionment except to castigate the federal decisions and deadlines, and allow that he was amenable to a special session. The legislature immediately adjourned the regular session and began a special session with just two weeks left before the federal court's reapportionment deadline. One day later, the house introduced a new bill; two days later they passed one and left the resolution of the matter to the senate.[35]

Once engaged, the senate considered two separate reapportionment plans. One, crafted by Ben Cherner of Birmingham, who subsequently died, and the University of Alabama Center for Business and Economic Research was consistent with the one-man, one-vote directive of the federal courts. But Cherner's plan, drawn principally from a computer model, was unpopular with his colleagues, primarily because it offered almost no protection for incumbents. The plan that the legislature passed, based on the recommendations of a committee led by Hugh Merrill and featuring very few potential races between existing legislators, elicited a skeptical reaction from Fred Gray, counsel for the plaintiffs in the case that had spawned the federal court ruling. Gray noted an excessively high population variance between some districts, announced that blacks could expect to win only half of the seats they expected to compete for under the terms of the federal plan, and that some districts, not surprisingly, were drawn for the sole purpose of reelecting incumbents. Wallace signed the bill anyway. Again more interested in themselves and their base of power than in meeting federal guidelines or improving the state, the Alabama legislature seemed intent on living up to a 1970 survey of state legislatures that dubbed the state lawmakers to be the worst in the country. A WSFA-TV editorial blistered the legislature for its self-serving and discriminatory plan: "When our legislators move under the gun of federal intervention the bills they pass tend to be filled with all sorts of escape clauses. The thinking seems to be: Although the handwriting is on the wall, let's see how much we can get away with. It's time that our representatives stop this sort of nonsense.... Either shape up, or plan on an early political retirement." Others echoed similar sentiments about the intractability and incompetence of the combined efforts of the legislative and executive branches, but the majority of the populace could not have been less interested in the reapportionment process. Integration stirred a host of deeply planted memories; fair representation did not.[36]

Because the governor and the legislature had not taken the federal guidelines seriously, the three-judge panel did not accept the substitute reapportionment plan. Wallace blasted the decision, calling the court plan "a most onerous and burdensome albatross around the necks of the people of Alabama." With the court overturning the legislature's plan, the reapportionment session was a complete flop, wasting both time and money. The regular session was not any better: "It has widely been widely rated," an *Advertiser* editorial declared on the eve of adjournment, "the worst legislature in years—some say the worst ever." Given the dubious reputation Alabama lawmakers had painstakingly crafted since 1819, the criticism was all the more bitter. And the inefficiency was compounded by the fact that the administration proposed an even more modest agenda than usual, fearful of taking a beating similar to the 1971 debacle.[37]

Yet another wasted legislative session was hardly news in Alabama. Wallace had called a blithering array of special sessions since 1963, and yet the state continued to face federal court orders for failure to achieve minimum standards in mental health, prisons, and welfare. Personality conflicts and lack of direction from the executive branch were particularly acute in the 1973 regular session, however. Lieutenant Governor Jere Beasley continued to vex the administration with his plan to expand the power of his office into a full-time job. With relations already strained because of Beasley's truculence during the 1971 session and his limited participation in the 1972 campaign after the shooting, Wallace was wary of his fellow Barbour County native. Frequently, Beasley flew across Alabama in a plane owned by the state's vocational education department, raising his name recognition and appearing to be a full-time lieutenant governor even if his job description had not been officially changed. "He's not supposed to do a damn thing," one administration floor leader in the senate snickered, "but sit up there and rule on senate procedures and I don't give a shit whether he opposes anything or approves of anything. He doesn't have a vote in this body unless we are tied."[38]

Though the administration plotted to mute Beasley or at least render him impotent, they could not rid themselves of him. He beat back attempts to reduce the number of committees in the senate and continued to send legislation to his own pet committee—Commerce, Transportation, and Common Carriers. Packed with his own handpicked slate of friends, Commerce became the easiest way to kill or delay bills when Beasley wanted to play politics. And the lieutenant governor had no trepidation about sending bills completely unrelated to commerce or transportation, such as an education capital outlay proposal, to that committee. Before the 1973 regular session even began, Beasley directed a dozen prefiled bills into Commerce's coffers. After the Alabama Development Office refused to allow him to use their airplane, Beasley sent a housing bill to Commerce for retribution. His reputation for hardball established, Beasley prepared to codify his power by asking for pay befitting a full-time second in command, an expanded office staff and expense account, and various other perquisites, even as he publicly disavowed any such plans. In addition, Beasley's bill provided the lieutenant governor with a nonvoting seat on all boards and committees that the governor served on, and placed the Alabama Development Office under his direct control. Though Beasley's staff had been expanded by resolution during the 1971 sessions, Attorney General Bill Baxley, an administration friend, had subsequently ruled that such changes must by created by an official legislative act. Speaker Sage Lyons, announcing his opposition to empowering Beasley, told reporters that Beasley threatened to block all legislation in the senate until he received his raise and expanded powers. "I have a lot of respect for the speaker," Beasley spun in response, "and I hope he won't let his personal feelings get involved. . . . I have no intention of letting personal feelings get in the way of the orderly opposition of the senate."[39]

Baxley's ruling threatened Beasley more than Lyon's machismo because the attorney general's opinion convinced the administration to return the lieu-

320 / Jeff Frederick

tenant governor to his previous salary of three hundred dollars per month. Beyond the necessity of hammering through a law to replace the moot resolution, Beasley understood that Baxley's ruling was more than just a legal opinion; it was a declaration of war between two young and aggressive lawyers, both of whom envisioned themselves occupying the governor's chair as soon as Wallace was finished with it. Beasley was already preparing for a gubernatorial campaign in the event that Wallace was too weak to run in 1974. He used a minor senate committee, Intergovernmental Cooperation, to expand his profile and tapped nearly a thousand people to various advisory boards. Insiders understood that these boards were rudimentary campaign organizations. And if he could get a ten-member office staff written into law, he would be more organized than Baxley or any other rival as soon as Wallace was through, be it 1974 or 1978.[40]

Though the administration preferred not to take a public position on Beasley's quest to transform his office, it was working feverishly behind the scenes. In addition to endorsing Baxley's ruling, Wallace made his feelings clear in private correspondence: "[It] is not a full-time office and its function is simply to preside over the sessions of the senate of the state of Alabama. Therefore this office does not have any function to perform when the legislature is not in session." Publicly, Wallace told reporters that Beasley's office was a matter for the legislature to decide and that he had no interest in the issue at all. Beasley attempted to convince Alabamians that he was not involved in trying to push through his package: "I've been too busy with other things to think about that." But behind the scenes, Beasley's assistant, Wayne McMahan, was actively lobbying legislators to make his boss a full-time lieutenant governor. Needing a respite during the fracas, Wallace traveled to Auburn to see a Pat Boone concert that included a duet, "Jesus Loves Me," between the headline act and Cornelia Wallace.[41]

In the middle of the legislative session, a Montgomery television station, WSFA-TV, summed up the ramifications of the Wallace-Beasley feud: "A lieutenant governor with this authority could play havoc with the legislative process. If the second in command and the governor were to work in concert it could spell disaster for any legislator who may wish to oppose the executive branch of government—and if the two executives were in disagreement it could mean the stalling of any legislation at all." The legislature needed no such prompting to be ineffective. As one former legislator noted, his three goals as a lawmaker were to "one, kill bad legislation; two, kill bad legislation; and, three, make sure I achieved the first two." Already socially and fiscally conservative, the legislature's various factions—urban, rural, black—were drowned in a sea of poor leadership and special interest clout. The net result was that a state riven with economic and educational problems—the typical Alabama student was still about two years behind the national average in educational performance—continued to drift farther behind regional and national averages. In 1973, Alabamians flocked to see the film *Walking Tall,* which featured Sheriff Buford Pusser rescuing his small southern town. Sadly, no such official was available to rescue state government in Alabama.[42]

The 1973 session was particularly disastrous because of the severity of need in Alabama. State Highway Department director Ray Bass notified the Governor's Fiscal Study Committee prior to the start of the regular session that annual debt service requirements had topped $41 million, resulting in a debt-coverage ratio that would prevent deficit financing for future road construction unless a new revenue stream was added. The Department of Pensions and Security faced the potential of a $132 million cut in federal matching funds, even as caseloads were increasing by as many as three thousand families per year. The budget request submitted by the administration called for no additional funds and no new case managers. Various economic indices indicated that poverty in Alabama was actually getting worse. A study by the Center for Business and Economic Research at the University of Alabama found that per capita income in Alabama, as a percentage of national income, was decreasing. The report traced the gap to the lack of skilled workers and the never-ending story that the available jobs were in low wage industries. A report by the Alabama League of Aging Citizens concluded that older Alabamians supported by fixed incomes were ingesting a "diet of death" characterized by high food prices, meatless meals, and such limited transportation that they could not take advantage of food stamps. State troopers continued to be reassigned to monthly duty performing tasks outside their job description for which the Department of Public Safety was not compensated. Alabama students received an average appropriation of $2.44 per student for the so-called free textbook program, the smallest allocation of any southeastern state and only 44 percent of the funding in the second to last state. As a result, Alabama parents continued to pay for books—when they could find them—because too many classes were still sharing a few books among a room full of students. One Alabamian could not control his outrage. "It is a crying shame," a writer who identified himself only as "citizen" wrote to his governor, "for the children of Cleveland School to have to use old warn [*sic*] out books and not have enough books to go around. . . . You PROMISED that the state would furnish the books." In spite of the state's penurious approach and the cavalcade of textbook system failures, Wallace asked state education superintendent Leroy Brown and finance director Taylor Hardin to investigate the possibility of the state providing free books to private school students.[43]

Rhonda, a six-year-old Alabamian, wrote Wallace expressing her sense of urgency at the paucity of textbooks in her classroom: "Please help me get some textbook's. I am just six year's old and I would like to learn to read and write." Even if Rhonda could already write and, considering the possibility that her bleat was politically inspired by her parents or teachers, her penmanship and grammatical deficiencies are textbook examples of first-grade work. The text- book issue was one of few examples when Alabamians looked beyond the gov- ernor's wheelchair and vented some real rage—though they, and he, did almost nothing else about it. "The parents of this state," Mrs. Terak Till demanded, "were promised free textbooks for their children.... Now, however, the parents are learning of the state's intention of reneging on this promise. Such action can only result in widening the credibility gap between the state government and its citizens ... [and] this is just another example of the empty promises made by the state officials who find it politically expedient." The textbook pro- gram, nearly a decade after being launched, remained a complete mess.[44]

The problems of inadequate resources plagued nearly every department in state government. The administration was fully aware that budget shortfalls and federal court orders required a more proactive approach, yet it took very few steps to address the root causes of grave problems. A survey of prison health care by the Medical Association of Alabama cited the need for a massive influx of money in order to address wanton hygiene problems including substandard toilets and no isolation areas for prisoners with communicable diseases. Prison guards—inadequate in number according to federal court records—were be- ing paid just over $5,000 annually. The officers requested a guaranteed an- nual wage of at least $6,000. Montgomery County sheriff M. S. Butler joined the chorus of law enforcement officers begging the administration to provide funds and end the corrections staff nightmare. "Meet some of their immediate needs," Butler urged Wallace concerning state prison guards, "such as con- structing a cat walk over the cell blocks, pay raises for the guards, and segre- gating the [trusties] and prisoners who are on the Work Release Program from the other prisoners." Alabama Law Enforcement Planning Agency director Bo Davis called the funding of prisons a "crisis" and cited future revenue prob- lems as potentially more acute: "The minimum standards for medical ser- vices and mental health services [in state prisons] mandated by the federal court action in the *Newman vs. Alabama* case are but a prelude to the addi- tional minimum standards and requirements likely to become mandatory in the foreseeable future." Alabama was so derelict in providing medical care to prisoners that, in an October 1972 court order, Frank Johnson called the ram- pant neglect "barbarous and shocking to the conscience."[45]

Riots were legion at the state's major maximum security facilities. Prison overcrowding was so severe that prisoners were forced to sleep on cots or on the floor in aisles and hallways. Draper, Atmore, and Holman prisons were de- signed to house 1,900 inmates collectively; as of January 1974, the combined population was 2,693, 141 percent of capacity. In a May 1973 altercation at Holman, 4 prisoners captured and stabbed a guard; an August 1973 riot left 17 injured; and a January 1974 outburst was led by 64 inmates and left a guard and a prisoner dead. Overwork, underpay, and deadly conditions made it next to impossible to recruit prison guards and forced administrators to put off firing bad employees in light of their already thin ranks. While the governor held fast to a no-new-taxes pledge, continued to preach law and order, and decried reports of new prisons he characterized as veritable hotels, others in the state sensed that the crowded conditions were certain to lead to more violence within the prison walls. "We have to remember," civil rights lawyer and state representative Fred Gray urged, "that they are still human beings." Gray, hardly a favorite of the administration, could be expected to make critical comments, but the state Board of Corrections was equally dissatisfied with the administration's commitment to the prison system. "We . . . are of the opinion," a board-backed memorandum to the governor noted, "that Alabama's penal system is and has been for some time, in a state of crisis insofar as the funding necessary to fulfill our legal and moral obligations to the confined is concerned."[46]

Even successful rehabilitation programs designed to curb recidivism were in dire need of adequate funding. The 1972–73 annual report of the Work Release Program indicated that 80 percent of inmates admitted to the program remained employed with the same firm after being paroled. The following year, the number of prisoners completing work release increased from 136 to 334 with an average weekly salary of $132, more than some prison guards were earning. Corrections tripled the number of state facilities offering work release employment, maximizing a quarter million dollar grant from the Law Enforcement Planning Agency. Even so, an internal report characterized the system as "hamstrung" by limited state financial support.[47]

One Board of Corrections study estimated the basic financial requirements in order to meet minimum state and federal standards. According to the report, the Corrections appropriation for fiscal year 1974 was $11.126 million, $1.048 million *less* than the previous year and $1.476 million *less* than estimated expenses. The same study identified 1975 requirements for the state penal system at $24.088 million. In no uncertain terms, Alabama was funding its prisons at less than 50 percent of basic needs. As the stream of federal court orders continued to appear, the administration's public reaction continued to be a mixture of excoriating federal judges for coddling lawbreakers and claiming the prison system was operating satisfactorily. Many in the state echoed the administration's stance on prison reform. "I believe," Jesse Scarbrough wrote Wallace, "that the federal courts will continue to establish guidelines and release convicted criminals. However, they will never grant relief in the busing of school children."[48]

As Alabama struggled to meet minimum standards in corrections, national rankings continued to reveal the state's inability to make much progress in education. Alabama teachers, despite virtually doubling their salaries over the previous decade, earned an average of $8,105 in fiscal year 1971–72, 76 percent of the national average, and more than $2,500 less than the typical American teacher. As measured in terms of annual gross income, Alabama teachers were actually falling farther behind their peers. Ten years earlier, the typical teacher in the Heart of Dixie had made $1,348 less than the national average. Alabama students continued to receive the smallest amount of per pupil funding in the country. In Wallace's first year in office, 1963–64, education received 27 percent of state revenue; in 1972–73, education continued to receive 27 percent. Despite the administration's regular recitations of Alabama's industrial growth, the state remained forty-eighth in per capita income, an indication that the state's school systems were not equipped to work miracles in the classroom or prepare skilled workers to land high wage jobs. For all of the Wallace policies and rhetoric about making dramatic improvements in education, the state continued to tread water.[49]

Vocational education and job preparedness were particularly problematic in Alabama. A Citizen's Advisory Board on Commerce and Industrial Development report indicated much work remained to be done if Alabama workers, who were statistically older than employees in other southeastern states, were to be seen as a competitive advantage. The board advocated more funds, as did every other agency of state government, but made more specific recommendations as well. A "rapid-response" team was needed to train employees for new or expanding industries; a master state manpower training policy was necessary to coordinate the actions of state and local vocational education agencies; and a more comprehensive effort by the department of education was required to transform students into marketable workers.[50]

The problems of vocational education were significant enough and divisive incidents made matters worse. According to testimony in an AEA report to the State Department of Education, Opelika State Vocational and Technical College director Dorsey Haynes ran his trade school like an absolutist czar. The report suggested that Haynes fired or demoted teachers at will. In one instance, Haynes fired a teacher, citing court-ordered mandates to hire blacks for the purpose of achieving a racial balance. Yet the replacement teacher that Haynes hired was white. Student testimony indicated that students and faculty alike were expected to spend class time working on projects for Haynes, his friends, and relatives, including installing cassette players, laying carpet, repairing boats, and painting automobiles. In some cases, these items were soon sold, with some of the school's faculty and administrators pocketing the profits. A partial list of charges against Haynes compiled by the *Montgomery*

Advertiser included registering state vehicles in his own name, requiring the school staff to repair his Winnebago, removing parts from state cars to put in his niece's car, and purchasing junk vehicles only to sell them for personal profit as soon as students had repaired them. Several students complained that 75 to 90 percent of class time was taken up with teachers performing their own outside work instead of mentoring students.[51]

No agency suffered from the continuing lack of leadership as much as mental health. Ironically, Wallace, in front of reporters and on the hustings, regularly referred to mental health improvements as a lasting testament to the accomplishments of Governor Lurleen. "I want a bronze plaque put up in the mental health centers," the governor ordered Building Commissioner Hugh Adams, "stating that the facility was authorized in the administration of Governor Lurleen Wallace and finished in the administration of Governor George Wallace." But in the end, Lurleen's initiatives provided very few changes to the essential culture of the mental health system and George failed to make it a priority. Administration critics realized that mental health funding rarely influences voters en masse. Apologists cited the need to minimize taxation in a state defined by too much poverty. Somewhere in between lies the reality: instead of crafting solutions, the administration preferred to blame the meddling federal government for mental health problems.

Court-ordered mental health improvements and fire code violations necessitated substantial renovations to facilities at Bryce, Partlow, and Searcy. A systematic review of facilities in August 1971 indicated that the state required a substantial infusion of resources in order to meet minimum standards of the American Psychiatric Association. Construction and renovations at Bryce alone were estimated at $51.465 million. Projected costs at Searcy, $25.134 million, and Partlow, $1.240 million, were also significant. Fire safety inspections revealed glaring deficiencies: lack of fire escapes, defective wiring, insufficient quantities of fire extinguishers, as well as risky practices including lighting cigarettes with clothes irons.[52]

The Board of Mental Health, an agency that earned plenty of scorn for their own ineffective leadership, constantly lobbied the administration for more funds. At one point, pressure on the board became so intense that they were forced to issue a press release to deny accusations that board members had never visited the state's mental health institutions. Even so, the board and director Stonewall Stickney reacted immediately to the costly fire code renovation estimates. "The department of mental health," Stickney notified the board, "at this point does not have anything like this amount in its capital outlay funds." Stickney argued that the board was not only not expanding its services but that they were in immediate danger of cutting back even further. Mental health workers and advocates circulated a petition calling on the administration to provide emergency revenue: "We are of the opinion that unless a special session is called at once and sufficient funds are provided, that the result will be irreparable damage to the program for the mentally handicapped in Alabama." Doubtless, the chronic mismanagement of mental health in Alabama began long before Wallace entered the political fray. But the fact remains that the Wallace administration's initiatives never approached minimum standards, regional or national averages, or court-ordered requirements.[53]

Mental Health chairman Paul Burleson summarized the administration's failure to provide the necessary leadership and resources: "Some of the conditions at Bryce and Searcy Hospitals and at Partlow School are gravely in need of improvement and the conditions . . . in some areas are deplorable. . . . As is the case with most state other state-funded institutions, a lack of money has been and still is the main problem." A 1970 American Psychiatric Association study, long after Lurleen Wallace's supposed breakthrough in mental health, ranked Alabama last in per patient expenditures for resident patients. Contractor mistakes compounded the limited funding. Some change orders were relatively minor, a few thousand dollars to alter building plans for one reason or another. Others were more substantial, including a January 1973 change that cost the state an additional $1,660,812. Alabamian Connie Chamberlain wrote the governor to express her sentiment that the mental health situation was so moribund that she favored the drastic action of raising taxes. An administration letter to Alabamian Carol Dunlop is an excellent example of the administration's disinterest in real reform. "I know from personal tours," some aide wrote with Wallace's name on May 22, 1972—a date when the governor was on his back in a hospital room in Silver Springs, Maryland—"and from those of my advisors that conditions have been substantially improved and that we are well on the way to providing an environment that will give maximum treatment opportunities." At the time of the supposed improvements, the state was under a court order and was facing periodic inspections from a federally sponsored Human Rights Committee to determine if Alabama was continuing to violate the civil rights of patients by providing the equivalent of medieval care.[54]

Though the administration made some funds available, they never considered the complete and comprehensive overhaul required to make Alabama mental health care as good as peer states. A 1971 study revealed that Alabama was spending $7.55 per patient, 51 percent of the national average and 61 percent of the southeastern average. The standard of care was so low that rumors about mental health treatment reached legendary status. "How pleasantly surprised I was," University of Alabama student Suzy Roberts, a volunteer at Partlow, wrote Wallace, "at the conditions I found there. I honestly expected cages, whips, and outhouses as everyone I talked to does." Stickney urged Wallace to allow him to bring in an expert consultant from the National Institute of Mental Health to modify the state's program in order to meet changing needs. The administration marked the written plea NAN—no answer needed. Still, Wallace made time to write Director Stickney about adding a company owned by one of his supporters to the mental health bid list and involved himself in a dispute about whether a blind doctor could continue to go coon hunting on the grounds of Bryce.[55]

Personality conflicts, managerial incompetence, and poor leadership exacerbated the lack of funding and the administration's reluctance to make mental health a priority. Inadequate education was another factor; one federal court order required the state to hire fifty-six full-time psychiatrists for state mental health facilities at a time when only sixty-five were licensed in the entire state. One conflict, a nasty spat between Commissioner Stickney and Bryce superintendent James Folsom—a distant cousin of Cornelia Wallace—characterized the internecine nonsense that wasted time, money, and resources, and left Alabama patients in poor hands. Folsom resigned in August 1972, citing managerial incompetence: "I could no longer work in an atmosphere where my every action was being construed as disruptive and I was very upset about the lack of concern of other mental health officials to our pressing problems." The not so thinly veiled charge that Stickney was the biggest problem in mental health elicited an immediate reaction from the commissioner who blasted Folsom and promised he was on the verge of firing him anyway. An anonymous mental health employee told the *Montgomery Advertiser* that the conflicts were about to explode even further: "We're sitting atop a volcano that's going to erupt any day into another state mental health crisis." The tumult caused Jere Beasley, no stranger to a fight himself, to call for calm. "We should not be airing our internal problems with the newspapers in the state," the lieutenant governor suggested. "We're gonna have to get off this feuding, fussing, and fighting." The bickering was made worse, in some ways, because of the optimistic but inaccurate pronouncements about mental health progress that had been publicly disseminated in previous months. "For Partlow State School," a 1972 *Alabama Mental Health and Retardation Review* article boasted, "the year 1971 will be remembered as a year of accomplishments. Many new and innovative programs were begun which reflect the current thinking of experts in the field of mental health."[56]

In the Folsom-Stickney dispute, 250 of Folsom's backers, patients and staff alike, demonstrated and called for Stickney to resign. Other supporters circulated petitions, wired, and wrote the governor asking him to reinstate Folsom at Bryce. Wallace met with Folsom to still the waters but refused to take a public position in favor of either Stickney or Folsom. Folsom's exit made the most noise, but five other top officials had quit within the preceding four months. If Wallace refused to make his feelings known, the Board of Mental Health did not. At a September 1972 meeting, barely a month after Folsom quit, the board asked Stickney for his resignation. "A change in administration," chairman Paul Burleson declared, "would be in the best interest at this time for the mentally ill and retarded." Stickney retorted that he had no plan to resign and that the board would have to fire him. A little over a week later, they did. Stickney's termination was only one in a litany of woes during four brutal years in his life: federal court orders, the accidental death of his wife, a devastating fire that destroyed his house, and his son's arrest on drug charges.[57]

In their periodical, *Alabama Mental Health and Retardation Review,* the Board of Mental Health tried to distance themselves from the personality battles, contending the raw emotion of the situation was caused by a complex set of factors for which Stickney could not be held accountable: "One could, however, with justification, ask: 'Where were all the people who apparently have suddenly found so many quick and easy answers—the eagle-eyed reporters who run a few feet ahead of the pack—when these deplorable conditions were developing?' . . . Is Doctor Stickney responsible? . . . Of course not." Who was responsible for the deplorable deterioration of mental health care in Alabama? It is beyond the parameters of this book to make such an analysis, and the definitive history of the mental health system in Alabama has yet to be written. One thing is certain, however. Opponents and supporters of both Folsom and Stickney, federal court judges, and visiting experts all concluded that the state suffered from a lack of political leadership, a woefully inadequate budget, and little or no regulation and monitoring.[58]

Rumors and reports of administration corruption compounded problems caused by the frightening level of inefficiency in state government. Throughout the Wallace era, state road building had been dominated by politics. "Every public road is a political road," Wallace Highway Department director Ray Bass later admitted to the Associated Press. "It's not a myth. Caesar had the same problem. It's always been a fact that road decisions tend to favor areas where the support came from." As usual, Gerald Wallace was in eye of the storm. The Alabama Bar Association developed a code of ethics they might have named "the Gerald Wallace provision"; it outlawed taking fees without offering services—a notorious Wallace practice. A Highway Department scandal centered on nearly one hundred thousand dollars of equipment that was purchased but never received by the state. The vendor, Machinery and Supplies, had only one customer, the Highway Department, and employees admitted that they never delivered any parts to the government. Reams of phony purchase orders, delivery receipts, and memoranda assigning the parts to various department locations indicated that the corruption involved numerous state employees. One employee recalled instances of purchasing whiskey and delivering it to state employees. Court testimony included evidence from state Highway Department officials that they took direct orders from Gerald Wallace. Telephone records indicated a volume of conversation between Gerald and Ruby Latham, de facto head of the firm. In December 1972, Gerald was driving a Jeep registered to Machinery and Supplies when he crashed the vehicle in Montgomery. In the context of the growing Watergate investigation, the governor noted the mess in his own state: "Confidence in government at all levels is at a low ebb at this time." As the Machinery and Supplies scandal unraveled, eventually leading to four indictments, Jesse Gann, one of the governor's executive assistants and a Baptist minister, resigned in disgrace after being charged with drunken driving, disrupting a state-sponsored seminar on drug use, and reportedly firing his pistol in the capitol. During the same month that some state officials faced trial for their involvement in the Machinery and Supplies scandal, Seymore Trammell, ringleader of the corrupt forces in the first Wallace administration, was paroled from prison.[59]

Good Intentions

Even as decades of inattention to policy began to take its toll in Alabama, the administration launched a few initiatives designed to address structural problems in the lives of ordinary Alabamians. Wallace and insurance commissioner John Bookout partnered with BlueCross to develop a low-cost health insurance plan for the working poor. Launched on statewide television in the spring of 1972, the Alabama Health Care Plan provided a sixty-day period of open enrollment that was subsequently extended one additional month. Wallace himself promoted the plan on both radio and television, and BlueCross committed $90,000 in order to publicize it. Bookout expected a large enrollment in the program, given the amount of marketing and the number of eligible individuals and families: "Governor Wallace, the participating companies, and my department put [a] great deal of time and effort into creating this program and we certainly feel that it will benefit many unfortunate people in the state."[60]

The program was well designed for the target group of "near-poor." Any Alabamian not covered by either Medicaid or an employee plan, and earning less than $4,000 per year was automatically eligible. Each dependent to be included in the plan merited an additional $600 exemption to the income threshold. As a result, a family of five was eligible as long as the annual household income was less than $6,400. And the premiums were reasonable. Single coverage was available for as low as $4.75 per month with a $500 annual deductible. Even with an optional lower deductible, $250, a family could be covered for as little as $16 per month. Fifteen separate companies and countless representatives of those firms in branch offices across the state were authorized to write polices. Though the firms received a tax incentive for participating in the program, they made no profit on the policies themselves. Alabama Association of Life Underwriters president Roy Blackburn promised Wallace that his trade association would inform as many consumers as possible about the plan.[61]

The governor used the plan as part of his panoply of campaign promises during the rough-and-tumble 1970 tussle with Albert Brewer and deserves credit for fulfilling the pledge. After his inauguration, numerous letters continued to pour into Montgomery urging Wallace to keep his word and further demonstrating the urgent need for such a plan. "Can you give me some information," Mrs. J. C. Butts, a diabetic, wrote to the governor, "on some insurance companies that offer insurance to people who can not possibly pay those high rates? My husband is retired, I am only 58 years of age, therefore I cannot get coverage from Medicare. . . . My husband's total income is $253.86 a month and [he] is under the care of a cardiologist." Mrs. B. F. Simms had a similar tale of woe: "I would . . . like to know how I can get in the Heart Clinic in Birmingham, as I can't afford a doctor. I owe a large bill to a doctor and I quit going because I could not pay my bill. I needed him once very bad and he refused to see me. I hate to owe this bill but I can't pay it." Carl McEwen summarized the need and the reality of life for many Alabamians: "I pick up an odd job once in a while and make a dollar or two but nothing I can depend on. My wife and I both have bad health and are unable to do hard work and that is the only kind of work to do around here."[62]

Despite the administration's efforts and the demonstrable needs of Alabamians whose lives in the mines, mills, and dirt were no match for the cost and availability of medical care in the state, the plan flopped. By April 1972, only 1,155 applications for membership had been filed with only 69 percent completed correctly. Since 10,000 policyholders were needed to allow the program to function properly, the administration was concerned. "If the program has not improved," Bookout warned Wallace, "we will work out a conversion program whereby subscribers can convert to a low cost policy of some sort with Blue Cross and some other companies." By June, only 1,600 had enrolled in a state where nearly half a million people were eligible. By the end of 1972, fewer than 3,200 subscribers had been accepted and BlueCross, though agreeing to provide service to any new customers, had abandoned any interest in additional promotion. Only ten claims had been paid. The State Insurance Department was reduced to mailing out second applications to Alabamians who had inquired about the program earlier in the year. Two years later, reflecting on the program, Harry Pennington described the health care plan as "the biggest failure of this administration."[63]

The Alabama Health Care Plan, arguably the best-intentioned program of

Wallace's entire gubernatorial career, failed for several reasons. Some Alabamians may have been too proud to sign up for coverage for the poor. The South had fashioned a rural culture of self-reliance above all else and hardened a conceptualization of masculinity based on toughness and adaptability. These cultural and gender issues were stronger in many households than any medical or economic realities. It is also true that some of the working poor who could have used the insurance were illiterate, unaware of its existence, or unable to phone or visit an agent or government official. No amount of promotion short of door-to-door visits could have reached all the eligible Alabamians. But a deeper analysis would also place some of the blame on the people's largely accurate perception that state government was incapable of offering much help. An overstated but essentially accurate synopsis of the history of state government in Alabama would note that, for many Alabamians, nothing very useful ever came out of Montgomery. To lay this blame at the feet of George Wallace would be disingenuous; Alabama politicians had set a standard of underperformance long before the governor arrived on Goat Hill. Yet to absolve Wallace of any responsibility in the creation of a political culture that suggested the governor and legislature could not be counted on to do much to change lives in Alabama would be equally reckless. Wallace took an existing political culture and froze it in time. His perpetual campaigning, indifference to policy, and scapegoating of the federal government led to one conclusion: the job of the governor was to cuss the liberals and the Yankees and echo the memories deeply entrenched in the minds of white southerners. To expect anything more was foolhardy since a white Alabamian should never believe, the political culture suggested, that adequate textbooks, medical care, assistance for the poor, and mental health treatment for the state's vulnerable were remotely as important as standing up for states' rights and keeping property taxes low. Wallace did not create this belief, but at a time when poor, white Alabamians might have been ready to question its veracity, he reminded them what was, and was not, the mission of state government.

Despite the administration's vitiation of state government, Wallace continued to reveal the multiple aspects of his personality that combined to make him the most interesting political personality in twentieth-century southern politics. Even as he battled paraplegia and pain, steered clear of the most pressing policy issues, and quietly began planning a 1974 campaign for reelection, Wallace continued to reach out and touch the lives of ordinary Alabamians who had been crushed in various ways. "Carlton Allen Thomas Jr., age 29, . . . drowned," the governor wrote to legal advisor Bill Jackson, "trying to save the life of James Breedlove who lost control of his car. He could not swim and in trying to get Breedlove out, who eventually was saved, he drowned. We have a medal that can be awarded . . . I want it awarded to this man and papers drawn up properly." On another occasion, Wallace intervened to get a combat re-assignment for an Alabama soldier serving in Vietnam whose wife and seven children had undergone a series of tragedies back home in Weaver, Alabama. Wallace made a point to urge aide Mills Cowling to place a longstanding state employee on the official merit system roster in order to upgrade his salary and retirement benefits. Touched by the plight of the elderly and the unemployed, Wallace worked, behind the scenes, to find jobs and benefits for many Ala-bamians who contacted him directly. And Wallace was insistent that support-ers, and even relatives and friends of supporters, receive a letter from the gov-ernor at a time of bereavement. While this doubtless helped him maintain a connection to some of the state's voters, he performed these acts of human kindness without seeking any publicity.[64]

After the assassination attempt, Wallace was particularly attuned to folk battling paraplegia and quadriplegia. At Birmingham's Spain Rehabilitation Center, Wallace encountered a young girl who had been on the back of a mo-torcycle with her boyfriend when the bike crashed into a tractor-trailer. Un-able to deal with their daughter's quadriplegia, her parents virtually aban-doned her. The boyfriend, who walked away with only scratches, soon deserted her as well. Wallace visited her every day that he was at Spain and called her frequently after he left. When she died, Wallace was crushed. "He was just heartbroken," Peggy remembered, "because there she was all alone and her grandparents couldn't get to the places that she needed to be. Someone needed to come in and there was just not a program like that set up in Alabama." At Wallace's insistence, the legislature later created a home assistance program for disabled patients. And as a matter of personal philosophy, Wallace spoke often to people from all over the country coming to grips with paralysis and to groups gathering research funds.[65]

Even as the governor's complex personality included a sporadic desire to help the state's most vulnerable, campaigning and preparing to campaign re-mained the most important focus of his administration. As early as Octo-ber 1972, Charles Snider and Wallace were devising an electoral calculus for the 1976 presidential race. "Governor Wallace has a chance to help restructure the Democratic Party," executive assistant Mickey Griffin averred in a lengthy memorandum. The George McGovern debacle in 1972 convinced Wallace that the political mainstream was shifting currents and he might be able to end up in the middle of the national waters instead of lilting to the far right bank. In fact, political polls identified Wallace as one of the early favorites to be the Democratic nominee in 1976, along with Massachusetts senator Ted Kennedy who traveled to Alabama to meet with the governor in 1973. Even McGovern admitted Wallace represented a growing number of Americans: "The hand-writing was probably on the wall the day Wallace was shot. President Nixon capitalized on that opportunity with a candidacy that was really tailor-made to attract Wallace voters." In no uncertain terms, McGovern believed that Wallace's incapacitation prevented a Wallace third-party run in 1972 that would have split the Nixon vote and put the South Dakotan in the oval office. Working behind the scenes within days of Richard Nixon's reelection, Wallace forces managed to oust McGovernite Jean Westwood as Democratic National Chairman and ushered in the centrist Robert Strauss.[66]

As the Wallace team contemplated fund-raising, mailing lists, and campaign strategy, it was increasingly clear that the governor would be a gubernatorial candidate in 1974. Wallace began taking some cautious steps to change his profile from virulent segregationist to respectable social conservative. In August 1972, the governor hired Linda Johnson, an African American woman, to work in the office as a temporary employee. Johnson, the first black employee in the governor's suite since 1959, answered phones and ran miscellaneous errands. A year later, Wallace crowned Terry Points homecoming queen at the University of Alabama, the first black to win the coveted title. That same year the governor began courting black voters more obviously. Appearing before the Southern Conference of Black Mayors at a meeting in Tuskegee, Wallace received a standing ovation and posed for countless pictures after his thirty-minute speech. Flashing a self-deprecating sense of humor not always visible on the stump, Wallace brought the crowd to roaring laughter. "Perhaps this is no time to discuss busing," he deadpanned, "but I would like to say a few words about Alabama's school bus system." But the tagline that emerged from this meeting and would be on display for Wallace's remaining years in the political arena was more straightforward: "We are all God's children. I have never opposed any of our citizens achieving the American dream."[67]

Factually inaccurate based on any exhaustive review of the first decade of Wallaceism in Alabama, the statement nonetheless carried a great deal of weight when delivered by a man wearing glasses thick as Coke bottles, using a hearing aid, and being rolled onto the stage in a wheelchair. Wallace himself understood his physical limitations and increasingly referred to them in public. "I can't walk, hear, or see very good," he joked to a group of Washington-based reporters. "I might wind up in a nursing home before the next election . . . but I got eight years to serve up here before I can do that." R. M. Stienz spoke for many in Alabama's African American community in a letter she wrote to Wallace in 1973: "Perhaps you have had time to reflect and understand how God has given you a second chance to undo some of the evils you have put into motion and that it was a white man who crippled you for life." Wallace continued to receive letters from the lunatic white supremacist fringe, including missives suggesting he adopt a plan for castration and sterilization of undesirables, and deport all blacks to Rhodesia because they were planning a population conspiracy based on breeding "like Rabbits." "Kick the niggers out of the University of Alabama," another Alabamian counseled. "Dismiss 'em for something and don't let anyone tell you [that] you have to dishonor the legal traditions of the people of Alabama." These tired old rants notwithstanding, Wallace no longer courted these voters actively, advocated public policy that would entice them to his camp, nor reached out directly to them to distribute campaign material or transport like-minded folk to the polls.[68]

At the same time that Wallace began to elevate his profile—albeit slightly— within the black community, increasing numbers of whites came to embrace some of Wallace's old school message on race, particularly the idea that southerners were not the only Americans to develop a white supremacist ethos. "George Wallace has been saying for years," Nieman Journalism Fellow and North Carolinian Ned Cline assessed in the *Boston Globe*, "the North was worse than the South in racial attitudes. . . . A year at Harvard watching the politicos of Boston barricade themselves against the realities of busing to achieve racial desegregation has convinced me Wallace was right, albeit for the wrong [meaning, political] reasons."[69]

African Americans noticed Wallace's subtle changes. Charles Evers, whose brother, Medgar, had been gunned down a decade earlier in Mississippi, released a statement that he would support Wallace on a presidential ticket in 1976. Though Evers was criticized for his statement by those pointing to Wallace's middling record of appointing African Americans to state positions, he noted in correspondence that a majority of the responses to his announcement were favorable. "I have been responsible," Wallace wrote in a carefully phrased letter that underwent a least two drafts, "for the appointment of more than 140 blacks to these various boards and agencies throughout our state, including key positions at the Selective Service Boards, the Law Enforcement Planning Agency, the Manpower Advisory Council, the Youth Services Board, and the five-member Educational Television Commission." Whether those positions were, in fact, "key" is problematic. Wallace rarely, if ever, attended meetings of those boards and there is no evidence that he relied on the counsel of any African Americans during his second elected term. And other correspondence from the administration featured different statistics on the appointment of African Americans to state agencies. "Governor Wallace," Assistant Legal Advisor Curtis Redding wrote to an inquirer, "has appointed over seventy black[s] to commissions and boards throughout the state." Just the same, the very inclusion of minorities in state government—no matter how insignificant the post—represents a change.[70]

At a February 21, 1974, press conference announcing his candidacy to be elected for an unprecedented third term—after the longstanding succession provision had been changed—Wallace spoke directly to black Alabamians:

"The people of Alabama are good people, compassionate people. We're going to show the nation that all the people of Alabama can live together in a spirit of peace and harmony. There has never been any other aim by myself as governor nor the people of Alabama. Sometimes we may have been misinterpreted." The post-Laurel George Wallace was a kinder, gentler Wallace, a governor occasionally interested in policy and creating a legacy. The rhetoric was softer, the appeal was wider, and to some extent, the intentions were better. But Wallace's history in office and his perpetual campaigning make it difficult not to look past the mellow verbiage and directly at the reality of a planned presidential campaign in two years. It is also true that, shortly after his narrow win over Albert Brewer in 1970, Wallace told reporters he would never again run for governor of Alabama. Ever the political animal, Wallace changed positions and tacked slightly left, at least on the issue of race.[71]

Though the administration took steps to woo black Alabamians as early as 1972, these actions were not necessary in order to be reelected in 1974. In late 1971 and early 1972 when Wallace was powerless to combat the legislature and the patina of being a working governor had disappeared in yet another national campaign, Wallace's hopes for another term were dicey. Albert Brewer, still smarting from the bitter 1970 campaign, had his campaign files on active status and was mulling a second crack at Wallace. Other potential candidates were testing the waters. But after the shooting, Wallace was unbeatable. Beloved again, the object of sympathy across the region, Wallace had even crept onto the list of the ten most admired men in America. State Republican Party chairman Richard Bennett saw the writing on the wall ten months before the 1974 general election, declaring that the GOP should not even run a candidate. The 1974 campaign was the easiest, least taxing, and least active campaign in Wallace's political career.[72]

State senator Eugene McLain was the only serious candidate to challenge Wallace in the 1974 race, and he was only token opposition. McLain focused his campaign on Wallace's disinterest in governance, citing federal court orders for prisons and mental health care, high unemployment, and allegations of corruption. "Getting a good education," McLain declared, "is the first step in getting a good job. Yet fifty percent of our adult population doesn't have the benefit of a high school diploma and more than twenty percent of our children who start first grade do not complete high school." The veteran legislator ridiculed Wallace's industrial development pronouncements as inaccurate or outright falsehoods and noted the state's increasing number of workers unable to find industrial jobs. Some of the optimistic figures on new and expanded industry, McLain reasoned, were from firms that Wallace knew had no intention of coming to Alabama. McLain's charges were quickly countered by Red Bamberg, director of the Alabama Development Office—the state's industry hunters. "They're usually so taken aback," the governor's friend claimed of industrial prospects, "that they accept immediately and we find it's not too hard to interest them in Alabama. I consider Governor Wallace the most useful attraction we've had in bringing in new industries."[73]

McLain charged that Alabama continued to add low-wage, low-skill industry at a time when other southern states were resisting such ventures. "I don't think we should allow anyone to take advantage of our southern people," Georgia governor Jimmy Carter exclaimed at a conference on southern economic development; "the first thing I tell them is if you're looking for cheap labor, we don't want you." McLain's plan to separate the industrial development function from political appointees, turn its daily operation over to trained professionals, and court high-skill, high-wage industry attracted no attention from the body politic. Contextually, the difference between Alabama and peer states in the South was striking. Alabama was still courting any industry; other states had moved past unskilled work and were climbing on board the Sunbelt technology bandwagon.[74]

Contrary to the raucous campaigns of 1958, 1962, and 1970, and the curiosity of the 1966 race, the 1974 campaign featured an incumbent whose appearances were confined almost exclusively to the weekends—quite a statement given the governor's desire to bathe in the cameras and lights and hear the roar of the crowd. One *Birmingham News* report suggested that Wallace had skillfully used federal revenue-sharing funds over the previous three years as his best campaign device. As it had been doing for a decade, the administration put Wallace front and center every time good news was available to be delivered. In the case of revenue sharing and Alabama Law Enforcement Planning Agency (ALEPA) grants, Wallace held photo opportunities where he would distribute checks to local officials, even though the recipients had been notified of their awards weeks or months before. In the case of ALEPA, the governor had numerous opportunities to hand out checks and slap the backs of thankful constabularies. According to a 1973 ALEPA memorandum, the state distributed 645 separate grants in that year alone. Federal revenue-sharing funds in that same fiscal year included a total appropriation of $67.5 million, a tidy sum considering Wallace had great scope in allocating those funds, without so much as a check or balance from the legislature.[75]

Wallace was in such a comfortable position during the 1974 campaign that his forces spent more time preparing for the 1976 presidential race than the gubernatorial election. Conservative fund-raiser Richard Viguerie raised $2 million between August 1973 and August 1974, retiring the debt from 1972 and stockpiling a tidy surplus. A March 1974 memorandum from campaign director Charles Snider made no mention of the governor's race even though the primary was only six weeks away. Instead, Snider updated the governor about additional ways to raise money for the 1976 race, including selling Wallace's likeness on silver bars and medallions. Eventually, the campaign sold George Wallace watches, George Wallace coins, George Wallace posters, and countless other baubles that are no doubt available at antique stores, flea markets, and church bazaars all over the state of Alabama to this day.[76]

Every message McLain tried to deliver to the voters was turned back by Wallace. "Every single dollar that has been spent," the governor retorted to allegations of corruption, "has been spent honestly. I've been an honest governor. . . . I promise you four years of honest government, if elected." When McLain accused Wallace of spending too much time campaigning across America, Wallace simply told the people that he did it for them, taking five bullets and convincing the country that Alabama "is in the mainstream of American life." And Wallace continued to convince Alabamians to look past sister states and regional and national averages, and simply compare Alabama to itself. "For the first time in history," a 1974 campaign brochure touted, "Alabama in 1973 passed the billion dollar figure for a single year in announced capital investment. The total . . . almost doubled the 1972 figure, itself a record, and continued the great decade of industrial progress." The campaign was so humdrum that Wallace had no need to pay entertainers like Roy Clark up to seventy-five hundred dollars as in the 1970 campaign to draw a crowd. The people of Alabama yawned through the 1974 campaign because no force in the state, Bear Bryant included, could have beat George Wallace in a wheelchair that year. The election was held just the same and the governor garnered 65 percent of the vote in the primary and 83 percent in the November general election. Alabama had elected George Wallace for the third time—four counting Lurleen—but it remained to be seen whether it had elected the same ole George Wallace or not.[77]

10

Stuck in Neutral / 1974–1978

For George Wallace, the fall of 1974 was as full of promise as the colorful bursts of autumn-blooming azaleas and flowering trees that splashed red, white, and purple hues across the state's lush green backdrop. Battling constant pain—emotionally and physically—Wallace nonetheless basked in the glow of the easiest gubernatorial campaign of his life and anticipated a looming presidential campaign that found him in the favorite's role for the first and only time in his life; a September Gallup poll placed the Alabama governor ten points ahead of his nearest rivals. Gerald Ford's September pardon of former President Richard Nixon cast a pall over his administration only one month into his presidency. In a brash interview with *Washington Post* columnist David Broder, Wallace continued to play the part of an unreconstructed antagonist of the federal government and the national media: "You fellows keep writing about the New South and you mention four or five governors—but never me. But I carried all the counties in Florida in 1972 and that's a New South state if ever there was one. I went to North Carolina and beat Terry Sanford, the symbol of the New South. I beat him bad." Wallace had no intention of prepackaging himself strictly for national party consumption. He sensed a looming shift in the attitudes of voters as the Vietnam and Watergate dramas continued to unfold. "Let me tell you," he exclaimed, "the New South is just as tired of the central government flim-flam—of giveaways and bureaucracy—as the Old South was. Naturally people change, but the people in the South are less tolerant of big government interfering in their lives now than they were four years ago. They're tired of it."[1]

On a chilly January morning, Wallace took the oath of office for an unprecedented third time. Though the wind was not as biting and the air not as unforgiving as in 1963, Wallace warmed the assembled throng with a thirty-minute address chock-full of reasons to be proud to be an Alabamian—a trademark theme of his entire political career: "My fellow Alabamians, who have labored so long, so hard and with such perseverance, and determination to make this the great state that it is. It is you to whom I am responsible and it is for you and for you alone that I must and will perform the duties of this great office." Though the governor refrained from the strident remarks that characterized his first inaugural, he referred to a panoply of changes in the state in the twelve years since he last drew a line in the dirt and defied the federals to alter the state's longstanding policy of racial separation. "Our citizens have been subjected to many difficult and trying experiences," the governor declared, "but, as is usually the case, adversity has made us a more dedicated and unified people. We find in our state today a determination on the part of all our people to work untiringly and in unison for the betterment of Alabama." Whether the state was as united as the governor suggested was problematic, but the social changes in Alabama continued to develop: fifteen black lawmakers prepared to enter the legislature; numerous black Alabamians marched in the ceremonies; and the historically black Alabama State University Choir entertained through song.[2]

Though the inaugural remarks contained only the usual nugget about the governor continuing to express his voice in national affairs, the administration was already anticipating the next campaign. Wallace brimmed with confidence as one piece of good news after another rolled in concerning the prospects for the 1976 presidential campaign. Massachusetts senator Edward Kennedy dropped out of the race before it even began. Small donations, the bread and butter of every Wallace campaign, continued to trickle in one, five, ten, and twenty dollars at a time. The fund-raising form mailed to potential donors pulled no punches. "Dear Governor Wallace," the document, full of boxes indicating the amount of the enclosed check, read, "I appreciate all of the sacrifices you have made to send the liberals and socialist politicians a message. I am enclosing my contribution to help you try and save our beloved America." In time, Paul Weyrich, influential in the nascent movement of social conservatives into the political process, began to work with the campaign. "How does it feel," Wallace boasted to Democratic National chair Robert Strauss at a meeting in Kansas City, "to be shaking hands with the leading candidate." A December 1976 study, "The Wallace Prospect"—compiled by Ernest Ferguson—concluded that Wallace was likely to enter the 1976 convention with more committed delegates than any other candidate. The momentum created by polls and fund-raising reached such a zenith that the campaign cautioned itself to avoid gloating. "So the game plan now," an internal memorandum warned, "is to downwind polls as it is too early for the polls to reflect what is happening in politics. If we brag about the polls and where we stand, we then stand to get hurt more when the polls reflect a drop."[3]

Nothing pleased Wallace more than the acts of fealty that accompanied his sudden status as front-runner. National reporters traveled to Montgomery to ingratiate themselves to the governor. Gary Hart, George McGovern's campaign director and later a Colorado senator, traveled to Montgomery to talk politics with Wallace at the mansion. Richard Nixon visited Alabama twice and Vice President Spiro Agnew, according to the governor, "has been to Alabama so many times I thought he had an office here." At regional and national meetings, Wallace was the jewel of the red carpet. "I don't have to go to Washington and New York anymore," Wallace boasted; "now they come to us." Paralysis notwithstanding, life seemed so grand and the future so bright that Wallace's spirits were not even dampened when a fire ravaged the state's sixty-seven-year-old governor's mansion. Though he was not in the mansion at the time of the fire—probably started when a cigarette ignited flammable refinishing materials—Wallace shook off thoughts of how he would have escaped from the upstairs living quarters and quietly relocated to the guest house. The guest quarters were poorly maintained and hardly fitting for a governor and his family: the roof leaked, the carpet was heavily stained and mildewed, and the ceiling was damaged and discolored.[4]

The campaign even fanned rumors of discussions between Wallace and officials connected with California governor Ronald Reagan. The two pillars of the New Right, some social conservatives averred, could form a third party that would topple both the Democrats and the Republicans, and return America to a position of unquestioned military strength, minimal taxation, and pre–Warren court values of school prayer, states' rights, capital punishment, and rigid strictures against abortion. When Reagan ventured to Cullman County, Alabama, to speak at a chamber of commerce meeting in early 1975, Wallace introduced the former actor and set off a new round of speculation. "Nothing is inconceivable," Wallace told inquiring scribes who could not resist the temptation of speculating about a Wallace-Reagan political marriage. The two conservative titans met briefly in a Cullman motel room. After Reagan's speech, the always-chatty Cornelia Wallace remarked to reporters that Reagan's speeches were quite similar to her husband's talking points during the 1972 campaign. The talk of a partnership, however, was mostly one-sided, even though the *Nation* discussed the possibility in print. Reagan aide Michael Deaver denied any dialogue on a political partnership, and Reagan further scuttled the subject: "It is very difficult for me to see how such a ticket could come together."[5]

Wallace operative Mickey Griffin—assigned by the governor to work directly with the national Democratic Party—made enough headway to position Wallace forces more significantly on key committees than ever before. Admittedly partisan, Griffin nonetheless reflected the prevailing sentiment among Wallace forces two years before the next presidential election. "He is an American hero," Griffin surmised of his boss; "he is the visible candidate.

Wallace would be an asset to any nominee, if being the candidate himself is taken away from him or escapes him. The governor can give complex answers in simple language. He doesn't con the people; he communicates with them. Ever hear of detente? Who in Pisgah, Alabama, knows what detente is? But they want to know and George Wallace talks the language of the folks in Pisgah."[6]

But beneath the allure of dreams of 1600 Pennsylvania Avenue—late 1974 and 1975 are the only years that Wallace felt he had a legitimate shot at becoming president—were more painful lessons for Alabama and its governor. Wallace anticipated zooming ahead of his segregationist past and earning the respect of the American body politic, but instead, by 1976, the governor was stuck in neutral, unable to escape the memory created by his own past, unable to make much of a difference in Alabama, unable to run for another term as governor in 1978, and eventually kicked aside to the political curb. The promise of the fall of 1974 shattered in the pieces of a broken marriage, more legislative battles, the inevitable failure of another presidential bid, and a Senate campaign that never gained much traction. By the end of 1978, with Wallace a lame duck and seemingly finished as a political personality, the optimism had turned into sadness, and the most dynamic personality in Alabama political history was more likely to be pitied than worshiped.

Utility Battles

Within the state, Wallace was more intrigued by locking horns with the state's major utilities—Alabama Power, Alagasco, and South Central Bell—than most any other matter. Tucked in the panoply of 1970 campaign promises was a pledge by Wallace to wage war against the utilities. Supposedly led by nameless and faceless bureaucrats, the major utilities, to many Alabamians, were coldly indicative of money-grubbing, corporate abusers. To his credit Wallace kept his word from 1970 and fought nearly every rate increase request during the decade. With desegregation a certainty and mainstream Alabamians gradually adjusting themselves to the idea of blacks and whites sharing buses, water fountains, and schoolhouses, Wallace, usually aware of the next political trend before most anyone else, attacked rising utility prices as unnecessary and unfair. "I assure you," Wallace promised Alabamians upset at rising phone bills, "that I am going to do everything in my power to prevent any increase in the telephone rates of this company even to the point of appealing to the Supreme Court of Alabama if necessary." No one thing bound Alabamians—Methodists and Baptists, Auburn and Alabama fans, Mountain Brook residents and trailer park dwellers, three-piece-suit wearers and those who worked with their name printed above the pocket on their shirt—together like the common disgust at opening the monthly envelope for their utilities. Wallace was so renowned for his antiutility campaign that people wrote Jere Beasley during Wallace's hospitalization in Maryland to make sure the acting governor was just as vigilant as the elected one.[7]

This sentiment was abundantly clear to the governor who kept steady tabs on the major themes of incoming mail. "On behalf of ourselves and many others," Mr. and Mrs. V. A. Scott wrote to Wallace, "who, like ourselves, are facing retirement and will have to live on a low fixed income which will barely cover the necessities of life, we wish to lodge a strong protest against the rate increase recently requested by the Alabama Power Company." The Scotts promised Wallace that they lived a Spartan life without central air conditioning or a clothes washer or dryer, only a modicum of television viewing, and never more than two cooked meals per day: "Yet in spite of [this] our Alabama Power bill for July 1972 was $24.43; for August, $26.60; for September, $30.82 and for October, $25.98. It seems completely unreasonable that the Alabama Power Company can charge the rates they charge for the services rendered—and now they want more." Other Alabamians expressed similar sentiments. "It seems that we senior citizens on a fixed income," Mr. and Mrs. W. K. Ustick complained, "will be forced to deny ourselves of the necessities of life to pay for these bills."[8]

The rising rates, in conjunction with Wallace's steady drumbeating, turned popular sentiment against Alabama Power. Though the company had been active in Alabama communities and charities for decades, it also had appropriately earned a reputation, among politicians seeking reelection, as a powerful interest group. According to historian Wayne Flynt, as the firm increased its capacity and customer base from the 1920s forward, it also increased its influence on Goat Hill. Though most Alabamians rarely complained about Alabama Power's exhaustive lobbying efforts, the higher monthly bills made such discussion more commonplace. "I am tired of seeing Reddy Kilowatt on television," Joseph Levin moaned in a missive to Alabama Power president Joseph Farley. "I am tired of seeing full page newspaper ads propagandizing the Power Company's plight if rates don't rise; I am tired of seeing high-paid lobbyists hanging around the capitol seeking to influence pro–Power Company legislation; I am damned sick and tired of a monopoly which can't even function properly in a competition free vacuum." Even if some Alabamians found Power Company advertising unsavory, the PSC ruled the practice was acceptable. The ads were also a lot less common than critics alleged. According to the PSC, 1971 advertising represented only 0.41 percent of Alabama Power's total operating revenue.[9]

Three decades later, even the most laconic jeremiads about thirty-dollar power bills seem laughable. But situated in the context of Alabama's mind-numbing poverty, increases in monthly utility expenditures, especially for fixed-income folks were significant. And for Alabama families trying to raise children, lost in a free textbook system that was never especially free, and facing a decade where the manufacturing plants they had given their lives to began to take on plywood windows, the monthly budget left little room for higher electric, gas, and phone expenditures. At the same time, Alabamians were facing higher unemployment and gasoline prices, as well as skyrocketing interest rates—the prime rate topped 12 percent in January 1975. And for many rural Alabamians, some of whom were still subject to party-line telephone systems, the increased utility fees did not necessarily reflect improved services. One Alabamian reacted with glee upon leaving the state since he had spent the past twelve months asking for a telephone that South Central Bell was unable to provide. The governor's office consistently reminded Alabamians that Wallace was fighting hard to keep those bills as low as possible. Even correspondence from the Office of Consumer Protection contained a rejoinder about Wallace's steadfast refusal to bow to the greedy wishes of the megalomaniacal power companies: "I am sure you realize that Governor Wallace for the past several years has consistently opposed the increases granted to the utility companies in Alabama. . . . Please be assured that Governor Wallace is doing all in his power to help the elderly, disabled, and handicapped citizens, and he will continue his fight to bring about a reduction in the high cost of utilities."[10]

One of the administration's initial targets was the fuel pass-on charge, sometimes termed energy cost adjustment. As the cost of energy skyrocketed during the 1970s, utilities had to pay more for the raw materials—oil, coal, natural gas, and others—that they needed to generate and distribute electricity to both commercial and residential end users. One Alabama Power official, Vice President Alan Barton, estimated that 82 percent of the state's electricity was generated by coal. As a percentage of monthly electric bills, energy pass-on costs could be quite high. A sample Alabama Power bill for December 1976 was only $32.63, but included an energy cost adjustment of $8.19, some 25 percent of the total charge. Though consumers viewed the pass-on charges as a new phenomenon, they actually date to the mid-1960s, a time when the governor was decidedly less vociferous about utility rates. The charges had not been itemized on bills until 1975, but had been legal for the previous decade, when they were lumped into a more generic monthly notice. Consumers objected even as the utilities attempted to explain their own financial plight, the panoply of energy costs beyond their control, and the need for enough operating income to build more facilities and ultimately lower costs through economies of scale. All of the administration rancor motivated some Alabamians to become more involved in governmental proceedings. Although PSC meetings had barely attracted flies in the past, as many as a thousand or more people showed up for rate request hearings after Wallace elevated the issue.[11]

Even as many ordinary Alabamians were struggling with higher bills, the utility companies faced their own hardships. As a matter of simple business practices, rising oil and coal costs had to be passed on to the consumer. "I feel that one of the biggest problems facing us as a company," an Alabama Power worker wrote to public service commissioner Kenneth Hammond, "is the education of the public as to why the cost of electricity has risen so sharply. As you know, the increased costs of our fuel alone is more than the average customer understands." And to generate enough power for future service needs, many of the utilities—most prominently Alabama Power—required a substantial commitment to new production and distribution facilities. From a simple mathematical standpoint, if the billions of dollars of new industrial growth that Wallace and the Alabama Development Office had crowed about for a decade was in fact a reality, utility companies were surely faced with rising demands for energy. According to Public Service Commission records, from 1971 to 1973, Alabama Power added at least 78,854 new customers. "It is an undisputed fact," the PSC concluded during one rate increase hearing, "that the company must build additional generating capacity to serve the ever-expanding need of present and future demand from all classes of customers." Perhaps more importantly for Alabama Power, the PSC concluded that internal earnings were insufficient to finance the construction of new facilities. Rate increases, then, were not just profit-taking, they were essential at a time when Alabama Power had a minimum of $1.2 billion committed to construction.[12]

The public debate pitted Wallace and Alabama consumers against the utility companies and business progressives who understood that industry could not relocate to Alabama if the electric, gas, and telephone infrastructure was insufficient to handle the increased load. "I . . . fail to understand," James Phipps wrote to Wallace, "how you expect the Alabama Power Co. and the South Central Telephone Co. to be able to build the plants needed to supply the industry you claim to have brought, or will bring, into Alabama. . . . We want to have industry thrive and provide jobs for our sons and daughters and certainly industry will not locate in a climate of 'get the big dogs' and where there is a good chance for 'brownouts' in years to come." Many union representatives, other spokesmen for workers, and trade associations supported the position of corporate management when it came to endorsing rate increases. "We are afraid," Hobert Williams, president of the Alabama State Building and Construction Trades Council warned, "the position that you are taking on the Public Service Commission's decision regarding utility rates will start a no-growth situation which Alabama cannot afford." Wallace, who traditionally sought to court union favor in order to woo votes, found himself at odds with labor leaders over his quest to prevent rate hikes.[13]

Wallace's principal strategy in forestalling utility increases was threefold:

complain loudly in public and in correspondence about rate increases; fund legal challenges whenever possible; and propose legislation designed to reduce the possibility of rate hikes. The first component of the plan was simple, despite the governor's health woes. Periodic ceremonial duties gave Wallace the opportunity to tell reporters that the utilities did not understand "the serious nature of this situation and the plight of the people." The staff was able to offer replies to correspondence that stressed Wallace's resolve against rising rates. "The governor announced," assistant T. Jeff Davis wrote as a common refrain to Alabamians complaining about energy prices, "his firm stand in opposition to this increase, declaring that present rates are excessive and that continued rate increases must be stopped."[14]

The second component of the Wallace utility war was a series of legal challenges to all rate increase requests. Wallace filed formal requests with the federal government, asking the attorney general to investigate South Central Bell's telephone prices. Since the beginning of his second elected term in 1971, Wallace had entrusted attorney Maurice Bishop with the task of litigating appeals to PSC rulings and filing additional challenges within the court system. "I have had the finest rate attorney defending and protesting the rate increases," Wallace bragged to supporters, "for every utility for the last number of years. . . . Maurice Bishop of Birmingham is one of the finest most intelligent and knowledgeable men in this field. . . . The record will show the amount of millions of dollars he has saved the public by his knowledge." Though his litigation rarely persuaded authorities to overturn rate increases, Bishop was able to delay the process enough to help Wallace politically and strap the utilities financially.[15]

Bishop and the administration even challenged Alabama Power's program of donating funds to various charities. Eventually, the PSC concurred, ruling that voluntary charitable giving by public utilities of funds that included fuel cost pass-on charges was improper. The utilities cast the issue as a matter of firms wishing to be good community partners; the administration painted the donations as an example of giving away other people's hard-earned money in ways and amounts that consumers had no control over. The raw politics of the matter favored the utilities. "One of the things," Dotson Nelson Jr. wrote to Wallace, "which has kept our country great has been generosity of this type. I certainly hope that you will use your good office to have this rethought and consider the effects that this would have upon such worthy things as the United Way." Gene Bromberg expressed similar sentiments to the governor: "I am very discouraged to read that the Public Service Commission wants to deny the public utilities the right to make pre-tax, voluntary, charitable contributions. . . . The tax payer will bear the burden."[16]

Administration supporters were surprised that the antiutility battle extended to the issue of charitable donations and used Wallace's own rhetoric from the freedom-of-choice school battles of the past. "That decision," Frank Spain argued, "strikes a blow at the heart of the American concept of freedom of choice, for without the support of corporations, including the utilities, we will have only one single governmental system." Others, such as H. B. Yielding, suggested that eliminating the philanthropy was the worst way imaginable to "try to reduce the cost of operating a public utility." Bishop and the administration were undeterred. "The issue involved is rather simple," the barrister summarized, "whether the utility should be permitted to donate consumer funds or their own. It is easy to give away the other man's money. Now the utilities will have the opportunity to give away their own money." Bishop suggested, optimistically, that the political fallout was negligible: "In any event, I know the decision has been almost universally approved by the consumers of Alabama."[17]

The legal strategy to prevent the PSC from increasing rates went farther than paying for an attorney to file legal appeals. PSC investigator Chris Whatley was "loaned" to the administration to assist Bishop and others in the executive branch fighting against Alabama Power. Whatley spent so much time working for the administration that the Public Service Commissioners had to ask Wallace in writing to return him. Eventually, Wallace tapped Whatley to join the Public Service Commission as a commissioner. With Whatley and Jim Zeigler—a former consumer advocate—joining the PSC, the administration's agenda received a longer look. On at least one occasion, Commissioner Zeigler asked for a $54 million rate cut for Alabama Power, based largely on arguments crafted by Bishop.[18]

The third component of the antiutility campaign included proposing legislation to curb specific utility practices. The administration crafted a package of bills written by Bishop and designed to attack the utilities, and Wallace called a special session to force the legislature to consider it. The package included eight bills—the governor called it "a tool" for the PSC—including cutting the pass-on charge, creating a special attorney to represent the public in rate matters, rate refunds, a plan to alter the complicated procedure for calculating the rate base, and a provision directing all appeals of PSC decisions immediately to the Alabama supreme court. Some of the utility package took on the trappings of a witch hunt; one bill was proffered that would mandate full financial disclosure of income for all utility employees making in excess of fifteen thousand dollars per year. Jere Beasley, often at odds with the governor, called the utility session "the most important session of the Alabama Legislature that I've been involved in over the last five years." Less than a week after Wallace called the special session into order, Alabama Power announced a layoff of 1,775 workers.[19]

The reaction to the administration's utility package was almost universally negative. Industry experts suggested that the bills would provide little of the immediate rate relief that Wallace had been crowing about since 1970. PSC research essentially mirrored much of Alabama Power's own findings: six of the eight provisions of the administration package were disastrous and the rest were not likely to encourage much expansion of electrical capacity, the critical component of meeting future demand and ultimately stabilizing the market. A *Montgomery Advertiser* report termed one administration floor leader as "embarrassed" at the prospect of supporting the bills. The bills passed the more malleable house but failed to survive the more independent senate.[20]

The legislature's reluctance to embrace the administration utility package provided deep cover for Wallace when consumers continued to face rising prices throughout the inflationary 1970s. "A minority of those in the Senate killed all the legislation through filibusters," Wallace reminded upset consumers, implying that his package would have softened rates. "The governor has only certain limits of authority in the matter, but I have done the best I could do and shall continue to do all that I can, under the statutes of Alabama and the Constitution of Alabama. My sympathies lie with those who will be oppressed by high rate bills, especially those with a small income." In another letter, Wallace assured an interested Alabamian that his plan would have checked utility greed: "The utility package which I offered would cut down on some of the wastage in public utilities and allow more efficient and economic utilization of our energy resources. Unfortunately, no relief was forthcoming at that time."[21]

A study conducted by the Alumax Corporation reflected the growing concern among industry insiders about future power requirements and the administration's attitude toward utilities. The report, written in 1976, cited the "unfavorable regulatory climate in Alabama" and concluded that the existing electrical capacity in the state would be insufficient as early as 1979: "The adequacy of future power availability is dependent on Alabama Power's ability to obtain prompt, reasonable, and responsible rate relief from the PSC, or the courts, if necessary to enable Alabama Power to raise capital funds to continue the planned electric system expansion program." Other companies planning possible expansions were equally concerned. "Regardless of whether we locate in Alabama," Herbert Clough, a senior official with a firm considering constructing a $400 million facility in the state counseled, "we urge a realistic regulatory attitude in order to insure a reliable future power supply for Alabama's householders and industry alike."[22]

A typical response by the administration to rate increase requests was to criticize them as unreasonable: "Certainly I would agree that future power needs must be anticipated and productive facilities constructed. . . . But unless something is done to curb increasing electric rates, air conditioning and electric heat for a number of our citizens will become little more than a dream." Even so, a PSC ruling cited research compiled by Alabama Power that concluded that rates must be raised to allow for the construction of additional capacity: "The company's estimates of demands upon its system [have] proven historically accurate herein and also in proceedings for several certificates of convenience and necessity for large generating plants and associated transmission facilities currently under construction." The same ruling included a warning about Alabama Power's ability to generate future capacity without increasing prices. According to historian Leah Rawls Atkins, the Wallace anti-utility campaign left Alabama Power much closer to financial collapse than most Alabamians realized.[23]

Over time, the state's media began to question the administration's utility battle. An Anniston radio station, WDNG, blasted Wallace, citing General Motors' reluctance to construct two new facilities in Tuscaloosa because of the utility climate. "Some politicians," a 1976 commentary announced, "find it popular with much of the public to jump on Alabama Power Company by saying that this company is trying to gouge the little man and make huge profits. If enough people continue to fall for this sham, the day may come when brown outs and black outs are common place. Who will the people blame then?"[24]

Continuity and Change in Public Policy

While the utility battle raged, Wallace took steps to make state government more diverse. Annie Laurie Gunter, the first woman appointed to the Wallace cabinet back in 1972, was moved from coordinator of highway safety to director of the Consumer Protection Agency. Though Alabama highways were notorious for fatal accidents, coordinating administration safety policy had very little cachet and the post was considered a minor one. The state's official move to the 55 mph speed limit was unpopular, though it contributed to 172 fewer highway deaths in its inaugural year. Jesse Lewis replaced Gunter at Highway Safety, becoming the first African American to hold a cabinet post under Wallace. One possible explanation for the appointment can be found in Wallace's 1976 presidential strategy, which sought to target black voters. "We intend to demonstrate Alabama is a moving state," an internal memorandum stated in identifying criteria for winning black votes, "that does not deny rights and opportunities by showing progress during the Wallace administrations." Even so, it is just as likely that Wallace was ready to begin welcoming change, even in his own administration. The same month as Lewis received his post, Wallace accepted an honorary doctorate from Alabama State, sharing the stage with civil rights veteran Ralph Abernathy. Tuskegee mayor Johnny Ford, a former Nixon supporter and suddenly a Wallace man, praised

Wallace: "My governor has been fair and judicious to all Alabamians, rich or poor, black or white. This is 1975. This is a new day, this is a New South."[25]

Wallace's more public gestures of racial reconciliation came later—late 1970s and early 1980s apologies to John Lewis, Jesse Jackson, and others are the most famous—but his initial steps toward those whom he had earlier tried to keep segregated came in his third elected term. As historian Dan Carter has concluded, it is impossible to know the exact motivations of a man whose inner core was so molded by a life of southern politics. And George Wallace's personality had many facets, some exaggerated, others mostly hidden. Yet no dispute is possible on two pivotal matters: Wallace understood the electoral necessities of courting black voters for future campaigns, presidential, gubernatorial, or senatorial, and Wallace understood pain as well as any person living in Alabama. From May of 1972 until his death in 1998, George Wallace lived in constant, numbing, emotionally draining, hopeless pain with only the flimsiest hopes of ephemeral relief. His life became one gigantic pharmacological cocktail, leaving him with side effects as exhausting as his spinal injury itself.[26]

Stephan Lesher, the author of an authorized and comparatively sympathetic biography of Wallace, believes Wallace's racial epiphany was based on the need for votes, a quest to separate his conservatism from his racist past, and self-reflection: "Alone and crippled, forced to introspection for the first time in his life, he realized that though he had purported to be the champion of the poor and the helpless, he had trampled on the poorest and most helpless of all his constituents—the blacks." Some of Lesher's details are wrong, even if his larger point suggests some of the complexity of Wallace. The governor, in fact, was frequently introspective: after his 1958 defeat, before the stand at the schoolhouse door at Foster Auditorium, after the violence at the Edmund Pettus Bridge in Selma, after Lurleen died, during executions, after the 1968 campaign was over, after trailing in the 1970 primary, and on several other occasions. During most of these moments of soul-searching, Wallace had little to gain politically by embracing change. Is it simply coincidence that a man driven by politics opened his arms to the African American community when they had something to offer him?[27]

But if, as Dan Carter says, many people hold fast to the optimism inherent in a truly penitent Wallace begging forgiveness for the pain he caused, plenty of evidence actually exists for such a conclusion. From 1974 until his death, Wallace was softer, less hyperbolic, more interested in his children and his God, and more inclusive in his personal and professional politics. His 1974 and 1982 gubernatorial victories included sizable support by black Alabamians. Others, like Judge Frank Johnson, who found the apologies too little and too late can steel themselves against a redeemed Wallace with an awareness of the physical and psychological scars that linger unspoken across the state. History pales in comparison to the power of memory, especially in a state like Alabama where the lessons of kinfolk carry more weight than the research and writing of scholars. In the end, Wallace had his own reasons for reaching out to black Alabamians, some genuine and heartfelt, others shaped by a new political reality. Other southern politicians usually cast in a more progressive light, such as Jimmy Carter, took on the trappings of segregationist rhetoric in order to get themselves elected. So if Wallace was overtly political in his apologias, he was not the only one.[28]

If the inclusion of blacks into the governor's cabinet was a clear sign of change, much of the rest of the third elected term is symbolic of continuity and mediocrity. Highway director Ray Bass predicted his department would soon face a $117 million shortfall, largely the result of accumulated debt over the previous two decades of bond bills and the failure to provide new revenue streams. According to Bass, the use of bonds, though helpful in road construction, created a major fiscal problem. "Our ratio of debt service to revenue," Bass admitted, "has been reduced to the point where additional authorizations for bond sales will require a major tax increase in order to finance the debt service and maintain a favorable debt service to revenue ratio." Bass halted road construction and repairs, including seven major projects across the state, cut interstate projects to the bone, and laid off so many Highway Department employees that the governor was sued for unfair termination practices. By way of comparison, Alabama spent $1,973 per mile of road for basic maintenance costs; neighbors Georgia, $3,444, and Tennessee, $5,723, spent considerably more. Nationally, on average, states allocated 35 percent of their total highway budget to repairs; Alabama spent only 19 percent.[29]

If the state's road system was on the verge of being bankrupt, the forests were not in much better shape. Though Wallace was sympathetic to the state's foresters in keeping the state's property tax rates low, he did little to alter his precedent of nonsupport for forest fire protection. And as was the case with the highway department, mental health, prisons, and several other key departments, the governor was regularly warned that major changes needed to be made in order to prevent an emergency. "The thing that concerns me," Alabama Forestry Association executive vice president J. Hilton Watson cautioned, "is that even though we may have prevented a holocaust last week, there is a good possibility that we might be facing one in the near future." Throughout a dangerously dry period in early 1977, conservation officials struggled to minimize millions of dollars of damage to an important industry. "Our problems at this point," a wildlife situation report explained, "are caused in part by not having adequate manpower and equipment. Without some type of relief through changing weather conditions or assistance from other agencies, the State of

Alabama will suffer a severe loss through wildfires." This report could have been written in 1963, so little had changed over the previous fourteen years.[30]

According to an Alabama Forestry Commission memorandum, resources allocated to conservation fire control had actually been slashed over the preceding years, not expanded. "We have reduced," G. A. Gibbs, chairman of the commission complained, "approximately 20% of our fire control personnel over the last few years. This reduction of forces, already completely inadequate to meet the needs of the forest fire control in the State of Alabama, is part of our history we must live with." Gibbs also suggested that the pitiful funding of forestry left the agency so strapped that he was not sure "how long we can operate before we must close down the operation for lack of funds." The legislature passed 7.5 percent salary increases, but funding never accompanied the authorization.[31]

Significant fire destruction, undoubtedly exacerbated by insufficient manpower and equipment, wracked Alabama in 1976, 1977, and 1978. One estimate indicated that a three-week stretch of fires in 1976 caused $142 million in losses. A 1977 Southeastern States Forest Fire Compact Commission report declared the damage in Alabama that year to be the worst in the region. A rash of fires in the spring of 1978 was so dangerous—once again the state suffered worse damage than any other southeastern state—that the administration issued a no-burn order that, at least temporarily, resulted in Alabama citizens being asked to refrain from using their barbeque grills. "The forest fire situation seems to be getting worse," Wallace admitted. "Find out what we should do other than the No Burn Order. Should we have some guardsmen fighting the fire? Would that be feasible? I am not sure whether they have the equipment or not?"[32]

An Alabama Forestry Association survey of southeastern states indicated that Alabama had made virtually no progress since 1963 in protecting a $2.5 billion industry. In fact, the number of state fires and amount of damage had increased dramatically through the 1970s. Alabama spent $320,000 per million acres of commercial forest land, while peer states—Georgia ($517,302), Florida ($1,055,493), Mississippi ($738,360), and Tennessee ($535,968)—allocated substantially more resources for conservation and development. Among Alabama's neighbors, only Georgia had more commercial forest land. The average annual forestry budget of the four adjacent states was $12.6 million; Alabama's annual appropriation was $6.7 million, 53 percent of the peer state average. Compounding the inability to protect one of the state's few growing industries was the reality that the state was under a federal court order to hire African Americans as conservation officers.[33]

While Conservation Department issues had not changed much since 1963, mental health was undergoing a flurry of changes. Bryce Hospital underwent its fourth management reorganization in four years. New Mental Health director Taylor Hardin, a lightning rod to be sure, fired Partlow superintendent Richard Buckley, touching off a firestorm of "he said, she said" over the lack of progress at the state's institutions. The move to regional and community mental health facilities provided an avalanche of new buildings and satellite offices. Even so, the state was serving a smaller percentage of the population in 1976 than it was in 1970, and none of the state's major mental health institutions were accredited by the Joint Commission on Accreditation of Hospitals.[34]

Alabama prisons continued to be grossly overpopulated; the facility at Mt. Meigs was at 132 percent of capacity, with inmates continuing to sleep on the floor, yet 106 new prisoners were relocated to the prison. The total system continued to run at nearly twice the recommended capacity. "We simply don't know where we're going to put these people," spokesman John Hale admitted. Board of Corrections chairman Thomas Staton, noting that his department was receiving about 43 percent of the resources it needed, begged for revenue-sharing funds, additional legislative appropriations, and every other funding source short of a bake sale. "The Board of Corrections," Staton noted, admitting that another federal court order was a distinct possibility, "and its employees are straining every mental, financial, spiritual, and physical resource to make the Alabama prisons safe places for humane confinement. . . . The needs are immediate and conditions are explosive and deteriorating badly." And this was not a new situation. Corrections officials had pleaded for additional funds for decades and, as recently as November 1974 Commissioner L. B. Sullivan had characterized the prison system as "in a state of crisis." Sullivan cited a bevy of problems including more prisoners, antiquated facilities and vehicles, and an annual prison guard turnover of nearly 40 percent. Despite these glaring needs, Wallace continued to pledge that new taxes would not be tolerated. The Corrections budgets for fiscal years 1975 and 1976 provided only $415,000 for additional construction.[35]

Wallace's response to the continual litany of prison issues was to blame liberals for wanting to coddle prisoners. A class action suit claiming that Alabama prisons were so inhumane that they violated the Eighth Amendment was met with disgust. "We are going to throw the prisoners away, to the penitentiaries of this state," Wallace blasted. "We've tried what the sob sisters wanted." When further clarification from the court mandated that prison commissaries should be staffed by certified dieticians and prisoners should have access to new razor blades for shaving, Wallace lashed out again: "If the federal courts were as concerned about people put in cemeteries of Jefferson County as they are with people shaving, things would be in a good deal better condition." At the time of Wallace's retort, a *Wall Street Journal* report indicated some alarming conditions, even for a state with a notorious prison reputation. As many as five prisoners were housed in a four-by-eight-foot cell, with buckets for toilets, and some prisoners singled out for special punishment received only one meal per day and one hour of exercise every eleven days. A check of two thousand prisoners revealed only forty that had not been seriously injured over the previous two years. Less than 9 percent of Holman inmates were enrolled in an education or vocational program. A *Newsweek* probe identified twenty-seven inmates who had been killed during the previous two years. "I would rather be caught with a knife by a guard," one inmate maintained, "than be caught without one by another inmate." An Alabama Advisory Committee to the U.S. Civil Rights Commission determined that race played a role in assigning inmates and providing discriminatory treatment. Blacks, according to the study, were routinely assigned to the most infamous state facilities with whites disproportionately assigned to newer prisons. The Advisory Committee also noted the lack of black or female members on the State Board of Corrections and estimated the recidivism rate among Alabama prisoners to be at 67 percent. "It isn't that the recidivist rate is high," University of Alabama professor Charles Slack summarized, "that is amazing. It's appalling. . . . What is amazing is that the other third somehow make it without coming back."[36]

Eventually, Frank Johnson agreed with the petitioners, declaring the state prisons "cruel and unusual punishment" and setting various timelines for the state to meet minimum guidelines. The decision could hardly be labeled activist since a Board of Correction lawyer, Robert Lamar Jr., admitted that some prisons were in clear violation of the Constitution. Yet almost immediately, the administration and its supporters wailed about the additional costs—judged by some to be in excess of $150 million—necessary to turn state penal facilities into veritable hotels. "A state is not at liberty," the federal judge reasoned in anticipation of the all-too-familiar complaint, "to afford its citizens only those constitutional rights which fit comfortably within its budget." In his ruling, Johnson described a "rampant violence and jungle atmosphere" that unfortunately, given his previous judgements, came as no surprise. Few who had heard the tales of rampant rat and roach infestation would have found the prisons acceptable, and longtime prison critics rejoiced that yet another federal court order might finally force the state to take meaningful action. "It is pleasant to know," Frances Kent wrote to Johnson, "[that] your pompous little governor has been called to task for something for a change." Undeterred, Wallace lapsed into Confederate-speak: "Just another example of the federal court trying to run our state." More analytically, representative Gerald Dial unintentionally summed up the reality of administration policy over the preceding years: "Building roads gets votes. Improving prisons doesn't."[37]

Wallace continued to turn the heat up on Johnson, declaring that "thugs and federal judges" were threatening the state by rendering it too soft on criminals and vowing not to call a special session to raise money for prison reform. "A vote for George C. Wallace," the governor retorted, "might give a political barbed wire enema to some of the federal judges in this country. . . . We are blameless in this order. There has been no intentional neglect of prisoners in Alabama." Despite the rhetoric, the administration had been warned by Corrections officials a year before Johnson's decision that such a ruling could be forthcoming. "I and the other members of the Board of Corrections," Staton cautioned, "feel that we face a truly desperate situation, of potential intense embarrassment to us and to the governor. Drastic action is needed fast."[38]

Johnson's ruling spurred several exposés, including a detailed study by the *Birmingham News*. The same month that Birmingham native Louise Fletcher won the Academy Award for her portrayal of maniacal Nurse Ratched in *One Flew over the Cuckoo's Nest,* her hometown newspaper reported no rehabilitation was possible in state prisons that featured one working toilet for every two hundred inmates, a pipe in a wall serving as a shower, and inmates using metal vegetable cans as drinking cups for water and homemade prison hooch. Because most of the facilities utilized dormitory sleeping arrangements with multiple cots instead of individual cells, rapes were commonplace, and the guards were so severely outnumbered that they dared not venture into inmate areas once lights were out at ten o'clock. The media attention caused some to vent their frustration not at Johnson, but at the governor. "I am ashamed and discouraged," John Prewitt wrote to Wallace, "by your reaction to Judge Johnson's order concerning our penal institutions. In the name of humanity and our mother state, please re-examine your values." Prewitt's advice notwithstanding, Wallace's public sentiment did not change, conflating the separate issues of victim's rights and humane treatment of prisoners into one issue. "I certainly join with you in your thoughts about this subject," Wallace wrote to L. J. Racey who was concerned about prisoners receiving an education and other benefits, "and have frequently spoken out against the coddling of criminals. . . . Somewhere along the line, we have lost sight of the real values in our society, as victims should not have to continue to pay the price brought on by convicted felons.[39]

Though he had struggled with capital punishment decisions during his first term, Wallace became an outspoken advocate for executing criminals even while he publicly forgave Arthur Bremer for sentencing him to life in a wheelchair. Wallace signed a bill passed by the state legislature reinstating capital punishment. Ideologically, Wallace justified his position by citing the death penalty as a deterrent to crime and victims' rights as an important consideration long overlooked. "I believe," the governor predicted, "that we will soon be seeing a return of capital punishment throughout the United States as it is the only effective deterrent of serious and heinous crimes." His preference for capital punishment was so pronounced that his correspondence included the rejoinder that a constitutional amendment would be in order should the Supreme Court outlaw the practice. As a Methodist, Wallace's position was in contrast to the official United Methodist Church statement: "The use of the death penalty gives official sanction to a climate of violence. Any government undermines its moral authority when it presumes upon the prerogatives of God by taking human life in response to criminal deeds."[40]

Even if the death penalty was not popular with orthodox Methodists, it resonated with other Alabamians. "We are all potential future victims of maniacs," Charles Owens declared in a letter to the governor, "unless you use your authority and ability to have murders eradicated permanently. So what if 85% of murders are committed by blacks, then put them to death." Though he believed executions prevented some crimes from occurring, Wallace did not consider gun registration as a deterrent to crime: "I am opposed to federal legislation which would enforce the registration of guns by our citizens. . . . Those who do not obey the present laws against murder, robbery, and assault are not likely to obey a gun control or registration law. These people would remain armed while the law-abiding citizen would be restricted." And Wallace often noted that he was shot in Maryland, a state with gun registration laws, though Bremer's gun had been purchased in Wisconsin. In a state where the opening of deer season is as eagerly anticipated as Christmas, any limitations on gun purchasing were sure to be unpopular.[41]

The governor made only token efforts to link pornography to his anticrime agenda. Despite its reputation as the buckle on the Bible Belt, Alabama witnessed a growth in the amount of adult entertainment media available in the state, including material featuring minors. A *Birmingham News* report identified four Birmingham businesses that trafficked in child pornography and a host of others that sold material featuring teenagers and adults. "We'd like to make a strong push to get this kind of material out of the city," an undercover vice operative admitted, "but we just don't have the manpower to do it." In Madison County, private clubs featuring go-go dancing became small havens for prostitution, drug use, gambling, and violence. A grand jury report noted that thirteen-year-old girls were among the entertainers routinely permitting paying customers to "fondle their bodies." The same grand jury concluded that as many as one hundred private clubs, supposedly nonprofit according to the law, operated in the Huntsville area alone. Wallace himself was the victim of a publicity stunt by at least one pornographic magazine. *Screw Magazine* put the governor's likeness, without his permission, on the back page of a February 1976 issue, provoking understandable outrage. "I want to assure you," Wallace aide Curtis Redding wrote to angry supporters, "that Governor Wallace at no time has given his permission for his name or picture to be used to endorse this magazine. As a matter of fact, Governor Wallace has spoken out many times against magazines such as this."[42]

The 1976 Presidential Campaign

Nationally, conservatives took note of Wallace's list of talking points. "It's parochial schools, pornography, drugs, crime, busing, quotas in union shops," former Nixon speechwriter Pat Buchanan summarized. "I don't know that anybody but George Wallace is talking about those things." As Dan Carter has demonstrated, Wallace's "genius was his ability to voice his listeners' sense of betrayal—of victimhood—and to refocus their anger." Whether Wallace was the "most influential loser in twentieth-century American politics," as Carter has suggested, or the "most influential outsider" as Buchanan noted in 1976 is open to debate. That many of his themes were coopted by a future generation of mostly Republican politicians is not.[43]

Although prison reform bashing, capital punishment sound bites, and anti-gun control comments were eagerly greeted by many supporters, the timing of Johnson's prison ruling was particularly problematic for the governor. Three days before the decision, the country singer Grandpa Jones kicked off Wallace's first rally of the 1976 presidential campaign in Boston. With comely Wallace girls collecting donations, the governor treated the antibusing Bostonians to a chorus of big-government taunts. "In 1976," Wallace crowed, "the big issue is whether the great middle class can survive the trend toward big government." Press reports noted that the defiant Wallace who stalked the stage and hammered home points with clenched fists was gone. The crowds were polite, not raucous, reserved, not frenzied. George Wallace was no longer the most charismatic politician in America. Dan Carter has described a Wallace appearance prior to the Laurel shooting as "palpably sexual, bizarrely blending the sacred—God, Mother, and Country—and the profane, with calls for violence and retribution." The 1976 crowd dynamics still merged the creative and destructive elements but with a comparatively antiseptic whisper, not a bellowing Rebel Yell. The message, then, was similar, but the messenger was forever changed. "Like he's said before," George Wallace Jr. commented in response to scribes who noted the difference in performance, "he's paralyzed from the waist down, but too many men running for president are now paralyzed from the neck up." Cornelia Wallace was more circumspect. In handwritten marginalia, she jotted down her thoughts on Wallace's suddenly vincible stump presence: "He's got to perform better . . . never know where the hell he's going. I don't have any confidence in him."[44]

Less than three weeks later, the Iowa caucuses were won by a southern governor, but a Georgian—Jimmy Carter—not Wallace, garnered the victory. As much as Carter leaped onto the national stage as a surprise candidate, the Wallace campaign had taken stock of him much earlier, even though it had identified Washington senator Henry "Scoop" Jackson as the candidate to beat. "Even newspapers in his home state have ragged him about his candidacy," an internal Wallace campaign memorandum noted, "[but Carter] is not to be underestimated in the energy department. He has picked up a sort of Wallace issue package." Carter had, in fact, been beating the electoral bushes across the country for a few years, much like he had campaigned ceaselessly for four years after losing the 1966 gubernatorial primary in Georgia. Carter was understandably ebullient in beating Wallace in Iowa, since Wallace had appeared to be the front-runner for the previous eighteen months. "At this moment," Carter chirped, "in a two-man race, I would beat George Wallace. [His support] is like a rock. He can't take it away but it doesn't grow very much."[45]

The Iowa caucuses gave the first indication to Wallace that he was still unelectable in a national race. Wallace placed fourth in the Oklahoma caucuses, even though the campaign spent some last-minute money on an advertising blitz. At a time when Wallace was clearly distancing himself from his segregationist past, West Virginia Klan leader Dale Reusch announced he hoped to be Wallace's vice president. Few took notice of the West Virginian, but it was another reminder of the support Wallace had traditionally attracted. Edmund Muskie dismissed the governor, fund-raising notwithstanding: "I don't really regard him as part of the current crop. His time has passed." Even the news from Mississippi was not very positive. Expected to command up to two-thirds of that state's delegates, Wallace won only a plurality of 49 percent. In South Carolina, Wallace placed first in delegate counts as well, but captured only 27.8 percent of the total compared to Carter's 23.4 percent. Even more troubling for Wallace was that he had outspent Carter five to one and made more personal appearances in the Palmetto State. Health and energy issues prevented Wallace from venturing to each state. And where he did campaign, he continued to book the large arenas and halls that he filled in 1968 and 1972. Yet, empty seats became more commonplace as it grew apparent that the Wallace road show was not quite the same. Carter won a surprising victory in New Hampshire—Wallace did not even campaign in the Granite State, even though the Democratic standard-bearer in the general election since 1952 had won there—and the Georgian began to speak more confidently: "[It is] now quite possible that I can beat Wallace in Florida." For Wallace to have any momentum, a strong showing in Massachusetts and Florida was essential.[46]

Despite Massachusetts' reputation for liberalism, the economic downturn of the mid-1970s coupled with the fractious Democratic Party, McGovern's crushing defeat in 1972, and the strength of the busing issue in certain key geographic areas gave Wallace a fighting chance for victory. Wallace spent considerable time and money in the Bay State and in fact he doubled his vote count from 1972 in that state, racking up five-to-one vote count advantages in antibusing strongholds like South Boston. Yet the Alabama governor placed second overall to Jackson, even though some aides had privately predicted a signature victory. Typically, Wallace claimed victory in the face of defeat: "The American people are beginning to realize that big government cannot solve all their problems. The Democratic establishment is shaken up tonight. I've run so well in an impossible state." In fact, his words are strikingly similar to the governor's analysis of his efforts in the 1964 presidential campaign. The only difference was that he entered the 1976 campaign believing he could actually win.[47]

Jackson, understandably, had a far different assessment of the meaning of the Massachusetts primary. "I think," the Washington senator proclaimed, "it was a victory for rational thinking on the busing issue. I think Wallace failed. He had only one issue, and he beat it all the time. In order to be credible he has to win in the North. He lost his chance to win the nomination in Massachusetts." Polls indicated that honesty in government, creating new jobs, and balancing the national budget were the dominant issues. Post-Watergate politics had moved past the simple question of whether government could solve structural problems. In fact, every single president elected since the Nixon resignation campaigned largely on the premise that government should be smaller, more agile, and more responsible, even if, once in office, all these presidents actually expanded the size and some of the roles of government.[48]

Wallace certainly deserves some credit, along with Watergate and the failures of the Vietnam War, in creating these changing expectations of the federal government. But voters now demanded a measure of honesty and character, real or perceived as the case may be, in their presidents as well as a handful of important solutions they could believe in. Wallace was an expert at identifying problems, but he rarely elaborated anything other than simple answers to complex questions as governor or as a presidential candidate. "We ought to have bombed them out of existence up in North Viet Nam," he declared in a 1975 statement concerning his policy on the war. "People say that would be barbaric, but if we had done it when some of us first said it, it wouldn't have cost one-tenth or one-fifteenth the lives that have been lost—and we would have won." Such comments made for good sound bites but were not comprehensive solutions to the problem of America's longest war.[49]

Even his own campaign staff noted that the vague generalities with which the governor spoke were hard to codify. "Frankly, this is a difficult task for me," aide Bert Haltom complained when trying to translate some of Wallace's statements into formal platform proposals. "The governor's position papers . . . are helpful but he generalizes so much it is hard for me to translate his stand on some important issues into Platform Committee position paper caliber." And the governor's track record in Alabama indicated to many voters that he could not be counted on to find answers to complex questions. These realities combined with the wheelchair and his 1960s reputation kept Wallace's national plans stuck in neutral.[50]

Two years after the 1976 campaign was over, Wallace insisted his wheelchair was a major reason he failed to win the nomination. "When I was running for the Democratic presidential nomination," the governor wrote in an exclusive *Washington Post* essay, "many cited my condition as a reason to vote against me. The party hierarchy calculatingly used this against me. . . . I still think, looking back, that I would have been on the Democratic national ticket had I not been shot. Only painful experience prevents me from joking that I don't know which would have been preferable." Others in the inner circle felt the same; the wheelchair was the culprit. Cornelia concurred, believing the image of the wheelchair was too powerful to overcome. "I think George's campaign organization let him down," she told *Parade Magazine*. "For TV they should've shown him swimming in the pool, driving the boat at the lake. They could've stood him in his braces or leaned him up against a fence post on the farm and had him say 'this is where I was brought up. My father was a dirt farmer.' "[51]

Even southerners were no longer sold on the idea that Wallace was the best choice to run against Gerald Ford in 1976. A September 1975 poll of seven states of the Old Confederacy placed Wallace comfortably ahead of Carter. A January 1976 poll still placed Wallace at the top, though his margin had narrowed. By March, Carter had moved almost fourteen points ahead of Wallace, making Florida the governor's last chance to resuscitate his campaign. To make matters worse, the March poll revealed that southerners preferred both Ford and Reagan, nonsouthern Republicans, to Wallace. The 1976 primary in Florida, a state that the governor carried impressively in 1972, was effectively the last stand for Wallace's presidential aspirations.[52]

Wallace diversified his appeal in Florida, adding anti-Castro and antiabortion rhetoric to his staple diet of anticrime, antibusing, and anti–big government. Cuban Americans were energized voters in South Florida, and no candidate could be expected to win their support without offering some tough talk about the Communist leader of their homeland. "I've learned that a man of courage like George Wallace," Ruben Mendiola, who campaigned for the governor in Florida, declared "is needed to stop Communism. Governor George Wallace is the only political figure of his time who has the necessary qualifications to destroy Communism." Wallace's prolife position was an attempt to appeal to the state's sizable Catholic vote at a time when many of his rivals were openly courting Jewish voters. Wallace, in fact, endorsed more than a reversal of the *Roe v. Wade* decision. "I am in support of a Constitutional Amendment," he noted in correspondence, "which would protect the lives of unborn children and would nullify the Supreme Court decision on abortions." Wallace also campaigned against state and federal funds, typically through Medicaid, being used to pay for the procedure. In Alabama, however, abortion laws were actually more lenient than in Florida, with abortion-on-demand available in Birmingham.[53]

Carter attacked Wallace's Alabama record with a vengeance during the Florida primary: "Alabama has the most regressive tax structure in the country and federal courts there are running many aspects of state government." These charges had been tried before, by northeastern politicians, liberal Democrats, journalists, and college professors, and had usually failed to sway southern voters. But coming from a Georgian who represented many of the South's traditions—military service and agriculture—they took root. "Wallace hasn't solved many problems in Alabama," Carter railed, "and thus can't be trusted to do any better for the nation." Here was another southern boy, albeit one with good hair and an easy smile, telling Florida voters that the symbol of a white South for more than a decade, George Wallace, could not measure up to the demands of a modern South. Floridians agreed, delivering a victory for Carter and dealing Wallace a final blow. The governor sounded defiant, noting he had no plans to leave the race and terming Florida too "cosmopolitan" to be considered a southern state. Privately, the campaign staff knew it was over.[54]

Most of the remaining funds and energy were sunk into North Carolina, a state Wallace won in 1972 with 50 percent of the vote. Wallace took a harder line in attacking Carter as "warmed-over McGovern," and he taped several commercials that were harshly critical. Withal, Carter crushed Wallace 54 percent to 35 percent and the Wallace campaign immediately laid off thirty-one workers. By May, only two reporters traveled with the campaign. "Naturally your chances diminish each time you lose a primary," Wallace reflected. "I'm glad to see that the other candidates have moved to the issues I started in 1972." Hecklers began taunting Wallace cruelly, showing up at a rally in Wisconsin in wheelchairs and wearing Arthur Bremer masks. With one defeat after another, Wallace was forced to campaign in Alabama during the state's primary, something he had never before been compelled to do. "In 1972," he told Alabamians at a campaign stop, "they didn't stop us with bullets. And in 1976 they launched the strongest spike and smear campaign against you and me and Alabama in the history of this country to stop our thoughts from being heard." The risk of losing in Alabama was such a potential embarrassment that the campaign used endorsements from state football legends Bear Bryant and Shug Jordan and urged conservative voters not to cross party lines in support of Reagan. Wallace won in Alabama, but carried barely 50 percent of the Democratic vote.[55]

The Alabama primary was little more than a last chance for Wallace to claim a victory before quitting the race. The twenty-six-passenger plane the campaign had used since January was exchanged for a seven-seater. Four years and two days after being shot, Wallace returned to Maryland to campaign briefly. Queried by scribes about what might have been, Wallace responded optimistically if not necessarily accurately: "If that [the shooting] had not happened, I would be here as president of the United States." A few weeks later, Wallace threw in the towel and endorsed Carter after a late-night phone conversation with the Georgian. On June 13, 1976, Carter, as a sign of respect, flew to Montgomery to meet with Wallace and prepare a statement of party unity. "People who have been in this political game a long time," the governor mused, "have to learn that you can't win every time and I lost. The people voted for Carter."[56]

Some Wallace supporters found Carter unworthy of Wallace's vetting. "If Jimmy Carter is elected," O. M. Herring of Opelika wrote to Wallace, "and I am pretty sure he will be, we can look for a Negro vice-president for he is obligated to them now and he is going to have to pay off for all those kisses he has been passing out among them, and in that case by some cruel act of fate, this country could be left with a Negro president." By endorsing Carter, a fellow southerner but a moderate by definition, Wallace was seen by some as breaking faith. For the diehard Wallace voter, the governor's support for Carter seemed to be a disavowal of the previous twelve years of backlash rhetoric, particularly about the liberal nature of the national Democratic Party. "I did not see one item in the platform that you have espoused over the last six or eight years," Thomas Nolder scolded. "I am truly disappointed in your behavior. Had I known that you would 'sell out' and put party ahead of principle when it came down to the wire, I never would have supported you all of these years." Even Cornelia seemed disappointed by her husband's championing of Carter: "Don't get me started on Jimmy Carter. There is such a thing, you know, as honor in your word."[57]

In the 1976 presidential election, Carter carried Alabama and all of the states of the Old Confederacy save Virginia. Surprisingly, given the conventional wisdom about the Solid South, Carter and Adlai Stevenson (1952) were the only Democratic candidates to win all of Alabama's electoral college votes in the last half of the twentieth century. Could the Georgian have won the presidency without the efforts of George Wallace? Wallace's endorsement was not instrumental in 1976 to a Carter victory, though it did provide a measure of party unity—something the party had enjoyed very little of since 1964, largely because of Wallace himself. And though the governor did campaign for Carter in Florida, Mississippi, and Alabama, his impact was not pivotal. Just the same, Carter was quick to give credit to Wallace: "Within forty-eight hours after Governor Wallace withdrew and threw his support to me, I had more than 1,700 delegate votes. It was Wallace who put me over the top." And over the previous twelve years, Wallace had introduced the nation to the concept that a person from the Deep South could be taken seriously as a candidate.[58]

Though he was a team player in actively supporting his party's nominee for the first time in decades, Wallace was devastated that his own presidential ambitions were effectively dashed before spring had even sprung. With no chance to run for another gubernatorial term in 1978, Wallace, officially finished as a national presence, was left to ponder his own possibilities in a career that seemed to be over. The only electoral possibility for the governor who had run for something eight times since 1962 was a Senate race, something he had strongly considered in 1966, but not since. Such a position was problematic though, since senators were often expected to attend committee meetings and show up to cast votes. And Wallace had demonstrated very little interest in governance since his time in the Alabama legislature. Aides prepared for a Senate run in 1978 for John Sparkman's seat, even though the possibility did not excite Wallace much. "I see myself as governor for nearly three more years in Alabama," he told *Parade Magazine,* "and then, of course, my political career will probably be over. . . . I would not run for office again." Cornelia Wallace offered her own speculation about her husband's next career move: "He may be in the U.S. Senate, or he might be appointed to the U.S. Supreme Court, or he may just retire and lecture and tour and write."[59]

George and Cornelia

Cornelia had some plans of her own. Stoking comparisons to Lurleen's campaign, Cornelia let it be known to reporters that she was not ruling out her own bid for governor in 1978. While Lurleen had been a reluctant political warrior—agreeing to run because she deeply loved her husband, warts and all, and knew he needed the seat of power in Montgomery in order to run his 1968 presidential bid—Cornelia did not have a reluctant bone in her body. She craved the limelight and enjoyed speaking to reporters even when her comments exasperated the governor. But the biggest reason that Wallace had no intention of fronting another stand-in was that their marriage was falling apart.[60]

Cornelia's interest in the spotlight went beyond the possibility of running for governor. Using a ghostwriter, she completed a book, *C'nelia,* which achieved modest success, including excerpts published in *Good Housekeeping.*

Though she deferred on the text, Cornelia personally selected most of the book's twenty-eight photographs, preferring action shots of her on horseback, playing tennis, and water-skiing. Cornelia promoted the book on television, including the *700 Club, Tomorrow, Mike Douglas,* and *Dinah Shore* programs. Though advanced press promised the book would "make some news with some of its revelations," it was more style and glitz than substance.[61]

Her business savvy was not rooted in academic knowledge but in an inherent urge for self-promotion. The book was sold at Wallace presidential rallies, even though George—despite claims that he was an unofficial editor—was largely uninvolved. Her publisher, A. J. Holman, a division of J. B. Lippincott, sought access to the Richard Viguerie–produced campaign mailing list to spur sales. Cornelia also made overtures about producing her own line of tennis clothes. In contemplation of kick-starting a recording career, she ordered sheet music of the most popular musicians of the time including Peter Frampton and John Denver. Her youthful and attractive appearance—she was photographed driving a NASCAR pace car and flying in a jet fighter—offered a striking contrast to her husband's wheelchair-bound image.[62]

Cornelia always made for good copy. She told reporter Lloyd Shearer that Wallace initially cautioned her against marrying him. "You don't want to marry me," she recalled Wallace telling her during their 1970 courtship. "Someday I'll be in a wheelchair." According to Shearer's report in *Parade Magazine,* Cornelia was undeterred: "That wouldn't bother me because I'm looking for a man who can't get away." While this story seemed heartwarming, other public comments in the same article seemed disjointed. Cornelia claimed her husband was shot as part of a conspiracy, even though little evidence for one existed. "I think that while Bremer was staying at the Waldorf-Astoria Hotel in New York," she claimed, "someone with strong telepathic [*sic*] tuned in on him, maybe two or three rooms away, and sent strong thought waves out which said, 'Arthur Bremer, you're very sick, very sick, very sick. George Wallace is making you sick. If you want to be well again, you must get rid of George Wallace.'"[63]

Cornelia suffered from her own cavalcade of health issues, battling headaches, persistent hay fever, kidney infections, abdominal bleeding, and painful reactions to oral contraceptives as an adult after enduring malaria as a child. As a result, she scheduled frequent medical tests and scheduled a variety of medical and dental appointments for the children. At one point, Cornelia requested that the entire mansion staff be tested for tuberculosis. Despite regular warnings from her physicians to stop smoking, Cornelia struggled with quitting. At times, her cravings became so intense that she fired off memoranda to the mansion staff, demanding they go to the store to pick up cartons of Benson and Hedges Menthols or Salem Long Lights. Even though she was a size six, at least one of her physicians counseled her to take a rigorous exercise program more seriously in order to build endurance. And at least one physician who reviewed her medical records was not convinced her maladies were entirely pathological. "She did have some upper GI [gastrointestinal] complaints," William Ferrante observed, "which subsided after she settled some domestic problems."[64]

Lurleen Wallace had used a light touch with the mansion staff, often preferring to do much of the cooking and cleaning herself. In contrast, Cornelia was much more demanding, wanting even the slightest request followed to exact detail, though she was rarely interested in assisting in the completion of the daily chores. "Please keep Wesson oil, gallon size, in the kitchen," she ordered the kitchen staff. "Also keep a large bottle of Crisco oil. The spinach was not right. See if you can get some American spinach." She could be equally adamant about precise performance of laundering duties: "Please wash the table napkins by themselves. Do not wash them with any of the clothes as they are coming back to the table smelling like body odor. Also do not put them in the dryer with any other clothes." On another occasion she sent a directive that a "chrome two-prong hook" be mounted in the guest house bathroom "in the center of the door exactly five feet from the floor." While this sort of persnickety behavior might be expected to surface now and again over seven years in the mansion, all of the preceding examples took place within a month of each other, along with requests to separate her leopard housecoat and summer clothes from her winter wardrobe, return a bathing suit to a store, and go to the store to pick up fingernail polish remover. Cornelia's relationship with the staff is best illustrated by a terse memo she sent in 1976 to all mansion employees: "The sign in the elevator and at the top of the stairs still applies: do not come to the second floor unless you have called and gotten permission first."[65]

Cornelia's idiosyncracies would have been tolerated easily by the family had she been more interested in being an attentive mother figure for the young Lee Wallace. It is, of course, a physical impossibility to be in two places at one time, and Cornelia's preference was to be in the middle of the action, not supervising homework and playing with the children. On at least one occasion, Cornelia directed a memorandum to the "trooper who picks children up after school this afternoon," indicating a minimal level of involvement in the daily care of Lee and her two boys, Jim and Josh.[66]

Equally frustrating to some family members and the staff was Cornelia's expectation that staff members would perform duties most Alabama children did for themselves. "Please get Mary Black and Strawberry to go through Jim and Josh's closets. I am thoroughly disgusted with the way their clothes are being kept. Their Sunday suits are not matched up with the pants, ties, or shirts. Their shoes and closets are filthy and are not organized a all. . . . I expect the closets and drawers to be perfectly straight when I check them Monday afternoon." All over Alabama, mothers had similar complaints about the rooms and closets and dresser drawers of their children. Yet those women directed their maternal wrath at their children, expecting them to clean up the mess. "No one unpacked my suitcase or my dirty clothes," she moaned on another occasion, "even my dry cleaning from the hanging bag." Given her love of clothes—the family had several charge accounts at Montgomery department stores, which often meant making only minimum payments or receiving late notices—unpacking Cornelia's luggage could be quite a chore.[67]

Considering Wallace's failed presidential bid and the mounting stress in the family from their personal differences in age and expectations, it is little wonder that the marriage disintegrated. George had suggested to Cornelia that they quietly divorce after the shooting, though no indication exists that she considered it. But by September 1977, the marriage was in tatters—evidence exists that the couple had not shared a bedroom in years—and Cornelia moved out. Both filed separately for divorce within three days. Rumors swirled that Cornelia had retained noted attorney F. Lee Bailey, though he did not take the case. As the divorce trial loomed, Cornelia spent eight days at St. Margaret's Hospital for what her physician and attorney described as "mental and physical exhaustion." Wallace claimed that his second wife had bugged his telephone. Cornelia later admitted to recording his conversations, which she said included illicit discussions between the governor and former love interests. For his part, Wallace claimed that Cornelia had been engaged in a series of affairs with state troopers.[68]

When word of the tapes leaked out, an angry Wallace attempted spin control to no avail. "There were some tapes," the governor allowed, "and a device. That's all that was involved. No one has been harmed. No one has been hurt. This happened in my bedroom between me and my wife. What happens between me and my wife, as long as it doesn't affect the State of Alabama or my service as governor, remains between my wife and myself." According to Dan Carter, the governor's aides collected hundreds of tapes and deposited them in the Alabama River. A decade earlier, word of the tapes might have remained out of the newspapers. But with journalism's impact on exploding the inconsistencies of the Vietnam War and the unraveling of the Watergate mess, newspaper reporters had a stronger sense of mission. And this story was just too juicy to resist.[69]

The specter of a trial with loads of unflattering gossip leaking into the press threatened to publicly embarrass both Wallaces. A settlement was announced ten minutes before the morning of the trial. Cornelia received a $75,000 alimony payment—roughly one-third of Wallace's net worth of $209,000—a lot on Lake Martin, and most of the gifts given to the couple during their seven years of marriage. A *Montgomery Advertiser* editorial speculated that the agreement was cobbled together when Wallace feared Cornelia's attorneys would investigate his brother Gerald. In his office at the capitol with a picture of Cornelia on the wall, the governor resisted efforts by reporters to delve into the messy details: "I think both of us preferred to settle the matter rather than having all of you folks looking into our personal and private matters."[70]

After the divorce, Cornelia attempted to launch an entertainment career. "I'm going to work," the new divorcée announced. "I don't know exactly what I'm going to do, but people will be seeing a lot more of me from now on." She traveled to Plains, Georgia, to meet with Billy Carter who later introduced her to his agent, Tandy Rice. Cornelia and Rice floated a number of possibilities for her future: commercials, acting in television and movie productions, her own talk show, another book, and modeling. Rice admitted he was not quite sure of Cornelia's talents, characterizing her simply as a "media happening." She managed to make an appearance on *Good Morning America,* but could not make much headway on a career as a celebrity.[71]

With nothing left to do, Cornelia launched a brief campaign for governor. Her official paperwork was filed fifteen minutes before the deadline. "Three years ago," she declared, "there was a lot of talk about my running for governor, but like everyone else, I was disillusioned by it [politics] and I wanted to get away from it." In a moment of complete honesty, Cornelia told reporters one of her reasons for seeking the highest office in the state was that she did not have "a rich husband or a father to support me." Evidence suggests, however, that Cornelia had begun another relationship. "I always like being with you," she confided in her journal of an unknown paramour. "You give me a lot of pleasure that you are unaware of. I hope we can see each other from time to time." Another entry implied the relationship was progressing: "You were presumptuous in assuming I wanted a commitment from you. I am not ready for that at this time. Everything in my life needs to be free flowing, non-binding, and non-restrictive."[72]

Cornelia informed reporters that her uncle, former governor Jim Folsom, had encouraged her to run and that the current governor of Alabama had offered her some political advice: change her name on the ballot to Mrs. George C. Wallace. "We agreed it would increase my vote," Cornelia chirped. "This may be the last time George Wallace's name appears on the ballot in Alabama and it is a fitting tribute to the man I was married to for seven years." As for his endorsement of her candidacy, Folsom was unequivocal: "She's a damned liar." A month after starting the comical fling at politics, Cornelia withdrew, citing reneged financial commitments as her undoing: "I am running this campaign at my own personal expense and to continue without the help of friends who have not fulfilled their obligations for financial contributions to me, places a hardship on me." With a handful of brief exceptions, Cornelia then slipped out of the public eye.[73]

Senator Wallace?

With his professional and personal life coming apart at the seams, Wallace was left with only one option: campaign. Campaigning was the only part of Wallace's life that was comforting. The roar of an Alabama crowd, the admiration of throngs of well-wishers clamoring to shake his hand, and the sense that all eyes were fixed on him were the one true addiction in Wallace's life. The racial animus—part Deep South socialization and part political opportunism—were just means to an end. The workaday world of department meetings, ceremonial functions, and tussles with the legislature were nothing more than distractions to be tolerated. Campaigning was all that George Wallace had left. "I'm leaning toward running for the U.S. Senate in 1978," the governor told scribes in the aftermath of Carter's defeat of Ford. "That's not to say I'm announcing, but I certainly lean in that direction."[74]

Parsing through the tangle of precampaign statements of George Wallace can be an exhausting chore. In nearly every campaign beginning in 1966, Wallace claimed he would not run, he might run, he was considering running, he was examining his options, he had yet to consider whether he was running, he was leaning toward running, he was too busy to think about running, and he would not rule out running, And then, of course, he would announce that he was a candidate. The 1978 Senate campaign was no different in its genesis.

But Wallace's grip on the state's voters was more tenuous than at any time since 1958. Several factors account for Wallace's declining popularity. His control over the legislature had been virtually nonexistent since 1971. Eight campaigns from 1962 to 1976 had convinced many Alabamians that it was time for someone else to govern who was interested in performing the actual duties of the office and not jetting around the country trying to get other men's jobs. And Alabamians, in light of rising unemployment, inflation, and interest rates, and continuing federal court orders, were beginning to question whether the governor was making much of a difference. Wallace brushed aside suggestions that his divorce would hurt him politically. But for some Alabamians who grew up listening to Wallace badger judges and rivals about their alleged moral relativism and situational ethics, the messy separation and divorce mattered. Most importantly, the Alabama polity had real reservations about whether Wallace was physically capable of performing the work.[75]

The governor's approval rating among likely Alabama voters slipped to 48 percent, with a disapproval rating that was up to 38 percent and climbing. A poll commissioned by the governor summarized his uphill climb to be elected in 1978. "Obvious weaknesses, in addition to health, are his length of service in office, his lack of empathy for youth, women, and blacks and a feeling on the part of some voters that he is not completely to be trusted." For the campaign, the fact that Wallace was no longer viewed in Alabama as someone who could be trusted was particularly damaging. For his entire political career, he had made a point of telling Alabamians that he represented their values, their beliefs, and their traditions. He had reminded them at every touchdown of his plane in Montgomery that they, the rank-and-file working-class Alabama citizens, were just as cultured, just as smart, just as refined, and just as good as anybody in the country. If Alabamians were no longer soothed by Wallace's appeals to their feelings of inferiority, then the governor was in real trouble. A decade after the civil rights tumult subsided, outsiders still did not think much of Alabama, and some Alabamians were ready to begin changing that image. A survey commissioned by the state Democratic Party revealed that 50.7 percent of Alabama voters agreed that "Alabama state politics is pretty corrupt."[76]

Looking deeper, the poll identified a number of key changes. In previous years, Wallace had performed remarkably well on election day with Alabama women. But by the late 1970s, the female Alabama electorate had begun to shift. Wallace's token appointments of women and his criticism of abortion and the Equal Rights Amendment did not attract younger women to him. Though Wallace was usually well versed in poll numbers, his stance against the ERA ran counter to a state Democratic Party survey that indicated 64.7 percent of state voters approved of the proposed amendment. A decade earlier, when politicians were still considered celebrities and Wallace was the virtual equivalent of a rock star, young voters and children had flocked to his rallies. But by 1978 Wallace was a debilitated middle-aged man, and politics was more likely to bore young people than excite them. To the youngest voting demographic, he was just another old politician that their parents cared about but they did not. "The race for the U.S. Senate promises to be a tough uphill battle for Governor George Wallace," the poll assessed, "who appears to be politically vulnerable at this point in time." Another poll, this one conducted among University of Alabama students, indicated Howell Heflin, not the governor, was the preferred choice of Capstone students.[77]

Heflin offered Wallace his stiffest competition since the 1970 gubernatorial primary against Albert Brewer. The giant Tuscumbia native had been elected Alabama supreme court chief justice in 1970 and had worked feverishly to modernize the state's archaic court system. Heflin had organized a Citizens Conference for judicial reform while president of the State Bar Association. That body produced a rough blueprint for change that would create some uniform standards for state and local courts. "We had too many little laws," Justice Hugh Maddox recalled; "we had no uniform rules of procedure. Every little court had it's own rules, myriads of rules." Alabama had suffered the opprobrium of the national legal community when the state's quickie divorce mill—it was easier for a couple, and more lucrative for state lawyers, to get a divorce in Alabama than anywhere else in the country—was exposed. After beating former governor John Patterson in 1970, Heflin began to take steps to implement reform including creation of a Department of Court Management, reducing the lengthy backlog of cases on the docket, and eventually, revising the judicial article in the state constitution. Heflin's reputation had been quietly built on change, not preserving a status quo hardened by the traditions and memories of a distant past.[78]

Heflin declined a chance to run for reelection in 1976, indicating that he had plans for either a gubernatorial or senatorial bid in 1978. With Jere Beasley and Bill Baxley angling for the governor's office, and Albert Brewer contemplating another bid, Heflin focused on a Senate seat. After visiting John Sparkman in Washington, Heflin emerged from the meeting content that the state's senior senator would not run again. Heflin's early polls revealed a sizable lead for Wallace—45 percent to 17—but also suggested that the governor's support was capped at 45 percent and could drop quickly under the right circumstances. The governor's own poll placed the race much closer, 41 percent to 36, with much of his support coming from the state's union members and working poor. Heflin succeeded in raising money from the AFL-CIO and other labor organizations, another ominous sign for Wallace. In addition, the governor raised only $85,987 in the first quarter of 1978, a figure that was substantially less than Heflin's $210,992.[79]

At a National Governor's Conference in Washington D.C., Wallace confessed that his star was not shining as brightly as before. "I'm not the main attraction anymore," the governor noted to those scribes still drawn to him. "[California governor Jerry] Brown's running for president. I got knocked out of it in Maryland." Reporters noted a clear difference in the two years since the last presidential campaign had ended. The governor's increasingly poor hearing was the most noticeable change. "He was like an old man," one congressional staffer observing the conference proceedings confided. More than a few athletes continued to enter the arena when they should have gracefully retired. Muhammad Ali, arguably the greatest boxer of all time, lost decisions to Leon Spinks in 1978 and Trevor Berbick in 1981—lesser lights that he would have dispatched quickly in his prime. Johnny Unitas, arguably the greatest quarterback in history, limped to his finish line, throwing only ten touchdown passes versus twenty-two interceptions over the final three seasons of his great career. In the same vein, perhaps Wallace, as much a competitor in his sport if not as accomplished as either Ali or Unitas, continued when he should have devoted his remaining years to repairing relationships with family and friends.[80]

Speculation in Alabama as early as mid-April suggested that Wallace would bow out of the Senate race. Rumors suggested that Wallace would accept an endowed chair at the University of Alabama, write a book, or hit the lecture circuit to create a retirement nest egg, something he had never shown much interest in. A number of factors created this conjecture. Though the administration attempted to keep the governor's medical condition out of the spotlight, Wallace battled recurrent urinary tract infections, was hospitalized for a broken leg, had major hearing and vision problems, and maintained limited working hours. While the wheelchair made it impossible for Wallace to be beaten in the 1974 gubernatorial race, it had proven to be a major impediment to voters in 1976. A 1978 poll indicated that Alabama voters were concerned that Wallace was too frail for another elected office: "If he hopes to win, he must conduct a massive campaign and organizational effort, dissuading many voters from the belief that newer, younger, healthier candidates can better serve Alabama in the U.S. Senate."[81]

Another major factor was Wallace's reluctance to relocate to Washington, D.C. Though he promised reporters that he would earn instant seniority in the Senate because of his name and reputation, the reality was that Wallace would be but one of a hundred senators. And senators spent most days performing the sort of activities that Wallace had so detested as governor: staff meetings, issues analysis, caucuses, committee assignments, party functions, and crafting policy. The workday of a senator was incongruent with Wallace's interests and his skill set. Combined with the reality of learning a new city, finding an apartment or house that could meet his special needs, and being eight hundred miles from Montgomery, a life in Washington, D.C., seemed like a lonely existence. Simply put, Wallace was interested in being elected senator from Alabama, but had no interest in being one.[82]

Another factor complicated Wallace's actions during the 1978 Senate race: whether he would continue to have the protection and care of two state troopers. The administration pressured the legislature to provide two full-time bodyguards for Wallace's use, a service expected to cost about two hundred thousand dollars per year when all expenses were totaled. Some press corps insiders had speculated that Wallace's interest in the Senate was primarily a ploy to have a paid staff at his beck and call. A *Montgomery Advertiser* editorial summarized why the troopers were so important to the governor: "Without those two troopers, Wallace would be a virtual invalid, lying in bed from dawn to dusk. Such a dreary existence would be a veritable seventh circle of Hell for a man of Wallace's unique temperament and needs." Alabama voters had mixed feelings about providing Wallace troopers after he left the governor's office. Some appreciated his years of service; others, less sympathetic, felt his paralysis had occurred during a personal campaign, not while conducting the duties of his office.[83]

It is also true that by April 1978 it was more likely that Wallace would lose, than win. On May 16, 1978, six years and a day after he was shot in Maryland, the governor bowed out of the Senate race, effectively retiring: "Having thought all day yesterday and last night and today, I want to make this announcement to you. I've decided, I will not be a candidate for the U.S. Senate. . . . Although I feel I could win the U.S. Senate seat, my conclusion in the last few days is to retire." Wallace offered no reason for quitting and advisor Elvin Stanton refuted suggestions, then and now, that health or fear of losing were motivating factors. A day after bowing out, Wallace was still opaque: "I just changed my mind. I decided I did not want to run. I could have won this seat. I have no doubt about that." Not surprisingly, Heflin did not believe Wallace: "I expect the possibility of losing a political race in his home state preyed on his mind, though he would never admit that he was afraid to lose." Whatever his reason for withdrawing from the race, some Alabamians claimed victory for Wallace anyway. "Governor Wallace is a very shrewd man," Walter Yarn wrote in a letter to the editor of the *Montgomery Advertiser,* "and I personally feel that he used this senate race to obtain lifetime protection from the State of Alabama. Outwitting the legislators on Capitol Hill is nothing new for Governor Wallace, but there again, look at what he has to outwit."[84]

The entire exit from the Senate race against Heflin would have been more graceful had the governor been consistent in the month after bowing out. On June 1, 1978, Jim Allen—former lieutenant governor under Wallace in his first term and the junior senator from Alabama—died suddenly from a heart attack. As a matter of law, Governor Wallace was charged with appointing an interim senator until a special election could be held. The best time for the special election would be during the looming general election. In other words, Wallace suddenly had another Senate seat opening to ponder for himself. Speculation was rampant, including a wild scenario in which Wallace would resign and new governor Jere Beasley would appoint him to fill Allen's vacant seat. What remained clear once the rumormongering subsided was that Wallace was seriously considering running for Allen's seat, no matter who was appointed to fill it. "It seems," aide Billy Joe Camp rationalized, "the people of Alabama have realized more and more that come January they will not have an experienced voice in the U.S. Senate." Qualifying papers were drafted.[85]

Maryon Allen, Senator Allen's widow, made it clear that she wanted to be appointed to the position. Wallace complied. After considering a run for the seat for another thirteen days, Wallace again announced he would not be a candidate. "This does not mean that I am retiring from politics," the governor asserted, though he seemingly had. "I expect to remain active for years to come and will continue my interest and my concerns that affect Alabama and the nation." For the first time since 1962, George Wallace would not be a candidate in the primary or general election of a major Alabama political campaign. And just to make sure Alabamians were thoroughly confused as to whether he was retired or not, Wallace denied, as he had done before, that he would be a candidate. He told reporters that he would never run for elective office in Alabama again. The governor even termed speculation that he might run in 1982 "just silliness."[86]

Even without Wallace, the election season of 1978 was a raucous one. With all the attention focused on Attorney General Bill Baxley, former governor Albert Brewer, and Lieutenant Governor Jere Beasley, Fob James came from the back of the pack to win the governor's race. Most of the administration backed Baxley; George Jr. actively worked for the attorney general's campaign and Wallace publicly endorsed Baxley in the runoff against James. While Wallace could not get Baxley elected, he did manage to throw Beasley to the political curb, something the governor and his staff pointed to with pride. A reflective Beasley reached out to Wallace, hoping to salvage a strained relationship born of two politicians with sizable egos and substantial ambition. "Now that I'm going back to private life," Beasley handwrote in a letter to Wallace, "there is no reason why we can't be friends. . . . I accept my part of the blame for this that I am due. I sincerely tried to work with you and wanted to do so. . . . I hope that our families can be friends in the future." Wallace remained distant from Beasley until the final years of his life.[87]

Wallace endorsed James for the general election, which the former Auburn football player won easily. "Fob you're going to make the best governor Alabama ever had," Wallace announced on election night, "and that's saying a lot because I haven't been so bad myself." In a carefully worded letter sent as he prepared to leave office, Wallace pledged to support his replacement: "Whatever small part I, as a citizen, can play in helping you, I will be happy to do so. You have only to call upon me. I usually am not at a loss of words to express myself but it is . . . difficult to adequately describe my true feelings concerning your attitude toward me and the kindnesses shown by you and your family." As he prepared for inauguration, James promised to turn to Wallace for advice.[88]

End of the Road, Part 1

Wallace's final months in office were surprisingly effective. After being pushed around by the legislature for most of the term, Wallace called the solons into special session five weeks before the primary to consider property tax legislation. In bluster reminiscent of the early 1960s, Wallace dared the legislators not to pass his package of bills: "If anybody wants to call my hand on this tonight, I may just go out before the people of Alabama and tell them who you are." If the property tax lid bill—legislation designed to slash homeowner rates and cap tax rates on certain property—failed to pass, Wallace promised some "political funerals on September 5." The entire package passed in a few days with only minor cosmetic changes.[89]

While the last special session of the third elected term featured some of the old trademark Wallace power, it was the governor's continued commitment to spinal cord patients that served as his best accomplishment. "The State of Alabama, like most other states," Wallace wrote early in 1975, "has not done all that it should have done over the years for these miserable people, but I propose to correct that in the next session of our legislature." He did. The Alabama Program for Spinal Cord Injuries provided home care, medical equipment and supplies, transportation, and home modification for quadriplegic and paraplegic Alabamians. Low-income patients were targeted for admission into the program. Given the legislature's well-deserved reputation for disinterest in the state's most vulnerable citizens, it is nearly impossible to imagine this program touching as many lives as it did without the impetus of George Wallace. The George C. Wallace Urology Rehabilitation and Research Center was created at UAB to study the unique bladder function problems of spinal cord patients.[90]

Wallace testified frequently or sent written statements to private and governmental groups concerned with the plight of homebound patients. His testimony was often heartfelt. "It strikes me," Wallace told a congressional subcommittee considering an appropriation for regeneration research, "that this entire field is ready to be ignited if only we can appreciate what opportunities exist scientifically as to what is involved for the nation in terms of cost. I strikes me that this sum is quite modest. Frankly when I see other fields like cancer research receive considerably over one hundred times as much as paraplegia research, I have to ask myself, 'Do people really understand what it's like to be a paraplegic?' "[91]

And Wallace did more than just start a program. He personally intervened in a number of instances to help paralysis victims through letters, telephone calls, visits, and using his contacts to arrange for services. "As you may know," Wallace wrote Reba Thompson, "I too, have been unable to walk for some time. Since my injury, I believe that I am more conscious of the infirmities of others. And this, I strongly believe—we can rise above such physical limitations with God's love and the care and concern of our families and friends." Wallace, though he battled his own depression, was particularly dynamic when it came to encouraging young victims of spinal cord injuries to forge through the adversity and create a meaningful life despite the paralysis. "Younger people," the governor wrote to a parent of a spinal cord injury patient, "seem to have more stamina and strength and make a better comeback than some of us who are older. Certainly there is no reason to expect that he does not have a bright future ahead of him and that he can make many rewarding contributions to society and his [fellow men]."[92]

For many paraplegics, Wallace was an inspiration. "I fell and broke my back in three places, lower lumbar 1-2-3," Alvin McConnell wrote to the governor. "I have no use of my bowels or kidneys. I am taking drugs by the bushels, but it doesn't seem to help too much. Won't you please tell me what you do for pain. I see you on t.v. and admire you very much for your courage. I ask myself, 'Is it worth living? . . . . Won't you answer my letter? It may give me a little encouragement to go on living." It is impossible to assess how much encouragement Wallace was able to provide. But given the physical and emotional challenges facing paralysis victims, a phone call, letter, or visit from a famous person in a similar predicament must have provided some measure of comfort.[93]

Continuing his work for spinal cord patients seemed a natural fit for Wallace as he prepared to leave the governor's office. He agreed to become director of development for Rehabilitation Resources at UAB, a position that would allow him to use his contacts to raise money for the hospital where he had received so much care after returning to Alabama. "I know that I will be working in an area of great interest and concern to me," he said in a news release, "and I feel I can make a meaningful contribution." A new home in Montgomery was built to better care for his special needs. The mansion staff completed an inventory of personal items as Wallace wanted to begin moving boxes to his new home and office as early as August 1978. Letters of support poured in from around the country from people as disparate as presidential advisor Hamilton Jordan and actor David Soul of *Starsky and Hutch* fame.[94]

As the calendar turned and Fob James took the oath of office, fifty-nine-year-old George Wallace, private citizen, prepared to chart a new course away from the world of politics. He had no firm plans save the position at UAB and an agreement to lead a tour through the Holy Land with anyone willing to pay $1,295 to join him. A reflective Wallace took stock of the experiences of the past sixteen years. "[Race] was not the intention of the whole matter in the first place," he stated of the contentious era he dominated. "It was the government we were fighting. It wasn't a fight against black people. . . . Segregation is over and it's better that it is over . . . and it's not coming back." According to the *Birmingham News,* Wallace was another thing that was not coming back. In their year-end review, the newspaper characterized the governor as "retiring from political life." As smart as their writers and editors were, they should have known to never say never when it came to George Wallace and politics.[95]

11
The Last Campaign / 1982–1987

While 1978 closed without the satisfying feeling of winning an election, the new year came with none of the typical encumbrances for George Wallace. Gone was the responsibility of navigating through the swarms of federal court orders. As a former governor, Wallace had no need to huddle with floor leaders or plot an administration legislative package. No appointments needed to be made and no department meetings were on the schedule. Reporters found Fob James's transition to power more appealing than keeping pace with his predecessor. Wallace had been kicked off the front page.

Wallace occupied his time with his fund-raising position at UAB and by offering occasional lectures there and at Auburn University at Montgomery. His standard of living was comfortable; between his salary at UAB and perquisites created by the legislature for his unofficial position as "governor's councillor," Wallace made in excess of $86,000 per year. This was more money than Wallace had ever made in his life, and more than enough to live on comfortably, particularly since he had so few nonmedical expenses. The AUM lectures paid a handsome $500 per day, though a *Montgomery Advertiser* report suggested Wallace was only compensated for eighteen such appearances. According to a partial listing of 1979 financial records, the former governor's biggest monthly living expenditure may have been the purchase of his trademark cigars. Total state cost for Wallace, including security, office space, essentials, and a staff of six troopers, right-hand man Elvin Stanton, and two secretaries, was approximately $350,000 per year. Coming off the breakneck pace of nine campaigns since 1962—including the aborted 1978 senatorial race—the slower pace would have been a welcome relief to many politicians closing in on their sixtieth birthday. But Wallace was not content to slip quietly off to political retirement. Though the burdens of governance were gone, so was the stimulation of raw, retail politics, Wallace's raison d'être. Over the course of the first four-year term in two decades without access to power, Wallace grew increasingly depressed, lost physical strength, and became more isolated. By 1982, friends and associates were eager to get Wallace back into electoral politics, convinced his deteriorating health and spirits would be buoyed by a new campaign.[1]

Elvin Stanton who remained a trusted associate and employee of Wallace during the interregnum period of 1979 to 1982 witnessed the change in Wallace firsthand. "Those were really three of the hardest years that George Wallace ever faced . . . being out of office and not being in the spotlight. Any governor or politician who is defeated or quits . . . the faucet turns off . . . and there is no drip, drip after that. . . . The rush is gone but it happens instantaneously." For a time, Wallace used contacts with the Carter administration to land some federal grants for UAB, though the work never interested him much.[2]

Part of the reason a new campaign could even be considered was because of the general ineffectiveness of Fob James. The former Republican-turned-Democrat—he later reversed course yet again and returned to the GOP—overcame endorsements of his opponents by luminaries including Wallace and Bear Bryant to defeat more celebrated figures Bill Baxley, Albert Brewer, and Jere Beasley. But governing was another matter, and James lacked administrative skills and had little interest in the protocol and patience associated with steering legislation into law. On paper, James seemed like a southern governor straight out of central casting. Carrying a family name fashioned from Confederate icons Nathan Bedford Forrest and John Bell Hood, Forrest Hood James had been a college football star at Auburn and served in the army. With his father and a family friend, James created Diversified Products, a sporting goods company whose major product line consisted of plastic barbells and dumbbells. By the time the company was sold in 1977, James had become a wealthy man and his liquidity allowed for an extensive media campaign in the 1978 primary. James, the dark horse, ran away from the field, placing first in the primary, winning the runoff by a large margin, and crushing Republican Guy Hunt—himself a future governor—in the general election.[3]

Popularity at the polls and a splashy inaugural theme—James promised a New Beginning—do not necessarily translate into gubernatorial success. With every James administration victory—better federal relations, appointment of blacks into more prominent government posts—came several defeats including failure to pass much of his agenda of constitutional reform, home rule, and unearmarking of state funds. And James could be his own worst enemy. He failed, unbelievably, to sign a package of twenty-five crime bills passed by the legislature within the ten-day period provided by law. Worn down by the mud and the blood of governance, James, extremely unpopular after declaring a 15 percent proration, declined to run for reelection in 1982. "What you saw tonight," a WSFA editorial by Bob Ingram noted of James's announcement that he was staying out of the fray, "is the stuff of which history is made. An incumbent governor, a governor with a stronger constituency than some of you might realize, one who could legally seek a second term if he desired, who said thanks, but no thanks. No politician worthy of the name would ever have made such a decision but whoever said Fob James was a politician." As governor, James's intentions may have been noble, but he was unable to overcome the legions of special interest groups that dominated Alabama politics and unwilling to practice the political art of compromise. Even James's sympathetic biographer dubbed him "perhaps the most stubborn man who has held the office of governor in Alabama."[4]

Ingram's editorial inadvertently summarized one of the major differences between James and Wallace. While neither were especially productive at policy, Wallace could instinctively turn any piece of bad news into a political opportunity. James had no such éclat. James was even wont to blame himself for state problems, something Wallace would never have done. "That's not a money problem, that's a management problem," he admitted concerning the state's funding shortfall. "I'm the problem, because I couldn't get the unearmarking and fringe benefit package passed." James's travails, the moribund Alabama economy, and the encouragement of numerous friends and previous associates made Wallace reconsider political retirement and wage one last campaign. "Actually Fob James elected George Wallace the last term," Stanton posited. "People would come to visit the [former] governor . . . three years later and were saying 'George we really need you back in there. You know what we got up there [as governor] we can't live with that."[5]

Two plus decades after first winning office, Wallace's last campaign seems replete with a host of symbolism. Only a run for governor could lift the sagging spirits and broken body of the state's most recognizable politician. Campaigning was lifeblood to Wallace in ways that family and faith and sense of place were to other Alabamians. That his last race was for governor, not president, typifies Wallace's lasting impact as a political figure. Though he was surely influential in national politics, it remains a mathematical fact that in four races for the presidency, Wallace garnered a total of forty-six electoral college votes. Though Jimmy Carter traded on the Wallace name in 1976, no other serious candidate considered Wallace mainstream enough to embrace him as part of a national campaign. Wallace was a part of the supporting cast that realigned national politics—collapse of the New Deal Democratic coalition, the migration of much of the white South to the Republican Party, ascendancy of the New Right—but he was the main attraction in an Alabama political drama whose effects continue to be felt today. Alabama's political culture, as the state surveys the first decade of the twenty-first century is typified by an outdated constitution, a legislative process dominated by special interests, a reluctance to embrace change, a frightening level of inefficiency, an economy generally

ranked in the bottom 10 percent of all states, antagonism for the federal government, and ample contempt for those who think the current schools, tax
system, and intellectual climate could be improved. And while George Wallace
is not responsible for the creation of all these political machinations and characteristics, each of them became more entrenched, more accepted, and more
resistant to reform because of a quarter century of Wallaceism.[6]

The last campaign would also provide one final attempt for Wallace to cull
a positive legacy for himself. Upon leaving office in January 1979, Wallace announced his greatest achievements were the junior college system, the growth
of industry in Alabama, and the more subjective plaudit that "everybody is
saying [now] the things I was saying." And while he hoped Alabamians would
remember fondly the raises in teacher salaries and his wife's interest in mental
health, ordinary folks in Eutaw, Guntersville, and Enterprise were more likely
to recall the stand in the schoolhouse door, the protracted cussin' at the federal
government, and quite possibly the refrain from the first inaugural: "segregation now, segregation tomorrow, segregation forever."

Given that de jure segregation was finished and de facto segregation increasingly rare, Wallace, if he could win another term, had one last opportunity
to reshape himself in the image he first cast as a legislator—compassionate,
benevolent, and interested in the state's working-class families. He had one
last campaign to convince Alabamians he had been a good governor. In his
1983 inaugural program, Wallace touted his first gubernatorial term as "an
era of progress unequaled in Alabama history." In the same publication, Wallace claimed credit for unprecedented industrial development; low unemployment and property taxes; free textbooks; the growth of the state's community colleges, technical schools, and universities; obtaining federal funds for
the Tennessee-Tombigbee waterway; and turning tourism into a $1 billion a
year economic juggernaut. Campaign advertising in 1982 reflected this sentiment. "What we do need is George Wallace as governor again," one spot read.
"He is a compassionate man who understands the needs of the average working man and woman. He cares about *all* our people—young and old, rich and
poor, black and white."[7]

Caring for those people and crafting a public policy designed to mitigate
the troubles in their lives was sure to be no easy task. State funds were stretched
so perilously thin that some analysts suggested as many as sixty thousand
teachers would have to be laid off in 1983. And the government could expect
less revenue than in fiscal year 1982. "Every school system in this state will have
fewer education personnel next year unless the economy improves," Education Superintendent Wayne Teague predicted. Nearly 20 percent of the state's
128 local school systems needed to borrow money just to provide the basic services required to complete the school year. And apparently all the sound and

fury of the previous decades of industrial development press releases signified nothing. State retirement director David Bronner suggested Alabama's industrial climate "was in the worst shape they've been in since the Depression." One long-range budget estimate for 1984–85 projected basic appropriation needs of $729,597,592 and expected revenues of $475,061,071, a 35 percent shortfall. After seeing comprehensive assessments of how inflation, interest rates, unemployment, and declining tax revenues were effecting the Alabama economy, Wallace admitted in correspondence that the problems were "monumental.... As one with many years of experience in state government, I cannot recall a time in our past when any legislature has been confronted with more problems than the members of the 1983 legislature." In late February, months before the official campaign began, unemployment in Alabama reached 14.7 percent.[8]

It is a curious thing that southerners can do two seemingly contradictory things and think nothing of the dichotomy. It seems a historical surety that many of the same southerners dancing and catting at the honky-tonks on Saturday night were filling pews on Sunday morning. The most religious region of the country was also the place most likely to witness disputes being settled through violence. Lovers' quarrels and romantic triangles, sociologist John Shelton Reed has documented through FBI statistics, are twice as likely to result in murder in the South than elsewhere in the country. One might aptly term this curious phenomenon of inconsistencies Southern Confusion Syndrome and document it in any of a thousand ways. For Wallace, claiming credit for creating a robust Alabama economy during his previous terms, while bemoaning the horrible condition of Alabama industry and employment as he campaigned to be returned to his old job is a classic case of Southern Confusion Syndrome. If Wallace had created so many meaningful jobs for Alabamians could they have all disappeared so quickly under the weight of the James administration? Could all of Wallace's vaunted industrial development and his carefully constructed image of Alabama as a business-friendly environment have evaporated so soon? If Wallace had been such an economic magnet as governor, why was the state continuing to wallow far below the national average in most economic indices? Wallace's contrasts, both boastful and mournful at the same time, seem striking today, but it did not seem to bother many Alabamians who eagerly embraced rumors of another campaign.[9]

Economic malaise notwithstanding, Wallace and some advisors began making plans as early as the fall of 1981 for him to run. After a meeting with administration veterans and a few stalwart donors at the Holiday Inn East in Montgomery, Wallace agreed to test the waters by commissioning a poll. Woody Anderson, Jimmy Faulkner, and a few other friends provided some working capital to pay for the polling, which indicated that the governor's health was not as significant a factor in the minds of Alabama voters as previously believed. Perhaps sensing Wallace was preparing to unseat him, James fired an occasional barb at his predecessor before officially announcing he would not seek a second term: "When I entered office I found a state government that didn't care about the taxpayers, about the schoolchildren, about you, about poor people. Nepotism, cronyism, buddyism were rampant. I found a big bully that was the system itself." While James's points had some validity, his popularity had crashed so precipitously that few paid attention. Wallace began quietly raising money, holding periodic meetings, and discussing the best ways possible to court black voters. The 1982 competition promised to be formidable with Lieutenant Governor George McMillan, Bill Baxley, and Speaker Joe McCorquodale all contemplating entering the fray, and Emory Folmar, the conservative Republican mayor of Montgomery, likely awaiting the Democratic primary winner in the general election. McQuorquodale and McMillan had developed particularly potent power bases during James's term.[10]

The possibility of running another race for governor clearly energized Wallace emotionally, though initially he had to be talked into it. Wallace continued to cite his age and injuries when admirers came to call and asked him to enter the race. George Jr. compared his father to Winston Churchill, telling him that he was too young to retire. "I'd say," George Jr. recalled years later, "it sounds like to me they want you to run for governor again. . . . You are younger than Churchill when he made his comeback. I used to give him that Churchill line and he always liked that. He would say, 'I am aren't I.'" Stanton recalled that Wallace was worried that one last run would be too much of an imposition on supporters who had gone to bat financially for the governor time and time again. Some trusted advisors had already cautioned Wallace not to run and risk losing the race and his reputation à la Jim Folsom. Over time, and like in 1958 and 1970 when a cautious Wallace needed regular pep talks, he came to believe he should run and he could win. "Wallace seems to be back in pretty good health," advertising executive John Hartsfield surmised, "and he's talking good. Somebody said that he's feeling good and he's talking good and he may run. Somebody else said 'You've got it backward: he's feeling good and talking good because he is running.'" Behind the scenes, fund-raising letters were mass mailed with the message a combination of the old fire and brimstone Wallace and the kinder, gentler Wallace of more recent vintage. "Alabama is a different place," the text of one form letter soliciting funds read. "When I say different I do not mean geography. I'm talking about the people, the very alive sense of the free enterprise system and belief in God that we have here in Alabama. I'm talking about the fact that we stood and fought for our rights while the liberals and intellectuals thumbed their noses at us." Son-in-law Jim Parsons served as campaign treasurer and organized a system of perquisites for donors including gold, silver, and bronze lapel pins, embossed membership cards, and opportunities to meet and greet the candidate himself.[11]

The year 1982 proved to be a pivotal one for two Alabama legends. As George Wallace prepared to step back on the stage for what would prove to be his last time, University of Alabama football coach Paul "Bear" Bryant decided to retire. As historian Andrew Doyle has noted, both Wallace and Bryant gave Alabamians reason to feel pride, but often with different outcomes: "George Wallace attracted headlines and stirred deep emotions, but he invariably lost his quixotic battles. Alabamians who had been given so few reasons to feel pride in their native state saw Paul Bryant as a warrior who turned those mere slogans into tangible flesh-and-blood reality." While neither championed racial change, Bryant's team played against integrated universities in bowl games as early as 1966 and eventually the Crimson Tide recruited black athletes. Alabama lore suggests Bryant told friends he would not be the first Southeastern Conference coach to recruit African American players, but would not be the third either, an indication he had no interest in becoming a pioneer but would not hold fast to white supremacy if it put him at a competitive disadvantage. Yet as great as Bryant's teams were on the gridiron in their glory years, he too had seemingly aged suddenly. His 1982 team lost three conference games—something not seen in twelve years—and even lost a nonconference game to Southern Mississippi. Despite his six official national championships—ardent Tide fans claim even more—Bryant announced he had "done a poor job of coaching."[12]

Wallace and Bryant were friendly, conversing occasionally on the telephone or in person when the governor attended Tide games or when the two attended the same charity event. Neither was especially easy on subordinates. Wallace chewed up staffers with demanding campaign schedules and rarely paused to say thank you. "It was assumed," Stanton recalled of the twenty-four-hour-a-day availability that Wallace expected, "if you signed on for the team, it's like being in the Army . . . you have a tour of duty and that comes first and you miss a lot of those things and a lot of families suffer." Bryant could be tough on assistant coaches, but players were more likely to tremble before his expectations. "I don't want ordinary people," Bryant bellowed; "I want people who are willing to sacrifice and do without a lot of those things ordinary students get to do. That's what it takes to win." Bryant's practices could be brutal, and especially early in his career, reporters and rival coaches considered Bryant too aggressive and his teams too violent, even for a game defined by physicality and rough play.[13]

As Bryant turned the coaching reins over to a former player, Ray Perkins, only to die less than a year later, George Wallace prepared to enter the political ring again. Wallace accepted a few speaking engagements in order to gauge his comfort level with the Alabama body politic. Another engagement was in the offing as well. Lisa Taylor, a platinum blond former model and television commercial actress, became the third Mrs. George Wallace in 1981, capping a long if unusual courtship. The couple first met when Lisa teamed with her sister Mona and appeared at 1968 Wallace presidential rallies to perform their country music stylings as "Mona and Lisa." According to Wallace biographer Stephen Lesher, Taylor claimed to have fallen in love with Wallace in 1968. Wallace later told Lesher that Taylor called him shortly after his divorce from Cornelia was finalized in 1978 and proposed marriage. By 1981 Wallace "finally gave in" and the paraplegic former governor and the thirty-two-year-old-divorcee—three decades younger than her groom—married.[14]

The 1983 Inaugural Book of George Wallace described Taylor's "unpretentious graciousness and quiet charm" as her defining characteristics. Quiet charm, apparently, is in the eye of the beholder. After she appeared with her husband at a gala affair at the Alabama Music Hall of Fame, the *Birmingham News* described Taylor's haute couture on the red carpet as a "froufrou Vegas vision in a cream colored sheath gown with petal brocade and plumes of cream boa feather." Taylor also became involved in a major squabble with her ill father over a portion of family land she had claimed for herself. According to historian Dan Carter, who compared Taylor's physical appearance to Dolly Parton, while James Taylor was comatose in the hospital, Taylor and her siblings divided several million dollars worth of land between themselves. After her father, James, made a remarkable recovery, Lisa steadfastly refused to return her portion to him, sparking a brief public relations fiasco. Shortly after moving into the mansion, Lisa skipped a morning coffee date with wives of the state's legislators, causing another brief firestorm.[15]

The marriage disintegrated quickly, though the parties waited until Wallace left office for the last time in 1987 to formally divorce. The Wallace children were no great fans of the marriage, but generally they subsumed their feelings hoping that their father would find happiness wherever possible. Eventually, Lisa Wallace tried her hand at politics, running for state treasurer as a Republican in 2004. Her venture was unsuccessful despite her ability to attract the endorsement of the Conservative Christians of Alabama political action group for her "strong prolife" position.[16]

Wallace winnowed a portion of the field before the race ever began. Former attorney general Bill Baxley hoped to avenge his 1978 defeat and announced first that he would run only if Wallace did not, then pivoted, suggesting that he intended to run no matter Wallace's intention. Over dinner in 1981, with Baxley and George Jr., Wallace made it clear to Baxley that he was leaning toward running and that the former attorney general ought to take appropriate steps to get out of the way. As George Jr. remembered the conversation, "Baxley said 'Well, governor, I'm organizing, I'm speaking and traveling, I'm getting ready to run now and people are talking about you running.' . . . And dad says, 'You need to do that Bill, you organize.' And he says, 'Well, governor, what do you think you are going to do?' and Dad says, 'I'm going to keep the door open this wide' with that cigar in his mouth. And I'm sitting here and I looked at Bill and I said, 'If you don't know that he's telling you he's going to run for governor, you need to have your head examined.' . . . I think Bill got the message."[17]

Baxley ran for lieutenant governor that year.

The principal threats to another Wallace term were McMillan and McCorquodale. Both tailored their message to appeal to voters concerned about the stagnate economy and Alabama's unfavorable image. A 1984 study by the Fantus Company, two years after the election, confirmed that McMillan and McCorquodale were on to something. "The real problem," the final report suggested, "lies in the failure to develop positive alternatives for longstanding negative impressions." The Fantus Company found a number of other serious deficiencies in the Alabama economy including poor management-labor relations, insufficient venture capital, and inadequate government approaches to economic development, and cited as particularly negative the state's "personal income taxes, financing costs, environmental regulation, industrial site availability, health care, and the state's colleges and universities." Specifically, Fantus recommended that the state create a more balanced tax structure, make a major investment in public education, and do whatever necessary to "project a positive state image." Both McMillan and McCorquodale argued that the single greatest impediment to an improved state reputation was George Wallace. Alabamians were not convinced.[18]

While McMillan and McCorquodale were highlighting Wallace as the problem, the former governor was arguing that his experience was essential if Alabama was going to create the jobs necessary to boost the economy. Alabama's 14.7 percent unemployment rate in February 1982—the national unemployment rate was 9.7 percent—made jobs the most important issue of the campaign. According to Bureau of Labor statistics, the unemployment rate in December 1982 was the highest the state experienced in the twenty-nine-year period between 1976 and 2005. Unemployment in Birmingham reached a staggering 15.6 percent in October; in Gadsden, more than one in five had no work. On the stump and after taking office Wallace depicted himself as a proven industry hunter whose track record indicated he would bring jobs to the state: "I have personally written, introduced, or supported the passage of many pieces of legislation designed to help industry. Some examples include industrial revenue bond financing, ad valorem tax exemptions, sales tax exemptions . . . inventory tax exemptions . . . grants for water and sewer projects, construction of access roads to plant sites, [and] tax exemptions on pollution control machinery."[19]

While Wallace targeted blacks and union members in the 1982 campaign, he also continued to attract many of his previous supporters, "I was a states' rights man," Claude McClearen told the *Birmingham News,* noting that the issues of the past were not the main issues of the 1982 campaign. "The main driving point [in 1982] has been jobs—getting people working. Segregation was a point in the past, but we must forget that now and learn how to put meat and potatoes on people's tables." As he had done in most of his previous gubernatorial campaigns, Wallace picked a single theme and hammered it home repeatedly. In 1962 that theme was integratin' federal judges like Frank Johnson; in 1970, the theme was busing; the 1974 campaign was so lopsided that Wallace did not need speeches, let alone themes; in 1982 the issue was jobs. McClearen and countless other Wallace voters wore buttons that identified them as a "Wallace crony," lampooning charges by McMillan and McCorquodale that previous Wallace administrations had been especially lucrative for the governor's friends and donors. And every step of the way, Wallace and his surrogates touted his proven track record at landing jobs for Alabama workers. "He knows how to bring new industry and jobs to Alabama," a frequently published newspaper advertisement promised.[20]

Whether Alabamians embraced Wallace as their Democratic standard-bearer for a fourth time solely because they believed he would bring jobs to the state is problematic, though Wallace insiders insist that was the case. Equally as likely is the possibility that Alabamians thought state government was incapable of making much of an impact in their lives and they would be served just as well by electing someone they had first embraced twenty years earlier. In the absence of an attractive alternative, many whites and a growing number of black Alabamians found Wallace—no longer a menacing figure who was threatening the federal government, drawing lines in the dust, or tossing gauntlets at tyrannical judges and social engineers—as comfortable as an old shoe. The other candidates, McCorquodale and McMillan, piled up clout in the legislature, dollars for the campaign, and newspaper endorsements, but they made few inroads with the body politic. Wallace garnered 43 percent of the primary vote, dispatching McCorquodale and leaving only McMillan to defeat in the runoff.[21]

While the governor won all but six counties in the primary—Clarke, Dallas, Jefferson, Lee, Montgomery, and St. Clair—the results were misleading. In many counties, the combined McMillan and McCorquodale vote, the collective anti-Wallace tally, far outpaced Wallace. Together, McCorquodale and McMillan tallied 121,416 more votes than the governor. While black Alabamians were warming to the governor's cacophony of apologies for segregation and traditional supporters were considering the possibility that Wallace was healthy enough to perform the job, not all the state's registered voters were convinced. In order to win another term, Wallace would have to siphon off a significant number of votes from McCorquodale or such minor candidates as Jim Folsom, running yet again, and Reuben McKinley. Stated more simply, if all 1,268,251 Alabamians who voted in the primary cast ballots in the runoff, Wallace would need to find an *additional* 208,657 supporters in order to beat McMillan.[22]

Wallace was generally upbeat and amiable with reporters during the runoff campaign, even if the old magic was only evident in episodic bursts. Polls continued to indicate that the governor's health was not nearly the negative issue that many inside the campaign expected it to be. McMillan continued to blame previous Wallace actions and policies for creating an unfavorable business climate that resulted in Alabama ranking second to last in unemployment. But critical attacks on a man in a wheelchair seemed excessive to some Alabama voters. In the end, Wallace's narrow 23,759-vote victory margin was due to several factors: Alabamians were comfortable with him; voter turnout in the runoff actually declined 22 percent, allowing Wallace to win even though he only added 86,734 votes between the primary and the runoff; and George McMillan failed to energize enough voters who believed the economy could be different with him, not Wallace, in charge. Despite the Wallace candidacy and his ballyhooed public apologies for exploiting race in the past, Alabamians largely yawned through this election season. McMillan endorsed Wallace, though McCorquodale crossed party lines and championed Republican challenger Emory Folmar, the mayor of Montgomery, as did former governor Albert Brewer.[23]

Folmar was the most formidable Republican challenger for the governorship since Jim Martin had been crushed by Lurleen Wallace in 1966. A pistol-toting, highly decorated, former army infantry officer, Folmar was the first serious candidate since John Patterson in 1958 to be more socially conservative than Wallace. It was a strange turn of events for the governor, but the 1982 general election illustrated the greatness of Wallace as a practitioner of the art of politics. The very voters he had so methodically snubbed in past campaigns— white moderates, economic progressives, and African Americans—became the core of his support. Few politicians in American history have so skillfully reinvented themselves. In fact, Wallace had done it several times already, evolving from economic liberal state legislator to moderate gubernatorial candidate to race-baiting governor to sympathetic invalid to repentant elder statesman. And Wallace found ways to work with old rivals, such as Paul Hubbert of AEA, as well as disgruntled former associates like Bill Jones who assisted in developing a strategy to beat Folmar. Wallace campaigned in black churches, singing "Amazing Grace! How sweet the sound, that saved a wretch *like me*" and wooing dark-skinned voters that two decades earlier he privately accused of being spear-throwing cannibals. While Wallace might have lost to a more progressive candidate or even to Folmar if the economy had been more vigorous, the fact remains that he won an unprecedented fourth term, largely on the strength of accumulating an overwhelming majority of black votes. Even so, Alabamians were either apathetic about the race or assumed that Wallace would win: more Alabamians voted in the Democratic primary than in either the runoff or the general election. Conditioned by past performance to expect little real change from their government, many Alabamians, despite poverty and joblessness, found no reason to go to the polls, though the lines could not have been very long at most locations.[24]

Folmar, who was endorsed by the *Birmingham News* and the Moral Majority, carried only five counties, Jefferson, Lee, Madison, Montgomery, and St. Clair, and totaled less than 40 percent of the vote. Wallace avoided a televised debate with Folmar during the campaign, preferring not to be photographed near the vigorous Montgomery mayor and hoping to avoid the type of gaffe that could reverse his sizable lead. But in the days before the general election, Wallace's health reappeared as an issue, foreshadowing four difficult and illness-plagued years. Folmar had largely overlooked Wallace's health as an issue—following the same tack as McMillan and McCorquodale—thinking it below the belt to make light of a paraplegic. As the polls opened, the governor suffered from what his staff identified as laryngitis, a common problem for candidates who had been in full throat for months. Yet Wallace had not barnstormed the state in 1982 as he had done in 1962 and 1970, something that would have explained his hoarseness. The *Birmingham News* reported that the governor was actually battling a 105-degree fever. Had the press published the reports of the fever the weekend before the election, some Alabama voters might have had second thoughts about electing a sixty-three-year-old in questionable health. "This will end," Wallace told state scribes inquiring about his health troubles. "I'm still strong and healthy." But he was neither.[25]

Lost amid a sea of ironies in the 1982 election, was the support Wallace—economically progressive at least when compared to Folmar—received from disaffected Reagan Democrats. Reagan won a narrow victory in Alabama in 1980 over Jimmy Carter and later became a beloved conservative icon across many parts of the South but was exceedingly unpopular in the state during the 1982 gubernatorial campaign, largely because of the floundering economy. "It is fairly clear that President Reagan's programs," a *Birmingham News* editorial noted a day after Wallace's 1982 win, "to stabilize the economy and check the power and growth of the federal government were not enthusiastically endorsed." Folmar suffered at the polls as Alabama voters began to momentarily rethink their gradual realignment to the party of Lincoln. Republican congressman Albert Lee Smith was swept aside by Democrat Ben Erdreich despite outspending him three to one. Two years later as the economy began to improve, Reagan's popularity began to soar and he easily crushed Walter Mondale in the 1984 election in Alabama. Wallace, not coincidentally, failed to support Mondale, the Democratic candidate, writing one supporter that "I will not be involved in any campaign that is not in the best interest of Alabama." If George Wallace is responsible for a conservative transformation of American politics, as historian Dan Carter suggests, then it seems highly ironic that Wallace's last victory was aided by Reagan's early economic failings.[26]

In Sickness and in Health

George Jr., Elvin Stanton, Bill Jackson, Henry Steagall, Bill Rushton, and others comprised the administration's transition team. Distracting the press from the governor's declining health allowed the new brain trust time to focus on another sick patient, the state's woeful economy. The advisors compiled a report, urging Wallace to "take prompt remedial action to prevent a collapse of the state's financial structure." With the state already at 15 percent proration, Wallace was about to take the reins with little or no money available for Medicaid, unemployment compensation, or mental health, and less-than-projected revenues and interest income from state deposits. On top of all of this gloomy economic news, Wallace was already facing conflict within the state legislature. "Before the cock crows thrice," representative Alvin Holmes wailed about Wallace, "he's started to embark on the same things he did back in the sixties to people in Alabama. Everything he has promised us to get our support [from blacks] he has vetoed." Holmes, one of seventeen African Americans in the state house of representatives, later termed the governor's appointment of Ray Bass to be director of the Highway Department an "insult" and characterized Bass as a man with a "deep-seated hatred for black people." Joe Reed was less brash, but no less clear; he expected results for African Americans in Alabama: "The burden of proof is still on the governor. But there are signs that the governor wants to make sure all elements of society have a fair share of democracy." The honeymoon of the fourth elected term was indeed short.[27]

On the day when Wallace took the oath of office to be governor of the State of Alabama for the final time, a *Montgomery Advertiser* report suggested that the administration was pondering a tax hike, something that would have been considered anathema in years past. Though the administration did not confirm these intentions, the report was an admission that years of inefficiency and mismanagement had caught up to the state in the midst of an unemployment crisis. Wallace's fourth inaugural address was decidedly less strident than his first, and more compassionate and forthright than any of the previous three: "I have held the hand of the unemployed. . . . I have looked into the faces of the hungry . . . and I have heard the desperate pleas of parents who could not care properly for their children."[28]

The speech did not stir much press coverage outside of the state or many passions inside it, but in many ways it was the finest of Wallace's forty-year career in Alabama politics. The circus atmosphere of the past was gone, and the simple twenty-three-minute remarks expressed a level of understanding and grace that had been largely absent from Wallace's past administrations. "For many people," Wallace proclaimed, "these are the lean years of their lives. And as governor of Alabama, I call for relief. And I shall call for relief again and again and again. In the years ahead, I will be calling on all of you, rich and poor, young and old, male and female alike for your help in rebuilding Alabama."[29]

Wallace's call to action was inspirational.

We recognize and applaud the desires of those of great individual wealth to build among us monuments to high culture and entertainment. We recognize and applaud the great temples of worship and Christian education that religious denominations seek to build and assert upon our landscape to glorify almighty God. But for God's sake, let us also hear the sighs of the hungry and the cold among us. Let us do unto the least of these and God will reward us with his blessings in his way in his time.

No one can be rich as long as there are those among us who are hungry. Any nation that forgets its poor will lose its soul. When we turn to each other, we can view the future not with despair, but with hope.[30]

Conceptually, the appeal to the common Alabamian was nothing new. But previous appeals had been shallow and based on Wallace's trademark brand of militant populism: Alabamians are just as good and refined as people anywhere; Alabamians do not have to take orders from Washington liberals, federal judges, or power-hungry presidents; Congress is conspiring to change your way of life. These past speeches and their divisive themes were nothing more than government by sloganeering. The 1983 inaugural was proof that Wallace's near quarter century of rule in Alabama could have been different. He could have reshaped the state's history of interest group dominance and systematic inattention to the state's most vulnerable. But by 1983, he was no longer powerful enough or popular enough to enact major change. Instead, his last term began the way his first term had ended: no constitutional revision, no economic empowerment for some of the poorest people in all America, an education system that paled in comparison to the rest of the country, and mental health, prison, and patronage practices that continued to elicit federal supervision.

According to journalist Clarke Stallworth, Wallace contemplated offering a 1963 inaugural that was remarkably similar to the actual 1983 address. Stallworth quoted Wallace floor leader Pete Matthews just days before the infamous 1963 speech was delivered: "I just left George's office and he showed me the inaugural speech. After all that racist talk in the campaign, he's now talking about all of us working together, black and white." Of course Wallace never delivered the speech that Matthews, now deceased, supposedly read. Instead of embracing a different Alabama, Wallace vowed "segregation today, segregation tomorrow, segregation forever." But if such a speech existed—there is no hard copy of the document in any of the collections of Wallace administration material—it further demonstrates the tragedy of George Wallace. By 1983, the start of the last campaign, a campaign to reshape the Wallace legacy and the state of Alabama, the governor had virtually no power over the state legislature, only fleeting bursts of the energy and stamina necessary to pull off such a miracle, and little leverage against the interest groups that dominated the political economy.[31]

Interest groups had ruled the state for decades before Wallace made his first political speech in Alabama. The Farm Bureau, Alabama Cooperative Extension Service, Forestry Association, Cattlemen's Association, Milk Producers, and other agricultural groups held so much sway with legislators that the lobbyists actually sat on the floor of the legislature during official sessions. During Frank Dixon's administration in the early years of World War II, the governor wrote Alabama Cooperative Extension Service leader P. O. Davis, a former Farm Bureau official, with a request: "Will you have somebody to draw up the type of appeal that you think I should make," a telling example of how interest groups dictated state policy.[32]

According to political scientist Clive Thomas, Alabama is one of only nine states where interest groups are dominate, not merely complementary or subordinate forces. Political scientist David Martin has noted that Alabama has more than forty regulatory boards whose members disproportionately come from the very industries they are entrusted with monitoring. Wallace may have been reluctant to contest interest group hegemony, but he was shrewd enough to keep a running total of which lobbyists were contributing to which legislators' campaign war chests. Wallace's own fund-raising indicates the level of support interest groups provided him in the 1982 campaign; not surprisingly, the Farm Bureau, trial lawyers, and various labor unions were key contributors.[33]

Interest groups notwithstanding, Wallace attacked the state's financial crisis shortly after taking office. A special session of the legislature was called, conducted, and adjourned within two weeks of the inauguration. The session yielded an increased oil and gas severance tax to return the state to within 85 percent of budgeted funding. Others funds were shifted in order to make state Medicaid coffers temporarily solvent again. A second special session was scheduled to address reapportionment and Wallace boldly told the AEA, which had supported him in 1982, not to count on teacher raises in the immediate future. The administration began the process of appointing more minorities to government positions and kept fastidious statistics documenting the improvements. Among the notable African Americans serving in the administration was Hezekiah Wagstaff, assistant press secretary, and Delores Pickett, a one-time actress, as director of the Department of Minority Affairs. By 1984, blacks filled nearly a quarter of all state government positions, a level commensurate with the state's total black population and much higher than the paltry 2 percent of civil service jobs held in 1970.[34]

But aside from this brief outpouring of legislative and executive branch efficiency, the governor and the state were saddled with serious issues. Twice within a month Wallace was hospitalized, once for diverticulitis and again for a reaction to medication. Press reports in the *Montgomery Advertiser* noted swirling rumors that Wallace was seriously ill. Increasingly deaf, Wallace used selective hearing when necessary in order to avoid long answers to taxing questions proffered by nosy reporters. The combination of illness, unavailability, and physical decline led to a growing belief that Wallace was not only increasingly frail but that he was suffering from high levels of anxiety. The illnesses and pain were significant enough for Wallace to miss the wedding of his twenty-one year-old daughter, Lee, who wore her mother Lurleen's diamond ring and watch during the ceremony. Less than a week later, Wallace poked fun at himself and the reporters who were already speculating that he would not last all four years of his term: "To you press people, the funeral is not until next week."[35]

Even as Wallace was still able to fire off a quip or two when necessary, state legislators were beginning to question his ability to perform either the spirit or the letter of the job. "George Wallace is not running the state now," Alvin Homes alleged, "and he didn't run it the last time he was governor." Representative James Caldwell echoed Holmes: "I really can't say how he's doing or anything about it. I can't communicate with the governor's office in rumors." Press reports indicated Wallace was broaching the possibility of resignation, though administration stalwarts like Billy Joe Camp flatly denied such thoughts. Camp, Elvin Stanton, Henry Steagall, Bill Rushton, and others found themselves taking on larger roles within the daily affairs of state government. Reluctantly, Ham Hutchinson, Wallace's personal physician, noted the obvious: the intense pain and constant setbacks had left Wallace depressed. Even this admission was couched in political terms as the doctor insisted much of the emotional distress of the governor was related to the state's troubled economy. "Whether you believe it or not," Hutchinson told the *Montgomery Advertiser,* "he is very sensitive and it worries him to think about people being cold without heat or not having enough to eat."[36]

Over the remaining years of the final term, a slow trickle of reports left a picture of a largely incapacitated governor struggling to stay strong enough to function. Wallace was in and out of the hospital so much that thirty-three of the first eighty-one nights of the final term were spent in various hospitals. Medication—including corgard, lasix, desyrel, Ascendin, methadone, and opiate derivatives—was added and sometimes subtracted in order to alleviate pain and record accurate test results. Throughout the governor's last four years in office, he continued to undergo a variety of surgical procedures including an exploratory spinal operation to alleviate phantom pain, a colonoscopy to remove a small polyp, and various treatments to correct a racing heartbeat, fevers, chronic urinary tract infections, and persistent cold and flu symptoms. All the while, Wallace's hearing grew worse until associates were virtually shouting at the governor even when only a few feet away. "Wallace's hearing problems," *Journal-Advertiser* columnist Kendal Weaver noted, mean that "his aides almost [invariably] have to repeat any lengthy question for him—sometimes [making] communication difficult in the news conference setting." Age spots on his hands grew increasingly noticeable and the governor's gray eyebrows made him looker older and more feebler. By July 1986, a *Florence Times Tri-Cities Daily* report suggested that the governor had spent most of the previous three months in bed, the result of chronic ulcers and open sores.[37]

Press reports optimistically described a typical Wallace day at the office as beginning around 1:00 p.m. With the morning taken up with physical therapy, reading the state's major newspapers, and telephone calls, the actual workday at the mansion included appointments from 2:00 until 5:00. By 5:30 p.m., Wallace was en route back to the mansion for more phone calls and some dictation. And while the administration reminded Alabamians whenever possible that their governor could lift weights, crank a handheld bicycle device, and perform sit-ups, the strain of constantly defending their boss's ability to perform was becoming increasingly difficult. "Probably forty percent of my work week," Camp complained to reporters pressing for more details, "was spent on matters that would be considered rumors."[38]

The negative press reports and conjecture surrounding Wallace's health demonstrate some significant changes in how the media operated by the last term. Early in his political career, Wallace's infidelity and personal foibles never made it into print. But by 1978—long after the Vietnam War, Watergate, and other national, regional, and local scandals had soured the press on running interference for politicians—Wallace's crumbling relationship with Cornelia was front page news. By 1983, reporters were discussing the weakness of the governor's handshake and his fitness to serve. "It . . . [is] appropriate to ask," Bob Ingram posited on a WSFA-TV 12 editorial in Montgomery, "who will be in charge of state government. . . . The answer: Elvin Stanton, Billy Joe Camp, Henry Steagall, Ken Wallis . . . the governor's closest aides." Bill Ruston offered his resignation as director of the Alabama Development Office after word of a previous conviction for writing bad checks hit the news wire. Wallace refused the offer, but negative coverage continued to pepper the administration. The Alabama press corps, formerly forgiving, was now sinking its teeth into every aspect of an aging governor presiding over a lethargic economy.[39]

A May 1983 *Montgomery Advertiser* editorial blistered the administration for its failure to replace the old Wallace cronies with a younger, more educated, and more professional palace guard. During the campaign, Wallace had promised to turn state government over to a new breed of administrator: "Wallace . . . in a press conference . . . surrounded with fresh, youthful supporters [said] these would be his cronies during this term. . . . Now, six months after the election, the Wallace cronies are looking remarkably familiar and the governor is passing out political plums as if they were his private property." Other electronic and print outlets were equally critical.[40]

The administration made several highly questionable appointments. Former administration civil defense director and Wallace friend C. J. Sullivan was tapped to study the effects of thunderstorms on mobile homes. The job came with a cushy $45,000 annual salary, not much less than Wallace's own compensation of $61,474. Wallace supporter Robert Beard was given a position in charge of renovating Montgomery's Garrett Coliseum, even though his own supervisor admitted that the new employee did not possess the experience or expertise necessary to perform the work. Hubert Taylor, Wallace's brother-in-law, was named to a six-year term on the court of criminal appeals. Wheeler Foshee, a longtime Wallace supporter and recent parolee who had served prison time for mail fraud, was named assistant director of the state Department of Aeronautics. Neither the position, which included an annual salary of $38,000, nor the appointee was endorsed by the department's director, James Rowe. In the midst of a series of crises at Auburn University that made President Hanly Funderburk tremendously unpopular, Wallace realigned the board of trustees in an effort to prop up the embattled Funderburk. Bob Harris, a Funderburk critic, was not reappointed, and supporters of the Auburn president, Red Bamberg and Bobby Lowder, were selected to join the trustees. Lowder, who had business ties with football coach Pat Dye at the time, became the unquestioned leader of the board and a source of considerable controversy. Throughout the

Montgomery banker's tenure, the board of trustees had been routinely criticized for micromanagement and placing athletic results ahead of academic excellence. Historian Wayne Flynt has characterized Lowder's tenure on the board as detrimental to the university: "I would describe Lowder as a control freak who is obsessed with Auburn football, and whose time on the Auburn Board was characterized by conflict, votes of no confidence, and perpetual turmoil."[41]

These appointees were only part of an evolving administration strategy for curbing state unemployment: increase the size of government. In the first five months of his final term, Wallace added 700 new employees to the state payroll. The outgoing James administration had presided over a reduction in the number of state government employees, cutting 1,477 positions in four years. Over the course of 1983, the Wallace administration hired some 1,400 people, including the 700 new positions, most of which became permanent slots. Even as the governor continued to hire at his historical rate of roughly 1,000 new positions per year, he blamed other factors for his inability to hire even more. "At the change of this administration and even before that," he wrote to job-seeker Kathy Moon Kreps in 1986, "there was a hiring freeze because of a shortage of funds. . . . Again, at the present time, there is no hiring with the state as a result of the new incoming administration and the freeze on employment. . . . The truth of the matter is that I no longer have the influence that I did have because this administration is ending." Though most of the plum positions were filled by supporters, the face of state government was changing. Of the nearly 3,000 appointments in the first thirty-two months of the final term, 27.2 percent went to women, and 15 percent were filled by minorities.[42]

Success Stories

Despite the governor's poor health and questionable appointments, the administration enjoyed a handful of notable accomplishments. With an eye toward attracting industry—in periods of relative health the governor ventured overseas to Europe and the Far East seeking foreign investments—Wallace endorsed the idea of creating a state supercomputer. "The computers which are hooked into our state government's computer network," the governor wrote in a 1985 column, "can make more than five million calculations per second. That is fast. . . . But it isn't fast enough to meet the growing needs of scientific and industrial research." It is unclear who first presented the idea of the supercomputer—staffer Elvin Stanton insists it was Wallace's own idea—but the governor steered it into reality by using an executive order to create the supercomputer network authority. No matter whose idea it was, it was an effort to make Alabama a leader at a time when the state lagged behind much of the rest of the nation in most measurable categories. Wallace placed the super-computer in Huntsville, a logical choice given that city's mixture of technology and industry. At the time, Huntsville's Cummings Research Park was among the nation's largest in land and employees.[43]

Wallace also assembled a coalition of legislators to pass his oil and gas package. To his credit, Wallace advocated the creation of a trust that secured $347.5 million from oil and gas leases. Wallace fought off a host of legislators who wanted to spend the money on various pet projects. "I am opposed to that," Wallace wrote of the plan to spend the money immediately, "because once you open the door it is difficult to close. It is imperative to put as much as we can into the trust so it will draw as much interest as possible. We can take care of those special projects later." This save-first attitude was a radical departure for Wallace who had aggressively sought to pass major bond issues and then control the immediate allocation of the funds earlier in his career. "We have a very unique opportunity," Wallace told legislators at the opening of the special session called to consider the issue, "to provide a legacy for future generations of Alabamians. This legacy will survive us and serve as a constant and consistent reminder to posterity of our concern about the future economic health of our state."[44]

Wallace partnered with Lieutenant Governor Bill Baxley on the package, even though Baxley had already announced he was running for governor in 1986 and Wallace had yet to rule out a reelection bid. In addition, Baxley was intent on redirecting some of the accrued interest to public safety. Even so, Baxley helped shepherd the bill out of the senate, a body notoriously hostile to Wallace, and scheduled numerous press conferences and interviews across the state to urge its passage.[45]

Wallace remained above partisan politics in naming his appointees to the committee created to oversee the investment of the windfall oil and gas funds. Jimmy Lee, Louis Willie, and Winton "Red" Blount were three of the governor's choices to comprise the committee and none could be described as a Wallace crony. Blount in particular, a Republican who had served as postmaster for Richard Nixon at a time when the president had funneled four hundred thousand dollars in campaign funds to support Albert Brewer, had been considered a Wallace opponent for some time. Even Bob Ingram, more critical of Wallace in the final term than during previous administrations, praised Wallace for avoiding politics with the oil and gas committee.[46]

Archaic provisions of the state's constitution required the legislation to be brought before Alabama voters as a constitutional amendment. Wallace won passage of the amendment, despite calls by some interest groups to revisit the matter so that they could have the oil and gas funds earmarked for their own pet projects. By applying the interest income directly to the general fund, the state was able to minimize a broader array of budgetary shortfalls for mental health, prisons, and other programs that had traditionally drawn the ire of federal courts.[47]

Continuing Issues

Prisons, an aspect of Alabama government that had been under near constant federal court orders for more than a decade, were eventually released from federal scrutiny during the final Wallace administration. Though the federal courts were finally convinced that the state was taking meaningful steps to correct the festering prison problems, internal prison studies indicated that Alabama prisons were disproportionately filling up with black inmates. Of the 50 prisoners on death row, 34 were black. Those awaiting execution took no solace in the fact that during the 1983 execution of prisoner John Louis Evans, Yellow Mama, the state's outdated electric chair, charred and burnt the convict's body, which was left smoldering long after Evans was declared dead. Blacks made up 58.8 percent of the total prison population. Among female inmates, almost twice as many were black as white. Given the fact that a quarter of the state's population was black, the propensity of arrests of African Americans was mathematically dubious. Equally incongruous was the fact that the state's measurable crime rate dropped by 20 percent in the first five years of the 1980s, yet the prison population was still growing. In the ten years before 1985, the prison population tripled and by the midway point of the decade, 55.1 percent of all inmates were serving sentences of fifteen years or more. As a result of a 1980 law mandating life without parole for certain offenders, the number of state prisoners serving such permanent sentences grew from 17 in 1980 to 328 in 1985. Even with the opening of a new correctional facility in Limestone county, the state's prison population remained nearly 300 inmates over capacity.[48]

Wallace remained detached from the prison situation but did speak out on a few related issues. Alabama highways, long considered death traps because of the small number of troopers engaged in traffic enforcement, continued to be a frequent scene of fatal accidents. Wallace urged the legislature to respond to the crisis by passing a mandatory seat belt law. "I do not personally like the idea of government mandating individual actions," the governor concluded in a message to the state senate, "but in many instances, government and reason must rise above idealistic philosophy, particularly when the lives, health, and safety of citizens . . . are at stake." Wallace also used the power of his office to make public appeals to prevent abortion without parental notification, curb drug abuse, and catch deadbeat dads who failed to pay child support. "I believe," Wallace railed in a column probably ghostwritten by Elvin

Stanton or Associated Press reporter Rex Thomas, "and I feel that a vast majority of Americans would agree, that the death penalty would be an appropriate punishment for the narcotics bosses and the punishment would serve as the most effective deterrent." Despite the governor's interest, Alabama highways continued to be dangerous, the distribution and use of drugs continued to rise, and too many fathers failed to honor their moral and legal obligations to their children.[49]

The state's biggest obligation to children, an adequate education system, was still mediocre. Despite a flurry of bond issues, new junior colleges and trade schools, and teacher raises throughout the first three Wallace terms, the state was statistically no better than when Wallace took office in 1963. By the mid 1970s, even the state's education administrators were admitting as much. "I know we're low on the totem pole in education," State Board of Education member Christine Drake admitted. "We've got a long way to go." Wayne Teague, the state's top education official, echoed similar sentiments: "Alabama's public schools have never been extravagant with the taxpayer's money. They couldn't afford to be. We've been playing catch-up with the rest of the country for too long as far as school finances are concerned."[50]

The relationship between finances and education had changed very little, despite the emergence of the Alabama Education Association as a powerful interest group. Though the AEA agitated for more funding to be applied to the Special Education Trust Fund and had successfully prevented Wallace administration attempts to redirect education funds and borrow money from the teacher's retirement system, the popular opinion of the AEA, in political circles, was that their first mission was to cajole the legislature into raises for teachers. The state's colleges and universities often found themselves in conflict with K through 12 schools for limited funds, like two hungry dogs fighting for table scraps. As a result, educators and citizens were unable to effectively work together against other entrenched interest groups who balked at higher taxes and often had the ear of the Wallace administration. The net effect of the limited funding and internecine education wars was that well-intentioned programs had no chance to succeed. "Confidence in public education has lessened in recent years," Teague admitted in an annual superintendent's report.[51]

Reading instruction, for example, was labeled a priority as early as 1973 when the legislature declared that improved reading skills were the number one priority for state schools. By 1977, the state was no longer allocating money to test the reading readiness or proficiency of first grade students. The state's own report on reading in the mid-1970s concluded that "reading achievement continued its downward spiral." By 1975, only five school systems in the state were producing eighth graders who could read at the national average baseline, and only three systems met the same standard for tenth graders. The study identified three critical factors in the state's failure to produce students who could read competently: income level, amount of property tax in the school district, and the amount of income tax in the school district. But beyond the dollars and cents deficiencies, the report concluded that the state was poorly coordinating reading initiatives among its schools, teachers, and students. By the 1980s, the state's dropout rate was frighteningly high, and too few high-skill, high-wage industries were seriously considering an Alabama workforce that was underprepared for such work. Wallace acknowledged that functionally illiterate adults earned less money, were statistically more likely to require welfare services or end up in prison, and had "real trouble finding any kind of job." By his own conservative estimate, Alabama had two hundred thousand such adults who "cannot read the label on a medicine bottle . . . cannot read the help wanted ads in a newspaper. And if they do find a job, they cannot fill out the application." A 1984 report by an outside consultant, the Fantus Company, laid much of the blame for the state's stagnant economy at the feet of the state's poorly performing schools. According to Fantus, the state "failed to keep pace" in public education, had too few skilled workers, had insufficiently prepared students to become competent workers, and had a substandard amount of financial support for schools.[52]

In 1984, the same year that the Fantus Company wrote its report, Teague prepared "A Plan for Excellence," an assessment of the state's education system and strategic initiative for the future. In his report, Teague identified insufficient per pupil expenditures, lack of capital outlay, bitter federal relations, and high pupil-teacher classroom ratios. "Materials provided to Alabama's classrooms," he admitted, "are woefully inadequate. . . . The time for talk is over. We must now turn our attention to planning solutions for our identified problems." Teague, whether he knew it or not, had deftly identified the most grievous problem with state education: the propensity to complain vociferously about the problems without ever attempting to implement or pay for the solutions. A quick analysis of education initiatives in other states in the mid 1980s, compiled for the administration by UAB assistant vice president for governmental relations G. William Croker, revealed peer states were aggressively looking for new revenue streams to improve their schools. Arkansas, Tennessee, Kentucky, Georgia, Louisiana, Florida, and Virginia had implemented or proposed major tax increases that were targeted for education. And if Wallace did not believe the Fantus report or his own superintendent, the U.S. Bureau of Census confirmed many of the findings.[53]

Wallace's final term in office may have been his best effort for improving education in Alabama. The administration pushed the legislature to provide two separate 15 percent raises for teachers, bringing them closer than ever to national averages. Instead of just floating a bond issue or two and then allocating many of those dollars to support his pet junior college system—though the administration again relied on deficit financing for capital outlay—the governor advocated some real reform efforts and pushed, albeit unsuccessfully, for new revenue sources for education. Wallace's education reform bill of 1984 was designed to increase teacher salaries; implement a statewide kindergarten program; augment math, science, and computer science curricula; attract a pool of highly qualified undergraduate students to the teaching profession; and establish a commission to implement further reforms. "This is not a typical reform committee," a governor's press release declared, "and they are not going to come up with a lot of reform theories. They are people who have the assignment to take the results of numerous blue-ribbon committees and turn them into real educational reform." Even so, the Education Reform Commission met several times, developed their own political rivalries, and failed to meet most of Wallace's expectations for real change.[54]

As usual, implementation of any plan to improve the state's schools was dependent on finding sufficient funds. Prior to 1984, Alabama schoolchildren were selected to attend kindergarten through a lottery system, since so few schools offered classes. Adding kindergarten programs in every school system of the state was a fundamental component of Teague's "Plan for Excellence." And though Wallace championed more educational reform in the last term than in any of his previous administrations, he failed to propose adequate resources in his budget request. "Your budget proposal," Teague wrote to Wallace, "which the House Ways and Means Committee will soon consider, is, in my opinion, inadequate in its allocation of teacher units for kindergarten instruction. . . . Kindergarten must be funded and monies you have allocated for the State Department of Education must remain if we are to carry out the mandates of our plan." Kindergarten had been identified as an integral part of changing the education culture in Alabama and the administration placed it fourth in its long list of priorities.[55]

A detailed study of the state's bleak financial picture was compiled by Wallace's trusted confidant Henry Steagall. In the assessment delivered before a joint legislative hearing, Steagall identified fourteen core elements of education that demanded additional revenue in order to be satisfactory. Steagall included school library assistance, increases in health insurance coverage for educators, new school buses, replacement of damaged buildings, and removal of asbestos in older schools in his list of priorities. Despite Steagall's testimony, too little money was available to fix problems in a political culture where raising property or income taxes was practically sacrilegious.

In his final term, Wallace advocated a variety of increased taxes, some regressive, others more progressive. As usual, Wallace turned first to regressive tax increases on cigarettes, beer, and gambling proceeds. By 1983, Alabama had the highest percentage of state and local beer taxes in the nation, and its gasoline and vehicle taxes were much higher than the national average. And by 1986, some economic trends embraced by many consumers—falling interest rates and declining gasoline prices—had a negative effect on Alabama's general fund, which was dependent on oil and gas revenue and the interest from certain deposits. An assessment of the state's tax system by a task force assembled by Wallace concluded that the state's taxes on gasoline, tobacco, and a handful of other items were unusually high and that property tax rates were unusually low. This information was hardly groundbreaking: these problems had been recognized for decades. No matter how many task forces, committees, and university groups complained about the state's shaky financial status, Alabama interest groups managed to keep property taxes and personal and corporate income taxes low. As a result, Alabama students were consistently challenged to do more with less than any other groups of American students.[56]

Yet again, plans to alter the tax system were quickly turned back by the legislature, which wanted no part of tax hikes so close to an election. Predictably, some continued to moan about waste and excessive spending, and demand that the state simply tighten its belt a little further. Wallace, bursting into tears at a press conference, declared Alabama had no more fat to trim and reiterated his intention to call a special session and force the legislature to create some new sources of revenue. But again, Wallace, in the twilight of his political career, no longer had the power or the popularity to force the legislature to act on his wishes. "I think as far as going to Montgomery and looking at nothing but a tax proposal," Senate Rules Committee chair Charles Bishop challenged, "that will fail in the senate. . . . I don't think the senate is going to listen to the same old junk." The state, already in proration, faced another round of deeper cuts. A *Montgomery Advertiser* editorial, looking past the plight of schools, teachers, and students, noted the effects that failure to find more money would have on the state's people: "The state will likely have to turn away poor mothers who want day care services for their kids, but instead will have to leave their jobs and go on welfare. Some mental patients will eventually be denied care. . . . The impact on prenatal services to expectant mothers could be devastating."[57]

But Wallace could not hammer together a coalition to pass the gambling tax despite making it a point of emphasis in the regular session of the legislature and then calling a special session to push it through. "I'm dead serious," he promised, publicly pondering the idea of calling the legislature back into session for a third time, "about this tax on gambling. I don't like this philosophy of taxing other things but not gambling." Eventually the legislature passed a plan to provide some $2 million per year for education by taxing concessions at the state's three dog tracks, hardly more than a token gesture for the state's schools. Even that was a major achievement in a state where citizens

like Duron Smith wrote letters to newspapers demanding that public education be abolished. "If all education was private," Smith announced in a missive to the *Montgomery Advertiser,* "as it should be, this letter would be unnecessary. The free market would take care of all problems of funding and there
would be no 'controversial' matters such as sex education and religious teaching to tear the system apart. Governments have no more constitutional obligation to educate children than to feed and clothe them." Smith's views were
not indicative of all Alabamians, but they buttressed the political philosophy
of too many interest groups in Alabama that placed low taxes next to godli-
ness, or perhaps even before it. As a result, too many Alabamians viewed Auburn University tailback Bo Jackson's Heisman Trophy as the state's most significant educational accomplishment in the decade.[58]

The administration, with the strong backing of AEA, did convince the legislature to pass a merit pay plan for teachers known as the "career ladder."
Conceptually, the idea allowed school systems to reward outstanding teachers
while terminating those that could not meet minimum standards. In reality,
a good idea became another opportunity for the AEA to exert its influence, as
a majority of the committee designed to create an evaluation plan were state
teachers. "Well, what's wrong with that," Wallace bellowed in response to carping critics of his close relationship with AEA and the decision to stack the
evaluation committee with its members. "Why shouldn't teachers have a voice
in judging the work performance of other teachers?" Other observers were less
thrilled that the AEA was driving the evaluation process. "What's that old line
about the fox guarding the hen house?" Bob Ingram chirped in a WSFA editorial.

While campaigning for the presidency had sidetracked every previous gubernatorial term, Wallace was too incapacitated and too marginalized to get
involved in the 1984 presidential race. Even so, Alan Cranston, John Glenn, and
Walter Mondale attempted to garner a Wallace endorsement in hopes that it
might boost their sagging images in the South. Former president Jimmy Carter
lobbied Wallace to support Mondale. "I hope you will not consider it presumptuous of me," Carter wrote recalling past Wallace-Carter political alliances, "to
consider it advantageous for us to continue this close relationship, at least to
the extent of discussing the candidates and issues as they pertain to the South-
land." Going further and apparently with a straight face, Carter continued to
posit Mondale, the liberal Minnesotan, as the embodiment of what a southerner should look for in a presidential candidate: "I also know from my intensive relations with him in the White House that he is dedicated to good solid
southern principles. ... My hope is that you can endorse Fritz." Wallace endorsed no candidate in the 1984 campaign, though word leaked out that he was
not inclined to vote Democratic in November.[59]

By mid 1985, the administration was considering the possibility of running for reelection in 1986. In brief bursts of five or ten minutes, enough Wallace magic could appear to remind voters and observers that no Alabamian had comparable political skills. "Campaigns always bring out the best in Wallace," Bob Ingram noted after a particularly jubilant Wallace exulted in a legislative victory and parried successfully with the assembled scribes. "They cause the juices to flow and his were flowing Wednesday. He was winking at his buddies, giving them a knowing grin and all the while coming up with some pretty good one-liners for the media." For Ingram and other informed onlookers, Wallace was preparing to run for governor, yet again.[60]

End of the Road, Part 2

Polls released in the summer of 1985, however, revealed an electorate increasingly characterized by Wallace fatigue. Both the *Birmingham News* and its rival, the *Birmingham Post-Herald,* released surveys that indicated Alabamians no longer believed Wallace was fit enough to be governor and that it was time for someone else to run the state. By early 1986, a Davis, Penfield, and Associates poll suggested that Wallace's numbers were weak, likely to decline even further, and unlikely to be sufficient for him to even make a runoff in the Democratic primary. Sixty percent of those polled believed Wallace was too frail to be governor. Rumors swirled that Wallace, unable to compete with younger candidates like Lieutenant Governor Bill Baxley, former lieutenant governor George McMillan, and Attorney General Charles Graddick in the Democratic primary season, might opt to run as an independent. After months of speculation, Wallace finally squelched that possibility: "I have nothing to do with any petition and I would not accept the petition. I would not run as an independent under any circumstances."[61]

By April, it was increasingly clear that Wallace would be a bigger underdog in 1986 than at any other time in his political career. On Wednesday April 2, 1986, Wallace rode to the house chambers in the old state capitol carrying two speeches written by aide Elvin Stanton. One set of remarks announced his candidacy for reelection; the other declared the end of his political career. Years later, Stanton summed up the ambivalence much of the palace guard felt about the decision: "We had to weigh out what was good for him and a lot of us thought that if he would run and serve, it would be good for his health as far as longevity because he'd be politically active. At the same time, we had noticed a decline in his health." Faced with the real possibility of defeat and reflecting on declining eyesight, near total hearing loss, constant pain, and numerous hospitalizations over the previous years, Wallace retired: "After much prayerful consideration, I feel that I must say that I have climbed my last political mountain. . . . But for now, I must pass the pick to another climber and say 'Climb on. Climb on to higher heights. Climb on until you reach the very peak.' Then look back and wave at me. For I, too, will still be climbing."[62]

The crowd of three hundred supporters stood in stunned disbelief. Though they were hearing something they had known was likely, the words still surprised them: George Wallace was finally finished in Alabama politics. Grown men including security personnel bawled like babies. "They are crying, they are crying," Stanton remembered, "because it was truly the end of an era." Wallace was equally sad, weeping and pausing often as he haltingly stumbled through his speech. "He knew what it meant," Stanton summarized, "and I think it was the most emotional speech I've ever seen him give. Far more emotional than standing in the schoolhouse door or a lot of the campaign speeches that I sit back and relish. But that one got to everyone's heart." A quarter century of Wallace dominance, for better or worse, was over.[63]

Balance Sheet

From 1963 to 1986, George Wallace used his rare collection of political skills and unmatched popularity in the state to advance his own political career. For most of the journey, it was difficult to identify the policies that Wallace cared most about. "Well I don't know what that would be," Jere Beasley admitted when queried about the governor's core beliefs. "It's really a difficult question to answer. Probably shouldn't be, but he enjoyed hearing those hands clap and just the adoration of the people. He thrived on it." Policy and governance always took a backseat in the Wallace administration to campaigning. "Hell he didn't want to have to fool with it," McDowell Lee declared. "It was just, 'y'all take care of that.'" Fuller Kimbrell concurred: "If he had used more of his ability to do more for the state instead of putting so much attention to national politics, he'd have been a better governor. And then if he'd tried to stop some of the bad things that happened, you know, instead of sitting by a lot, it would have made a difference for Alabama."[64]

Wallace presided over an array of new educational programs. He created a system of trade schools and junior colleges that undoubtedly created opportunities for some Alabamians to earn employment skills and prepare for matriculation at a four-year college. Funding levels and teacher salaries increased, and financially strapped parents benefited from the textbook system. Unfortunately, the administration was better at passing legislation than administering programs. The textbook system was woefully underfunded and mismanaged, beset by political considerations, and too often more concerned with the lifestyle of the book's author than the process of getting books into the classroom. The junior colleges and trade schools spiraled out of control, reflecting political expediencies instead of comprehensive planning. All the while, seg-regated education, whether in public or private schools, was a higher priority than quality education.[65]

By the time Wallace was more interested in lasting reform, he was physically unable to make it happen, especially when it came to wrangling more dollars for state programs. A political culture predicated on high amounts of regres-sive taxes, low property and income tax, and special interest group power was too powerful for the aging Wallace to topple. "During his last term," a *Mont-gomery Advertiser* editorial noted, "he has been one of the few politicians will-ing to stand up to Alabama's abysmal tax structure which strangles the poor and middle class; he tried but he failed."[66]

Of all the tragedies associated with a quarter century of Wallaceism, per-haps this is the most tragic, more lasting than the appeals to racism and the patronage scandals, the litany of federal court decisions and the endless cam-paigning: George Wallace wasted much of his potential. On his best day, he was empathetic to the plight of people whose lives were one paycheck or wel-fare check from disaster. At his best, Wallace understood that Alabama needed better schools, better jobs, and a government that was responsive to the needs of victims, mental health patients, and other vulnerable folk no matter their race, religion, or creed. But those days, cast against the context of four elected terms plus part of one for his first wife, pale in comparison to the days in which Wallace focused only on campaigns and votes. At some point, an effec-tive governor has to govern, make difficult choices, and lead all the people. For Wallace, a boy who dreamed of becoming governor, policy and change were never as important as they should have been. Wallace, in ways no other Ala-bama governor has ever been able to consider, could have made Alabama a jewel of the Deep South, a place characterized by a diverse economy, schools as good as the national average, and a political system where interest groups were complementary, not dominating forces.

Ultimately the biggest tragedy of Wallaceism in Alabama is the question of what might have been. What if Wallace had used his considerable skills to soften the racial atmosphere instead of inflame it? What if Wallace had re-formed the regressive tax code? What if Alabama under the leadership of a charismatic figure like George Wallace had reshaped its prisons, and mental health system, and state constitution? Could Wallace have challenged the sta-tus quo and reshaped Alabama to become the "Athens of the South" that he claimed it was becoming? The answers to these questions are debatable. Sadly, Wallace, the most powerful and popular governor in state history, preferred to use his gifts and political capital to enhance his own standing. "Our hope now," an exasperated Julia Riggs Houchens wrote in February 1971, "is that real leadership will replace the need for political maneuvering." The politics of perpetual campaigning, however, usually led to maintaining the status quo, not advancing the state. Squandered opportunities are sometimes more painful than egregious mistakes.[67]

The administration was effective at recruiting low-wage, low-skill industry to the state. Wallace, in particular, was an expert salesman, wooing prospects with his charisma and using various state agencies to build roads, bridges, and airstrips in order to close deals. Like all consummate politicians, Wallace had superior interpersonal communication skills. "He would go to Mobile," Elvin Stanton recalled, "and he would see somebody that I didn't have any idea who it was, but he had met that person maybe one time three years ago and had a conversation and he would say, 'Well hello, Rita, how is your granddaddy? Is he still operating the sawmill or did he retire?' . . . That person would leave there thinking that George Wallace was the best friend that family had ever had." While this skill was useful on the campaign trail, it also translated effectively into industrial development. Industrial prospects straddling the fence about site location believed their decision was the most important thing in Wallace's world.[68]

Even so, the administration rarely targeted high-skill, high-wage prospects, preferring to trumpet the state's low wages, industry-friendly labor climate, and sweetheart deals created by the Wallace and Cater Acts. As a result, Alabama never matched the infrastructure and education environment that allowed cities like Atlanta, New Orleans, Tampa, and Charlotte to become Sunbelt commercial meccas. "Despite Wallace's Populist rhetoric," historian Pete Daniel concluded, "he did little for the average Alabamian. . . . As the agricultural system moved from sharecropping to agribusiness, the dispossessed received little aid from the governor." Press releases and stump speeches about industrial expansion made Alabamians feel good about their governor, but a decade later they had little to show for it. As quickly as industry came to Alabama for low wages and lucrative incentives, it left for Third World nations when a better deal came along. Tax breaks and special arrangements meant most new industries contributed little more than paychecks to their employees. Complementary businesses sprang up to provide groceries and jeans for blue-collar workers and their kin but dried up as soon as the mill shut down. "One of the problems we face," Wallace's son-in-law, former justice Mark Kennedy surmised, "is while other states were growing into the New South and looking at tax reform and constitutional reform, we were not. This is one of the legacies that Governor Wallace and his administration [left]. And we'll be paying for that for another generation."[69]

The blue-collar and lower middle-class core supporters that Wallace banked on embraced Wallaceism even if the administration's record was uneven. The governor's connection with Alabamians was never about policy or performance.

It was more personal than that. Wallace reached into the collective memories of everyday Alabamians and vowed to stand up for their culture and values, keep them independent of federal meddling, and tell the world they were just as good as anyone else. In a sense, Wallace's best political skill was understanding the mentality of his constituents and telling them what *they* wanted to hear. As a result, Wallace was more of an emotional spokesman than a leader. The emotional peak of a Wallace campaign rally was not when he told the throng what he wanted to do for them, it was when he reminded them that he believed what they believed. Wallace told white Alabama that its beliefs were reasonable, rational, and responsible. It mattered little that old-age pensions were insufficient to pay food and rent, that mental health facilities were substandard, and that social workers had twice the legal caseload. What mattered was that Wallace understood words like "tradition" and concepts like southern morality. He forged a connection that survived after segregation fell, after he was confined to a wheelchair, and after presidential campaigns became distant memories. The connection is evident in tens of thousands of letters to the governor from people asking for everything from legal advice to the best way to get a septic tank fixed. To many Alabamians, Wallace was family, and they spoke and wrote to him accordingly.

Race was inextricably linked to the actions and rhetoric of the administration. The term "racist" carried a black and white demarcation in later decades that belies the shades of gray inherent in southern race relations during the civil rights movement. It was an era when died-in-the-wool racists, often but not always garbed in Klan regalia, burned crosses and churches and sowed the "strange fruit" immortalized by singer Billie Holiday. Based on this rubric, Wallace was not a racist, though he was a segregationist who believed, as did most Deep South whites of a similar age, that white folks were superior to blacks. "I don't think he believed in hanging people," McDowell Lee summarized, "but he would use popular issues any way he could for his benefit." The caveat that his words and deeds were done for political expedience hardly mitigates the consequences, unintended or not. In the end, an opportunist is no better than a racist, and less honest.[70]

Wallace was the centrifugal force of Alabama, defining the social, cultural, and political context around which nearly every issue revolved. At his best, Wallace, raised in the throes of the Depression, understood the hardships facing the state's rural poor. "There wasn't anybody down there during those times," Lee noted of Barbour County, "that had a heck of a lot of money. And he saw the poverty and what not having anything could mean and do to people." Wallace had a heart for the state's most vulnerable, for the "little man." And he understood that government could be a force for change. On many occasions, Wallace reached out to help individuals find work or get competent medical care. Yet more often than not, he chose to follow the klieg lights and search for the roar of the crowd rather than help Alabama reach its full potential.[71]

George Wallace was a complex man. He could be either a free-spending liberal or a social conservative based on the times and the issue. He was the most skillful politician in the post–World War II South. He gave a voice to millions of disaffected Americans who believed that the federal government was intruding where it had no business. He helped reshape modern conservatism so completely that a new political order was created. He never profited personally from his tenure in office, and accumulating wealth was never a motivation. Yet his greatest and most troubling legacy is that he left Alabama in the same place that he found it in 1963. To be sure, racial segregation was gone, but the Alabama economy was still a step or two behind peer states in most measurable categories. "I think that there were some issues," Kennedy reflected, "that I would have done a lot differently and I think that there were a lot of things that were done during those fifteen or twenty years that he was in power that probably were not good for this state. But was he a good governor? I say that he was effective, that he was loved in this state. He brought Alabama to the attention of a lot of people, both good and bad."

In 1998, Wallace's body gave way to twenty-six years of pain and paralysis caused by Arthur Bremer's bullets. His last decade of life had been painful and he had increasingly spent his days reading from a device that magnified his Bible. Visitors would drop by now and again, but Wallace in the winter of his life was not much of an attraction for the newest breed of Alabama politicians. Widowed from his first wife, divorced from his second and third, never as close to his children as an old man might desire, Wallace died understanding pain and separation and loss in ways that he had never imagined on a January day in 1963 when he took the oath of office for the first time.

As Wallace's body lay in state in September 1998, news reporters and television crews crowded around the capitol to interview black and white Alabamians. Asked to define his legacy, some folks noted his 1963 inaugural address, the junior college system, or his transformation from racial demagogue to apologetic paraplegic. But more often than not, the masses who waited in line to pay their final respects to the governor could not quite come to grips with their feelings. Wallace had been their governor, and they loved him even as they were still not quite sure what to make of him. Until the state addresses the core issues it faced in 1963—issues that remain in the twenty-first century—Alabama will never be able to turn the page on the Wallace years.

Appendix: People Interviewed

All interviews were conducted by the author and are in his possession.

Allen, Julia, 27 July 2001
Beasley, Jere, 24 July 2001, Montgomery, Ala.
Brewer, Albert, 14 and 21 August 2001; 14 August 2002, Birmingham, Ala.
Doss, Chriss, 14 August 2002, Birmingham, Ala.
Dunkelberger, Jane, 9 February 2000 (not recorded), Auburn, Ala.
Ewing, Ed, 21 August 2002, Montgomery, Ala.
Hall, Emma, 8 February 2000 (not recorded), Opelika, Ala.
Hubbert, Paul, 24 July 2002, Montgomery, Ala.
Ingram, Bob, 7 June 2001, Montgomery, Ala.
Jones, Bill, 8 July 1999, Woodville, Ala.; 1 March 2000 (not recorded), Auburn, Ala.; 26 July 2002, Birmingham, Ala.
Jones, Jean, 8 July 1999, Woodville, Ala.; 1 March 2000 (not recorded), Auburn, Ala.
Kennedy, Mark, 30 August 2002, Montgomery, Ala.
Kennedy, Peggy Wallace, 2 August 2001, Montgomery, Ala.
Kimbrell, Fuller, 25 May 2001, Tuscaloosa, Ala.
Lee, McDowell, 2 August 2001, Montgomery, Ala.
Maddox, Hugh, 18 September 2002, Montgomery, Ala.
Martin, David L., 16 February 2000 (not recorded), Auburn, Ala.
Patterson, John, 7 August 2001, Montgomery, Ala.
Smith, June, 7 March 2000 (not recorded), Auburn, Ala.
Stanton, Elvin, 28 August 2002, Montgomery, Ala.
Turnham, Pete, 25 July 2002, Auburn, Ala.
Wallace, George, Jr., 7 August 2002, Montgomery, Ala.

Notes

Preface

1. Rick Bragg, *All Over but the Shoutin'* (New York: Vintage Books, 1997), 61.

2. George Wallace to Dede Smith, 10 June 1966, SG22416; George Wallace to Tom Harris, 30 August 1966, SG22417, all in Administrative Files of Governor George C. Wallace (hereafter Admin. Files Gov. G. Wallace), Alabama Department of Archives and History (hereafter ADAH).

3. Among the best works on the civil rights movement that include some assessment of Wallace are E. Culpepper Clark, *The Schoolhouse Door: Segregation's Last Stand at the University of Alabama* (New York: Oxford University Press, 1995); Glenn T. Eskew, *But for Birmingham: The Local and National Movements in the Civil Rights Struggle* (Chapel Hill: University of North Carolina Press, 1997); and Robert J. Norrell, *Reaping the Whirlwind: The Civil Rights Movement in Tuskegee* (Chapel Hill: University of North Carolina Press, 1998).

4. Marshall Frady, *Wallace,* 2nd ed. (New York: New American Library, 1976); Stephan Lesher, *George Wallace: American Populist* (New York: Addison-Wesley, 1994); Dan T. Carter, *The Politics of Rage: George Wallace, the Origins of the New Conservatism, and the Transformation of American Politics* (New York: Simon and Schuster, 1995).

5. "Stand Up for America," 1968 campaign flyer, in author's possession.

6. "Keep Alabama Southern," 1958 campaign flyer of Judge George Wallace, George C. Wallace Collection, LPR 124, box 43, ADAH; *Birmingham News,* 10 May 1962; *Montgomery Advertiser,* 22–23 May 1962, 4 April 1986; *Huntsville Times,* 13 May 1962.

7. *New York Times,* 15 September 1998, quoted in Rick Bragg, *Somebody Told Me* (Tuscaloosa: University of Alabama Press, 2000), 144.

8. Interview, George Wallace Jr.; interview, Mark Kennedy.

Chapter 1

1. Frank Lawrence Owsley, "The Irrepressible Conflict," in *I'll Take My Stand: The South and the Agrarian Tradition* by Twelve Southerners (New York: Harper and Brothers, 1930) 61–91.

2. W. J. Cash, *The Mind of the South* (1941; New York: Vintage Books, 1991), 380–84; David E. Alsobrook, "William D. Jelks," in *Alabama Governors: A Political History of the State,* ed. Samuel L. Webb and Margaret E. Armbrester (Tuscaloosa: University of Alabama Press, 2001), 140–46; William Warren Rogers, Robert David Ward, Leah Rawls Atkins, and Wayne Flynt, *Alabama: The History of a Deep South State* (Tuscaloosa: University of Alabama Press, 1994), 345–54.

3. Wayne Flynt, *Poor but Proud: Alabama's Poor Whites* (Tuscaloosa: University of Alabama Press, 1989), 256–58; Rogers, Ward, Atkins, and Flynt, *Alabama,* 351; Joel Williamson, *A Rage for Order* (New York: Oxford University Press, 1986), 53–57. Williamson notes that Washington "retreated from an overt and exciting claim to perfect equality, and, whatever his goals were in his own mind, he seemed to white people to settle for substantially less. Thus leadership in the white world, North and South, felt safe with Washington, and they applauded the expansion and consolidation of his power in the black world."

4. Sheldon Hackney, *Populism to Progressivism* (Princeton: Princeton University Press, 1969); Rogers, Ward, Atkins, and Flynt, *Alabama,* 355–75.

5. Rogers, Ward, Atkins, and Flynt, *Alabama,* 369–75; David Allan Harris, "Braxton Bragg Comer," in *Alabama Governors,* 150–56; Flynt, *Poor but Proud,* 262.

6. Robert J. Norrell, "Labor at the Ballot Box: Alabama Politics from the New Deal to the Dixiecrat Movement," *Journal of Southern History* 57, no. 2 (May 1991): 201–34; Wayne Flynt, "Bibb Graves," in *Alabama Governors,* 174; Samuel L. Webb, "Hugo Black, Bibb Graves and the Ku Klux Klan: A Revisionist View of the 1926 Alabama Democratic Primary," *Alabama Review* 57, no. 4 (October 2004): 243–73. For more on the Klan in Alabama during the first half of the twentieth century, see Glen Feldman, *Politics, Society, and the Klan in Alabama, 1915–1949* (Tuscaloosa: University of Alabama Press, 1999).

7. James Agee and Walker Evans, *Let Us Now Praise Famous Men* (Boston: Houghton Mifflin, 1939), 211; Flynt, *Poor but Proud,* 281–332; Norrell, "Labor at the Ballot Box," 214–15.

8. Flynt, "Bibb Graves," 173–79; Norrell, "Labor at the Ballot Box," 215–34; John Hayman with Clara Ruth Hayman, *A Judge in the Senate: Howell Heflin's Career of Politics and Principle* (Montgomery: New South Books, 2002), 57.

9. Norrell, "Labor at the Ballot Box," 216–34.

10. Ibid., 224–34; William D. Barnard, *Democrats and Dixiecrats: Alabama Politics, 1942–1950* (Tuscaloosa: University of Alabama Press, 1974), 120–46; Kari Frederickson, *The Dixiecrat Revolt and the End of the Solid South, 1932–1968* (Chapel Hill: University of North Carolina Press, 2001), 133–86.

11. Stephan Lesher, *George Wallace: American Populist* (New York: Addison-Wesley, 1994), 118–26; Dan T. Carter, *The Politics of Rage: George Wallace, the Origins of the New Conservatism, and the Transformation of American Politics* (New York: Simon and Schuster, 1995), 90–96; Marshall Frady, *Wallace* (New York: Meridian Books, 1970), 122–27. The painful lesson was learned when Wallace lost the 1958 gubernatorial election to John Patterson. It was then that he uttered the now famous epiphany: "Well boys, no son-of-a-bitch will ever out-nigger me again." There is some disagreement among scholars about the exact wording, but all agree to the theme behind the quote, regardless of the specific words.

12. V. O. Key, *Southern Politics in State and Nation* (New York: Alfred A. Knopf, 1949), 36–43.

13. Ibid., 45–56.

14. Ibid., 54–57; David Martin, "Alabama," in *Interest Group Politics in the Southern States,* ed. Ronald J. Hrebenar and Clive S. Thomas, 255–67 (Tuscaloosa: University of Alabama Press, 1992); Anne Permaloff and Carl Grafton, *Political Power in Alabama: The More Things Change . . .* (Athens: University of Georgia Press, 1995); interview, Chriss Doss; interview, Pete Turnham.

15. *Birmingham News,* 5 November 1967. Jackson's official title was executive secretary.

16. Carter, *Politics of Rage,* 17–23; Birmingham News, *Wallace: A Portrait of Power* (Birmingham: Birmingham News, 1998), 19–21; Lesher, *George Wallace,* 19–23.

17. Lesher, *George Wallace,* 19–22; Carter, *Politics of Rage,* 20–23.

18. Lesher, *George Wallace,* 26.

19. Ibid., 23; Carter, *Politics of Rage,* 26.

20. Lesher, *George Wallace,* 23–30; Birmingham News, *Wallace,* 21.

21. Carter, *Politics of Rage,* 27–29; Lesher, *George Wallace,* 30–32.

22. Carter, *Politics of Rage,* 29–30; Lesher, *George Wallace,* 16–32.

23. Interview, Bill Jones, 26 July 2002.

24. Carter, *Politics of Rage,* 31; Lesher, *George Wallace,* 33–36.

25. Lesher, *George Wallace,* 36–43; George Wallace Jr., as told to James Gregory, *The Wallaces of Alabama: My Family* (Chicago: Follet, 1975), 17.

26. Carter, *Politics of Rage,* 51–53; Lesher, *George Wallace,* 42–46; Frady, *Wallace,* 84.

27. Lesher, *George Wallace,* 46–49.

28. Ibid., 48–51; interview, Bob Ingram. According to the historian Dan Carter, the boardinghouse was the same one Wallace endured while a senate page.

29. Carter, *Politics of Rage,* 54–56; Lesher, *George Wallace,* 50–53.

30. Lesher, *George Wallace,* 55–62; Carter, *Politics of Rage,* 59–67.

31. Carter, *Politics of Rage,* 66–69.

32. Interview, McDowell Lee; Carter, *Politics of Rage,* 74–75; Lesher, *George Wallace,* 65–67; Mark M. Carroll, "George Corley Wallace, Jr., in the 1947 Legislature: Folsomite or Bourbon?" (master's thesis, University of Houston, 1990).

33. Carl Grafton and Anne Permaloff, *Big Mules and Branchheads: James E. Folsom and Political Power in Alabama* (Athens: University of Georgia Press, 1985); George Sims, *The Little Man's Big Friend: James E. Folsom in Alabama Politics, 1946–1958* (Tuscaloosa: University of Alabama Press, 1985).

34. Carroll, "George Corley Wallace Jr."; Carter, *Politics of Rage,* 75–78; Wallace and Gregory, *The Wallaces of Alabama,* 31–32; Lesher: *George Wallace,* 106. One of the patients in the state's miserable tubercular facilities was Gerald Wallace. "The conditions," Gerald recalled, "were horrible at the time I went into the county hospital. There were eight and ten patients crowded into each ward, and the patients had to look after the other patients, since there was not enough care. Many patients died while they were in the ward with the others."

35. "Alabama an Ideal Location for Industry," Admin. Files Gov. G. Wallace, SG22379, ADAH; Lesher, *George Wallace,* 86–87. The Wallace Act is separate from the similarly worded Cater Act that allowed municipalities to form their own industrial development corporations for bond financing and construction. The Wallace and Cater Acts were used for luring General Motors, Chrysler, Proctor and Gamble, Michelin, and Monsanto to the state.

36. Lesher, *George Wallace,* 75–77.

37. Ibid., 89–91; Carter, *Politics of Rage*, 78–80.

38. Lesher, *George Wallace*, 90–91; Carter, *The Politics of Rage*, 79–80; Wallace and Gregory, *The Wallaces of Alabama*, 37–41. Historian Dan Carter quotes a family friend who observed Wallace's interaction with his wife: "Hell he'd dole out about $5 a week and expect her to buy groceries and keep herself and the kids clothed and when she'd complain that it wasn't enough, he'd grump around for two or three days about how much money she was wasting." George Jr. reflected the ambivalence the children had about their father and the love they had for their mother: "All of my life I've wanted to prove myself to my dad because he's so strong. . . . In my eyes, my dad could do anything. . . . Because of his frequent absences, I think I relied more on my mother for company. She and I were very close. I believe she tried to fill the gap that was caused by his being gone so much."

39. Lesher, *George Wallace*, 91–96; David Frost, *Witness to Injustice* (Jackson: University Press of Mississippi, 1995), 73–75; Stephen Fayer, Daniel McCabe, and Paul Stekler, "George Wallace: Settin' the Woods on Fire," *The American Experience*, PBS documentary, produced by Daniel McCabe and Paul Stekler, Midnight Films and Big House Productions, 2000; interview, Pete Turnham; interview, McDowell Lee, Montgomery, Alabama. Frost's book reflects the ambivalence many Alabama blacks had for Wallace: "As I said before, I think Governor Wallace is a very fine person. I get in trouble with some colored people for saying that because they still don't like Governor Wallace. I voted for Governor Wallace back yonder because I knew that he don't mean all that stuff he was saying. He was saying that to get elected."

40. *Birmingham World*, 6 July, 10 July 1957; Carter, *Politics of Rage*, 82–85; Howell Raines, *My Soul Is Rested* (New York: G. P. Putnam's Sons, 1977), 56.

41. Lesher, *George Wallace*, 101–7; Carter, *Politics of Rage*, 82–87.

42. Interview, John Patterson; interview, Bob Ingram; Bill Jones, *The Wallace Story* (Northport, Ala.: American Southern, 1966), 5–7; Lesher, *George Wallace*, 110–27; Carter, *Politics of Rage*, 90–96.

43. Numan V. Bartley and Hugh D. Graham, *Southern Elections: County and Precinct Data, 1950–1972* (Baton Rouge: Louisiana State University Press, 1978), 9–10; Jones, *The Wallace Story*, 13; Carter, *Politics of Rage*, 90–96; interview, John Patterson.

44. George Wallace to Joseph Maxwell, 13 May 1958, Admin. Files Gov. G. Wallace, SG22370, Alabama Department of Archives and History; Lesher, *George Wallace*, 128–29; *Birmingham World*, 10 May, 17 May 1958.

45. *Birmingham World*, 17 May 1958; "Bruce Henderson for Governor," campaign brochure, box 6, J. Bruce Henderson Papers, ADAH; Jones, *The Wallace Story*, 14–15; Carter, *Politics of Rage*, 91–92; Raines, *My Soul Is Rested*, 305; interview, John Patterson. Henderson's campaign material indicated how quickly race had become the dominant issue in Alabama politics: "We have no hope unless we require our candidates for governor and other high offices to promise to support only the electors who will not vote for the nominees who have pledged themselves to the national Negro bloc voters to integrate the white South. We need men in high office who will support only those who have pledged themselves to vote for a Democrat of national stature and who understand and sympathize with the peculiar racial problems of the South. Give me your confidence and your mandate. Let me time the enactment of new segregation machinery, give me a sovereignty commission to implement and

advertise the building of a white political voting bloc in Alabama and the South and we will put our schools and our state and the South beyond the reach of integration. Nothing! Nothing! Nothing! could have caused me to run for governor of Alabama except the certain knowledge that unless we are able to stop the present trend of surrender to integration, that my 11 grandchildren and their children and your grandchildren will not be safe from destruction by integration."

46. Interview, John Patterson; Raines, *My Soul Is Rested,* 304–11; Lesher, *George Wallace,* 124–25; Carter, *Politics of Rage,* 94–95; Jones, *The Wallace Story,* 13–18.

47. Bartley and Graham, *Southern Elections,* 13–14; Lesher, *George Wallace,* 125; Carter, *Politics of Rage,* 96. Wallace won sixteen counties: Barbour, Bullock, Coffee, Colbert, Cullman, Dale, Franklin, Geneva, Henry, Houston, Lauderdale, Macon, Mobile, Montgomery, Pike, and Walker. Interestingly, Wallace drew about an equal number of counties from the traditionally white hill country and Wiregrass strongholds of the old reformist Populist insurgency as from his native and traditionally conservative Black Belt.

48. Carter, *Politics of Rage,* 97–100; Lesher, *George Wallace,* 129–33.

49. Lesher, *George Wallace,* 133–36; Carter, *Politics of Rage,* 98–101.

50. Tinsley E. Yarbrough, *Frank Johnson and Human Rights in Alabama* (Tuscaloosa: University of Alabama Press, 1981), 67–68; Lesher, *George Wallace,* 134–39; Carter, *Politics of Rage,* 100–103.

51. *Birmingham News,* 27 January 1959; *Birmingham Post-Herald,* 27–28 January 1959; *Montgomery Advertiser,* 27–28 January 1959; Carter, *Politics of Rage,* 102–3; Lesher, *George Wallace,* 138–40; Carl Elliott Papers, box 5502, W. S. Hoole Special Collections, University of Alabama.

52. Interview, Bob Ingram; *Birmingham News,* 2 May, 6 May 1962; Carter, *Politics of Rage,* 103. Privately, Wallace was more vindictive, holding a grudge against Johnson for his mocking ruling. "He's a no-good goddamn lying son-of-bitching race-mixing bastard," Wallace fumed.

53. *Huntsville Times,* 6 May 1962; *Montgomery Advertiser,* 4 May, 6 May, 23 May, 26 May 1962.

54. *Montgomery Advertiser,* 17 May, 28 May 1962; *Birmingham News,* 11 May 1962; *Huntsville Times,* 16 May 1962.

55. *Huntsville Times,* 16 May 1962; *Birmingham News,* 16 May, 23 May 1962; interview, George Wallace Jr. Some of the rumors bordered on the grotesque, foreshadowing a tactic used in 1970 against Albert Brewer and occasionally against Wallace himself by frustrated opponents. The less sensational rumors claimed that deGraffenreid was Autherine Lucy's lawyer, an atheist, and receiving financial support from the Kennedys. DeGraffenreid attributed their genesis to the "Barbour County Rumor Mill."

56. *Montgomery Advertiser,* 12 May, 25–27 May 1962; *Birmingham News,* 28 May 1962.

57. *Birmingham News,* 13 May 1962; *Montgomery Advertiser,* 17 May 1962.

58. Billy Graham to Frank Boykin, 28 May 1965, Admin. Files Gov. G. Wallace, SG22387, ADAH; Mary Hawkins to Bruce Henderson, 29 July 1960, and Bruce Henderson to Mary Hawkins, 2 August 1960, box 6, J. Bruce Henderson Papers, ADAH; *Birmingham News,* 13 May 1962; Peter Kohn, *The Cradle: Anatomy of a Town, Fact and Fiction* (New York: Vintage Press, 1969), 48–50; *Alabama Baptist,* 3 May, 10 May, 31 May 1962, 28 February, 2 May,

16 May, 20 June, 27 June, 11 July, 8 August, 15 August, 5 September, 19 September 1963. Macon's attacks on minority groups were directed at other Protestant denominations but left no doubt he was also referring to civil rights activists.

59. Bartley and Graham, *Southern Elections,* 16; *Huntsville Times,* 27 May 1962.

Chapter 2

1. Table SA30, Regional Economic Information System, Bureau of Economic Analysis, U.S. Department of Commerce, Economics and Statistics Administration; and Table SA05, Regional Economic System, Bureau of Economic Analysis, U.S. Department of Commerce, Economics and Statistics Administration. For an excellent analysis of poverty in Alabama see Wayne Flynt, *Poor but Proud: Alabama's Poor Whites* (Tuscaloosa: University of Alabama Press, 1989).

2. Interview, John Patterson.

3. Interview, John Patterson.

4. Virginia Van Der Veer Hamilton, *Lister Hill: Statesman from the South* (Chapel Hill: University of North Carolina Press, 1987); Ivo Hall Sparkman, *Journeys with the Senator* (Huntsville: Strode, 1977); *Memorial Addresses and Other Tributes in the Congress of the United States on the Life of John Sparkman: Ninety-ninth Congress, Second Session* (Washington, D.C.: U.S. GPO, 1986); Carl Elliott and Mike D'Orso, *The Cost of Courage: The Journey of the American Congressman* (New York: Doubleday, 1992).

5. Interview, John Patterson; *Mobile Register,* 28–29 November 1962.

6. Albert Burton Moore, *History of Alabama* (1934; Tuscaloosa: University Book Store, 1951), I used the 1934 edition; A. B. Moore to George Wallace, 19 July 1963, and statement of A. B. Moore on the Reasons for the Commemoration of the Civil War, in Admin. Files Gov. G. Wallace, SG22362, ADAH; Walter Fleming, *Civil War and Reconstruction in Alabama* (New York: Columbia University Press, 1905); Eric Foner, *Reconstruction: America's Unfinished Revolution, 1863–1877* (New York: Harper and Row, 1988); "Alabama Color Book," Admin. Files Gov. G. Wallace, SG22374, ADAH; interview, Bob Ingram; *Mobile Register,* 30 November 1962; *Montgomery Advertiser,* 15 June 1963.

7. *Montgomery Advertiser,* 9 January, 16 January 1966.

8. Wayne Flynt, *Alabama Baptists: Southern Baptists in the Heart of Dixie* (Tuscaloosa: University of Alabama Press, 1998); and William Warren Rogers, Robert David Ward, Leah Rawls Atkins, and Wayne Flynt, *Alabama: The History of a Deep South State* (Tuscaloosa: University of Alabama Press, 1994), 549; *Alabama Baptist* 31 May 1962, 27 June, 15 August, 19 September 1963; and *Mobile Register,* 13 April 1963.

9. Bruce Henderson to Mary Hawkins, 2 August 1960, box 6, J. Bruce Henderson Papers; Billy Graham to Frank Boykin, 28 May 1965, and Frank Boykin to Billy Graham, 1 June 1965, Admin. Files Gov. G. Wallace, SG22387; Mary Hawkins to Bruce Henderson, 29 July 1960, box 6, J. Bruce Henderson Papers, all in ADAH; and, interview, John Patterson.

10. "Sermon of Minister O. B. Porterfield at the Cleveland Avenue Church of Christ," O. B. Porterfield Papers, SPR 103; "Holy Week and the Civil Rights Demonstrations at the Churches: A Sermon-Address delivered by Dr. Robert Strong," Admin. Files Gov. G. Wallace, SG22387, all in ADAH.

11. *Mobile Register,* 25 January 1963; Rogers, Ward, Atkins, and Flynt, *Alabama,* 548; Statewide Oral History project, Alabama Center for Higher Education, interview no. 148, Dr. S. Q. Bryant interviewed by Robert Parker, Hollis Burke Frissell Library, Tuskegee University Archives, Tuskegee, Ala. For more on the Scottsboro case see Dan T. Carter, *Scottsboro: A Tragedy of the American South* (Baton Rouge: Louisiana State University Press, 1979).

12. "Statement of John P. Kohn to the Board of Revenue," 9 November 1964, Hugh Maddox Papers, LPR 103, box 1, ADAH; and Dan T. Carter, *Politics of Rage: George Wallace, the Origins of the New Conservatism, and the Transformation of American Politics* (New York: Simon and Schuster, 1995), 15.

13. Interviews, Albert Brewer; Earl Morgan to Ed Rodgers, 28 June 1963, Admin. Files Gov. G. Wallace, SG22364, ADAH.

14. Interviews, Albert Brewer.

15. *Montgomery Advertiser,* 1 January 1963; Carter, *Politics of Rage,* 9–11; "Inaugural Address of Governor George C. Wallace," Governor's Speeches: George Wallace, Lurleen Wallace, Albert Brewer, M94.1398, ADAH.

16. Carter, *Politics of Rage,* 10; *Montgomery Advertiser,* 3 November 1963. Inaugural events correspondence from various advertising agencies to George Wallace, SG22367; memorandum from Bill Jones to Bob Kendall, 11 December 1963, SG22375; memorandum from Bill Jones to Jack Ward, 25 March 1963, SG22363; memorandum from Bill Jones to Jack Ward, 24 May 1963, SG22364; memorandum to All Department Heads from Governor George C. Wallace, undated, SG22373; "Creed for Wallace Cabinet Members," SG22373 all in Admin. Files Gov. G. Wallace; and interviews, Bill Jones.

17. George Wallace to Howard K. Smith, 9 October 1962, SG22377; various telegrams from George Wallace to the Alabama Congressional Delegation, SG22368, all in Admin. Files Gov. G. Wallace, ADAH.

18. Executive order no. 1, 15 January 1963, Admin. Files Gov. G. Wallace, SG22362, ADAH; *Montgomery Advertiser,* 11 March 1964. Wallace's staff in March 1964 had eleven employees and a monthly payroll of $8,636. In contrast, John Patterson's staff as he left office had eleven employees and a monthly payroll of $8,982. Wallace relished any appearance, proper or not, that his administration was more cost-efficient than his rivals. In reality, an *Advertiser* report found that if the total number of employees that were actually working full-time for the governor were added to the payroll, the monthly payroll would have actually been $11,797.

19. Carl Grafton and Anne Permaloff, "James E. Folsom," in *Alabama Governors: A Political History of the State,* ed. Samuel L. Webb and Margaret E. Armbrester (Tuscaloosa: University of Alabama Press, 2001), 197–205. For more on Folsom see William D. Barnard, *Dixiecrats and Democrats: Alabama Politics, 1942–1950* (Tuscaloosa: University of Alabama Press, 1974); Carl Grafton and Anne Permaloff, *Big Mules and Branchheads: James E. Folsom and Political Power in Alabama* (Athens: University of Georgia Press, 1985); and, George Sims, *The Little Man's Big Friend: James E. Folsom in Alabama Politics, 1946–1958* (Tuscaloosa: University of Alabama Press, 1985).

20. Interview, Bob Ingram; *Montgomery Advertiser,* 4 August 1963. "Map of Alabama Counties Prohibiting the Sale of Alcoholic Beverages," SG22382; Mrs. Graham Shaddix et al.

to George Wallace, 23 January 1963, SG22370; George Wallace to Mrs Graham Shaddix, 6 February 1963, SG22370; and George Wallace to Mrs. L. E. Miles, 6 February 1963, all in Admin. Files Gov. G. Wallace, SG22370, ADAH. *Montgomery Advertiser,* 30 May 1963.

21. Sirotte, Permutt, Friend, and Friedman to Mitchell Rogovin, Office of Commissioner of Internal Revenue Service, 4 April 1963, Admin. Files Gov. G. Wallace, SG22382, ADAH.

22. Ed Dannelly to George Wallace, 1 May 1963; George Wallace to Ed Dannelly, 3 May 1963; Robert K. Bell to George Wallace, 13 August 1963; George Wallace to Leonard C. Johnson, 25 September 1963; and, memorandum from George Wallace to Herman Whisenant, 13 September 1963, all in Admin. Files Gov. G. Wallace, SG22362, ADAH.

23. Executive order no. 2, 15 January 1963, Admin. Files Gov. G. Wallace, SG22362, ADAH; *Montgomery Advertiser,* 1 March, 8 March, 13 March, 27 March 1963; John Tyson to George Wallace, 7 March 1963; Houston Feaster to George Wallace, 14 March 1963; and H. Austill Pharr to George Wallace, 15 March 1963, all in Admin. Files Gov. G. Wallace, SG22363, ADAH.

24. *Mobile Register,* 17–18 January 1963; *Montgomery Advertiser,* 28 February 1963; Wallace quote to Seymour Trammell, reference interview transcripts, "George Wallace: Settin' the Woods on Fire," www.pbs.org/wgbh/amex/wallace/filmmore/reference/interview/index.html. For a discussion of the Populist movement as a reasoned economic plan see Lawrence Goodwyn, *The Populist Moment: A Short History of the Agrarian Revolt in America* (New York: Oxford University Press, 1978).

25. Seymour Trammell as quoted in "George Wallace: Settin' the Woods on Fire," *The American Experience,* PBS.

26. Wallace was privately encouraged to run for president by some Alabamians even before he was inaugurated as governor. Publicly, he was linked to the possibility of being the standard bearer for the State's Rights party as early as March 1963. Although he did not take these suggestions seriously at first, the exposure he received as the leading anti-integration spokesman in the South and a leading critic of the Civil Rights Act quickly convinced him he had a platform for national campaigns. Publicly, he maintained that he had no interest in other offices, though privately the machinery for running in a limited number of 1964 primaries was already being assembled. Since he was chronically underestimated by intellectuals, political rivals in the North, and the national media, Wallace was able to make favorable impressions, especially in the eyes of his supporters. His instincts were reinforced with a flood of favorable letters that inundated the governor's office and came from every state in the Union.

27. *Montgomery Advertiser,* 12 February, 19 February, 3 March, 6 March, 9 March 1963; interview, Fuller Kimbrell; and interview, John Patterson.

28. *Montgomery Advertiser,* 10 March, 15 March 1963; interview, Bob Ingram; interview, McDowell Lee.

29. *Montgomery Advertiser,* 15–17 March, 14–16 April 1963.

30. Ibid., 14–20 April, 28 April 1963; *Birmingham News,* 13 April 1963. Various memorandums and correspondence from George Wallace, October 1962, SG22372; telegram from E. C. Kantrell to George Wallace, 13 April 1963, SG22364; and, telegram from Joe Russell to George Wallace, 13 April 1963, SG22364, all in Admin. Files Gov. G. Wallace, ADAH. When

Wallace officially reinstated the Mobile I-10 project, his press release hailed the work of the county's four representatives, the city governing bodies of Mobile, Prichard, and Chickasaw, and the Mobile County Commission. Senator John Tyson was completely left out. For more, see press release and telegrams of George C. Wallace on Mobile I-10 Project, Admin. Files Gov. G. Wallace, SG22364, ADAH.

31. *Montgomery Advertiser,* 19 April 1963.

32. Interview, Fuller Kimbrell.

33. George Wallace to Ed Rodgers, 26 July 1963, SG22365; "Tentative Allocations Wallace Municipal Aid Program," May 1963, SG22364; George Wallace to Senator Albert H. Evans and Representative Roswell Doggett, 15 July 1963, SG22364; memorandum from Cecil Jackson to Bob Kendall, 9 December 1963, SG22375; and, Elton B. Stephens to George Wallace, 25 September 1963, SG22365, all in Admin. Files Gov. G. Wallace, ADAH.

34. George Wallace to Seymore Trammell, 15 April 1963, SG22364; George Wallace to Richard Stone, 26 March 1963, SG22364; George Wallace to Seymore Trammell, 25 February 1963, SG22364; various letters and memorandums from George Wallace, SG22363–404; George Wallace to Richard Stone, 25 September 1963, SG22363; memorandums from Richard Stone to George Wallace, 26 September 1963, SG22363; Earl Morgan to Al Lingo, 12 July 1963, SG22367, all in Admin. Files Gov. G. Wallace, ADAH. The administrative files are replete with patronage intervention by Wallace on behalf of friends. Wallace occasionally got so involved with minutiae that he was writing and reviewing memos concerning custodians at junior colleges.

35. Interview, John Patterson; *Birmingham News,* 2 July 1950, 20 August 1955; interview, Fuller Kimbrell; interview, Julia Allen; various correspondence to George Wallace, 29 April, 5 June, 28 June 1963, Admin. Files Gov. G. Wallace, SG22364, ADAH; Sandra Baxley Taylor, *Me 'n' George: A Story of George Corley Wallace and His Number One Crony, Oscar Harper* (Mobile: Greenberry Press, 1988); various monthly reports of encumbrances and liquidations from the Department of Finance, Admin. Files Gov. G. Wallace, SG22367 and SG22368, ADAH.

36. Asa Rountree, "Report of Alabama's 1963 Airport Construction Program"; "Alabama Aviation News," August and July 1963 newsletters; "Special Activities Report for the Week of April 28–May 4," all in Admin. Files Gov. G. Wallace, SG22362, ADAH.

37. Asa Rountree to George Wallace, 29 May 1963; Rountree, "Report of Alabama's 1963 Airport Construction Program," all in Admin. Files Gov. G. Wallace, SG22362, ADAH.

38. *Montgomery Advertiser,* 18 October 1963; interviews, Albert Brewer.

39. State of Alabama Planning and Industrial Development Board, "Alabama: An Ideal Location for Industry," Admin. Files Gov. G. Wallace, SG22379, ADAH.

40. Cooper Green to Earl Morgan, 22 October 1963, SG22378; memorandum from Phillip Hamm to Earl Morgan, 24 October 1963, SG22378; E. R. Dickson to George Wallace, 25 March 1963, SG22366; Cooper Green to Hans J. Greven, 3 March 1963, SG22366, all in Admin. Files Gov. G. Wallace, ADAH.

41. *Montgomery Advertiser,* 9 April 1963. "State of Alabama Department of Education Superintendents and Teachers Salary Survey Report, School Year 1963–1964," Admin. Files Gov. G. Wallace, SG22363, ADAH. Alabama spent $202 per pupil (black and white combined) while the national average was over $400.

42. Department of Education State Summary from Annual Report, 1963, Admin. Files Gov. G. Wallace, SG22373, ADAH.

43. Truman Pierce, "A Look at Alabama and Her Future," Admin. Files Gov. G. Wallace, SG22363, ADAH.

44. Pierce, "A Look at Alabama," Admin. Files Gov. G. Wallace, SG22363, ADAH.

45. Pierce, "A Look at Alabama," Admin. Files Gov. G. Wallace, SG22363, ADAH.

46. *Montgomery Advertiser,* 24 March 1963; Rogers, Ward, Atkins, and Flynt, *Alabama,* 611.

47. *Montgomery Advertiser,* 28–29 March, 5 April 1963.

48. Interviews, Albert Brewer; *Montgomery Advertiser,* 31 March, 5–6 April, 8 April 1963.

49. *Montgomery Advertiser,* 15–19 April, 24 April 1963.

50. Ibid., 25–28 April, 30 April, 1–3 May, 7 May 1963.

51. David J. Garrow, *Bearing the Cross: Martin Luther King Jr. and the Southern Christian Leadership Conference* (London: Vintage Books, 1993), 231–65.

52. Interviews, Albert Brewer; *Montgomery Advertiser,* 28 March, 7 May 1963; 4 February 1964; interview, Bob Ingram.

53. Confidential memorandums from Austin Meadows to Junior College Presidents, 8 April 1966, Admin. Files Gov. G. Wallace, SG22404, ADAH.

54. Southern Regional Education Board press release, 10 February 1963, SG22364; Report of the Southern Regional Education Board, 28 March 1963, SG22364; Bob Ingram, "1963 Report of the Southern Regional Education Board," SG22364; *Montgomery Advertiser,* 25 May 1963; press release of A. R. Meadows, State Superintendent of Education, 19 December 1963, SG22373; undated marginalia written by Cecil Jackson on letter from Raymond Hurlburt to Cecil Jackson, SG22364, all correspondence and reports in Admin. Files Gov. G. Wallace, ADAH.

55. Minutes of the 5 August 1963 Board of Education meeting, Admin. Files Gov. G. Wallace, SG22364, ADAH; *Montgomery Advertiser,* 6 August 1963.

56. *Montgomery Advertiser,* 22 January, 5 February, 27 March, 6 June 1963; George Wallace to Bob Kendall, 25 March 1963, SG22363; George Wallace to Bob Kendall and Ed Rodgers, 10 June 1963, SG22364; George Wallace to Ed Rodgers, 1 April 1963, SG22364, all correspondence in Admin. Files Gov. G. Wallace, ADAH.

57. Interviews, Albert Brewer.

58. E. Culpepper Clark, *The Schoolhouse Door: Segregation's Last Stand at the University of Alabama* (New York: Oxford University Press, 1995), 153; *Montgomery Advertiser,* 15 May, 16 July 1963; interviews, Albert Brewer.

59. Clark, *Schoolhouse Door,* 246; interviews, Albert Brewer.

60. *Montgomery Advertiser,* 2 April 1963; telegram from George Wallace to Lister Hill and John Sparkman, 1 April 1963, Admin. Files Gov. G. Wallace, SG22368, ADAH.

61. *Montgomery Advertiser,* 3 April, 5 April, 10 April, 17 April 1963; telegram from George Wallace to Lister Hill and John Sparkman, Admin. Files Gov. G. Wallace, SG22368, ADAH.

62. Interview, John Patterson.

63. Wesley Critz George, "The Biology of the Race Problem" (Montgomery: Commission of the Governor of Alabama, 1962), 15–31, 84–86; Herbert C. Sanborn, "Summa Jus, Summa Injuria," typescript, undated, all in Admin. Files Gov. G. Wallace, SG22395, ADAH.

64. Interview, John Patterson; Gunnar Myrdal, *The American Dilemma: The Negro Problem and Modern Democracy* (New York: Harper, 1944); Carleton Stevens Coon, *The Origin of Races* (New York: Knopf, 1962); Carleton Putnam, *Race and Reason* (Washington, D.C.: Public Affairs Press, 1961).

65. Undated memorandum from Bill Jones to Adjutant General Alfred Harrison; George Wallace to Richmond Flowers, 6 May 1963, all in Admin. Files Gov. G. Wallace, SG22362, ADAH.

66. For more on Richmond Flowers see John Hayman, *Bitter Harvest: Richmond Flowers and the Civil Rights Revolution* (Montgomery: Black Belt Press, 1996). Useful biographies of Judge Johnson are Tinsley E. Yarborough, *Judge Frank Johnson and Human Rights in Alabama* (Tuscaloosa: University of Alabama Press, 1981); Jack Bass, *Taming the Storm: The Life and Times of Judge Frank M. Johnson and the South's Fight over Civil Rights* (New York: Doubleday, 1993); Frank Sikora, *The Judge: The Life and Opinions of Alabama's Frank M. Johnson, Jr.* (Montgomery: Black Belt Press, 1992); and Robert F. Kennedy, *Judge Frank M. Johnson* (New York: Putnam, 1978).

67. Susanetta R. Harris to Richmond Flowers, 17 October 1963, SG22373; Mrs. Anna B. Ross to Richmond Flowers, 8 April 1964, SG22383; and, Harry P. Gamble Sr. to Earl Morgan, 10 June 1963, SG22362, all in Admin. Files Gov. G. Wallace, ADAH.

68. Jeff Frederick, "Stand by Your Man: Race, Alabama Women, and George Wallace in 1963," *Gulf South Historical Review* 18, no. 1 (Fall 2002): 47–75; Bob Ingram, "Panel Presentation Comments," Alabama Studies Symposium, July 20, 2001, Montgomery, Alabama.

69. Inaugural Address of Governor George C. Wallace, Speeches of Governor George C. Wallace, Lurleen B. Wallace, and Albert Brewer, reel no. 2, in author's possession; *Mobile Register*, 14 January 1963; Stephan Lesher, *George Wallace: American Populist* (New York: Addison-Wesley, 1994), 165; Strom Thurmond to George Wallace, 15 August 1963, SG22368; telegram from George Wallace to Strom Thurmond, 21 August 1963, SG22368; George Wallace to Lester Maddox, 24 August 1964, SG22381, all correspondence in Admin. Files Gov. G. Wallace, ADAH. For more on the Dixiecrats see Kari A. Frederickson, *The Dixiecrat Revolt and the End of the Solid South, 1932–1968* (Chapel Hill: University of North Carolina, 2001). For more on Strom Thurmond see Jack Bass and Marilyn W. Thompson, *Ol' Strom: An Unauthorized Biography of Strom Thurmond* (Atlanta: Longstreet, 1998), and Nadine Cohadas, *Strom Thurmond and the Politics of Southern Change* (Macon: Mercer University Press, 1993). For more on Lester Maddox see Bob Short, *Everything Is Pickrick: The Life of Lester Maddox* (Macon: Mercer University Press, 1999), and Bruce Galphin, *The Riddle of Lester Maddox* (Atlanta: Camelot, 1968).

70. Association of Citizens' Council, "The Citizens' Council," tract no. 65759L (Greenwood, Miss.: Association of Citizens' Councils, 1954), 1–5, box 6, J. Bruce Henderson Papers, ADAH; interview, John Patterson; interview, Jere Beasley; interview, Bob Ingram. For more on the Citizens' Councils see Neil R. McMillen, *The Citizens' Council: Organized Resistance to the Second Reconstruction, 1954–1964* (Champaign: University of Illinois Press, 1971), and Hodding Carter, *The South Strikes Back* (Garden City, N.Y.: Doubleday, 1959).

71. Association of Citizens' Council, "The Citizens' Council," tract no. 65759L (Greenwood, Miss.: Association of Citizens' Councils, 1954), 4, box 6, J. Bruce Henderson Papers, ADAH.

72. Memorandum from Bruce Henderson to the trustees of the Alabama Foundation,

20 February 1961, box 7; Leonard Wilson to Bruce Henderson, 27 January 1961, box 6; Leonard Wilson, "Suggested Program for the State Citizens' Council Organization," undated, box 6, all in J. Bruce Henderson Papers, ADAH.

73. Form letter from George Wallace to New Citizens' Council Member, 5 November 1963, SG22383; telegram from Jefferson County Citizens' Council to George Wallace, 12 September 1963, SG22368; telegram from George Wallace to Jefferson County Citizens' Council, 13 September 1963, SG22368; George Wallace to Houston Feaster, 16 March 1963, SG22383; miscellaneous 1963 correspondence to George Wallace, SG22362–64, all in Admin. Files Gov. G. Wallace, ADAH.

74. *Montgomery Advertiser,* 22 July 1963; *Mobile Register,* 21 November 1962, 11 January, 7 March, 18 April 1963.

75. *Montgomery Advertiser,* 8 April, 16– 17 July 1963.

76. Ibid., 16 October 1963.

77. C. Carroll Pierce to Bob Cleckler, [no month or day] 1963, SG22362; telegram from Willard Wirtz to George Wallace and marginalia written by Cecil Jackson, 13 March 1963, SG22362; telegram from George Wallace to Carl Elliot, 24 April 1963, SG22368; telegram from Sam Gibbons, 15 March 1963, SG22363; George Wallace to Charles Cooper, 13 May 1963, SG22365, all in Admin. Files Gov. G. Wallace, ADAH.

78. *Montgomery Advertiser,* 17 October 1963.

79. Ibid., 17–19 October, 21 October, 28 October, 7–8 November 1963; various correspondence and memorandums, Admin. Files Gov. G. Wallace, SG22372, ADAH.

80. Lesher, *George Wallace,* 164–236; interviews, Bill Jones; interviews, Albert Brewer.

81. Clark, *Schoolhouse Door,* 224–37; *Montgomery Advertiser,* 30–31 May, 1–2 June, 4 June, 6–9 June, 12 June 1963; telegram from George Wallace to Frank Rose, 12 June 1963, Admin. Files Gov. G. Wallace, SG22368, ADAH. To Wallace's credit, no major violence occurred that day in Tuscaloosa or at the University Extension Center in Huntsville. Wallace appeared on television and sent a telegram to the state's major newspapers asking for peace and for the citizens of the state to stay away from the campus. Telegram of George Wallace to various newspapers, 5 June 1963, Admin. Files Gov. G. Wallace, SG22368, ADAH.

Chapter 3

1. *Montgomery Advertiser,* 9 December, 20 December, 29 December 1963, 1–2 January 1964.

2. Ibid., 29 December 1964.

3. John Carnett to George Wallace, [received January 1964], Admin. Files Gov. G. Wallace, SG22373, ADAH.

4. *Montgomery Advertiser,* 5 April, 19 April, 25–26 April, 12 August 1964.

5. "The Civil Rights Movement," Speech of George Wallace in Atlanta, Georgia, 4 July 1964, Essential Documents in American History, Essential Documents, 1492–present, p. 1, item number 9709120870.

6. "Confidential Industrial Prospects Report: North Central U.S.," February 1964, SG22378; George Wallace to Jim Clark, undated, SG22379; Cooper Green to George Wallace, 28 May 1964, SG22379, all in Admin. Files Gov. G. Wallace, ADAH.

7. *Montgomery Advertiser,* 23 January 1964; minutes of the meeting of the Committee of 100, 29 January 1964, Admin. Files Gov. G. Wallace, SG22414, ADAH.

8. "Alabama Social Welfare Annual Report, 1962–63," Department of Pensions and Security, SG22378; minutes of the 9 December 1964 Unemployment Compensation Committee Meeting, SG22390, all in Admin. Files Gov. G. Wallace, ADAH; and *Montgomery Advertiser,* 1 September 1963, 16 March 1964.

9. Highlights of the 1963–64 Fiscal Year, memorandum from Ruben King to State Board of Pensions and Security; State of Alabama Department of Pensions and Security 1964, Admin. Files Gov. G. Wallace, all in SG22378, ADAH; *Montgomery Advertiser,* 22 January 1964.

10. Ruben King to George Wallace, 3 April 1963, Admin. Files Gov. G. Wallace, SG22366, ADAH.

11. Ruben King to George Wallace, 3 April 1963, Admin. Files Gov. G. Wallace, SG22366, ADAH.

12. Ruben King to George Wallace, 3 April 1963, Admin. Files Gov. G. Wallace, SG22366, ADAH; Ruben King to George Wallace, 8 August 1963, Admin. Files Gov. G. Wallace, SG22366, ADAH.

13. Memorandum from George Wallace to Susie West, 2 March 1964, SG22378; memorandum from George Wallace to Ruben King, 22 December 1964, SG22392; Ruben King to Miss Josie Mae Randolph, 31 December 1964, SG22392, all in Admin. Files Gov. G. Wallace, ADAH. Unfortunately for Miss Randolph, King was unable to resume her payments for assistance to the blind.

14. *Montgomery Advertiser,* 1 September, 3 September 1963.

15. Mrs. Louis Anderson to George Wallace, 20 August 1963; Mrs. Fletcher King to George Wallace, 29 August 1963, all in Admin. Files Gov. G. Wallace, SG22374, ADAH.

16. M. H. Woodard to George Wallace, 12 September 1963; George Wallace to M. H. Woodard, 18 September 1963, all in Admin. Files Gov. G. Wallace, SG22363, ADAH.

17. George Wallace to M. H. Woodard, 18 September 1963, Admin. Files Gov. G. Wallace, SG22363, ADAH; *Birmingham News,* 5–15 September 1963; *Montgomery Advertiser,* 11 April, 31 July 1964.

18. Executive order no. 9 of the governor of Alabama, 2 September 1963, Admin. Files Gov. G. Wallace, SG22363, ADAH.

19. *Mobile Register,* 7 September, 10–11 September, 20 September 1963; *Montgomery Advertiser,* 1 September, 3 September, 5–7 September 1963; *Birmingham News,* 1–11 September 1963.

20. *Mobile Register,* 7 September, 10 September 1963; *Montgomery Advertiser,* 7 September, 10 September 1963; *Huntsville Times,* 1–14 September 1963. Tricia Miree to George Wallace, 3 September 1963, Admin. Files Gov. G. Wallace, SG22374, ADAH. Several state newspapers pressured the Wallace administration to keep the schools open including the *Montgomery Advertiser, Selma Times-Journal, Birmingham News,* and *Huntsville Times.*

21. Telegram from James Rea to George Wallace, 2 September 1963, Admin. Files Gov. G. Wallace, SG22374, ADAH; *Montgomery Advertiser,* 3 September 1963.

22. *Montgomery Advertiser,* 11 September 1963.

23. Ibid., 13 September, 20 September, 4 October, 8 October, 13 October, 30 October 1963.

Telegram from George Wallace to John Segrest, 12 September 1963, SG22368; and, Martha C. Oliver, "A Report to You," 1965 Macon Academy Newsletter, SG22374, all in Admin. Files Gov. G. Wallace, ADAH.

24. Martha Oliver, "A Report to You," Macon Academy Newsletter, Admin. Files Gov. G. Wallace, SG22374, ADAH; *Montgomery Advertiser,* 2 November 1963. Tuition in 1964 was $20 per month per student; in 1965 it was $22 per month per student. The 1964–65 annual budget was $99,981, of which $61,200 was allocated from tuition and $38,781 from outside sources including special contributions, scholarships, sponsors, and out-of-county tuition rates that were as high as $35 per month per student.

25. Telegram from George Wallace to Wayne McLendon, 12 September 1963, Admin. Files Gov. G. Wallace, SG22374, ADAH.

26. George Wallace to John Segrest, 3 September 1964; Frances Wadsworth to George Wallace, 25 September 1964; Harry F. Weyher to John Segrest, 11 December 1964, all in Admin. Files Gov. G. Wallace, SG22374, ADAH; *Montgomery Advertiser,* 30 October 1963, 23 December 1964; various memorandums, SG22374; various correspondence from George Wallace to Charles Cooper, SG22377, all correspondence in Admin. Files Gov. G. Wallace, ADAH. Draper supported eugenics and other racially charged pseudoscientific ideas through the Pioneer Fund, where he served on the board of directors for forty-five years.

27. *Montgomery Advertiser,* 5–7 September, 9 September, 16–18 September, 20 September; *Birmingham News,* 16–18 September 1963.

28. Interview, McDowell Lee; *Montgomery Advertiser,* 16 September, 3 October, 8 October 1963; Wayne Flynt, "The Ethics of Democratic Persuasion and the Birmingham Crisis," *Southern Speech Journal* 35 (Fall 1969): 40–53.

29. *Montgomery Advertiser,* 8 January, 10–11 January 1964.

30. Ibid., 10 January, 24 January, 26 January 1964.

31. Ibid., 27 January 1964.

32. Ibid., 27 January, 31 January, 4 January, 15 February 1964; "Statement of Governor George C. Wallace," 3 February 1964, Admin. Files Gov. G. Wallace, SG22374, ADAH.

33. *Chicago Sun-Times,* 6 February 1964; *Montgomery Advertiser,* 6 February 1964; transcript of 10 February 1964 press conference of Governor George C. Wallace, Admin. Files Gov. G. Wallace, SG22374, ADAH; *Montgomery Advertiser,* 27 June 1964.

34. Transcript of 10 February 1964 press conference of Governor George C. Wallace; statement of George C. Wallace, 3 February 1964; J. A. Gordon to George Wallace, 6 February 1964, all in Admin. Files Gov. G. Wallace, SG22374, ADAH; *Montgomery Advertiser,* June 19, 1964.

35. *Montgomery Advertiser,* 12 February 1964.

36. Ibid., 19 February, 21 February, 17 March, 26 March 1964; Resolution of the Alabama State Board of Education, 18 February 1964, Admin. Files Gov. G. Wallace, SG22374, ADAH.

37. *Montgomery Advertiser,* 21 April, 24 April, 23 May, 26 May 1964.

38. Ibid., 18–22 September 1964.

39. *Montgomery Advertiser,* 18 September, 20 September, 22 September.

40. State of Alabama Department of Education Annual Report of 1964, Admin. Files

Gov. G. Wallace, SG22374, ADAH; *Montgomery Advertiser,* 4 October 1964; *Mobile Press,* 22 September 1964.

41. *Montgomery Advertiser,* 13 December 1964; minutes of the State Board of Education Meeting, 10 December 1964, SG22386; press release of the Textbook Study Committee of the Alabama Society of the Daughters of the American Revolution, 20 July 1964, SG22374, minutes and press release in Admin. Files Gov. G. Wallace, ADAH.

42. *Birmingham News,* 3 July 1964.

43. Ibid., 3 July, 8–9 July 1964.

44. Opinion of the Supreme Court of Alabama, October Term 1963–64, *George C. Wallace et al. v. Paul R. Malone,* 19 July 1964; Elton B. Stephens to George Wallace, 20 July 1963, all in Admin. Files Gov. G. Wallace, SG22374, ADAH.

45. Resolution of the Alabama Board of Education, 1 October 1963; Austin Meadows, Superintendent of Education to Paul R. Malone, 5 November 1963, all in Admin. Files Gov. G. Wallace, SG22374, ADAH; *Montgomery Advertiser,* 10 October 1963.

46. Telegram from Paul R. Malone to George Wallace, 21 June 1964, Admin. Files Gov. G. Wallace, SG22374, ADAH; *Montgomery Advertiser,* 23 June, 3 July, 9 July 1964.

47. *Montgomery Advertiser,* 9 July 1964; Harvey Elrod, Deputy Attorney General, to Earl C. Morgan, Admin. Files Gov. G. Wallace, SG22374, ADAH.

48. *Montgomery Advertiser,* 1–2 October, 10 October, 10 December 1964; interview, McDowell Lee; and interviews, Albert Brewer.

49. Minutes of the State Board of Education Meeting, 10 December 1964, Admin. Files Gov. G. Wallace, SG22386, ADAH; *Montgomery Advertiser,* 10 October, 13 November, 17 November, 13 December 1964.

50. Mrs. James M. Sizemore to George Wallace, 7 December 1964, Admin. Files Gov. G. Wallace, SG22387, ADAH.

51. A. F. Lee, Commissioner of the State of Alabama Board of Corrections, to Jimmy Noles, 2 April 1964, Admin. Files Gov. G. Wallace, SG22372, ADAH; *Tulsa Tribune* 19 November 1964.

52. *Tri-Cities Daily,* 15–16 November 1964; *Montgomery Advertiser,* 31 May 1964.

53. Various correspondence to George Wallace; memorandum from George Wallace to Frank Lee, 15 April 1964; memorandum from Earl Morgan to all State Government Department Heads, May 1964, all in Admin. Files Gov. G. Wallace, SG22372, ADAH; *Montgomery Advertiser,* 20 March 1964.

54. *Montgomery Advertiser,* 19 June, 24 June 1964; "Final Report of the Study Commission investigating the use of Convict Labor on State Highways," 7 October 1964, SG22385; Frank Lee to Mrs. John Bugler, 22 June 1964, SG22372; George Wallace to Mrs. John Bugler, 18 June 1964, SG22372, all in Admin. Files Gov. G. Wallace, ADAH.

55. "Final Report of Study Commission Investigating Use of Convict Labor on State Highways," 7 October 1964, Admin. Files Gov. G. Wallace, SG22385, ADAH.

56. "Final Report of Study Commission Investigating Use of Convict Labor on State Highways," 7 October 1964, Admin. Files Gov. G. Wallace, SG22385, ADAH; *Montgomery Advertiser,* 30 June, 1 August 1964.

57. *Montgomery Advertiser,* 1–2 July 1964.

58. Ibid., 31 July 1964; Colleen Ann Bugler to George Wallace, 16 June 1964; a mother to George Wallace, 15 June 1964, all in Admin. Files Gov. G. Wallace, SG22372, ADAH.

59. State of Alabama Twenty-Fourth Annual Statistical Report of the State Board of Pardons and Paroles, October 1, 1962–September 30, 1963; memorandum from L. B. Stephens to George Wallace, 24 May 1963, all in Admin. Files Gov. G. Wallace, SG22366, ADAH.

60. *Montgomery Advertiser,* 31 July 1964; "Final Report of Study Commission Investigating the Use of Convict Labor on State Highways," 7 October 1964, Admin. Files Gov. G. Wallace, SG22385, ADAH.

61. *Montgomery Advertiser,* 3 November, 7 November 1963, 16 June 1964.

62. Ibid., 4–5 January 1964; interviews, Albert Brewer.

63. *Montgomery Advertiser,* 25–26 July, 30 July 1964. One day before announcing the plan to call the special session, Wallace assured the media, "I haven't made any decision about that at all," *Montgomery Advertiser,* July 24 1964. Not everyone was quick to jump on Goldwater's bandwagon. Alabamians, particularly those in the northern part of the state, were reminded of the chronology of the senator's views on TVA: 1957, "TVA was conceived in socialism, born during a period of economic chaos and has been nurtured and expanded in deceit"; 1961, "We should sell TVA to private interests even if we could get only $1 for it"; 1963, "I am quite serious in my opinion that TVA should be sold"; and 1963, "I meant it then. I mean it now." Citizens for TVA Inc., Admin. Files Gov. G. Wallace, SG22382, ADAH.

64. *Montgomery Advertiser,* 31 July, 1 August, 3–6 August 1964.

65. Constitution of the State of Alabama, 1901; *Montgomery Advertiser,* 6 August 1964.

66. *Montgomery Advertiser,* 7 August 1964.

67. Ibid., 7–9 August, 16 August 1964.

68. Ibid., 16 August, 19–23 August, 26 August, 29 August 1964.

69. Roster of State Democratic Executive Committee of Alabama, SG22403; Roster of State Democratic Steering Committee of Alabama, SG22363; Frank Mizell to George Wallace, 13 February 1963, SG22364; Freida Billingsley, Secretary of the Alabama Democratic Campaign Steering Committee, 27 May 1963, SG22363, all in Admin. Files Gov. G. Wallace, ADAH.

70. *Montgomery Advertiser,* 2–3 December 1963.

71. Ibid., 24 June 1964; John Bailey to George Wallace, 25 February 1964, Admin. Files Gov. G. Wallace, SG22372, ADAH.

72. *Montgomery Advertiser,* 23 July, 4 August 1964.

73. Ibid., 22 August 1964; Testimony Prepared for Delivery by George C. Wallace before the Platform Committee of the National Democratic Convention, 21 August 1964, Admin. Files Gov. G. Wallace, SG22373, ADAH.

74. Testimony Prepared for Delivery by George C. Wallace before the Platform Committee of the National Democratic Convention, 21 August 1964, Admin. Files Gov. G. Wallace, SG22373, ADAH.

75. Testimony Prepared for Delivery by George C. Wallace before the Platform Committee of the National Democratic Convention, 21 August 1964, Admin. Files Gov. G. Wallace, SG22373, ADAH; *Cross and the Flag* (August 1964): 19.

76. *Montgomery Advertiser,* 22–24 August 1964; report of Jess Lanier about the Alabama

Delegations Activities at the 1964 Democratic National Convention, undated, Admin. Files Gov. G. Wallace, SG22373, ADAH.

77. Report of Jess Lanier about the Alabama Delegations Activities at the 1964 Democratic National Convention, undated; telegram from George Wallace to Jess Lanier, 24 August 1964, all in Admin. Files Gov. G. Wallace, SG22373, ADAH. Roy McCord, Ethel McCord, Reuben Newton, Sue Newton, Harold Morris, Ester Hannay, and Don Hawkins were the Alabamians who signed the oath.

78. Report of Jess Lanier about the Alabama Delegation's Activities at the 1964 Democratic National Convention, undated, Admin. Files Gov. G. Wallace, SG22373, ADAH; "Proposed Organization of Alabama Delegates to Democratic National Convention," August 1964; "Mr. [Goodwin's] Statement to the Alabama Caucus"; Resolution of the Alabama Legislature, 25 August 1964, all in Admin. Files Gov. G. Wallace, SG22373, ADAH; *Montgomery Advertiser,* 28 August, 26 September 1964.

79. *Montgomery Advertiser,* 30 August, 3 September 1964; press release of the Tennessee-Tombigbee Waterway Development Authority, September 1964, Admin. Files Gov. G. Wallace, SG22382, ADAH.

80. W. D. Malone to George Wallace, 29 December 1962, Admin. Files Gov. G. Wallace, SG22364, ADAH; William A. Degregorio, *The Complete Book of U.S. Presidents* (New York: Wings Books, 1993), 515, 553-54. In 1960, six of the eleven from the unpledged slate were elected.

81. Memorandum from Bill Jones to Eli Howell, 8 July 1964, SG22381; "Stand Up for America," paid political advertising by friends of Governor George C. Wallace, SG22373; Stanley Pospisil to George Wallace, 14 September 1963, SG22364; *Dan Smoot Report* 9, no. 24 (17 June 1963); George Wallace to Stanley Pospisil, 12 November 1963, SG22364; John Grenier to George Wallace, 15 October 1963, SG22364; George Wallace to Calvin Poole, 10 July 1964, SG22372; I. J. Scott to George Wallace, 21 May 1964, SG22373, political ad and correspondence in Admin. Files Gov. G. Wallace, ADAH.

82. "Vote for Unpledged Electors and Support Governor George C. Wallace, Stand Up for America," paid political advertising by friends of Governor George C. Wallace; "Outline for Elector Campaign"; "Stand Up for America Sample Ballot," all in Admin. Files Gov. G. Wallace, SG22373, ADAH. The unpledged electors were Lieutenant Governor Jim Allen, Pell City newspaper editor Edmund Blair, Speaker of the House Albert Brewer, State Senator Albert Evans, former Attorney General McDonald Gallion, former Director of Industrial Relations Jack Giles, former Birmingham Mayor Arthur Hanes, State Senator Pete Matthews, Montgomery Attorney Frank Mizell, and Opelika contractor Jud Scott.

83. "Stand Up for America Sample Ballot," paid political advertisement by Phil Holmes, Mobile, Alabama; "Vote for Unpledged Electors and Support Governor George C. Wallace," paid political advertising by friends of Governor George C. Wallace, all in Admin. Files Gov. G. Wallace, SG22373, ADAH; *Montgomery Advertiser,* 22 June 1964.

84. Cecil Jackson to Bull Connor, 10 December 1963, SG22372; Leonard Wilson, Executive Secretary of the Citizen's Councils of Alabama, 18 March 1964, SG22373; I. J. Scott to George Wallace, 14 August 1964, SG22373; special memorandum of the Hudson-Thompson company to all Hudson-Thompson employees, 29 April 1964, SG22373, all in Admin. Files Gov. G. Wallace, ADAH.

85. *Montgomery Advertiser*, 6–8 May, 11 May, 13 May, 17 May, 3–4 June, 7 June 1964; interviews, Albert Brewer; interviews, Bill Jones; memorandum from Cecil Jackson to Jim Solomon, 8 June 1964, and Mary G. Allen to George Wallace, 4 June 1964, in Admin. Files Gov. G. Wallace, SG22372, ADAH.

86. John Grenier to George Wallace, 22 February 1963, SG22379; telegram from Jim Martin to George Wallace, 19 October 1964, SG22373, all in Admin. Files Gov. G. Wallace, ADAH.

87. *Montgomery Advertiser*, 16–17 September 1964.

88. Ibid., 6 September, 29 October, 1 November, 8 November 1964; memorandum from Earl Morgan to George Wallace, 30 September 1964, Admin. Files Gov. G. Wallace, SG22373, ADAH.

89. *Montgomery Advertiser*, 4–5 November, 7–8 November, 10 November, 13 November, 15 November 1964.

90. Ibid., 20 November 1964.

Chapter 4

1. *Montgomery Advertiser*, 3 January, 4 February 1965.

2. Ibid., 3 January 1965.

3. Code of Alabama (Charlottesville: Michie, 1958), title 36, sec. 58 (60); *Montgomery Advertiser*, 4 August 1965. Al Lingo to Cecil Jackson, 22 April 1963, SG22367; Earl Morgan to Al Lingo, July 12 1963, SG22367; "1963–64 29th Annual Report of the Department of Public Safety," SG22393, all in Admin. Files Gov. G. Wallace, ADAH.

4. Al Lingo to Cecil Jackson, 22 April 1963, Admin. Files Gov. G. Wallace, SG22367, ADAH.

5. Memorandum from Captain R. W. Godwin and Lieutenant W. B. Painter to Albert J. Lingo, 25 January 1963; Earl Morgan to Al Lingo, 11 March 1963, all in Admin. Files Gov. G. Wallace, SG22367, ADAH.

6. "Individuals Active in Civil Disturbances," Admin. Files Gov. G. Wallace, SG22393, ADAH; *Montgomery Advertiser*, 14 March 1965.

7. *Montgomery Advertiser*, 3–5 January, 16 June 1965. Ruben King and Phil Hamm were the others who refused to sign the pledge.

8. Mary Stanton, *From Selma to Sorrow: The Life and Death of Viola Liuzzo* (Athens: University of Georgia Press, 1998), 209–10. Glenn T. Eskew, *But for Birmingham: The Local and National Movements in the Civil Rights Struggle* (Chapel Hill: University of North Carolina Press, 1997), 301–2, 390; Robert J. Norrell, *Reaping the Whirlwind: The Civil Rights Movement in Tuskegee* (Chapel Hill: University of North Carolina Press, 1998) 145; Lee E. Bains, "Birmingham 1963: Confrontation over Civil Rights," in *Birmingham, Alabama, 1956–1963: The Black Struggle for Civil Rights*, ed. David J. Garrow (Brooklyn: Carlson, 1989), 192, 199.

9. S. Jonathan Bass, *Blessed Are the Peacemakers: Martin Luther King Jr., Eight White Religious Leaders, and the "Letter from Birmingham Jail"* (Baton Rouge: Louisiana State University Press, 2001), 180; Stephen L. Longnecker, *Selma's Peacemaker: Ralph Smeltzer and*

Civil Rights Mediation (Philadelphia: Temple University Press, 1987), 34–35; *Washington Post,* 3 August 1964.

10. *Montgomery Advertiser,* 13–17 March 1965; Citizens Council File, 1965, SG22383; Petitions in Support of Al Lingo, SG223936; various letters to George Wallace, 15–21 March 1965, SG22394, all in Admin. Files Gov. G. Wallace, ADAH.

11. Lester Wingard to George Wallace, 11 March 1965, SG22394; George Wallace to Lester Wingard, 17 March 1965, SG22394; H. F. Dunning to George Wallace, 17 March 1965, SG22397, all in Admin. Files Gov. G. Wallace, ADAH.

12. *Montgomery Advertiser,* 5 January 1964; 16 June 1965; Mobile County Sheriff Ray Bridges to George Wallace, 21 June 1965, Admin. Files Gov. G. Wallace, SG22394, ADAH; *Mobile Register,* 20 June 1965.

13. Contracts for Employment of Additional Police Force, 11 May 1963 and 7 June 1963, SG22363; Claude Kelly, Director of the Alabama Department of Conservation to George C. Wallace, 8 April 1965, SG22384; Hugh Maddox to Claude Kelley, 28 April 1965, SG22384, all in Admin. Files Gov. G. Wallace, ADAH.

14. John Spaulding, Executive Secretary of the Alabama Wildlife Federation to George Wallace, 26 March 1965; Claude Kelley to Cecil Davis, President of the Sportsmen's Club, 29 March 1965, all in Admin. Files Gov. G. Wallace, SG22384, *Montgomery Advertiser,* 22 October, 5 November 1963.

15. "Alabama Forest Facts," Fall 1963, Produced by the State of Alabama Planning and Industrial Development Board, SG22371; Claude Kelley to George Wallace, 8 May 1963, SG22362; draft of letter written by Claude Kelley, undated, SG22362; memorandum from Claude Kelley to George Wallace, 8 August 1963, SG22362; Claude Kelley to Jack Greer, 8 May 1963, SG22362; memorandum from J. M. Stauffer to Claude Kelley, 3 May 1963, SG22362, all in Admin. Files Gov. G. Wallace, ADAH.

16. Claude Kelley to Gardner Bassett, 8 May 1963; Claude Kelley to George Wallace, 2 May, 8 May 1963; memorandum from Claude Kelley to Conservation Department Section Chiefs, 12 February 1963, all in Admin. Files Gov. G. Wallace, SG22362, ADAH.

17. *Montgomery Advertiser,* 23–24 October, 30–31 October, 3 November 1963; memorandum from Fred Robertson, Director of the Auburn University Cooperative Extension Service, to All County Agents, 22 October 1963, Admin. Files Gov. G. Wallace, SG22362, ADAH. Concerning the inability to turn back small fires, on one October day alone, the number of active fires grew from 74 to 93.

18. L. W. Parker to Claude Kelley, 2 May 1963; Minutes from Advisory Board of Conservation Meeting, 5 February 1963; Hugh Mahon to George Wallace, 21 February 1963; memorandum from J. M. Stauffer to Claude Kelley, 14 February 1963, all in Admin. Files Gov. G. Wallace, SG22362, ADAH.

19. Claude Kelley to George Wallace, 2 May 1963; memorandum from J. M. Stauffer to Claude Kelley, 3 May 1963, all in Admin. Files Gov. G. Wallace, SG22362, ADAH.

20. Marion Leach to Alabama Certified Tree Farmers, 1 March 1963; Minutes from Advisory Board of Conservation Meeting, 5 February 1963, all in Admin. Files Gov. G. Wallace, SG22362, ADAH. Leach was chairman of the Alabama Tree Farm Committee.

21. Minutes of the Advisory Board of Conservation Meeting, 19 February 1964, SG22371;

Montgomery Advertiser, 22 March 1964, 7 August 1965; Joe Graham, President of the Alabama Forest Products Association to Claude Kelley, 5 March 1964, SG22367; Claude Kelley to Joe Graham, 13 March 1964, SG22367, minutes and correspondence in Admin. Files Gov. G. Wallace, ADAH.

22. Various 1964 contracts between the state of Alabama and Conservation Department vendors, correspondence between Claude Kelley and George Wallace, all in Admin. Files Gov. G. Wallace, SG22372, ADAH.

23. Memorandum from Claude Kelley to George Wallace, 12 May 1964; memorandum from the Department of Conservation to State Park employees, undated and untitled; memorandum from Laurence H. Marks, Chief of the Division of State Parks, to Claude Kelley, 8 September 1964, all in Admin. Files Gov. G. Wallace, SG22367, ADAH.

24. John Spaulding to George Wallace, 26 March 1965; Claude Kelley to Cecil Davis, 29 March 1965; minutes of the Conservation Board Meeting of 17 February 1965, all in Admin. Files Gov. G. Wallace, SG22384, ADAH.

25. Memorandum from Bill Jones to Ed Ewing, 5 February 1964; Ed Ewing to Bill Jones, 19 February 1964, all in Admin. Files Gov. G. Wallace, SG22379, ADAH.

26. [A state employee] to George Wallace, 22 May 1963, SG22365; [a Kilby prison guard] to George Wallace, 1 February 1963, SG22363; various letters from Charles Woods to George Wallace, SG22363; memorandum from Earl Morgan to George Wallace, 28 June 1963, SG22363; testimony of inmate Jack Earl Robbins to Board of Corrections, 15 May 1963, SG22363; Frank Lee to George Wallace, 14 May 1963, SG22363; T. Earle Johnson to George Wallace, 4 April 1963, SG22363; R.S. Watson to Charles Woods, 21 March 1963, SG22363, all in Admin. Files Gov. G. Wallace, ADAH.

27. Thomas Crawford, Acting President United Mine Workers District 20 to George Wallace, 26 September 1963, SG22365; "The Alabama Merit System 1963 Annual Report of the State Personnel Department," SG22366; minutes of the Unemployment Compensation Committee Meeting of 9 December 1964, SG22390, all in Admin. Files Gov. G. Wallace, ADAH; Philip Crass, *The Wallace Factor* (New York: Mason Charter Books, 1976), 79; memorandum from George Wallace to Arlis Fant, Director of Labor, 28 September 1964, SG22376; unnumbered executive order of Governor George C. Wallace, SG22408, all in Admin. Files Gov. G. Wallace, ADAH.

28. *Birmingham Post-Herald,* 23 February 1963. T. B. Britt, "A Treatise on Some of Alabama's Economic Ills," undated typescript, SG22365; "1965–1967 Alabama Education Association Legislative Program," SG22386; George Wallace to W. L. Grubbs, 10 February 1964, SG22376; minutes of meeting of the Board of Control of the Employees Retirement System, 6 May 1963, 30 October 1963, 14 May 1964, 28 October 1964, SG22380; George Wallace to Gene Loop, 5 November 1965, SG22408, all in Admin. Files Gov. G. Wallace, ADAH.

29. Various correspondence of Arlis Fant, SG22376; "Activities of the Department of Labor, October 1, 1962–September 30, 1963," SG22376; "Creed for Wallace Cabinet Member," SG22373, all in Admin. Files Gov. G. Wallace, ADAH.

30. Memorandum from George Wallace to Arlis Fant, 13 November 1964; Arlis Fant to W. J. McDowell, Business Representative of the Sheet Metal Workers Local 48, 15 December 1964, all in Admin. Files Gov. G. Wallace, SG22390, ADAH.

31. "Twentieth Annual Report of the Department of Labor of the State of Alabama,

1962–1963," SG22376; Twenty-first Annual Report of the Department of Labor of the State of Alabama, SG22390; Arlis Fant to Mrs. R. J. Bagwell, 2 February 1966, SG22408; *Montgomery Advertiser,* 19–20 September, 7 November 1966; telegram from W. L. Hopper to Claude Kelley, 13 September 1966, SG22408; Major General Alfred C. Harrison, Adjutant General to W. L. Hopper, 15 September 1966, SG22408; various correspondence, SG22385; memorandums from Cecil Jackson to Hugh Maddox, 17 January 1966, SG22408, all reports and correspondence in Admin. Files Gov. G. Wallace, ADAH; *Birmingham News,* 4–13 January 1966.

32. *Montgomery Advertiser,* 3–4 April 1965; *Wall Street Journal,* 1 July 1965; various correspondence, Admin. Files Gov. G. Wallace, SG22383, ADAH.

33. "Sales Trends Report for the Month of April 1965," *Jobbers News and Products,* May 1965. Press release of the Governor's Office of the State of Alabama, 15 April 1965, SG22394; various correspondence to George Wallace, SG22383; T. B. Britt, "A Treatise on Some of Alabama's Economic Ills," unpublished and undated, SG22365, all in Admin. Files Gov. G. Wallace, ADAH. *Montgomery Advertiser,* 3 April, 12 May 1965; Mrs. A. J. Helton and Mrs. H. E. Thornton to George Wallace, undated, and George Wallace to Mrs. A. J. Helton and Mrs. H. E. Thornton, 26 August 1965, in Admin. Files Gov. G. Wallace, SG22383, ADAH. As for his religion, Wallace was a Methodist but accepted an honorary degree from fundamentalist Bob Jones University in 1964. Interestingly enough, a year later Bob Jones University was accredited by the state Board of Education for teacher education. Minutes of the State Board of Education Meeting, 29 June 1965, Admin. Files Gov. G. Wallace, SG22386, ADAH.

34. *Montgomery Advertiser,* 5 January, 9–10 January 1965.

35. Ibid., 12 January, 23 January, 4 February, 11 February 1965.

36. Ibid., 11 February, 14 February 1965. The first special session was called for highway bond legislation; the second, for education; the third, for redistricting; and the fourth, for passage of the Wallace amendment, which would have prevented the executive, legislative, and judicial branches of the federal government from interfering in public education within the states.

37. Proclamation by the Governor to Convene the Legislature, 10 February 1965, Hugh Maddox Papers, LPR 103, box 3, ADAH; *Montgomery Advertiser,* 14–17 February 1965.

38. *Montgomery Advertiser,* 16 February, 19 February, 21–22 February, 27 February 1965; various telegrams and letters to George Wallace; memorandum from Hugh Maddox to Bill Jones, 3 March 1965, correspondence in Admin. Files Gov. G. Wallace, SG22395, ADAH.

39. *Montgomery Advertiser,* 25–26 February, 28 February, 10 March, 12 March 1965. Meadows, in testimony before the senate, later admitted that he sold his sample copies for personal profit. The superintendent claimed he was "just following a practice used for more than forty years," and noted the inadequacy of his $10,000 annual salary.

40. *Montgomery Advertiser,* 4 March, 18 March, 23 March 1965.

41. Truman M. Pierce, *Alabama Schools in 1965* (Auburn: Auburn University School of Education, 1965), Alabama Collection, Auburn University, Auburn, Ala.; *Montgomery Advertiser,* 1–3 March 1965. Pierce's report is also in Admin. Files Gov. G. Wallace, SG22386, ADAH.

42. Pierce, *Alabama Schools in 1965,* Alabama Collection, Auburn University, Auburn, Ala.; *Montgomery Advertiser,* 1–3 March 1965.

43. Pierce, *Alabama Schools in 1965,* Alabama Collection, Auburn University, Auburn, Ala.; *Alabama Municipal Journal* 22, no. 5 (November 1964).

44. *Montgomery Advertiser,* 1–2 April, 9 April, 13–15 April, 21 April 1965; "1965–1967 Alabama Education Association Legislative Program," Admin. Files Gov. G. Wallace, SG22386, ADAH.

45. *Montgomery Advertiser,* 17 April, 21–24 April, 28 April 1965.

46. Ibid., 19 February, 21 February, 27 February, 8 March, 11 March, 13 March 1965; Stephan Lesher, *George Wallace: American Populist* (New York: Addison-Wesley, 1994), 339. Some books with a broader emphasis on the 1965 voting rights campaign in Selma are Stanton, *From Selma to Sorrow;* Frank Sikora, *Selma, Lord, Selma* (Tuscaloosa: University of Alabama Press, 1997); *Civil War to Civil Rights: A Pictorial History of Selma, Alabama* (Portland: Pediment, 1998); Taylor Branch, *Pillar of Fire: America in the King Years, 1963–1965* (New York: Simon and Schuster, 1998); Beatrice Siegel, *Murder on the Highway: The Viola Liuzzo Story* (New York: Macmillan, 1993); Charles W. Eagles, *Outside Agitator: Jon Daniels and the Civil Rights Movement in Alabama* (Chapel Hill: University of North Carolina Press, 1993); U.S. National Park Service, *Selma to Montgomery National Trail Study, April 1993: A Study of the Voting Rights March* (Washington, D.C.: Department of the Interior, 1993); J. L. Chestnut, *Black in Selma: The Uncommon Life of J. L. Chestnut* (New York: Farrar, Straus, and Giroux, 1990); Stephen L. Longenecker, *Selma's Peacemaker: Ralph Smeltzer's Civil Rights Mediation* (Philadelphia: Temple University Press, 1987); Charles Fager, *Selma 1965: The March That Changed the South* (Boston: Beacon Press, 1985); and David J. Garrow, *Protest at Selma: Martin Luther King Jr. and the Voting Rights Act of 1965* (New Haven: Yale University Press, 1978).

47. *Montgomery Advertiser,* 5 February, 11 February, 4 March 1965; Wayne Flynt, "The Ethics of Democratic Persuasion and the Birmingham Crisis," *Southern Speech Journal* 35 (Fall 1969): 40–53.

48. *Montgomery Advertiser,* 13 March 1965.

49. Ibid., 4 March 1965.

50. Ibid., 12 March 1964, 4 March 1965. State Sovereignty File, SG2238; miscellaneous correspondence, SG22393; Cecil Jackson to Al Lingo, 13 July 1964, SG22381, all in Admin. Files Gov. G. Wallace, ADAH.

51. *Montgomery Advertiser,* 17 March 1965.

52. Statement of Governor George Wallace, 16 March 1965, SG22395; telegram from George Wallace to President Lyndon Johnson, 18 March 1965, SG22395, all in Admin. Files Gov. G. Wallace, ADAH; *Montgomery Advertiser,* 18–19 March 1965.

53. *Montgomery Advertiser,* 18–22 March, 24–31 March, 28 April 1965. Wallace received countless letters from Alabamians fearful that Graham was coming to Alabama on a mission to promote integration. Many of the letters urged Wallace not to attend any of the acclaimed evangelist's services. Wallace met with Graham in his office but attended no services. Graham did come to the state and spoke before integrated crowds, but he concentrated mostly on saving souls and did not take on the issue of integration. Publicly, Graham took a middle path: "There is no doubt that certain demonstrations have helped dramatize the problem and have aroused the conscience of the nation, however some of the

extreme elements that accompany these demonstrations have had a tendency to get out of hand."

54. Ibid., 30 March, 4 April, 22 April 1965.

55. Ibid., 15 April, 21 April, 28 April, 1 May, 23 May 1965; "Statement for Selma Film," Admin. Files Gov. G. Wallace, SG22397, ADAH; various memorandums between Cecil Jackson, Earl Morgan, and Ed Ewing, Admin. Files Gov. G. Wallace, SG22397, ADAH.

56. Report of the Alabama Legislative Commission to Preserve the Peace, 1964, SG22384; Report of the Alabama Legislative Commission to Preserve the Peace, 1965, SG22384; *Montgomery Advertiser,* 30 June 1965; memorandums from Hugh Maddox to George Wallace, 5 October 1965, SG22416; memorandums from Hugh Maddox to Eli Howell, 5 October 1965, SG22416, all reports and correspondence in Admin. Files Gov. G. Wallace, ADAH. State sovereignty funds were used in at least two cases, Bessemer and Bibb County.

57. *Montgomery Advertiser,* 31 December 1963, 13 September 1964. Richard Morphew to George Wallace, 27 January 1965; Report on the Citizens' Councils of America Leadership Conference by O. D. Johnson of Pierce County, Georgia, undated; various Citizens' Council correspondence, all in Admin. Files Gov. G. Wallace, SG22383, ADAH.

58. *Montgomery Advertiser,* 8 May, 16 May 1965; Lesher, *George Wallace American Populist* 337–45, 353.

59. *Montgomery Advertiser,* 21 May, 11 June, 11 August, 13 August, 3 September, 8 September, 29 September 1965; Crass, *The Wallace Factor,* 80.

60. George Wallace to the NAACP, 2 July 1965; Roy Wilkins to George Wallace, 8 July 1965, all in Admin. Files Gov. G. Wallace, SG22392, ADAH.

61. State of Alabama Planning and Industrial Development Board, 1965 year-end report, 4 January 1966, SG22393; file memorandum from Cecil Jackson, 17 May 1965, SG22394; Speech of Leonard Beard to the Birmingham Rotary Club, 30 January 1963, SG22366; Thornton, Farish, and Gauntt Incorporated to Cecil Jackson, 6 May 1965, SG22394; George Wallace to Ernest Harris, 15 March 1965, SG22393; memorandum from Leonard Beard to George C. Wallace, 13 December 1965, SG22393; memorandum from Leonard Beard to George Wallace, 9 December 1965, SG22393, all in Admin. Files Gov. G. Wallace, ADAH; *Birmingham News,* 22 August 1965; *Mobile Register,* 23 May 1963; *Montgomery Advertiser,* 6 June 1965.

62. Cooper Green to Leonard Beard, 4 December 1964; Leonard Beard to George Wallace, 8 December 1964; Frank Boykin to Mr. D. S. Leslie, 10 February 1965; Frank Boykin to George Wallace, 10 February 1965; George Wallace to Frank Boykin, 4 March 1965, all in Admin. Files Gov. G. Wallace, SG22394, ADAH.

63. State of Alabama Planning and Industrial Development Board 1965 Year End Report, 4 January 1965, Admin. Files Gov. G. Wallace, SG22393, ADAH; William Warren Rogers, Robert David Ward, Leah Rawls Atkins, and Wayne Flynt, *Alabama: The History of a Deep South State* (Tuscaloosa: University of Alabama Press, 1994), 578–84; interview, Jere Beasley; *Montgomery Advertiser,* 19 September 1965.

64. *Montgomery Advertiser,* 17 April 1965.

65. Ibid., 2 May, 5 May, 7 May, 9 May 1965.

66. Ibid., 25 July 1964, 13 May, 2 June, 19 June, 17 July, 21 July, 13 September 1965; Crass, *The Wallace Factor,* 78.

67. *Montgomery Advertiser,* 23–24 July, 11 August, 27 August 1965.

68. Ibid., 23 July, 8 August, 15 August, 20 August, 31 December 1965.

69. *Mobile Register,* 15 May 1963; *Montgomery Advertiser,* 9–10 August, 13 August, 22 August, 31 December 1965.

70. Various correspondence of George Wallace, Admin. Files Gov. G. Wallace, SG22395; memorandum from Eli Howell to George Wallace, undated, SG22397; *Philadelphia Sunday Bulletin,* 21 February 1965; *Mobile Register,* 4–5 September, 7 September, 12 September, 15 September 1965; George Wallace to Eli Howell, 29 December 1965, SG22416, all correspondence in Admin. Files Gov. G. Wallace, ADAH.

71. *Montgomery Advertiser,* 10–11 September, 17 September, 19 September 1965.

72. Ibid., 23–24 September, 17 October 1965.

73. Ibid., 26 September, 5 October 1965.

74. Ibid., 22 November 1963. The succession provision can be found in article 5, sec. 119 of the 1901 Constitution.

75. *Mobile Register,* 18 August, 28 August, 7 September 1963.

76. *Montgomery Advertiser,* 12 April, 24 May, 5–7 August, 9 August, 11–12 August, 14 August, 16 August, 29 August 1965; interview, John Patterson. Wallace tallied 212,068 votes, 43 percent of the total vote in Maryland, and won sixteen counties. In all, ten separate U.S. senators campaigned against him in Maryland.

77. *Montgomery Advertiser,* 10 September, 12 September 1965.

78. Interview, Bob Ingram; *Montgomery Advertiser,* 12 September 1965; Carter, *Politics of Rage,* 264–72; Lesher, *George Wallace American Populist,* 352–55; Stephen Fayer, Daniel McCabe, and Paul Stekler, "George Wallace: Settin' the Woods on Fire," *The American Experience,* PBS documentary, produced by Daniel McCabe and Paul Stekler, Midnight Films and Big House Productions, 2000.

79. *Montgomery Advertiser,* 5 May, 12 July 1965; *Biographical Directory of the United States Congress,* online version, www.bioguide.congress.gov.

80. *Montgomery Advertiser,* 18 July, 30 September, 1 October, 8 October 1965; interviews, Albert Brewer; interviews, Bill Jones; interview, John Patterson. Wallace had previously been on the record as vowing not to call a special session for the sole purpose of altering the gubernatorial or senatorial succession provisions. Surprisingly, once the actual melee began, his opponents did not accuse him of breaking earlier pledges or waffling on the issue.

81. *Montgomery Advertiser,* 12 September, 3 October 1965.

82. Ibid., 16 October 1965, *Birmingham News,* 30 September–24 October 1965; *Birmingham Post-Herald,* 30 September–24 October 1965; *Tuscaloosa News,* 1–27 October 1965; *Huntsville Times,* 30 September–24 October 1965.

83. *Montgomery Advertiser,* 2–3 October 1965.

84. Ibid., 2 October 1965; interviews, Bill Jones.

85. J. Bruce Henderson to Wallace Malone, 2 October 1965, J. Bruce Henderson Papers, box 7, ADAH.

86. *Montgomery Advertiser,* 3–4 October, 6 October 1965. The house passed the succession bill by a vote of 74 to 23. Despite the relative ease of passage, Wallace opponents in the house were emboldened to challenge the governor as they had never been in the past. John Casey characterized Speaker Albert Brewer's chair rulings as "a display of raw political

power. [This is] the most daring and open power grab in the history of Alabama," *Montgomery Advertiser,* 6 October 1965

87. *Montgomery Advertiser,* 7–10 October 1965; interview, John Patterson; interview, McDowell Lee; interviews, Bill Jones; interview, Bob Ingram.

88. *Montgomery Advertiser,* 16–17 October 1965; interview, Bob Ingram. Opponents Ed Horton from Florence, Roscoe Roberts from Huntsville, and Larry Dumas from Birmingham appeared with Wallace at succession rallies. Roberts's experience was particularly hair-raising, with the local police saving him from a sure beating. The number of senators in opposition to succession varied during the fight. In general, fourteen senators were identified with the antisuccession position. These fourteen represented mostly urban areas including the seven most populous counties: Jefferson, Mobile, Montgomery, Madison, Tuscaloosa, Calhoun, and Etowah.

89. *Montgomery Advertiser,* 8 October, 10 October 1965; interview, Bob Ingram.

90. *Montgomery Advertiser,* 8 October, 10 October, 16 October, 19–22 October 1965; interview, John Patterson.

91. Ibid., 23–24 October 1965; J. L. Lewis to George Wallace, 10 November 1965; George Wallace to J. L. Lewis, 15 November 1965, correspondence in Admin. Files Gov. G. Wallace, SG22408, ADAH; interviews, Albert Brewer; interview, Bob Ingram; interview, John Patterson.

Chapter 5

1. *Montgomery Advertiser,* 2 January, 4–6 January 1966; *Birmingham News,* 4–5 January 1966. In the last five months of 1965, more than seventy thousand black Alabamians registered to vote.

2. *Montgomery Advertiser,* 9 January, 16 January 1966; various correspondence concerning the Alabama Rooster, Admin. Files Gov. G. Wallace, SG22373, ADAH.

3. I. J. Scott to Roy Mayhall, 24 September 1965, Admin. Files Gov. G. Wallace, SG22385, ADAH.

4. State Democratic Executive Committee Records, box 103, ADAH; *Montgomery Advertiser,* 22–23 January 1966; *Birmingham News,* 22–23 January 1966.

5. State Democratic Executive Committee Records, box 103, ADAH; *Montgomery Advertiser,* 23 January 1966.

6. "Statement of Principles of Alabama Democratic Party," 22 January 1966, Admin. Files Gov. G. Wallace, SG22403, ADAH; *Montgomery Advertiser,* 23 January 1966.

7. State Biographical Sketch, Surname File no. 580-M871293, ADAH.

8. Interview, Bob Ingram; *Birmingham News,* 25 July 1954; *Selma Times-Journal,* 24 July 1954; *Montgomery Advertiser,* 20 May, 22 May 1955, 27 April 1963; *Birmingham News,* 3 September 1967.

9. George Wallace to A. W. Todd, 28 March 1963, SG22362; A. W. Todd to George Wallace, 29 March 1966, SG22362; "Cooperative Survey of Alabama Fruits, Vegetables, and Nuts," *Progress Report of the Department of Agriculture and Industries,* July 1963, SG22362; scheduling memorandums, undated, SG22382, all in Admin. Files Gov. G. Wallace, ADAH; *Montgomery Advertiser,* 11 June 1965, 15 February 1966.

10. Dewey W. Grantham, *The South in Modern America: A Region at Odds* (Fayetteville: University of Arkansas Press, 2001), 260–61; "Alabama Personal Income by Major Source and Earnings by Industry," table SA05, Regional Economic Information System, Bureau of Economic Analysis, Center for Government Services, Auburn University, Auburn, Ala.; *Mobile Register,* 3 May, 23 May 1963; *Montgomery Advertiser,* 18 October 1963.

11. *Montgomery Advertiser,* 1 May, 6 May, 10 May, 13 May, 17 May 1964; "Alabama Wall Downed: Don't Block Imports, U.S. Judge Orders State," *National Provisioner* (6 June 1964): 16–17. Various correspondence to George Wallace in May 1964, SG22370; various 1964 Docks Department correspondence and memorandums, SG22373; "Report on Beef Imports Created from a Joint Meeting by the Commissioners of Agriculture from Alabama, Florida, Georgia, Mississippi, and Louisiana and the Respective States' Cattlemen's Association," 9 April 1964, SG22370; memorandum from Doyle Connor, Commissioner of Agriculture State of Florida on Five-State Report on Beef Imports, 22 April 1964, SG22370, all in Admin. Files Gov. G. Wallace, ADAH.

12. *Montgomery Advertiser,* 29 May, 3 June, 18 June, 23 June, 1 August 1964; "Alabama Wall Downed: Don't Block Imports, U.S. Judge Orders State," *National Provisioner* (6 June 1964): 16–17.

13. *Montgomery Advertiser,* 25 September, 5 October 1964, 21 January, 9 February, 22 May, 26 June 1966.

14. Minutes of the Board of Agriculture Meeting, 13 November, 13 December 1966, 12 February 1964, Admin. Files Gov. G. Wallace, SG22370, ADAH; *Montgomery Advertiser,* 21 January, 13 February, 13 March 1966.

15. *Alabama Journal,* 10 October 1962, 28 April 1964; *Montgomery Advertiser,* 14 January 1963; Philip Crass, *The Wallace Factor* (New York: Mason Charter, 1976), 232–33; Alabama State Docks Department Annual Report for 1961, Admin. Files Gov. G. Wallace, SG22363, ADAH.

16. Alabama State Docks Department Annual Report to the Governor for Fiscal Year ending September 30, 1963"; Statement of Earnings by Fiscal Year Ended September 30 1963; *Montgomery Advertiser,* 1 January 1964; Mylan Engel to George Wallace, September 1962, all reports and correspondence in Admin. Files Gov. G. Wallace, SG22363, ADAH.

17. *Montgomery Advertiser,* 31 July, 13 November, 16 November, 27 December 1964, 27 December 1965, 26 March 1966. Houston Feaster to George Wallace, 1 September 1964, SG22373; press release of the State Docks Department, undated, SG22373; Houston Feaster to George Wallace, 27 August 1963, SG22363, all in Admin. Files Gov. G. Wallace, ADAH. See also Alabama State Docks Department Annual Reports for 1964–1966, Admin. Files Gov. G. Wallace, ADAH.

18. Ludger Lapeyrouse to Houston Feaster, 18 February 1964; A. W. Todd to George Wallace, 24 February 1964; telegram from A. W. Todd to Houston Feaster, 28 February 1964; Houston Feaster to Dewitt Reams, 6 May 1964, all in Admin. Files Gov. G. Wallace, SG22373, ADAH; *Mobile Register,* 18 February 1964. Feaster also cited the possibility of declining grain prices if the elevator was turned over to a single private concern but nevertheless indicated political factors as the "first" reason for keeping the elevator in state control.

19. H. L. Holman to Houston Feaster, 26 September 1963, SG22363; George Wallace to Buddy Crawford, 5 April 1963, SG22363; Earl Morgan to Houston Feaster, 5 April 1963,

SG22363; various correspondence from Houston Feaster, SG22373; Riley Smith to Houston Feaster, 21 August 1963, SG22363; George Wallace to Houston Feaster, 23 August 1963, SG22363; Theodore J. Richter to George Wallace, 17 May 1963, SG22363, all in Admin. Files Gov. G. Wallace, ADAH.

20. Various correspondence and memorandums, Docks Department file, Admin. Files Gov. G. Wallace, SG22385, SG22363, ADAH.

21. J. A. Russell to Mr. Olin Brooks, 17 February 1966, Admin. Files Gov. G. Wallace, SG22403, ADAH; Surname Files, file no. M844533, print no. 00756, ADAH; Crass, *The Wallace Factor,* 232–33.

22. Various correspondence to George Wallace; Mrs. George F. Comer, President of the Leroy, Alabama PTA, to George Wallace, 23 September 1966, all in Admin. Files Gov. G. Wallace, SG22387, ADAH; *Birmingham News,* 22 December 1968, 15 January, 22 March 1969; *Montgomery Advertiser,* 20 September, 31 October 1966; final decree of the Circuit Court of Montgomery County, Alabama case nos. 3728 and 36753–63, *Seymore Trammell v. Scott, Foresman, and Company,* June 1966, Admin. Files Gov. G. Wallace, SG22387, ADAH.

23. Free Textbook Act; various correspondence between George Wallace and Hugh Maddox, all in Admin. Files Gov. G. Wallace, SG22387, ADAH.

24. *Birmingham News,* 10 June 1966; Jimmy Jones to the Alabama State Textbook Committee, undated; Hugh Maddox to George Wallace, 10 January 1967; George Wallace to Cecil Jackson, 30 May 1967, all correspondence in Admin. Files Gov. G. Wallace, SG22405, ADAH.

25. Minutes of the meeting of the Alabama Trade School and Junior College Authority, 12 May 1964, 14 May, 17 September 1965, 10 January, 9 February, 20 April, 18 May, 6 July 1966, Admin. Files Gov. G. Wallace, SG22404, ADAH; Laws of the Legislature of Alabama, special session 1965, act 243, 331–43.

26. *Montgomery Advertiser,* 27 July, 31 August 1966.

27. Various legislative correspondence, Admin. Files Gov. G. Wallace, SG22410, ADAH; memorandums from George Wallace to Charles Cooper, 17 February, 9 May, 10 May, 29 June, 12 July 1966, Admin. Files Gov. G. Wallace, SG22410, ADAH; *Alabama Municipal Journal,* August 1966, 35; *Montgomery Advertiser,* 8 January, 21 March, 5 June, 31 July, 4 August, 12 August 1966. Women jury service bills had been proposed in previous sessions, although Wallace had never publicly supported them or worked behind the scenes to get them passed. The jury bill was passed with a provision that it be voted on by the public in a referendum, even though federal law mandated allowing women to serve beginning in 1967.

28. Memorandum from George Wallace to Leonard Beard, 13 December 1965, SG22393; memorandum from Leonard Beard to George Wallace, 9 December 1965, SG22393; *Business Week,* 22 January 1966, 122; *Wall Street Journal,* 19 January 1966; various photocopies of industrial development advertisements, SG22414; memorandum from George Wallace to Leonard Beard, 7 February 1966, SG22413; Greg Symons to George Wallace, 18 January 1966, SG22414; George Wallace to Greg Symons, 28 January 1966, SG22414, all advertisements and correspondence in Admin. Files Gov. G. Wallace, ADAH.

29. Carter, *Politics of Rage,* 306–7; *Montgomery Advertiser,* 25 February, 22 March, 8 August, 30 August 1966. George Wallace to Charles Cooper, 9 August 1966, SG22410; George

Wallace to William Westmoreland, 9 December 1965, SG22417, in Admin. Files Gov. G. Wallace, ADAH.

30. *South Bend (Ind.) Tribune,* 30 May 1966; "Home Is the Soldier," *Newsweek,* 6 June 1966; *Los Angeles Times,* 30 May 1966; *Boston Globe,* 30 May 1966; George Wallace to Mrs. Earl Chaffinch, 17 June 1966, Admin. Files Gov. G. Wallace, SG22412, ADAH.

31. Memorandum from Blue Barber to Ed Ewing and Jack House, 11 March 1966; memorandum from Ed Ewing to Blue Barber, 23 March 1966; Byron Causey to George Wallace, 24 January 1966, all in Admin. Files Gov. G. Wallace, SG22417, ADAH.

32. Tom Harris to George Wallace, 11 August 1966; George Wallace to Tom Harris, 30 August 1966; John Doar, Assistant Attorney General, Civil Rights Division to Tom Harris, 5 August 1966; signed compliance form of Tom Harris, undated, all in Admin. Files Gov. G. Wallace, SG22417, ADAH. Harris complained that the problem originated in part because a black customer received a hamburger with a pickle despite ordering a plain burger.

33. Legislative reference memorandum on Alabama laws concerning marriage and intermarriage, 18 February 1966, SG22410; Roberta Hahn to George Wallace, 11 February 1966, SG22410; George Wallace to Dede Smith, 10 June 1966, SG22416, all in Admin. Files Gov. G. Wallace, ADAH.

34. Various correspondence to George Wallace, SG22387–417; WASP to George Wallace, 25 March 1966, SG22416, all in Admin. Files Gov. G. Wallace, ADAH; Carter, *Politics of Rage,* 300; Sandra Baxley Taylor, *Me 'n' George: A Story of George Corley Wallace and His Number One Crony, Oscar Harper* (Mobile: Greenberry Press,1988), 39; *Montgomery Advertiser,* 9 February 1966.

35. *Montgomery Advertiser,* 5 January, 17 February 1965. See chapter 4 of this book for a discussion of the educational legislation passed during the 1965 special session.

36. *Montgomery Advertiser,* 2 March, 7 March, 10 March 1965, 22 September 1964.

37. Ibid., 5 May, 7 May, 12–13 May, 23 May, 3 September, 8 September 1965.

38. Ibid., 29 September, 3 October 1965, 7 April 1966.

39. Ibid., 7 April 1966.

40. Ibid., 8 April 1966.

41. Ibid., 12 May 1966; interviews, Albert Brewer.

42. *Montgomery Advertiser,* 12 May, 21–22 May, 29 May, 4 June 1966.

43. Ibid., 7 June, 9 June 1966. A few superintendents went on record opposing such mass meetings, including the leaders of school systems in Huntsville, Florence, and Decatur.

44. Ibid., 31 May 1966.

45. Ibid., 12 June, 17 June, 19 June, 23 June, 28 June 1966. By the end of June, a new HEW report noted that 82 of the state's 146 hospitals had been cleared for Medicare patients.

46. Ibid., 2 July, 6 July, 20 July, 26–27 July 1966.

47. Ibid., 3 June, 28 July, 6 August, 13 August, 30 August, 31 December 1966.

48. Ibid., 12–14 August 1966.

49. Ibid., 19 August, 26 August, 28 August 1966.

50. Ibid., 20 August 1966.

51. Ibid., 21 August, 23–24 August 1966.

52. Ibid., 24–29 August 1966.

53. Ibid., 10– 11 September, 13 September, 18 September, 22 September 1966; Bruce Henderson to George Wallace, 25 August 1966, box 6, J. Bruce Henderson Papers, ADAH.

54. *Montgomery Advertiser,* 24–25 September, 1 October, 6 October, 29–30 November, 21 December, 23 December, 30 December 1966.

55. Stephan Lesher, *George Wallace: American Populist* (New York: Addison-Wesley, 1994), 352.

56. *Montgomery Advertiser,* 27 August, 24 October, 27–28 October 1966; Carter, *Politics of Rage,* 272; Lesher, *George Wallace,* 355–56.

57. Lesher, *George Wallace,* 356; Carter, *Politics of Rage,* 272–77; interview, John Patterson; *Montgomery Advertiser,* 16 February 1966.

58. Carter, *Politics of Rage,* 277; draft of complaint, *George Wallace v. Roy Mayhall,* Agnes Baggett, and Perry Hooper, Hugh Maddox Papers, LPR 103, box 3, ADAH; *Montgomery Advertiser,* 28 October 1966.

59. Taylor, *Me 'n' George,* 77–91; Carter, *Politics of Rage,* 277; *Montgomery Advertiser,* 5 November, 9 November, 11 November 1966.

60. Carter, *Politics of Rage,* 277–78; Jack House, *Lady of Courage: The Story of Lurleen Burns Wallace* (Montgomery: League Press, 1969), 44.

61. Carter, *Politics of Rage,* 277–81; memorandum from George Wallace to all department heads, undated, Admin. Files Gov. G. Wallace, SG22373, ADAH; interview, Bob Ingram.

62. Interviews, Bill Jones; Carter, *Politics of Rage,* 278–79; *Montgomery Advertiser,* 28 November, 9 January 1966.

63. *Montgomery Advertiser,* 9 January, 11–12 January 1966; Carter, *Politics of Rage,* 278–79; Lesher, *George Wallace,* 356–57.

64. *Montgomery Advertiser,* 31 December 1965; 23 January, 25–26 January, 30 January, 9–10 February, 13 February 1966; Carter, *Politics of Rage,* 280; *Gadsden Times,* 20 February 1966.

65. Interviews, Bill Jones; interview, Jere Beasley; interviews, Albert Brewer, interview, Bob Ingram; interview, June Smith; *Montgomery Advertiser,* 16 October 1966; Carter, *Politics of Rage,* 273–80.

66. Interviews, Bill Jones; interviews, Albert Brewer; Carter, *Politics of Rage,* 281; Stephen Fayer, Daniel McCabe, and Paul Stekler, "George Wallace: Settin' the Woods on Fire," *The American Experience,* PBS documentary, produced by Daniel McCabe and Paul Stekler, Midnight Films and Big House Productions, 2000. See also House, *First Lady of Courage* and Anita Smith, *The Intimate Story of Lurleen Wallace: Her Crusade of Courage* (Montgomery: Communication Unlimited, 1969). There is some disagreement among scholars and contemporaries about whether George forced Lurleen to run. I would argue that Lurleen loved her husband and her decision was based on how badly she knew he wanted to run for president. Consequently, pressure, if it was applied at all, was unnecessary.

67. *Montgomery Advertiser,* 10–11 February, 13 February 1966; Carter, *Politics of Rage,* 279–80.

68. *Montgomery Advertiser,* 3 December 1963, 11 February 1966; interview, Bob Ingram.

69. John F. Kraft, Inc., "Study of Voter Attitudes in Alabama," June 1964, in author's possession.

70. Kraft, "Study of Voter Attitudes in Alabama," June 1964.

71. Kraft, "Study of Voter Attitudes in Alabama," June 1964; *Montgomery Advertiser,* 6 March 1966.

72. *Montgomery Advertiser,* 19–20 February, 22 February, 29 March, 9 April, 23 April 1966. Numerous national media outlets covered all or part of the campaign including *Newsweek,* the *Los Angeles Times, Saturday Evening Post, New York Times,* and *Washington Post.*

73. *Montgomery Advertiser,* 22 February, 24–25 February 1966; *Birmingham News,* 24 February, 25 February 1966; *Huntsville Times,* 24–25 February 1966; *Mobile Register,* 24–25 February 1966. Lurleen's announcement was quick and to the point: "Ladies and gentlemen, I will be a candidate for governor of Alabama." She went on to note, "my election would enable my husband to carry out his programs for the people of Alabama. We will continue the type of administration that has proved to be in the best interest of all the people of this state." Lurleen also coronated her husband as her number one advisor and announced she planned to pay him $1 per year.

74. *Montgomery Advertiser,* 27 January, 30 January, 1 February, 24 February, 25 February, 3 March 1966; Carter, *Politics of Rage,* 11–12. All told, thirteen black candidates ran in local Barbour County elections in 1966.

75. *Montgomery Advertiser,* 12 January, 2 March, 15 March, 22 March, 14 April, 17 April 1966; Carter, *Politics of Rage,* 285. Powell had shared a boardinghouse with Wallace at the University of Alabama.

76. *Montgomery Advertiser,* 2 March, 17–18 April 1966; Carter, *Politics of Rage,* 285.

77. *Montgomery Advertiser,* 1 February, 9 February, 2 March, 6 March, 24 April, 1 May, 15 May 1966.

78. *Montgomery Advertiser,* 2 March, 9 March, 27 March, 3 April, 7 April, 17 April 1966. Questioned by a Goodwater shoe repairman about what he was promising the voters this year, Folsom responded in characteristic fashion: "Whatever they want; just like everybody else—roads, babysitters—anything."

79. *Montgomery Advertiser,* 9 March, 3 April, 7 April, 10 April, 27 April 1966.

80. Ibid., 12 February, 28 February, 1–2 March 1966.

81. Ibid., 10 March, 22 March, 24 March, 28 March, 31 March, 8 April 1966.

82. Ibid., 5 April, 8 April, 10 April, 17 April, 23–24 April 1966. Lurleen was kept away from joint candidate appearances primarily because George would not have been allowed to speak.

83. Anne Permaloff and Carl Grafton, "John Patterson, 1959–1963," in *Alabama Governors: A Political History of the State,* ed. Samuel L. Webb, and Margaret E. Armbrester (Tuscaloosa: University of Alabama Press, 2001), 210–15 ; *Montgomery Advertiser,* 2 March, 5 March 1966; interview, John Patterson.

84. *Montgomery Advertiser,* 8 March, 13 March, 17 March, 20 March, 27 March 1966; interview, John Patterson.

85. Ibid., 30–31 March, 1 April, 3 April, 5 April, 8 April, 15 April, 17 April, 21 April, 23–24 April, 28–29 April 1966; interview, John Patterson.

86. *Montgomery Advertiser,* 26 February, 13 March, 17 March, 24 March 1966.

87. Ibid., 9 March, 1 April, 4 April, 7 April, 16 April, 29 April, 1 May 1966. Flowers's best line in the campaign concerned Wallace's denunciation of communism and reluctance to

use the word segregation on the stump. "The only reason he talks communism," Flowers snapped, "is because there aren't 228,000 communists registered to vote in Alabama."

88. Carter, *Politics of Rage,* 285–86; William Warren Rogers, Robert David Ward, Leah Rawls Atkins, and Wayne Flynt, *Alabama: The History of a Deep South State* (Tuscaloosa: University of Alabama Press, 1994), 523; *Montgomery Advertiser,* 2 October, 4 October 1965, 27 March, 1 May 1966; interviews, Bill Jones; "Alabama at the Crossroad," political pamphlet of Carl Elliot, Admin. Files Gov. G. Wallace, SG22403, ADAH. For more on Carl Elliot see, Carl Elliot Sr. and Michael D'Orso, *The Cost of Courage: The Journey of an American Congressman* (New York: Doubleday, 1992).

89. *Montgomery Advertiser,* 2 October 1965, 27 February, 17 March, 24 March, 27 March 1966; "Alabama at the Crossroad," political pamphlet of Carl Elliot, Admin. Files Gov. G. Wallace, SG22403, ADAH. Elliot won the support of organized labor throughout the state and earned the endorsement of the Alabama Labor Council, the first time the council had ever given its blessing to a single gubernatorial candidate. Wallace supporters had a sense of humor if nothing else. Elliot had promised a big paper mill for the town of Cordova while he was still in Congress. The mill never relocated. During the campaign, anonymous fake checks for $100 to $500 came to Elliot from the "Cordova Paper Company."

90. *Montgomery Advertiser,* 27–28 March, 17 April, 28–29 April, 1 May 1966. Jefferson County had 234,000 registered voters. The next largest county, Mobile, had 130,000.

91. *Montgomery Advertiser,* 19 March, 27 March 1966; interview, Bob Ingram. Numerous unrecorded conversations with Alabamians, 1999–2002.

92. Kraft, "Study of Voter Attitudes in Alabama," June 1964. Lurleen's campaign slogan was "Stand Up for Alabama."

93. *Montgomery Advertiser,* 5 March, 19–20 March, 23 March 1966; Carter, *Politics of Rage,* 281–90. A sample five-day campaign schedule: Monday March 21, Phenix City 10 a.m., Opelika 11:30 a.m., Alexander City 3:30 p.m., Fairfax 7:30 p.m.; Tuesday March 22, Coldwater 10 a.m., Sylacauga 11:30 a.m., Childersburg 2 p.m., Sycamore 3:30 p.m., Talladega 7 p.m.; Wednesday March 23, Pell City 10:30 a.m., Oneonta 1 p.m., Arab 3 p.m., Albertville 5 p.m.; Thursday March 24, Roanoke 10 a.m., Wedowee 11 a.m., Ashland 12 p.m., Heflin 3:30 p.m., Anniston 7 p.m.; Friday March 25, Thomasville 1 p.m., Grove Hill 2:30 p.m., Jackson 4 p.m., Leroy 7 p.m.

94. *Montgomery Advertiser,* 31 March, 6 April, 9 April, 12 April, 16 April 1966.

95. Ibid., 19 March, 26 April, 1–2 May 1966; interview, Bob Ingram.

96. Ibid., 1 May, 4 May 1966.

97. *Dothan Eagle,* 4 May 1966; *Evergreen Courant,* 4 May 1966; *Clayton Record,* 4 May 1966; *Lee County Bulletin,* 4 May 1966. The *Birmingham News* was less ecstatic: "Alabamians in majority had their emotional fling Tuesday. They showed 'em. They showed LBJ, showed Katzenbach, showed the beatniks, showed the Negroes, showed the 'liberal' press, showed everybody. And they changed reality not one whit."

98. *Montgomery Advertiser,* 4–15 May 1966.

99. John Kohn to Jim Martin, 17 May 1966; Jim Martin to B. Baxley, 27 July 1966; John Schuler to Glen Curlee, 30 September 1966, all in Admin. Files Gov. G. Wallace, SG22403, ADAH; *Montgomery Advertiser,* 10 July, 12–13 July, 16 July, 23–24 July, 30–31 July 1966. Martin floated a trial balloon in the days before the start of the state Republican convention about

switching to the senate race. Grenier lined up delegates to block Martin's expected move. In the end, Martin chose not to create an open rift in the party and sentenced himself to certain defeat. In the weeks and months after the election, the Martin-Grenier feud went public anyway. Thurmond gave the keynote address at the state convention. Goldwater pledged to come to Alabama to help defeat George Wallace.

100. *Montgomery Advertiser*, 26 September, 28–29 September, 2 October, 8 October 1966; Carter, *Politics of Rage*, 290–91.

101. *Montgomery Advertiser*, 14 October, 26 October, 30 October, 9–11 November 1966; *Greensboro Watchman*, 7–14 October 1966.

Chapter 6

1. *Birmingham News*, 29 December 1966; 1 January, 8 January, 15 January 1967. To minimize confusion, Governor Lurleen Wallace will be referred to as "Lurleen," and Governor George Wallace as either "George" or "Wallace."

2. Interview, George Wallace Jr.; *Birmingham News*, 8 January, 15–16 January 1967; *Huntsville Times*, 2 February 1967; Melvin Kacharos to J. F. Rea, 2 February 1967, Administrative Files of Governor Lurleen Wallace (hereafter Admin. Files Gov. L. Wallace), SG22408, ADAH. George Wallace cited the inappropriateness of a statewide celebration in light of the Vietnam War as his reason for canceling the inaugural ball. Cynics, then and now, suggest that he did not want to risk the public embarrassment of having a black man ask his wife to dance or that he could not bear the thought of all the attention being on Lurleen.

3. Alabama Department of Archives and History Web site, www.archives.state.al.us/conoff/awtodd.html; interview, John Patterson; *Birmingham News*, 4 August, 9 August, 25 August 1968, 24 February, 28 February, 10 March 1969, 27 March, 1 April, 22 April 1970; John Hayman, *Bitter Harvest: Richmond Flowers and the Civil Rights Revolution* (Montgomery: Black Belt Press, 1996); *Birmingham Post-Herald*, 16 September 1969; *Montgomery Advertiser*, 28 January 1974; Carl Elliot to Bill Jones, 28 November 1967, Carl Elliot Papers, box 5643, W. S. Hoole Library, University of Alabama, Tuscaloosa, Ala.

4. Anita Smith, *The Intimate Story of Lurleen Wallace: Her Crusade of Courage* (Montgomery: Communications Unlimited, 1969), 1–6.

5. Stephan Lesher, *George Wallace: American Populist* (New York: Addison-Wesley, 1994), 370–86; Smith, *The Intimate Story of Lurleen Wallace*, 19–23; interview, George Wallace Jr.; interview, Ed Ewing; *Birmingham News*, 10 May 1967.

6. *Birmingham News*, 26 February 1967; Mrs. Annie Pipkin to Lurleen Wallace, 24 January 1968, SG22446; Lurleen Wallace to Annie Pipkin, 6 February 1968, SG22446; Mrs. Loy Logan to Lurleen Wallace, 17 June 1967, SG22431; Lurleen Wallace to Mrs. L. Logan, 23 June 1967, SG22431, all in Admin. Files Gov. L. Wallace, ADAH.

7. John Foraker to Lurleen Wallace, 24 January 1967; Lurleen Wallace to John Foraker, 27 January 1967; John Jones to Lurleen Wallace, undated; Lurleen Wallace to John Jones, 20 March 1967, all in Admin. Files Gov. L. Wallace, SG22431, ADAH.

8. Interview, George Wallace Jr.; interview, Mark Kennedy and Peggy Wallace Kennedy. "I realized at an early age," George Jr. recalled, "that [my father] was unique, that he

had become a national figure and I tried to pretty much handle it, but I had to handle it on my own."

9. Interview, Mark Kennedy and Peggy Wallace Kennedy.

10. Interview, Bill Jones; interview, George Wallace Jr.

11. Memorandum from George Wallace to Rex Roach, 16 August 1967, SG22428; memorandum from George Wallace to Rex Roach, undated, SH22428; memorandum from George Wallace to Rex Roach, 14 February 1967, SG22428; John Price to George Wallace, 22 November 1966, SG22422; memorandum from George Wallace to Hugh Maddox, 5 October 1967, SG22438, all in Admin. Files Gov. L. Wallace, ADAH.

12. Interview, Mark Kennedy and Peggy Wallace Kennedy; interview, George Wallace Jr.

13. Interview, Mark Kennedy and Peggy Wallace Kennedy; interview, George Wallace Jr.

14. Interview, George Wallace Jr.; interview, Mark Kennedy and Peggy Wallace Kennedy.

15. Interview, George Wallace Jr.

16. *Birmingham News,* 16 January, 25 January, 23 April 1967.

17. Ibid., 16–17 January 1967; interview, Julia Allen; interview, Ed Ewing; Speech of Governor Lurleen B. Wallace before the Legislature of Alabama, 30 March 1967, Admin. Files Gov. L. Wallace, SG22453, ADAH.

18. Ester Peterson to George Wallace, 10 July 1963; Report of Subcommittee on Employment Policies and Practices in State and Local Government; Salary Level and Occupational Distribution of Men and Women Employed under the Merit System, April 1964; minutes of the meetings of the Governor's Commission on the Status of Women, 15 November 1963, and 14 February, 12 May, 11 August 1964, all in Admin. Files Gov. L. Wallace, SG22438, ADAH.

19. Interview, Ed Ewing; *Birmingham News,* 8 January, 16–17 January 1967; memorandum from Cecil Jackson to Eli Howell, 13 February 1967; Lurleen Wallace to Mrs. Josephine Morris, 17 February 1967; Hugh Maddox to Bill Nichols, undated; Lois Miles to Lurleen Wallace, 20 January 1967, all correspondence in Admin. Files Gov. L. Wallace, SG22426, ADAH.

20. Minutes of the Meeting of the Alabama Mental Health Board, 19 January 1967, Admin. Files Gov. L. Wallace, SG22426, ADAH; *Birmingham News,* 5 February, 7 February 1967.

21. *Birmingham News,* 26–27 February 1967; *Alabama Mental Health Newsletter* 18, no. 13 (March 1967); Jack House, *Lady of Courage: The Story of Lurleen Burns Wallace* (Montgomery: League Press, 1969), 94–95; minutes of the meeting of the Alabama Board of Mental Health, 22 December 1966; Murray Hall to Lurleen Wallace, undated, Mrs. Carl Hill to Lurleen Wallace, 27 February 1967, minutes and correspondence in Admin. Files Gov. L. Wallace, SG22426, ADAH.

22. Mary Cox to Lurleen Wallace, 26 February 1967; Ruby McQueen to Lurleen Wallace, 25 February 1967; Becky Jagoe to Lurleen and George Wallace, 25 July 1967; Master Sergeant Roy Jolley to Lurleen Wallace, undated, all in Admin. Files Gov. L. Wallace, SG22426, ADAH.

23. *Birmingham News,* 28 February, 1–2 March 1967; Leah Rawls Atkins, correspondence with author.

24. Sworn affidavit of Karl Prussion, 26 July 1965, Admin. Files Gov. L. Wallace, SG22426, ADAH; transcript of Richard Cotten radio broadcast, in *Richard Cotten's Conservative Viewpoint,* vol. 5, sec. 4; partial photocopy of Kenneth Goff, ed., *Brainwashing: A Synthesis of the Russian Textbook on Psychopolitics* (n.p., n.d.), Admin. Files Gov. L. Wallace, SG22426, ADAH; *Borger News Herald,* 16 June 1963.

25. H. L. Hunt to George Wallace, 9 August 1967; George Wallace to H. L. Hunt, 18 August 1967, all in Admin. Files Gov. L. Wallace, SG22426, ADAH.

26. Mrs. H. W. Gill to Ernest Stone, 2 March 1968; Milton Cutchen, "Deception by Design: An Evaluation of Moral Re-Armament by the 'Up with People' Movement," February 1968, all in Admin. Files Gov. L. Wallace, SG22442, ADAH.

27. Mrs. H. W. (Elsie) Gill to George Wallace, 1 August 1967; Hugh Maddox to Charles Cargile Jr., undated, all in Admin. Files Gov. L. Wallace, SG22426, ADAH. The administration did not support an Interstate Mental Health Compact partially because of criticism that the state would be abandoning some of its power.

28. *Birmingham News,* 2 March 1967.

29. Ibid., 2–3 March, 5–6 March, 8 March, 10 March, 12 March 1967. I asked numerous insiders in Lurleen's administration if she ever initiated any policies her husband did not approve. In every case, the answer was no.

30. Ibid., 3 March, 10–12 March, 15 March 1967.

31. Ibid., 5 February, 10 February, 19 April, 25 April 1967.

32. Reuben Jackson to George Wallace, 30 May 1967; William Killough to Lurleen Wallace, 7 March 1967; George Wallace to Reuben Jackson, 6 June 1967, all in Admin. Files Gov. L. Wallace, SG22427, ADAH; *Birmingham News,* 9 March, 28 March, 7 April 1967.

33. *Birmingham News,* 10 February 1967.

34. Ibid., 1 March, 3 March, 22 March, 21 April 1967; 56th Annual Report of the Alabama State Highway Department, October 1, 1966 to September 30, 1967, Admin. Files Gov. L. Wallace, SG22427, ADAH.

35. *Birmingham News,* 26 March, 28 March 1967.

36. Ibid., 7–8 April, 11 April 1967. The altered bill allocated 88 percent of the car tag increase to the Highway Department and 12 percent to cities and counties. The gas tax redistribution bill allocated 45 percent for bond financing, 33 percent to counties on a population basis, 12 percent to municipalities, and 10 percent for equal distribution to every county.

37. Ibid., 12 April, 18–19 April, 22–23 April 1967.

38. Ibid., 25–28 April, 1 May 1967.

39. Ibid., 28 April, 30 April, 1 May 1967.

40. Ibid., 2–3 May 1967; Carolyn Rayborn to Lurleen Wallace, 5 May 1967, Admin. Files Gov. L. Wallace, SG22427, ADAH. The final bill reallocated the gasoline tax to provide 45 percent for bond financing and 55 percent to counties and municipalities. Cities received 10 percent of the 55 percent share. Of the county funds (45% of the 55% nondebt service share), 25 percent was allocated on an equal basis and 75 percent on a population basis with each county assured of receiving no less than $550,000. The bill also allowed for all funds to be distributed entirely on a population basis after the 1970 census was completed.

41. *Birmingham News,* 2–3 May 1967; Robert Jaeger to George Wallace, 25 May 1967; George Wallace to Robert Jaeger, 1 June 1967; George Wallace to Representative Quinton Bowers, 22 June 1967, all correspondence in Admin. Files Gov. L. Wallace, SG22427, ADAH.

42. *Birmingham News,* 30 April, 3 May 1967.

43. Notice of hearing, U.S. Department of HEW in the matter of the Alabama Department of Mental Health, Alabama Mental Health Board, Bryce Hospital, Searcy Hospital, and Partlow State School and Hospital, docket no. MCR-44, served 12 January 1967, and Decree of Enjoinment, U.S. District Court for Middle District of Alabama, *Anthony Lee et al. v. Macon County Board of Education,* 22 March 1967, in Admin. Files Gov. L. Wallace, SG22423, ADAH; *Birmingham News,* 13–14 January, 23–24 March 1967; statement of Governor George C. Wallace, 12 January 1967, Admin. Files Gov. L. Wallace, SG22433, ADAH.

44. Interview, George Wallace Jr. Notice of hearing, U.S. Department of HEW in the matter of the Alabama Department of Mental Health, Alabama Mental Health Board, Bryce Hospital, Searcy Hospital, and Partlow State School and Hospital, docket no. MCR-44, served 12 January 1967, SG22426; statement of Governor George C. Wallace, 12 January 1967, SG22433, all in Admin. Files Gov. L. Wallace, ADAH; *Birmingham News,* 13 January, 14 January 1967. In oral history, George Wallace Jr. described his mother as "philosophically . . . in agreement. . . . And while she agreed with him on those things, she did so because that had been her socialization and upbringing."

45. Alabama Social Welfare Annual Report, 1965–66; Ruben King to Alton Turner, 1 June 1967; Comparative Caseload Data for October 1966 and November 1966, Alabama Department of Pensions and Security; Alice Crim to George Wallace, 15 September 1966; Ruben King to Alice Crim, 10 October 1966; campaign brochure of Alabama Old Age Pension Association, all in Admin. Files Gov. L. Wallace, SG22433, ADAH.

46. *Birmingham News,* 13 January 1967. Memorandum from Hugh Maddox to MacDonald Gallion, 6 February 1967, SG22426; Respondents Answer to Notice of Hearing of HEW, docket no. MCR-44, SG22426; statement of Governor Lurleen B. Wallace on action of Secretary Gardner, undated, SG22453; brief of *Frank Lee v. Caliph Washington,* Supreme Court of the United States, SG22421; decree of the three-judge federal panel, *Lee v. Washington,* 12 December 1966, SG22421; Nicholas Hare to Hugh Maddox, 1 November 1967, SG22421; Nicholas Hare to George Wallace, 15 November 1967, SG22421; Nicholas Hare to Frank Lee, 12 March 1968, SG22421; decision of the U.S. Supreme Court, *Lee v. Washington et al.,* October Term 1967, 11 March 1968, SG22421, all in Admin. Files Gov. L. Wallace, ADAH; *New York Times,* 8 November 1967.

47. *Birmingham News,* 16 January, 24 January 1967. Telegram from Paul Johnson to Lurleen Wallace, 26 January 1967; press release of Senator Lister Hill, 21 January 1967; statement of Governor Lurleen B. Wallace, undated, all in Admin. Files Gov. L. Wallace, SG22453, ADAH.

48. Telegram from Ralph Abernathy to Lurleen Wallace, 19 January 1967, Admin. Files Gov. L. Wallace, SG22453, ADAH.

49. *Memphis Press-Scimitar,* 26 January 1967; *Birmingham News,* 25–26 January 1967.

50. *Birmingham News,* 25–26 January 1967. George Wallace to Russell Long, 27 January 1967; Bull Connor to George Wallace, 27 January 1967; Mrs. Annie Collier to Lurleen Wallace, 31 January 1967, all in Admin. Files Gov. L. Wallace, SG22433, ADAH.

51. *Birmingham News,* 22–24 March, 26 March, 30 March, 22 July 1967; decree of Enjoinment, U.S. District Court for Middle District of Alabama, Eastern Division, *Anthony Lee et al. v. Macon County Board of Education,* 22 March 1967, Admin. Files Gov. L. Wallace, SG22423, ADAH.

52. Press release of the State Department of Education, 10 January 1967, SG22422; A Statistical Presentation for Alabama Sovereignty Commission, Alabama School Statistics 1962–67, 29 August 1968, SG22453; Joe Reed to Ernest Stone, 7 February 1967, SG22422; Hugh Maddox to Mike Book, 24 February 1967, SG22422, all in Admin. Files Gov. L. Wallace, ADAH.

53. Ernest Stone to Hugh Maddox, 15 February 1967, SG22422; Hugh Maddox to Ernest Stone, 24 February 1967, SG22422; State Summary of Education from Annual Report, 1966, SG22423; National Education Association, "Wilcox County, Alabama: A Study of Social, Economic, and Educational Bankruptcy," June 1967, SG22423, all in Admin. Files Gov. L. Wallace, ADAH.

54. National Education Association, "Wilcox County, Alabama: A Study of Social, Economic, and Educational Bankruptcy," June 1967, Admin. Files Gov. L. Wallace, SG22423, ADAH.

55. *Birmingham News,* 28–30 March 1967.

56. Telegram from Mrs. A. Ben Conolly to Lurleen Wallace, 23 March 1967; Alan Burns to Lurleen Wallace, 30 March 1967; Robert and Nell Payne to Lurleen Wallace, 26 March 1967; telegram from Lurleen Wallace to College and University Presidents, 27 March 1967, all in Admin. Files Gov. L. Wallace, SG22423, ADAH.

57. Speech of Lurleen Wallace before the Legislature of Alabama in Joint Session, 30 March 1967, Admin. Files Gov. L. Wallace, SG22453, ADAH; *Birmingham News,* 31 March 1967.

58. Speech of Lurleen Wallace before the Legislature of Alabama in Joint Session, 30 March 1967, Admin. Files Gov. L. Wallace, SG22453, ADAH.

59. *Birmingham News,* 31 March, 1–2 April 1967. Telegram from John Bell Williams to Lurleen Wallace, 15 April 1967; Lurleen Wallace to John Bell Williams, undated; telegram from John McKeithen to Lurleen Wallace, 13 April 1967, all in Admin. Files Gov. L. Wallace, SG22423, ADAH.

60. Mrs. J. W. Battle to Lurleen Wallace, 31 March 1967; Albert Branscomb to Lurleen Wallace, 29 March 1967; Lurleen Wallace to Albert Branscomb, 11 April 1967; C. H. Clark to Lurleen Wallace, 11 May 1967; Hugh Maddox to C. H. Clark, 17 May 1967, all in Admin. Files Gov. L. Wallace, SG22423, ADAH.

61. Interview, Hugh Maddox; *Thunderbolt* no. 83 (November 1966); W. T. Pickel to George Wallace, 6 September 1967, SG22424; George Wallace to W. T. Pickel, 8 September 1967, SG22424; George Johnston to George Wallace, undated, SG22423; George Wallace to George Johnston, 17 May 1967, SG22423; *Birmingham News,* 3 September 1967; L. C. Courton to George Wallace, undated, SG22429; Robert Macqueen to George Wallace, undated, SG22429; George Wallace to Robert Macqueen, 25 February 1966, SG22429; interviews, Bill Jones; Mrs. Hester Skinner to George Wallace, 3 July 1963, SG22365, all correspondence in Admin. Files Gov. G. Wallace, ADAH.

62. Klavern 59 to Lurleen Wallace, 13 April 1967, SG22423; Mitchell Howard to George

Wallace, 18 April 1966, SG22429; Hugh Maddox to Mitchell Howard, 24 November 1966, SG22429; George Wallace to Ira Clarkson, SG22429; Byron de la Beckwith to George Wallace, 2 July 1967, SG22422; Cecil Jackson to Byron de la Beckwith, 19 July 1967, SG22422; Mrs. Beth Ransdell to George Wallace, 5 March 1968, SG22440; George Wallace to Mrs. Beth Ransdell, 8 March 1968, SG22440, all in Admin. Files Gov. L. Wallace, ADAH.

63. Hugh Maddox to George Wallace, 23 May 1967, Admin. Files Gov. L. Wallace, SG22423, ADAH; *Birmingham News,* 6 April, 12 April 1967.

64. *Birmingham News,* 1 April 1967; speech by Lurleen Wallace to the Alabama League of Municipalities Convention, 11 April 1967, Admin. Files Gov. L. Wallace, SG22453, ADAH.

65. *Birmingham News,* 5–6 April 1967.

66. Ibid., 5–7 April 1967.

67. Ibid., 8 April, 17 August, 26 August, 29 August 1967; Agenda of the Meeting of the Alabama Board of Education, 24 March 1967, Admin. Files Gov. L. Wallace, SG22423, ADAH. For more on Morris Dees see his autobiography, *A Season for Justice: The Life and Times of Civil Rights Lawyer Morris Dees* (New York: Charles Scribner's Sons, 1991).

68. *Birmingham News,* 5–7 April, 16 April 1967; telegram from Al Siegal to Lurleen Wallace, 7 April 1967, Admin. Files Gov. L. Wallace, SG22423, ADAH; transcript of interview with Harry Philpott, ed. Dwayne Cox and Kayla Barrett (Auburn: Auburn University, 1992), Oral History Collection, Auburn University, Auburn, Ala.

69. *Birmingham News,* 16–18 April 1967; George Wallace to John McKeithen, 10 April 1967; telegram from Lurleen Wallace to John McKeithen, Robert McNair, Dan Moore, Claude Kirk, Buford Ellington, Edward Breathitt, Winthrop Rockefeller, Mills Goodwin Jr., and John Connally, 11 April 1967; Claude Kirk to Lurleen Wallace, 13 April 1967, all correspondence in Admin. Files Gov. L. Wallace, SG22444, ADAH.

70. *Birmingham News,* 11–13 April, 15–16 April 1967.

71. Ibid., 31 March, 14 April, 18 April 1967; *Mobile Register,* 7–9 April 1967; Speech of Lurleen Wallace for Governor's Day at the University of Alabama, 28 April 1967, Admin. Files Gov. L. Wallace, SG22453, ADAH.

72. *Birmingham News,* 26 April, 26 May 1967; Explanatory Letter from the Clarke County Board of Education Superintendent Norman Loper to Parents, 1 May 1967, Admin. Files Gov. L. Wallace, SG22423, ADAH.

73. *Birmingham News,* 3 May, 5 May, 16 May, 5 June 1967; Hugh Maddox to Freddy Broyles, 11 October 1966, SG22424; Charles P. Hayes to Dr. J. E. Jackson, 2 February 1967, SG22424; memorandum from Hugh Maddox to Jake Jordan, 1 June 1967, SG22425, all correspondence in Admin. Files Gov. L. Wallace, ADAH.

74. *Birmingham News,* 2 May, 5–7 May, 11 May, 5 June 1967.

75. Ibid., 27 May, 5 June, 17 June, 21 June, 26–28 June 1967; transcript of interview with Harry Philpott.

76. *Birmingham News,* 10 July, 14 July, 16 July, 23 July, 3 August, 22–23 August, 27 August 1967.

77. Press release of Lurleen Wallace, undated, SG22424; decree of enjoinment, 22 March 1967, U.S. District Court for the Middle District of Alabama, *Anthony Lee v. Macon County Board of Education,* SG22423, all in Admin. Files Gov. L. Wallace, ADAH; *Birmingham News,* 27 August 1967.

78. Teacher choice form of the Anniston City Schools; Birmingham city school choice forms of Donald Jones, Nanette Burbage, and Margaret Bowman, all in Admin. Files Gov. L. Wallace, SG22424, ADAH.

79. Hugh Maddox to Mrs. Paul Wheeler, 21 September 1967; Hugh Maddox to W. T. Carey, undated; Lurleen Wallace to Golda Grant, 21 September 1967; Mrs. Ralph Kirkland to Lurleen Wallace, 7 September 1967; Hugh Maddox to Mrs. Ralph Kirkland, 22 September 1967; telegrams from Lurleen Wallace to the presidents of the Alabama Congress of Parents and Teachers, Alabama Education Association, Alabama Principals Association, and Alabama State Bar, 5 September 1967, all in Admin. Files Gov. L. Wallace, SG22424, ADAH.

80. Mrs. Maymie Brennan to Lurleen Wallace, 5 September 1967; Lurleen Wallace to Mrs. Maymie Brennan, 28 September 1967, all in Admin. Files Gov. L. Wallace, SG22424, ADAH.

81. Millard Harkrider to Lurleen Wallace, 12 September 1967; Mrs. Steve Holliday to Lurleen Wallace, 3 September 1967; Lurleen Wallace to Mrs. Steve Holliday, 8 September 1967; John L. Robinson to George Wallace, 8 September 1967; Laurence Gunnison to Lurleen Wallace, 3 September 1967, all in Admin. Files Gov. L. Wallace, SG22424, ADAH.

82. *Birmingham News,* 4 September, 6 September, 9–10 September, 17 September, 28 October 1967.

83. S. Douglass Smith,"The Case for Comprehensive State Planning," Alabama Department of Finance Study, 16 August 1967, Admin. Files Gov. L. Wallace, SG22425, ADAH.

84. Ralph Swofford to Hugh Maddox, 6 June 1967; Lurleen Wallace to Frank Sloan, 6 June 1967; Frank Swofford to Hugh Maddox, 10 July 1967; Lurleen Wallace to Frank Sloan, 10 July 1967, all in Admin. Files Gov. L. Wallace, SG22422, ADAH; Bruce J. Reynolds, "A History of African-American Farm Cooperatives, 1938–2000," USDA/RBS/Cooperative Services, www.agecon.ksu.edu/accc/ncr194/Events/2001meeting/Reynolds01.pdf; *Birmingham News,* 11–12 May, 14 May, 30 May, 11 June, 9 July 1967. For more on Alabama's relationship with the federal Office of Economic Opportunity see Susan Youngblood Ashmore, "Carry it On: The War on Poverty and the Civil Rights Movement in Alabama, 1964–1970," (PhD diss., Auburn University, 1999).

85. *Birmingham News,* 19 February, 31 July 1967. George Wallace to Richard Stone, 1 February, 1 March 1967, SG22425; George Wallace to Jake Jordan, 1 February 1967, SG22425; George Wallace to Taylor Hardin, 4 February 1967, SG22425; George Wallace to Seymore Trammell, 14 February, 23 February 1967, SG22425; George Wallace to Mills Cowling, 1 March, 4 April 1967, SG22425; George Wallace to Ruben King, 7 June 1967, SG22433, all in Admin. Files Gov. L. Wallace, ADAH.

86. *Birmingham News,* 26 July, 3 August, 1 September, 3 September, 17 September 1967; interview, Ed Ewing; interview, George Wallace Jr. Draft of proposed mental health legislation, SG22426; minutes of the 16 March and 18 April 1967 meeting of the Alabama Board of Mental Health, SG22426; Hugh Maddox to Douglas Ethridge, 5 October 1967, SG22445; WSFA-TV 12 editorial, 19 April 1968, SG22445; press release of the Governor's Office, 5 December 1967, SG22445, all in Admin. Files Gov. L. Wallace, ADAH. *Newsletter of the Montgomery County Association for Mental Health* 4. no.5 (May 1968).

87. Speech of Lurleen Wallace to the Medical Association of Alabama, 21 April 1967, Admin. Files Gov. L. Wallace, SG22453, ADAH.

88. *Montgomery Advertiser*, 11 January 1966; *Birmingham News*, 15 January, 27 June, 2 July, 10 July, 15 July 1967; Smith, *The Intimate Story of Lurleen Wallace*, 14–18; House, *Lady of Courage*, 99; Lesher, *George Wallace*, 382; Dan T. Carter, *The Politics of Rage: George Wallace, the Origins of the New Conservatism, and the Transformation of American Politics* (New York: Simon and Schuster, 1995), 308–9.

89. *Birmingham News*, 12 July, 23 July, 3 August, 14 August 1967; Smith, *The Intimate Story of Lurleen Wallace*, 24–25.

90. *Birmingham News*, 12 September, 14–15 September, 10 October 1967; Smith, *The Intimate Story of Lurleen Wallace*, 24–28.

91. *Birmingham News*, 1–2 November 1967; Smith, *The Intimate Story of Lurleen Wallace*, 29–31.

92. B*irmingham News*, 17 November, 19 November, 21–22 November, 4–5 December 1967; Lesher, *George Wallace*, 382; interview, Hugh Maddox; interview, Ed Ewing.

93. *Birmingham News*, 7 December, 10 December 1967; interview, Hugh Maddox.

94. *Birmingham News*, 2 January, 4–5 January, 8–10 January 1968; Smith, *The Intimate Story of Lurleen Wallace*, 32; Carter, *Politics of Rage*, 317–18.

95. *Birmingham News*, 11 January 1968; Smith, *The Intimate Story of Lurleen Wallace*, 37–42, 95; Lesher, *George Wallace*, 382–83; interview, Ed Ewing.

96. *Birmingham News*, 23 February, 27–28 February, 1 March, 2 March, 4 March, 11–12 March, 27 March 1968.

97. Interview, Ed Ewing; Lesher, *George Wallace*, 383; interviews, Albert Brewer; Smith, *The Intimate Story of Lurleen Wallace*, 103.

98. *Birmingham News*, 7 May 1968; Lesher, *George Wallace*, 384.; interview, George Wallace Jr.; interview, Peggy Wallace Kennedy and Mark Kennedy.

Chapter 7

1. Interviews, Bill Jones; interview, Ed Ewing; *Birmingham News*, 7 May, 8 May.

2. Interviews, Bill Jones; Jack House, *Lady of Courage: The Story of Lurleen Burns Wallace* (Montgomery: League Press, 1969), 151–64; Anita Smith, *The Intimate Story of Lurleen Wallace: Her Crusade of Courage* (Montgomery: Communication Unlimited, 1969), 109–20; Dan T. Carter, *The Politics of Rage: George Wallace, the Origins of the New Conservatism, and the Transformation of American Politics* (New York: Simon and Schuster, 1995), 321; Stephan Lesher, *George Wallace: American Populist* (New York: Addison-Wesley, 1994), 384–85; *Birmingham News*, 7–10 May 1968. Before Lurleen, Jefferson Davis was the only dignitary to lie in state at the capitol.

3. Lesher, *George Wallace*, 385–86; interviews, Bill Jones; interview, Hugh Maddox; interview, Ed Ewing; interview, Elvin Stanton.

4. *Birmingham News*, 8–9 May 1968; interview, Peggy Wallace Kennedy; interviews, Albert Brewer.

5. *Birmingham News;* 12 May 1968; interview, Bob Ingram.

6. Interview, Bob Ingram. Even after the Brewer administration returned the Finance Department to legal guidelines and bid procedures, Wallaceites continued to earn many of the asphalt bids. Ingram recalls Oscar Harper and Fuller Kimbrell continuing to receive

bids because their operations had become so large that they could afford to undercut the competition. "God knows," Ingram noted, "some of our people didn't bid low and they were hurt. . . . I hope it didn't hurt us [politically] because we were just trying to do it right."

7. Interviews, Albert Brewer.

8. Interviews, Albert Brewer; interview, Bob Ingram.

9. Interview, Julia Allen; interviews, Albert Brewer; interview, Bob Ingram.

10. Interviews, Albert Brewer; *Birmingham News,* 19 May, 22–23 May, 22 June 1968; Carter, *Politics of Rage,* 322; interview, George Wallace Jr.

11. Albert Brewer to Cecil Jackson, 20 October 1967; George Wallace to Albert Brewer, 13 November 1967; Albert Brewer to Thornton Fleming, R. S. Waters, Raymond Baker, E. M. Frazier, Redus Collier, V. L. Greenwell, 2 November 1967, all in Albert Brewer Papers, box 5 ADAH; *Birmingham News,* 22 May, 3–4 September 1968.

12. *Birmingham News,* 12 May, 15–16 May, 23 May 1968; Melba Till Allen to Albert Brewer, 27 May 1968, and Albert Brewer to Melba Till Allen, 29 May 1968, Administrative Files of Governor Albert Brewer (hereafter Admin. Files Gov. Brewer), SG22439, ADAH.

13. *Birmingham News,* 16 May, 2 June, 26 June, 7 September 1968; B. G. Thornton to Albert Brewer, and Hugh Maddox to B. G. Thornton, Admin. Files Gov. Brewer, SG22640, ADAH.

14. *Birmingham News,* 23 January 1969; memorandum from Albert Brewer to All Department Heads, 28 June 1968; memorandum from Albert Brewer to Alfred Harrison, 11 September 1968; interviews, Albert Brewer; memorandum from Albert Brewer to Bob Ingram, 2 December 1968; memorandum from Bob Ingram to Joe Graham, 3 December 1968; Mrs. Sim Wilbanks to Albert Brewer, 1 August 1968; Albert Brewer to Mrs. Sim Wilbanks, 2 August 1968, all correspondence in Admin. Files Gov. Brewer, SG22640, ADAH.

15. *Birmingham News,* 31 May, 7–8 December 1968; interviews, Albert Brewer; Cecil Jackson to Ruben King, 7 May 1968, Admin. Files Gov. Brewer, SG22449, ADAH.

16. *Birmingham News,* 23–24 July, 28 July, 30 July 1968. Herman Ross to Albert Brewer, 3 July 1969, SG22455; T. C. Almon to Albert Brewer, 10 March 1970, SG22636; Albert Brewer to Houston Feaster, 30 March 1970, SG22636; Houston Feaster to Albert Brewer, 3 March 1970, SG22636; memorandum from Robert Cleckler to Albert Brewer, 27 September 1968, SG22448, all in Admin. Files Gov. Brewer, ADAH.

17. Interview, Bob Ingram.

18. *Birmingham News,* 26 November, 8 December 1968; *Huntsville Times,* 6 December 1968. ABC chairman Dewitt Reams later admitted that Milsapp received money as a liquor agent.

19. *Birmingham News,* 27 November, 29 November, 1 December 1968; interviews, Albert Brewer; Albert Brewer to Winston Carter, 6 January 1969; Albert Brewer to Mr. and Mrs. H. J. Morris, 6 January 1969; Albert Brewer to Bill Burton, 16 December 1968; Albert Brewer to Mrs. Ethel Bain, 2 January 1969, all correspondence in Admin. Files Gov. Brewer, SG22455, ADAH.

20. Interviews, Albert Brewer.

21. *Birmingham News,* 19 January, 28 March 1969.

22. Carter, *Politics of Rage,* 369; *Birmingham News,* 28 March 1969.

23. *Birmingham News,* 28 March, 14–15 July, 4–5 September 1969.

24. Interviews, Bill Jones; interview, Ed Ewing; *Birmingham News,* 24 August 1969.

25. Interviews, Bill Jones; interview, Ed Ewing; Carter, *Politics of Rage,* 364–65; *Birmingham News,* 27 October, 1 November 1968.

26. *Birmingham News,* 2 May, 12 May, 15 May 1969; Carter, *Politics of Rage,* 352–54; Lesher, *George Wallace,* 418. The *Birmingham News* offered a gushing appraisal of Brewer's first year in office: "His performance during that year rates high marks. . . . Brewer has 'come across' as an intelligent, level-headed, honest, poised young executive, and important to him in full view of his expressed interest in seeking a full term in office next year, this good impression has been absorbed, not only outside the state but by Alabamians who previously knew of him only as a legislator and lieutenant governor."

27. Interviews, Albert Brewer.

28. Interviews, Albert Brewer; *Birmingham News,* 10 July, 27 August, 20 November 1969; Curtis Adams to Albert Brewer, 6 October 1969, Admin. Files Gov. Brewer, SG22650, ADAH.

29. *Birmingham News,* 20 August, 15 November, 26 November, 16 December 1969, 11 January, 13–14 January 1970. Lolley's attorney, former legislator Vaughn Hill Robison, called George Wallace and Jim Allen as witnesses.

30. Draft of executive order no. 15; memorandum from Bob Cleckler to Kate Simmons, 24 October 1969, all in Admin. Files Gov. Brewer, SG22640, ADAH; *Birmingham News,* 12–13 September, 24 September 1969; memorandum from Howell Heflin to members of the Alabama Ethics Commission, 30 October 1969, Admin. Files Gov. Brewer, SG22640, ADAH.

31. Memorandum from Albert Brewer to Richard Holmes, 29 October 1969; Legal Opinion of James Solomon, Solomon to Richard Holmes, 31 December 1969, all in Admin. Files Gov. Brewer, SG22640, ADAH.

32. Proposed Committee Appointments of Alabama Ethics Commission; Richard Dominick to Howell Heflin, 6 November 1969; Howell Heflin to Justice Pelham Merrill and James Carter, undated; Howell Heflin to Albert Brewer, 6 January 1970, all in Admin. Files Gov. Brewer, SG22640, ADAH.

33. Report and Recommendations of the Committee on Ethics in the Executive Branch; Final Report of the Legislative Ethics Committee of the Alabama Ethics Commission; Final Report of the Committee on Ethical Conduct of Lobbying Interests, all in Admin. Files Gov. Brewer, SG22640, ADAH.

34. Community Planning Division Newsletter of the Alabama State Planning and Industrial Development Board, May 1969; R. G. Kendall to James Somerall, 16 April 1969, all in Admin. Files Gov. Brewer, SG22627, ADAH; *Birmingham News,* 5, April, 9 April 1969.

35. Various memorandums and correspondence from Albert Brewer, SG22621; minutes of board meeting of the State Planning and Industrial Development Board, 26 November 1968, SG22621; William Oppold to Albert Brewer, 7 August 1969, SG22627; Albert Brewer to Ed Mitchell, 15 August 1969, SG22627; Albert Brewer to William Oppold, 21 August 1969, SG22627; Jim Hunter to Albert Brewer, 22 August 1969, SG22627; Albert Brewer to William Oppold, 26 August 1969, SG22627; memorandum from Ed Mitchell to Albert Brewer, 18 April 1969, SG22627, all in Admin. Files Gov. Brewer, ADAH.

36. Interviews, Albert Brewer; *Birmingham News,* 18 July 1968; memorandum from Hugh Maddox to Albert Brewer, 15 January 1969, Admin. Files Gov. Brewer, SG22640, ADAH.

37. Albert Brewer to Arthur Youngblood, 27 June 1968; press release of the Department of Conservation, 2 July 1968; Report Covering the Investigation of a Fish Kill at Locust Fork of Black Warrior River, 13 July 1968; Investigation of a Fish Kill below Eslava Creek Sewage Treatment Plant on Dog River in Mobile, undated; Preliminary Report of a Fish Kill on Dog River, 18 July 1968; Preliminary Report on Fish Kills Reported in the Mobile Area, 30 July 1968, all in Admin. Files Gov. Brewer, SG22454, ADAH; *Montgomery Advertiser,* 4 August 1968.

38. Archie Hooper to Charles Kelley, 2 July 1968; Preliminary Report of an Investigation of a Fish Kill; Paul Traina to Archie Cooper, 10 July 1968; Charles Kelley to Claude Kelley, 2 July 1968, all in Admin. Files Gov. Brewer, SG22454, ADAH.

39. Telegram from E. Bruce Trickey to Albert Brewer, date unclear; *Birmingham News,* 20 July 1968; Max Edwards to Lurleen Wallace, 29 February 1968; statement for the Alabama Water Improvement Commission by Geigy-McIntosh, statement and correspondence in Admin. Files Gov. Brewer, SG22454, ADAH.

40. Hugh Maddox to C. E. Green, 6 May 1968; Albert Brewer to John DiPlacido, 28 June 1968; Leonard Beard to Hugh Maddox, 7 March 1968, all in Admin. Files Gov. Brewer, SG22454, ADAH. Secretary of the Interior Morris Udall did not approve Alabama's water pollution guidelines. At a subsequent meeting of the Alabama Water Improvement Commission, a decision was made to avoid compromising on dissolved oxygen ratios, temperature requirements, and nondegradation standards.

41. Albert Brewer to Dr. Ira Myers, 11 July 1968; minutes of the meeting of the Alabama Water Improvement Commission, 26 July 1968; Ira Myers to MacDonald Gallion, 2 August 1968; Ira Myers to Albert Brewer, 6 August 1968; Ira Myers to Lambert Mims, 31 July 1968; Ira Myers to the Mobile County Commission, 31 July 1968, all in Admin. Files Gov. Brewer, SG22454, ADAH; *Birmingham News,* 14 July, 1 August, 5 August 1969.

42. Philip Green to Albert Brewer, 17 July 1968; Robert E. Jones to Albert Brewer, 26 July 1968; Ray Scott to Albert Brewer, 19 July 1968; Ray Scott to B.A.S.S. members, undated, all in Admin. Files Gov. Brewer, SG22454, ADAH.

43. E. O. Eddins to Albert Brewer, 18 September 1968; Albert Brewer to E. O. Eddins, 27 September 1968; Albert Brewer to Dr. Ira Myers, 9 September 1968, all in Admin. Files Gov. Brewer, SG22454, ADAH.

44. *Birmingham News,* 15 May, 13 July, 13 August, 22 August 1969; Tulah Davis to Albert Brewer, 3 October 1970, Admin. Files Gov. Brewer, SG22655, ADAH.

45. *Birmingham News,* 15 May, 13 July, 13 August, 22 August 1969; interviews, Albert Brewer; interview, Chriss Doss; Earl Mallick to Dr. A. H. Russakoff, 25 April 1969, Admin. Files Gov. Brewer, SG22455, ADAH.

46. Dr. Charles Pittman and the University of Alabama Chemistry Department to Albert Brewer, 14 July 1969, Admin. Files Gov. Brewer, SG22455, ADAH.

47. *Birmingham News,* 14 September 1969, 1 July, 8 July 1970; various correspondence of Albert Brewer on air and water pollution, 1970, Admin. Files Gov. Brewer, SG22655, ADAH.

48. *Birmingham News,* 7–8 July, 10 July, 13 July, 29 July, 14 August, 3 September, 1 October, 22 October 1970; Tulah Davis to Albert Brewer, 3 October 1970, Admin. Files Gov. Brewer, SG22655, ADAH.

49. *Birmingham News*, 7 September 1969; interviews, Albert Brewer; press release of the Governor's Office, 29 December 1969, Admin. Files Gov. Brewer, SG22657, ADAH.

50. *Birmingham News*, 24 August 1969; Gordon E. Harvey, *A Question of Justice: New South Governors and Education, 1968–1976* (Tuscaloosa: University of Alabama Press, 2002), 52–53, 60–63; interviews, Albert Brewer.

51. *Birmingham News*, 7 September 1969.

52. Ernest Stone to Albert Brewer, 14 May 1968; Albert Brewer to Ernest Stone, undated; Hugh Maddox to Sara Pugh, 27 August 1968, all in Admin. Files Gov. Brewer, SG22443, ADAH; *Birmingham News*, 23 May 1968.

53. Interviews, Albert Brewer; *Birmingham News*, 1 June, 12–14 June 1968; Harvey, *A Question of Justice*, 22–24, 43; minutes of the meeting of the Alabama State Board of Education, 12 June 1968, Admin. Files Gov. Brewer, SG22443, ADAH.

54. *State Department of Education News*, 11 July 1968; Bob Cleckler to Mrs. Ellington, 17 October 1968; memorandums from Albert Brewer to Ernest Stone, 7 October 1968; Ernest Stone to Albert Brewer, 22 October 1968; Free Textbook Program Summary, all correspondence in Admin. Files Gov. Brewer, SG22443, ADAH.

55. *State Department of Education Newsletter*, 11 July 1968; R. L Saunders, "Why Are Good, Qualified Teachers Leaving Alabama," reprinted in *Birmingham News*, 4 September 1969. James Davis to Albert Brewer, 27 May 1969, SG22459; Report of the Alabama Education Association, SG22458; Albert Brewer to Ernest Stone, 5 November 1968, SG22458; Ernest Stone to Albert Brewer, 23 August 1968, SG22448, all in Admin. Files Gov. Brewer, ADAH. The teacher flight issue was desperate. Twenty-eight percent of graduates entering teaching left the state. Of that group, 40 percent went to Georgia and 27 to Florida. The median age of Alabama teachers was rising every year. More than one-third of state teachers were fifty years old or older. Eighty percent of teachers were female, and Saunders's report indicated that gender imbalance was unlikely to change until major salary adjustments were made.

56. Harvey, *A Question of Justice*, 45–46. Tom Gloor to Albert Brewer, 28 August 1968, SG22459; Tom Gloor to H. B. Woodward, 10 September 1968, SG22459; Albert Brewer to Tom Gloor, 10 September 1968, SG22459; memorandum from Hugh Maddox to Bob Inman, 7 October 1968, SG22458, all in Admin. Files Gov. Brewer, ADAH; *Birmingham News*, 12 September 1968.

57. Report of the Alabama Education Study Commission, Admin. Files Gov. Brewer, SG22460, ADAH; *Birmingham News*, 15 January, 26 January, 16 February, 18 March 1969.

58. Report of the Alabama Education Study Commission, Admin. Files Gov. Brewer, SG22460, ADAH; *Birmingham News*, 15 January, 31 January, 28 March 1969; transcript of Oral History of Harry Philpott, Special Collections, Auburn University, Auburn, Ala.

59. Albert Brewer to the National Education Association, 14 November 1968, SG22458; Hugh Maddox to the U.S. Department of Health, Education, and Welfare, 14 November 1968, SG22459; Carl E. Wedekind to High Maddox, 31 October 1968, SG22459; Report of the Legislative Committee to the AEA Assembly of Delegates, SG22458, all in Admin. Files Gov. Brewer, ADAH; interviews, Albert Brewer; Harvey, *A Question of Justice*, 59.

60. Transcript of oral history of Harry Philpott, Special Collections, Auburn Univer-

sity, Auburn, Ala.; Albert Brewer to Jess Griffin and the Capital City Jaycees, 4 October 1968, Admin. Files Gov. Brewer, SG22458, ADAH; *Birmingham News*, 6 February, 2 April, 1 May 1969; Harvey, *A Question of Justice*, 58–63.

61. *Birmingham News*, 3–5 May 1969; Harvey, *A Question of Justice*, 60; transcript of oral history of Harry Philpott, Special Collections, Auburn University, Auburn, Ala.

62. Oliver Quayle Company, "A Study of the Political Climate in Alabama," study no. 1212, March 1969; Penetration Research Limited, "A Study of the Political Climate in Alabama," wave 2, study no. 769, September 1969, all in private collection of Albert Brewer. Penetration Research is an arm of the Quayle Company.

63. Penetration Research Limited, "A Study of the Political Climate in Alabama," wave 2, study no. 769, September 1969, in private collection of Albert Brewer; *Birmingham News*, 11 May 1969.

64. Penetration Research Limited, "A Study of the Political Climate in Alabama," wave 2, study no. 769, September 1969, in private collection of Albert Brewer; *Birmingham News*, 22 August 1968; Harvey, *A Question of Justice*, 22–24.

65. *Birmingham News*, 29 August 1969; *Montgomery Advertiser*, 29 August 1969; *Valley-Times News*, 29 August 1968. Memorandum from Ernest Stone to Albert Brewer, 6 September 1968; C. C. "Bo" Torbert to Albert Brewer, undated; Albert Brewer to C. C. Torbert, 3 September 1968; memorandum from Ernest Stone to Albert Brewer, 9 September 1968; Pro Rata Share of Insurance Valuation of Buildings for Grades to be Closed during 1969–70, all in Admin. Files Gov. Brewer, SG22443, ADAH; Harvey, *A Question of Justice*, 19–29.

66. *Birmingham News*, 29 August 1969; *Dothan Eagle*, 30 August 1968. Albert Brewer to W. P. Chastain. 5 September 1968, SG22443; Albert Brewer to Jake Bromberg, 10 September 1968, SG22443; Albert Brewer to Mrs. Richard Knox, 29 August 1969, SG22459; Albert Brewer to Richard Lowe, 6 November 1969, SG22460, all in Admin. Files Gov. Brewer, ADAH.

67. *Birmingham News*, 30 August 1968; Harvey, *A Question of Justice*, 29. Telegram from Albert Brewer to School Superintendents, 24 October 1969; Albert Brewer to Raymond Christian, 20 May 1969; Raymond Christian to Albert Brewer, 23 May 1969, all in Admin. Files Gov. Brewer, SG22459, ADAH.

68. Albert Brewer to Carl Herbert Lancaster, 21 October 1968, Admin. Files Gov. Brewer, SG22459, ADAH.

69. *Birmingham News*, 3–4 September 1969.

70. Ibid., 8 September 1969; interviews, Albert Brewer.

71. *Birmingham News*, 28 September, 26 October 1969; interviews, Albert Brewer; interview, Bob Ingram.

72. Interviews, Bill Jones; *Birmingham News*, 1 December, 2 December 1969.

73. *Birmingham News*, 3 December, 15 December, 18 December 1969, 19 January, 21 January, 1 February, 23 February, 26 February 1970; Lesher, *George Wallace*, 432–38; Carter, *Politics of Rage*, 384–89, 407–14; interview, Bob Ingram.

74. *Birmingham News*, 15 December, 18 December 1969.

75. Carter, *Politics of Rage*, 387; Oliver Quayle and Company, "A Survey of the Political Climate in Alabama," wave 3, study no. 1286, January 1970, in private collection of Albert Brewer.

76. *Birmingham News*, 7 January, 15 January, 21 January, 4 February, 9 February 1970.

77. Ibid., 23–26 February 1970; Harvey, *A Question of Justice,* 40–41.

78. *Birmingham News,* 26 February 1970.

79. Oliver Quayle Company, "A Survey of the Political Climate in Alabama," wave 3, study no. 1286, January 1970, in private collection of Albert Brewer; interviews, Albert Brewer.

80. *Birmingham News,* 27 February, 12 March, 15 March, 22 March, 26 March 1970; interviews, Albert Brewer.

81. *Birmingham News,* 5 April, 27 April, 3 May 1970; Numan V. Bartley and Hugh D. Graham, *Southern Elections: County and Precinct Data, 1950–1972* (Baton Rouge: Louisiana State University Press, 1978), 21–22.

82. Penetration Research Limited, "A Survey of the Political Climate in the State of Alabama," wave 4, study no. 785, March 1970, in private collection of Albert Brewer.

83. Carter, *Politics of Rage,* 386; *Birmingham News,* 15–16 March, 19–20 March, 22 March, 22 April 1970.

84. *Birmingham News,* 15 March, 17 March, 21–22 March, 24 March, 27 March, 31 March, 5 April, 9 April, 12 April, 15–16 April, 19 April 1970; Penetration Research Limited, "A Survey of the Political Climate in the State of Alabama," March 1970, and Oliver Quayle and Company, "A Survey of the Political Climate in the State of Alabama," wave 5, study no. 1324, April 1970, all in private collection of Albert Brewer.

85. *Birmingham News,* 21 April, 24 April, 3 May 1970; interviews, Albert Brewer; interview, Elvin Stanton.

86. Oliver Quayle and Company, "A Survey of the Political Climate in the State of Alabama,"April 1970, in private collection of Albert Brewer; *Birmingham News,* 4 May, 6 May 1970; Bartley and Graham, *Southern Elections,* 21–22. Primary voting totals are as follows: Brewer, 428,146; Wallace, 416,443; Woods, 149,887; Carter, 15,441; all others, 9,763.

87. Interview, Mark Kennedy and Peggy Wallace Kennedy; *Birmingham News,* 7 May 1970.

88. Interviews, Albert Brewer; interview, Bob Ingram; author's collection of 1970 campaign material; Carter, *Politics of Rage,* 393–95.

89. Interview, Bob Ingram; interviews, Albert Brewer; interview, George Wallace Jr.; *Birmingham News,* 22 May 1970; Penetration Research Limited, "A Study of the Political Climate in Alabama," wave 6, study no. 798, May 1970, in private collection of Albert Brewer.

90. Bartley and Graham, *Southern Elections,* 21–22. In the runoff, Wallace received 559,832 votes to Brewer's 525,951.

Chapter 8

1. *Birmingham News,* 3–7 June 1970; *Los Angeles Times,* 4–5 June 1970; *Washington Post,* 4–5 June 1970; *Washington Star,* 4–5 June 1970.

2. *Birmingham News,* 2–June, 17 June 1970; interviews, Albert Brewer.

3. Jeff Frederick, "The Gubernatorial Campaigns of Jimmy Carter" (master's thesis, University of Central Florida, 1998).

4. Interview, Chriss Doss; interview, Jere Beasley; interviews, Albert Brewer; *Birmingham News,* 11 June 1970, 10 January 1971.

5. *Birmingham News*, 8 September, 23 September, 5 December 1970.

6. Ibid., 18 June, 21 June, 25 June, 28 August, 16 September, 1 October, 4 November 1970; interviews, Albert Brewer.

7. Interviews, Albert Brewer.

8. *Birmingham News*, 17–19 January 1971.

9. Stephan Lesher, *George Wallace: American Populist* (New York: Addison-Wesley, 1994), 453–57; *Birmingham News*, 16 September 1970; interview, Mark Kennedy and Peggy Wallace Kennedy.

10. *Birmingham News*, 26 December 1970, 14–15 January, 2 February, 18 February, 11 August, 16 October, 23 November 1971; Lesher, *George Wallace*, 457; interview, Elvin Stanton; interview, George Wallace Jr.

11. Interview, Chriss Doss; Lesher, *George Wallace*, 456–57.

12. Interview, Elvin Stanton; interview, Peggy Wallace Kennedy; interview, George Wallace Jr.

13. *Birmingham News*, 11 November, 30 November, 1–2 December, 7 December 1970, 19 January, 21 January, 14 March, 4 April, 31 October 1971; interview, Jere Beasley. Beasley denies that he was the Wallace candidate but admits "I did take advantage . . . of the public's perception that I was."

14. *Birmingham News*, 17 February 1971. Statement of Mrs. S. A. Cherry to the State Board of Education, undated; Mrs. S. A. Cherry to George Wallace, undated; Vernon St. John to Leroy Brown, 18 February 1971, all in Admin. Files Gov. G. Wallace, SG22658, ADAH.

15. *Birmingham News*, 11 March, 24 March, 27 March, 30 March, 1 April 1971.

16. Ibid., 12 April, 14–15 April, 18 April 1971.

17. Ibid., 21 April, 25 April, 28 April, 4 May, 21 November 1971.

18. Ibid., 2–4 May 1971; interview, Elvin Stanton.

19. *Birmingham News*, 13 January, 21 January, 2 March, 21 March, 4 April 1971; interview, Jere Beasley.

20. *Montgomery Advertiser*, 5–6 May 1971; *Birmingham News*, 5–6 May 1971.

21. *Birmingham News*, 21 April 1971. "A Message from the Governor as a Suggestion to the Parents and Guardians of Students Who Expect to Attend the Public Schools of Alabama this Fall," undated, SG22660; George Wallace to Ira Price, 31 August 1971, SG22659, all in Admin. Files Gov. G. Wallace, ADAH.

22. *Birmingham News*, 14 August 1971. Executive order no. 21, SG22659; Karl Berger to George Wallace, 30 August 1971, SG22659; Charles Millican to George Wallace, 18 August 1971, SG22659; Walter Givhan to George Wallace, 13 August 1971, SG22675, all in Admin. Files Gov. G. Wallace, ADAH.

23. Reverend J. M. Drummond to George Wallace, 19 February 1971; George Wallace to J. M. Drummond, 1 March 1971, all in Admin. Files Gov. G. Wallace, SG22658, ADAH; *Birmingham News*, 28 September, 22 October 1970.

24. Statement of Governor George C. Wallace on Busing, 6 August 1971, Admin. Files Gov. G. Wallace, SG22659, ADAH; *Save Our Schools*, newsletter of the Liberty Lobby, 20 September 1971.

25. Memorandum from George Wallace to Leroy Brown, 1 March 1971, SG22658; John

Harris to Leroy Brown, 26 March 1971, SG22658; Leroy Brown to John Harris, 31 March 1971, SG22659; memorandum from John Harris to George Wallace, 8 April 1971, SG22659; L. G. Walker to O. P. Richardson, 6 April 1971, SG22659; George Wallace to John Harris, 9 April 1971, SG22659; George Wallace to Leroy Brown, 30 August 1971, SG22659; memorandum from Lewis McGee to John Harris, 15 November 1971, SG22675, all in Admin. Files Gov. G. Wallace, ADAH.

26. Memorandum from Leroy Brown to Harry Pennington, 27 July 1971; memorandum from Leroy Brown to Local School Superintendents, 23 July 1971; "Information on Schools Closed by Federal Court Orders and Schools Reopened," State Department of Education Form; memorandum from Harry Pennington to George Wallace, 27 July 1971; George Wallace to John Mitchell, 29 June 1971, all in Admin. Files Gov. G. Wallace, SG22659, ADAH.

27. *Birmingham News,* 2 July, 22 July 1971; interview, Paul Hubbert. Hal Dutch to George Wallace, 4 August 1971; Bobbie Robinson to George Wallace, 18 August 1971; Louis R. Bryant to George Wallace, 4 August 1971; Frank Earnest to Paul Hubbert, 16 August 1971; memorandum from George Wallace to Tom Drake and Pete Matthews, 31 August 1971; Henry Rembert to George Wallace, 17 August 1971, all in Admin. Files Gov. G. Wallace, SG22718, ADAH.

28. *Birmingham News,* 22 July, 14 August, 17 August, 26 August, 4 September, 8 September, 15 September 1971. Bill McCollough to George Wallace, 20 August 1971; George Wallace to William McCollough, 31 August 1971, all in Admin. Files Gov. G. Wallace, SG22659, ADAH.

29. *Swann v. Charlotte-Mecklenburg Board of Education, Supreme Court Reporter* 91, no. 14 (15 May 1971), SG23443; Act no. 1418, the Alabama Anti-Busing Law, Acts of Alabama, Regular Session 1971; "Sequence of Events Leading to the Decision of Judge Pointer," Wallace Administration Research, SG22675; George Wallace to J. D. Logan, 10 March 1971, SG22658, all in Admin. Files Gov. G. Wallace, ADAH.

30. *Birmingham News,* 20–21 October 1971. Memorandum from George Wallace to John Harris, 31 August 1971, Admin. Files Gov. G. Wallace, SG22659; *Dothan Eagle,* 27 October 1971; "Sequence of Events Leading to the Decision of Judge Pointer," Wallace Administration Research, and John Harris to William Baxley, 30 November 1971, in Admin. Files Gov. G. Wallace, SG22675, ADAH.

31. *Birmingham News,* 4 December 1971. Statement of Governor George Wallace, 9 December 1971; telegrams from George Wallace to Tom Bevill and Bob Jones, 13 December 1971; statement of the Alabama Republican Party, undated, all in Admin. Files Gov. G. Wallace, SG22675, ADAH.

32. Minutes of the State Board of Education meeting, 30 April 1971, Admin. Files Gov. G. Wallace, SG22659, ADAH; *Birmingham News,* 6 March, 19 March 1971.

33. *Birmingham News,* 2 June, 18 June 1971; press release of the State of Alabama Education Study Commission, 17 June 1971, Admin. Files Gov. G. Wallace, SG22659, ADAH.

34. Interview, Paul Hubbert. For more on the weakness of the AEA in its early years, see James Howard Mason Jr., "The Alabama Education Association and Its Influence on Legislative Decisions Regarding Education in the State of Alabama, 1965–1972" (PhD diss., Auburn University, 1973).

35. Interview, Paul Hubbert; *Birmingham News,* 25 June 1971.

36. Defendant Report of the Court, 23 September 1971; William Tarnower, Consultation

Report of Bryce Hospital, all in Admin. Files Gov. G. Wallace, SG22662, ADAH. Other estimates identify the national average at $14.89 per day, reducing the Alabama per diem to 46 percent of the national average.

37. William Tarnower, Consultation Report of Bryce Hospital; Glenn E. Morris, Consultation Report of Bryce Hospital, all in Admin. Files Gov. G. Wallace, SG22662, ADAH.

38. *Birmingham News*, 25 June, 30 June 1971; interview, Paul Hubbert; *Alabama School Journal*, 1 July 1971; Mason, "The Alabama Education Association and Its Influence on Legislative Decisions Regarding Education in the State of Alabama, 1965–1972," 112–14.

39. Interview, Paul Hubbert.

40. Interview, Paul Hubbert; Guy Kelley to George Wallace, 29 June 1971, and minutes of the State Board of Education Meeting, 22 July 1971, in Admin. Files Gov. G. Wallace, SG22659, ADAH; *Birmingham News*, 23 July 1971.

41. Interview, Paul Hubbert.

42. *Birmingham News*, 12 August, 20 August 1971; interview, Paul Hubbert.

43. Interview, Chriss Doss; *Birmingham News*, 21 August, 10–11 September, 24 September 1971.

44. *Birmingham News*, 25 July, 23 September, 3 November 1971; interview, Chriss Doss.

45. *Birmingham News*, 14 July 1971; interview, Jere Beasley.

46. Interviews, Albert Brewer; interviews, Bill Jones; interview, Jere Beasley.

47. *Birmingham News*, 14–16 July, 20 July, 17 September 1971; *Montgomery Advertiser*, 5 February 1972; interview, Jere Beasley; Hugh Morrow III to George Wallace, 15 July 1971, Admin. Files Gov. G. Wallace, SG22658, ADAH.

48. *Birmingham News*, 16 September, 21 September, 3 October 1971; *Mobile Register*, 3 October, 10 October 1971. James Grigg to George Wallace, 22 October 1971; memorandum from George Wallace to John Harris, 26 October 1971; George Wallace to Sage Lyons, 26 October 1971; George Wallace to William McClure, 9 November 1971, all in Admin. Files Gov. G. Wallace, SG22698, ADAH.

49. William Ruckelshaus to George Wallace, 16 February 1971, SG22655; Barbara Lampe to George Wallace, 25 February 1971, SG22655; Ira Myers to George Wallace, 29 April 1971, SG22655; Ira Myers to William Ruckelshaus, 28 April 1971, SG22655; George Wallace to William Ruckelshaus, 4 March 1971, SG22670, all in Admin. Files Gov. G. Wallace, ADAH.

50. Analysis and Criticism of the Alabama Air Pollution Control Act of the 1969 Regular Session, act no. 1135; George Wallace to Richard Ayres, 20 May 1971; John Daniel to Harry Pennington, 13 May 1971, all in Admin. Files Gov. G. Wallace, SG22655, ADAH; *Birmingham News*, 28 July 1971. Daniel, an attorney in the Public Health Department, drafted Wallace's letter to Ayres.

51. *Birmingham News*, 1 September, 4 September 1971. Suggested Alabama Air Pollution Control Law, revised 4 March 1971, SG22655; Alabama Air Pollution Control Act, act no. 1135, Regular Session 1969, SG22655; Alabama Air Pollution Control Act of 1971, act. no. 769, SG22673; Robert L. Duprey, "Comments on Proposed Alabama Air Pollution Control Bill," SG22655, all in Admin. Files Gov. G. Wallace, ADAH.

52. The Water Improvement Commission Act, act. no. 1260, approved 22 September 1971, Admin. Files Gov. G. Wallace, SG22673, ADAH.

53. *Birmingham News*, 1 September, 16 November 1971; Harry Smith to George Wallace,

11 November 1971, Admin. Files Gov. G. Wallace, SG22673, ADAH; *Mobile Register,* 3 October 1971.

54. Frances Luke to George Wallace, 11 November 1971; J. E. Powell to George Wallace, 11 November 1971; Mrs. R. J. Smith to George Wallace, 12 November 1971; *Birmingham News,* 8 November, 15 November 1971; Jack Ravan to George Wallace, 23 May 1972, all correspondence in Admin. Files Gov. G. Wallace, SG22673, ADAH.

55. John Hayman with Clara Ruth Hayman, *A Judge in the Senate: Howell Heflin's Career of Politics and Principle* (Montgomery: New South Books, 2002), 159–67; *Birmingham News,* 24 October 1971.

56. Interview, Hugh Maddox; interview, Jere Beasley; Hayman and Hayman, *A Judge in the Senate,* 174.

57. *Birmingham News,* 28–30 September 1971.

58. *Mobile Register,* 2–3 October, 5–6 October, 15 October 1971; *Montgomery Advertiser,* 1–3 October 1971.

59. Interview, Elvin Stanton; *Birmingham News,* 17 October, 24 October 1971.

60. *Birmingham News,* 28–29 October, 3 November 1971.

61. Memorandum from George Wallace to Billy Joe Camp, 28 October 1971; memorandum from George Wallace to Billy Joe Camp, 1 November 1971; memorandum from George Wallace to Billy Joe Camp, 22 October 1971, all in Admin. Files Gov. G. Wallace, SG22675, ADAH; *Birmingham News,* 7 December 1971.

62. *Birmingham News,* 7 November, 9–10 November, 14 November 1971.

63. Ibid., 16–17 November 1971; Mason, "The Alabama Education Association and its Influence on Legislative Decisions Regarding Education in the State of Alabama, 1965–1972," 113–14.

64. *Birmingham News,* 17–18 November 1971; interview, Paul Hubbert; Mason, "The Alabama Education Association and its Influence on Legislative Decisions Regarding Education in the State of Alabama, 1965–1972," 114.

65. *Birmingham News,* 19–20 November 1971; interview, Chriss Doss; interview, Paul Hubbert; Mason, "The Alabama Education Association and its Influence on Legislative Decisions Regarding Education in the State of Alabama, 1965–1972," 114–15.

66. *Birmingham News,* 20 November 1971.

67. Ibid., 21 November, 24 November, 1 December, 5 December, 12 December 1971; *Montgomery Advertiser,* 10 January 1972; press release of the Alabama Poultry Industry Association, undated, Admin. Files Gov. G. Wallace, SG22675, ADAH; interview, Jere Beasley.

68. *Birmingham News,* 30 June, 21 November, 28 November, 12 December 1971; Freda P. Roberts, "Supporting Our Schools with Property Tax," Google search: Martha Hornbeak, www.mcpss.com/.../Freda%20Roberts%20Presentation/property%20tax%20presentation. pdf; page no longer available.

69. Statement of Martha A. Hornbeak to the Senate Interim Committee, 28 October 1971, Admin. Files Gov. G. Wallace, SG22709, ADAH.

70. Statement and tabulation by counties of Democratic primary election, 5 May 1970, Admin. Files Gov. Brewer, SG22658, ADAH; Numan V. Bartley and Hugh D. Graham, *Southern Elections: County and Precinct Data, 1950–1972* (Baton Rouge: Louisiana State University Press, 1978), 19–22; *Race Relations Reporter* 2, no. 5 (15 March 1971).

71. George Wallace to Mrs. H. L. Spenard, undated, SG22669; George Wallace to Mrs. James J. Baker, 16 December 1971, SG22673, all in Admin. Files Gov. G. Wallace, ADAH.

72. Mr. and Mrs. R. L. Faust to George Wallace, 1 May 1971; Jack Busby to George Wallace, 23 April 1971; John Ripp to George Wallace, 1 April 1971; press release of the Alabama Consumer's Association, undated, all in Admin. Files Gov. G. Wallace, SG22669, ADAH.

73. Maurice Bishop to George Wallace, 13 March 1971; draft of Petition to Intervene before the Alabama Public Service Commission, March 1971; George Wallace to Mrs. H. L. Spenard, 20 May 1971; George Wallace to Annie L. Durrett, 3 June 1971; Testimony of George Wallace before the Legislative Interim Committee on Utility Rates and Procedures, undated; George Wallace to Ben Brown, 20 August 1971; George Wallace to John Mitchell, 20 August 1971; Ben Brown to George Wallace, 24 August 1971; George Wallace to W. J. Adkinson, 2 June 1971, all in Admin. Files Gov. G. Wallace, SG22669, ADAH.

74. *Birmingham News,* 1–2 December, 5 December, 8 December, 10 December, 12 December, 14–15 December, 17 December, 22 December 1971; *Montgomery Advertiser,* 5–7 January, 9–10 January, 13 January 1972.

75. *Montgomery Advertiser,* 13 January, 16 January, 19–20 January, 25–26 January, 1–2 February, 5 February 1972.

76. *Birmingham News,* 21 November, 19 December 1971; *Montgomery Advertiser,* 7 January, 19 March 1972; Lesher, *George Wallace,* 462–64.

77. *Birmingham News,* 22 December 1971; Dan T. Carter, *The Politics of Rage: George Wallace, the Origins of the New Conservatism, and the Transformation of American Politics* (New York: Simon and Schuster, 1995), 424–25; *Montgomery Advertiser,* 20–21 January, 23 January, 19 February 1972; "Selected Votes on Busing and Related Subjects, 1969, 1970, 1971," Admin. Files Gov. G. Wallace, SG22675, ADAH.

78. *Montgomery Advertiser,* 1–4 March, 15 March, 14 April, 27 April 1972; interview, Elvin Stanton; Carter, *Politics of Rage,* 425–26.

79. *Montgomery Advertiser,* 30–31 March, 2 April, 9 April 1972.

80. Carter, *Politics of Rage,* 427–28; *Montgomery Advertiser,* 3 April 1972; interview, Elvin Stanton.

81. Interview, Elvin Stanton; *Montgomery Advertiser,* 30 March, 5–6 April 1972.

82. Carter, *Politics of Rage,* 427–28; interview, Stanton.

83. Interview, Elvin Stanton; Carter, *Politics of Rage,* 415–36; Lesher, *George Wallace,* 479–81.

84. *Montgomery Advertiser,* 14–16 May 1972; Carter, *Politics of Rage,* 419–38; Lesher, *George Wallace,* 480–82.

Chapter 9

1. Interview, Elvin Stanton; Stephan Lesher, *George Wallace: American Populist* (New York: Addison-Wesley, 1994), 481–83; Dan T. Carter, *The Politics of Rage: George Wallace, the Origins of the New Conservatism, and the Transformation of American Politics* (New York: Simon and Schuster, 1995), 437–44; author's inspection of artifacts from shooting of George C. Wallace, June 24, 2004, ADAH; interview, Jere Beasley; *Washington Post,* 3 June 2005.

2. Interview, Peggy Wallace Kennedy; interview, George Wallace Jr; *Montgomery Advertiser,* 16 May, 30 June 1972; interview, Elvin Stanton.

3. *Montgomery Advertiser,* 16–18 May 1972; author's inspection of artifacts from shooting of George C. Wallace, 24 June 2004, ADAH; "George C. Wallace, Doctor's Bills 1972," George C. Wallace Collection, LPR 124, box 119, ADAH.

4. "Diagnosis Note on Wallace, Gov. George," undated from medical chart of George Wallace, George C. Wallace Collection, LPR 124, box 119, ADAH.

5. Interview, Elvin Stanton; Lesher, *George Wallace,* 483; *Montgomery Advertiser,* 18 May, 21 May, 23 May, 29–30 May, 9 June 1972.

6. Interview, Elvin Stanton; memorandum from Harry L. Pennington to Kate Simmons, 18 May 1972, George C. Wallace Collection, and memorandum from Bill Jackson to Harry Pennington, 31 May 1973 [*sic*], in LPR 124, box 119, ADAH. The date on the Jackson memo is clearly a typographical error; it was written in 1972. Stanton was not in Maryland at the time of the shooting but flew to Silver Springs shortly thereafter.

7. Interview, Jere Beasley; interview, Elvin Stanton; *Montgomery Advertiser,* 21 May, 3 June, 7 June 1972; memorandum from Harry Pennington to Bobby Bowick, 30 May 1972, Admin. Files Gov. G. Wallace, SG22697, ADAH.

8. Interview, Elvin Stanton; *Birmingham News,* 18 May–25 May 1972; *Montgomery Advertiser,* 18 May–25 May 1972.

9. *Montgomery Advertiser,* 23–24 May, 26 May 1972; Jesse Gann to Harry Pennington, 24 July 1972, Admin. Files Gov. G. Wallace, SG22697, ADAH.

10. *Montgomery Advertiser,* 24 May, 8 June 1972.

11. Ibid., 2 June, 4 June, 8 June, 13 June, 15 June, 18 June, 25 June 1972.

12. Ibid., 14 May, 1–2 June, 14 June, 18 June, 22 June, 28 June 1972.

13. Ibid., 20 June, 22 June, 25–26 June, 28 June, 1 July, 7–9 July 1972.

14. Ibid., 9 July, 11–12 July, 14 July 1972; *Birmingham News,* 11–14 July 1972; interview, Elvin Stanton; interview, George Wallace Jr.

15. Carter, *Politics of Rage,* 447–48; interview, George Wallace Jr; *Montgomery Advertiser,* 12 July 1972.

16. Memorandum from Jack Winfield to George C. Wallace, 16 December 1971, SG22717; memorandum from Jack Winfield to George C. Wallace, 27 December 1971, SG22717; confidential memorandum from Jack Winfield to George C. Wallace, 18 January 1972, SG22709; John Bookout to Jim Allen, 7 February 1972, SG22709; George Wallace to Jesse Gann, 29 November 1971, SG22697; George Wallace to Billy Joe Camp, 23 November 1971, SG22697, all in Admin. Files Gov. G. Wallace, ADAH.

17. *Montgomery Advertiser,* 15–16 July, 20 July, 25 July 1972.

18. Memorandum from George Wallace to Billy Joe Camp, 29 November 1971; memorandum from George Wallace to Billy Joe Camp, 29 November 1971; memorandum from Johnny Goff to Billy Joe Camp, 8 February 1973; memorandum from George Wallace to Jesse Gann, 29 November 1971; memorandum from George Wallace to Bobby Bowick, 17 November 1971; memorandum from George Wallace to Harry Pennington, 17 November 1971, all in Admin. Files Gov. G. Wallace, SG22697, ADAH.

19. Memorandum from George Wallace to Bobby Bowick, 4 October 1971, SG22697; memorandum from George Wallace to Harry Pennington, 11 January 1972, SG22697; "Policy

and Procedure Memorandum Number 3," undated, SG22704, all in Admin. Files Gov. G. Wallace, ADAH.

20. Memorandum from Elvin Stanton to Billy Joe Camp, 23 May 1973, Admin. Files Gov. G. Wallace, SG22697, ADAH.

21. Memorandum from George Mangum to Taylor Hardin, Harry Pennington, Jesse Gann, and Bobby Bowick, 13 December 1971; memorandum from George Mangum to George Wallace, Harry Pennington, Taylor Hardin, Jesse Gann, and Bobby Bowick, 13 December 1971, all in Admin. Files Gov. G. Wallace, SG22697, ADAH.

22. Memorandum from Johnny Goff to George Wallace, 15 June 1973; memorandum from George Wallace to Harry Pennington, 15 August 1973; memorandum from George Wallace to Harry Pennington, 30 August 1973; memorandum from George Wallace to Harry Pennington, undated; Billy Joe Camp to Johnny Goff, 17 November 1972, all in Admin. Files Gov. G. Wallace, SG22697, ADAH.

23. Memorandum from Johnny Goff to Harry Pennington, 4 December 1972; memorandum from Johnny Goff to George Wallace, 8 August 1973; "Projects Completed," undated direct mail report; Roy Smith to Harry Pennington, 22 February 1973; memorandum from Harry Pennington to Billy Joe Camp, 5 December 1972; memorandum from George Wallace to Billy Joe Camp, 25 October 1973, all in Admin. Files Gov. G. Wallace, SG22697, ADAH.

24. *Montgomery Advertiser,* 7 January, 14 January, 17 January, 22 January, 27–28 January 1973; *Health Today* (November 1973): 69.

25. *Health Today* (November 1973): 20–21; *Montgomery Advertiser,* 26 November 1972, 1 February 1973.

26. Letters to the editor from Clifford G. Wilkinson, Charles E. Cook, Freddie W. Ware, and Mr. and Mrs. T. O. Baty, *Montgomery Advertiser,* 11 February 1973; letter to the editor from Mr. and Mrs. David Slaughter, *Montgomery Advertiser,* 18 February 1973.

27. Letters to the editor from Richard Shelby and Harvey Crumhorn, *Montgomery Advertiser,* 11 February 1973; letter to the editor from Vennie Watkins, *Montgomery Advertiser,* 18 February 1973.

28. *Health Today* (November 1973): 20–23, 68–70; *Newsweek,* 26 February 1973, 29–30.

29. *Health Today* (November 1973): 20–23, 68–70; *Montgomery Advertiser,* 17 October, 28 December 1972; 27 February, 20 March, 6 May 1973; Billy Joe Camp to Roy Smith, 29 December 1972, Admin. Files Gov. G. Wallace, SG22697, ADAH.

30. *Montgomery Advertiser,* 17 October 1972.

31. *Newsweek,* 26 February 1973, 29; *Montgomery Advertiser,* 27 February, 2 March 1973.

32. *Newsweek,* 26 February 1973, 29; *Health Today* (November 1973): 20; *Montgomery Advertiser,* 4 March 1973; interview, Bill Jones; interview, Ed Ewing; interviews, Albert Brewer.

33. *Montgomery Advertiser,* 3 December, 17 December 1972; 4 April 1973.

34. Ibid., 4 January 1972, 2 March, 1 April, 4–5 April, 7 April 1973. The senate had more than a year to address the reapportionment issue and did very little themselves.

35. Ibid., 2–3 May, 5 May 1973.

36. Ibid., 1 April, 5 May, 11 May, 13 May, 16 May, 4 August 1973; WSFA-TV editorial, 23 July 1973, Admin. Files Gov. G. Wallace, SG22697, ADAH.

37. *Montgomery Advertiser,* 6 May, 5 August, 13 September 1973.

38. Interview, Jere Beasley; interview, Elvin Stanton; *Montgomery Advertiser,* 22 April 1973.

39. *Montgomery Advertiser,* 22 April, 2–3 May, 8 May, 16 August, 25 August 1973; editorial of WSFA-TV, Montgomery, 24 July 1973, Admin. Files Gov. G. Wallace, SG22697, ADAH.

40. *Montgomery Advertiser,* 18 March, 2 May 1973.

41. George Wallace to B. J. Barclay, 3 March 1972; George Wallace to Dwight Evans, 8 March 1972; George Wallace to Jim Averitt, 8 March 1972, all in Admin. Files Gov. G. Wallace, SG22696, ADAH; *Montgomery Advertiser,* 13 May, 16 May, 18 May, 25 May, 27 May 1973.

42. Editorial of WSFA-TV Montgomery, 24 July 1973, Admin. Files Gov. G. Wallace, SG22697, ADAH; *Montgomery Advertiser,* 16–17 June, 20 June 1973.

43. *Montgomery Advertiser,* 20 August, 3 November, 5 November 1972; *Birmingham News,* 3 March 1974. Minutes of the State Board of Pensions and Security, 21 September 1972, SG22705; "Proposed Biennial Budget of Department of Pensions and Security," 1 February 1973, SG22706; "Statement of Ruben King before Joint Interim Committee on Finance and Taxation," 19 March 1973, SG22706; memorandum from W. L. Allen to George Wallace, 22 August 1972, SG22709; memorandum from W. L. Allen to George Wallace, 14 November 1972, SG22710; Leroy Brown to John B. Ames, 18 February 1972, SG22718; Mrs. Fred Carter to George Wallace, 27 July 1972, SG22718; the "Citizen" of Cleveland, Alabama, to George Wallace, 27 March 1973, SG22718; memorandum from George Wallace to Leroy Brown, 14 February 1972, SG22718, all in Admin. Files Gov. G. Wallace, ADAH.

44. Rhonda to George Wallace, undated; Mrs. Terak Till to George Wallace, 2 August 1972, all in Admin. Files Gov. G. Wallace, SG22718, ADAH.

45. "Memorandum from Bill Jackson to Administrative Department Heads," 12 January 1973, SG22697; *Montgomery Advertiser,* 5 October 1972, 7 January 1973; memorandum from Bill Jackson to George Wallace, 30 August 1973, SG22696; M. S. Butler to George Wallace, 19 February 1974, SG22714; memorandum from Robert G. Davis to George Wallace, 30 November 1972, SG22696, all correspondence in Admin. Files Gov. G. Wallace, ADAH.

46. *Montgomery Advertiser,* 22 May, 9 August 1973; *Birmingham News,* 19–20 January, 22 January 1974; memorandum from the Board of Corrections to George Wallace, 29 November 1974, Admin. Files Gov. G. Wallace, SG23370, ADAH.

47. "Annual Report of the Work Release Program," October 1 1972 to September 30, 1973; "Annual Report of the Work Release Program," 1 October 1973 to 30 September 1974, all in Admin. Files Gov. G. Wallace, SG23370, ADAH.

48. "Actual Expenditures of Past Biennium and Estimated Expenditures for Biennium 1976–1977 of the Department of Corrections," undated, SG23370; "Budget Forms 1 and 2 of the Department of Corrections," undated, SG23370; Jesse Scarbrough to George Wallace, 3 October 1975, SG23371, all in Admin. Files Gov. G. Wallace, ADAH.

49. *Birmingham News,* 6 January 1974.

50. "Summary of Recommendations of the Citizen's Advisory Board on Commerce and Industrial Development," undated, Admin. Files Gov. G. Wallace, SG22694, ADAH.

51. *Montgomery Advertiser,* 24–25 October, 4 November, 13 December 1973.

52. "Estimate of Requirements for new Buildings and Renovations of Old Buildings at Bryce Hospital," 18 August 1971; "Estimate of Requirements for new Buildings and Renovations of Old Buildings at Searcy Hospital," 18 August 1971; "Estimate of Requirements for new Buildings and Renovations of Old Buildings at Partlow School and Hospital," 18 August 1971; "Report of Inspection of Grounds of Bryce Hospital," 3 August 1971, all in Admin. Files Gov. G. Wallace, SG22697, ADAH.

53. Press release of the Alabama Department of Mental Health, 16 March 1972, SG22698; Stonewall Stickney to Members of the Mental Health Board, 1 November 1971, SG22697; "Petition to the Honorable George C. Wallace, Governor of the State of Alabama, undated, SG22697, all in Admin. Files Gov. G. Wallace, ADAH.

54. *Alabama Mental-Health Retardation Review* 23, no. 6 (April 1972); Contract Change Order, 10 July 1972; Contract Change Order Number 4, 11 October 1972; Bill Jackson to Taylor Hardin, 20 March 1973; McCauley Associates to Saunders Construction. 22 January 1973; Connie Chamberlain to George Wallace; George Wallace to Carol Dunlop, 22 May 1972, all contract information and correspondence in Admin. Files Gov. G. Wallace, SG22698, ADAH.

55. Press release of the Alabama Department of Mental Health, 16 March 1972; Suzy Roberts to George Wallace, 21 February 1974; George Wallace to Stonewall Stickney, 13 April 1972; Stonewall Stickney to George Wallace, 24 July 1972; Ralph Adams to George Wallace, 8 December 1971; James Folsom to George Wallace, 20 December 1971; Claude Kelley to George Wallace, 27 December 1971, all in Admin. Files Gov. G. Wallace, SG22698, ADAH.

56. *Montgomery Advertiser*, 24–25 August, 27 August, 4 November 1972; *Alabama Mental Health-Retardation Review*, 23, no. 4 (1972); press release of Department of Mental Health, March 1972, in Admin. Files Gov. G. Wallace, SG22698, ADAH.

57. *Montgomery Advertiser*, 30 August, 9 September, 14–15 September, 22 September 1972; telegram from "We the employees and patients at Bryce Hospital" to George Wallace, [no day, no month] 1972; Mary McCool to George Wallace, 17 September 1972; Ruth Bolden to George Wallace, 18 September 1972; Staff of Bryce Hospital to James Folsom, 21 August 1972, all correspondence in Admin. Files Gov. G. Wallace, SG22698, ADAH.

58. *Alabama Mental Health-Retardation Review* 23, no. 6 (September 1972): 4.

59. *Montgomery Advertiser*, 17 November, 29–30 November, 19 December 1973, *Birmingham News*, 23 January, 30 January, 20 February 1974, 1 June 2005.

60. Memorandum from John Bookout to George Wallace, 27 November 1972; John Bookout to Lula Mae Whatley, 15 November 1972; John Bookout to Mrs. Mamie Schaeffer, 15 November 1972; John Bookout to Bob Villar, 8 June 1972, all in Admin. Files Gov. G. Wallace, SG22694, ADAH.

61. "The Alabama Health Care Plan"; editorial of WSFA-TV, 1 June 1972; Roy Blackburn to All Local Presidents of the Alabama Association of Life Underwriters, 19 May 1972, all in Admin. Files Gov. G. Wallace, SG22694, ADAH.

62. Mrs. J. C. Butts to George Wallace, 15 January 1972; Mrs. B. F. Simms to George Wallace, 13 January 1972; Carl W. McEwen to George Wallace, undated, all in Admin. Files Gov. G. Wallace, SG22694, ADAH.

63. Memorandum from John Bookout to George Wallace, 21 April 1972; "Summary of Applications to Alabama Health Care Plan," 21 April 1972; editorial of WSFA-TV, 1 June 1972;

memorandum from John Bookout to George Wallace, 27 November 1972; memorandum from Harry Pennington to Billy Joe Camp, 22 August 1974, all in Admin. Files Gov. G. Wallace, SG22697, ADAH.

64. Memorandum from George Wallace to John Harris, 29 November 1971, SG22697; memorandum from George Wallace to Jesse Gann, 11 November 1971, SG22697; memorandum from George Wallace to Jesse Gann, 4 December 1972, SG22697; Gladys Exurm to George Wallace, undated, SG22704; memorandum from George Wallace to Mills Cowling, 23 November 1971, SG22697; Ethel B. Tompkins to George Wallace, 16 July 1972, SG22704; George Wallace to Charles Snider, 2 April 1974, SG22697, all in Admin. Files Gov. G. Wallace, ADAH.

65. Interview, Peggy Wallace Kennedy.

66. Memorandum from Mickey Griffin to Harry Pennington, 4 October 1972, George C. Wallace Campaign Records, LPR 116, box 260, ADAH; *Montgomery Advertiser,* 12 November, 14 November, 10 December 1972; *Birmingham News,* 27 January 1974.

67. *Montgomery Advertiser,* 17 August, 17 November, 19 November 1973.

68. *Birmingham News,* 10 March 1974; R. M. Stienz to George Wallace, 12 April 1973; Wade Harness to George Wallace, 18 April 1973; "E. R." to George Wallace, 29 March 1973; Calvin Pruitt to George Wallace, 5 May 1974, all correspondence in Admin. Files Gov. G. Wallace, SG22699, ADAH.

69. *Boston Globe,* 29 May 1974.

70. Charles Evers to George Wallace, 25 July 1974; draft of George Wallace to Charles Evers, undated; George Wallace to Charles Evers, 31 July 1974; Curtis Redding to John Adam Watkin, 17 May 1974, all in Admin. Files Gov. G. Wallace, SG22693, ADAH.

71. *Birmingham News,* 22 February 1974.

72. Interviews, Albert Brewer; *Birmingham News,* 19 January, 20 February 1974.

73. *Birmingham News,* 5–6 January, 9 February, 25 February 1974.

74. *Charlotte Observer,* 19 August 1974; *Atlanta Constitution,* 19 August 1974; *Birmingham News,* 25–26 February 1974; Numan V. Bartley, *The New South, 1945–1980: The Story of the South's Modernization* (Baton Rouge, LSU Press, 1995), 437–60.

75. *Birmingham News,* 3 March 1974. Memorandum from Robert Davis to executive committee members of the state of Alabama Law Enforcement Planning Agency, 13 March 1973, SG22696; "Revenue Sharing First Quarter Operations, 1973–1974," SG22714; "General Revenue Sharing Allocations and Adjustments, United States Department of Treasury, July 1973," SG22714; "Report by the Congress, Revenue Sharing: Its Use by and Impact on State Governments, United States Department of the Treasury, August 1973," SG22714, all in Admin. Files Gov. G. Wallace, ADAH.

76. "Wallace Campaign Plans for the 1975-76 Period," document of the George C. Wallace campaign, George C. Wallace Campaign Records, LPR 116, box 260; memorandum from Charles Snider to George Wallace, 29 March 1974, Admin. Files Gov. G. Wallace, SG22697, all in ADAH.

77. *Birmingham News,* 29 March, 1–2 April, 7 May, 6 November 1974; 1974 campaign brochure of Governor George Wallace, box 42; Charles Snider to Richard Stone, 11 March 1970, box 114; Charles Snider to Richard Stone, 9 March 1970, box 114, all in George C. Wallace Collection, LPR 124, ADAH.

Chapter 10

1. *Birmingham News,* 28 September 1974; *Washington Post,* 11 September 1974.

2. *Montgomery Advertiser,* 20–21 January 1975.

3. *Birmingham News,* 9 September, 12 September, 26 December 1974; "Wallace Campaign Plans for 1975–76 Period," undated, George C. Wallace Campaign Records, LPR 116, box 260; Wallace campaign donation form, undated, Admin. Files Gov. G. Wallace, SG22719; Paul Weyrich to Charles Snider, 14 November 1975, George C. Wallace Campaign Records, LPR 116, box 259, all in ADAH.

4. *Birmingham News,* 3 May, 16 October, 25 December 1974; *Montgomery Advertiser,* 29 June 1975; Cornelia Wallace to Hugh Adams and Bruce Wyatt, 19 May 1975, and memorandum from James Solomon to Alabama State Building Commission, 18 October 1974, in Admin. Files Gov. G. Wallace, SG23367, ADAH.

5. *Montgomery Advertiser,* 22 March 1975; *Los Angeles Times,* 20 August 1975; *Nation* (13 September 1975): 201–4. Eli Howell to Charles Snider, 11 April 1975, George C. Wallace Campaign Records, LPR 116, box 282; various documents, Cornelia Ellis Snively Papers, LPR 137, box 5, all in ADAH; *Nation* (13 September 1975): 201.

6. *Birmingham News,* 27 May 1974.

7. George Wallace to Gaines B. Hall, 16 November 1971, SG22711; George Wallace to Philip Spann, 16 November 1971, SG22711; telegram from B. A. McConnell to Jere Beasley, 9 June 1972, SG22711, all in Admin. Files Gov. G. Wallace, ADAH.

8. Mr. and Mrs. V. A. Short to the Alabama Public Service Commission, copy to George Wallace, 7 November 1972, SG22711; Mr. and Mrs. W. K. Ustick to George Wallace, 12 January 1976, SG23392, all in Admin. Files Gov. G. Wallace, ADAH.

9. William Warren Rogers, Robert David Ward, Leah Rawls Atkins, and Wayne Flynt, *Alabama: The History of a Deep South State* (Tuscaloosa: University of Alabama Press, 1994), 447, 471; Joseph Levin to Joseph Farley, 23 August 1972, SG22711; Opinion and Order of the Alabama PSC, docket no. 16571, 13 December 1972, SG22711, all in Admin. Files Gov. G. Wallace, ADAH.

10. William Spencer to George Wallace, 9 October 1973, SG22711; John Sullivan to South Central Bell Telephone, 15 December 1975, SG23392; Annie Laurie Gunter to Harrell Johnson, 11 September 1974, SG22718, all in Admin. Files Gov. G. Wallace, ADAH; *Montgomery Advertiser,* 2 January 1975.

11. Alabama Power bill, name redacted, December 1976; *Montgomery Advertiser,* 7 March, 15 March 1975; James Williams to Alice Branton, 28 January 1976, bill and correspondence in Admin. Files Gov. G. Wallace, SG23392, ADAH.

12. J. R. Ivey to Kenneth Hammond, 18 February 1975, SG23392; PSC docket no. 16851 regarding Alabama Power, 28 January 1975, SG23392, all in Admin. Files Gov. G. Wallace, ADAH.

13. James Phipps to George Wallace, 1 June 1974, SG22719; telegram from Hobert Williams to George Wallace, 21 January 1977, SG23392; telegram from Bill Thrash to George Wallace, 24 January 1977, SG23392, all in Admin. Files Gov. G. Wallace, ADAH.

14. *Montgomery Advertiser,* 6 March, 29 June 1975; T. Jeff Davis to Anthony DeGiorgio, 24 February 1976, Admin. Files Gov. G. Wallace, SG23392, ADAH.

15. Elmer Bennett to George Wallace, 6 October 1971, SG22711; George Wallace to

Albert Dyess, 18 October 1976, SG23392; Maurice Bishop to George Wallace, 14 October 1976, SG23392, all in Admin. Files Gov. G. Wallace, ADAH.

16. Dotson Nelson Jr. to George Wallace, 19 July 1976; Gene Bromberg to George Wallace, 19 July 1976, all in Admin. Files Gov. G. Wallace, SG23392, ADAH.

17. Frank Spain to George Wallace, 15 July 1976; H. B. Yielding to George Wallace, 2 July 1976; Maurice Bishop to George Wallace, 15 July 1976, all in Admin. Files Gov. G. Wallace, SG23392, ADAH.

18. Memorandum from George Wallace to PSC, [date unclear] February 1971, SG22711; Bull Connor, Jack Owen, and Juanita McDaniel to George Wallace, 12 October 1971, SG22711; George Wallace to Connor, Owens, and McDaniel, 29 October 1971, SG22711; statement of C. C. Whatley to the Alabama PSC, 10 March 1976, SG23392, all in Admin. Files Gov. G. Wallace, ADAH; *Montgomery Advertiser,* 25 January 1975.

19. *Montgomery Advertiser,* 6 March, 11 March, 15 March, 18–19 March, 21 March, 26 March, 6 April 1975.

20. *Montgomery Advertiser,* 9 March, 23 March, 25 March 1975.

21. George Wallace to Albert Dyess, 18 October 1976; George Wallace to Douglas Weems, 26 January 1976, all in Admin. Files Gov. G. Wallace, SG23392, ADAH.

22. "Executive Summary of Alumax Study of Alabama Power Company's Capacity for the years 1979–1985," undated, but completed in 1976; Herbert Clough to George Wallace, 2 November 1976, all in Admin. Files Gov. G. Wallace, SG23392, ADAH.

23. George Wallace to Conrad Bostock, 11 January 1977, SG23392; Opinion and Order of the Alabama PSC, docket no. 16571, 13 December 1972, SG22711, all in Admin. Files Gov. G. Wallace, ADAH; personal communication, Leah Rawls Atkins.

24. Transcript of radio commentary of WDNG, 1 December 1976, Admin. Files Gov. G. Wallace, SG23392, ADAH.

25. *Montgomery Advertiser,* 2 January, 10 January, 5 February 1975; "Wallace Campaign Plan for the 1975–76 Period," George C. Wallace Campaign Records, LPR 116, box 260, ADAH.

26. Dan T. Carter, *The Politics of Rage: George Wallace, the Origins of the New Conservatism, and the Transformation of American Politics* (New York: Simon and Schuster, 1995), 13–15, 459–68; interview, George Wallace Jr; interview, Elvin Stanton.

27. Stephan Lesher, *George Wallace: American Populist* (New York: Addison-Wesley, 1994), 501.

28. Carter, *Politics of Rage,* 15; Randy Sanders, "The Sad Duty of Politics," *Georgia Historical Quarterly* 76, no. 3 (1992): 612–638; Jeff Frederick, "The Gubernatorial Campaigns of Jimmy Carter" (master's thesis, University of Central Florida, 1998), 104–9.

29. *Montgomery Advertiser,* 14 February 1975. Ray Bass to Alabama Legislators, 9 December 1974, SG23378; Ray Bass to Ella Parton, 19 September 1975, SG23379; memorandum from Ray Bass to George Wallace, 3 October 1974, SG23377; "Progress Report of Interstate System," 1 October 1974, SG23377; "Report of Ray Bass to Alabama Legislators," 2 May 1975, SG23378; *Larry Joe Cornelius et al. v. George C. Wallace,* U.S. District Court of Alabama, Northern Division, Civil Action no. 75-339-N, 25 September 1975, SG23379; "Bonded Indebtedness of the State of Alabama," 30 September 1973, SG23373, all in Admin. Files Gov. G. Wallace, ADAH.

30. J. Hilton Watson to George Wallace, 28 February 1977; Wildfire Situation Report,

18 February and 20 February 1977; C. W. Moody to George Wallace, 31 March 1978, all in Admin. Files Gov. G. Wallace, SG23409, ADAH.

31. G. A. Gibbs to George Wallace, 22 November 1977; memorandum from G. A. Gibbs to Employees of the Alabama Forestry Commission, 21 September 1977; "Motion passed by the Alabama Forestry Commission," 21 September 1977, all in Admin. Files Gov. G. Wallace, SG23409, ADAH.

32. *Montgomery Advertiser,* 8 April 1978. Eugene Keller to George Wallace, 11 November 1977; "Southeastern States Forest Fire Compact Commission Report," 29 June 1977; memorandum from George Wallace to Henry Steagall, 4 April 1978; George Wallace to Colonel E. C. Dothard, 4 April 1978, all in Admin. Files Gov. G. Wallace, SG23409, ADAH. The quote in text is from the Wallace to Steagall memo.

33. J. Hilton Watson to George Wallace, 28 October 1977; "Summary of Fire Control and Forestry Expenditure Comparisons of Surrounding States," [undated] 1977; Eugene Keller to George Wallace, 11 November 1977; Charles D. Kelley to Leila Dunn, 4 November 1977, all in Admin. Files Gov. G. Wallace, SG23401, ADAH.

34. *Montgomery Advertiser,* 13–14 February, 20 February 1975; "Alabama Department of mental Health Five Year Strategic Plan," 1976, Admin. Files Gov. G. Wallace, SG23383, ADAH.

35. *Montgomery Advertiser,* 13–16 February, 18 February, 20–21 February 1975. L. B. Sullivan to James Jordan, 29 November 1974; "State of Alabama Projected Expenditures for Correctional Facility Construction," Fiscal Years 1975 and 1976, all in Admin. Files Gov. G. Wallace, SG23370, ADAH.

36. *Wall Street Journal,* 28 August 1975; *Newsweek,* 26 January 1976; *Montgomery Advertiser,* 22 February 1975; *Birmingham News,* 2 November 1976.

37. *Birmingham News,* 13–15 January 1975; *St Louis Post-Dispatch,* 27 January 1976; Frances Kent to Frank Johnson, 25 March 1976, Admin. Files Gov. G. Wallace, SG23370, ADAH.

38. *Birmingham News,* 15 January, 25 January 1976; Thomas Staton to Harry Pennington, 9 January 1975, Admin. Files Gov. G. Wallace, SG23370, ADAH.

39. *Birmingham News,* 15 January, 25 January 1976. John Prewitt Jr. to George Wallace, 31 January 1976; George Wallace to L. J. Racey, 4 March 1976, all in Admin. Files Gov. G. Wallace, SG23370, ADAH.

40. George Wallace to Julie Holliday, 25 June 1976; George Wallace to Jane Blanc, 27 May 1976; George Wallace to Bonnie Wade, 9 April 1976; George Wallace to Trudon Price, 7 October 1974; George Wallace to Jack Sigleton, 30 March 1977; telegram from James K. Matthews, 30 November 1976, all in Admin. Files Gov. G. Wallace, SG23400, ADAH.

41. Charles Owens to George Wallace, 11 February 1977; George Wallace to Pat Fisher, 5 February 1976; George Wallace to Adrian Crane, 28 January 1977, all in Admin. Files Gov. G. Wallace, SG23400, ADAH; Carter, *Politics of Rage,* 419–37.

42. *Birmingham News,* 6 February 1977; "Madison County Grand Jury Report," August 1974, Admin. Files Gov. G. Wallace, SG23365, ADAH; *Screw Magazine,* 16 February 1976; Michael Arthur Rorer to George Wallace, 29 February 1976; Curtis Redding to Michael Arthur Rorer, 9 March 1976, all in Admin. Files Gov. G. Wallace, SG23413, ADAH.

43. *New York Times,* 1 February 1976; Carter, *From George Wallace to Newt Gingrich: Race in the Conservative Counterrevolution, 1963–1994* (Baton Rouge: LSU Press), xii–xv, 18–23; Carter, *Politics of Rage,* 468; *Arizona Republic,* 8 May 1976.

44. *Birmingham News,* 10–11 January 1975; Carter, *From George Wallace to Newt Gingrich,* 21; marginalia of Cornelia Wallace, undated, Cornelia Ellis Snively Papers, LPR 137, box 19, ADAH.

45. "Wallace Campaign Plan for the 1975–76 Period," George C. Wallace Campaign Records, LPR 116, box 260, ADAH; *Birmingham News,* 27 January 1976.

46. *Birmingham News,* 27 January, 4 March 1976; *New York Times,* 4–5 February, 8–9 February, 16 February, 25 February 1976.

47. *New York Times,* 1–3 March 1976; *Birmingham News,* 3 March 1976.

48. *New York Times,* 3 March 1976.

49. *National Review,* 9 May 1975.

50. Bert Haltom to Charles Snider, 4 June 1976, George C. Wallace Campaign Records, LPR 116, box 259, ADAH.

51. *Washington Post,* 4 June 1978; interview Elvin Stanton; interview George Wallace Jr.; *Parade Magazine,* 13 June 1976.

52. *New York Times,* 3 March 1976.

53. Ibid. J. B. McDonough Jr. to George Wallace, 1 July 1977; "Statement of Governor George C. Wallace on Abortion," 16 January 1976; Dianne Green to George Wallace, 5 July 1977; Melba Hentges to George Wallace, 27 July 1977; Penny Probst to George Wallace, 12 July 1977; Mary Ellen Gerstacker to George Wallace, 30 June 1977; Bill Black to George Wallace, 26 June 1977, all in Admin. Files Gov. G. Wallace, SG23415, ADAH.

54. *Birmingham News,* 5–6 March, 10 March 1976.

55. Ibid., 17 March, 19 March, 23–24 March, 31 March, 4 April, 7 April, 22 April, 27 April, 30 April, 1 May, 3 May, 5 May, 7 May 1976; "Speech of George Wallace before May 4, 1976 Primary," George C. Wallace Campaign Records, LPR 116, box 259, ADAH.

56. *Birmingham News,* 13 May, 18 May, 9 June, 13 June 1976; UPI Bulletin 052, 9 June 1976.

57. Judy Miller to George Wallace, undated, received 12 June 1976; O. M. Herring to George Wallace, 10 June 1976; Wayne Smith to George Wallace, 9 June 1976; Thomas Nolder to George Wallace, 21 June 1976, George C. all in Wallace Campaign Records, LPR 116, box 3, ADAH; *Parade Magazine,* 13 June 1976.

58. *Birmingham News,* 14 September, 17 September, 23 October 1976.

59. Ibid., 30 May 1976; "Preferences of Voters in the Race for U. S. Senator from Alabama, Confidential Report of a Public Opinion Survey conducted for George Wallace," George C. Wallace Campaign Records, LPR 116, box 259, ADAH; *Parade Magazine,* 13 June 1976; comments of Cornelia Wallace, undated, Cornelia Ellis Snively Wallace Papers, LPR 137, box 5, ADAH.

60. *Birmingham News,* 20 June 1976.

61. "Requests, Book Interviews, and Autograph Parties" undated; "Advertisement Copy of *C'nelia*"; "Subsidiary Rights Agreement no. SR 768H, "Cornelia Wallace and *Good Housekeeping,*" 6 November 1975, all in Cornelia Ellis Snively Wallace Papers, LPR 137, box 5 ADAH.

62. Robert D. McIntyre to Cornelia Wallace, 17 February 1976; Cornelia Wallace to Joe Booth, 1 December 1975; notes of phone conversation with Russell T. Hitt, undated; Murray Fisher to Cornelia Wallace, 7 August 1975; "Note to Mary's House of Music," undated; Dr. Kenneth Cooper to Cornelia Wallace, 20 August 1973, all in Cornelia Ellis Snively Wallace Papers, LPR 137, box 5 ADAH.

63. *Parade Magazine,* 13 June 1976.

64. "Patient Medical History of Mrs. Cornelia E. Snively," 1 July 1970, box 16; typed notes of Dr. George S. Peters, M.D., undated, box 16; various notes and memorandums concerning medical appointments, Summer 1977, box 17; Mrs. Wallace to Mrs. Fillingim, 14 May 1976, box 17; Dr. Kenneth Cooper to Cornelia Wallace, 20 August 1973, box 16; "Review of Notes by Dr. William Ferrante, 7 October 1968, box 16; memorandum from Mrs. Wallace, 6 May 1977, box 17; memorandum from Mrs. Wallace to Carl or Eddie, 14 December 1976, box 18, all in Cornelia Ellis Snively Papers, LPR 137, ADAH.

65. Memorandum from Mrs. Wallace to Kitchen, 30 May 1977; memorandum from Mrs. Wallace to Strawberry and Shirley, 1 June 1977; memorandum from Cornelia Wallace to Eddie Holcy, 27 June 1977; memorandum from Cornelia Wallace to Strawberry, 28 June 1977; memorandum from Mrs. George C. Wallace to kitchen, 30 June 1977; memorandum from Cornelia Wallace to Carl, 23 May 1977; memorandum from Mrs. Wallace to entire staff, 2 March 1976, all in Cornelia Ellis Snively Papers, LPR 137, box 17, ADAH.

66. Interview, George Wallace Jr.; memorandum from Mrs. Wallace to Troopers, 10 November 1976, Cornelia Ellis Snively Wallace Papers, LPR 137, box 17, ADAH.

67. Memorandum from Mrs. Wallace to Mrs. Fillingim, 3 May 1976; memorandum from Mrs. Wallace to Marilyn, undated, all in Cornelia Ellis Snively Wallace Papers, LPR 137, box 17; various statements of George and Cornelia Wallace, 1974 and 1975, George C. Wallace Collection, LPR 124, box 114, ADAH.

68. *Montgomery Advertiser,* 2 January, 4 January 1978.

69. *Birmingham News,* 6 September, 10 September 1976; Carter, *Politics of Rage,* 458.

70. *Montgomery Advertiser,* 5–6 January 1978.

71. Ibid., 11 February, 14 February, 18 May 1978.

72. Ibid., 13 July, 16 July 1978; "1978 Notebook of Cornelia Wallace," Cornelia Ellis Snively Wallace Papers, LPR 137, box 29, ADAH.

73. *Montgomery Advertiser,* 16 July, 9 August, 12 August 1978.

74. *Birmingham News,* 3 November 1976.

75. *Montgomery Advertiser,* 5 January 1976; Louis, Bowles, and Grove Incorporated, "Preferences of Voters in the Race for U.S. Senator from Alabama," George C. Wallace Campaign Records, LPR 116, box 259, ADAH.

76. Louis, Bowles, and Grove Incorporated, "Preferences of Voters in the Race for U.S. Senator from Alabama," George C. Wallace Campaign Records, LPR 116, box 259; Summary of Survey Results of State Democratic Party of Alabama, completed 18 February 1977, Admin. Files Gov. G. Wallace, SG23404, ADAH.

77. Frederick, "Stand by Your Man: Race, Alabama Women, and George Wallace in 1963," *Gulf South Historical Review* 18 (Fall 2002): 47–75; summary of survey results of State Democratic Party of Alabama, completed 18 February 1977, Admin. Files Gov. G. Wallace, SG23404, ADAH; Louis, Bowles, and Grove Incorporated, "Preferences of Voters in the Race for U.S. Senator from Alabama," George C. Wallace Campaign Records, LPR 116, box 259, ADAH; *Montgomery Advertiser,* 8 February 1978.

78. Interview, Hugh Maddox; John Hayman with Clara Ruth Hayman, *A Judge in the Senate: Howell Heflin's Career of Politics and Principle* (Montgomery: New South Books, 2001), 155–71.

79. Hayman and Hayman, *A Judge in the Senate,* 203–9; Louis, Bowles, and Grove Incorporated, "Preferences of Voters in the Race for U.S. Senator from Alabama," George C. Wallace Campaign Records, LPR 116, box 259; *Montgomery Advertiser,* 18 April 1978.

80. *Montgomery Advertiser,* 1 March 1978.

81. Ibid., 20 April, 19 July 1978; Louis, Bowles, and Grove Incorporated, "Preferences of Voters in the Race for U.S. Senator from Alabama," George C. Wallace Campaign Records, LPR 116, box 259.

82. Interview, Elvin Stanton.

83. *Montgomery Advertiser,* 20 April, 14 May, 18 May 1978.

84. Interview, Elvin Stanton; *Montgomery Advertiser,* 17–18 May, 21 May 1978; Hayman and Hayman, *A Judge in the Senate,* 209.

85. *Montgomery Advertiser,* 2 June, 4 June, 8 June, 25 June 1978.

86. Ibid., 9 June, 11 June, 22 June, 25 June, 28 September 1978.

87. Ibid., 6–7 September, 21–22 September, 27 September, 4 October; interview, Elvin Stanton; Jere Beasley to George Wallace, 12 October 1978, George C. Wallace Collection, LPR 124, box 40, ADAH.

88. *Montgomery Advertiser,* 8 October 1978; George Wallace to Fob James, undated; Fob James to George Wallace, 17 January 1979, all in George C. Wallace Collection, LPR 124, box 40, ADAH.

89. *Montgomery Advertiser,* 1 August, 3 August, 5 August 1978.

90. Wayne Teague to Barbara D. Bohn, 30 June 1977, SG23438; George Hudson to Mary Lou Taylor, 25 January 1977, SG23371; George Wallace to Mary Lou Taylor, 24 January 1977, SG23371; Mary Lou Taylor to George Wallace, 10 January 1977, SG23371; Governor George Wallace to Governor Dolph Briscoe, 19 March 1975, SG23438; "Proposal to Supply Specific Support for Alabama Rehabilitation Program for the Homebound," 20 January 1978, SG23438, all in Admin. Files Gov. G. Wallace, ADAH.

91. "Statement of Governor George C. Wallace on Need for an Additional $6 Million for Basic Research on Regeneration and Neuro Prosthesis of the Central Nervous System," 30 April 1977, Admin. Files Gov. G. Wallace, SG23438, ADAH.

92. George Wallace to Reba Thompson, 5 December 1975; George Wallace to Mrs. Dale Winemiller, 19 May 1975, all in Admin. Files Gov. G. Wallace, SG23392, ADAH.

93. Alvin McConnell to George Wallace, 9 March 1977, Admin. Files Gov. G. Wallace, SG23438, ADAH.

94. *Montgomery Advertiser,* 10 October 1978; Bettye Fink to Derryl Gordon, 9 November 1977, SG23413, and George Wallace to Derryl Gordon, 22 August 1978, in SG23408, Admin. Files Gov. G. Wallace, ADAH; Hamilton Jordan to George Wallace, undated, and David Soul to George Wallace, 1 February 1979, in George C. Wallace Collection, LPR 124, box 40, ADAH.

95. *Montgomery Advertiser,* 8 December 1978; *Birmingham News,* 1 January 1979.

Chapter 11

1. *Montgomery Advertiser,* 8 January, 25 February 1982; interview, Elvin Stanton; Stephan Lesher, *George Wallace: American Populist* (New York: Addison-Wesley, 1994), 496–97; cigar

receipts of George Wallace from Eli Witt Company and HavaTampa Wholesale Center, various dates in 1979, George C. Wallace Collection, LPR 124, box 50, ADAH. Records indicate Wallace spent as much as $1,000 on cigars in 1979.

2. Interview, Elvin Stanton.

3. *Montgomery Advertiser*, 21 September, 4 October, 8 November 1978; William H. Stewart, "Forrest 'Fob' James Jr., 1979–1983, 1995–1999" in *Alabama Governors: A Political History of the State*, ed. Samuel L. Webb and Margaret E. Armbrester (Tuscaloosa: University of Alabama Press, 2001), 243–44; Sandra Baxley Taylor, *Governor Fob James: His 1994 Victory, His Incredible Story* (Mobile: Greenberry, 1995), 53–74.

4. Lesher, *George Wallace,* 497; Stewart, "Forrest 'Fob' James Jr." 245, *Birmingham News,* 31 December 1982; WSFA-TV editorial of Bob Ingram, 8 July 1982, Administrative Papers of Governor Fob James, SG22496, ADAH; Taylor, *Governor Fob James,* 417. For more on the history of interest groups in Alabama see Jeff Frederick, "Divide and Conquer: Interest Groups and Political Culture in Alabama, 1929–1971," in *History and Hope in the Heart of Dixie: Essays in Honor of Wayne Flynt* (Tuscaloosa: University of Alabama Press, 2006).

5. *Birmingham News,* 2 November 1982; interview, Elvin Stanton.

6. For another interpretation of Wallace's greatest impact on American politics see Dan T. Carter, *Politics of Rage: George Wallace, the Origins of the New Conservatism, and the Transformation of American Politics* (New York: Simon and Schuster, 1995).

7. Inaugural book of Governor George C. Wallace, January 1983, Administrative Files of Governor Fob James, SG22496, ADAH; *Birmingham News,* 1 November 1982.

8. *Birmingham News,* 1 November 1982; "Chart 3: State General Fund Budget Requests Compared to Estimated Available Funds FY 1984–85," presentation of Henry B. Steagall to Joint Legislative Budget Hearings, 10 January 1984, SG5022, and George Wallace to Gary Aldridge, 22 July 1983, SG4767 in Admin. Files Gov. G. Wallace, ADAH; *Montgomery Advertiser,* 26 February 1982.

9. John Shelton Reed, *My Tears Spoiled My Aim and Other Reflections on Southern Culture* (Orlando: Harcourt Brace, 1994), 85.

10. *Montgomery Advertiser,* 13 January, 24 January, 2 February 1982; interview, Elvin Stanton; Taylor, *Governor Fob James,* 239–94.

11. *Montgomery Advertiser,* 2 February 1982; interview, George Wallace Jr.; interview, Elvin Stanton; campaign fund-raising from George Wallace to "friend," [undated] 1982, and memorandum from Jim Parsons to George Wallace, 6 May 1982, in Administrative Files of Governor Fob James, SG22496, ADAH.

12. Andrew Doyle, "An Atheist in Alabama Is Someone Who Doesn't Believe in Bear Bryant: A Symbol for an Embattled South," in *The Sporting World of the Modern South,* ed. Patrick Miller, 247–67 (Urbana: University of Illinois Press, 2002); *Birmingham News,* 31 December 1982.

13. Interview, George Wallace Jr.; interview, Bill Jones; Doyle, "An Atheist in Alabama," 254–60; www.espn.go.com/classic/biography/s/Bryant_Bear.html.

14. Lesher, *George Wallace,* 496–97.

15. Inaugural Book of Governor George C. Wallace, January 1983, Administrative Files of Governor Fob James, SG22496, ADAH; Undated *Birmingham News* clipping, Admin.

Files Gov. G. Wallace, SG4757, ADAH; Carter, *Politics of Rage,* 462–63; *Cullman Times,* 19 May 1983; *Birmingham News,* 21 May 1983.

16. Lesher, *George Wallace,* 497; Carter, *Politics of Rage,* 463; interview George Wallace Jr.; interview Peggy Wallace Kennedy and Mark Kennedy; www.ccofal.org/alabama/june25.phtml.

17. Interview, George Wallace Jr.

18. Fantus Company, "State of Alabama: Comparative Business Climate Analysis," 29 June 1984, Admin. Files Gov. G. Wallace, SG4757, ADAH.

19. George Wallace to Charles Reed, 15 June 1983, Admin. Files Gov. G. Wallace, SG4726, ADAH; *Montgomery Advertiser,* 26 February, 31 December 1982; George Wallace col. no. 205, week of December 21, 1986, Admin. Files Gov. G. Wallace, SG4208, ADAH. National unemployment rate per www.infoplease.com/ipa/A0104719.html. Bureau of Labor unemployment statistics per www.bls.gov/web/lauhsthl.htm.

20. *Birmingham News,* 1–3 November, 31 December 1982.

21. Lesher, *George Wallace,* 497.

22. "1982 Democratic Primary Results," www.sos.state.al.us/downloads/dl3.cfm?trgturl= election/general/eagovernor1946-2002.xls&trgtfile=eagovernor1946-2002.xls.

23. Interview, Elvin Stanton; "1982 Democratic Run-Off Results," www.sos. state.al.us/downloads/dl3.cfm?trgturl=election/general/eagovernor1946-2002.xls&trgtfile= eagovernor1946-2002.xls; *Birmingham News,* 31 December 1982; *Montgomery Advertiser,* 16 January 1983.

24. "1982 Democratic Primary Results," "1982 Democratic Run-Off Results," "1982 General Election Results," www.sos.state.al.us/downloads/dl3.cfm?trgturl=election/general/ eagovernor1946-2002.xls&trgtfile=eagovernor1946-2002.xls; interview, Paul Hubbert; interviews, Bill Jones; *Montgomery Advertiser,* 16 January 1983.

25. *Birmingham News,* 2–4 November 1982; *Montgomery Advertiser,* 27 February 1983.

26. *Birmingham News,* 3–4 November 1982; Carter, *Politics of Rage,* 465–68; George Wallace to Stephen Brewer, 30 July 1984; Edna Alexander to George Wallace, 16 May 1984; George Wallace to Edna Alexander, 30 July 1984, all correspondence in Admin. Files Gov. G. Wallace, SG4743, ADAH.

27. *Birmingham News,* 4 November, 8 November 1982; *Montgomery Advertiser,* 1 January, 16–17 January 1983.

28. *Montgomery Advertiser,* 18 January 1983; "1983 Inaugural Address of Governor George C. Wallace," Author's Collection of the Speeches of George and Lurleen Wallace.

29. "1983 Inaugural Address of Governor George C. Wallace," in author's possession.

30. "1983 Inaugural Address of Governor George C. Wallace," in author's possession.

31. *Birmingham Post-Herald,* 16 April 2005.

32. Minutes of the Board of Trustees Meeting of Auburn Polytechnic Institute, March 1, 1937, RG AU521; Biographic Sketch of Posey Oliver Davis, undated, Records of the Alabama Cooperative Extension Service, RG71, box 7; Governor Frank Dixon to P. O. Davis, October 6, 1942; Records of the Alabama Cooperative Extension Service, RG 71, box 82; "Suggested Press Release of Governor Frank Dixon," undated, Records of the Alabama Cooperative Extension Service, RG 71, box 82, all in Auburn University Archives and Special

Collections, Auburn, Ala.; Cox, "Luther N. Duncan, the Extension Service, and the Farm Bureau, 1921–1932," 184–97.

33. Frederick, "Divide and Conquer"; Clive S. Thomas, "Change Transition, and Growth in Southern Interest Group Politics," in *Interest Group Politics in the Southern States,* ed. Ronald J. Hrebenar and Clive S. Thomas, 342–43 (Tuscaloosa: University of Alabama Press, 1992); David Martin, "Alabama: Personalities and Factionalism," in *Interest Group Politics in the Southern States,* 252–54; interview, Jere Beasley; "Political Contributions Made to Candidates in 1982 Elections," 1 June 1983, and contributions to campaign of George Wallace, undated, in Admin. Files Gov. G. Wallace, SG5022, ADAH.

34. *Montgomery Advertiser,* 1 February, 6 February, 9–10 February, 16 February 1983; "Wallace Administration Appointments from 1-8-83 through 9-30-85," Admin. Files Gov. G. Wallace, SG5025, ADAH; *New York Times,* 12 February 1984.

35. *Montgomery Advertiser,* 21–22 February, 27 February, 11 March, 13 March, 19 March 1983.

36. Ibid., 17 March, 19–21 March, 23 March, 2 April 1983.

37. Press release of the Office of the Governor, 31 October 1985, Admin. Files Gov. G. Wallace, SG2967, ADAH; *Birmingham News,* 31 December 1984, 31 December 1985; *Montgomery Advertiser,* 22 February, 29 May 1983; *Birmingham Post Herald,* 5 November 1986; *Florence Times and Tri-Cities Daily,* 13 July 1986.

38. Robert Ingram, "The Issue of Wallace's Health," WSFA-TV editorial, 17 July 1985, SG4757, Admin. Files Gov. G. Wallace, ADAH; *Florence Times and Tri-Cities Daily,* 8 May 1983; *Birmingham News,* 8 May 1983.

39. Robert Ingram, "The Issue of Wallace's Health," WSFA-TV editorial, 17 July 1985, SG4757, Admin. Files Gov. G. Wallace, ADAH; interview, Bob Ingram; *Montgomery Advertiser,* 23 February, 26 February 1983.

40. *Montgomery Advertiser,* 13 May 1983.

41. Ibid., 2 February, 6 February, 23 February, 26 February, 2 April, 13 May 1983; *Alabama Journal,* 5 June 1983; *Birmingham News,* 17 May 1983; personal communication, Wayne Flynt.

42. *Montgomery Advertiser,* 4–5 June 1983; *Columbus Enquirer,* 9 June 1983; George Wallace to Kathy Moon Kreps, 29 December 1986, SG8401, and Wallace administration Internal Appointment Statistics, 8 January 1983 through 30 September 1985, SG5025, in Admin. Files Gov. G. Wallace, ADAH.

43. Press release of the Office of the Governor, undated, SG5023; Wallace col. no. 131, 21 July 1985, SG4757; Thomas Bartlett to George Wallace, 6 September 1985, SG4756; press release of the Office of the Governor, 23 September 1985, SG2967; "The State of Alabama Supercomputer Project, Huntsville Position," undated, SG4758, all in Admin. Files Gov. G. Wallace, ADAH; *Huntsville Times,* 10 July 1985.

44. Proclamation of the Governor of Alabama, 23 January 1985, SG5023; Wallace col. no. 92, 21 October 1984, SG4757; Wallace col. no. 109, 17 February 1985, SG4757; Message of Governor George Wallace to the Special Session of the Legislature, 23 January 1985, SG5024, all in Admin. Files Gov. G. Wallace, ADAH.

45. Bill Baxley to George Wallace, 18 January 1985, SG5023; "List of Press Conferences of

Lieutenant Governor Baxley for Oil and Gas Fund Constitutional Amendment," undated, SG4758, all in Admin. Files Gov. G. Wallace, ADAH.

46. Robert Ingram, "The Excellent Wallace Appointments," WSFA-TV 12 editorial, 11 February 1985, Admin. Files Gov. G. Wallace, SG4757, ADAH.

47. Wallace col. no. 109, 17 February 1985, Admin. Files Gov. G. Wallace, SG4757, ADAH.

48. "Department of Corrections Annual Report," 30 September 1982; "Department of Corrections Annual Report for 1985," all in Admin. Files Gov. G. Wallace, SG4719, ADAH; *Montgomery Advertiser,* 23 April, 25 April 1983.

49. "Message from the Governor to the Alabama Senate," undated, SG5024; Wallace Henley to George Wallace, 26 March 1984, SG5022; Wallace col. no. 115, 31 March 1985, SG4757; memorandum from Rex Thomas to Elvin Stanton, 24 October 1986, SG4708; Wallace col. no. 116, 7 April 1985, SG4757, all in Admin. Files Gov. G. Wallace, ADAH.

50. *Alabama Education* 1, no. 2 (October 1977); *Alabama Education* 1, no. 4 (December 1977).

51. "Superintendent's Report on Education in Alabama," May 1976, Alabama Department of Education Files, SG13269, ADAH.

52. "The Status of Reading Instruction in Alabama Schools in 1977"; "1973 Report of State Department of Education to Alabama Legislature"; State Department of Education and Alabama Education Study Commission, "The Status of Reading Instruction in Alabama Schools, 1976: A Report to the Legislature," all in Alabama Department of Education Files, SG013238; Wallace col. no. 117, 14 April 1985; Fantus Company, "State of Alabama Comparative Business Climate Analysis," 29 June 1984, all in Admin. Files Gov. G. Wallace, SG4757, ADAH.

53. Wayne Teague, "A Plan for Excellence, Alabama's Public Schools: A Report to the Alabama State Board of Education, Governor George C. Wallace, to the Legislature and the People of Alabama," 12 January 1984, SG4741; G. William Croker to Billy Joe Camp, 1 March 1984, SG5022; "State Support for Education: A Summary of Recent Actions and Proposals," unpublished document, SG5022; Fantus Company, Exhibits 43, 47, Summary of Census Department Records, SG4757; Fantus Company, exhibits 44–46, Summary of U.S. Department of Education Records, SG4757, all in Admin. Files Gov. G. Wallace, ADAH.

54. Press release of the governor's remarks, 26 March 1984, SG5025; "Summarization of Education Reform Bill of 1984," SG5025; memorandum from Rex Cheatam to George Wallace, 30 October 1985, SG4732; minutes of the Governor's Education Reform Commission, 10 August 1984, SG4732; Governor's Education Reform Commission, "Education Reform in Alabama: The Road to Excellence," SG4732, all in Admin. Files Gov. G. Wallace, ADAH.

55. Wayne Teague, "A Plan for Excellence, Alabama's Public Schools: A Report to the Alabama State Board of Education, Governor George C. Wallace, to the Legislature and the People of Alabama," 12 January 1984, SG4741; "Summarization of Education Reform Bill of 1984," Admin. Files Gov. G. Wallace, SG5025; Wayne Teague to George Wallace, 12 April 1984, SG4741, all in Admin. Files Gov. G. Wallace, ADAH.

56. Governor's Task Force on Economic Recovery, "The Effect of Alabama's Tax System on Economic Development: Analysis and Policy Options," SG5022; Governor's Remarks for

the Special Session of the Legislature, 8 September 1986, SG13103, all in Admin. Files Gov. G. Wallace, ADAH.

57. "State and Local Beer Taxes Nationwide," typescript of Governor's Task Force on Economic Recovery, 1 December 1983, Admin. Files Gov. G. Wallace, SG5022, ADAH; *Montgomery Advertiser,* 7 March, 9 September 1986.

58. *Montgomery Advertiser,* 22 September, 25 September, 26 December 1986; *Gadsden Times,* 28 September 1986; *Birmingham Post-Herald,* 10 September 1986; *Anniston Star,* 19 September 1986; *Florence Times Tri-Cities Daily,* 2 July 1986.

59. John Glenn to George Wallace, 26 May 1983; Alan Cranston to George Wallace, 24 January 1983; Jimmy Carter to George Wallace, 31 January 1984, all in Admin. Files Gov. G. Wallace, SG4743, ADAH.

60. Robert Ingram, "Acting Like a Candidate," WSFA-TV editorial, 17 May 1985, Admin. Files Gov. G. Wallace, SG4757, ADAH.

61. Robert Ingram, "The Wallace Polls," WSFA-TV editorial, 12 June 1985, Admin. Files Gov. G. Wallace, SG4757, ADAH; *Montgomery Advertiser,* 14 March 1986.

62. Interview, Elvin Stanton; *Montgomery Advertiser,* 3 April 1986; *Birmingham News,* 3 April 1986.

63. Interview, Elvin Stanton; *Montgomery Advertiser,* 3 April 1986; *Birmingham News,* 3 April 1986.

64. Interview, Jere Beasley; interview, McDowell Lee; interview, Fuller Kimbrell.

65. Memorandum from George Wallace to Leroy Brown, 12 July 1971; Report of the Department of Education on Appropriations for Education from 1962 to 1971, 16 July 1971, all in Admin. Files Gov. G. Wallace, SG22659, ADAH.

66. *Montgomery Advertiser,* 3 April 1986.

67. Julia Riggs Houchens to George Wallace, 10 February 1971, Admin. Files Gov. G. Wallace, SG22659, ADAH.

68. Interview, Elvin Stanton.

69. Pete Daniel, *Standing at the Crossroads: Southern Life in the Twentieth Century* (Baltimore: Johns Hopkins University Press, 1996), 211; interview, Mark Kennedy.

70. Interview, McDowell Lee.

71. Interview, McDowell Lee.

Index